PERL™, CGI, AND JAVASCRIPT® COMPLETE

SYBEX **SAN FRANCISCO ▸ PARIS ▸ DÜSSELDORF ▸ SOEST ▸ LONDON**

Associate Publisher: Richard Mills

Contracts and Licensing Manager: Kristine O'Callaghan

Acquisitions and Developmental Editor: Denise Santoro Lincoln

Compilation Editors: Jeff Gammon, Kathy Grider-Carlyle

Editors: Pat Coleman, Valerie Perry, Vivian Perry, Marilyn Smith, Kris Vanberg-Wolff

Compilation Technical Editor: Anthony Lincoln

Technical Editors: David Medinets, Piroz Mohseni, Rima Regas, David Shank, David Wall

Compilation Production Editor: Teresa Trego

Production Editors: Susan Berge, Katherine Cooley, Brenda Frink, Kim Goodfriend, Elizabeth Hurley, Shannon Murphy, Gemma O'Sullivan, Lisa Reardon, Rebecca Rider, Duncan Watson, Kim Wimpsett

Book Designer: Maureen Forys, Happenstance Type-O-Rama

Electronic Publishing Specialist: Kris Warrenburg

Graphic Illustrator: Andrew Benzie and Tony Jonick

Proofreaders: Nanette Duffy, Andrea Fox, Amey Garber, Camera Obscura, Laurie O'Connell, Suzanne Stein

Indexer: Nancy Guenther

Cover Designer: Design Site

Cover Photographer: Michel Tcherevkoff Ltd./Image Bank

Library of Congress Card Number: 00-105390

ISBN: 0-7821-2780-0

Trademarks

Acknowledgments

This book incorporates the work of many people, inside and outside Sybex.

Richard Mills, Associate Publisher, originated the idea of an inexpensive compilation encompassing Perl, CGI, and JavaScript. Acquisitions and Developmental Editor Denise Santoro Lincoln got the project up and running and defined the book's overall structure and contents. Jeff Gammon edited and adapted all the chapter material for publication in this book, and Kathy Grider-Carlyle edited the reference sections. Anthony Lincoln worked to ensure the technical accuracy and cohesiveness of the contents.

A large team of talented individuals helped to put together the various books from which *Perl, CGI, and JavaScript Complete* was compiled: Maureen Adams, Cheryl Applewood, Peter Kuhns, Suzanne Rotondo, and Denise Santoro-Lincoln worked on acquisition and development; Pat Coleman, Valerie Perry, Vivian Perry, Marilyn Smith, and Kris Vanberg-Wolff all contributed to editing; David Medinets, Piroz Mohseni, Rima Regas, David Shank, and David Wall provided technical edits; and Susan Berge, Katherine Cooley, Brenda Frink, Kim Goodfriend, Elizabeth Hurley, Shannon Murphy, Gemma O'Sullivan, Lisa Reardon, Rebecca Rider, Duncan Watson, and Kim Wimpsett supplied production editing expertise.

A special thanks to the *Perl, CGI, and JavaScript Complete* production team: Production Editor Teresa Trego; Book Designer Maureen Forys; Electronic Publishing Specialist Kris Warrenburg; Proofreaders Nanette Duffy, Andrea Fox, Amey Garber, Camera Obscura, Laurie O'Connell, and Suzanne Stein; and Indexer Nancy Guenther, all of whom pooled their talents to produce the handsome book you're now reading.

Finally, our most important thanks go to the contributors who agreed to have their work excerpted into *Perl, CGI, and JavaScript Complete*: Eric C. Herrmann, James Jaworski, Deborah S. Ray, Eric J. Ray, Joseph Schmuller, and Erik Strom. Additionally, new material was provided by James Jaworski, who wrote the JavaScript reference section, and Nathan Moser, who wrote the two Perl reference sections. Without the efforts of this talented group, this book would not exist.

CONTENTS AT A GLANCE

CONTENTS

Part II ▸ Advanced JavaScript   139

Chapter 5 ▫ Processing Forms   141

Part IV ▸ Building Web Applications with Perl   401

Appendix C □ Standard Perl Modules   797

INTRODUCTION

This 1,000-page compilation of helpful information from five of Sybex's successful books provides comprehensive coverage of Perl, CGI, and JavaScript, which are indispensable scripting languages for anyone interested in creating dynamic, interactive Web sites. This book was created with these goals in mind: to offer at an affordable price a thorough guide covering the most important features and uses of Perl, CGI, and JavaScript, and to acquaint you with some of our best authors—their writing styles and teaching skills, and the level of expertise they bring to their books—so you can easily find a match for your interests. Whether you're a beginner or an experienced programmer, *Perl, CGI, and JavaScript Complete* is designed to provide all the essential information you'll need to understand and skillfully use the languages, including hands-on, step-by-step instructions, real-world examples, and insightful tips. At the same time, this book invites you to explore the even greater depths and wider coverage of material in the original books.

If you've read other how-to computer books, you understand that there are many possible approaches to the task of creating and transforming Web pages. The books from which *Perl, CGI, and JavaScript Complete* was compiled represent a range of the approaches to teaching that Sybex and its authors have developed—from the quick, concise *No experience required* style to the extremely thorough *Mastering* style. These books also address readers at different levels of computer experience. As you read through various chapters of this book, you'll see which approach works best for you. You'll also see what these books have in common: a commitment to clarity, accuracy, and practicality.

You'll find in these pages ample evidence of the high quality of Sybex's authors. Unlike publishers who produce "books by committee," Sybex authors are encouraged to write in individual voices that reflect their own experience with the evolution of the computing technology. Nearly every book represented here is the work of a single writer or a pair of close collaborators; when Eric Herrmann, for example, says, "Personally, I am not a big fan of most HTML editors because I think they try to do too much...," you know you are getting the benefit of *his* direct experience. Likewise, all the chapters are based on their authors' firsthand testing of prerelease software and subsequent expertise with the final product.

In adapting the various source materials for inclusion in *Perl, CGI, and JavaScript Complete*, we've preserved these individual voices and perspectives. Chapters were edited only to minimize duplication and to update or add cross-references so that you can easily follow a topic across chapters.

Who Can Benefit from This Book?

Perl, CGI, and JavaScript Complete is designed to meet the needs of a wide range of users. The books from which this book is compiled are each targeted to a specific audience:

▶ *Mastering JavaScript and JScript* is aimed at savvy HTML users who want to take the next step and learn to write JavaScript programs that will make their Web sites come alive. This is the most comprehensive tutorial and reference available, with information on both Netscape and Microsoft's enhancements of JavaScript. The book starts with everything beginners need to know and then moves on to more advanced topics, such as scripting ActiveX components, working with plug-ins, building multimedia applications, and interfacing with CGI programs.

▶ *Dynamic HTML: Master the Essentials* is a revolution for Web site designers, allowing precise control of the layout of interactive Web pages. This "teach yourself" book was written for the millions of Webmasters, designers, and HTML newbies who want to quickly incorporate Dynamic HTML into their own pages. Covering both the Microsoft and Netscape implementations, this book gives readers the skills they need to use DHTML's most useful features—layering, Cascading Style Sheets, using object models, and working with JavaScript, VBScript, ActiveX controls, and Java. Readers learn by working through scores of practical examples.

▶ *Mastering HTML 4: Premium Edition* is ideal for those looking for comprehensive coverage at an unbeatable value—everything in *Mastering HTML 4*, plus 200 entirely new pages and a CD packed with code, a searchable HTML reference, and powerful Web utilities! Special topics only available in the Premium Edition include XML and DOM, expanded DHTML coverage, an update on HTML development tools, and productivity enhancement tips throughout. Enjoy both print and electronic versions of the popular "Master's Reference" to HTML tags, style sheets, JavaScript, HTML special characters, and HTML color codes. This is as comprehensive as it gets!

▶ *Perl CGI Programming: No experience required* provides the fastest way for newcomers to learn Perl and CGI programming for enhancing and creating open, interactive Web sites. Learn to create valuable, interactive CGI Web forms, including catalogs, search engines, order forms, database referencing, and user feed-back scripts. The platform- and browser-independent presentation provides real-world examples and complete step-by-step instructions for learning and using Perl. *Perl CGI Programming: No experience required* is currently out of print, so this book you're holding provides you with five chapters that are difficult to obtain elsewhere.

▶ *Mastering Perl 5* is the answer for those who are looking for a fast and effective tool for learning the most popular language for building interactive applications for the Web. Unlike the leading books, it's designed for non-programmers and readers who aren't Unix gurus and is written in the classic, unintimidating Mastering style. It also specifically addresses the fastest-growing audience for Perl: Windows NT and 98 users. Each section of the book has a "JumpStart" opener that allows readers to learn by doing; they are walked through a complex example that illustrates key Perl concepts.

So, if it seems as if this book contains something for everybody, we've achieved what we started out to do. Whether you're a SOHO (small-office/home-office) programmer working with a stand-alone computer or on a simple peer-to-peer network with no administrators or technical staff to rely on or you're an experienced Web developer, you'll find information you can use in this book.

Although you certainly could read this book from beginning to end, you may not need to read every chapter. The Contents at a Glance, the Table of Contents, and the Index will help you find specific topics, as will the information in the next section.

How This Book Is Organized

Perl, CGI, and JavaScript Complete has five parts, consisting of 16 chapters and three reference sections.

Part I: JavaScript Fundamentals　The four chapters in this part of the book are designed to teach you the fundamentals of JavaScript and get you up and running with your own JavaScript programs.

Part II: Advanced JavaScript　The purpose of the chapters in this part of the book is to introduce you to more advanced JavaScript tasks, such as processing forms, using hidden fields and cookies, and interfacing your JavaScript programs with CGI programs.

Part III: Perl and CGI Fundamentals   Part III then introduces you to Perl and CGI programming. You'll learn how to write your first program, debug programs in general, and use Perl and CGI in the real world (such as dealing with files, bringing your counter to the Web, and running your counter). You'll also learn how to create real-world HTML forms with Perl.

Part IV: Building Web Applications with Perl   Part IV is where the real Perl fun begins. You'll learn how to quiz and poll your visitors, create a guest book for your Web site, and monitor Web site activity. You'll also learn all about e-mail programs and protocols and Unix and Windows e-mail solutions for your Perl programs. This section of the book will also introduce you to using Perl with databases, show you how to create a database table and import data, introduce you to the SQL language, and teach you how to create an Internet connection to a database.

Part V: JavaScript and Perl References   Part V provides you with three comprehensive JavaScript and Perl references. The JavaScript objects, Perl functions, and Perl modules references found in this section are essential resources to learning JavaScript, CGI, and Perl development.

A Few Typographical Conventions

When an operation requires a series of choices from menus or dialog boxes, the ➢ symbol is used to guide you through the instructions, like this: "Choose Programs ➢ Accessories ➢ System Tools ➢ System Information." The items the ➢ symbol separates may be menu names, toolbar icons, check boxes, or other elements of an application—any place you can make a selection. Also, when you notice the ➡ arrow in a line of code, it's indicating that the line is actually a continuation of the preceding line.

This typeface identifies Internet URLs and HTML code, and **boldface type** is used whenever you need to type something into a text box.

You'll find these types of special notes throughout the book:

TIP

You'll see many tips—quicker and smarter ways to accomplish a task, which the authors have based on many, many months spent using the scripting languages.

NOTE

You'll see these Notes, too. They usually represent alternate ways to accomplish a task or some additional information that needs to be highlighted.

WARNING

In a very few places you'll see a Warning like this one. When you see a Warning, pay attention to it.

YOU'LL ALSO SEE "SIDEBAR" BOXES LIKE THIS

These boxed sections provide added explanation of special topics that are noted briefly in the surrounding discussion but that you may want to explore separately. Each sidebar has a heading that announces the topic so you can quickly decide whether it's something you need to know about.

So Where Can I Get These Great Books?

Most of the Sybex books used to compile *Perl, CGI, and JavaScript Complete* are available at book and computer stores worldwide. If you can't find a book you're looking for (or can't easily get to a bookstore), don't worry. Sybex books are available for purchase online at the Sybex Web site, at

    http://www.sybex.com

or through online booksellers, such as Fatbrain (previously known as Computer Literacy), at

    http://www.fatbrain.com

and Amazon.com, at

    http://www.amazon.com

For More Information...

See the Sybex Web site, www.sybex.com, to learn more about the books that went into *Perl, CGI, and JavaScript Complete*. On the site's Catalog page, you'll find links to just about any book you're interested in.

We hope you enjoy this book and find it useful. Happy computing!

PART i

JavaScript Fundamentals

CHAPTER 1
LEARNING THE FUNDAMENTALS

Imagine being able to create interactive multimedia adventure games that anyone can play over the World Wide Web. Imagine being able to create animated product catalogs that not only help your customers find the products they want but enable them to purchase them using secure online payment systems. Imagine being able to create database applications for use by your company's sales force from one end of the country to another via the company's intranet. With Java Script, you no longer have to imagine, you can do it all.

Adapted from *Mastering JavaScript and JScript*, by James Jaworski

ISBN 0-7821-2492-5   925 pages $39.99

JavaScript is a new and powerful programming language for the World Wide Web. It not only enables the development of truly interactive Web pages, it is also the essential glue that integrates *Java applets*, *ActiveX Controls*, *browser plug-ins*, *server scripts*, and other Web *objects*, permitting developers to create *distributed applications* for use over the Internet and over corporate *intranets* as well.

If all the terms in the preceding paragraphs are a bit confusing to you, you've come to the right place to begin your involvement with JavaScript and the world of interactive Web page development. In this chapter, I will provide all the background information you need to begin mastering the JavaScript language. I'll start with the concepts that are essential to understanding the operation of the World Wide Web.

NEW

NOTE

JavaScript is supported by Netscape Navigator, Microsoft Internet Explorer, and Opera Software's Opera Browser. As such, it is an important tool for both current and future Web development. Throughout this book I will be emphasizing the scripting capabilities provided by Navigator 4.5 (JavaScript 1.3) and Internet Explorer 5 (JScript 5). The Opera 3.5 browser only supports JavaScript 1.1, which is a small subset of the scripting capabilities supported by Navigator and Internet Explorer.

THE WEB

The World Wide Web, or simply *the Web* for short, is one of the most popular services provided via the Internet. At its best, it combines the appeal of exploring exotic destinations with the excitement of playing a video game, listening to a music CD, or even directing a movie, and you can do it all by means of an intuitive, easy-to-use, graphical user interface. Probably the most appealing aspect of the Web, however, is the fact that it isn't just for spectators. Once you have some experience with Web *authoring tools*, you can publish yourself—and offer over the Web anything you want to make available, from your company's latest research results to your own documentary on the lives of the rich and famous.

A little history: What exactly *is* the Web? The Web is the collection of all browsers, servers, files, and browser-accessible services available through the Internet. It was created in 1989 by a computer scientist named Tim Berners-Lee; its original purpose was to facilitate communication between research scientists. Berners-Lee, working at the *Conseil*

Européen pour la Recherche Nucléaire (CERN), the European Laboratory for Particle Physics, located in Geneva, Switzerland, designed the Web in such a way that documents located on one computer on the Internet could provide links to documents located on other computers on the Internet.

To many, the most familiar element of the Web is the *browser*. A browser is the user's window to the Web, providing the capability to view Web documents and access Web-based services and applications. The most popular browsers are Netscape's Navigator and Microsoft's Internet Explorer, the latest versions of which both support JavaScript. Both browsers are descendants of the *Mosaic* browser, which was developed by Marc Andreessen at the National Center for Supercomputing Applications (NCSA), located at the University of Illinois, Urbana-Champaign. Mosaic's slick graphical user interface (GUI, pronounced "gooey") transformed the Web from a research tool to the global publishing medium that it has become today.

Today's Web browsers extend Mosaic's GUI features with multimedia capabilities and with *browser programming languages* such as Java and JavaScript. These programming languages make it possible to develop Web documents that are highly interactive, meaning they do more than simply connect you to another Web page elsewhere on the Internet. *Web documents created with JavaScript contain programs*—which you, as the user of a browser, run entirely within the context of the Web pages that are currently displayed. This is a major advance in Web publishing technology. It means, for one thing, that you can run Web-based applications without having to install any additional software on your machine.

In order to publish a document on the Web, it must be made available to a Web *server*. Web servers retrieve Web documents in response to browser requests and forward the documents to the requesting browsers via the Internet. Web servers also provide gateways that enable browsers to access Web-related applications, such as database searches and electronic payment systems, as well as other Internet services, such as Gopher and Wide Area Information Search (WAIS).

The earliest Web servers were developed by CERN and NCSA. These servers were the mainstay of the Web throughout its early years. Lately, commercial Web servers, developed by Netscape, Microsoft, and other companies, have become increasingly popular on the Web. These servers are designed for higher performance and to facilitate the development of complex Web applications. They also support the development of server-based applications using JavaScript and Java. Code written in these languages can be integrated very tightly with the server, with the result that server-side programs are executed very efficiently.

Because the Web uses the Internet as its communication medium, it must follow Internet communication *protocols*. A protocol is a set of rules governing the procedures for exchanging information. The Internet's Transmission Control Protocol (TCP) and Internet Protocol (IP) enable worldwide connectivity between browsers and servers. In addition to using the TCP/IP protocols for communication across the Internet, the Web also uses its own protocol, called the HyperText Transfer Protocol (HTTP), for exchanges between browsers and servers. HTTP is used by browsers to request documents from servers and by servers to return requested documents to browsers. Figure 1.1 shows an analogy between the English language and telephony protocols over the phone system on the one hand, and HTTP and TCP/IP over the Internet, on the other hand. Browsers and servers communicate via HTTP over the Internet in the same way that an American and an Englishman would communicate via English over a phone system.

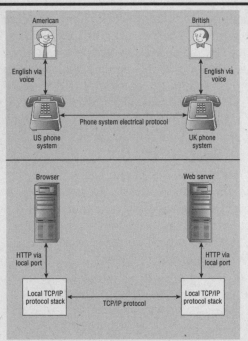

FIGURE 1.1: An analogy. Browsers and servers communicate via HTTP over the Internet in the same way that an American writer and a British editor would communicate via English over a phone system.

THE HYPERTEXT MARKUP LANGUAGE

The HyperText Markup Language, or HTML, is the *lingua franca* of the Web. It is used to create Web pages and is similar to the codes used by some word processing programs, notably WordPerfect.

HTML uses ordinary ASCII text files to represent Web pages. The files consist of the text to be displayed and the *tags* that specify *how* the text is to be displayed. For example, the following line from an HTML file shows the text of a title between the appropriate title tags.

```
<TITLE>Mastering JavaScript and JScript</TITLE>
```

The use of tags to define the elements of a Web document is referred to as *markup*. Some tags are used to specify the title of a document, others are used to identify headings, paragraphs, and hyperlinks. Still others are used to insert forms, images, multimedia objects, and other features in Web documents.

NOTE

This book assumes that you already have a working knowledge of HTML. This section briefly reviews the important aspects of the language. If you have not used HTML, you should also check out the links to HTML tutorials and reference information located on the Web page for *Mastering JavaScript and JScript* (ISBN 0-7821-2492-5) at http://www.sybex.com.

Tags always begin with a left angle bracket, <, and end with a right angle bracket, >. The name of the tag is placed between these two symbols. Usually, but not always, tags come in pairs, to surround the text that is marked up. Such tags are referred to as *surrounding* tags. For example, HTML documents begin with the <HTML> tag and end with the </HTML> tag. The first tag of a pair of tags is referred to as the *beginning* or *opening* tag, and the second tag of the pair is referred to as the *ending* or *closing* tag. The ending tag has the same name as the beginning tag except that a / (a forward slash character) immediately follows the <.

Other tags, known as *separating* tags, do not come in pairs, and have no closing tags. These tags are used to insert such things as line breaks, images, and horizontal rules within marked up text. An example of a separating tag is the <HR> tag, which is used to insert a horizontal rule (a line) across a Web page.

Both surrounding and separating tags make use of *attributes* to specify properties of marked-up text. These attributes and their *attribute values*, if any, are included in the tag. For example, a horizontal rule 10 pixels wide may be specified using the following tag:

```
<HR SIZE="10">
```

The above HR tag contains a SIZE attribute that is assigned an attribute value of 10.

NOTE

Attributes and attribute values are placed in the opening tag of a pair of surrounding tags.

Listing 1.1 contains a sample HTML document that illustrates the use of tags in marking up a Web page. Figure 1.2 shows how Netscape Navigator displays this HTML document. The <HTML> and </HTML> tags are used to identify the beginning and end of the HTML document. The document contains a head, identified by the <HEAD> and </HEAD> tags, and a body, identified by the <BODY> and </BODY> tags. The document's head contains a title that is marked by the <TITLE> and </TITLE> tags. (The title appears at the top of the Navigator window.)

Listing 1.1: Example HTML Document

```
<HTML>
<HEAD>
<TITLE>This text is the document's title.</TITLE>
</HEAD>
<BODY>
<H1 ALIGN="CENTER">This is a centered heading.</H1>
<P>This is the first paragraph.</P>
<P>This is the second paragraph.</P>
<HR SIZE="10">
<P ALIGN="CENTER">This paragraph is centered
➥ and below the horizontal rule.</P>
</BODY>
</HTML>
```

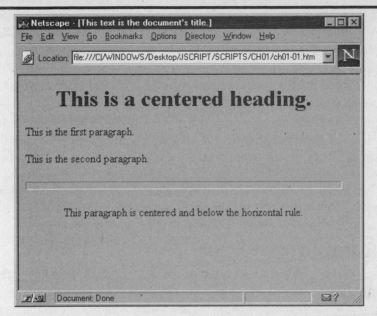

FIGURE 1.2: A browser display of the HTML document shown in Listing 1.1

Here are a few items to notice within this listing:

► The document's body contains a Heading 1 that is marked by the `<H1>` and `</H1>` tags. The opening `<H1>` tag uses the `ALIGN` attribute to center the heading.

► Two paragraphs immediately follow the heading. These paragraphs are marked by the paragraph tags `<P>` and `</P>`.

► Following these two paragraphs is a horizontal rule with its `SIZE` attribute set to 10.

► The last element of the document's body is a paragraph that uses the `ALIGN` attribute to center the paragraph.

The Development of HTML

HTML was originally developed by Tim Berners-Lee at CERN. Since then, it has evolved through several major revisions. Each revision adds new tags that increase the expressive power of the language. For example, HTML 2 added the capability to include forms within Web documents, and HTML 3.2 added tags for tables and tags that support the use of JavaScript and Java.

NEW

As of this writing (winter 1998), HTML 4 is the latest official version of HTML. HTML 4 adds support for international text, greater accessibility, more flexible tables, generic objects, printing, and advanced style sheets.

Although HTML is periodically standardized, the language continues to grow as the result of new tags, attributes, and attribute values that browser developers introduce. Because Netscape and Microsoft hold the largest share of the browser market, they have taken the lead in defining new additions to HTML. These additions are not part of the official HTML language, so they are referred to as *extensions*. Most extensions are eventually integrated into the official version of HTML.

Cascading Style Sheets

Style sheets provide the capability to control the way in which HTML elements are laid out and displayed. For example, you can use style sheets to control the color, font, and spacing used with different HTML elements. Support for Cascading Style Sheets, or CSS, was developed by the World Wide Web consortium and introduced with HTML 3.2, and additional CSS support was added in HTML 4. *Cascading* refers to the capability to use multiple levels of style sheets for a document where one level of style may be used to define another.

Two levels of Cascading Style Sheets have been defined. CSS1 is a simple style sheet mechanism that allows basic styles (for example, fonts, colors, and spacing) to be associated with HTML elements. CSS1 is an outgrowth of HTML 3.2 and is supported by Internet Explorer 3 (and later), Navigator 4 (and later), as well as other browsers. CSS2 builds on CSS1 and adds support for media-specific style sheets, content positioning, downloadable fonts, table layout, internationalization, automatic counters and numbering, and other capabilities.

In addition to CSS1 and CSS2, Navigator 4 introduced JavaScript style sheets, or JSS. JSS is similar to CSS1 and makes styles available as JavaScript properties.

HELPER APPLICATIONS

Most graphical Web browsers provide support for viewing images in common graphics formats, such as Graphics Interchange Format (GIF) and

Joint Photographic Experts Group (JPEG). Some can even play audio files. However, most browsers do not provide much more than that in terms of multimedia features. Instead of building larger, more complicated browsers to handle many different file formats, browser developers use *helper applications*. When a browser encounters a file type that it does not know how to handle, it searches its list of helper applications to see if it has one that is capable of dealing with the file. If a suitable helper is found, then the browser executes the helper and passes it the name of the file to be run. If an appropriate helper cannot be found, then the browser prompts the user to identify which helper to use, or to save the file for later display.

External Viewers and Plug-Ins

Early helper programs operated independently of the Web browser. These programs, referred to as *external viewers*, were executed separate from the browser and created their own windows to display various types of files. Netscape and Microsoft developed the capability for their second-generation browsers to use *plug-in* or *add-in modules*, which not only execute automatically when needed but display their output in the browser window. Since then, numerous companies have developed plug-in modules to support everything from the three-dimensional worlds created by the Virtual Reality Modeling Language (VRML) to CD-quality audio.

Plug-in modules are generally quicker to load and more efficient than external viewers. Because they execute with the browser, they can be accessed from within the browser environment. Netscape provides the capability to control plug-in modules from Java and JavaScript code via its LiveConnect toolkit. Microsoft provides a similar capability through its Internet Explorer Object Model.

Using MIME Types to Identify Helpers for File Formats

So far, I've described how browsers use helper applications to display different types of files, but how does a browser know which helpers to use for a given file? The answer lies in MIME types.

MIME stands for Multipurpose Internet Mail Extensions. MIME was originally developed as a standard for including different types of files in electronic mail. It was subsequently adopted by Web servers and browsers to identify the types of files referenced in a Web page.

MIME identifies file types using a *type/subtype* naming scheme. Examples of common MIME types are text/plain, text/html, image/gif, and video/quicktime. The first component of a MIME type identifies the general type of a file, while the second part identifies the specific type within the general category. For example, the text/plain and text/html types both belong to the text category, but they differ in their subtypes. Table 1.1 lists some common MIME types.

TABLE 1.1: Example MIME Types

MIME TYPE	DESCRIPTION
text/plain	Generic ASCII text file
text/html	Text file containing HTML
image/gif	Image in Graphics Interchange Format
image/jpeg	Image in Joint Photographic Experts Group format
audio/x-wav	File containing sounds stored in the Windows audio file format
video/mpeg	Video in the Moving Pictures Experts Group format
video/quicktime	Video in the Apple QuickTime format
Application/octet-stream	Raw (unformatted) stream of bytes
Application/x-javascript	File containing JavaScript source code

Web servers contain configuration files that match file extensions with their MIME types. For example, files that end with the extensions .htm or .html are associated with the text/html MIME type and files that end with .jpg, .jpe, or .jpeg are associated with the image/jpeg MIME type.

Browsers also contain configuration information about MIME types. This information is used to map MIME types to the helper application that displays files of that type.

When a browser requests a file from a Web server, the server uses the file's extension to look up the file's MIME type. The server then identifies the file's MIME type to the browser. The browser uses the file's MIME type to determine which helper application, if any, is to be used to display the file. If the file is to be displayed by an external viewer, the browser waits until the file has been completely received before launching the viewer. If the file is to be displayed by a plug-in, the browser launches the plug-in and passes the file to the plug-in as the file is received. This enables the plug-in to begin displaying the file before it is fully loaded, which is an important capability of audio and video streaming applications.

UNIFORM RESOURCE LOCATORS (URLs)

A *Uniform Resource Locator*, or URL, is the notation used to specify the addresses of an Internet file or service. You have probably seen numerous examples of URLs. They are included in TV commercials, they're shown on billboards, and they appear in magazine ads. I've even heard people announce them, slash by slash and dot by dot, on the radio. Examples of URLs include `http://home.netscape.com`, `http://www.microsoft.com`, and `ftp://ftp.cdrom.com`.

A URL always contains a *protocol identifier,* such as `http` or `ftp`, and a host name, such as `home.netscape.com`, `www.microsoft.com`, or `ftp.cdrom.com`, which appear in the preceding examples. Commonly used protocol identifiers are `http`, `ftp`, and `gopher`. The protocol identifier is also referred to as a *scheme*. When writing a URL, the protocol identifier is followed by `://` and then the host name of the computer to which the protocol applies. (In URLs, path names are written using forward slash (/) characters, rather than back slash (\ ) characters.) For example, to access the main home page of Microsoft on the host named `www.microsoft.com`, you would use the URL `http://www.microsoft.com`. To access the root directory of the File Transfer Protocol (FTP) server hosted at `ftp.cdrom.com`, you would use the URL `ftp://ftp.cdrom.com`.

In addition to the host name, the URL can specify the path and file-name of a file to be accessed by adding a single / character followed by the name. For example, from the Sybex Web site, follow the link to my home page for *Mastering JavaScript and JScript*, which is located in the `javascript` subdirectory of my Web server's root directory, in the file `index.htm`. The URL for this file is therefore:

```
http://www.jaworski.com/javascript/index.htm
```

(Actually, because my Web server is set up to use the filename `index.htm` by default, it can be omitted from the URL. The URL `http://www.jaworski.com/javascript` would be sufficient to locate the file.)

NOTE

URLs may also contain additional addressing components, such as a port name before the path and filename, and a file offset after the filename.

THE FILE PROTOCOL IN URLS

Your browser can use the file protocol to access files located on your local machine. Suppose the file `test.htm` was located on your Window 95 Desktop. The path to this file would be `c:\windows\desktop\test.htm`. To open the file with your browser, you would use the following URL:

```
file://localhost/C|/WINDOWS/Desktop/test.htm
```

The host name `localhost` in the preceding URL is used to refer to the local file system and may be omitted safely. The slash following `localhost`, however, should be retained. The preceding URL could thus be written as follows:

```
file:///C|/WINDOWS/Desktop/test.htm
```

Note that in both preceding examples the C: drive designation that you are probably most familiar with from DOS conventions is written as C| instead.

THE HYPERTEXT TRANSFER PROTOCOL (HTTP)

HTTP is the protocol used for communication between browsers and Web servers. HTTP uses a request/response model of communication. A browser establishes a connection with a server and sends URL requests to the server. The server processes the browser's request and sends a response back to the browser.

A browser connects with a Web server by establishing a TCP connection at port 80 of the server. (This is the default port unless another is specified in the URL.) This port is the default address at which Web servers "listen" for browser requests. Once a connection has been established, a browser sends a request to the server. This request specifies a request method, the URL of the document, program, or other resource being requested, the HTTP version being used by the browser, and other information related to the request.

Several request methods are available. GET, HEAD, and POST are the most commonly used ones.

The GET method is used to retrieve the information contained at the specified URL. This method may also be used to *submit* data collected in an HTML *form* (the topic of Chapter 5, "Processing Forms") or to invoke a Common Gateway Interface program (a topic I discuss in the following section). When the server processes a GET request, it delivers the requested information (if it can be found). The server inserts at the front of the information an HTTP header that provides data about the server, identifies any errors that occurred in processing the request, and describes the type of information being returned as a result.

The HEAD method is similar to the GET method except that when a Web server processes a HEAD request it only returns the HTTP header data and not the information that was the object of the request. The HEAD method is used to retrieve information about a URL without actually obtaining the information addressed by the URL.

The POST method is used to inform the server that the information appended to the request is to be sent to the specified URL. The POST method is typically used to send form data and other information to Common Gateway Interface (CGI) programs. The Web server responds to a POST request by sending back header data followed by any information generated by the CGI program as the result of processing the request.

NEW

The current version of HTTP is HTTP 1.1. It incorporates performance, security, and other improvements to the original HTTP 1. A new version of HTTP, referred to as HTTP-NG, is currently being defined. (The *NG* stands for "next generation.") The goal of HTTP-NG is to simplify the HTTP protocol and make it more extensible.

COMMON GATEWAY INTERFACE PROGRAMS

The *Common Gateway Interface* is a standard that specifies how external programs may be used by Web servers. Programs that adhere to the Common Gateway Interface standard are referred to as CGI programs. CGI programs may be used to process data submitted with forms, to perform database searches, and to support other types of Web applications such as clickable image maps.

A browser request for the URL of a CGI program comes about as the result of a user clicking a link or submitting a form. The browser uses HTTP to make the request. When a Web server receives the request, the Web server executes the CGI program and also passes it any data that was submitted by the browser. When the CGI program performs its processing, it usually generates data in the form of a Web page, which it returns via the Web server to the requesting browser.

The CGI standard specifies how data may be passed from Web servers to CGI programs and how data should be returned from CGI programs to the Web server. Table 1.2 summarizes these interfaces. In Chapter 5, "Processing Forms," and Chapter 7, "Interfacing JavaScript with CGI Programs," you'll study CGI and learn how to create CGI programs.

TABLE 1.2: CGI Summary

METHOD OF COMMUNICATING	INTERFACE	DESCRIPTION
Command-line arguments	Web server to CGI program	Data is passed to the CGI program via the command line used to execute the program. Command-line arguments are passed to CGI programs as the result of ISINDEX queries.
Environment variables	Web server to CGI program	A Web server passes data to the CGI program by setting special variables, referred to as environment variables, that are available to the CGI program via its environment.

CONTINUED ➡

TABLE 1.2 continued: CGI Summary

METHOD OF COMMUNICATING	INTERFACE	DESCRIPTION
Standard input stream	Web server to CGI program	A Web server passes data to a CGI program by sending the data to the standard character input stream associated with the CGI program. The CGI program reads the data as if it were manually entered by a user at a character terminal.
Standard output stream	CGI program to Web server	The CGI program passes data back to the Web server by writing it to its standard output stream (for example, to a terminal). The Web server intercepts this data and sends it back to the browser that made the CGI request.

JAVA APPLETS

The Java language, developed by Sun Microsystems, Inc., has realized tremendous popularity in the last few years. Although it was originally developed as a language for programming consumer electronic devices, Java has increasingly been adopted as a hardware- and software-independent platform for developing advanced Web applications. Java may be used to write stand-alone applications, but a major reason for its popularity is its ability to develop programs that can be executed by a Web browser.

The Java programs that can be executed by the Web browser are called *applets* rather than applications, because they cannot be run outside of the browser's own window. (*Application* usually implies a complete, stand-alone program.) Programmers create Java applets using built-in programming features of the Java Developer's Kit (JDK). Web pages, written in HTML, reference Java applets using the <APPLET> tag, in much the same way that images are referenced using the <IMAGE> tag. When a Web page that references a Java applet is loaded by a browser, the browser requests the applet code from the Web server. When the browser receives the applet code, it executes the code and allocates a fixed area of the browser window. This area is identified by attributes specified with the <APPLET> tag. The applet is not allowed to update the browser display or handle events outside of its allocated window area.

By way of comparison, JavaScript provides access to the entire Web page, but does not support many of the more advanced, object-oriented programming features of Java.

Netscape Navigator and Microsoft Internet Explorer provide the capability for JavaScript scripts to load Java applets, access Java objects, and invoke their methods.

ACTIVEX — MICROSOFT OBJECTS

ActiveX is Microsoft's approach to executing objects other than Java applets in Internet Explorer. The name *ActiveX* was used to make it seem like a new and innovative technology. However, ActiveX is nothing more than Component Object Model (COM) objects that can be downloaded and executed by Internet Explorer. COM traces its origin back to the Object Linking and Embedding (OLE) technology of Microsoft Windows 3.1.

COM objects are instances of *classes* (object types) that are also organized into *interfaces*. Each interface consists of a collection of *methods* (functions). COM objects are implemented inside a *server* (dynamic-link libraries, operating system services, or independent processes) and are accessed via their methods. The *COM library* provides a directory of available COM objects. Over the many years since Windows 3.1, many software components have been developed as COM objects.

ActiveX components are simply COM objects that implement a specific type of interface. They are important in that they provide a means for the large base of COM objects to be reused within Internet Explorer. They also allow older languages, such as C++ and C, to be used to build components for Web applications.

While ActiveX components allow the use of legacy software in Internet Explorer, they also present some drawbacks. The most significant drawback is that ActiveX is only supported by Internet Explore 4 and 5. No other browser (including earlier versions of Internet Explorer) is able to use ActiveX. ActiveX has also been criticized for its poor security. An ActiveX component is not required to behave in a secure manner like a Java applet or JavaScript script. In fact, it has been demonstrated that

ActiveX components can be used to steal or modify sensitive information or completely wipe out a user's system. Microsoft has countered this vulnerability by allowing ActiveX components to be digitally signed. This does not prevent ActiveX components from violating security, but, in some cases, it can be used to determine whether a particular Web site is responsible for causing damage.

ActiveX components are useful in intranet applications where all users of a particular company are required to use Internet Explorer and the components are signed by the company or a trusted developer. Because the Internet Explorer Object Model allows ActiveX components to be accessed from JavaScript, JavaScript scripts can be used to integrate the ActiveX components into the intranet applications.

A BRIEF HISTORY OF JAVASCRIPT

Often, one programming language will evolve from another. For example, Java evolved from C++, which evolved from C, which evolved from other languages. This is also the case for JavaScript. Netscape originally developed a language called *LiveScript* to add a basic scripting capability to both Navigator and its Web-server line of products; when it added support for Java applets in its release of Navigator 2, Netscape replaced LiveScript with JavaScript. Although the initial version of JavaScript was little more than LiveScript renamed, JavaScript has been subsequently updated with each new release of Navigator.

NOTE
Although JavaScript bears the name of Java, JavaScript is a very different language that is used for a very different purpose.

JavaScript supports both Web browser and server scripting. Browser scripts are used to create dynamic Web pages that are more interactive, more responsive, and more tightly integrated with plug-ins, ActiveX components, and Java applets. JavaScript supports these features by providing special programming capabilities, such as the ability to dynamically generate HTML and to define custom event-handling functions.

JavaScript scripts are included in HTML documents via the HTML <SCRIPT> tag. When a JavaScript-capable browser loads an HTML document containing scripts, it evaluates the scripts as they are encountered. The scripts may be used to create HTML elements that are added to the displayed document or to define functions, called *event handlers,* that respond to user actions, such as mouse clicks and keyboard entries. Scripts may also be used to control plug-ins, ActiveX components, and Java applets.

Microsoft implemented JScript in its Internet Explorer 3. The scripting capability of Internet Explorer 3 is roughly equivalent to Navigator 2. Netscape introduced JavaScript 1.1 with Navigator 3 and JavaScript 1.2 with Navigator 4. JavaScript 1.1 added a number of new features, including support for more browser objects and user-defined functions. JavaScript 1.2 added new objects, methods, and properties, and support for style sheets, layers, regular expressions, and signed scripts.

Netscape also supported server-side scripting with its LiveWire and LiveWire Pro (renamed to LiveWire Database Service) features of its Enterprise and FastTrack Web servers. On the server side, JavaScript is used to more easily develop scripts that process form data, perform database searches, and implement custom Web applications. Server-side scripts are more tightly integrated with the Web server than CGI programs.

Microsoft introduced its version of JavaScript, referred to as JScript, in Internet Explorer 3. JScript is tightly coupled to Internet Explorer and allows almost all HTML elements to be scripted. JScript is compatible with JavaScript 1.2. Microsoft also included server-side JavaScript support with its Internet Information Server (IIS). It later developed a more general approach to server-side scripting with its Windows Scripting Host and remote scripting technologies. Remote scripting allows Internet Explorer to remotely execute scripts on a server and receive the server script outputs within the context of a single Web page.

Netscape and Microsoft submitted their scripting languages to the European Computer Manufacturers Association (ECMA) for standardization. ECMA released the Standard ECMA-262 in June of 1997. This standard describes the ECMAScript language, which is a compilation of the best features of JavaScript and JScript. An updated version of this standard was released in June of 1998.

Microsoft worked closely with ECMA and updated Internet Explorer 4 and JScript (JScript 3.1) to achieve ECMAScript compliance. Navigator achieved ECMAScript compliance with JavaScript 1.3, which is supported in Navigator 4.06 and 4.5.

Internet Explorer 5 introduced JScript 5, which provides additional scripting capabilities, such as the `try - catch` statement. This statement provides advanced error handling support and is included in the latest version of ECMAScript (Standard ECMA-262, edition 3).

While Netscape and Microsoft were busy introducing new versions of their browsers and scripting languages, another JavaScript-compatible browser was launched by Opera Software (http://www.operasoftware.com). Opera browsers 3.2 and 3.5 both support JavaScript 1.1.

Another JavaScript-related standardization effort was initiated by the World Wide Web Consortium to standardize the basic objects that are made available by browsers when processing HTML and XML documents. This effort resulted in a specification known as the Document Object Model (DOM) Level 1. It provides a standard set of objects for representing HTML and XML documents, a standard model of how these objects can be combined, and a standard interface for accessing and manipulating them. The DOM is like an application programming interface (API) for HTML and XML documents. However, the DOM is not a complete API in that it does not specify the events that occur when a user interacts with an HTML or XML document (and methods for handling them). At this time, neither Navigator nor Internet Explorer satisfy the requirements of the DOM.

LIVEWIRE AND LIVEWIRE DATABASE SERVICE

LiveWire is a graphical environment for developing and managing Web sites. Netscape created it for use with their servers. One of LiveWire's features is that it supports the development of server-side programs using the JavaScript language. These programs are used in the same way as CGI programs, but they are more closely integrated with Web servers and the HTML pages that reference them. The LiveWire Database Service provides the capability to connect server scripts to databases. Server scripts access databases using the industry-standard Structured Query Language (SQL).

Server-based JavaScript programs are compiled with HTML documents into a platform-independent bytecode format. When a Web browser requests a compiled document, it is translated back into HTML format and sent out to the browser. The server-based scripts remain with the server and are loaded to perform any server-side processing. The HTML document loaded by the browser communicates with the server-side scripts to implement advanced Web applications that are distributed between the browser, server, and other server-side programs, such as database and electronic commerce applications.

LiveWire provides a number of programming objects that JavaScript scripts can use to implement CGI-style programs. These objects simplify the communication between browsers, Web servers, and server-side scripts.

Active Server Pages, Windows Scripting Host, and Remote Scripting

Microsoft's Active Server Pages (ASP) is a server-side scripting environment that is similar to LiveWire. You can use it to include server-side scripts and ActiveX components with HTML pages. The combined HTML and script file is stored as an ASP file. When a browser requests the ASP file from your Web server, the server invokes the ASP processor. The ASP processor reads through the requested file, executes any script commands, and sends the processing results as a Web page to the browser. ASP pages can also invoke ActiveX components to perform tasks, such as accessing a database or performing an electronic commerce transaction. Because ASP scripts run on the Web server and send standard HTML to the browser, ASP is browser independent.

Microsoft introduced ASP with Internet Information Server (IIS) version 3. It also works with IIS 4, Personal Web Server for Windows 95, and Peer Web Server for Windows NT Workstation.

As a result of the success of ASP, Microsoft developed Windows Scripting Host (WSH), a technology that allows scripts to be run on Windows 95, 98, and NT 4. WSH is language independent and supports JScript, VBScript, and other languages. It allows scripts to be executed from the Windows Desktop or a console (MS-DOS) window. WSH scripts are complete in themselves and do need to be embedded in an HTML document. WSH is an exciting technology in that it extends the capabilities of JScript beyond the Web to the Windows Desktop and operating system. WSH scripts can be used to replace MS-DOS scripts and provide the capability to take full advantage of the Windows GUI, ActiveX, and operating system functions in JScript scripts.

NOTE
WSH can be freely downloaded from Microsoft's Web site at `http://msdn .microsoft.com/scripting/`.

Microsoft's latest addition to scripting technology is referred to as *remote scripting*. Remote scripting enables client-side scripts, running on Internet Explorer, to execute server-side scripts, running on IIS. This lets Internet Explorer and IIS perform simultaneous processing and communicate with each other within the context of a Web page, allowing the page to be dynamically updated with server information without having to be reloaded. This frees the user from having to reload a Web page during the execution of a Web application and provides for a higher degree of interaction between the browser and Web server. For example, with remote scripting, a Web server can validate form data and provide the user with feedback while the user is still filling out the form.

Remote scripting allows browser/server communication to be accomplished in either a synchronous or an asynchronous manner. When synchronous communication is used, a client-side script executes a server-side script and waits for the server-side script to return its result. When asynchronous communication is used, the client-side script executes the server-side script and then continues with its processing without waiting for the server-side script to finish.

NOTE
Remote scripting can be freely downloaded from Microsoft's Web site at `http://msdn.microsoft.com/scripting/`.

INTRANETS, EXTRANETS, AND DISTRIBUTED APPLICATIONS

In the last couple of years, corporations have begun to look at ways of deploying TCP/IP networks inside of their companies to take advantage of the full range of standards-based services provided by the Internet. These "company-internal internets" have become known as *intranets*. Intranets may be private networks that are physically separate from the Internet, internal networks that are separated from the Internet by a firewall, or simply a company's internal extension of the Internet.

Companies deploy intranets so that they can make Internet services available to their workers. E-mail, Web browsing, and Web publishing are the most popular of these services. Many companies make Web servers available for their employees' intranet publishing needs. These intranet Web servers allow departments, groups, and individuals within a company to conveniently share information while usually limiting access to the information published on the intranet to company employees.

The popularity of intranets as a way of communicating and of sharing information within a company has brought about a demand for more powerful and sophisticated intranet applications. The eventual goal is for the intranet to provide a common application framework from which a company's core information processing functions can be implemented and accessed. Netscape, Sun, Microsoft, and other Web software providers are focusing on the intranet as the primary application framework for the development of business software.

Because of its client/server architecture and user-friendly browser software, the Web is the perfect model for implementing these common intranet application frameworks. The approach taken by Netscape, Microsoft, and other Web software developers is to use the Web browser as the primary interface by which users connect to the intranet and run intranet and extranet applications. These applications are referred to as *distributed applications* because their execution is distributed in part on the browser (via JavaScript, Java, ActiveX, XML, and other languages); in part on the server (via CGI programs and JavaScript and Java server-side programs); and in part on database and other enterprise servers.

Distributed intranet and extranet applications use HTML, JavaScript, Java, XML, and other languages for programming the browser-based user interface portion of the distributed application. They also use JavaScript and Java to perform server-side programming. Other server-side components may be written in Java, C++, or other languages and made available as Common Object Request Broker Architecture (CORBA) or Distributed Component Object Model (DCOM) objects. These objects may also be accessed from JavaScript.

In many distributed application development approaches, Java is seen as a key technology for developing the components of distributed applications, and JavaScript is seen as the essential glue that combines these components into fully distributed Web-based intranet and extranet applications.

SUMMARY

This chapter covered the concepts that are essential to understanding the operation of the Web. You learned about Web development languages, such as HTML, Java, and JavaScript. You also covered related Web technologies, such as HTTP, CGI, LiveWire, ASP, and remote scripting. You should have a basic understanding of how these elements work together to develop Web applications.

Part i

CHAPTER 2

WORKING WITH JAVASCRIPT

JavaScript started as "LiveScript," a scripting language that Netscape developed. Independently, Sun Microsystems had developed Java, formerly "Oak," as a language to control consumer electronic devices. Because of its power and efficiency, Java found a home on the Internet as a language for small programs called "applets."

Adapted from *Dynamic HTML: Master the Essentials*, by Joseph Schmuller

ISBN 0-7821-2277-9   607 pages $29.99

Along the way, Netscape and Sun joined forces and turned LiveScript, later named "LiveWire," into a subset of Java. Ultimately, Netscape changed the name to JavaScript, and the rest is history. JavaScript resembles Java syntactically, but as a scripting language, it's interpreted, as is VBS, rather than compiled, as is Java.

In its effort to gain a firm foothold on the Web, Microsoft developed its own flavor of JavaScript, and called it JScript. Microsoft's implementation has a few enhancements designed to take advantage of IE.

JavaScript Syntax

JavaScript syntax differs from VBScript syntax. In JavaScript, a line ends with a semicolon. Thus, JavaScript has no need for a continuation character: Until it encounters a semicolon, the JavaScript interpreter considers everything to be part of one line.

Here's another difference. A procedure in VBScript is either a function, if it returns a value, or a subroutine, if it doesn't. In JavaScript, every procedure is a function, whether it returns a value or not. In a JavaScript function, curly brackets surround the code. The left curly bracket follows the function's argument list, and the right curly bracket is the last character in the function. You may have seen functions before, but for completeness, here's what the format looks like:

```
function functionName(argument1, argument2) {
    statement 1;
    statement 2;
        .

        .

    statement n;
}
```

One other difference is crucial. If you're used to programming in VBScript, you've probably adopted a loose outlook about uppercase and lowercase letters. VBScript is *case-insensitive*, meaning that "a" and "A" are equivalent. JavaScript, however, is *case-sensitive*, so that "a" and "A" are most decidedly not the same.

Comments in VBScript begin with an apostrophe. In JavaScript, you indicate a one-line comment by two slashes: //. JavaScript ignores anything on the same line that follows the two slashes. You can have a comment that spans more than one line. A multiline comment begins with /* and ends with */.

VARIABLES

Here are some rules to follow when you name variables in JavaScript:

- ► The name must start with an alphabetic character (a-z or A-Z) or an underscore (_).
- ► The rest of the name can contain any letter, any digit, or an underscore.
- ► A variable's name can't contain a space.
- ► Avoid JavaScript *reserved words* as the names of variables.

A Word about Reserved Words

A reserved word is a word set aside for a particular purpose. Some reserved words are terms in JavaScript, others are terms in Java. Here they are:

abstract	else	if	new	static
try	boolean	extends	implements	null
super	typeof	break	false	import
package	switch	var	byte	final
in	private	synchronized	void	case
finally	instanceof	protected	this	while
catch	float	int	public	throw
with	char	for	interface	reset
throws	do	function	long	return
transient	double	goto	native	short
true				

The names of built-in functions and objects are also reserved.

Creating Variables

JavaScript programmers typically use variables without declaring them, although, strictly speaking, this isn't good programming practice. If you want to declare a variable explicitly, use var. This reserved word is the equivalent of the VBS dim statement. As in VBS, explicit declaration helps avoid conflicts in variable creation.

Use var when you declare variables in a script for animation:

```
var glblTimer;
var glblAnimationStartedFlag = 0;
```

As you can see, two uses of var are possible. One declares the variable, the other declares the variable and sets an initial value.

Notice also the glbl prefix. I use it to indicate that a variable's scope is global. Functions throughout a SCRIPT element can refer to a global variable. To make a variable global, you declare it prior to any function. A local variable, on the other hand, is created inside the body of a function, and only that function can refer to it.

To shorten the number of lines in your script, JavaScript allows you to declare more than one variable with a single var statement:

```
var x, y, z;
```

Variable Types

Because JavaScript is a *loosely typed* language, you don't have to specify the type of data a JavaScript variable will hold when you declare it.

JavaScript has three types of variables:

▶ Numeric variables—contain numbers (e.g., var numberOfWords = 78)

▶ String variables—contain text between quotation marks (e.g., var myName = "Joseph")

▶ Boolean variables—contain logical statements (e.g., true or false)

JavaScript treats the reserved word null as an "empty" variable.

When you put some data into a variable, in effect you define it to be a numeric, a string, or a boolean.

In a script, you can put different types of data into a variable at different times, thus changing that variable's sub-type. You have to be careful when you do this, however, because you can get unexpected results. Here's an example:

```
var numFirst = 17;
var numSecond = 76;
var numSum;
numSum = numFirst + numSecond;
```

These lines of code result in 93 as the value for numSum. If you keep the value of numSecond as is and change the type of numFirst to a string, however,

```
varNumFirst = "17";
```

then

```
numSum = numFirst + numSecond;
```

gives the string "1776" as the value for numSum. Why? That last expression for numSum now sees the string "17" as the value for numFirst and automatically turns numSecond into the string "76". In that context, the +, which added the two numbers together in the first numSum expression, becomes the concatenation operator.

NOTE

Concatenation describes the linking of two or more strings. The + operator can act as the addition operator for a set of numeric variables, but it will act as the concatenation operator if one variable is a string.

NOTE

typeof() is a useful function built into JavaScript. It returns a string indicating its argument's type.

A Word about Numbers

VBScript has types of numerical variables. JavaScript, on the other hand, has one—the numeric. This type holds both integers and floating point numbers. The numbers can be in scientific notation, like 8.765e15 or 6.54e-19. Numbers can also be octal (base 8) or hexadecimal (base 16). If the JavaScript interpreter encounters a number with a leading 0, it interprets it as a base 8 number. If the interpreter encounters a number with a leading 0 followed by an x, it interprets it as a hexadecimal.

A Word about Strings

Inside a string, you can place special characters that tell the JavaScript interpreter to perform specific actions or to interpret a character in a special way. For example, you can add a long string to a text area, like this:

```
function info(event){
textArea = document.forms[0].elements["textareaEventInfo"];
textArea.value = "target: " + event.target.name + "\ n"
    + "which: " + event.which + "\ n"
    + "modifiers: " + event.modifiers + "\ n"
    + "type: " + event.type + "\ n"
    + "screenX: " + event.screenX + "\ n"
    + "screenY: " + event.screenY + "\ n"
    + "pageX: " + event.pageX + "\ n"
    + "pageY: " + event.pageY;
}
```

The special character here is "\ n", which tells the interpreter to move to the next line in the text area before displaying the next part of the string.

The backslash is the signal for the advent of a special character. Sometimes the backslash indicates that a punctuation mark used for one purpose should be interpreted another way. For example, if you want to include a double quote as part of a string (and not as the beginning or end of a string), precede it with a backslash. Table 2.1 shows the JavaScript special characters.

TABLE 2.1: JavaScript Special Characters

Symbol	What it is
\ \	Backslash
\ '	Single quote
\ "	Double quote
\ b	Backspace
\ f	Form feed

CONTINUED →

TABLE 2.1 continued: JavaScript Special Characters

Symbol	What it is
\ n	New line
\ r	Carriage return
\ t	Tab

CREATING OBJECTS

JavaScript enables you to create new objects. You use the reserved word new to do this. The format is

```
var variableName = new ClassName;
```

This tells the JavaScript interpreter that you're creating a new instance of ClassName and you're calling it variableName. In JavaScript, strings, numbers, and arrays are objects. When you create a new instance of one of these types, as in

```
var stringName = new String("DHTML Master the Essentials");
```

it's the same as

```
var stringName = "DHTML Master the Essentials";
```

Sometimes you have no choice but to use new, as in the next section.

CREATING ARRAYS

Sometimes you want to refer to a set of items that are similar in some way, and you'd like to be able to refer to them as "the first one," "the second one," and so forth, without giving each one a unique name. In these cases, the *array* is the appropriate structure to use.

Simple Arrays

As an example of how JavaScript handles arrays, consider the array called SportNames, which holds the names of sports in this order: "Baseball," "Basketball," "Bowling," "Football," "Hockey," "Soccer," and "Track." I've put this array into Table 2.2. As you can see, the index corresponds to the row, and we begin numbering indices from 0 rather than from 1 (this is called *zero-based indexing*).

TABLE 2.2: The SportNames Array

Index	Sport
0	"Baseball"
1	"Basketball"
2	"Bowling"
3	"Football"
4	"Hockey"
5	"Soccer"
6	"Track"

NOTE

In JavaScript 1, position 0 holds the length of the array, and the first item goes into position 1. In JavaScript 1.1 (and later) and in JScript, you put the first item in position 0.

With this array, we refer to "Baseball" as sportNames[0] and to "Football" as SportNames[3]. (Note the use of square brackets, rather than parentheses, as in VBScript.)

In JavaScript (beginning with version 1.1), an array is an object. Every array is an instance of the Array class. As you saw in the preceding section, you use the reserved word new to create a new instance of a class. Thus, we would create the SportNames array object with the statement

```
var sportNames = new Array(7);
```

NOTE

It's customary in JavaScript to begin object names with lowercase letters.

This code would create the array and insert the items:

```
var sportNames = new Array(7);
sportNames[0] = "Baseball"
sportNames[1] = "Basketball"
sportNames[2] = "Bowling"
sportNames[3] = "Football"
sportNames[4] = "Hockey"
sportNames[5] = "Soccer"
sportNames[6] = "Track"
```

JavaScript's built-in Array object gives you another way to initialize an array:

```
var sportNames = new Array("Baseball", "Basketball",
➡ "Bowling", "Football", "Hockey", "Soccer", "Track");
```

It also gives you another way to refer to an array-item. These two expressions

```
sportNames[3]
sportNames["Football"]
```

are equivalent. With a string index, as in the second expression, the array-item becomes a property of the SportNames object. So the statement

```
sportNames.Football
```

is equivalent to the other two. This statement, however,

```
sportNames.3
```

generates an error.

Complex Arrays

To carry our example forward, suppose we add a column to the table—a column that denotes whether or not the sport is in the Olympics. Table 2.3 shows the layout.

TABLE 2.3: Expanding the SportNames Table

INDEX	SPORT	OLYMPIC SPORT?
0	"Baseball"	Yes
1	"Basketball"	Yes
2	"Bowling"	No
3	"Football"	No
4	"Hockey"	Yes
5	"Soccer"	Yes
6	"Track"	Yes

We can represent this kind of table in a *multidimensional* array.

A JavaScript multidimensional array is an array of arrays. To make a two-dimensional array out of Table 2.3, we can consider each row as an array, and then combine those arrays into another array:

```
var baseball = new Array("Baseball", "Yes");
var basketball = new Array("Basketball", "Yes");
var bowling = new Array("Bowling", "No");
var football = new Array("Football", "No");
var hockey = new Array("Hockey", "Yes");
var soccer = new Array("Soccer", "Yes");
var track = new Array("Track", "Yes");
var sportNames = new Array(baseball, basketball, bowling,
➡ basketball, bowling, football, hockey, soccer, track);
```

In this array, you'd refer to "Bowling" as sportNames[2][0]. Note the syntax of the two sets of brackets. The statement sportNames[2,0] generates an error.

Array Methods

The Array object provides three methods:

- join(separator)—returns a string that holds all the array-items, with the value of separator as the separator between consecutive elements
- reverse()—reverses the order of the array-items
- sort()—sorts the array-items

JAVASCRIPT OPERATORS

JavaScript contains a full set of operators for comparisons, for logical operations, and for arithmetic. Table 2.4 shows the comparison operators.

TABLE 2.4: The JavaScript Comparison Operators

OPERATOR	NAME
==	Equality
!=	Inequality
<	Less Than
>	Greater Than
<=	Less Than Or Equal To
=>	Greater Than Or Equal To

Notice that the Equality comparison operator (==) is different from the symbol (=) that assigns a value to a variable. Table 2.5 presents the JavaScript logical operators, and Table 2.6 presents the arithmetic operators.

TABLE 2.5: JavaScript Logical Operators

OPERATOR	WHAT IT MEANS
!	NOT
&&	AND
||	OR

TABLE 2.6: JavaScript Arithmetic Operators

OPERATOR	NAME
+	Addition
–	Subtraction
*	Multiplication
/	Division
%	Modulus
++	Increment
–	Decrement
–	Negation

Each of the last three operators is a *unary* operator, an operator that works on one entity. The expression `variableName++` is equivalent to

```
variableName = variableName + 1;
```

and `variableName––` is equivalent to

```
variableName = variableName – 1;
```

NOTE

JavaScript also has a set of bitwise logical operators. You'll probably have little use for them, so I won't cover them in this chapter.

Assignment Operators

The equal sign (=) is the JavaScript assignment operator. You can combine this operator with arithmetic and logic operators, as Table 2.7 shows.

TABLE 2.7: Combining the Assignment Operator with Arithmetic and Logic Operators

COMBINATION	WHAT IT MEANS
x += y	x = x + y
x -= y	x = x - y
x *= y	x = x * y
x /= y	x = x / y
x %= y	x = x % y
x |= y	x = x | y
x &= y	x = x & y

PROGRAM FLOW

JavaScript gives you a number of ways to choose an alternative when your script encounters a choice point.

switch

JavaScript's switch is analogous to the VBS Select Case statement. It enables your program to perform a test and then, based on the result, pick one of several possible paths, called cases. Within each path, you can have a number of lines of code. When the program finishes going through the code for that path, your program exits the switch if it encounters a break statement.

Imagine an expression called testExpression with the possible values of "baseball", "football", "basketball", or "hockey". The switch would look like this:

```
switch(testExpression) {
    case "baseball" :
        statement 1;
        statement 2;
        statement 3;
        break;
    case "football" :
        statement 4;
        statement 5;
        break;
    case "basketball" :
        statement 6
        statement 7
        statement 8
        statement 9
        break;
    case "hockey" :
        statement 10;
        break;
    default :
        statement 11;
        break;
}
```

Note the final case, default, which executes if textExpression isn't one of the indicated values.

What happens if you don't include break? All the statements that follow the matching case will execute, even though they're within different cases.

You'll work through an exercise with switch later in this chapter.

if

JavaScript's if statement is straightforward:

```
if (conditional expression) {
    statement 1;
    statement 2;
}
```

If the conditional expression evaluates to true, statement 1 and statement 2 execute. If not, they don't.

else

else extends the if statement. It specifies code to execute if the conditional expression evaluates to false:

```
if (conditional expression) {
    statement 1;
    statement 2;
}
else {
    statement 3;
    statement 4;
}
```

Another Kind of *if*

Sometimes a program has to set the value of a variable as the result of evaluating a conditional expression. Here's a shorthand way to do this:

```
variableName = (conditional expression) ?
➥ firstValue : secondValue
```

If the conditional expression evaluates to true, firstValue is set as the value of variableName. If the conditional expression evaluates to false, secondValue is set as the value of variableName.

MAKING CODE REPEAT

Like VBScript, JavaScript provides a set of options for making code repeat.

for

The for loop is a fundamental way to make code repeat. Here's the format:

```
for (starting expression; conditional expression;
➡ update expression) {
    code that runs if the conditional expression
➡ evaluates to true
}
```

Here, for example, is a for example:

```
<HTML>
<HEAD>
<SCRIPT>
function forExample() {
    for (i = 0; i < 10; i++) {
        document.forms[0].elements[0].value =
        document.forms[0].elements[0].value + "\ n" +
            "the value of i is: " + i;
    }
}
</SCRIPT>
<TITLE> </TITLE>
</HEAD>
<BODY onload = forExample()>
<FORM>
<TEXTAREA Rows = 15 Cols = 30>
</TEXTAREA>
</FORM>
</BODY>
</HTML>
```

If you were to open this file (we'll call it forExample.htm for future reference) in Navigator or in IE, you would see

```
the value of i is: 0
the value of i is: 1
the value of i is: 2
the value of i is: 3
the value of i is: 4
the value of i is: 5
```

```
the value of i is: 6
the value of i is: 7
the value of i is: 8
the value of i is: 9
```

in the TEXTAREA. As you can see, the for loop stops executing when i gets to 10 because the conditional expression i < 10 is no longer true.

NOTE

If the expression document.forms[0].elements[0].value looks strange to you, refer to the "Browser Objects" section in Chapter 4.

while

The while loop is another frequently used way of repeating code. The general format is:

```
while (conditional expression) {
    code that executes while the
        ➥ conditional expression is true
}
```

To produce the same output as in the for example, the SCRIPT should look like this if you're using while:

```
<SCRIPT>
var i = 0;
function whileExample() {
    while (i < 10) {
        document.forms[0].elements[0].value =
        document.forms[0].elements[0].value + "\ n" +
            "the value of i is: " + i;
        i++;
    }
}
</SCRIPT>
```

And change the <BODY> tag to:

```
<BODY onload = whileExample()>
```

do while

The do while loop, new in JavaScript 1.2, guarantees that code will execute at least once. In this loop, the conditional expression appears after the code to be executed:

```
do {
    code to execute
}
.while (conditional expression)
```

The code in do executes, and control then moves to while. If the conditional expression evaluates to true, control moves back to do. The process continues until the conditional expression evaluates to false.

To use this type of loop to produce the output in the for example, the SCRIPT is:

```
<SCRIPT>
var i = 0;
function dowhileExample() {
    do {
        document.forms[0].elements[0].value =
        document.forms[0].elements[0].value + "\ n" +
            "the value of i is: " + i;
        i++;
    }
    while (i < 10)
}
```

Change the <BODY> tag to:

```
<BODY onload = dowhileExample()>
```

A Special *for* Loop

JavaScript provides for...in, a for loop that enables you to examine the properties of an object or the elements of an array. The format is

```
for property in object {
code to execute
}
```

To show you how this loop works, here's an exercise that combines some of the knowledge you acquired in this chapter. You're going to create a page that IE and Navigator can both open. The particular browser that opens it will determine the page heading. The script will use the for...in loop to access the properties of the browser's window object, and the document.write method will display those properties and any defined values.

In your text editor, create a page called forinExample.htm. In the HEAD element, create a SCRIPT, and in the SCRIPT element type

```
function forinExample() {

}
```

The first part of the function is a switch statement. The test expression for the switch is the window.navigator.appName property. The switch statement works in conjunction with the case statement, covered previously. It evaluates an expression and attempts to match it to a set of case labels. For more information about the window.navigator.appName object, refer to "Browser Objects" in Chapter 4. This property holds a string that indicates which browser opened the page. The case statements use the document.write method to put an appropriate header on the Web page:

```
switch (window.navigator.appName) {
    case "Microsoft Internet Explorer" :
        document.write("<CENTER><H1>IE Window Object
Properties</H1><HR></CENTER><BR>");
        break;
    case "Netscape" :
        document.write("<CENTER>
➡ <H1>Navigator Window Object
    Properties</H1><HR></CENTER><BR>");
        break;
    default :
        break;
}
```

Next, we set up the for...in loop that accesses the window object's properties and displays them on the page:

```
var property;

for (property in window) {
    document.write("The " + property +
➡ " of window is: " +
    window[property] + "<BR>")
    }

}
```

The expression window[property] takes advantage of the JavaScript equivalence between object.property and the array reference object["property"] that I mentioned earlier in the section on arrays. Notice that we use the concatenation operator along with the HTML <BR> tag. This is like concatenating "\ n" at the end of a string—it will cause the next result to appear on the next line in the display.

Add the appropriate HTML:

```
<TITLE>Accessing the Window Object</TITLE>
</HEAD>
<BODY onload = forinExample()>
</BODY>
</HTML>
```

In the <BODY> tag, the inline call to forinExample() starts things off when the page loads.

Figure 2.1 shows this page in IE, and Figure 2.2 shows the page in Navigator.

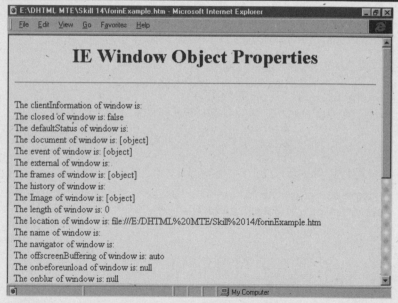

FIGURE 2.1: forinExample.htm in IE shows the properties of the IE window object.

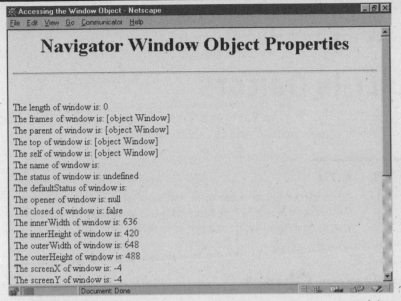

FIGURE 2.2: `forinExample.htm` in Navigator shows the properties of the Navigator window object.

Note the different headings in the pages. Also, you'll see how the properties of the `window` object differ between the two browsers. Not all the properties will have values, but it's still an instructive exercise.

break and *continue*

JavaScript provides mechanisms for getting out of a loop and for advancing to the next iteration of a loop. The break statement, which you saw in the section on `switch`, immediately moves control outside of a loop. `continue` moves to the next iteration.

A quick modification to `forExample.htm` provides an example of `continue`:

```
function forExample() {
    for (i = 0; i < 10; i++) {
        if (i % 2 == 0) { continue}
        document.forms[0].elements[0].value =
        document.forms[0].elements[0].value + "\ n" +
            "the value of i is: " + i;
    }
}
```

The `if` statement tests the remainder of dividing `i` by 2. If the remainder is 0, `continue` advances to the next iteration of the `for` loop. The net effect is to display only odd values of `i`.

Built-In Objects

In JavaScript, `String`, `Date`, and `Math` are objects built into the language. Each of these objects provides useful methods.

NOTE

All JavaScript objects have three methods: `eval`, which evaluates a string of JavaScript code; `toString`, which converts an object to a string; and `valueOf`, which converts an object to a primitive value.

The *String* Object

The `String` object provides a full set of methods for manipulating strings, as shown in Table 2.8.

TABLE 2.8: Methods of the String Object

Method	What It Does
`anchor(name)`	Turns the string into an HTML anchor tag, using name as the anchor's name
`big()`	Changes the string's text to a big font
`blink()`	Changes the string's text to a blinking font
`bold()`	Changes the string's text to a bold font
`charAt(index)`	Finds the character in the string at the (zero-based) index position
`fixed()`	Changes the string's text to a fixed-pitch font
`fontcolor(color)`	Changes the string's text to a specified color

CONTINUED →

TABLE 2.8 continued: Methods of the String Object

METHOD	WHAT IT DOES
fontsize()	Changes the string's text to a specified size
indexOf(character,from)	Searches the string for the first occurrence of character, returning its position in the string. You can optionally start the search at from.
italics()	Changes the string's text to italics
lastIndexOf(character,from)	Searches backward through the string to find the last occurrence of character
link(href)	Turns the string into an HTML link tag, with href as the anchor name
small()	Changes the string's text to a small font
split(sep)	Returns an array created by splitting the string into separate sections at each occurrence of the string sep
strike()	Changes the string's text to a strikethrough font
sub()	Changes the string's text to a subscript font
substring(start,finish)	Returns a substring of the string beginning at start and ending at finish
sup()	Changes the string's text to a superscript font
toLowerCase()	Changes the string's text to lowercase
toUpperCase()	Changes the string's text to uppercase

How do you use these methods? Here's an exercise to show you. You're going to create a JavaScript function that incorporates some of these methods and uses the document.write() method to display the results on a Web page.

In your text editor, create a SCRIPT element that initializes a new string:

```
var s = new String("DHTML Master the Essentials");
```

Next, start a function called stringThings that takes an argument called stringName. This argument will hold a string:

```
function stringThings(stringName) {
```

Eventually, we'll call stringThings with s as the argument.

Have the first line of the function use document.write() to display the string:

```
document.write(stringName + "<BR>");
```

Now we'll add three lines. The first italicizes the string,

```
document.write(stringName.italics() + "<BR>");
```

the second makes it bold,

```
document.write(stringName.bold() + "<BR>");
```

and the third shows how you can put methods together to produce a composite result:

```
document.write(stringName.bold().italics().fontsize(25) +
"<BR>");
```

That last line makes the string bold and italic, and gives it a font size of 25 pixels.

Now let's turn the string into an array. This line breaks up the string wherever a space occurs and displays the resulting segments as the items in an array:

```
document.write(stringName.split(" ") + "<BR>");
```

This line forms the array and sorts the array-items:

```
document.write(stringName.split(" ").sort() + "<BR>");
```

This line forms the array and reverses the order of the array-items:

```
document.write(stringName.split(" ").reverse() + "<BR>");
```

Finally, add a line that returns and displays a substring. This expression will give you a surprising result, as you'll see in a moment:

```
document.write(stringName.substring(1,4) + "<BR>");
```

Finish off the function and the SCRIPT element:

```
}
</SCRIPT>
```

Add this HTML:

```
<TITLE>String Things</TITLE>
```

```
</HEAD>
<BODY onload = stringThings(s)>
</BODY>
</HTML>
```

The in-line function call in <BODY> activates stringThings() when the page opens. It calls the function with s as the argument, and s is the newly created string "DHTML Master the Essentials".

Here's the whole stringThings.htm file:

Listing 2.1: stringThings.htm

```
<HTML>
<HEAD>
<SCRIPT>
var s = new String("DHTML Master the Essentials");
function stringThings(stringName) {
    document.write(stringName + "<BR>");
    document.write(stringName.italics() + "<BR>");
    document.write(stringName.bold() + "<BR>");
    document.write(stringName.bold().italics().fontsize(25)
+ "<BR>");
    document.write(stringName.split(" ") + "<BR>");
    document.write(stringName.split(" ").sort() + "<BR>");
    document.write(stringName.split(" ").reverse() +
"<BR>");
    document.write(stringName.substring(1,4) + "<BR>");
}
</SCRIPT>
<TITLE>String Things</TITLE>
</HEAD>
<BODY onload = stringThings(s)>
</BODY>
</HTML>
```

Figure 2.3 shows the page in IE. (It looks the same in Navigator.)

Note the lines that display arrays. In each array, the items appear in a comma-delimited list.

The last line shows that surprising result I mentioned. With the arguments to substring set at 1 and 4, you would expect the function to return HTML. Instead, it returns HTM.

NOTE

You would see a quirky little difference between IE and Navigator if you were to go into the `stringThings.htm` file and delete + `"<BR>"` from the final `document.write()`. You could then reopen the page in IE and see all the `document.write()` results displayed, or you could reopen the page in Navigator and see that the final `document.write()` doesn't appear.

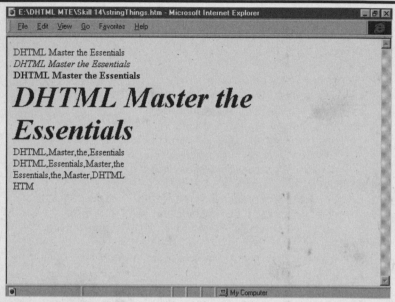

FIGURE 2.3: `stringThings.htm` in IE shows the results of applying String methods.

The *Math* Object

The JavaScript `Math` object has methods that you can use to build calculations into your scripts. Table 2.9 shows these methods.

TABLE 2.9: Methods of the Math Object

METHOD	RETURNS...
abs()	A number's absolute value

CONTINUED ➡

TABLE 2.9 continued: Methods of the Math Object

METHOD	RETURNS...
acos()	A number's arc cosine in radians
asin()	A number's arc sine in radians
atan()	A number's arc tangent in radians
ceil()	An integer equal to or immediately above a number
cos()	A number's cosine
exp()	e to a specified power
floor()	An integer equal to or immediately below a number
log()	A number's natural logarithm
max()	The larger of two numbers
min()	The lesser of two numbers
pow()	The value of a base to a specified power
random()	A pseudo-random number between 0 and 51
round()	A number rounded to the nearest integer
sin()	A number's sine
sqrt()	A number's square root
tan()	A number's tangent

Here are some examples that show how to use these methods:

```
var x, y, z;
y = Math.sqrt(x);
z = Math.pow(x,y);
x = Math.random();
```

The Math object has some useful properties—constants that can come in handy. Table 2.10 presents these properties.

TABLE 2.10: Properties of the Math Object

PROPERTY	MEANING	APPROXIMATE VALUE
E	Base of natural logarithms	2.718
LN2	Natural logarithm of 2	0.693
LN10	Natural logarithm of 10	2.302
LOG2E	Logarithm of e to base 2	1.442
LOG10E	Logarithm of 10 to base 2	0.434
PI	Ratio of circumference of a circle to its diameter	3.1416
SQRT1_2	Square root of .5	0.707
SQRT2	Square root of 2	1.414

The *Date* Object

The JavaScript Date object gives you the capabilities for working with times and dates. Table 2.11 shows its methods.

TABLE 2.11: Methods of the Date Object

METHOD	WHAT IT DOES
getDate()	Returns the day of the month in the Date object
getDay()	Returns the day of the week
getHours()	Returns the hours
getMinutes()	Returns the minutes

CONTINUED ➡

TABLE 2.11 continued: Methods of the Date Object

METHOD	WHAT IT DOES
getMonth()	Returns the month
getSeconds()	Returns the seconds
getTime()	Returns complete time
getTimeZoneOffset()	Returns the number of hours difference between Greenwich Mean Time and the time zone in the computer running the script
getYear()	Returns the year
parse()	Returns the number of milliseconds between the date and January 1, 1970 00:00:00
setDate()	Sets the Date object's day of the month
setHours()	Sets the hours
setMinutes()	Sets the minutes
setMonth()	Sets the month
setSeconds()	Sets the seconds
setTime()	Sets the complete time
setYear()	Sets the year
toGMTString()	Changes the Date object's date into a string in Greenwich Mean Time
toLocalString()	Changes the Date object's date into a string
UTC()	Returns a date in terms of the number of milliseconds since January 1, 1970 00:00:00

Part i

ALERTING, CONFIRMING, AND PROMPTING

We end this discussion of JavaScript with a look at three boxes that JavaScript provides for communicating with the user. These boxes are analogous to VBScript's MsgBox.

The first, alert, presents a message and a button, as shown in Figure 2.4.

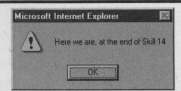

FIGURE 2.4: The JavaScript alert box presents a message and a button referencing Skill 14 from *Dynamic HTML: Master the Essentials*.

The second, confirm, presents a message and two buttons, as shown in Figure 2.5.

FIGURE 2.5: The confirm box presents a message and two buttons.

Finally, as shown in Figure 2.6, the prompt box presents a message, a text box for user entry, two buttons, and a wide area.

FIGURE 2.6: The prompt box presents a message referencing the skills from *Dynamic HTML: Master the Essentials*, a text area for user data entry, and two buttons.

SUMMARY

JavaScript is a very rich scripting language. It provides a wealth of control structures, operators, built-in functions, objects, and flexibility. Some say that if you learn JavaScript, you'll have a leg up if you then try to learn Java. I'm not sure this is true, but one thing's certain: Mastering JavaScript will give you control over objects that bring a Web page to life.

NOTE

For more information on the Netscape version of JavaScript, visit http://developer.netscape.com/library/documentation/communicator/jsguide4/index.htm **and** http://developer.netscape.com/library/documentation/communicator/jsref/index.htm. **For more information on the Microsoft version, visit** http://www.microsoft.com/jscript/us/jslang/jstoc.htm **and** http://www.microsoft.com/jscript/us/jstutor/jstutor.htm.

Part i

CHAPTER 3

ADDING JAVASCRIPT

U sing JavaScript, you can add some pizzazz to your pages, taking them from ho-hum pages to ones that react to visitor actions, process and check information that visitors provide, and even deliver information appropriate to each visitor. With the increasingly sophisticated nature of the Web, you often need these kinds of attractions to hold visitors' attention and to keep them coming back.

Adapted from *Mastering HTML 4: Premium Edition*, by Deborah S. Ray and Eric J. Ray

ISBN 0-7821-2524-7   1,216 pages $49.99

For example, you can use JavaScript to change a button's color when the mouse cursor moves over it. This draws visitors' eyes to the button and indicates that they can follow this link to something new. Or, you can display a message in the status bar to give visitors more information about the link, such as "Follow this to our new catalog!" Highlighted links help visitors know what to expect at the end of the link.

You can also use JavaScript to validate forms before visitors submit them. For example, you can use JavaScript to ensure that a visitor completes an e-mail field before actually submitting the form, as shown in Figure 3.1. In addition, you can use JavaScript to change images based on visitor action or to provide fancy, form-based navigation links.

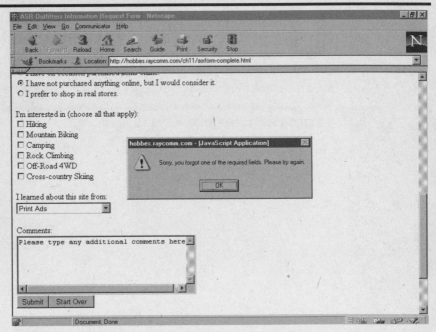

FIGURE 3.1: You can use JavaScript to validate form input.

In this chapter, we'll look at what JavaScript is and how to use it, and, with some examples, we'll show you how to include JavaScript scripts in your HTML documents. We'll start with simple scripts and then build on them. We will concentrate on basic JavaScript capabilities (JavaScript 1.1 and some of 1.2 and 1.3), which is a good compromise between high functionality and broad browser acceptance.

ADDING JAVASCRIPT TO YOUR DOCUMENT

You can add JavaScript to your page in three ways:

- ▶ Embed the JavaScript in the page.
- ▶ Place the JavaScript in the document head.
- ▶ Link to JavaScript stored in another file.

TIP

The options for placing JavaScript closely resemble the options for placing Style Sheets.

Table 3.1 lists and describes the HTML tags and attributes you use to add a JavaScript script.

TABLE 3.1: JavaScript Tags and Attributes

TAG/ATTRIBUTE	DESCRIPTION
<SCRIPT>	Identifies the script section in the document.
LANGUAGE="JavaScript"	Specifies the scripting language. This attribute is deprecated but often used.
TYPE="text/javascript"	Provides the script MIME type.
SRC="..."	Optionally specifies the location of an external script.
<NOSCRIPT>	Provides content for nonscript-capable browsers.
<!-- //-->	Comment tags hide the contents of the script from nonscript-capable browsers.

Embedding JavaScript

If you're adding a fairly short JavaScript script, your best bet is to embed it in the HTML document, in the code that the JavaScript affects. For example, you can embed a JavaScript script that adds the current date to your document because this particular script is only a few lines long.

Embedding works like this: When visitors open your page, their browser "reads" your HTML source document line by line. If your HTML code includes JavaScript within the document body, the browser performs the actions as it reads the page. For example, if the <BODY> tag includes a JavaScript script, the first task the browser completes is running the script. Or, if you include a JavaScript script in the first actual text of the document, the browser runs the script as soon as it gets to the text.

Let's embed a JavaScript script that prints the current time and date as the page loads. The JavaScript statement—in this case, the whole script—is document.write(Date()). Here are the steps:

1. Start with the following HTML code:

```
<!DOCTYPE HTML PUBLIC
 "-//W3C//DTD HTML 4.0-Transitional//EN">
<HTML>
<HEAD>
<TITLE>The Date Page</TITLE>
</HEAD>
<BODY>
<H1>Welcome!</H1>
</BODY>
</HTML>
```

2. Add an introductory sentence, like this:

```
<!DOCTYPE HTML PUBLIC
 "-//W3C//DTD HTML 4.0-Transitional//EN">
<HTML>
<HEAD>
<TITLE>The Date Page</TITLE>
</HEAD>
<BODY>
<H1>Welcome!</H1>
<P>Today's date is:
</P>
</BODY>
</HTML>
```

3. Add <SCRIPT> tags where you want the script:

```
<BODY>
```

```
<H1>Welcome!</H1>
<P>Today's date is:
<SCRIPT>

</SCRIPT>
</P>
```

4. Add the TYPE= attribute to specify the script's MIME type:

```
<BODY>
<H1>Welcome!</H1>
<P>Today's date is:
<SCRIPT TYPE="text/javascript">

</SCRIPT>
</P>
```

5. Add comment tags to hide the script from browsers that do not recognize scripting. Include the standard HTML comment tags (<!-- and -->), and preface the closing HTML comment tag with a // to hide the comment from the JavaScript interpreter. The complete comment tag looks like this:

```
<BODY>
<H1>Welcome!</H1>
<P>Today's date is:
<SCRIPT TYPE="text/javascript">
<!--
// -->
</SCRIPT>
</P>
```

6. Add the actual JavaScript statement:

```
<SCRIPT TYPE="text/javascript">
<!--
document.write(Date());
// -->
</SCRIPT>
```

That's it! The resulting page looks like this:

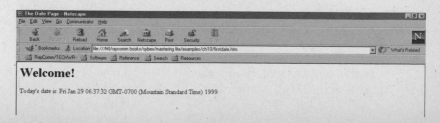

Using this method, the initial "Today's date is" text appears in all browsers, regardless of whether they support JavaScript. Browsers that don't support JavaScript display Today's Date Is and a blank. To hide the script from browsers that don't support JavaScript, simply replace the JavaScript statement as shown in the following code. In this way, visitors will either see it or not, but they won't see a lead-in with an unfulfilled promise. You get the same effect in JavaScript-capable browsers and nothing at all in non-JavaScript browsers.

```
<SCRIPT TYPE="text/javascript">
<!--
document.write("Today's date is: " + Date());
// -->
</SCRIPT>
```

You are not restricted to a single JavaScript statement, and you can embed several statements through the page source. These additional statements display information about the visitor's browser in the document:

```
<!DOCTYPE HTML PUBLIC
➡ "-//W3C//DTD HTML 4.0-Transitional//EN">
<HTML>
<HEAD>
<TITLE>The Date Page</TITLE>
</HEAD>
<BODY>
<H1>Welcome!</H1>
<P>
<SCRIPT TYPE="text/javascript">
<!--
document.write("Today's date is: " + Date());
// -->
</SCRIPT>
</P>
<P>
<SCRIPT TYPE="text/javascript">
<!--
document.write("You appear to be using " + navigator.appName
➡ + " version " +        navigator.appVersion + ".")
// -->
</SCRIPT></P>

</BODY>
</HTML>
```

In this script as well, the JavaScript is interpreted line by line as it appears in the HTML source. In the new statement, the text strings, such as "You appear to be using" and "version," are combined with properties of the navigator object—that is, with characteristics of the browser—to display the line shown. The resulting page from this example looks like this:

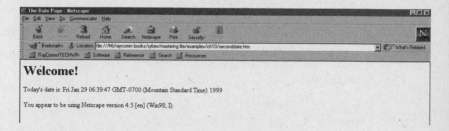

Embedding is a great way to start adding JavaScript to your page. You can use this technique alone or combine it with others.

TIP

If you choose to embed the JavaScript, you'll need to provide for older browsers that don't support it.

Adding a JavaScript Block in the *<HEAD>*

If you repeatedly use JavaScript within documents, consider placing it in the document <HEAD> tag. Collecting individual statements in one place creates a function; creating functions in the <HEAD> tag is convenient and easy to troubleshoot.

In the following examples, we'll show you how to move the JavaScript statements in the preceding example from the body of the document into the document head. Here's the code to start with:

```
<!DOCTYPE HTML PUBLIC
"-//W3C//DTD HTML 4.0-Transitional//EN">
<HTML>
<HEAD>
<TITLE>The Date Page</TITLE>
</HEAD>
<BODY>
<H1>Welcome!</H1>
<P>
<SCRIPT TYPE="text/javascript">
<!--
document.write("Today's date is: " + Date());
```

```
// -->
</SCRIPT>
</P>
<P>
<SCRIPT TYPE="text/javascript">
<!--
document.write("You appear to be using " + navigator.appName
➡ + " version " +      navigator.appVersion + ".")
// -->
</SCRIPT></P>

</BODY>
</HTML>
```

This HTML document includes two JavaScript sections. One displays the current date and time, and the other displays the name and version number of the visitor's browser. You include the command in the document <HEAD> tag and then run the function from the document body. Here are the steps:

1. Add the <script> tags to the document <HEAD>, like this:

```
<HEAD>
<TITLE>The Date Page</TITLE>
<SCRIPT>

</SCRIPT>
</HEAD>
```

2. Add the TYPE= attribute to specify that the script is a JavaScript:

```
<HEAD>
<TITLE>The Date Page</TITLE>
<SCRIPT TYPE="text/javascript">

</SCRIPT>
</HEAD>
```

3. Add comment tags (<!– //–>) to hide the script from other browsers. Don't forget the //!

```
<HEAD>
<TITLE>The Date Page</TITLE>
<SCRIPT TYPE="text/javascript">
<!--

// -->
</SCRIPT>
</HEAD>
```

Remember, we're putting the script in the document head, so it will not display anything in the browser window. You have to place instructions within the document body to do anything with the script.

4. To make the JavaScript statement that displays the date into a function, name it and place it in inside brackets ({ }). In this example, the name is `printDate`. Add the function name (`printDate`) and { }.

```
<SCRIPT TYPE="text/javascript">
<!--
function printDate() { }
// -->
</SCRIPT>
```

5. Add the JavaScript statement within the brackets. Use what you used within the document body, which was `document.write("Today's date is: " + Date());`.

```
<SCRIPT TYPE="text/javascript">
<!--
function printDate() {document.write("Today\ 's date is:
➨ " + Date());}
// -->
</SCRIPT>
```

6. To call (activate or run) the function from the document body, add your <SCRIPT> tags within the <BODY> tags, as shown here:

```
<BODY>
<H1>Welcome!</H1>
<P>
<SCRIPT TYPE="text/javascript">
<!--

// -->
</SCRIPT>
</P>
</BODY>
```

7. Add `printDate()`, which is the name you gave the function, within the tags.

```
<BODY>
<H1>Welcome!</H1>
<P>
<SCRIPT TYPE="text/javascript">
<!--
printDate()
```

```
// -->
</SCRIPT>
</P>
</BODY>
```

The resulting page looks similar to the following:

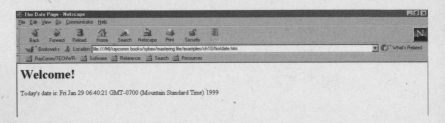

TIP

If you separate the JavaScript script into its own section, enclose it with comment marks <!-- and //-->. Not all browsers can interpret JavaScript, and the comment marks instruct these browsers to ignore the JavaScript section. JavaScript-enabled browsers will see past the comment marks and recognize the <SCRIPT> tags.

Linking JavaScript

If you plan to use script functions in several documents, consider placing them in a separate file, and refer to that file from your document. You can build, test, and store working JavaScript code in one location and use it in several Web pages. You can also share this code with others who can link it into their documents.

The linked document is simply a text file that includes all your variable definitions and functions. You can even copy the functions from the headers of your existing HTML documents if you want. If this document also includes variables and functions that you don't need for the Web page, the browser uses what it needs, as it is called.

To continue with our date example, you can make a functions.js document that contains the following text:

```
function printDate() {  document.write(Date()) }
```

This linked document does not need any special headings or tags. It simply includes the definitions for the variables and functions. You can then link to the script with the following code from the document <HEAD> (including all the surrounding tags):

```
<HEAD>
<TITLE>The Date Page</TITLE>
<SCRIPT SRC="functions.js" TYPE="text/javascript">
<!--
// -->
</SCRIPT>
</HEAD>
```

Now, by including this reference to your functions document, you can access any functions from any document you create.

You can include as many functions or variable definitions within your functions document as you like. Alternatively, you can reference multiple external scripts by including additional <SCRIPT> tags.

Providing for Older Browsers

As you add JavaScript to your pages, you must accommodate older browsers that cannot interpret JavaScript, as well as browsers in which JavaScript is not enabled. If you include a JavaScript script in the <HEAD> tag or if you link the JavaScript script from a separate document, you've already provided for older browsers because these don't show up in the document body.

If you embed the JavaScript script, however, you must make sure the script doesn't show up. The best way to accommodate older browsers is to make sure that text dependent on the JavaScript (such as "Today's date is") is part of the JavaScript statement. You might recall from the example that the embedded code looks like this:

```
<SCRIPT TYPE="text/javascript">
<!--
document.write("Today\'s date is: " + Date());
// -->
</SCRIPT>
```

However, if you want to give additional information to script-incapable browsers (rather than just hiding information from them), you can also use the <NOSCRIPT> tag and include alternative text. For example, if you have a form that uses JavaScript to validate input, you might add a statement to the top of the form, within a <NOSCRIPT> tag, that warns users of

non-JavaScript browsers that their responses won't be validated and that
they should be particularly careful to proofread their responses:

```
<H2>Personal Information Form</H2>
<NOSCRIPT>
<P>Please be very careful to proofread your responses.
➡ If any information is incorrect (particularly your
➡ e-mail address), we'll be unable to contact you.
➡ </P></NOSCRIPT>
Please enter your name and address below:<BR>
```

In this example, the JavaScript-enabled browser displays only the Personal Information Form heading, followed by "Please enter your name
and address below"; other browsers will also display the "Please be very
careful to proofread your responses. If any information is incorrect (particularly your e-mail address), we'll be unable to contact you."

For a small amount of JavaScript or for JavaScript that isn't essential
to the content of your document, using the <NOSCRIPT> tag is a convenient way to deal with both situations. If you have more complex
JavaScript applications on your page, you'll need to identify visitors'
browsers and automatically direct them to the correct page.

TIP

See Matt's Script Archive on the Web at www.worldwidemart.com/scripts/
for server-side means of identifying browsers and redirecting them appropriately.

ADDING EVENT HANDLERS

JavaScript relies heavily on event handlers, which react to visitor actions
by running statements or calling JavaScript functions. Event handlers
provide visitors with additional information by reacting to what they're
doing on the page—moving their mouse, clicking a button, or selecting
options on a form. JavaScript's event handlers react to these events by
doing whatever you tell them to do. For example, with the onMouseOver
and onMouseOut event handlers, you can change the information in your
status bar, flash an alert box, or change an illustration. Figure 3.2 shows
an alert box triggered by an onMouseOver event.

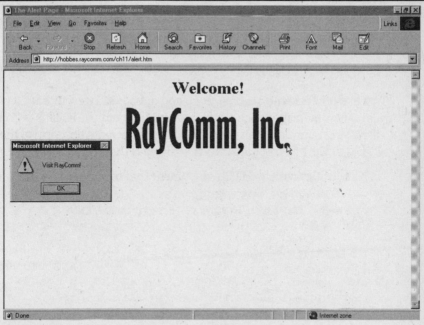

FIGURE 3.2: One of the most common JavaScript event handlers is onMouseOver.

NOTE

JavaScript provides a variety of event handlers that can react to visitor actions. In this chapter, however, we discuss only a couple of them.

Using *onMouseOver* and *onMouseOut* Events

You commonly use an onMouseOver event with anchor tags (<A>) to provide additional information about the link. The onMouseOut event, then, generally undoes what the onMouseOver event does.

Using these event handlers, you can, among other things, implement timed status bar events, swap images, and alert visitors. We'll show you how in the next few sections. First, though, let's look at how to add the onMouseOver and onMouseOut event handlers.

TIP

Unfortunately, neither Internet Explorer 3 or earlier nor Netscape Navigator 2 or earlier recognize the onMouseOut event. If your visitors use these browsers, consider using a separate function to clear the status bar, as described below.

Let's now add the onMouseOver and onMouseOut event handlers to display a new message in the status bar and then remove it. This is handy for displaying information in the status bar that is more descriptive than the URL that the browser automatically displays there. Here are the steps:

1. Start with an HTML document that includes a link, like this:

   ```
   <!DOCTYPE HTML PUBLIC
   ➥ "-//W3C//DTD HTML 4.0-Transitional//EN">
   <HTML>
   <HEAD>
   <TITLE>Status Bar</TITLE>
   </HEAD>
   <BODY>
   <H1>Welcome!</H1>
   <A HREF="http://www.raycomm.com/">
   Visit the RayComm, Inc., site.</A>
   <P>
   </BODY>
   </HTML>
   ```

2. Add the onMouseOver event handler to the <A> tag:

   ```
   <A HREF="http://www.raycomm.com/" onMouseOver=" ">
   Visit the RayComm, Inc., site.</A>
   ```

3. Add window.status= to the event handler. The window.status= property specifies what appears in the status bar.

   ```
   <A HREF="http://www.raycomm.com/"
   ➥ onMouseOver="window.status= ">
   Visit the RayComm, Inc., site.</A>
   ```

4. Add the text that will appear in the status bar, enclosed in single quotes (' '). You use single quotes because the window status statement itself is enclosed in double quotes, and you must nest unlike quotes within each other.

   ```
   <A HREF="http://www.raycomm.com/"
   ➥ onMouseOver="window.status='Check us out!' ">
   Visit the RayComm, Inc., site.</A>
   ```

5. Add a semicolon (to indicate the end of the statement), and add return true to the end (just before the closing quotes).

This essentially tells the JavaScript interpreter that the function is complete and to do it.

```
<A HREF="http://www.raycomm.com/"
➡ onMouseOver="window.status='Check us out!';
➡ return true">
Visit the RayComm, Inc., site.</A>
```

If you try this, you'll see that the "Check us out!" statement appears in the browser status bar after you move the cursor over the link. The statement stays in the status bar, which probably isn't what you want.

To restore the status bar after the cursor moves away from the link, simply add the onMouseOut event handler, like this:

```
<A HREF="http://www.raycomm.com/"
onMouseOver="window.status='Check us out!'; return true"
onMouseOut="window.status=''; return true">
Visit the RayComm, Inc., site.</A>
```

Using Timed Status Bar Text Events

JavaScript includes a timer method that allows you to set up timed events. For example, you can use it in conjunction with the onMouseOver event handler to display the status bar text for a period of time and then clear it. Although the timer is a bit more complicated than the onMouseOut event handler, it is more universal. It keeps the status bar text you set from remaining in the status bar, even with older browsers. More browsers will understand the timer method than will understand the onMouseOut event handler.

In general, the function we need to clear the status bar text should do two things:

▶ Set the status bar text to a specific text string.

▶ Wait for a specified time, and then clear the status bar again.

Because this function is slightly more involved than resetting the status bar onMouseOver event, we create the script in the document head, as shown earlier in this chapter. Here's how:

1. In an HTML document, add the <SCRIPT> and comment tags in the document head:

```
<!DOCTYPE HTML PUBLIC
➡ "-//W3C//DTD HTML 4.0-Transitional//EN">
<HTML>
<HEAD>
```

```
<TITLE>Status Bar</TITLE>
<SCRIPT TYPE="text/javascript">
<!--

// -->
</SCRIPT>
</HEAD>
<BODY>
<H1>Welcome!</H1>
<A HREF="http://www.raycomm.com/">
Visit the RayComm, Inc., site.</A>
<P>
</BODY>
</HTML>
```

2. Name the function SalesPitch and add the needed brackets:

```
<SCRIPT>
<!--
function SalesPitch() {  }
//-->
</SCRIPT>
```

3. Add the window.status statement to set the status bar. The return true won't strictly be needed, but it also won't hurt anything and might be useful later

```
<SCRIPT>
<!--
function SalesPitch() {
    window.status="Check us out!"; return true;
}
//-->
</SCRIPT>
```

4. Add the new method, setTimeout. Within the parentheses, the first parameter sets the window status to null (' '), and the second specifies to wait 3000 milliseconds (3 seconds). The return true is, in this case, needed to tell the Java-Script interpreter that it's done.

```
<SCRIPT>
<!--
function SalesPitch() {
    window.status="Check us out!";
    setTimeout("window.status=''",3000); return true;
}
//-->
</SCRIPT>
```

That's it! With this SalesPitch script in the document header, you need only call the script from the link in the document with an onMouseOver statement, as shown here.

```
<A HREF="http://www.raycomm.com/"
➥ onMouseOver="SalesPitch(); return true">
```

The `return true` business at the end serves only to tell the JavaScript interpreter that the statement is done and that the interpreter should act on it. In this example, the function displays the required text in the status bar, waits 3 seconds, and then clears the status bar.

NOTE

In most of these examples, we show fairly generic JavaScript. If you are using objects, methods, properties, or event handlers from early versions of JavaScript, you don't need to add the version to the JavaScript language attribute. But, if you are using a later version with expanded capabilities, such as onMouseOut, and functions are defined in the document, include the number within the `<SCRIPT>` tags, as in LANGUAGE= "JavaScript1.2".

TIP

Add comments to your JavaScript to track what the script does. This is useful for future reference and helpful to people with whom you share your JavaScript functions. Add your name and the name of your JavaScript to the document source.

ADDING A LITTLE EXCITEMENT TO THE PAGE LOAD

Just as events can respond to a visitor's mouse actions, events can occur when the page loads or unloads. However, anything time consuming (such as playing a sound) or intrusive (such as displaying a welcome alert) can irritate visitors far more than impress them with your technical skills.

We suggest that you perform actions with the onLoad or onUnload events only if visitors will expect it in the context of the page or for other reasons.

Swapping Images

You can use the onMouseOver and onMouseOut event handlers to change linked images when the mouse cursor moves over them.

WARNING

Unfortunately, this technique works only with Netscape Navigator 3 or later and Internet Explorer 4 or later. Older browsers don't recognize images as objects.

To change an image when the mouse moves over it, you need an anchor tag (<A HREF="...">) and two versions of the image—one is the standard presentation, and the other is the highlighted presentation. When the page initially loads, the standard image is visible. Then, when the mouse moves over the image, the highlighted image replaces the standard image. Finally, when the mouse cursor moves away again, the images change back. Conceptually, the process is the same as changing the status bar text in the preceding example; however, instead of changing the status bar, you swap images.

To set up images to swap, you first need a pair of images that are precisely the same size but visually different.

Next, you need a link using an image in your document. The image tag must also have a NAME= attribute so that JavaScript can identify and refer to it. We'll use the following sample document:

```
<!DOCTYPE HTML PUBLIC
 "-//W3C//DTD HTML 4.0-Transitional//EN">
<HTML>
<HEAD>
<TITLE>Image Swap</TITLE>
</HEAD>
<BODY BGCOLOR="FFFFFF" TEXT="000000" LINK="0000FF"
 VLINK="800080" ALINK="FF0000">
<CENTER>
<A HREF="http://www.raycomm.com/"><IMG SRC="image1.gif"
 WIDTH="50" HEIGHT="10" BORDER="0" NAME="catbtn"></A>
</CENTER>
</BODY>
</HTML>
```

Two images, cleverly titled image1.gif and image2.gif, are available to swap within the image tag, which is called catbtn. To identify the image, you refer to it by name (catbtn) and src, which is a property of the `catbtn` image object. For example, to change the image (but not change it back), you can use a statement such as the following:

```
onMouseOver="catbtn.src='image2.gif'; return true"
```

In the context of the `<IMG>` tag, the `onMouseOver` statement looks like this:

```
<A HREF="http://www.raycomm.com/"
➥ onMouseOver="catbtn.src='image2.gif'; return true">
<IMG SRC="image1.gif" WIDTH="50" HEIGHT="10" BORDER="0"
➥ NAME="catbtn"></A>
```

The `catbtn.src` changes the source property of the `catbtn` object to `image2.gif`; it had previously been set to `image1.gif`.

Similarly, to change the image back when the cursor moves away, use an `onMouseOut` statement with the opposite image setting, as shown here:

```
<A HREF="http://www.raycomm.com/"
➥ onMouseOver="catbtn.src='image2.gif'; return true"
➥ onMouseOut="catbtn.src='image1.gif'; return true">
<IMG SRC="image1.gif" WIDTH="50" HEIGHT="10" BORDER="0"
➥ NAME="catbtn"></A>
```

For a series of images, you use a series of `if` statements in a function to make the changes. Using `if` statements keeps your HTML code easier to read and makes it easier to change your script later. You can easily add more statements to reshuffle images in different contexts by using a function like this:

```
function switcher(place) {
if (place==1) document.catbtn.src="image2.gif";
if (place==2) document.catbtn.src="image1.gif";
}
```

The `if` statements check for the value of place and change the image accordingly. You call this function from the body of your document with code, as shown below. Instead of placing the full change function in the `<A>` tag, you place `switcher()` in the attribute value.

```
<A HREF="http://www.raycomm.com/">
<IMG SRC="image1.gif" ALIGN="" WIDTH="50" HEIGHT="10"
➥ BORDER="0" onMouseOver="switcher(1)" ALT="" NAME="catbtn"
➥ onMouseOut="switcher(2)">
</A>
```

If your visitors use the newest versions of Netscape Navigator or Internet Explorer and you want to do more—such as change the image and change the status bar—you can use a `switch` statement, as shown here:

```
function switcher(place) {
```

```
switch (place) {
    case(1): document.catbtn.src="image2.gif";
        window.status="Second Image";
        break;
    case(2): document.catbtn.src="image1.gif";
        window.status="First Image";
        break; } }
```

Using this technique, you can list all the options. Like the if statements above, the switch statement lists each option and the action to take. In a switch statement, each option is a case.

In this example, the first line calls the function and includes the number for the variable place. You use place in the switch statement, which has two cases. If place is equal to one, use case(1). Therefore, case(1) sets the source property for the image named catbtn (catbtn.src) to image2.gif. When you place an image element, you insert an HTML tag just as you do for the if statement:

```
<A HREF="http://www.raycomm.com/">
<IMG SRC="image1.gif" ALIGN="" WIDTH="50" HEIGHT="10"
➥ BORDER="0" onMouseOver="switcher(1)" ALT=""
➥ NAME="catbtn" onMouseOut="switcher(2)">
</A>
```

You may have noticed that the switch from the if statement switcher function to the case statement switcher function requires no changes within your HTML code. When you place JavaScript functions in the document head, you can make changes without editing all the tags in your code.

Using *onClick* and *onChange* Event Handlers

In addition to onMouseOver and onMouseOut event handlers, you can use onClick and onChange event handlers, which are activated when visitors click an object or a button or change a form field. Including these event handlers is similar to using the onMouseOver and onMouseOut event handlers. You can use the onChange or the onClick event handler to set link destinations in forms, among other things.

Alerting Visitors with *onClick*

A handy use for the onClick event is an alert box (see Figure 3.3), which is a small dialog box that contains a message and an OK button. For example, an alert could be an expanded note about the object, such as "Come to this page for more news on this year's programs!"

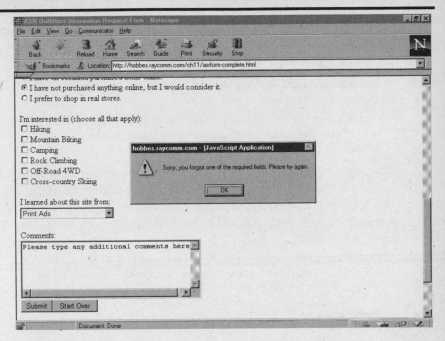

FIGURE 3.3: Alert boxes are a handy way to give visitors information.

At its simplest, you can combine an event handler (to start the process) with an alert, like this:

```
<IMG SRC="infolink.jpg" onClick="alert('Visit RayComm!');
➥ return true">
```

Visitors see the accompanying dialog box and must click OK to proceed. Alerts can be quite irritating, however, so use them only in conjunction with buttons or other actions so that visitors can make a conscious choice. For example, as shown in Figure 3.3, you can combine the alert with form validation information and base the alert pop-up on the visitor's form responses.

Setting Link Destinations in Forms

One of the handiest JavaScript functions is setting link destinations in forms to direct visitors to information based on their selections in the form. For example, if a form contains a Course Offered selection list, visitors can select courses that interest them, and you can programmatically set the destination of a jump to meet the needs of the selections. You can also use JavaScript to set destinations so that when your visitors click buttons or perform other actions on the page, the script opens new pages, just as a traditional link would. This technique can add visual interest to your pages as well as let you interactively produce new pages for your visitors.

Minimally, to set destinations and activate links, use the `onClick` event handler, as shown here.

```
<FORM><INPUT TYPE="radio" NAME="lesson" VALUE="Lesson 1"
➥ CHECKED onClick="self.location='lesson1.htm'">
➥ Lesson 1: Getting Started<BR></FORM>
```

The `self.location='someurl.htm'` entry opens the file `someurl.htm` in the same window when a visitor clicks the radio button. If you want the document to open in a separate window, the process is similar. For example, to open `lesson1.htm` in another frame, called `main`, you can use the following:

```
<INPUT TYPE="radio" NAME="lesson" VALUE="Lesson 1"
➥ CHECKED onClick=" parent.main.location='lesson1.htm'">
➥ Lesson 1: Getting Started
```

NOTE

The `parent.main.location` object name refers to the parent document (in this example, that would be the frameset document, then the `main` object [frame] within it, then the location property of the frame).

A single jump can also lead to a variable destination—the document opened depends on the visitor's selection from a list. For example, your document contains catalog information, such as pictures, product descriptions, and prices. A visitor clicks a category to open the correct page of your catalog. Visitors might also select activities from a list such as this.

```
<FORM>
<SELECT NAME="Activity"
➥ onChange="setLink(this.selectedIndex)">
    <OPTION>Hiking
    <OPTION>Camping
    <OPTION SELECTED>Mountain
    <OPTION>Sailing
    <OPTION>Winter
</SELECT>
</FORM>
```

The onChange event handler passes information to a function called setLink. The selectedIndex property is the position in the list (starting with zero!) of the current selection in the list. So, this.selectedIndex is the numeric value that represents the position in the current list of the value selected.

A relatively simple function setLink, located in the document head, assigns the final URL to the page properties and loads the new URL:

```
<SCRIPT>
function setLink(num) {
        if (num == 0) { self.location="hiking.html"}
        if (num == 1) { self.location="camping.html"}
        if (num == 2) { self.location="mountain.html"}
        if (num == 3) { self.location="sailing.html"}
        if (num == 4) { self.location="winter.html"}   }
</SCRIPT>
```

With this type of scripting, it's easier to figure out what's going on, it's easier to make changes later, and it's easier to accommodate unique, nonsequential names, such as newmountainbikes.html or augustactivities.html.

Using the *onSubmit* Event Handler

One of the most common uses for the onSubmit event handler is to validate form input. You can verify that visitors fill in required fields, that they make required selections, or that they fill in an appropriate combination of fields. Suppose you provide a form that lets visitors purchase a product, T-shirts. You can use JavaScript to verify that visitors include their mailing address, provide a credit card number, and specify a color. If you lack any of this input from visitors, you won't be able to complete the order.

The following examples, based on the ASR Outfitters general information form, show a couple of approaches to form validation. These examples assume a form with NAME="survey". If your form is named differently, please adjust accordingly. You can also substitute form[0] for the name of the first form within your page.

You can use the following generic script to loop through your form and check for forgotten or omitted values:

```
<script language="JavaScript">
<!--
function checkOut() {
for (x=0; x<document.survey.elements.length; x++){
        if (document.survey.elements[x].value == "") {
```

```
                    alert("Sorry, you forgot one of the required
➡ fields. Please  try  again.")
                    break;     }
                    }
              return false;
          }
   //-->
   </script>
```

To check your form, use onSubmit="checkout(this.form) in your
<FORM> tag. The script looks through each of the fields in your form to
see if any are completely empty and then, if any are empty, flashes an
alert with the text:

```
   Sorry, you forgot one of the required fields.
➡ Please try again.
```

It then exits.

If some fields need to be filled and some don't or if you need to check
specific values, you can do so. For example to ensure that the first name
field (called firstname) is filled out and not too short (fewer than two
characters), add the following if statement to the script:

```
   if (document.survey.firstname.value.length <= 2){
       alert("Please enter your first name.")
       return false}
```

The complete script would then look like this:

```
   <script language="JavaScript">
   <!--
   function checkOut() {
   for (x=0; x<document.survey.elements.length; x++){
       if (document.survey.elements[x].value == "") {
             alert("Sorry, you forgot one of the required
➡ fields. Please try again.")
             break;      }
             }
             return false;
   if (document.survey.firstname.value.length <= 2){
       alert("Please enter your full first name.")
       return false}
       }
   //-->
   </script>
```

You can continue adding other conditions in the same way.

One of the more complex validation problems involves e-mail
addresses. Although more complex scripts are available, you'll probably

find that a basic check to ensure that the address includes something, an @ sign, and something else will suffice:

```
<script language="JavaScript">
<!--
function checkOut() {
for (x=0; x<document.survey.elements.length; x++){
    if (document.survey.elements[x].value == "") {
        alert("Sorry, you forgot one of the required
➥ fields. Please try again.")
        break;    }
        }
        return false;
if (document.survey.firstname.value.length <= 2){
    alert("Please enter your full first name.")
    return false}
if (document.survey.emailaddr.value.indexOf('@') == -1 ) {
    alert("Please correct your email address.
➥ It should look like you@domain.com")
return false}
    }
//-->
</script>
```

This addition verifies that the address contains an @ and that something after the @ exists. If you need more comprehensive validation, check out the scripts at the following Netscape site:

```
developer.netscape.com/library/examples/
➥ javascript/formval/overview.html
```

Tracking Visitors Using Cookies

Cookies are little objects that you can use to store information about visitors to your site, and that you can access with JavaScript. You can think of cookies as being high-tech name tags that identify your computer to a server computer. For example, if you visit the amazon.com Web site and purchase a book there, the amazon.com server deposits a cookie on your computer. Then, the next time you visit that site, the server looks around on your computer for the cookie so that it can identify you. The cookie on your computer is then matched up to information about you that is stored on the server, such as the information you provided, as well as, perhaps, the books you purchased. In this case, cookies can help make subsequent visits easier because visitors don't have to re-enter information.

Although the security risk to visitors is minimal, many people are (understandably) a little sensitive about having information stored about them and read by other computers. For that reason, browsers now offer visitors a lot of control over how cookies are handled. Early versions of Netscape Navigator simply accepted all cookies. Now, most browsers that recognize cookies warn visitors when a cookie is created and give visitors the option to accept or reject individual cookies.

Either way, the cookie information is not public property; the cookie stores information for you only, and not for public broadcast. It's like having a locker at the gym. Your locker may be in a room with other people's lockers, but only you have the key. Additionally, when the server looks on your computer for the cookie, it can only see and read the cookie it deposited, not other cookies, files, or information.

Cookies are not secret passageways into a visitor's computer, but rather a bookmark to identify where you and the visitor were in your adventure together. Creating a cookie is actually a bit of a cooperative venture in that the visitor answers prompts on the page and you save the information in a cookie.

If you want to track visitors to your Web site, you can, using two types of cookies:

► Session cookies, which endure only until a visitor closes the browser

► Persistent cookies, which endure until the expiration date you set

Session Cookies

Suppose you want to keep some information about a visitor's browsing session, such as the pages browsed or the products purchased. You can do so using *session cookies*. The JavaScript script not only records the visitor's session information, but also sends a message to the visitor when he or she arrives at and exits your site.

NOTE
This example shows some of the capabilities and power of cookies. It's also likely to irritate many visitors. Even if they know that cookies can be set and used, they likely don't want to be reminded of it overtly.

To implement session cookies, first create an empty cookie when the page loads. Start with a functional HTML document, such as the following:

```
<!DOCTYPE HTML PUBLIC "-//W3C//DTD HTML 3.2//EN">
<HTML>
<HEAD>
<TITLE>ASR Outfitters Cookie Form</TITLE>
</HEAD>
Cookie Bearing Document
</BODY>
</HTML>
```

Now, follow these steps:

1. Add a function to the document <HEAD> that sets the document cookie to the local time and date:

    ```
    <SCRIPT>
    <!--
    function homeMadeCookies () {
    var gotHere = new Date();
    document.cookie = gotHere.toLocaleString()}
    // -->
    </SCRIPT>
    ```

2. Initialize the cookie from the onLoad event handler, like this:

    ```
    <BODY onLoad="homeMadeCookies()">
    ```

The onLoad event handler starts the function called homeMadeCookies, which creates and places a value into the variable gotHere. From that information, the next line converts the GMT time to local time and stores that in document.cookie.

By setting up a second function, you can display a message when the visitor leaves. The fareWell function looks like this:

```
Function fareWell() {
var timedVisit = new Date();
    var tempTime = timedVisit.toLocaleString();
    alert("You got here at: " + document.cookie +
➡ " and now it's: " + tempTime); }
```

Then, by adding an onUnload event handler to the <BODY> tag, you can display the farewell message:

```
<BODY onLoad="homeMadeCookies()" onUnload="fareWell()">
```

The fareWell entry uses an alert to display a brief—cookie-based—message thanking the visitor, as shown here:

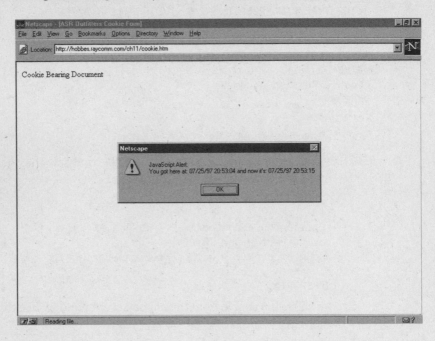

Persistent Cookies

You can also store information in cookies for a period of time. You use *persistent cookies* when you want to store information and use it in the future. For example, if a visitor fills out a form that includes his or her name and other personal information, you'd want to keep that information and use it when the visitor visits in the future. This is, for example, how the amazon.com site tracks your visits and seems to know things about you during subsequent visits.

Here are some facts you should know about persistent cookies:

- ▶ A browser retains a limited number of cookies. Netscape Navigator retains 300 cookies. Older cookies are discarded to make room for new ones.

- ▶ A cookie cannot be more than 4KB.

➤ You can have only 20 cookies per domain. If you're working from a large ISP, you might not be able to set cookies for all visitors.

These restrictions may not seem limiting at first, but they become so when the demand for feedback increases. Unlike session cookies, persistent cookies need an expiration date. After the cookie expires, a former visitor is treated as a new visitor.

NOTE

You'll find some outstanding scripts to manage cookies at Bill Dortch's hIdaho Design (www.hidaho.com). At this site, you'll find cookie.txt, which is code to build and read cookies, and cookies.htm, which is a working version of the code. We strongly recommend using these scripts, rather than developing your own.

Chapter 4
WORKING WITH OBJECTS

One of the most important features of JavaScript is that it is an object-based language. This simplifies the design of JavaScript programs and enables them to be developed in a more intuitive, modular, and reusable manner.

Adapted from *Mastering JavaScript and JScript*, by James Jaworski

ISBN 0-7821-2492-5   925 pages $39.99

This chapter describes JavaScript's support of objects and object-based programming. It introduces the JavaScript Object Model and summarizes the predefined JavaScript objects. It also shows how to create your own object types. When you finish this chapter, you'll be able to define and use objects in your Web pages.

WHAT ARE OBJECTS?

Most people know that objects are entities that exist in the real world of people, places, and things. But they also exist in the cyber world of computers and networking. Examples of real-world objects include you, the book you are reading, and the lamp that you use to provide you with light. Examples of cyber-world objects are the Web pages that you create and the individual HTML elements they contain. It is these types of objects that I will be discussing in relation to JavaScript.

An object consists of two things:

▶ A collection of *properties* that contain data

▶ *Methods* that enable operations on the data contained in those properties

When you view something as an object, you look at it in terms of its properties and methods. Table 4.1 identifies some of the properties and methods that could apply to the example objects mentioned in the previous paragraph.

TABLE 4.1: Examples of Objects, Properties, and Methods

OBJECT	PROPERTIES	METHODS
You (real-world object)	height weight hairColor	eat() exercise() grow()
This book (real-world object)	pages currentPage	turnPageForward() turnPageBackward() goToPage()
A lamp (real-world object)	onOffState	turnOn() turnOff()

CONTINUED ➡

TABLE 4.1 continued: Examples of Objects, Properties, and Methods

Object	Properties	Methods
A Web page (cyber-world object)	`title` `bgColor` `links`	`open()` `close()` `write()`
An HTML button (cyber-world object)	`name` `value`	`setLabel()`

You've already seen several examples of JavaScript objects. You've used the `document` object and its `write()` method in many of the scripts in previous chapters. You've also used the `alert()` method of the `window` object to display messages to the user. The fields of a form are also objects. You've seen how the `value` property of a field can be used to test and set the field's value. By the time you finish this chapter, you will have encountered all of the predefined JavaScript objects and learned how to create objects of your own.

NOTE

JavaScript is not a full object-oriented language—there are a few object-oriented programming features that it lacks. However, JavaScript is an object-based language, and provides several important object-oriented programming features. In order to learn why these features are important and how to use these features correctly, I'll begin by reviewing object-oriented programming in general and then identify which object-oriented programming features JavaScript supports.

WHAT IS OBJECT-ORIENTED PROGRAMMING?

The field of software engineering has evolved over the 50 or so years of the computer's existence. This evolution has brought about different approaches and strategies to the task of creating high-quality software while minimizing development time and costs. The most successful development approach currently in use is the object-oriented approach. This approach *models* the elements of a software application as objects— by modeling I mean object types are named, their properties are identified, and their methods are described. Once an object type is defined, it can then be used to create specific instances of other objects of that type and to construct other, more complex object types.

NOTE
Object-oriented programming is sometimes referred to by the acronym, OOP.

NOTE
An object type is referred to as a *class* in object-oriented languages such as Java and C++.

Object Types and Instances

An *object type* is a template from which specific objects of that type are created. It defines the properties and methods that are common to all objects of that type. For example, let's consider a person's mailing address as an object type. I'll name it `mailAddress` and give it the properties of `street-Address`, `city`, `state`, and `postalCode`. In addition to these properties, I'll define `changeAddress()` as a method for changing one person's address and `findAddress()` as a method for finding out another person's address. Don't worry about how I'm doing this—you'll learn that later—for this explanation just focus on what's being done.

When I define the `mailAddress` object type, I haven't specified anyone's address. I've only developed a template for the creation of an address—kind of like a blank Rolodex card. The address type can be *instantiated*, which is the programming term for creating a specific *instance* of that type of object; in this case it would mean creating a specific person's address record. This is similar to producing a Rolodex card, filling it in, and sticking it in the Rolodex.

The capability to define an object type from which specific object instances can then be created is a very basic but important feature of object-oriented software development.

Creating Object Types

While the definition and instantiation of object types is a basic feature of object-oriented languages, it is not the only feature these languages provide. The ability to use object types to define *other* object types is what really gives object-oriented programming its power. There are two major ways in which this is accomplished: through *object composition* and *inheritance*.

Object Composition

One approach to developing object types is to define primitive object types that serve as simple building blocks from which more complex types may be composed. This approach is referred to as *object composition*. Consider the process of building a house. At some point, somebody must construct the boards, nails, and glass panes that are used as the basic building blocks for constructing most homes. These building objects are assembled into more complex objects such as doors, windows, and prefabricated walls. These more complex objects are then, in turn, assembled into larger objects that eventually are integrated into a finished home. In the same way that boards, nails, glass panes, and other simple objects are used to construct a wide variety of different homes, simple object types are used in programming to create more complex object types which are eventually integrated into a final software application. For example, the mailAddress object may be used to create an employment application form, which is itself used to create a personnel database system.

Object composition is closely related to and depends on the capability to support *object reuse*. When an object type is defined, it is often very desirable that it be defined in such a way that it can be reused in other software applications. This simplifies the development of other applications and naturally leads to cost and schedule savings. The reuse of software objects is just as important as the reuse of technology in other engineering disciplines. Imagine the state of the automotive industry if the wheel had to be reinvented for every new type of car that's been developed.

Encapsulation—Packaging Objects   Software objects are reusable when they follow certain design principles. One of the most important of these principles is *encapsulation*. Encapsulation is the packaging of the properties and methods of an object into a container with an appropriately defined interface. The object's interface must provide the methods and properties that enable the object to be used in the manner that is intended, and must do it without providing methods or properties that would allow the object to be misused. If this abstract description is difficult to fathom, consider the interface of an automobile. Auto designers provide standardized steering, braking, and throttling capabilities in all cars, since these capabilities are basic to driving. However, no automobile manufacturer provides drivers with the capability to manually control the firing of spark plugs from the dashboard. Even if drivers were provided with this capability, they more than likely could not use it to any advantage.

Modularity and Information Hiding   Encapsulation depends upon two important concepts for its success. The first concept, *modularity*, refers to an object's being complete in and of itself and not accessing other objects outside their defined interfaces. Modular objects are said to be "loosely coupled," which means that dependencies between objects are minimized, and internal changes to an object do not require changes in other objects that make use of the object. The second concept, *information hiding*, refers to the practice of limiting information about an object to that which is required to use the object's interface. It is accomplished by removing information about the internal operation of an object from the object's interface.

Inheritance—A Hierarchical Approach to Object Design

The second major way of constructing object types from other object types is through *inheritance*. In this approach, higher-level, more abstract object types are defined from which lower-level, more concrete object types are derived. When a lower-level object type is created, it identifies one or more higher-level object types as its *parent* types. The *child* type inherits all of the properties and methods of its parents. This eliminates the need to redefine these properties and methods. The child type is free to redefine any of the methods that it inherits or to add new properties and methods. This enables the child type to tailor its inherited characteristics to new situations.

As an example, consider the various types of objects that may be constructed to implement a scrolling marquee. At the highest level, a `genericMarquee` may be constructed that has the basic properties `scrolledText` and `scrollRate`. It may provide basic methods, such as `startScrolling()` and `stopScrolling()`. From this generic marquee, more complex marquees may be created. For example,

horizontalMarquee and verticalMarquee object types may be constructed that add the property scrollDirection to those inherited from
genericMarquee. These, in turn, may be further refined into marquees
that use colored text and backgrounds. The properties textColor and
backgroundColor and the methods randomTextColor() and random-
BackgroundColor() could be added.

Using inheritance, more sophisticated, tailored object types can be created from those that are already defined. This is done by just adding the
properties and methods needed to differentiate the new objects from their
parents. Once a useful object type is created, it can then be reused many
times to create several child objects and numerous generations of offspring.

Classification and Inheritance   Object-oriented programming languages, such as Java and C++ (but not JavaScript), refer to an object's
type as its *class*, and provide the capability to develop child classes from
parent classes using inheritance. The resulting class structure is referred
to as a *classification scheme*. The classification schemes that result from
object-oriented development mimic those that are fundamental to the
way we as human beings acquire and organize knowledge. For example,
we develop general class names, such as *animal*, that we use to refer to
large groups of real-world objects. We then develop names of subclasses,
such as *mammal*, *bird*, and *insect*, which we use to refine our concept of
animal. We continue to develop more detailed classes that differentiate
between objects of the same class. The same sort of classification process
is carried out by developers of object-oriented programs.

Single and Multiple Inheritance   Part of the reason that inheritance
is a successful approach to object development is that it mimics the way
we acquire and organize knowledge—it is therefore *intuitive* to us. In addition to this, inheritance is *efficient*, because it only requires you to define
the properties and methods that are unique for an object's type.

Some languages, notably Java, enforce a more restricted form of inheritance, known as *single inheritance*. Single inheritance requires that a child
class have only one parent. However, a parent may have multiple children.
Since a child class inherits its properties and methods from a single parent, it is an exact duplicate of its parent before it adds its own unique
properties and methods.

Other languages, notably C++, support *multiple inheritance*. As you might expect, multiple inheritance allows child classes to inherit their properties and methods from more than one parent class. Multiple inheritance is much more powerful than single inheritance, because it allows independent, but complementary, branches of the class structure to be fused together into a single branch.

Multiple inheritance does, however, introduce some difficulties with respect to name resolution. Suppose that class C is the child of both class A and class B. Suppose also that both class A and B define different save() methods. Which of these two methods is inherited by class C? How does the compiler determine which method to use for objects of class C? Although it is certainly possible to develop naming schemes and compilers that resolve naming difficulties resulting from multiple inheritance, these solutions often require a significant amount of additional compilation and runtime processing.

Polymorphism—Many Methods with the Same Name   While at first it may appear to be undesirable to have many methods of the same name, the capability to do so is actually a feature of object-oriented programming. *Polymorphism* is the capability to take on different forms. It allows an object type to define several different implementations of a method. These methods are differentiated by the types and number of parameters they accept. For example, several different print() methods may be defined, each of which is used to print objects of different object types. Other print() methods may be defined which take a different number of parameters. The interpreter, compiler, or runtime system selects the particular print() method that is most appropriate for the object being printed. Polymorphism allows the programmer to use a standard method, such as print(), to perform a particular operation and to define different forms of the method to be used with different parameters. This promotes standardization and reusable software and eliminates the need to come up with many slightly different names to distinguish the same operation being performed with different parameters.

JavaScript's Object-Based Programming Features

In the previous section, you learned about the capabilities that are common to object-oriented programming languages. JavaScript does not support several of the capabilities described, but Java does support them. It is worth your while to become familiar with the object-oriented programming capabilities described in the previous section. That way, you'll be ready to eventually start learning how Java applets can be integrated with JavaScript scripts.

In this section, you'll learn which object-oriented programming capabilities JavaScript supports and how they are used to develop object-based JavaScript programs.

JavaScript is not a fully object-oriented programming language. It does not support the basic object-oriented programming capabilities of classification, inheritance, encapsulation, and information hiding. However, this is not as bad as it first appears. JavaScript is a scripting language, not a full programming language. The features that it does provide are geared toward providing a capability to quickly and easily generate scripts that execute in the context of a Web page or a server-side application.

JavaScript is referred to as an *object-based* language. It supports the development of object types and the instantiation of these types to create object instances. It provides great support for object composition, but only fair support for modularity and object reuse. Table 4.2 summarizes JavaScript's object-based programming capabilities.

TABLE 4.2: JavaScript's Object-Based Programming Capabilities

CAPABILITY	DESCRIPTION
Object types	JavaScript supports both predefined and user-defined object types. However, JavaScript does not provide capabilities for type enforcement. An object of any type may be assigned to any variable.
Object instantiation	Object types are instantiated using the new operator to create specific object instances.
Object composition	Object types may be defined in terms of other predefined or user-defined object types.

CONTINUED ➡

TABLE 4.2 continued: JavaScript's Object-Based Programming Capabilities

CAPABILITY	DESCRIPTION
	JavaScript code may be defined in a modular fashion, but JavaScript does not provide any features that enforce modular software development.
Object reuse	JavaScript software may be reused via the SRC attribute of the SCRIPT tag. Software may be made available for reuse via the Internet.
Information hiding	JavaScript does not provide any capabilities to support information hiding.
Encapsulation	Because JavaScript lacks information hiding capabilities, it cannot be used to develop encapsulated object types. Any method or property that is defined for a type is always directly accessible.
Inheritance	JavaScript does not provide any language features that support inheritance between object types.
Classification	Because JavaScript does not support inheritance, it cannot be used to develop a hierarchy of object types.
Polymorphism	JavaScript supports polymorphism using the arguments array for function definitions.

Although JavaScript does not provide all of the features of full object-oriented programming languages, such as Java, it does provide a suite of object-based features that are specially tailored to browser and server scripting. These features include a number of predefined browser and server objects and the capability to access related objects through the properties and methods of other objects. If this seems very abstract at this point, don't worry—you'll see several concrete examples of these features throughout this chapter.

THE JAVASCRIPT OBJECT MODEL

JavaScript supports a simple object model that is supported by a number of predefined objects. The *JavaScript Object Model* centers around the specification of object types that are used to create specific object instances. Object types under this model are defined in terms of properties and methods:

▶ Properties are used to access the data values contained in an object. Properties, by default, can be updated as well as read, although some properties of the predefined JavaScript objects are read-only.

▶ Methods are functions that are used to perform operations on an object. Methods may use the object's properties to perform these operations.

NOTE

This chapter describes the JavaScript Object Model as implemented by both Navigator and Internet Explorer. Each of these browsers provide additional browser-specific objects, methods, and properties.

Using Properties

An object's properties are accessed by combining the object's name and its property name as follows:

```
objectName.propertyName
```

For example, the background color of the current Web document is identified by the bgColor property of the predefined document object. If you wanted to change the background color to white, you could use the following JavaScript statement:

```
document.bgColor="white"
```

The preceding statement assigns the string "white" to the bgColor property of the predefined document object. Listing 4.1 shows how this statement can be used in an example script. Figure 4.1 shows the Web page that it produces. Several buttons are displayed with the names of different colors. When a button is clicked, the button's onClick event handler changes the background of the document by setting the document.bgColor property.

Listing 4.1: Using JavaScript Properties

```
<HTML>
<HEAD>
<TITLE>Using Properties</TITLE></HEAD>
<BODY>
<H1>Using Properties</H1>
<FORM>
<P><INPUT TYPE="BUTTON" NAME="red" VALUE="Red"
 ONCLICK='document.bgColor="red"'></P>
<P><INPUT TYPE="BUTTON" NAME="white" VALUE="White"
 ONCLICK='document.bgColor="white"'></P>
<P><INPUT TYPE="BUTTON" NAME="blue" VALUE="Blue"
 ONCLICK='document.bgColor="blue"'></P>
</FORM>
</BODY>
</HTML>
```

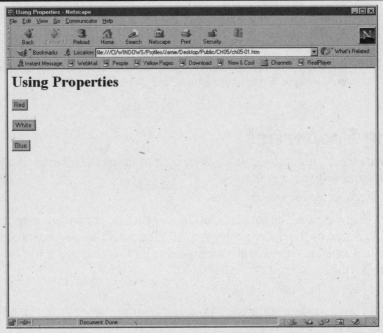

FIGURE 4.1: Using properties to change background colors (Listing 4.1)

Using Methods

An object's methods are accessed in the same manner as its properties:

```
objectName.methodName(parameterList)
```

The parameters, if any, are separated by commas. The parentheses must be used even if no parameters are specified. An example of a method invocation is

```
r=Math.random()
```

The random() method of the predefined Math object is invoked. This method returns a random floating-point number between 0 and 1. The number is then assigned to the r variable.

You have been using the methods of predefined JavaScript objects since your first script in Chapter 3, "Adding JavaScript." You've used the write() method of the document object to generate HTML entities that are written to the current document. You've also used the alert() method of the window object to display popup dialog boxes. In the next section, you'll be introduced to some of the objects that are automatically created by JavaScript-capable browsers. Later in this chapter, all of the predefined JavaScript objects will be introduced in summary form.

Creating Instances of Objects

Instances of objects of a particular object type are created using the new operator. You've previously used the new operator to create array objects. The same syntax is used to create objects of other types:

```
variable = new objectType(parameters)
```

The objectType(parameters) portion of the above statement is referred to as the *constructor*. Some object types have more than one constructor. Constructors differ in the number of parameters that they allow.

For example, Date is a predefined JavaScript object type. To create an instance of Date with the current date and time and assign it to the currentDate variable, you would use the following statement:

```
currentDate = new Date()
```

In the above statement, the Date() constructor does not take any parameters. The Date object type also allows object instances to be created for a specified date. For example, the following statement creates an instance of Date for January 1, 1999:

```
currentDate = new Date(99,1,1)
```

The constructor used in the above statement, Date(99,1,1), takes three parameters. The Date object type provides other constructors in addition to the ones described in this section. (The Date object type is formally introduced later in this chapter in the section, "The Date Object Type.")

BROWSER OBJECTS

When a Web page is loaded by a JavaScript-capable browser, the browser creates a number of JavaScript objects that provide access to the Web page and the HTML elements it contains. These objects are used to update and interact with the loaded Web page. Table 4.3 identifies these objects and summarizes their use.

TABLE 4.3: Browser Objects

OBJECT	USE
window object	To access a browser window or a frame within a window. The window object is assumed to exist and does not require the "window." prefix when referring to its properties and methods.
document object	To access the document that is currently loaded into a window. A document object refers to an HTML document that provides content—that is, one that has HEAD and BODY tags.
location object	To represent a URL. It can be used to create a URL object, access parts of a URL, or modify an existing URL.
history object	To maintain a history of the URLs accessed within a window.
frame object frames array	To access an HTML frame. The frames array is used to access all frames within a window.
link object links array	To access a text- or image-based source anchor of a hypertext link. The links array is used to access all link objects within a document. Internet Explorer combines the link object with the anchor object.
anchor object anchors array	To access the target of a hypertext link. The anchors array is used to access all anchor objects within a document.
image object images array	To access an image that is embedded in an HTML document. The images array is used to access all image objects within a document.

CONTINUED →

TABLE 4.3 continued: Browser Objects

Object	Use
`area` object	To access an area within a client-side image map.
`Applet` object `applets` array	To access a Java applet. The `applets` array is used to access all applets in a document.
`event` object `Event` object	To access information about the occurrence of an event. The `event` object provides information about a specific event. The `Event` (capitalized) object provides constants that are used to identify events.
`form` object `forms` array	To access an HTML form. The `forms` array is used to access all forms within a document.
`elements` object	To access all form elements (fields or buttons) contained within a form.
`text` object	To access a text field of a form.
`textarea` object	To access a text area field of a form.
	To access a set of radio buttons of a form or to access an individual button within the set.
`checkbox` object	To access a checkbox of a form.
`button` object	To access a form button that is not a submit or reset button.
`submit` object	To access a submit button of a form.
`reset` object	To access a reset button of a form.
`select` object `option` object	To access a select list of a form. The `option` object is used to access the elements of a select list.
`password` object	To access a password field of a form.
`hidden` object	To access a hidden field of a form.
`FileUpload` object	To access a file upload element of a form.
`navigator` object	To access information about the browser that is executing a script.
`screen` object	To access information about the size and color depth of a user's screen.

CONTINUED ⟶

TABLE 4.3 continued: Browser Objects

Object	Use
embed object embeds array	To access an embedded object. The embeds array provides access to all embedded objects in a document.
mimeType object mimeTypes array	To access information about a particular MIME type supported by a browser. The mimeTypes array is an array of all mimeType objects supported by a browser. Internet Explorer provides tacit support for mime-Types, returning an empty array.
plugin object plugins array	To access information about a particular browser plug-in. The plugins array is an array of all plug-ins supported by a browser. Internet Explorer provides tacit support for plugins, returning an empty array.

Table 4.3 summarizes the predefined objects that are created by a JavaScript-capable browser when a Web page is loaded. JavaScript also supports object types that are independent of the Web page that is loaded. These objects are described in the "Other Predefined Object Types" section later in this chapter.

The Browser Object Hierarchy

Your browser creates the objects presented in Table 4.3 as the results of Web pages that you design. For example, if you create a Web page with three forms, then the forms array will contain three form objects corresponding to the forms that you have defined. Similarly, if you define a document with seven links, then the links array will contain seven link objects that correspond to your links.

The browser objects are organized into a hierarchy that corresponds to the structure of loaded Web documents and the current state of the browser. This hierarchy is referred to as an *instance hierarchy*. The window and navigator objects are the highest-level objects in this hierarchy.

The *window* Object

The window object represents a browser window, and it has properties that are used to identify the objects of the HTML elements that comprise that window. For example, the frames array is a property of a window object. If the window uses the frame set tag to define multiple frames, then the frames array contains the frame object associated with each frame. The window's location property refers to the location object that contains the URL associated with the window. The window's screen property may be used to obtain the user's screen dimensions and color depth.

If a window contains displayable content, as opposed to a frame set tag, then the window object's document property refers to the document object associated with the window. The document object contains properties that reference objects that are displayed in the window. These properties include the links, anchors, images, and forms arrays. The links array identifies all link objects contained in a document. The anchors array identifies all named anchors. Link objects refer to the source of a hyperlink, while anchor objects refer to the named destinations of a link. The images, applets, and forms arrays identify all image, applet, and form objects contained in a document. A document's area property refers to an area within a client-side image map that is defined in the document. A document's history property refers to a history object that contains a list of URLs that the user has visited within a particular window.

NOTE

Internet Explorer combines the link and anchor objects. Both links and anchors can be accessed via the anchors array.

A document object's forms array identifies all form objects that are defined in the document. Although a document may define any number of forms, usually only one form is defined. The form object provides access to the individual elements defined for a particular form via the elements array. The elements array refers to text, textarea, radio, checkbox, button, submit, reset, select, password, hidden, and FileUpload form fields. These fields may also be individually accessed by their names. You'll learn how to use form-related objects in Chapter 5, "Processing Forms," and Chapter 7, "Interfacing JavaScript with CGI Programs."

The *navigator* Object

The navigator object, like the window object, is a top-level object in the browser hierarchy. The navigator object is used to describe the configuration of the browser being used to display a window. Two of its properties, mimeTypes and plugins, contain the list of all MIME types and plug-ins supported by the browser. Internet Explorer returns empty arrays for the mimeTypes and plugins properties.

Hierarchical Object Identifiers

Because your browser organizes the various objects of a Web page according to the instance hierarchy described in the previous section, a hierarchical naming scheme is used to identify these objects. For example, suppose an HTML document defines three forms, and the second form has seven elements. Also suppose the fifth element of the second form is a radio button. You can access the name of this radio button using the following identifier:

```
document.forms[1].element[4].name
```

The preceding identifier refers to the name of the fifth element of the second form of the current document. (Remember that array indices begin at 0.) You could display this name using the following statement:

```
document.write(document.forms[1].element[4].name)
```

NOTE

You do not have to identify the window object when you refer to the current window's properties and methods—your browser will assume the current window object by default. There is one exception, however: in event-handling code, it is the current document object that is assumed by default.

In most cases, you can refer to a property or method of a browser-created object by starting with document and using the property names of the objects that contain the object (such as links, anchors, images, and forms) to identify the object within the instance hierarchy. When you have named the object in this fashion, you can then use the object's property or method name to access the data and functions defined for that object.

Listing 4.2 provides an example of using hierarchical names to access the elements defined within a Web document. The document defines a number of functions in the document head. It begins by invoking the open() method of the window object to open a second browser window. This second window is assigned to the outputWindow variable and is used to write the description of the objects defined for the HTML document shown in Listing 4.2. The open() method takes two parameters—the URL of the document to be loaded in the window and a window name. Because you don't want to load a document at another URL, set the URL parameter to a blank string.

Listing 4.2: Using Hierarchical Object Identifiers

```
<HTML>
<HEAD>
<TITLE>Using Hierarchical Object Identifiers</TITLE>
<SCRIPT LANGUAGE="JavaScript"><!-
outputWindow = open("","output")
function setupWindow() {
 outputWindow.document.write("<HTML><HEAD><TITLE>Output
  Window</TITLE></HEAD><BODY>")
}
function describeBrowser() {
 outputWindow.document.write("<H2>Browser Properties</H2>")
 outputWindow.document.write(navigator.appCodeName+" ")
 outputWindow.document.write(navigator.appName+" ")
 outputWindow.document.write(navigator.appVersion+"<BR>")
 outputWindow.document.write(navigator.mimeTypes.length+
➥ " MIME
   types are defined. ")
 outputWindow.document.write(navigator.plugins.length+"
  plug-ins are installed.")
}
function describeWindow() {
 outputWindow.document.write("<H2>Window Properties</H2>")
 outputWindow.document.write("Frames: "+frames.length+
➥ "<BR>")
 outputWindow.document.write("URL: "+location.href+"<BR>")
}
function describeDocument() {
 outputWindow.document.write("<H2>Document Properties</H2>")
 describeLinks()
 describeForms()
}
function describeLinks(){
 outputWindow.document.write("<H3>Links</H3>")
 outputWindow.document.write("This document contains "
  +document.links.length+" links:<BR>")
 for(i=0;i<document.links.length;++i)
  outputWindow.document.write(document.links[i].href+"<BR>")
}
function describeForms() {
 outputWindow.document.write("<H3>Forms</H3>")
 for(i=0;i<document.forms.length;++i) describeForm(i)
```

```
     }
     function describeForm(n) {
      outputWindow.document.write("Form "+n+" has "
       +document.forms[n].elements.length+" elements:")
      for(j=0;j<document.forms[n].elements.length;++j)
       outputWindow.document.write("  "
        + document.forms[n].elements[j].name)
      outputWindow.document.write("<BR>")
     }
     function finishWindow() {
      outputWindow.document.write("<FORM><INPUT Type='button'
       Value='Close Window' onClick='window.close()'></FORM>")
      outputWindow.document.write("</BODY></HTML>")
     }
     // -></SCRIPT></HEAD>
     <BODY>
     <H1>Using Hierarchical Object Identifiers</H1>
     <P><A HREF="http://www.jaworski.com/javascript">Link to
       Mastering JavaScript and JScript home page.</A></P>
     <P><A HREF="http://home.netscape.com/">Link to Netscape's
     home page.</A></P>
     <FORM>
     <P><INPUT TYPE="TEXT" NAME="textField1"
      VALUE="Enter text here!"></P>
     <P><INPUT TYPE="CHECKBOX" NAME="checkbox1"
      CHECKED="CHECKED">I'm checkbox1.</P>
     <P><INPUT TYPE="CHECKBOX" NAME="checkbox2"> I'm
         checkbox2.</P><INPUT TYPE="SUBMIT" NAME="submitButton"
         VALUE="Click here!">
     </FORM>
     <SCRIPT LANGUAGE="JavaScript"><!-
     setupWindow()
     describeBrowser()
     describeWindow()
     describeDocument()
     finishWindow()
     // -></SCRIPT>
     </BODY>
     </HTML>
```

The setupWindow() function is used to generate the head of the second document and its opening body tag. It uses the outputWindow variable to select the second window as the target for writing. This function and other functions in the script write their output using statements of the following form:

```
     outputWindow.document.write()
```

These statements tell JavaScript to write to the document object of the window object identified by the outputWindow variable.

The describeBrowser() function displays some of the navigator object's properties to the second window. It also uses the outputWindow variable to select this window. It displays the appCodeName, appName, appVersion, and uses the length property of the mimeTypes and plugins arrays to determine the number of MIME types and plug-ins supported by the browser.

The describeWindow() function displays some properties of the original (first) window. It displays the number of frames defined by the window and the URL of the document loaded into the window. Since the window does not define any frames, the length of the frames array is 0. The href property of the window's location object is used to get the text string corresponding to the URL. The URL displayed when you execute the script will be different depending on the directory from which you run the files of this chapter.

The describeDocument() function displays some of the properties associated with the current document in the second window. It invokes the describeLinks() and describeForms() functions to perform this processing.

The describeLinks() function uses the length property of the links array to identify the number of links contained in the document. It then executes a for loop to display the URL associated with each of these links. The href attribute of the link object is used to get the text string corresponding to the URL.

The describeForms() function uses the length property of the forms array to iterate through the document's links and display each one. The displayForm() function is used to display each form.

The displayForm() function uses the length property of the elements array of each form object to identify the number of elements contained in a form. It takes a single parameter, identified by the n variable. This parameter identifies the index into the forms array of the form object being displayed. The name of each field element is displayed by referencing the name property of each object contained in the elements array of each form object identified in the forms array. This is a good example of using hierarchical object naming to access the lower-level elements of an HTML document.

The finishWindow() function appends the following HTML to the body of the document displayed in the second window:

```
<FORM>
<INPUT Type='button' Value='Close Window'
  onClick='window.close()'>
</FORM>
</BODY>
</HTML>
```

The form is used to create a button, labeled *Close Window*, that is used to close the second window. The onClick attribute of the INPUT tag is assigned the event handling code, window.close(), which is used to close the window upon clicking the button. The window object should be explicitly referenced in event handlers to ensure that the current window is closed and not the current document. The </BODY> and </HTML> tags are used to end the displayed document.

The main body of the HTML document defines two links—one to the *Mastering JavaScript and JScript* home page and one to Netscape's home page. The document then defines a form with four elements—a text field, two check boxes, and a Submit button.

The script contained in the main body of the document invokes the setupWindow(), describeBrowser(), describeWindow(), describe-Document(), and finishWindow() functions to display the contents of the first window in the second window referenced by the outputWindow object. This script is placed at the end of the document so that the various HTML elements of the document are defined when the script is invoked.

A second window is created to display the various properties of the document. The Web browser displays this second window as shown in Figure 4.2. When the user clicks the Close Window button, the original document, shown in Figure 4.3, is displayed. You can also use your browser's Window pull-down menu to switch between the two windows.

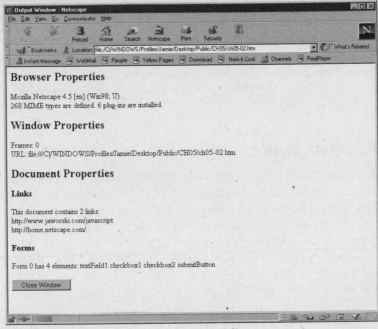

FIGURE 4.2: The output window (Listing 4.2)

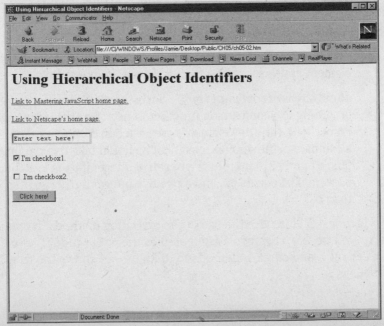

FIGURE 4.3: The original document window (Listing 4.2)

OTHER PREDEFINED OBJECT TYPES

In addition to the predefined browser objects discussed in earlier sections, JavaScript also provides general-purpose object types that support common operations. These object types (except the RegExp object type) are defined by the ECMAScript 1 specification and are described in the following sections.

The *Array* Object

The Array object allows arrays to be accessed as objects. The ECMAScript 1 specification defines two properties for the Array object: length and prototype. The length property identifies the length of an array. The prototype property is a property that is supported by all object types. It allows additional properties and methods to be defined for an object type. It is covered in the "Adding Properties and Methods to an Object Type" section later in this chapter.

ECMAScript 1 defines the following Array methods:

toString()   Returns a string version of an array. Array elements are separated by commas.

join(*separator*)   Returns a string version of an array. Array elements are separated by the *separator* string. If no separator is specified, a comma is used.

reverse()   Reverses the elements of an array; that is, the last element appears first and the first element appears last.

sort(*comparisonFunction*)   Sorts the elements of an array according to a comparison function. If no comparison function is specified, the array elements are sorted in dictionary order. If a comparison function is specified, it should take two parameters, p1 and p2, and return a negative integer if p1 is less than p2, zero if p1 equals p2, and a positive integer if p1 is greater than p2.

Listing 4.3 illustrates the use of the preceding methods. It creates an array of integers 0 through 10 and applies the toString(), join(':'), reverse(), and sort() methods to it. Figure 4.4 shows the results it displays.

Part i

Listing 4.3: Using the Methods of the *Array* Object

```
<HTML>
<HEAD>
<TITLE>Using Arrays</TITLE>
<SCRIPT LANGUAGE="JavaScript"><!-
// -></SCRIPT></HEAD>
<BODY>
<H1>Using Arrays</H1>
<SCRIPT LANGUAGE="JavaScript"><!-
myArray = [0, 1, 2, 3, 4, 5, 6, 7, 8, 9, 10]
document.write("myArray: "+myArray+"<P>")
document.write("myArray.toString(): "+myArray.toString()+
➡ "<P>")
document.write("myArray.join(':'): "+myArray.join(':')+
➡ "<P>")
document.write("myArray.reverse(): "+myArray.reverse()+
➡ "<P>")
document.write("myArray.sort: "+myArray.sort())
// -></SCRIPT>
</BODY>
</HTML>
```

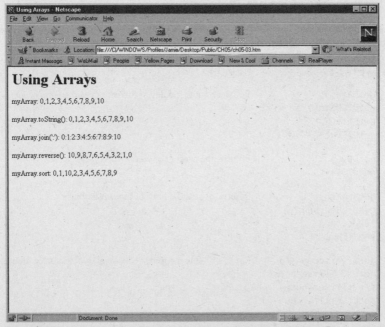

FIGURE 4.4: The results of applying Array methods (Listing 4.3)

The *Boolean* Object

The Boolean object allows Boolean values to be accessed as objects. It supports the prototype property and the toString() and valueOf() methods. The toString() method returns the string equivalent of a Boolean value. The valueOf() method returns *true* or *false* depending on the value of the underling object.

Boolean objects are created by identifying their value as an argument to the constructor:

```
myBoolean = new Boolean(false)
yourBoolean = new Boolean(true)
```

The *Date* Object

The Date object type provides a common set of methods for working with dates and times. These methods are summarized in Table 4.4. The methods with UTC in their name refer to Universal Coordinated Time, which is the time set by the World Time Standard. The Date object type supports the prototype property. Instances of the Date object type may be created with any of the constructors shown in Table 4.5. Listing 4.4 illustrates the use of the Date object type.

TABLE 4.4: Methods of the Date Object

Method	Description
getDate() getUTCDate() setDate() setUTCDate()	Returns or sets the day of the month of the Date object.
getDay() getUTCDay()	Returns the day of the week of the Date object.
getHours() getUTCHours() setHours() setUTCHours()	Returns or sets the hour of the Date object.
getMilliseconds() getUTCMilliseconds() setMilliseconds() setUTCMilliseconds()	Returns or sets the milliseconds value of the Date object.

CONTINUED ➡

TABLE 4.4: Methods of the Date Object

METHOD	DESCRIPTION
getMinutes() getUTCMinutes() setMinutes() setUTCMinutes()	Returns or sets the minutes of the Date object.
getMonth() getUTCMonth() setMonth() setUTCMonth()	Returns or sets the month of the Date object.
getSeconds() getUTCSeconds() setSeconds() setUTCSeconds()	Returns or sets the seconds of the Date object.
getTime() setTime()	Returns or sets the time of the Date object.
getTimeZoneOffset()	Returns the time zone offset (in minutes) of the Date object.
getYear() getFullYear() getUTCFullYear() setYear() setFullYear() setUTCFullYear()	Returns or sets the year of the Date object. The full year methods use four-digit year values.
toGMTString()	Converts a date to a string in Internet GMT (Greenwich Mean Time) format.
toLocaleString()	Converts a date to a string in *locale* format, which means the format commonly used in the geographical region in which the user is located.
toString()	Returns a string value of a Date object.
valueOf()	Returns the number of milliseconds since midnight January 1, 1970.
toUTCString()	Returns a string that represents the time in UTC.

TABLE 4.5: Date Constructors

CONSTRUCTOR	DESCRIPTION
Date()	Creates a Date instance with the current date and time.
Date(*dateString*)	Creates a Date instance with the date specified in the *dateString* parameter. The format of the *dateString* is "*month day, year hours:minutes:seconds*".
Date(*milliseconds*)	Creates a Date instance with the specified number of milliseconds since midnight January 1, 1970.
Date(*year, month, day, hours, minutes, seconds, milliseconds*)	Creates a Date instance with the date specified by the year, month, day, hours, minutes, seconds, and milliseconds integers. The year and month parameters must be supplied. If other parameters are included, then all preceding parameters must be supplied.

Listing 4.4: Using the *Date* Object

```
<HTML>
<HEAD>
<TITLE>Using the Date Object Type</TITLE>
</HEAD>
<BODY>
<H1>Using the Date Object Type</H1>
<SCRIPT LANGUAGE="JavaScript"><!-
currentDate = new Date()
with (currentDate) {
  document.write("Date: "+getMonth()+"/"+getDate()+"/"
➥ +getYear()
    +"<BR>")
  document.write("Time: "+getHours()+":"+getMinutes()+":"
    +getSeconds())
}
// -></SCRIPT>
</BODY>
</HTML>
```

The preceding document uses the methods of the Date object type to write the current date and time to the current document object. The currentDate variable is assigned a new Date object that is created using the new operator and the Date() constructor. A with statement is used to make the object stored with `currentDate` the default object for object references. The two `write()` method invocations use the `getMonth()`, `getDate()`, `getYear()`, `getHours()`, `getMinutes()`, and `getSeconds()` methods to access the various components of a `Date` object. Figure 4.5 shows the Web page generated by Listing 4.4.

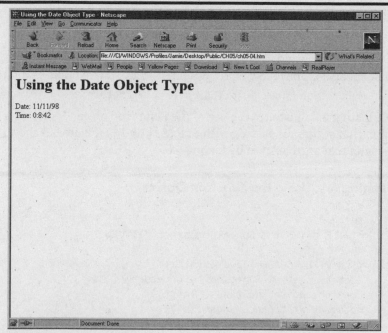

FIGURE 4.5: Using the Date object type (Listing 4.4)

The *Function* Object

The `Function` object allows functions to be accessed as objects. It can be used to dynamically create and invoke a function during a script's execution. The ECMAScript 1 specification identifies the `length` and `prototype` properties. The `length` property identifies the number of parameters defined for a function. Navigator and Internet Explorer define the `arguments` property and the `caller` property. The `arguments` property is an array that identifies the arguments that are passed to a function when it is invoked. The `caller` property identifies the function that invoked a particular function. Navigator also defines the `arity` property, which is identical to the `length` property.

The ECMAScript 1 specification defines the `toString()` and `valueOf()` methods. The `toString()` method returns a string representation of the function. The `valueOf()` method returns the function itself. Navigator also defines the `call()` and `apply()` methods, which can be used to invoke a `Function` object.

`Function` objects are created by supplying the function's parameters and body to the `Function()` constructor:

```
variable = new Function("p1", "p2", ..., "pn", "body")
```

The opening and closing brackets ({ and }) of the function body are not specified. The following function returns *x*-squared plus *y*-squared:

```
myFunction = new Function("x", "y", "return x*x + y*y")
```

Listing 4.5 illustrates the use of the `Function` object. It creates a function that surrounds a string with braces ([and]). Figure 4.6 shows the results that are displayed by Listing 4.5.

Listing 4.5: Using the *Function* Object

```
<HTML>
<HEAD>
<TITLE>Using the Function Object</TITLE>
<BODY><H1>
<SCRIPT LANGUAGE="JavaScript"><!-
addBraces = new Function("s","return '['+s+']'")
document.write(addBraces("This"))
document.write(addBraces("is"))
document.write(addBraces("a"))
document.write(addBraces("test."))
// -></SCRIPT>
</H1></BODY>
</HTML>
```

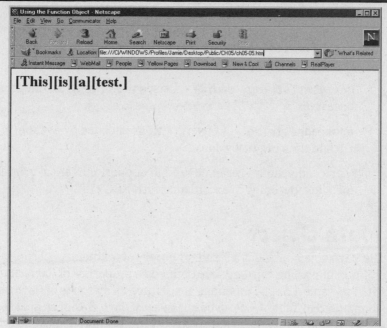

FIGURE 4.6: The results of the dynamically created function (Listing 4.5).

The *Global* Object

The ECMAScript specification defines the Global object to associate an object with the globally-accessible variables and functions defined in earlier versions of JavaScript. Navigator and Internet Explorer implement the Global object, but do not allow it to be explicitly created (via new Global()) or referenced (via "Global."). Instead, its properties and methods are referenced directly as global variables and functions.

The ECMAScript specification defines two constant properties: NaN and Infinity. The NaN constant means *not a number*. The Infinity property represents positive infinity. Methods defined for the Global object are as follows:

> **escape(*string*)**   Converts the *string* into a new string where certain characters are converted into escape sequences in accordance with RFC 1738.

> **eval(*x*)**   Evaluates and returns the value of the expression *x*.

> **isFinite(*number*)**   Returns *true* if *number* is finite and *false* otherwise.

isNaN(*number*)   Returns *true* if *number* is not a number and *false*, otherwise.

parseFloat(*string*)   Parses the *string* as a floating-point value.

parseInt(*string*, *radix*)   Parses the *string* as an integer of base *radix*.

unescape(*string*)   Converts strings encoded by escape() back to their original value.

The preceding methods can be used to support numerical tests and URL encoding/decoding in accordance with RFC 1738.

The *Math* Object

The Math object provides a standard library of mathematical constants and functions. The constants are defined as properties of Math, and are listed in Table 4.6. The functions are defined as methods of Math, and are summarized in Table 4.7. Specific instances of Math are not created because Math is a built-in object and not an object type. Listing 4.6 illustrates the use of the Math object; Figure 4.7 shows the Web page it generates.

TABLE 4.6: Math Properties

PROPERTY	DESCRIPTION
E	Euler's constant
LN2	The natural logarithm of 2
LN10	The natural logarithm of 10
LOG2E	The base 2 logarithm of *e*
LOG10E	The base 10 logarithm of *e*
PI	The constant *p*
SQRT1_2	The square root of _
SQRT2	The square root of 2

TABLE 4.7: Math Methods

METHOD	DESCRIPTION
abs(x)	Returns the absolute value of x
acos(x)	Returns the arc cosine of x in radians
asin(x)	Returns the arc sine of x in radians
atan(x)	Returns the arc tangent of x in radians
atan2(x,y)	Returns the angle of the polar coordinate corresponding to (x,y)
ceil(x)	Returns the least integer that is greater than or equal to x
cos(x)	Returns the cosine of x
exp(x)	Returns e^x
floor(x)	Returns the greatest integer that is less than or equal to x
log(x)	Returns the natural logarithm of x
max(x,y)	Returns the greater of x and y
min(x,y)	Returns the lesser of x and y
pow(x,y)	Returns x^y
random()	Returns a random number between 0 and 1
round(x)	Returns x rounded to the closest integer
sin(x)	Returns the sine of x
sqrt(x)	Returns the square root of x
tan(x)	Returns the tangent of x

Part i

Listing 4.6: Using the *Math* Object

```
<HTML>
<HEAD>
<TITLE>Using the Math Object</TITLE>
</HEAD>
<BODY>
<H1>Using the Math Object</H1>
<SCRIPT LANGUAGE="JavaScript"><!-
document.write(Math.PI+"<BR>")
document.write(Math.E+"<BR>")
document.write(Math.ceil(1.234)+"<BR>")
document.write(Math.random()+"<BR>")
document.write(Math.sin(Math.PI/2)+"<BR>")
document.write(Math.min(100,1000)+"<BR>")
// -></SCRIPT>
</BODY>
</HTML>
```

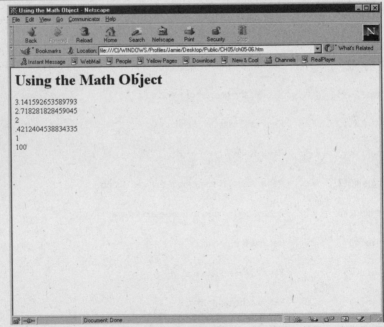

FIGURE 4.7: Example of using the Math object (Listing 4.6)

The *Number* Object

The Number object type allows numbers to be treated as objects. The ECMAScript 1 specification defines the following Number properties:

MAX_VALUE　The number is the maximum possible numeric value.

MIN_VALUE　The number is the minimum possible numeric value.

NaN　The number is not a number.

NEGATIVE_INFINITY　The number is negative infinity.

POSITIVE_INFINITY　The number is positive infinity.

prototype　The prototype property that is supported by all object types.

The preceding properties are used to identify numbers as having special characteristics. They are not normally used in scripts. Instead, use the properties and methods of the Global object.

The ECMAScript 1 specification defines the following Number methods:

toString(*radix*)　Returns a string that represents the number in base *radix*.

valueOf()　Returns the numeric value of the Number object.

Instances of the Number object are created by supplying a numeric value to the Number() constructor:

```
myNumber = new Number(123.456)
```

The *Object* Object

The Object object is the base object from which all other objects are derived. Its properties and methods are available to other object types.

The Object object supports the prototype and constructor properties. The constructor property identifies the name of the object's constructor.

The Object object supports the toString() and valueOf() methods. The toString() method converts an object to a string representation. The valueOf() method returns the primitive value (number, string, or Boolean) of an object if one is associated with the object. Otherwise, it returns the object itself.

`Object` objects can be created by supplying a number, string, Boolean value, or function in the `Object()` constructor. However, this is rarely done. Instead, it is better to use the constructor of the specific object type (that is, `Number()`, `String()`, `Boolean()`, or `Function()`).

The *String* Object

The `String` object type allows strings to be accessed as objects. It supports the `length` and `prototype` properties. The `length` property identifies the string's length in characters.

The `String` object type provides a set of methods for manipulating strings. The methods defined in the ECMAScript 1 specification are summarized in Table 4.8. Any JavaScript string value or variable containing a string value is able to use these methods. (Both Netscape and Internet Explorer define `String` methods in addition to those contained in Table 4.8.)

TABLE 4.8: String Methods

METHOD	DESCRIPTION
`charAt(index)`	Returns a string that consists of the character at the specified index of the string to which the method is applied.
`charCodeAt(index)`	Returns the Unicode encoding of the character at the specified index.
`fromCharCode(codes)`	Creates a string from a comma-separated sequence of character codes.
`indexOf(pattern)`	Returns the index of the first string specified by the *pattern* parameter that is contained in a string. Returns *-1* if the pattern is not contained in the string.
`indexOf(pattern, startIndex)`	Same as the previous method except that searching starts at the position specified by *startIndex*.
`lastIndexOf(pattern)`	Returns the index of the last string specified by the *pattern* parameter that is contained in a string. Returns *-1* if the pattern is not contained in the string.

CONTINUED ➡

TABLE 4.8 continued: String Methods

METHOD	DESCRIPTION
lastIndexOf(pattern, startIndex)	Same as the previous method except that searching starts at the position specified by *startIndex*.
split(separator)	Separates a string into an array of substrings based upon the *separator*.
substring(startIndex)	Returns the substring of a string beginning at *startIndex*.
substring(startIndex, endIndex)	Returns the substring of a string beginning at *startIndex* and ending at *endIndex*.
to LowerCase()	Returns a copy of the string converted to lowercase.
toString()	Returns the string value of the object.
toUpperCase()	Returns a copy of the string converted to uppercase.
valueOf()	Returns the string value of the object.

Listing 4.7 illustrates the use of the String object type. The script in the document body begins by defining the function displayLine(), which displays text followed by the <BR> tag. The displayLine() function is used to display several text strings that are modified using sample string methods. Figure 4.8 shows the Web page generated by Listing 4.7.

Listing 4.7: Using the *String* Object

```
<HTML>
<HEAD>
<TITLE>Using the String Object Type</TITLE>
</HEAD>
<BODY>
<SCRIPT LANGUAGE="JavaScript"><!-
function displayLine(text) {
 document.write(text+"<BR>")
}
s = new String("This is a test of the JavaScript String
➥ methods.")
 displayLine('s = '+s)
```

```
displayLine('s.charAt(1) = '+s.charAt(1))
displayLine('s.charCodeAt(1) = '+s.charCodeAt(1))
displayLine('s.indexOf("is") = '+s.indexOf("is"))
displayLine('s.lastIndexOf("is") = '+s.lastIndexOf("is"))
displayLine('s.substring(22,32) = '+s.substring(22,32))
displayLine('s.toLowerCase() = '+s.toLowerCase())
displayLine('s.toUpperCase() = '+s.toUpperCase())
split = s.split(" ")
for(i=0; i<split.length; ++i)
 displayLine('split['+i+'] = '+split[i])
// -></SCRIPT>
</BODY>
</HTML>
```

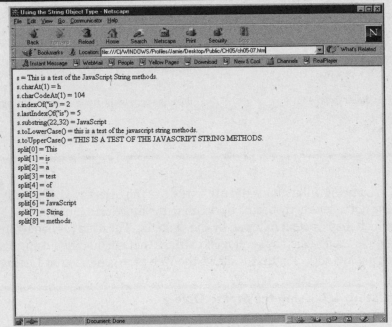

FIGURE 4.8: Using the String object (Listing 4.7)

Creating *String* Objects

`String` objects may be created in the same manner as other JavaScript objects using the new operator. For example, the variable `text` may be assigned the string `"I am a string"` using the following statement:

```
text = new String("I am a string")
```

The preceding statement is equivalent to:

```
text = "I am a string"
```

Regular Expressions and the *RegExp* Object

Support for *regular expressions* was introduced in JavaScript 1.2. Regular expressions are string expressions that describe a pattern of characters. They provide a powerful capability for finding patterns in text strings and performing search and replace operations on text. Regular expressions make use of a very compact, powerful, but somewhat arcane syntax. In JavaScript, regular expressions are implemented using the RegExp object, which is covered in Appendix A.

COLOR CONSTANTS

JavaScript defines a number of color constants that can be used with methods and functions that take color parameters. Some of these color constants are `"red"`, `"orange"`, `"yellow"`, `"green"`, `"blue"`, `"white"`, `"black"`, and `"brown"`. A complete list of the color constants can be found at `http://developer.netscape.com/docs/manuals/htmlguid/colortab.htm`.

DEFINING OBJECT TYPES

JavaScript provides the capability for you to define your own object types and create specific object instances. To create a new object type, you simply define a function that is used to construct specific instances of the object type. Essentially, this constructor function does two things:

► It assigns values to the object type's properties.

► It identifies other functions to be used as the object type's methods.

As an example of defining a new object type, we'll create the `table` object type. This object type will be used to create simple tables using JavaScript and write them to the current document.

Identifying and Assigning Properties

The first thing that we'll do is identify the properties of the `table` object type. The number of rows and columns of the table are obvious properties with which to start. Let's name these properties `table.rows` and `table.columns`. We'll also need to define a property to store the elements of the table. Let's call this property `table.data` and let it be an array of the following length:

```
table.rows * table.columns
```

Because HTML allows some table cells to be designated as header cells, let's also define the property `table.header` as an array of the same length as above, `table.rows * table.columns`, where each element is a Boolean value indicating whether a table cell is a header cell. Finally, let's define a property, `table.border`, that identifies the border width of the table. The following code shows how the table constructor would be defined using the items we just identified:

```
function table(rows,columns) {
  this.rows = rows
  this.columns = columns
  this.border = 0
  this.data = new Array(rows*columns)
  this.header = new Array(rows*columns)
}
```

As you can see, the `table()` constructor takes the parameters `rows` and `columns`, and assigns them to `this.rows` and `this.columns`. The `this` prefix is a special keyword that is used to refer to the current object. For example, the statement `this.rows = rows` assigns the value stored in the `rows` parameter to the `rows` property of the current object. Similarly, `this.columns = columns` assigns the `columns` parameter to the `columns` property of the current object. The parameters to the `table()` constructor do not have to be named *rows* and *columns*—they could have been named x and y. However, it is common to see parameters named after the object type properties to which they are assigned.

The border property of the current object is set to the default value of 0. This results in the creation of a borderless table. As mentioned earlier, the data and header properties are each assigned an array of size rows * columns.

In order to create an object that is an instance of the table object type, you use the new operator in conjunction with the table constructor. For example, the following statement creates a table of three rows by four columns and assigns it to the t variable:

```
t = new table(3,4)
```

Defining Methods

So far, we've defined the properties of the table object type. However, we'll need to define some methods to update the values of the data, header, and border properties and to write the table object to a document object.

Methods are defined by assigning the name of an already defined function to a method name in an object type constructor. For example, suppose the table_setValue() function is defined as follows. This function sets the value of the table cell at the specified row and column parameters to the value parameter.

```
function table_setValue(row,col,value) {
  this.data[row*this.columns+col]=value
}
```

We can use the previously defined table_setValue() function as the setValue() method of the table object type by including the following statement in the table constructor:

```
this.setValue = table_setValue
```

Note that trailing parentheses are not used in the preceding statement. The new table constructor is as follows:

```
function table(rows,columns) {
  this.rows = rows
  this.columns = columns
  this.border = 0
  this.data = new Array(rows*columns)
  this.header = new Array(rows*columns)
  this.setValue = table_setValue
}
```

An example of invoking the setValue() method for the table object stored in the t variable follows:

```
t.setValue(2,3,"Hello")
```

The preceding statement sets the table data value at row 2 and column 3 to "Hello".

Definition of the *table* Object

Listing 4.8 provides a complete definition of the table object. Note that functions must be defined before they can be assigned to a method name.

Listing 4.8: Definition of the *table* Object (*table.js*)

```
function table_getValue(row,col) {
 return this.data[row*this.columns+col]
}
function table_setValue(row,col,value) {
 this.data[row*this.columns+col]=value
}
function table_set(contents) {
 var n = contents.length
 for(var j=0;j<n;++j) this.data[j]=contents[j]
}
function table_isHeader(row,col) {
 return this.header[row*this.columns+col]
}
function table_makeHeader(row,col) {
 this.header[row*this.columns+col]=true
}
function table_makeNormal(row,col) {
 this.header[row*this.columns+col]=false
}
function table_makeHeaderRow(row) {
 for(var j=0;j<this.columns;++j)
  this.header[row*this.columns+j]=true
}
function table_makeHeaderColumn(col) {
 for(var i=0;i<this.rows;++i)
  this.header[i*this.columns+col]=true
}
function table_write(doc) {
 doc.write("<TABLE BORDER="+this.border+">")
 for(var i=0;i<this.rows;++i) {
```

```
      doc.write("<TR>")
      for(var j=0;j<this.columns;++j) {
       if(this.header[i*this.columns+j]) {
        doc.write("<TH>")
        doc.write(this.data[i*this.columns+j])
        doc.write("</TH>")
       } else{
        doc.write("<TD>")
        doc.write(this.data[i*this.columns+j])
        doc.write("</TD>")
       }
      }
      doc.writeln("</TR>")
     }
     doc.writeln("</TABLE>")
    }
    function table(rows,columns) {
     this.rows = rows
     this.columns = columns
     this.border = 0
     this.data = new Array(rows*columns)
     this.header = new Array(rows*columns)
     this.getValue = table_getValue
     this.setValue = table_setValue
     this.set = table_set
     this.isHeader = table_isHeader
     this.makeHeader = table_makeHeader
     this.makeNormal = table_makeNormal
     this.makeHeaderRow = table_makeHeaderRow
     this.makeHeaderColumn = table_makeHeaderColumn
     this.write = table_write
    }
```

Listing 4.8 adds the getValue(), set(), isHeader(), makeHeader(), make-Normal(), makeHeaderRow(), makeHeaderColumn(), and write() methods to the table definition introduced in the previous section.

The getValue() method returns the data value stored at a specified row and column. The set() method stores an array of values as the contents of a table. The makeHeader() and makeNormal() methods are used to identify whether a cell should or should not be a header cell. The makeHeaderRow() and makeHeaderColumn() methods are used to desig`nate an entire row or column as consisting of header cells. The write() method is used to write a table to a document object.

Using the *table* Object

Listing 4.9 provides an example of the use of the `table` object. The document's body contains a script that creates, initializes, and displays a three-row by four-column `table` object. Using the SRC attribute of the script tag, it includes the `table.js` file presented in the previous section. It begins by creating a `table` object and assigning it to the `t` variable. It then creates an array, named `contents`, that contains a list of values. The `set()` method is invoked to assign the contents array to the cells of the table stored at `t`. The table's `border` property is set to 4 pixels, and the cells of column 0 are designated as header cells. Finally, the `write()` method is used to write the table to the current document object. Figure 4.9 shows the Web page resulting from the script of Listing 4.9.

Listing 4.9: Using the *table* Object

```
<HTML>
<HEAD>
<TITLE>Defining Object Types</TITLE>
<SCRIPT LANGUAGE="JavaScript" SRC="table.js"><!-
// -></SCRIPT>
</HEAD>
<BODY>
<H1>Defining Object Types</H1>
<SCRIPT LANGUAGE="JavaScript"><!-
t = new table(3,4)
contents = new Array("This","is","a","test","of","the",
➡ "table",➡
  "object.","Let's","see","it","work.")
t.set(contents)
t.border=4
t.makeHeaderColumn(0)
t.write(document)
// -></SCRIPT>
</BODY>
</HTML>
```

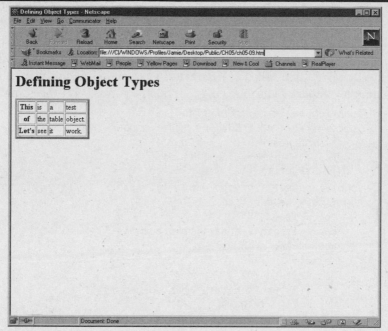

FIGURE 4.9: An example table (Listing 4.9)

Adding Properties and Methods to an Object Type

Object types that can be instantiated with the new operator are referred to as *instantiable* object types. They include all user-defined object types and most of the predefined object types. Examples of object types that are not instantiable are Math and Global. JavaScript provides the capability to add properties and methods to already defined instantiable object types via the prototype property.

For example, suppose we wanted to add a background color attribute to the table object type defined in previous section. We could add the new attribute with the following statement:

```
table.prototype.bgColor = "cyan"
```

The preceding statement uses the `prototype` property of the `table` object type to create a new property called `bgColor` to represent the background color of the table.

Now that we've defined the `bgColor` property, we should create an additional method called `colorWrite()` that writes a table using the `bgColor` property. The following function performs this processing:

```
function table_colorWrite(doc) {
  doc.write("<TABLE BORDER="+this.border+"BGCOLOR="
  +this.bgColor+">")
  for(var i=0;i<this.rows;++i) {
  doc.write("<TR>")
  for(var j=0;j<this.columns;++j) {
   if(this.header[i*this.columns+j]) {
    doc.write("<TH>")
    doc.write(this.data[i*this.columns+j])
    doc.write("</TH>")
   } else{
    doc.write("<TD>")
    doc.write(this.data[i*this.columns+j])
    doc.write("</TD>")
   }
  }
  doc.writeln("</TR>")
  }
  doc.writeln("</TABLE>")
}
```

We can use the `table_colorWrite()` function in the preceding listing as the `colorWrite()` method by including the following statement in our script:

```
table.prototype.colorWrite=table_colorWrite
```

Listing 4.10 updates the script shown in Listing 4.9 to make use of the new `bgColor` property and the `colorWrite()` method. Figure 4.10 shows the Web page that results from Listing 4.10. Note that we did not have to modify the original `table.js` file that is included via the SRC attribute.

TIP

Always create an object of the object type being modified before using the object type's `prototype` property. This will ensure that any new properties and methods are correctly added.

Listing 4.10: Updating an Object Type Definition

```
<HTML>
<HEAD>
<TITLE>Updating Object Types</TITLE>
<SCRIPT LANGUAGE="JavaScript" SRC="table.js"><!-
// -></SCRIPT>
</HEAD>
<BODY>
<H1>Updating Object Types</H1>
<SCRIPT LANGUAGE="JavaScript"><!-
function table_colorWrite(doc) {
 doc.write("<TABLE BORDER="+this.border+" BGCOLOR="+
this.bgColor+">")
  for(var i=0;i<this.rows;++i) {
  doc.write("<TR>")
  for(var j=0;j<this.columns;++j) {
   if(this.header[i*this.columns+j]) {
    doc.write("<TH>")
    doc.write(this.data[i*this.columns+j])
    doc.write("</TH>")
   } else{
    doc.write("<TD>")
    doc.write(this.data[i*this.columns+j])
    doc.write("</TD>")
   }
  }
  doc.writeln("</TR>")
  }
  doc.writeln("</TABLE>")
}
 t = new table(3,4)
 table.prototype.bgColor="cyan"
 table.prototype.colorWrite=table_colorWrite
 contents = new Array("This","is","a","test","of","the",
"table","object.",
  "Let's","see","it","work.")
 t.set(contents)
 t.border=4
 t.makeHeaderColumn(0)
 t.colorWrite(document)
 // -></SCRIPT>
</BODY>
</HTML>
```

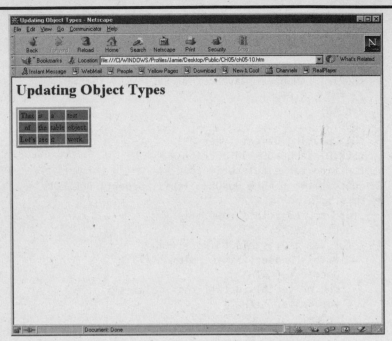

FIGURE 4.10: Tables with a background color (Listing 4.10)

DELETING PROPERTIES AND METHODS

The delete operator can be used to delete an element of an array. The delete operator can also be used to delete a property or method of a user-defined object. Its syntax is as follows:

```
delete objectName.propertyName
delete objectName.methodName
```

For example, suppose the myTable variable refers to a table object. The following statement deletes the header property of the object referenced by myTable:

```
delete myTable.header
```

There are few occasions in which it is desirable to delete a property or method of an existing object. As such, the delete operator is rarely used.

THE *EVENT, EVENT,* AND *ERROR* OBJECTS

In Chapter 3, "Adding JavaScript," you learned how to use event handlers to add functionality based on user actions such as clicks and mouseovers. JavaScript also provides event and error objects, which offer an added level of flexibility when creating event-based scripts.

An instance of the event object is created whenever an event occurs during the execution of a script. Navigator and Internet Explorer each define a different set of properties for the event object. Both browsers use the type property to identify the type of event that occurred and the screenX and screenY properties to identify the screen location at which the event occurred. Navigator and Internet Explorer also implement some similar properties with different names as summarized in Table 4.9.

TABLE 4.9: Similar Navigator and Internet Explorer Event Properties

NAVIGATOR PROPERTY	INTERNET EXPLORER PROPERTY	DESCRIPTION
pageX, pageY	clientX, clientY	The location of the event relative to the Web page
target	srcElement	The event source
which	button	The mouse button associated with the event
key	keyCode	The Unicode character code of the character corresponding to the key press
modifiers	altKey, ctrlKey, shiftKey	The state of the Alt, Control, or Shift keys

Part i

SUMMARY

This chapter described JavaScript's support of objects and object-based programming. It introduced the JavaScript Object Model and summarized the predefined JavaScript objects. It also showed you how to create your own objects and methods.

PART II
ADVANCED JAVASCRIPT

CHAPTER 5

PROCESSING FORMS

Forms provide you with an important capability for Web page development—they allow you to gather information from individuals who browse your Web pages. This is especially important if you use your Web site to advertise or sell your products. Forms make it easy to collect information from your Web page users. They provide a full range of graphical user interface (GUI) controls and they automatically submit the data they collect to your Web server. This data can then be processed by CGI programs, server-side JavaScript scripts built upon Netscape's LiveWire, server-side JScript scripts written as Microsoft's Active Server Pages, or other types of server-side scripts.

Adapted from *Mastering JavaScript and JScript*, by James Jaworski
ISBN 0-7821-2492-5   925 pages $39.99

JavaScript provides a number of features that can be used to enhance the forms that you develop for your particular Web applications. These features allow you to validate form data before it is submitted to your server and to exercise greater control of the interaction between your forms and Web users.

This chapter introduces the form object and discusses the JavaScript objects that are associated with form fields and GUI controls. It shows how to use the properties and methods of these objects, and how to handle form-related events. When you finish this chapter, you will know how to use JavaScript to create forms that perform local processing and will be able to use these forms to communicate with CGI programs.

NOTE

If you are unfamiliar with the HTML tags used to create forms, consult http://www.sybex.com. Use the catalog to access this book's Web page. From this page, follow the link to the author's home page, which will provide links to HTML tutorials and reference documents.

The *form* Object

JavaScript provides the form object to enable your scripts to interact with and exercise control over HTML forms. The form object is accessed as a property of the document object. Your browser creates a unique form object for every form that is contained in a document. These objects can be accessed via the document.forms[] array.

The form object is important because it provides you with access to the forms contained in your documents and allows you to respond to form-related events. Table 5.1 lists the properties of the form object as of JavaScript 1.3. These properties provide access to a form's attributes and allow you to work with a form's fields and GUI controls. In JavaScript 1.3, the form object provides three methods, handleEvent(), submit(), and reset(). The handleEvent() method is used to invoke a form's event handler for a specified event. The submit() and reset() methods are used to submit a form or reset a form's entries to their default values.

NOTE

The Internet Explorer object model defines additional properties and methods for the form object and the objects that are contained in a form. These properties and methods support Internet Explorer's implementation of DHTML.

TABLE 5.1: Properties of the form Object

PROPERTY	DESCRIPTION
action	Provides access to the HTML action attribute of the <form> tag
button	An object representing a button GUI control
checkbox	An object representing a checkbox field
elements	An array containing all the fields and GUI controls included in a form
encoding	Provides access to the HTML enctype attribute of the <form> tag
FileUpload	An object representing a file-upload form field
hidden	An object representing a hidden form field
length	Provides access to the length of the elements array
method	Provides access to the HTML method attribute of the <form> tag
name	Identifies the name of the form
password	An object representing a password field
radio	An object representing a radio button field
reset	An object representing a reset button
select	An object representing a selection list
submit	An object representing a submit button
target	Provides access to the HTML target attribute of the <form> tag
text	An object representing a text field
textarea	An object representing a text area field

Accessing Forms within JavaScript

Because form objects are properties of documents, they are accessed by referencing the documents in which they are contained. If you name a form when you create it, then you can access the form by its name. Forms are named using the form's name attribute. For example, if you create a form named employeeData you can access the form's method property using employeeData.method.

You can also use the forms property of the document object to access the forms contained in a particular document. The forms property is an array that contains an entry for each form contained in a document. Suppose that the employeeData form is the third form contained in the document loaded into the current window. You can access the form's method property using document.forms[2].method or document.forms["employeeData"].method.

Accessing Form Elements

A form may contain a wide variety of fields and GUI controls. These form components are referred to as *elements* of the form and are objects in their own right. Table 5.2 lists and summarizes the objects that may be contained in a form.

TABLE 5.2: The Objects That May Be Contained in a Form

Object	Description
button	A general-purpose button for implementing GUI controls
checkbox	A clickable field that allows multiple selections from within a group
FileUpload	A field that allows a user to specify a file to be submitted as part of the form
hidden	A field that may contain a value but is not displayed within a form
password	A text field in which the values that a user enters are hidden via mask characters

CONTINUED →

TABLE 5.2 continued: The Objects That May Be Contained in a Form

OBJECT	DESCRIPTION
radio	A clickable field that allows only a single selection from within a group
reset	A button that is used to reset the contents of a form to its default state
select	A list from which individual list items may be selected
submit	A button that is used to submit the data entered into a field
text	A single-line field for entering text
textarea	A multiline field for entering text

If the elements of a form are named using an HTML name attribute, then the element can be accessed using this name. For example, suppose that you have a form named form1 that contains a text field named ssn. You can access the value of this field using form1.ssn.value.

In most cases, you will access the elements of a form using the elements array property of the form object. This array contains an object for each element of a form. Suppose that the ssn field of the form1 form is the seventh element defined in the form. You can access the value of the ssn field using form1.elements[6].value.

The objects described in Table 5.2 reference the elements of a form and have properties and methods of their own as summarized in Tables 5.3 and 5.4.

TABLE 5.3: Properties of Form Elements

OBJECT	PROPERTY	DESCRIPTION
button	name	Provides access to the button's name attribute
	type	Identifies the object's type
	value	Identifies the object's value

CONTINUED ➡

TABLE 5.3 continued: Properties of Form Elements

OBJECT	PROPERTY	DESCRIPTION
checkbox	checked	Identifies whether the checkbox is currently checked
	defaultChecked	Identifies whether the checkbox is checked by default
	name	Provides access to the checkbox's HTML name attribute
	type	Identifies the object's type
	value	Identifies the object's value
FileUpload	name	Provides access to the object's name attribute
	type	Identifies the object's type attribute
	value	Identifies the object's value
hidden	name	Provides access to the object's name attribute
	type	Identifies the object's type
	value	Identifies the object's value
password	defaultValue	Identifies the object's default value
	name	Provides access to the object's name attribute
	type	Identifies the object's type
	value	Identifies the object's value
radio	checked	Identifies whether the radio button is currently checked
	defaultChecked	Identifies whether the radio button is checked by default
	name	Provides access to the object's name attribute
	type	Identifies the object's type
	value	Identifies the object's value

CONTINUED ➡

TABLE 5.3 continued: Properties of Form Elements

OBJECT	PROPERTY	DESCRIPTION
reset	name	Provides access to the object's name attribute
	type	Identifies the object's type
	value	Identifies the object's value
select	length	Identifies the length of the select list
	name	Provides access to the object's name attribute
	options	An array that identifies the options supported by the select list
	selectedIndex	Identifies the first selected option within the select list
	type	Identifies the object's type
submit	name	Provides access to the object's name attribute
	type	Identifies the object's type
	value	Identifies the object's value
text	defaultValue	Identifies the default text to be displayed in the text field
	name	Provides access to the object's name attribute
	type	Identifies the object's type
	value	Identifies the object's value
textarea	defaultValue	Identifies the default text to be displayed in the text area field
	name	Provides access to the object's name attribute
	type	Identifies the object's type
	value	Identifies the object's value

Part ii

NOTE

All form elements have the form property. This property references the form in which the element is contained. All form elements except the hidden element provide the handleEvent() method for directly invoking the element's event handlers.

TABLE 5.4: Methods of Form Elements

Object	Method	Description
button	click()	Simulates the button being clicked
	blur()	Removes focus from the button
	focus()	Gives focus to the button
checkbox	click()	Simulates the checkbox being clicked
	blur()	Removes focus from the checkbox
	focus()	Gives focus to the checkbox
FileUpload	blur()	Removes focus from the file-upload field
	focus()	Gives focus to the file-upload field
	select()	Selects the input area of the file-upload field
hidden	none	
password	blur()	Removes input focus from the password field
	focus()	Gives input focus to the password field
	select()	Highlights the text displayed in the password field
radio	click()	Simulates the clicking of the radio button
	blur()	Removes focus from the radio button
	focus()	Gives focus to the radio button

CONTINUED ➡

TABLE 5.4 continued: Methods of Form Elements

OBJECT	METHOD	DESCRIPTION
reset	click()	Simulates the clicking of the reset button
	blur()	Removes focus from the reset button
	focus()	Gives focus to the reset button
select	blur()	Removes focus from the selection list
	focus()	Gives focus to the selection list
submit	click ()	Simulates the clicking of the submit button
	blur()	Removes focus from the submit button
	focus()	Gives focus to the submit button
text	blur()	Removes focus from the text field
	focus()	Gives focus to the text field
	select()	Highlights the text in the text field
textarea	blur()	Removes focus from the text area
	focus()	Gives focus to the text area
	select()	Highlights the text in the text area

Listing 5.1 shows how the individual forms and form elements can be accessed in multiform documents. It creates the three-form document shown in Figure 5.1. When you click the Submit button of the first form, the onSubmit() handler invokes the displayFormData() function. Note that it does this in the context of a return statement. This causes the form submission to be aborted when displayFormData() returns a *false* value. This is always the case because displayFormData() always returns *false*.

Listing 5.1: Accessing the Elements of a Form (*formacc.htm*)

```
<HTML>
<HEAD>
<TITLE>Multiform Document Example</TITLE>
<SCRIPT LANGUAGE="JavaScript"><!--
function displayFormData() {
 win2=open("","window2")
 win2.document.open("text/plain")
 win2.document.writeln("This document has "+
  document.forms.length+" forms.")
 for(i=0;i<document.forms.length;++i) {
  win2.document.writeln("Form "+i+" has "+
   document.forms[i].elements.length+" elements.")
  for(j=0;j<document.forms[i].elements.length;++j) {
   win2.document.writeln((j+1)+" A "+
    document.forms[i].elements[j].type+" element.")
  }
 }
 win2.document.close()
 return false
}
// --></SCRIPT>
</HEAD>
<BODY>
<H1>Multiform Document Example</H1>
<FORM ACTION="nothing" onSubmit="return displayFormData()">
<H2>Form 1</H2>
<P>Text field: <INPUT TYPE="TEXT" NAME="f1-1"
 ~CAVALUE="Sample text"></P>
<P>Password field: <INPUT TYPE="PASSWORD" NAME="f1-2"></P>
<P>Text area field:
<TEXTAREA ROWS="4" COLS="30"
   NAME="f1-3">Write your novel here.</TEXTAREA></P>
<P><INPUT TYPE="SUBMIT" NAME="f1-4" VALUE="Submit">
<INPUT TYPE="RESET" NAME="f1-5"></P>
</FORM>
<HR>
<FORM>
<H2>Form 2</H2>
<P><INPUT TYPE="CHECKBOX" NAME="f2-1" VALUE="1"
➡ CHECKED> Check me!</P>
<P><INPUT TYPE="CHECKBOX" NAME="f2-1" VALUE="2"> No.
➡ Check me!</P>
```

```
<P><INPUT TYPE="CHECKBOX" NAME="f2-1" VALUE="3"> Check all
of us!</P>
<P><INPUT TYPE="RADIO" NAME="f2-2" VALUE="1"> AM</P>
<P><INPUT TYPE="RADIO" NAME="f2-2" VALUE="2" CHECKED> PM</P>
<P><INPUT TYPE="RADIO" NAME="f2-2" VALUE="3"> FM</P>
<INPUT TYPE="FILE" NAME="f2-3">
</FORM>
<HR>
<FORM>
<H2>Form 3</H2>
<INPUT TYPE="HIDDEN" NAME="f3-1">
<SELECT NAME="f3-2" SIZE="4">
<OPTION VALUE="">Item 1</OPTION>
<OPTION VALUE="">Item 2</OPTION>
<OPTION VALUE="" SELECTED>Item 3</OPTION>
<OPTION VALUE="">Item 4</OPTION>
<OPTION VALUE="">Item 5</OPTION>
</SELECT>
</FORM>
</BODY>
</HTML>
```

The displayFormData() function creates and opens a separate window and assigns the window object to the win2 variable. It then opens the window's document with a text/plain MIME type. It uses the forms array of the document object of the first window to determine how many forms are contained in the document. It then writes this information to the document contained in win2. Next, it identifies the number of elements in each form using the length property of the form's elements array. Finally, it displays the type property of each form element via win2, as shown in Figure 5.2.

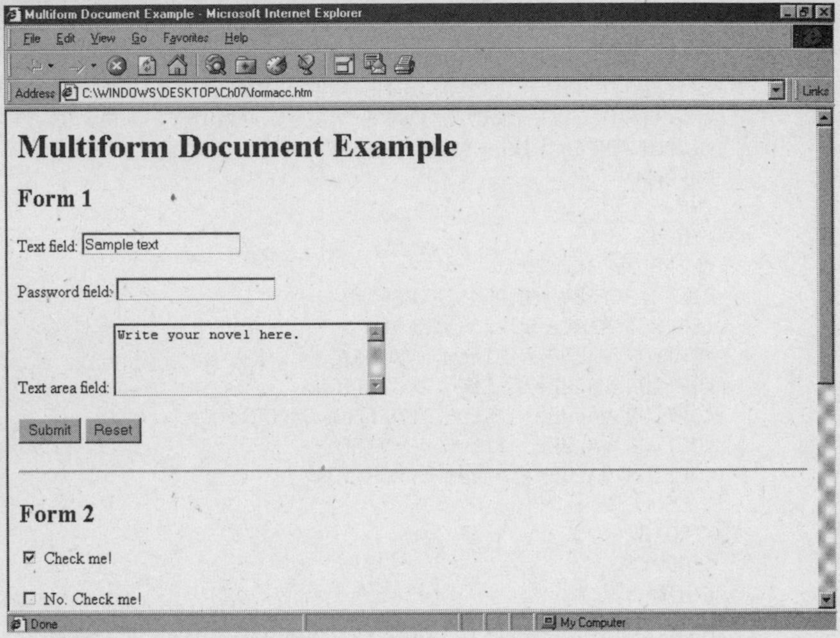

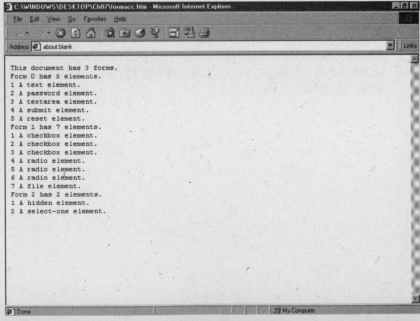

FIGURE 5.1: A multiform document (Listing 5.1)

FIGURE 5.2: A summary of the contents of the multiform document (Listing 5.1)

USING FORM EVENT HANDLERS

JavaScript's ability to handle form-related events is a very powerful tool for customizing form behavior. It allows you to control the user's interaction with your forms and to process form data as the user enters it. It also allows you to process form data locally at the user's browser, reducing the load on your communication bandwidth and on your Web server.

Form event handlers respond to events that indicate the user has performed an input action, such as filling in a text field, clicking a button, or submitting an entire form. These event handlers check the data entered by the user and then either prompt the user to correct any errors or provide the user with other feedback on the data that was entered. Form event handlers may also be used to adaptively present new forms to a user based upon the user's response to prior forms.

Responding to User Actions

If you have not already read Chapter 3, you should do so before continuing on in this chapter; event handlers, and specifically the onSubmit event handler, are covered in the "Adding Event Handlers" section in that chapter.

Clicks and checks   These are the most common types of form events. A user clicks a button or checks a checkbox to provide information or to perform an action. These events are handled by event-handling functions that provide feedback to the user on the results of the actions taken in response to the click or check.

Text changes   Text changes are another common type of form event. The user enters data into a text field or text area, an event is generated, and the event handler validates the user's entry and performs further processing based on the user's input.

List selection   When a user selects an item from a selection list, event-handling code is used to verify that the selection is consistent with other inputs and to perform any processing indicated by the selection.

Change of focus   Change-of-focus events occur when a form element, such as a text field or selection list, receives or loses the current input focus. These events usually do not require special event handling. However, JavaScript provides the capability to do so, when required.

Form submission and reset   These events are generated when a user clicks a submit or reset button. Form-submission events are typically handled by validating all of the data entered by the user, performing any local processing on that data, and then forwarding the data to a CGI program or other server-side script.

Because you have already covered form event handling in Chapter 3, I'm not going to bore you with any more trivial examples. Instead, we'll use JavaScript's event-handling capabilities to create a form-based Hangman game—something that is impossible to do in HTML alone.

If you're not already familiar with Hangman, here's a short description of the game. Hangman is a game where you try to guess a word, one letter at a time. You are initially presented with a word pattern where each letter of the word to be guessed is represented by an underscore (_) character. This tells you how many letters are in the word, but nothing more. When you guess a letter that is in the word, the underscore representing that letter is replaced by the letter you guessed correctly. This tells you that you've guessed the correct letter and shows you where the letter appears in the word. You continue to guess until you run out of guesses or you guess all of the letters of the word.

Your status in terms of guesses is depicted in a gallows—that's why it's called Hangman. Each time you guess incorrectly, a "body part" is added to the victim being hanged. You are only allowed seven incorrect guesses (head, upper and lower torso, two arms, two legs) before the game is over. The purpose of the game is not to be morbid, but to improve your word recognition skills.

Before going on to learn how the game is implemented using form event handling, you should play a few games. Start the game by opening hangman.htm from your browser. (The file is located on the Sybex Web site at www.sybex.com. To begin with, search for *Mastering JavaScript and JScript* on the Sybex site, and then click the link to that title that your search will yield. You then have access to information relating to the title from which this chapter was drawn. Click the Downloads link, read and accept the user license, click the Code link, select Chapter 7, and then save the file to an appropriate location on your computer. You will then have access to the hangman.htm file.) At startup, it presents the display shown in Figure 5.3.

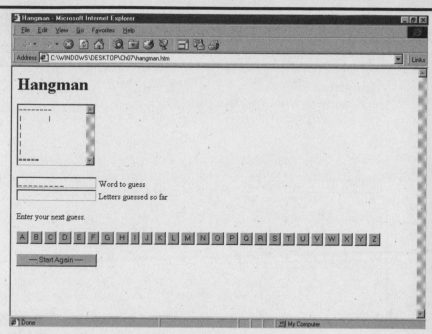

FIGURE 5.3: The Hangman opening display (Listing 5.2)

Play the game by clicking any of the buttons labeled *A* through *Z*. If you guess correctly, the game will display the position of the letter in the Word to Guess text field as shown in Figure 5.4. If you guess incorrectly, a part of your body will be hung in the gallows as shown in Figure 5.5. If you continue to guess incorrectly, your complete effigy will be hung (see Figure 5.6), an alert dialog box will tell you that you lost, and the game will start again. If you are clever enough to guess the word before you are hung, an alert dialog box will tell you that you won, and the game will start over. Clicking the Start Again button will immediately restart the game with a new word to guess.

NOTE

If you try to modify any of the form's text fields, an alert message will be displayed that tells you not to mess with that field.

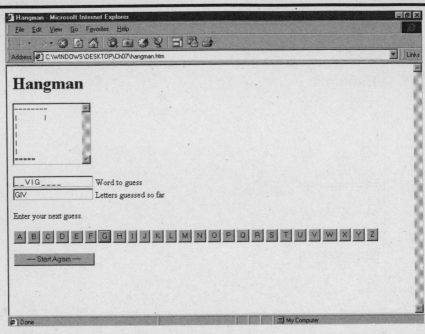

FIGURE 5.4: You guessed correctly (Listing 5.2)

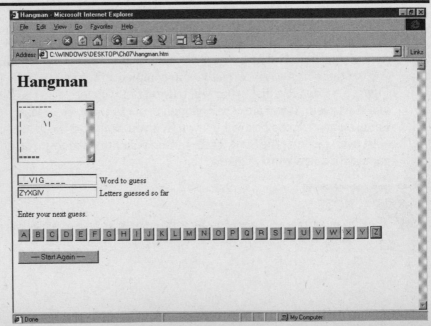

FIGURE 5.5: You guessed incorrectly (Listing 5.2)

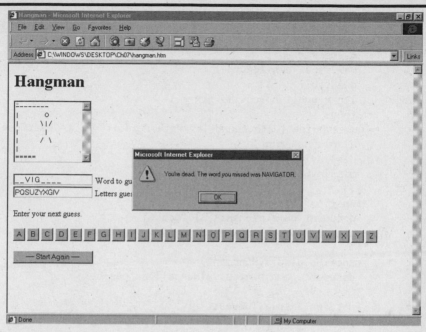

FIGURE 5.6: You're hung (Listing 5.2)

Listing 5.2 shows the contents of the hangman.htm file. This file is fairly long, but don't worry; I'll go over it one small piece at a time. The file contains two scripts: one in the document head and one in the document body. I'll start with the script in the document head because that's the part your browser processes first.

Listing 5.2: A JavaScript Hangman Game (*hangman.htm*)

```
<HTML>
<HEAD>
<TITLE>Hangman</TITLE>
<SCRIPT LANGUAGE="JavaScript"><!--
gallows = new Array("--------\n|        |\n|\n|\n|\n|\n=====",
"--------\n|      O\n|\n|\n|\n|\n=====",
"--------\n|      O\n|        |\n|\n|\n|\n=====",
"--------\n|      O\n|      \\\\|\n|\n|\n|\n=====",
"--------\n|      O\n|      \\\\|/\n|\n|\n|\n=====",
"--------\n|      O\n|      \\\\|/\n|        |\n|\n|\n=====",
"--------\n|      O\n|      \\\\|/\n|        |\n|      /\n|\n
➡ =====",
"--------\n|      O\n|      \\\\|/\n|        |\n|      / \\\\\n|\n
➡ =====")
```

```
  guessChoices = new
  Array("JavaScript","Navigator","LiveConnect","LiveWire")
  function startAgain() {
   guesses = 0
   max = gallows.length-1
   guessed = " "
   len = guessChoices.length - 1
   toGuess =
➥ guessChoices[Math.round(len*Math.random())] .toUpperCase()
   displayHangman()
   displayToGuess()
   displayGuessed()
  }
  function stayAway() {
   document.game.elements[3].focus()
   alert("Don't mess with this form element!")
  }
  function displayHangman() {
   document.game.status.value=gallows[guesses]
  }
  function displayToGuess() {
   pattern=""
   for(i=0;i<toGuess.length;++i) {
    if(guessed.indexOf(toGuess.charAt(i)) != -1)
     pattern += (toGuess.charAt(i)+" ")
    else pattern += "_ "
   }
   document.game.toGuess.value=pattern
  }
  function displayGuessed() {
   document.game.guessed.value=guessed
  }
  function badGuess(s) {
   if(toGuess.indexOf(s) == -1) return true
   return false
  }
  function winner() {
   for(i=0;i<toGuess.length;++i) {
    if(guessed.indexOf(toGuess.charAt(i)) == -1) return false
   }
   return true
  }
  function guess(s){
   if(guessed.indexOf(s) == -1) guessed = s + guessed
   if(badGuess(s)) ++guesses
   displayHangman()
```

```
displayToGuess()
displayGuessed()
if(guesses >= max){
alert("You're dead. The word you missed was "+toGuess+".")
 startAgain()
}
if(winner()) {
 alert("You won!")
 startAgain()
}
}
// --></SCRIPT>
</HEAD>
<BODY>
<H1>Hangman</H1>
<FORM NAME="game">
<PRE>
<TEXTAREA NAME="status" ROWS="7" COLS="16"
 ONFOCUS="stayAway()"></TEXTAREA>
</PRE><P>
<INPUT TYPE="TEXT" NAME="toGuess"
 ONFOCUS="stayAway()"> Word to guess<BR>
<INPUT TYPE="TEXT" NAME="guessed"
 ONFOCUS="stayAway()"> Letters guessed so far<BR>
<P>Enter your next guess.</P>
<INPUT TYPE="BUTTON" VALUE=" A " ONCLICK="guess('A')">
<INPUT TYPE="BUTTON" VALUE=" B " ONCLICK="guess('B')">
<INPUT TYPE="BUTTON" VALUE=" C " ONCLICK="guess('C')">
<INPUT TYPE="BUTTON" VALUE=" D " ONCLICK="guess('D')">
<INPUT TYPE="BUTTON" VALUE=" E " ONCLICK="guess('E')">
<INPUT TYPE="BUTTON" VALUE=" F " ONCLICK="guess('F')">
<INPUT TYPE="BUTTON" VALUE=" G " ONCLICK="guess('G')">
<INPUT TYPE="BUTTON" VALUE=" H " ONCLICK="guess('H')">
<INPUT TYPE="BUTTON" VALUE=" I " ONCLICK="guess('I')">
<INPUT TYPE="BUTTON" VALUE=" J " ONCLICK="guess('J')">
<INPUT TYPE="BUTTON" VALUE=" K " ONCLICK="guess('K')">
<INPUT TYPE="BUTTON" VALUE=" L " ONCLICK="guess('L')">
<INPUT TYPE="BUTTON" VALUE=" M " ONCLICK="guess('M')">
<INPUT TYPE="BUTTON" VALUE=" N " ONCLICK="guess('N')">
<INPUT TYPE="BUTTON" VALUE=" O " ONCLICK="guess('O')">
<INPUT TYPE="BUTTON" VALUE=" P " ONCLICK="guess('P')">
<INPUT TYPE="BUTTON" VALUE=" Q " ONCLICK="guess('Q')">
<INPUT TYPE="BUTTON" VALUE=" R " ONCLICK="guess('R')">
<INPUT TYPE="BUTTON" VALUE=" S " ONCLICK="guess('S')">
<INPUT TYPE="BUTTON" VALUE=" T " ONCLICK="guess('T')">
<INPUT TYPE="BUTTON" VALUE=" U " ONCLICK="guess('U')">
```

```
<INPUT TYPE="BUTTON" VALUE=" V " ONCLICK="guess('V')">
<INPUT TYPE="BUTTON" VALUE=" W " ONCLICK="guess('W')">
<INPUT TYPE="BUTTON" VALUE=" X " ONCLICK="guess('X')">
<INPUT TYPE="BUTTON" VALUE=" Y " ONCLICK="guess('Y')">
<INPUT TYPE="BUTTON" VALUE=" Z " ONCLICK="guess('Z')"><P>
<INPUT TYPE="BUTTON" NAME="restart"
```
➡ ```
VALUE="---- Start Again ----"
  ONCLICK="startAgain()">
<SCRIPT LANGUAGE="JavaScript"><!--
startAgain()
// --></SCRIPT>
</FORM>
</BODY>
</HTML>
```

The script defines two arrays, gallows and guessChoices, and eight functions—startAgain(), stayAway(), displayHangman(), display-ToGuess(), displayGuessed(), badGuess(), winner(), and guess(). Each of these is discussed in the following paragraphs.

# The *gallows* Array

This array contains eight string entries that correspond to the eight states that the gallows pole may be in: empty, head hanging, head and upper torso hanging, and so on. The strings may look very cryptic. That's because new lines are represented by the new-line character (\n) and back slashes are represented by a pair of back slashes (\\). These are the standard escape characters used by JavaScript, Java, C, and C++. Try decoding and drawing each of the strings in the gallows array to get a better feel for how these escape characters are used.

# The *guessChoices* Array

This array contains four words. These are the words that the user is required to guess. One word from this array is randomly selected for each play of the game. You can add or replace the words contained in this array to tailor Hangman with your own word list.

# The *startAgain()* Function

This function starts and restarts the Hangman game. It initializes variables used by the program and then invokes the functions required to display the hangman, show the word to be guessed, and display the letters that the user has already guessed. The guesses variable keeps track of
```

how many incorrect guesses the user has made. It is used to select which element of the gallows array is to be displayed. The max variable determines how many guesses the user can make before he or she is hung. The guessed variable is initialized to " " (one space) to indicate that the user has not yet guessed any letters.

NOTE
The value " " is used instead of "" (no space) because the indexOf() method of the string object does not work correctly for the value "".

The len variable is used to calculate the maximum array subscript of the guessChoices array. The toGuess variable is set to a randomly selected word in the guessChoices array. This word is then converted to uppercase. The displayHangman() function displays the hangman figure in the status text area. The displayToGuess() function displays the word being guessed in the toGuess text field. The displayGuessed() function displays the letters guessed by the user in the guessed text field. When the game is first started or restarted, the displayGuessed() function is used to blank out the guessed text field.

The *stayAway()* Function

This function is called by the onFocus event handlers of the form's text fields to warn the user not to mess around with these fields. This is to discourage the user from trying to change the content of these fields. Note that it moves the input focus to the "A" button before it displays the alert box.

The *displayHangman()* Function

This function displays the hangman character figure in the status text area. It does this by setting the value property of the status field of the game form of the current document to the gallows array entry corresponding to the number of incorrect guesses.

The *displayToGuess()* Function

This function displays a word pattern based on the word to be guessed and the letters the user has currently guessed. If a user has guessed a letter of the word, then that letter is displayed. Otherwise, an underscore character is displayed in place of the letter. It loops through each letter of the word contained in toGuess and uses the indexOf() method of the string object to determine whether that letter is contained in the guessed string. The word pattern is then written to the toGuessed text field.

The *displayGuessed()* Function

This function writes the value of the guessed variable to the guessed text field to inform the user of the letters that he or she has already tried. The guessed variable is updated each time a user makes a new letter guess.

The *badGuess()* Function

This function returns *true* if the letter represented by the s parameter is not in the word contained in the toGuess variable. It returns *false*, otherwise. It is used to determine whether the user has guessed incorrectly.

The *winner()* Function

This function checks each letter in the word contained in the toGuess variable and returns *false* if any letter is not in the string contained in the guessed variable. It returns *true* otherwise. It is used to determine whether the user has correctly guessed all letters of the toGuess word.

The *guess()* Function

This function is invoked whenever the user clicks a button with the letters A through Z. It is invoked by the button's onClick event handler and passes the letter associated with the button via the s parameter. Here's how it works:

1. The guess() function first checks to see if the letter is currently in the list of letters the user has already guessed, and adds the letter to the list if it is not.

2. It then checks to see if the letter is an incorrect guess, and increments the guesses variable accordingly.

3. Next, it invokes the appropriate functions to redisplay the form's text fields.

4. It then checks to see if the user has run out of guesses, and if so, alerts the user that he or she has been hung.

5. Finally, it invokes the `winner()` function to determine if the user has correctly guessed all letters of the `toGuess` word, and, if so, tells the user that he or she has won.

The form displayed by the browser is named game. It contains the text area named `status`, the text fields named `toGuess` and `guessed`, the buttons labeled *A* through *Z*, and the Start Again button. Each of these form elements performs event handling that supports the processing of the Hangman game. This event handling is as follows:

status, toGuess, and guessed   These fields handle the `onFocus` event by invoking the `stayAway()` function to tell the user to not mess with the field's contents.

A **through** *Z*   These buttons handle the `onClick` event by invoking the `guess()` function and passing as a parameter the letter associated with the button.

Start Again   This button invokes the `startAgain()` function to reinitialize the game's variables and restart the game.

The script contained in the document body contains the single statement, `startAgain()`, which initializes the variables used in the game and displays the contents of the form's text fields.

CLIENT-SIDE FORM PROCESSING

The Hangman game of the previous section is a great example of the power of local form processing. However, unless your sole purpose in Web programming is to entertain those who browse your Web page, you'll probably want to use forms to return some data to your Web server. This brings up the very important question of which processing should be performed locally via browser-side scripts and which should be performed on the server? For the most part, this question is easy to answer: "If it can be performed on the browser, then do it." It's a pretty good rule of thumb. However, as with most rules of thumb, there are cases that create exceptions to the rule. For example, if you don't want anyone to know how you process the form data, then don't do it locally on the browser. Anyone can figure out your processing approach by examining your JavaScript code. Another consideration is performance. If your Web application requires a time- or resource-intensive computation, you can avoid upsetting your user by having the data sent back to your high-performance server for processing. However, in most cases forms processing is short and quick, and no noticeable impact is made on browser performance.

WORKING WITH CGI SCRIPTS

Before the advent of JavaScript, the data the forms collected from users was submitted to Common Gateway Interface (CGI) programs. The CGI programs performed all processing on the form data and sent the results of that processing back to the browser so that it could be displayed to users. In this section, I'll show how to use JavaScript scripts to communicate with CGI programs. More importantly, I'll show how to use JavaScript to perform local processing of form data before sending the data to CGI programs.

Sending Form Data to a CGI Program

When a form sends data to a CGI program, it uses either the GET or POST method. These methods are specified by setting the method attribute of the form to either "get" or "post". If the GET method is used, the form encodes and appends its data to the URL of the CGI program. When a Web server receives the encoded URL, it passes the form data to the CGI program via a program variable known as an *environment* variable. If the POST method is used, the Web server passes the form's data to the CGI program via the program's standard input. The POST method is preferred over the GET method because of data size limitations associated with environment variables. The method property of the form object allows a form's method to be set within JavaScript.

A form's ACTION attribute specifies the URL of the CGI program to which a form's data is to be sent. The action property of the form object allows this URL to be set or changed within JavaScript. This allows a script to send a form's data to one of several CGI programs, depending upon the form's contents as entered by a user. For example, you can have a general-purpose form that collects information on users interested in your product line and then process that data in different ways depending upon the demographic data supplied by the user.

In most cases, form data is encoded using the URL encoding scheme identified by the following MIME type:

```
application/x-www-form-urlencoded
```

However, it is likely that another scheme

```
multipart/form-data encoding
```

will become popular because of its support for file uploads. This encoding scheme is discussed in RFC 1867, which can be found at the URL http://www.jaworski.com/javascript/rfc1867.txt. The encoding property of the form object identifies what encoding scheme was specified by the form's ENCTYPE attribute. The encoding property may also be used to change this attribute.

NOTE

An RFC (literally a Request for Comments) is a document that is used to describe a particular aspect of the Internet, such as a protocol standard or a coding scheme.

Performing Local Form Processing

Having covered the basic form properties that control a form's interaction with a CGI program, let's investigate how JavaScript can be used to locally process a form's data and then send the processed data to the Web server.

When a form is submitted, either as the result of a user clicking a submit button or the invocation of a form's submit() method, all of the data contained in the form's fields are sent to the Web server. This is both inefficient and undesirable because we can use JavaScript to preprocess a form's data.

The secret to using JavaScript to send processed form data to CGI programs is to use a *summary form* to hold the data that is the result of any local form processing. Once a form's data has been initially processed, it is put into a summary form, and then the summary form is sent to the CGI program for any additional processing that is required. Listing 5.3 illustrates this concept. A Web page is designed with two forms. The first form is visible to the user and is the form used to collect raw input data. This form is shown in Figure 5.7. It provides the user with four selection lists with which the user can select a particular type of automobile.

Listing 5.3: Using a Summary Form to Support Local Processing (*orderform.htm*)

```html
<HTML>
<HEAD>
<TITLE>Submitting the results of local form
➥ processing</TITLE>
<SCRIPT LANGUAGE="JavaScript"><!--
function processOrder() {
 order = ""
 order += document.orderForm.model.selectedIndex
 order += document.orderForm.doors.selectedIndex
 order += document.orderForm.color.selectedIndex
 sel = document.orderForm.accessories
 for(i=0;i<sel.length;++i)
  if(sel.options[i].selected) order += i
 document.submitForm.result.value = order
 document.submitForm.submit()
 return false
}
// --></SCRIPT>
</HEAD>
<BODY>
<H1>Select your next car:</H1>
<PRE>Model          Doors      Color     Accessories</PRE>
<FORM ACTION="" NAME="orderForm"
➥ ONSUBMIT="return processOrder()">
<SELECT NAME="model" SIZE="3">
<OPTION>Big Blob</OPTION>
<OPTION>Wild Thing</OPTION>
<OPTION>Penny Pincher</OPTION>
<OPTION>Class Act</OPTION>
</SELECT>
<SELECT NAME="doors" SIZE="3">
<OPTION>2 doors</OPTION>
<OPTION>4 doors</OPTION>
</SELECT>
<SELECT NAME="color" SIZE="3">
<OPTION>red</OPTION>
<OPTION>white</OPTION>
<OPTION>blue</OPTION>
<OPTION>black</OPTION>
<OPTION>brown</OPTION>
<OPTION>silver</OPTION>
<OPTION>pink</OPTION>
</SELECT>
```

```
<SELECT NAME="accessories" SIZE="3" MULTIPLE="MULTIPLE">
<OPTION>air conditioning</OPTION>
<OPTION>CD player</OPTION>
<OPTION>bigger engine</OPTION>
<OPTION>fancy dashboard</OPTION>
<OPTION>leather seats</OPTION>
</SELECT>
<P><INPUT TYPE="SUBMIT" NAME="order"
VALUE="I'll take it!"></P>
</FORM>
<FORM ACTION="http://www.jaworski.com/cgi-bin/echo.cgi"
      METHOD="POST" NAME="submitForm">
<INPUT TYPE="HIDDEN" NAME="result">
</FORM>
</BODY>
</HTML>
```

When the first form is submitted, the onSubmit event handler invokes the processOrder() function as the argument of a return statement. If the return statement returns *false,* then the form is not submitted. If the return statement returns *true,* then the form *is* submitted. Because processOrder() *always* returns *false*, the form will never be submitted. Instead, processOrder() fills in the invisible field in the second form and submits the second form to a CGI program located on my Web server. This CGI program is located at the URL http://www.jaworski.com/cgi-bin/echo.cgi. It merely echoes back any form fields that it has received from the browser. Figure 5.8 provides an example of the CGI program's output.

I'll summarize what I've covered so far. The first form is used to gather automobile selection data from the user. When the first form is submitted, processOrder() is invoked to process this data locally on the user's browser. processOrder() then inserts the processed data into the second form (named submitForm) and submits the second form to my Web server. The Web server then echoes the form fields back to the browser.

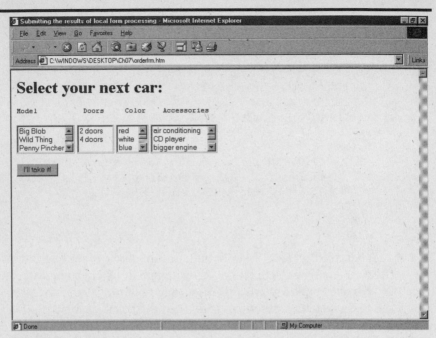

FIGURE 5.7: The form that is presented to the user (Listing 5.3)]

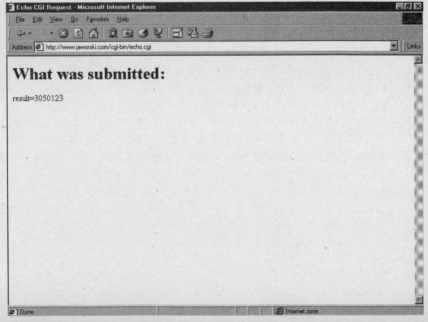

FIGURE 5.8: The form data that is echoed by the Web server (Listing 5.3)

The processing performed by processOrder() is quite simple, but it illustrates how locally processed form data can be sent to a Web server. Here are the steps:

1. processOrder() begins by setting the order variable to a string that contains the indices of the list items selected in the model, doors, and colors selection lists. Each of these three lists is a single-selection list.

2. For each item in the multiple-selection accessories list, processOrder() checks to see if the item has been selected, and appends the index of each selected accessories item to the string stored in the order variable.

3. The processOrder() function then sets the invisible results field of submitForm to the value stored in order. By doing so, it has placed all of the first form's results into a single field in submitForm.

4. The processOrder() function then invokes the submit() method of submitForm to send the result field to my Web server.

While you may not be impressed by the complexity of the processing performed by processOrder(), you should realize the value of the approach that it takes. This approach allows you to design your forms so that they are most appealing to your end users. When the user submits a filled-out form, you can process the form's results and send the results to your Web server in whatever format is most efficient for your CGI or other server-side programs.

SUMMARY

This chapter introduced the form object and discussed the JavaScript objects that are associated with form fields and GUI controls. It showed you how to use the properties and methods of these objects and how to handle form-related events. In the next chapter, you will learn how to enhance your forms by using hidden form fields and cookies.

Part ii

Chapter 6

Using Hidden Fields and Cookies

The Web was originally designed to be *stateless*, in the sense that all Web servers would process URL requests in the same manner, independent of any previous requests. This enabled the first Web servers to be fast and efficient by not requiring them to maintain information about the browsers requesting URLs. Browsers also operated in a stateless fashion, proccssing new URL requests independent of previous requests.

Adapted from *Mastering JavaScript and JScript,*
by James Jaworski
ISBN 0-7821-2492-5   925 pages $39.99

The stateless design of the Web works well in most cases. When a browser requests a particular Web page, the Web server that provides that page will serve it up to the browser in the same way every time. Similarly, all Web browsers requesting a particular Web page always request that page in the same way. However, there are situations in which you *want* the processing of one Web page to be dependent on the processing of previous pages. For example, you may want to enable a user to complete a series of forms in which the user's responses to the first form determine which forms are provided next. For instance, you may want to create a form that collects general information about the user, such as name and address, and link it to subsequent forms to collect more information. However, those forms will vary depending on what country the user has entered in the first form.

A number of capabilities have been successively introduced to enable Web applications to be built upon the stateless design of the Web. *Hidden form fields* were introduced first, followed by HTTP "cookies." These capabilities were introduced to allow CGI programs to maintain information about individual Web browsers. With JavaScript's support of browser-side scripting, the use of hidden fields and cookies can be taken to new levels.

In this chapter you'll learn how to use hidden fields and cookies to maintain browser state information and how you can use this information in your scripts to develop more capable and powerful Web applications. When you've finished this chapter, you'll be able to read and update hidden fields and cookies using JavaScript, and locally implement on the browser side much of the complex state-related processing that would otherwise be performed by server-side CGI programs.

MAINTAINING STATE INFORMATION

To gain a greater understanding of the problem of maintaining state information, let's explore the example discussed in this chapter's introduction. Suppose that you want to develop a Web page that presents a related series of forms to a user as follows:

Form One   Collects the user's name, address, phone number, and e-mail address.

Form Two   Asks the user which of your products he or she currently uses.

Form Three Asks the user to evaluate the products that he or she uses.

Say the user receives the first form, fills it out, and submits it. It goes to a CGI program located on your Web server. This CGI program processes the form's data and sends the second form to the user. The user fills out the second form and submits it. It goes to the same or perhaps a different CGI program on your server. When this CGI program receives the second form's data it has no way of knowing that the second form's data is related to the data of the first form. Therefore, it cannot combine the results of the two forms in its database. The same problem occurs with the CGI program that receives the third form's data.

There is a work-around to this problem. You can have the user enter some small piece of common information, like their e-mail address, in all three forms. When the second and third forms are submitted to your Web server, a CGI program can combine their data based upon the common e-mail address. This work-around allows your CGI programs to continue to operate in a stateless manner. However, your users suffer by having to reenter their e-mail address in all three forms. While this may not seem to be much of an inconvenience, it is noticeable, and it detracts from the appeal of your forms.

What would be even better is if your CGI program could somehow remember the e-mail address that was entered into the first form and attach it to the second and third forms that it sends to your browser. *Hidden form fields* (discussed next) were invented to provide CGI programs with this specific capability.

Using Hidden Form Fields

Hidden form fields are text fields that are not displayed and cannot be modified by a user. Forms with hidden fields are dynamically generated by CGI programs as the result of processing data submitted by other forms.

A CGI program sets a hidden field to a particular value when the server sends a form to a browser. When a user fills out and submits a form containing a hidden field, the value originally stored in the field is returned to the server. The server uses the information stored in the hidden field to maintain state information about the user's browser. To see how this works, let's examine how hidden fields can be used in the three-form example discussed in the previous section.

When a user fills out the name and address information and submits form 1, the CGI program on your server processes the form data by creating a record in a database and sending form 2 back to the user. However, instead of sending a static form 2, it dynamically *generates* a form 2 that contains a hidden field, with the field's value set to the e-mail address that was submitted in the first form.

When the user fills out and submits form 2, the hidden field (still with the user's e-mail address) is sent to your CGI program. Your CGI program can now relate the data of the second form to that of the first because they both have the same value in the e-mail address field. (This is true even though the user did not have to retype his or her e-mail address in the second form.) The same process is carried out for the third form, after which the CGI program sends back a Web page to the user, thanking him or her for filling out the forms.

JavaScript and Hidden Form Fields

At this point, you are probably wondering what any of this has to do with JavaScript. JavaScript's browser-side programming features take full advantage of and enhance the capabilities provided by hidden fields. With JavaScript, you can eliminate the need to send three forms back and forth between the user's browser and your CGI programs. A JavaScript script can perform the processing of all three forms locally on the user's browser and then consolidate the forms' results before sending them to a CGI program.

To see how JavaScript can use hidden fields to implement our three-form customer survey, take a look at the survey.htm file (Listing 6.1). This file uses the hidden form, control.htm, shown in Listing 6.2. If this file were opened on your browser, it would display the first form of a three-form series, as shown in Figure 6.1. You would then fill out this form and click the Next button. You would need to be sure to fill in the E-mail Address field; otherwise, you would receive the alert message shown in Figure 6.2.

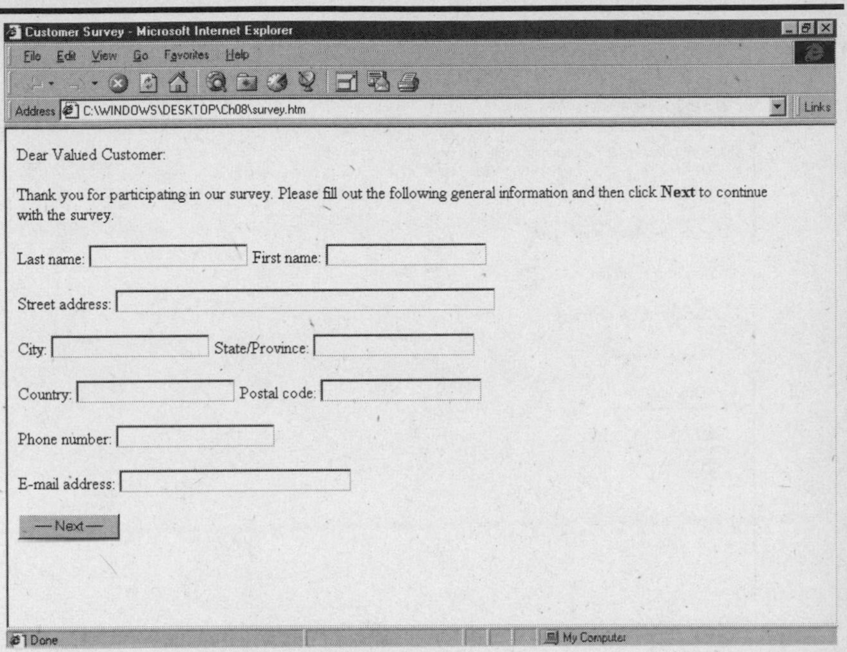

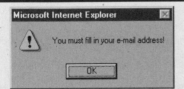

FIGURE 6.1: The first form of the customer survey asks the user to enter general name and address information. (Listing 6.3)

FIGURE 6.2: If the user skips the E-mail Address field, the form validation alert notifies the user that this information is necessary. (Listing 6.3)

After the Next button is clicked, the form shown in Figure 6.3 is displayed. This form asks you to identify which products you use. You would click on the check box of at least one of these fictitious products.

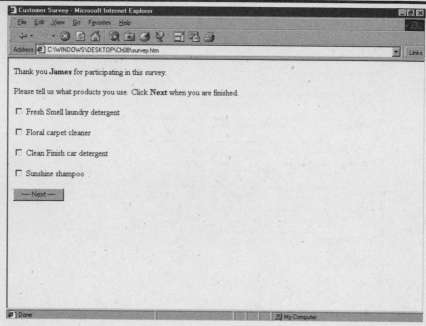

FIGURE 6.3: The second form of the customer survey asks users which products they use. (Listing 6.4)

NOTE

If you do not select at least one of the four products, the third part of the form will be skipped.

After the Next button of the second form is clicked, the third form is displayed, as shown in Figure 6.4. The third form asks you to evaluate the products that you selected in the second form. You would use the radio buttons to perform your product evaluation.

When the Next button on the third form is clicked, all of the values of the three forms are collectively sent to the CGI program located at http://www.jaworski .com/cgi-bin/thanks.cgi. This CGI program reads these values and then sends back the thank-you message shown in Figure 6.5.

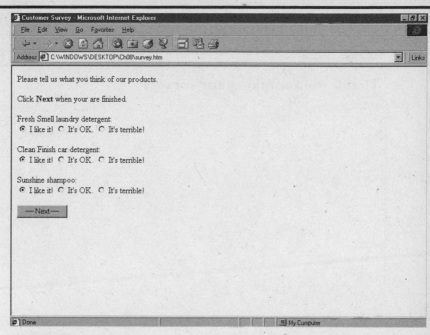

FIGURE 6.4: The third form of the customer survey asks customers how they like the products. (Listing 6.5)

The processing performed in the example all takes place on the user's browser. A CGI program is not required until after all three forms have been filled out. The values of these forms are stored in a separate invisible form that consists entirely of hidden fields. As the user completes each form, the values of the current form are stored in the hidden fields of the invisible form. When the user has completed the third form (or completed the second form without checking any products) the invisible form is submitted to the CGI program. This is much more efficient than having a CGI program process the results of each form separately.

TIP

If you were creating a real survey, you would dress up the form with graphics and a catchier layout.

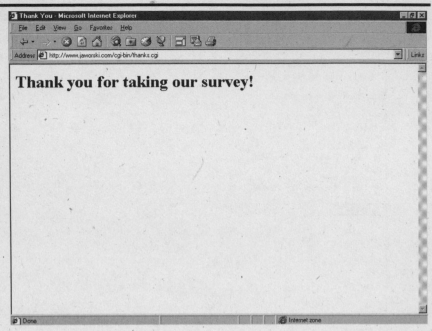

FIGURE 6.5: The thank-you message is displayed after the user completes the survey.

The `survey.htm` file shown in Listing 6.1 defines a two-frame set. The first frame loads the file `form1.htm` (Listing 6.3) and the second frame loads `control.htm` (Listing 6.2). The `Border` attribute of the frame set is set to 0 to avoid displaying a distracting border between frames.

Listing 6.1: Defining the Survey's Frame Set (*survey.htm*)

```
<HTML>
<HEAD>
<TITLE>Customer Survey</TITLE>
</HEAD>
<FRAMESET COLS="*,10" BORDER=0>
<FRAME SRC="form1.htm">
<FRAME SRC="control.htm">
</FRAMESET>
</HTML>
```

Listing 6.2: The Survey's Hidden Form (*control.htm*)

```
<HTML>
<HEAD>
<SCRIPT LANGUAGE="JavaScript"><!--
// --></SCRIPT>
</HEAD>
<BODY>
<FORM ACTION="http://www.jaworski.com/cgi-bin/thanks.cgi"
 NAME="controlForm"
 METHOD="post" TARGET="_top">
<INPUT TYPE="HIDDEN" NAME="lastName" VALUE="">
<INPUT TYPE="HIDDEN" NAME="firstName" VALUE="">
<INPUT TYPE="HIDDEN" NAME="street" VALUE="">
<INPUT TYPE="HIDDEN" NAME="city" VALUE="">
<INPUT TYPE="HIDDEN" NAME="state" VALUE="">
<INPUT TYPE="HIDDEN" NAME="country" VALUE="">
<INPUT TYPE="HIDDEN" NAME="zip" VALUE="">
<INPUT TYPE="HIDDEN" NAME="phone" VALUE="">
<INPUT TYPE="HIDDEN" NAME="email" VALUE="">
<INPUT TYPE="HIDDEN" NAME="products" VALUE="">
<INPUT TYPE="HIDDEN" NAME="evaluation" VALUE="">
</FORM>
</BODY>
</HTML>
```

The control.htm file defines a form with 11 hidden fields. Because all of the form's fields are hidden, the form is not displayed. These fields are filled in with the data collected by the three visible forms that are displayed to the user.

The form's NAME attribute is set to "controlForm". This allows the form to be referenced by name by the JavaScript code that executes with the forms contained in the first frame.

The form's ACTION attribute is set to the URL of my CGI program and its METHOD attribute is set to "post". When the form is submitted, this CGI program receives the data that has been stored in the hidden fields and returns a thank-you message to the user. The form's TARGET attribute is "_top". This causes the thank-you message to be displayed in the full window occupied by survey.htm rather than in the frame occupied by control.htm.

The form1.htm file displays the form shown in Figure 6.1 in the first frame of the frame set. It contains a single script that defines the processForm1() function. This function handles the onClick event that is generated when the user clicks the Next button. It sets the form1 variable to document.forms["formOne"] so that it can be used as a shortcut (to avoid having to retype the document prefix). It then checks to see if the email field is blank. If it is blank, then it displays an alert dialog box to the user; otherwise, it continues with its processing. The controlForm variable is used as a shortcut to the hidden form stored in the second frame. All of the fields from form1 are then copied into the hidden fields of controlForm. Finally, the form2.htm (Listing 6.4) file is loaded into the first frame and formTwo replaces formOne.

Listing 6.3: The First Form of the Survey (*form1.htm*)

```
<HTML>
<HEAD>
<TITLE>Customer Survey: General Information</TITLE>
<SCRIPT LANGUAGE="JavaScript"><!--
function processForm1() {
 form1 = document.forms["formOne"]
 if(form1.email.value=="")
  alert("You must fill in your e-mail address!")
 else {
  controlForm = parent.frames[1].document.controlForm
  controlForm.lastName.value=form1.lastName.value
  controlForm.firstName.value=form1.firstName.value
  controlForm.street.value=form1.street.value
  controlForm.city.value=form1.city.value
  controlForm.state.value=form1.state.value
  controlForm.country.value=form1.country.value
  controlForm.zip.value=form1.zip.value
  controlForm.phone.value=form1.phone.value
  controlForm.email.value=form1.email.value
  location.href="form2.htm"
 }
}
// --></SCRIPT>
</HEAD>
<BODY>
<P>Dear Valued Customer:</P>
<P>Thank you for participating in our survey. Please fill
out the following general information and then click
<B>Next</B> to continue with the survey.</P>
<FORM ACTION="" NAME="formOne">
<P>Last name: <INPUT TYPE="TEXT" NAME="lastName">
```

```
   First name: <INPUT TYPE="TEXT" NAME="firstName"></P>
   <P>Street address: <INPUT TYPE="TEXT" SIZE="50"
➡NAME="street">
   </P>
   <P>City: <INPUT TYPE="TEXT" NAME="city">
   State/Province: <INPUT TYPE="TEXT" NAME="state"></P>
   <P>Country: <INPUT TYPE="TEXT" NAME="country">
   Postal code: <INPUT TYPE="TEXT" NAME="zip"></P>
   <P>Phone number: <INPUT TYPE="TEXT" NAME="phone"></P>
   <P>E-mail address: <INPUT TYPE="TEXT" SIZE="30"
➡NAME="email">
   </P>
   <P></P>
   <INPUT TYPE="BUTTON" NAME="next" VALUE="---- Next ----"
   onClick="processForm1()">
   </FORM>
   </BODY>
   </HTML>
```

The form2.htm file displays the form shown in Figure 6.3. It contains two scripts—one in the document head and the other in the document body. The script in the document body is executed when the Web page is generated. This script is used to insert the first name of the user into the text that is displayed above the form.

Listing 6.4: The Second Form of the Survey (*form2.htm*)

```
<HTML>
<HEAD>
<TITLE>Customer Survey: Product Usage</TITLE>
<SCRIPT LANGUAGE="JavaScript"><!--
function processForm2() {
 controlForm = parent.frames[1].document.controlForm
 form2 = document.forms["formTwo"]
 products = ""
 if(form2.laundry.checked) products += "1"
 else products += "0"
 if(form2.carpet.checked) products += "1"
 else products += "0"
 if(form2.car.checked) products += "1"
 else products += "0"
 if(form2.shampoo.checked) products += "1"
 else products += "0"
 controlForm.products.value=products
 location.href="form3.htm"
}
```

```
// -->></SCRIPT>
</HEAD>
<BODY>
<SCRIPT LANGUAGE="JavaScript"><!--
document.write("<P>Thank you <B>"+
➡parent.frames[1].document.controlForm.firstName.value
➡+"</B> ")
document.writeln("for participating in this survey.</P>")
// -->></SCRIPT>
<P>Please tell us what products you use. Click <B>Next</B>
when you arefinished.</P>
<FORM NAME="formTwo">
<P><INPUT TYPE="CHECKBOX" NAME="laundry"> Fresh Smell
  laundry detergent</P>
<P><INPUT TYPE="CHECKBOX" NAME="carpet"> Floral carpet
  cleaner</P>
<P><INPUT TYPE="CHECKBOX" NAME="car"> Clean Finish car
  detergent</P>
<P><INPUT TYPE="CHECKBOX" NAME="shampoo"> Sunshine
  shampoo</P>
<P></P>
<P><INPUT TYPE="BUTTON" NAME="next" VALUE="---- Next ----"
➡onClick="processForm2()"></P>
</FORM>
</BODY>
</HTML>
```

The script in the document head defines the processForm2() function. This function handles the onClick event that is generated when the user clicks on the Next button. It sets the hidden products field of controlForm based upon the products the user has checked off. It then loads form3.htm (Listing 6.5) as the replacement for form2.htm in the first frame.

Listing 6.5: The Third Form of the Survey (*form3.htm*)

```
<HTML>
<HEAD>
<TITLE>Customer Survey: Product Evaluation</TITLE>
<SCRIPT LANGUAGE="JavaScript"><!--
function usesProducts() {
  productsUsed =
➡parent.frames[1].document.controlForm.products.value
  usage = new Array(productsUsed.length)
  productsInUse=false
  for(i=0;i<usage.length;++i) {
```

```
    if(productsUsed.charAt(i)=="0") usage[i]=false
    else{
     usage[i]=true
     productsInUse=true
    }
   }
   return productsInUse
  }
  function askAboutProducts() {
   document.writeln('<P>Please tell us what you think of our
➡products.</P>')
   document.writeln('<P>Click <B>Next</B> when you are
➡finished.</P>')
   document.writeln('<FORM NAME="formThree">')
   if(usage[0]){
    document.writeln('<P>Fresh Smell laundry detergent:<BR>')
    document.writeln('<INPUT TYPE="RADIO" NAME="laundry"')
    document.writeln('VALUE="like" CHECKED> I like it!')
    document.writeln('<INPUT TYPE="RADIO" NAME="laundry"')
    document.writeln('VALUE="ok"> It\ 's OK.')
    document.writeln('<INPUT TYPE="RADIO" NAME="laundry"')
    document.writeln('VALUE="dislike"> It\ 's terrible!')
    document.writeln('</P>')
   }
   if(usage[1]){
    document.writeln('<P>Floral carpet cleaner:<BR>')
    document.writeln('<INPUT TYPE="RADIO" NAME="carpet"')
    document.writeln('VALUE="like" CHECKED> I like it!')
    document.writeln('<INPUT TYPE="RADIO" NAME="carpet"')
    document.writeln('VALUE="ok"> It\ 's OK.')
    document.writeln('<INPUT TYPE="RADIO" NAME="carpet"')
    document.writeln('VALUE="dislike"> It\ 's terrible!')
    document.writeln('</P>')
   }
   if(usage[2]){
    document.writeln('<P>Clean Finish car detergent:<BR>')
    document.writeln('<INPUT TYPE="RADIO" NAME="car"')
    document.writeln('VALUE="like" CHECKED> I like it!')
    document.writeln('<INPUT TYPE="RADIO" NAME="car"')
    document.writeln('VALUE="ok"> It\ 's OK.')
    document.writeln('<INPUT TYPE="RADIO" NAME="car"')
    document.writeln('VALUE="dislike"> It\ 's terrible!')
    document.writeln('</P>')
   }
   if(usage[3]){
```

```
      document.writeln('<P>Sunshine shampoo:<BR>')
      document.writeln('<INPUT TYPE="RADIO" NAME="shampoo"')
      document.writeln('VALUE="like" CHECKED> I like it!')
      document.writeln('<INPUT TYPE="RADIO" NAME="shampoo"')
      document.writeln('VALUE="ok"> It\ 's OK.')
      document.writeln('<INPUT TYPE="RADIO" NAME="shampoo"')
      document.writeln('VALUE="dislike"> It\ 's terrible!')
      document.writeln('</P>')
    }
    document.writeln('<P></P><P>')
    document.writeln('<INPUT TYPE="BUTTON" NAME="next"')
    document.writeln('VALUE="---- Next ----" ')
    document.writeln(' onClick="processForm3()"></P>')
    document.writeln('</FORM>')
  }
  function processForm3() {
    controlForm = parent.frames[1].document.controlForm
    form3 = document.forms["formThree"]
    evaluation = ""
    for(i=0;i<form3.elements.length-1;++i)
      if(form3.elements[i].checked)
        evaluation += form3.elements[i].value + " "
    controlForm.evaluation.value=evaluation
    controlForm.submit()
  }
  // --></SCRIPT>
  </HEAD>
  <BODY>
  <SCRIPT LANGUAGE="JavaScript"><!--
  if(usesProducts()) askAboutProducts()
  else parent.frames[1].document.controlForm.submit()
  // --></SCRIPT>
  </BODY>
  </HTML>
```

The form3.htm file, unlike form1.htm and form2.htm, consists
almost entirely of JavaScript code. Most of the code is contained in the
script located in the document's head. A small script is contained in the
document's body. This script invokes the usesProducts() function to
determine whether the user had checked any products when they filled
out formTwo. If the user had checked at least one product, the askAbout-
Products() function is invoked to generate formThree. Otherwise, the
controlForm is submitted as is, without the user having to fill in
formThree.

The script in the document head defines three functions:

- ▸ usesProducts()
- ▸ askAboutProducts()
- ▸ processForm3()

These functions are discussed in the following subsections.

The *usesProducts()* Function

This function checks the hidden products field of controlForm to determine what products the user checked off when filling in formTwo. It initializes the usage array based upon this information. It sets productsInUse to *true* if the user has checked off any products in formTwo and to *false* otherwise. It then returns this value as a result.

The *askAboutProducts()* Function

This function generates the HTML content of formThree. It creates a short text introduction to the form, generates the <form> tag, and then generates a set of three radio buttons for each product the user selected in formTwo. It then generates a Next button for the form, setting the form's onClick event handler to processForm3(). Finally, it generates the closing </form> tag.

The *processForm3()* Function

This function handles the onClick event generated when the user clicks on the Next button after filling out formThree. It summarizes the radio buttons checked by the user and stores this summary in the hidden evaluation field of controlForm. It then submits the data contained in controlForm.

USING COOKIES

Hidden form fields were introduced to enable CGI programs to maintain state information about Web browsers. They work well in situations where the state information is to be maintained for a short period of time, as is the case when a user fills out a series of forms. However, hidden fields do not allow state information to be maintained in a *persistent* manner. That is, hidden fields can only be used within a single browser session. When a user exits the browser, the information contained in a hidden form field is lost forever.

Netscape developed the *cookie* as a means to store state-related and other information in a persistent manner. The information stored in a cookie is maintained between browser sessions; it survives when the user turns off his or her machine. Cookies allow CGI and other programs to store information on Web browsers for significantly longer time periods.

NOTE

Cookies are supported by Netscape Navigator, Internet Explorer, and most other major browsers.

A cookie consists of information sent by a server-side program in response to a URL request by the browser. The browser stores the information in the local cookie file ("the cookie jar") according to the URL of the CGI program sending the cookie. This URL may be generalized, based upon additional information contained in the cookie. Different browsers will store the cookie in different files. For example, Netscape Navigator stores cookies in a file named `cookies.txt`. Internet Explorer stores cookies in multiple files in the `\ windows\ cookies` directory.

WARNING

Internet Explorer 3 correctly processes cookies only when a document is read from the Web via an HTTP connection. In particular, it does not support cookies when a document is read from the local file system.

When a browser requests a URL from a Web server, the browser first searches the local cookie files to see if the URL of any of its cookies matches the URL that it is requesting. The browser then sends the Web server, as part of the URL request, the information contained in the matching cookie or cookies.

Cookies provide CGI programs with the capability to store information on browsers. Browsers return this information to CGI programs when they request the URL of the CGI program. CGI programs update cookies when they respond to browser URL requests. In this manner, a CGI program can use browsers to maintain state information and have the browsers return this information whenever they invoke the CGI program.

To get a better feel for how cookies work, let's revisit the three-form example introduced in the beginning of this chapter. The goal is to implement a sequence of forms in which each form expands upon the information gathered in previous forms. In order to do this, a CGI program must be able to relate the data received in later forms to that received in earlier forms. The solution is for the CGI program to identify related forms using data that is common to these forms. A person's e-mail address is a common example of this identifying data.

Cookies provide a persistent mechanism for storing identifying data. When a browser submits the first form (formOne, in the file form1.htm) to a CGI program, the CGI program responds by sending the second form (formTwo, in the file form2.htm) to the browser. A cookie containing the user's e-mail address accompanies this second form. When the browser submits formTwo, it returns any cookies that match the CGI program to which the form is submitted. This causes the user's e-mail address to be returned with the submitted formTwo data. The CGI program then sends the third form (formThree, in the file form3.htm) to the browser. When the user submits formThree, the browser again checks the local cookie file and sends any related cookies.

Cookies are obviously more powerful than hidden form fields. Since cookies can persist between browser sessions, they may be used to store permanent user data, such as identification information (e-mail address) and preferences (frames, background colors, and so on), as well as state information (the current page in an online book).

HOW IS INFORMATION STORED IN A COOKIE?

A cookie is created when a CGI program includes a Set-Cookie header as part of an HTTP response. This response is generated when a browser requests the URL of the CGI program. The syntax of the Set-Cookie header is:

```
Set-Cookie: NAME=VALUE
[; expires=DATE][; path=PATH][; domain=DOMAIN_NAME]
➥[; secure]
```

The NAME=VALUE field (discussed next) is required. The other fields are optional; however, they should all appear on the same line as the Set-Cookie header.

NOTE

More than one Set-Cookie header may be sent in a single HTTP response.

The *NAME=VALUE* Field

This field contains the essential data being stored in a cookie. For example, when used to store my e-mail address, it could appear as email=jamie @jaworski.com. A semicolon, comma, or white-space character is not allowed in the NAME=VALUE string per the cookie specification. Applications are free to develop their own encoding scheme for these strings.

The expires=*DATE* Field

This field specifies the expiration date of a cookie. If it is omitted, the cookie expires at the end of the current browser session. The date is specified in the following format:

Weekday, DD-Mon-YY HH:MM:SS GMT

Weekday is the day of the week. *DD* is the day of the month. *Mon* is the first three letters of the month. *YY* is the year (e.g., 97). *HH* is hours. *MM* is minutes. *SS* is seconds. The GMT time zone is always used. An example date is

Monday, 20-Sep-10 12:00:00 GMT

The above date is noon GMT on September 20th, 2010. Although cookies store the year in a two-digit year format, there is no year 2000 (Y2K) problem associated with them. Browsers accept the year 10 as the year 2010. If cookies are still around in the middle of the 21st century, then browsers of that era will need to be updated to support dates in the later part of that century.

TIP

Cookies that specify long-term user preferences should specify an expiration date of several years to help ensure that the cookies will be available as needed in the future. Cookies that specify short-term state information should expire in days, at which point the expired (stale) cookies are automatically destroyed.

The domain=*DOMAIN_NAME* Field

When a cookie is stored in the local file system, it is organized by the URL of the CGI program that sent the cookie. The `domain` field is used to specify a more general domain name to which the cookie should apply. For example, suppose the URL of the CGI program that sends a cookie has the domain *athome.jaworski.com*. A `domain=jaworski.com` field in a cookie would associate that cookie with all hosts in the *jaworski.com* domain, not just the single host *athome.jaworski.com*. The `domain` field cannot be used to associate cookies with top-level domains *.com*, *.mil*, *.edu*, *.net*, *.org*, *.gov*, and *.int*. Any domain name that is not part of the top-level domains (for example, *ca.us*) must include an extra subdomain. For example, *sd.ca.us* is allowed, but *ca.us* is not.

The path=*PATH* Field

This field is used to specify a more general path for the URL associated with a cookie. For example, suppose the URL of a CGI program is `http://www.jaworski.com/cgi-bin/js-examples/ch06/test.cgi`. The *path* of that CGI program is `/cgi-bin/js-examples/ch06/`. In order to associate a cookie with all of my CGI programs in this example, I could set `path=/cgi-bin`.

The *secure* Field

If the `secure` field is specified, then a cookie is only sent over a secure communication channel (HTTPS servers).

When a browser sends matching cookies back to a Web server, it sends an HTTP request header in the following format:

```
Cookie: NAME1=VALUE1; NAME2=VALUE2; ... NAMEN=VALUEN
```

NAME1 through NAMEN identify the cookie names and VALUE1 through VALUEN identify their values.

NOTE
You can find Netscape's original documentation on cookies at `http://www.netscape.com/newsref/std/cookie_spec.html`.

Using JavaScript with Cookies

Cookies provide a powerful feature for Web application development, but using them with CGI programs can be somewhat messy. You have to design your programs to send cookies via the HTTP response header and to receive cookies via the HTTP request header. While this is not difficult to implement, it means that more processing is performed on the server and not on the browser.

JavaScript, on the other hand, can take full advantage of cookies by reading and setting them locally on the browser, eliminating the need for the cookies to be processed by CGI programs. A JavaScript script can then forward any information the CGI program requires to perform its processing. By using JavaScript to maintain cookies and perform as much processing as possible on the browser, CGI programs can be greatly simplified, and in most cases, eliminated.

The cookie associated with a document is set using the document's `cookie` property. When you set a cookie, you must provide the same cookie fields that would be provided by a CGI program. For example, consider the following statements:

```
email="jamie@jaworski.com"
expirationDate="Thursday, 01-Dec-11 12:00:00 GMT"
document.cookie="email="+email+";expires="+expirationDate
```

These statements set the value of the `cookie` property of the current document to the string `"email=jamie@jaworski.com;` `expires=Thursday, 01-Dec-11 12:00:00 GMT"`. Note that the `expires` field is required to keep the cookie from expiring after the current browser session. `Domain`, `path`, and `secure` fields can also be used when a `cookie` property is set.

When the value of the cookie is retrieved using the statement

```
cookieString=document.cookie
```

the `cookieString` variable will be assigned the value `"email=jamie@jaworski.com"`. If multiple cookies had been set for the current document, then `cookieString` would contain a list of semicolon-separated `name=value` pairs. For example, consider the following statements:

```
email="jamie@jaworski.com"
firstName="Jamie"
lastName="Jaworski"
expirationDate="Thursday, 01-Dec-11 12:00:00 GMT"
```

```
document.cookie="email="+email+";expires="+expirationDate
document.cookie="firstName="+firstName
 +";expires="+expirationDate
document.cookie="lastName="+lastName+";expires="+
expirationDate
cookieString=document.cookie
```

The value of cookieString includes the name=value pairs of the email, firstName, and lastName cookies. This value is email=jamie @jaworski.com; firstName=Jamie; lastName=Jaworski.

NOTE

Bill Dortch provides a number of resuable cookie-processing functions at http://www.hidaho.com.

In order to get a feel for how cookies are accessed via JavaScript, take a look at the file cooktest.htm shown in Listing 6.6. It displays the form shown in Figure 6.6. This form allows you to enter the text of a cookie and then set the cookie by clicking the Set Cookie button. The new value of the cookie is displayed at the top of the Web page.

Listing 6.6: A Cookie Test Program (*cooktest.htm*)

```
<HTML>
<HEAD>
<TITLE>Cookie Test</TITLE>
<SCRIPT LANGUAGE="JavaScript"><!--
function updateCookie() {
 document.cookie=document.form1.cookie.value
 location.reload(true)
}
// --></SCRIPT>
</HEAD>
<BODY>
<SCRIPT LANGUAGE="JavaScript">
 <!--document.write("Your current cookie value is: '"+
   document.cookie+"'")// -->
</SCRIPT>
<FORM ACTION="" NAME="form1">
<P>Enter new cookie: <INPUT TYPE="TEXT" SIZE="60"
 NAME="cookie"></P>
<INPUT TYPE="BUTTON" NAME="setCookie" VALUE="Set Cookie"
 onClick="updateCookie()">
</FORM>
</BODY>
</HTML>
```

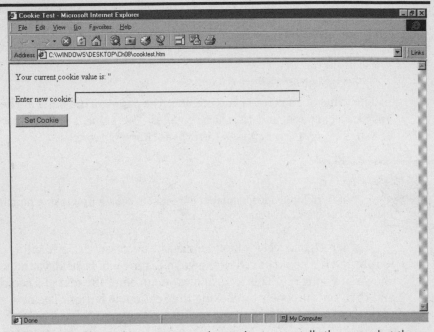

FIGURE 6.6: The cookie test program's opening screen tells the user what the current cookie value is and prompts him or her to enter a new cookie. (Listing 6.6)

To see how this script works, enter the cookie shown in Figure 6.7 and click on the Set Cookie button. The new cookie is displayed as shown in Figure 6.8. Experiment with this program by entering cookies with different or no expiration dates, terminating your browser, and restarting it to see what cookies have persisted between browser sessions.

The cookie test program is very simple. This attests to the power and flexibility with which JavaScript supports cookies. The program consists of two scripts—one in the document head and one in the document body. The script in the document body displays the current cookie values that are available to the document. The script in the document head handles the onClick event associated with the Next Cookie button by setting a cookie with the value entered by the user. It then reloads the current cooktest.htm document so that the updated cookie value is displayed. Note that the cookie test program runs locally without the need for a CGI program. For Web applications that do not require you to collect information from users, the combination of JavaScript and cookies can, in many cases, eliminate the need to develop CGI programs.

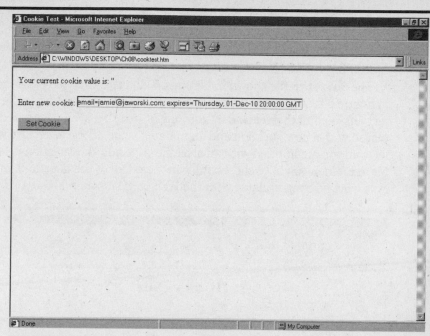

FIGURE 6.7: An example of how to enter the text of a cookie (Listing 6.6)

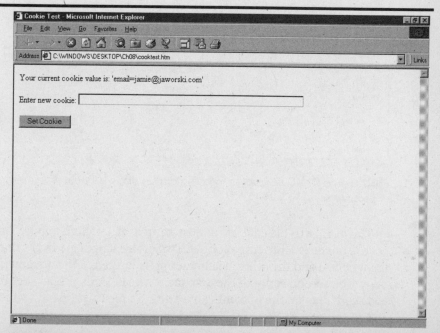

FIGURE 6.8: When the page reloads, the new cookie is displayed. (Listing 6.6)

Part ii

As another example of how JavaScript and cookies can be combined to build Web applications that execute entirely on the browser, we'll develop a JavaScript application that quizzes users about their understanding of historical facts.

The quiz.htm file shown in Listing 6.7 displays the Web page shown in Figure 6.9. When you click the radio button corresponding to the correct answer and then click the Continue button, the Web page is redisplayed with a new question and an updated score. If you select the wrong answer, you are notified with an alert message and the question is redisplayed. When you have successfully answered all of the questions in the quiz, you are congratulated with the Web page shown in Figure 6.10.

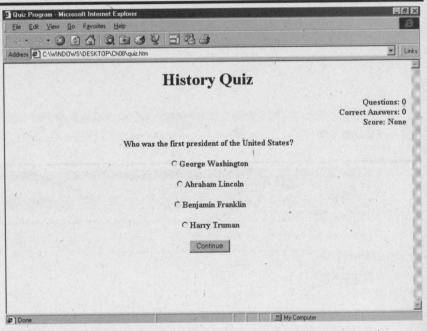

FIGURE 6.9: The Quiz Program opening display lists a quiz question and a group of possible answers. (Listing 6.7)

The quiz.htm file consists almost entirely of JavaScript code. This code is organized into three scripts. Two of the scripts are in the document's head and the other, a short script, is located in the document's body. The second script of the document's head loads the JavaScript code contained in the upcoming history.js file (Listing 6.8), which contains the questions that are used in the quiz. The quiz questions are contained in a separate file so that the quiz can be easily tailored to different sets of questions.

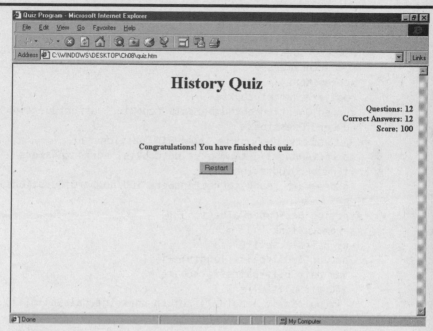

FIGURE 6.10: The Quiz Program final display tells users how well they scored. (Listing 6.7)

TIP

You can improve the quiz by adding graphics and links to related topics.

Listing 6.7: Quiz Program (*quiz.htm*)

```
<HTML>
<HEAD>
<TITLE>Quiz Program</TITLE>
<SCRIPT LANGUAGE="JavaScript"><!--
//Question object
function Question() {
  this.question=Question.arguments[0]
  var n=Question.arguments.length
```

```
  this.answers = new Array(n-2)
  for(var i=1; i<n-1; ++i)
   this.answers[i-1]=Question.arguments[i]
  this.correctAnswer=Question.arguments[n-1]
 }
 function readCookie() {
  currentQuestion=0
  numberOfQuestions=0
  correctAnswers=0
  score="None"
  cookie=document.cookie
  currentQuestion=getNumberValue(cookie,"currentQuestion")
  numberOfQuestions=
➥ getNumberValue(cookie,"numberOfQuestions")
  correctAnswers=getNumberValue(cookie,"correctAnswers")
  if(numberOfQuestions>0)
   score=Math.round(correctAnswers*100/numberOfQuestions)
 }
 function getNumberValue(s,n) {
  s=removeBlanks(s)
  var pairs=s.split(";")
  for(var i=0;i<pairs.length;++i) {
   var pairSplit=pairs[i].split("=")
   if(pairSplit[0]==n) {
    if(pairSplit.length>1) return parseInt(pairSplit[1])
    else return 0
   }
  }
  return 0
 }
 function removeBlanks(s) {
  var temp=""
  for(var i=0;i<s.length;++i) {
   var c=s.charAt(i)
   if(c!=" ") temp += c
  }
  return temp
 }
 function askNextQuestion() {
  document.writeln("<H4 ALIGN='CENTER'>"
   +qa[currentQuestion].question+"</H4>")
  displayAnswers()
 }
 function displayAnswers() {
  document.writeln('<FORM NAME="answerForm">')
```

```
  for(var ii=0;ii<qa[currentQuestion].answers.length;++ii) {
   document.writeln('<H4 ALIGN="CENTER">')
   document.writeln('<INPUT TYPE="RADIO" NAME="answer"> ')
   document.writeln(qa[currentQuestion].answers[ii])
   if(ii+1==qa[currentQuestion].answers.length) {
    document.writeln('<BR><BR><INPUT TYPE="BUTTON"')
    document.writeln('NAME="continue" VALUE="Continue" ')
    document.writeln(' onClick="checkAnswers()">')
   }
   document.writeln('</H4>')
  }
 document.writeln('</FORM>')
}
function checkAnswers() {
 var numAnswers=qa[currentQuestion].answers.length
 var correctAnswer=qa[currentQuestion].correctAnswer
 for(var jj=0;jj<numAnswers;++jj) {
  if(document.answerForm.elements[jj].checked) {
   if(jj==correctAnswer){
    correct()
     break
   } else{
     incorrect()
     break
   }
  }
  if(jj==numAnswers){
   incorrect()
   break
  }
 }
}
function correct() {
 ++currentQuestion
 ++numberOfQuestions
 ++correctAnswers
 updateCookie()
 location.reload(true)
}
function incorrect() {
 ++numberOfQuestions
 updateCookie()
 alert("Incorrect!")
 location.reload(true)
}
```

```
function updateCookie() {
 document.cookie="currentQuestion="+currentQuestion
 document.cookie="numberOfQuestions="+numberOfQuestions
 document.cookie="correctAnswers="+correctAnswers
}
function endQuiz() {
 document.cookie="currentQuestion=0"
 document.cookie="numberOfQuestions=0"
 document.cookie="correctAnswers=0"
 document.writeln('<FORM NAME="finishedForm">')
 document.write("<H4 ALIGN='CENTER'>")
 document.write("Congratulations! You have finished
➥ this quiz.")
 document.writeln('<BR><BR><INPUT TYPE="BUTTON"
➥ NAME="restart"
   VALUE="Restart" ')
 document.writeln(' onClick="restartQuiz()">')
 document.writeln("</H4>")
 document.writeln('</FORM>')
}
function restartQuiz() {
 location.reload(true)
}
// --></SCRIPT>
<SCRIPT LANGUAGE="JavaScript" SRC="history.js"><!--
// --></SCRIPT>
</HEAD>
<BODY>
<SCRIPT LANGUAGE="JavaScript"><!--
readCookie()
document.writeln("<H1 ALIGN='CENTER'>"+pageHeading+"</H1>")
document.writeln("<P ALIGN='RIGHT'><B>Questions: "
 +numberOfQuestions+"<BR>")
document.writeln("Correct Answers: "+correctAnswers+"<BR>")
document.writeln("Score: "+score+"</B></P>")
if(currentQuestion >= qa.length) endQuiz()
else askNextQuestion()
// --></SCRIPT>
</BODY>
</HTML>
```

We'll examine the code contained in the body of quiz.htm and then study the code in the document's head. After that, we'll cover history.js.

The Code in the Document Body

The code in the body of quiz.htm is very short. The readCookie() function is invoked to read the cookies associated with the document and use the cookie's name=value pairs to initialize the script's variables to the current state of the quiz. The cookies contain the number of the current question, the number of questions asked so far, and the number of correct answers. Next, the script creates a document heading based on the value of the pageHeading variable. (The pageHeading variable is initialized in history.js.)

The number of questions asked, number of correct answers, and quiz score are then displayed. The script checks to see if the value of currentQuestion is equal to or greater than the length of the qa array. (The qa array is also defined in history.js.) It is used to store all of the quiz's questions and answers. If the currentQuestion variable is greater than or equal to the length of the qa array, then all questions have been asked and the endQuiz() function is invoked to end the quiz. Otherwise, the askNextQuestion() function is invoked to present the user with another question.

The Code in the Document Head

The first script in the head of quiz.htm defines 12 functions. These functions are used as described in the following subsections.

The *Question()* Function   This function is used in history.js to create Question objects. It uses the arguments property of the function object to determine how many arguments were passed in the Question() invocation. The first argument is the text of the question. The last argument is an integer that identifies the correct answer. All arguments between the first and the last are used to define the answers to a question.

The *readCookie()* Function   This function reads the cookies of the current document and sets the currentQuestion, numberOfQuestions, and correctAnswers variables. It then uses these values to calculate the value of the score variable.

The *getNumberValue()* Function   This function is used by read-Cookie() to parse the cookie string s and return the value associated with a particular name n. It does this by removing all blanks from s and then splitting s by means of the field separator "; ". Having separated the string into name=value fields, it then separates these fields by "=". It checks to see if the name component of the split field matches n and returns the value associated with the name as an integer. If the name does not have a value it returns 0.

The *removeBlanks()* Function   This function removes all blanks contained in a string and returns this value as a result.

The *askNextQuestion()* Function   This function displays the current question in a centered Heading 4. It then invokes displayAnswers() to display the possible answers associated with this question.

The *displayAnswers()* Function   This function displays the possible answers of the current question as a form. A radio button is displayed with each answer. A Continue button follows the answers. The Continue button's onClick event handler is set to the checkAnswers() function.

The *checkAnswers()* Function   This function is invoked when a user answers a question and clicks on the Continue button. It determines how many answers are associated with a question and then checks the radio button of each answer to see if it is checked. When it finds a checked button, it determines whether the checked button is the correct answer. If the answer is correct, it invokes the correct() function; otherwise, it invokes the incorrect() function. If no radio buttons have been clicked, the incorrect() function is invoked.

The *correct()* Function   This function increments the currentQuestion, numberOfQuestions, and correctAnswers variables and invokes updateCookie() to write the values of these variables to the document's cookie jar. It then reloads the quiz.htm file to process the next question.

The *incorrect()* Function   This function increments the numberOfQuestions variable and invokes updateCookie() to write the value of this variable to the document's cookie jar. It then reloads the quiz.htm file to reprocess the same question.

The *updateCookie()* **Function** This function uses the document's cookie jar to temporarily store the program's state while the `quiz.htm` file is reloaded. It stores the values of the `currentQuestion`, `numberOfQuestions`, and `correctAnswers` variables.

The *endQuiz()* **Function** This function ends the quiz by setting the document's cookies back to their initial state. It then displays a form that congratulates the user for finishing the quiz and displays a Restart button so that the user can restart the quiz if she or he wishes. The `onClick` event handler for the Restart button is `restartQuiz()`.

The *restartQuiz()* **Function** This function handles the clicking of the Restart button by reloading the `quiz.htm` file so that the quiz may be restarted.

The Source File

Having gone through the description of `quiz.htm`, the `history.js` file (Listing 6.8) is easy to understand. It defines the `pageHeading` variable that is used to display the heading on each quiz page. It then creates the qa array. Each element of qa is a `Question` object. Twelve questions are defined. Feel free to add your own questions or delete the ones that I've created—you can change the entire content of the quiz by modifying `history.js`. You can also substitute your own question file for `history.js` by modifying the SRC attribute value of the second script of `quiz.htm`.

Listing 6.8: Quiz Questions (*history.js*)

```
//Heading displayed on the quiz page
pageHeading="History Quiz"
//Questions
qa = new Array()
qa[0] = new Question("Who was the first president
  of the United States?",
 "George Washington",
 "Abraham Lincoln",
 "Benjamin Franklin",
 "Harry Truman",
 0)
qa[1] = new Question("When did Columbus discover America?",
 "1249",
 "1942",
 "1492",
```

```
    "1294",
    2)
qa[2] = new Question("Who commanded the Macedonian army?",
    "Napoleon",
    "Alexander the Great",
    "Cleopatra",
    "George Patton",
    1)
qa[3] = new Question("Where did Davy Crockett lose his
➥life?",
    "The Spanish Inquisition",
    "The Alamo",
    "Miami, Florida",
    "On the Oregon Trail",
    1)
qa[4] = new Question("Who was the first man to
    walk on the moon?",
    "Louis Armstrong",
    "Buzz Armstrong",
    "Jack Armstrong",
    "Neil Armstrong",
    3)
qa[5] = new Question("Who wrote the <I>Scarlet Letter</I>?",
    "Michael Crichton",
    "Ernest Hemingway",
    "Nathaniel Hawthorne",
    "Charles Dickens",
    2)
qa[6] = new Question("Eli Whitney invented:",
    "Mad Cow Disease",
    "the Cotton Gin",
    "whisky",
    "the automobile",
    1)
qa[7] = new Question("Who was known as the King of the
➥Fauves?",
    "Salvatore Dali",
    "Henri Matisse",
    "Pablo Picasso",
    "Vincent Van Gogh",
    1)
qa[8] = new Question("Who discovered the force of gravity?",
    "Isaac Newton",
    "Galileo",
```

```
        "Copernicus",
        "Albert Einstein"
        ,0)
    qa[9] = new Question("Who created HTML?",
        "Tim Berners-Lee",
        "Marc Andreessen",
        "Bill Gates",
        "Jim Barksdale",
        0)
  qa[10] = new Question("Leonardo da Vinci was born in
    ➥Greece.",
        "True",
        "False",
        1)
    qa[11] = new Question("Louisiana was purchased from
    ➥France.",
        "True",
        "False",
        0)
```

This example shows how JavaScript can use cookies to create a complex Web application without the use of a CGI program. All of the cookie processing is performed locally on the browser.

COMPARISON — COOKIES VS. HIDDEN FORM FIELDS

Now that you've learned how both hidden fields and cookies can be used to maintain state information, you may be wondering which one you should use and when. In general, cookies are the preferred option because they allow persistent storage of state information, whereas hidden fields do not. However, cookies may not be the right choice for all applications. Table 6.1 summarizes the trade-offs between cookies and hidden fields.

TABLE 6.1: Cookies vs. Hidden Fields

TRADE-OFF	COOKIES	HIDDEN FIELDS
Ease of use	Requires cookie string parsing	Requires form setup and access
Browser support	Navigator, Internet Explorer, other browsers	Almost all browsers

CONTINUED ➡

TABLE 6.1 continued: Cookies vs. Hidden Fields

TRADE-OFF	COOKIES	HIDDEN FIELDS
Server support	May not be supported by some servers	Supported by all servers
Performance	Slower—requires disk I/O	Faster—implemented in RAM
Persistent storage	Supported	Not Supported
Availability	Maximum cookie storage may be reached	No practical storage limitation

Both cookies and hidden fields are easy to use; however, both also have some coding overhead associated with them. Cookie strings need to be parsed when they are read. Hidden fields require invisible forms to be set up. As far as ease of use is concerned, I prefer cookies because all of the setup processing is performed in JavaScript.

Even though cookies are supported by Navigator, Internet Explorer, and other browsers, they are not supported by all browsers. On the other hand, hidden fields are supported by all HTML 2–compatible browsers.

Not all Web servers support cookies, though they do support hidden form fields. Cookies are not as performance efficient as hidden fields because cookie operations require disk I/O to the local cookie file. However, in most applications this performance difference is not noticeable.

Cookies provide persistent storage. That is their biggest advantage and why they were developed in the first place. If you require persistent storage, then you have to use cookies.

Cookies may not always be available to your scripts. The cookie specification states that a browser cannot claim that it is cookie capable unless it provides a minimum cookie storage capacity of 300 (currently, this limit is not a problem for most browsers). However, with the increase in cookie popularity, it could be an issue in the future. In addition, most browsers limit the number of cookies that can be stored for a given domain. Netscape Navigator 4 has a 20-cookies-per-domain limit and Internet Explorer 3 has a single-cookie-per-domain limit. Hidden fields do not have any practical limits.

SUMMARY

In this chapter you learned how to use hidden fields and cookies to maintain browser state information. You learned how JavaScript enhances the capabilities that both hidden fields and cookies provide by maximizing local processing and reducing the need for CGI programming.

CHAPTER 7

INTERFACING JAVASCRIPT WITH CGI PROGRAMS

The Common Gateway Interface (CGI) is the standard for communication between Web servers and server-side Web programs. Netscape, Microsoft, and most other Web servers support the Common Gateway Interface. Thus, for the most part, Web application designers can develop server-side programs that will work regardless of the particular type of Web server used at a Web site. If you want to write a server-side program that will have the greatest portability, then develop it as a CGI program or a Java servlet.

Adapted from *Mastering JavaScript and JScript*,
by James Jaworski
ISBN 0-7821-2492-5   925 pages $39.99

In this chapter, you'll learn how CGI programs work. We'll cover the types of Web applications in which CGI programs are used. On the one hand, you'll learn how to interface JavaScript scripts with CGI scripts, and on the other hand, you'll learn how to use CGI programs to generate JavaScript code. When you finish this chapter, you'll know how to combine JavaScript scripts with CGI programs in your Web applications.

WHEN TO USE CGI PROGRAMS

When creating a Web application, perform as much processing as is reasonably possible on the browser, rather than on the server, to conserve precious communication bandwidth and server-processing resources. Any processing that is performed locally reduces the load on your Web server.

However, for some Web applications, server-side processing is absolutely essential. These applications include any that collect and store data about multiple users (for example, online registration forms and customer surveys). Applications that require significant database support (for example, large catalogs and search engines) also fall into this category.

CGI programs provide the interface between Web browsers and online databases. They also provide gateways to other online services, such as Gopher and WAIS (though, admittedly, the popularity of these services has declined with the rise of the World Wide Web). Any Web application that requires server-side storage or access to non-Web resources is a potential candidate for the use of a CGI program.

HOW CGI PROGRAMS WORK

CGI programs (also referred to as CGI scripts) are the external programs I was talking about when I said that the CGI is a standard interface for communication between Web servers and external programs. The CGI specification identifies how data is to be passed from a Web server to a CGI program, and back from the CGI program to the Web server.

NOTE
Refer to Chapter 5, "Processing Forms," for a discussion and examples of using CGI programs with forms.

The following points summarize how the CGI works:

▶ A browser requests a CGI program by specifying the CGI program's URL. The request arises as the result of the user submitting a form or clicking a link. (The browser may insert into the URL a query string or extra path information.)

▶ When a Web server receives a URL request, it determines whether the URL refers to a CGI program. Most Web servers identify CGI programs by the path in which they are located or by their filename extension. For example, all files in the path /cgi-bin/ or with the extensions .CGI or .PL could be considered CGI programs.

▶ When a Web server identifies a request for a CGI program, it executes the CGI program as a separate process and passes any data included in the URL to the program.

▶ The CGI program performs its processing and then returns its output to the Web server. The conventions defined by the CGI specification determine how CGI programs receive data from and return data to Web servers. These conventions are described in the following sections.

The overall process is depicted in Figure 7.1.

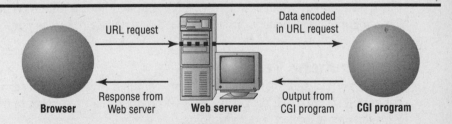

FIGURE 7.1: Web servers communicate with external programs using the conventions of CGI.

Getting Data from the Web Server

When a CGI program is executed, one of its first tasks is to determine what data was passed to it by the Web server. This data may be passed in the following ways:

- Command-line arguments
- Environment variables
- The program's standard input stream

Command-line arguments and the standard input stream are supported by almost all programming languages. Environment variables are less commonly used outside of Web applications. The following subsections describe when and how CGI programs receive data via each of these mechanisms.

Command-Line Arguments

Command-line arguments are parameters that are passed to programs via the command line that is used to execute the program. For example, the following command line executes the search program and passes it the string news as an argument:

```
search news
```

HTTP ISINDEX queries are the means of passing data to CGI programs as command-line arguments. CGI programs read the command-line arguments via the mechanisms provided by the programming language in which they are written. For example, the C programming language provides the argc and argv variables for accessing command-line arguments. The Perl programming language provides the @ARGV array for the same purpose.

Environment Variables

Environment variables are the primary mechanism by which Web servers communicate with CGI programs. All CGI programs can receive data from Web servers via environment variables.

Environment variables are variables that are external to a program's execution. They are used to define the environment in which a program executes. Table 7.1 identifies the environment variables defined by CGI version 1.1. The most important of these variables are CONTENT_LENGTH, which identifies the number of bytes that are passed via standard input, and PATH_INFO and QUERY_STRING, which identify data that is passed via extra path information or a query string.

TABLE 7.1: Environment Variables Used by CGI

ENVIRONMENT VARIABLE	DESCRIPTION
AUTH_TYPE	The authentication scheme used to validate the user requesting access to a Web page.
CONTENT_LENGTH	The number of characters that have been passed via standard input.
CONTENT_TYPE	The MIME type associated with the data available via standard input.
GATEWAY_INTERFACE	The version of the CGI specification supported by the server.
HTTP_*	The contents of the various HTTP headers received by the Web server. "HTTP_" is prepended to the name of the header. For example, the ACCEPT header is represented by the HTTP_ACCEPT environment variable, and the USER_AGENT header is represented by the HTTP_USER_AGENT variable.
PATH_INFO	The extra path information added to the URL of the CGI program.
PATH_TRANSLATED	The full path name that was translated from the URL by the Web server.
QUERY_STRING	The query string portion of the URL.
REMOTE_ADDR	The IP address of the host associated with the requesting browser.
REMOTE_HOST	The name of the host associated with the requesting browser.
REMOTE_IDENT	The verified name of the host associated with the requesting browser.
REMOTE_USER	The name of the user associated with the requesting browser.

Part ii

TABLE 7.1 continued: Environment Variables Used by CGI

ENVIRONMENT VARIABLE	DESCRIPTION
REQUEST_METHOD	The method associated with the browser request: GET, POST, HEAD, and so on.
SCRIPT_NAME	The path and name of the CGI program.
SERVER_NAME	The name of the Web server host.
SERVER_PORT	The HTTP port number (usually 80) used by the Web server.
SERVER_PROTOCOL	The name and version of the protocol used by the requesting browser to submit the request.
SERVER_SOFTWARE	The name and version number of the Web server software.

The environment variables shown in Table 7.1 are available to all CGI programs regardless of whether the CGI program was executed as the result of an ISINDEX query, a form submission, or the clicking of a hyperlink.

Many programming languages provide special mechanisms for accessing environment variables. For example, Perl provides the $ENV array, and C provides the getenv() library function. Because the capability to read environment variables is important for any nontrivial CGI programs, it should be a primary consideration when selecting a CGI programming language.

TIP

Some Web servers, such as Netscape servers, define server-specific environment variables in addition to those defined by the CGI. If you want your CGI programs to be portable between Web servers, you should not use these server-specific environment variables.

Reading Query String Data   When data is passed to a CGI program via the QUERY_STRING environment variable, the data is encoded using the following conventions. These coding conventions are referred to as *URL coding:*

- ▸ Spaces are replaced by plus (+) signs.

- ▸ Other characters may be replaced by character codes of the form %*xx* (with the *xx* being replaced by two hexadecimal digits). For example, %2a is used to encode a plus sign.

CGI programs must decode the data passed via the QUERY_STRING variable. This is accomplished by replacing plus signs with spaces, and sequences of the form %*xx* with their character equivalent. This decoding is known as *URL decoding.*

NOTE

JavaScript provides the escape() and unescape() functions to support URL encoding and decoding. The escape() function takes a single string parameter and returns a URL-encoded version of the string. The unescape() function takes a single string parameter and returns the URL-decoded version of the string.

Form Data Coding   In addition to query string encoding, other application-specific codings may be used. For example, form data is encoded as a sequence of name=value pairs, separated by ampersands (the & symbol), with name being replaced by the form field's name attribute and value being replaced by the field's value when submitted by the user. Any equals signs or ampersands appearing in the data are encoded using the %xx hexadecimal coding scheme covered in the previous section.

When the form uses the GET method, form data is passed to CGI programs via the QUERY_STRING environment variable. When the form uses the POST method, form data is passed to the CGI programs via standard input. The use of standard input is covered in a later section of this chapter.

CGI programs should decode form data by using the ampersands to separate the query string into name=value pairs, using the equals signs to separate the name and value portions, and then decoding the name and value portions using the URL decoding conventions.

NOTE

If a query string does not have data in the form of name=value pairs, then most Web servers assume that the requested URL is an ISINDEX query, and pass the query string as a command-line argument.

Reading Extra Path Data   Extra path information is data that is added to a URL as additional path information following the path to the CGI program. The extra path information is passed to a CGI program using the PATH_INFO environment variable. For example, in the following URL, http:/www.jaworski.com/cgi-bin/echo-query/extra/path/ info, the path /extra/path/info that follows echo-query would be passed to the echo-query program via PATH_INFO as "/extra/path/ info". Extra path information is an easy way to send fixed information to CGI programs. It is usually used with non-form URLs.

TIP

If you intend to use extra path information to send data to CGI programs, you should use URL-coding to ensure that the data is correctly processed by Web browsers and servers.

The Standard Input and Output Streams

Standard input refers to the keyboard input received by character-mode programs, such as non-graphical DOS programs and UNIX and Windows NT command-line programs. Relatedly, *standard output* refers to the visible output produced by these programs: characters that are displayed on the console monitor (in this context, this would normally be the *server's* console window, not the user's).

NOTE

The physical console of olden days has been replaced by a command-line console window on modern windowing systems.

In addition to treating users' input and output in standard ways, most operating systems have the capability of allowing command-line programs to run in an environment where the user's keyboard and display monitor can be *simulated*. This means that input other than the user's keyboard input (for instance, a query string or extra path information in a URL, or data from a browser form) can be *redirected* to a program *as* standard input. The program can process the data regardless of the fact that the data came from some source other than the standard source (keyboard input). Similarly, a program's output can be redirected by a server to the user's browser as though it were standard output to the server's own console display. Web servers make use of this redirection capability to process posted form data, as shown in Figure 7.2.

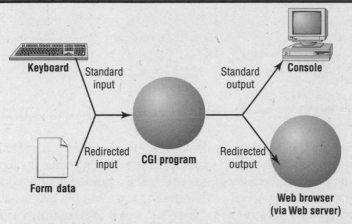

FIGURE 7.2: Web servers redirect the standard input and output streams of CGI programs to support browser/CGI program communication.

When the POST method is used to submit a form, the form's data is sent by the Web server to a CGI program as standard input to the CGI program. When a Web server creates a process to execute a CGI program, it redirects the form's data to the standard input stream of the CGI program. This data appears to a CGI program as if it were typed by a user at a keyboard. (*Note:* The amount of data that can be redirected in this manner is subject to limitation. You can use the CONTENT_LENGTH environment variable to identify the number of bytes to be made available via standard input.)

The output of the CGI program is returned to the Web server so that it can be redirected to the user's browser. By redirecting standard input and output, the Web server allows CGI programs to be designed using the simple character-stream approach common to DOS and UNIX programs. Almost all programming languages provide capabilities to read data from the standard input stream and write data to the standard output stream.

Sending Data Back to the Web Server

A CGI program returns data to the requesting browser via the Web server. In all cases, it returns the data by writing it to the standard output stream. The output of the CGI program must begin with a header line, followed by a blank line, and then by the data to be displayed by the browser. The header line usually consists of a `Content-type` header that specifies the MIME type of the data returned by the CGI program. In most cases, the MIME type will be `text/html`, as shown in the following example:

```
Content type: text/html
<HTML>
<HEAD>
<TITLE>CGI Results</TITLE>
</HEAD>
<BODY>
<H1>It worked!</H1>
</BODY>
</HTML>
```

The header line does not have to be a `Content-type` header; a CGI program can instead return a `Location` header that specifies the name of a URL to be loaded. For example, consider the following program output. The `Location` header specifies that the `results.htm` file that is located at the partial URL `/javascript/results.htm` is to be returned as the result of the CGI program's execution.

```
Location: /javascript/results.htm
blank line
```

TIP

When using a `Location` header, be sure to follow it by a single blank line, even if the header is the entirety of your script.

Using Nonparsed Header Programs

As mentioned in the previous section, CGI programs normally return data to the requesting browser via the Web server, which takes care of providing all of the required HTTP headers. It is possible, however, for CGI programs to bypass the Web server and return data directly to the requesting browser. Of course, when you do this, your CGI program is then responsible for providing all of the required headers.

CGI programs that bypass the Web server and return data directly to Web browsers are referred to as *nonparsed header programs*. Most Web servers require nonparsed header CGI programs to begin with the characters nph- (*nph* followed by a hyphen) to help servers differentiate between regular CGI programs and nonparsed header programs.

When should you use nonparsed header programs? The answer is almost never. By going through the Web server, your CGI programs can be designed much more simply and easily. The only time it makes sense to bypass the Web server is when your CGI program returns a large amount of data and you don't want the server to delay transmission of the data to the browser.

THE GENERAL DESIGN OF A CGI PROGRAM

Now that you've learned how CGI programs receive data from and return data to Web servers, we'll cover the general design of typical CGI programs.

Most CGI programs are *transaction oriented*. They receive input data from a browser, perform processing based on the data received from the browser, and return the results of the processing to the browser. The way that a CGI program reads and processes its data depends on the way that is requested by a browser.

ISINDEX Queries

The CGI program looks for input data by checking its command-line arguments. If it does not have any data, then it returns a Web page containing an ISINDEX tag to the requesting browser. This allows the user to submit data to the CGI program. If the CGI program does contain data in its command-line arguments, then it decodes the data using URL decoding, processes the ISINDEX query, and sends the results of the query to the requesting browser.

Form Processing

CGI programs that process form data access the form data in different ways depending on whether the form is submitted using the GET or POST method. If the form is submitted via the GET method, then the form data is read from the QUERY_STRING variable. If the form is submitted via the POST method, then the form data is read from the standard input stream.

When the form data has been read, it is decoded and processed. The data returned by the CGI program can consist of other forms, other Web pages, or files of other MIME types.

Server-Side Image-Map Queries

CGI programs that process image-map queries read the coordinates of the user's click from the QUERY_STRING environment variable. These programs perform their processing based on the coordinates of the click and a map file. The map file associates image regions with URLs.

The particular map file to be used can be specified as extra path information. The image-map program returns the URL associated with the coordinates of the user's click.

Using Custom Hyperlinks to Invoke CGI Programs

Some CGI programs may be invoked as the result of the user clicking a hyperlink. Data may be passed to the CGI program via a query string or extra path information contained in the URL. The CGI program uses command-line arguments and environment variables to access this data. It performs its processing and then returns its output to the browser.

A SHELL SCRIPT EXAMPLE

By now, you are probably anxious to see an example of a CGI program. Listing 7.1 provides a CGI script written in the Linux shell programming language. Don't worry if you don't understand Linux shell programming; the script only uses the echo and cat commands. The first line of the script identifies the file as a shell script. The second line writes the Content-type header to standard output. The third line writes the required blank line to standard output. Subsequent lines write an HTML document to standard output.

The first part of the document identifies the command-line arguments that are passed to the CGI program. The $# variable identifies the number of command-line arguments, and the $* variable identifies the values of these arguments.

Listing 7.1: The *echo-query* Script

```sh
#!/bin/sh
echo Content-type: text/html
echo
echo "<HTML>"
echo "<HEAD>"
echo "<TITLE>Echo CGI Request</TITLE>"
echo "</HEAD>"
echo "<BODY>"
echo "<H1>CGI Request</H1>"
echo "<H2>Command Line Arguments</H2>"
echo "<P>Number of command line arguments: $#</P>"
echo "<P>Command line arguments: "$*"</P>"
echo "<H2>Environment Variables</H2>"
echo "<PRE>"
echo AUTH_TYPE = $AUTH_TYPE
echo CONTENT_LENGTH = $CONTENT_LENGTH
echo CONTENT_TYPE = $CONTENT_TYPE
echo GATEWAY_INTERFACE = $GATEWAY_INTERFACE
echo HTTP_ACCEPT = "$HTTP_ACCEPT"
echo HTTP_USER_AGENT = "$HTTP_USER_AGENT"
echo PATH_INFO = "$PATH_INFO"
echo PATH_TRANSLATED = "$PATH_TRANSLATED"
echo QUERY_STRING = "$QUERY_STRING"
echo REMOTE_ADDR = $REMOTE_ADDR
echo REMOTE_HOST = $REMOTE_HOST
echo REMOTE_IDENT = $REMOTE_IDENT
echo REMOTE_USER = $REMOTE_USER
echo REQUEST_METHOD = $REQUEST_METHOD
echo SCRIPT_NAME = "$SCRIPT_NAME"
echo SERVER_NAME = $SERVER_NAME
echo SERVER_PORT = $SERVER_PORT
echo SERVER_PROTOCOL = $SERVER_PROTOCOL
echo SERVER_SOFTWARE = $SERVER_SOFTWARE
echo "</PRE>"
echo "<H2>Standard Input</H2>"
cat
echo "</BODY>"
echo "</HTML>"
```

The second part of the returned document identifies the environment variables that are passed to the CGI program. These variables are referenced by prepending a $ to the name of the environment variable.

The last part of the returned document identifies the data that is sent to the CGI program via the standard input stream. The `cat` command is used to read CONTENT_LENGTH characters from standard input and write them to standard output.

NOTE

The echo-query program shown in Listing 7.1 is accessible via the URL http://www.jaworski.com/cgi-bin/echo-query.cgi.

If you were to use the echo-query script, you would need to create an HTML document to access the script's URL. Listing 7.2 provides such a document. It contains a link to echo-query with both extra path information and a query string appended.

If you were to open cgi-test.htm with your browser, you would see the Web page displayed in Figure 7.3. Figure 7.4 shows the Web page that would be returned if you were to click the link to the CGI program. Note the value of the QUERY_STRING and PATH_INFO variables.

TIP

The echo-query script is a useful tool for testing your links in order to see how the data they encode is passed to a CGI program.

Listing 7.2: Accessing the *echo-query* Script (*cgi-test.htm*)

```
<HTML>
<HEAD>
<TITLE>CGI Test</TITLE>
</HEAD>
<BODY>
<A HREF="http://www.jaworski.com/cgi-bin/echo-query.cgi/
➥ extra/path/info?f1=v1&f2=v2">
Click here to access echo-query</A>
</BODY>
</HTML>
```

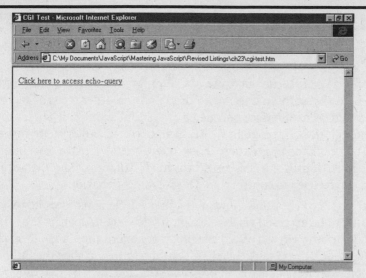

FIGURE 7.3: The Web page generated by `cgi-test.htm` (Listing 7.2)

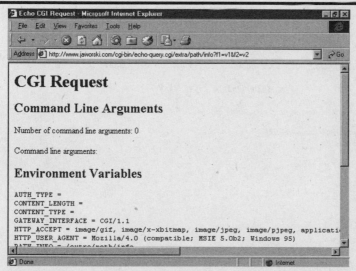

FIGURE 7.4: The results returned by echo-query (Listing 7.2)

Part ii

Interfacing JavaScript Scripts with CGI Scripts

JavaScript scripts can make use of CGI programs to access online databases, to access Internet services, or to perform other types of server-side processing. The interface between a JavaScript script and a CGI program is through the CGI program's URL. Scripts can use the URL to invoke a CGI program and pass data to it as a query string or extra path information. If a CGI program is accessed via an HTML form, then the form's data can be used to control the CGI program's behavior.

The js2cgi.htm file, shown in Listing 7.3, demonstrates how CGI programs can be accessed via JavaScript. If you were to open js2cgi.htm with your browser, you would see that it generates the HTML form shown in Figure 7.5. If you were then to fill out the form and click the Submit button, your form data would be sent to the add2db.cgi CGI program at the URL http://www.jaworski.com/cgi-bin/add2dbcgi, and the Web page shown in Figure 7.6 would be displayed.

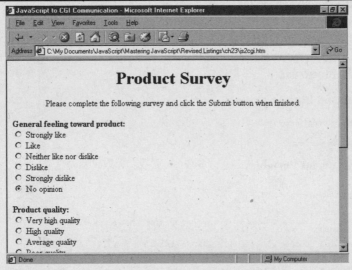

FIGURE 7.5: Using JavaScript to process a form's data and send it to a CGI program (Listing 7.3)

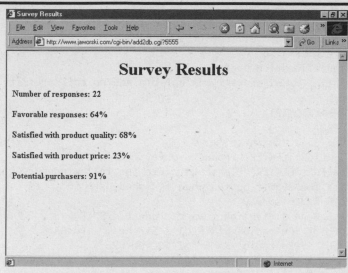

FIGURE 7.6: The survey results are displayed using JavaScript generated by a CGI program (Listing 7.5).

The js2cgi.htm file consists of an HTML form with four sets of radio buttons. The user clicks the radio buttons to fill out the product survey. The sendToCGI() function handles the onClick event of the Submit button by determining which buttons were selected and creating a four-character text string (stored in the results variable) that summarizes the form's data. For example, suppose a user selected the third value of the first set of radio buttons, the fourth value of the second set, the first value of the third set, and the last value of the last set. The value of the results variable would be *2305*.

The value of the results variable is appended to the URL of the CGI program as a query string, and the href property of the current window's location object is set to the URL. This causes the URL of the CGI program to be requested.

Listing 7.3: Interfacing JavaScript with a CGI Program (j&2cgi.htm)

```
<HTML>
<HEAD>
<TITLE>JavaScript to CGI Communication</TITLE>
<SCRIPT LANGUAGE="JavaScript"><!--
function sendToCGI() {
  results=""
```

Part ii

```
  surveyForm=window.document.survey
  for(var i=0;i<surveyForm.length-1;++i)
   if(surveyForm.elements[i].checked)
     results+=i%6
  window.location.href=
   "http://www.jaworski.com/cgi-bin/add2db.cgi?"+results
}
// --></SCRIPT>
</HEAD>
<BODY BGCOLOR="white"">
<H1 ALIGN="CENTER">Product Survey</H1>
<P ALIGN="CENTER">Please complete the following survey and
click the Submit button when finished.</P>
<FORM NAME="survey">
<P><B>General feeling toward product:</B><BR>
<INPUT TYPE="radio" NAME="g1"> Strongly like<BR>
<INPUT TYPE="radio" NAME="g1"> Like<BR>
<INPUT TYPE="radio" NAME="g1"> Neither like nor dislike<BR>
<INPUT TYPE="radio" NAME="g1"> Dislike<BR>
<INPUT TYPE="radio" NAME="g1"> Strongly dislike<BR>
<INPUT TYPE="radio" NAME="g1" CHECKED> No opinion<BR>
</P>
<P><B>Product quality:</B><BR>
<INPUT TYPE="radio" NAME="g2"> Very high quality<BR>
<INPUT TYPE="radio" NAME="g2"> High quality<BR>
<INPUT TYPE="radio" NAME="g2"> Average quality<BR>
<INPUT TYPE="radio" NAME="g2"> Poor quality<BR>
<INPUT TYPE="radio" NAME="g2"> Very poor quality<BR>
<INPUT TYPE="radio" NAME="g2" CHECKED> No opinion<BR>
</P>
<P><B>Product pricing:</B><BR>
<INPUT TYPE="radio" NAME="g3"> Price is very high<BR>
<INPUT TYPE="radio" NAME="g3"> Price is high<BR>
<INPUT TYPE="radio" NAME="g3"> Price is about right<BR>
<INPUT TYPE="radio" NAME="g3"> Price is low<BR>
<INPUT TYPE="radio" NAME="g3"> Price is very low<BR>
<INPUT TYPE="radio" NAME="g3" CHECKED> No opinion<BR>
</P>
<P><B>Purchase plans:</B><BR>
<INPUT TYPE="radio" NAME="g4"> Plan to purchase<BR>
<INPUT TYPE="radio" NAME="g4"> May purchase<BR>
<INPUT TYPE="radio" NAME="g4"> May purchase if price is
  lowered<BR>
<INPUT TYPE="radio" NAME="g4"> May purchase if quality is
  improved<BR>
<INPUT TYPE="radio" NAME="g4"> Do not plan to purchase<BR>
```

```
<INPUT TYPE="radio" NAME="g4" CHECKED> No opinion<BR>
</P>
</TABLE>
<INPUT TYPE="BUTTON" VALUE="Submit"
 onClick="sendToCGI()">
</FORM>
</BODY>
</HTML>
```

When my Web server receives the URL request for add2db.cgi, it executes the Perl script shown in Listing 7.4. Because the query string passed by js2cgi.htm is a single value and not a name=value pair, my Web server assumes that the request is an ISINDEX query and passes the data contained in the URL's query string as a command-line argument.

The add2db.cgi script works as follows. The first line identifies the location of the Perl interpreter. The second line opens the file db.txt with append access. This means that anything written to db.txt will be appended to the end of the file. The third line writes the value of the command-line argument to the db.txt file. This value is the four-character form processing result that was appended to the URL of add2db.cgi. The fourth line writes a new line character to db.txt. The fifth line closes the db.txt file, and the last line returns the file located at http://www .jaworski.com/javascript/results.htm as the result of the CGI program's processing. Figure 7.6 shows how results.htm is displayed.

Listing 7.4: A Perl Program That Stores the Form Data on the Server (*add2db.cgi*)

```
#!/usr/bin/perl
open (OUTPUT, ">>db.txt");
print OUTPUT @ARGV;
print OUTPUT "\ n";
close (OUTPUT);
print "Location: /javascript/results.htm\ n\ n";
```

RETURNING JAVASCRIPT FROM CGI PROGRAMS

One of the more powerful techniques of integrating client-side JavaScript scripts with CGI programs is to use CGI programs to return JavaScript code. In doing so, your Web applications become more dynamic and efficient by allowing browsers to perform some of the CGI program's processing.

Instead of responding with a static Web page, your CGI programs are able to perform the minimum amount of server-side processing and return a JavaScript script that completes the application processing on the browser.

The following example shows how CGI programs can be used to return JavaScript code. This example builds on the add2db.cgi example of the previous section.

In the last line of Listing 7.4 the results.htm file is returned to complete the processing of add2db.cgi. Listing 7.5 shows the contents of results.htm. It contains two scripts in the document head. The first script includes JavaScript code from the URL http://www.jaworski.com/cgi-bin/getdb.cgi. But this is the URL of a CGI program. Listing 7.6 shows the source code of getdb.cgi.

Because the output of getdb.cgi is crucial to the operation of results.htm, we'll examine the operation of getdb.cgi before continuing with the discussion of results.htm. The file getdb.cgi is a Perl script that summarizes the data contained in db.txt and returns its results as a JavaScript array. Recall that each line of db.txt is a four-digit value that describes the data entered into the form shown in Listing 7.3. The getdb.cgi script reads through db.txt and counts how many times radio buttons 1 through 6 are selected for survey topics 1 through 4. This results in a 24-value array. A 25th value is added that identifies the number of lines in db.txt.

getdb.cgi performs its processing as follows:

Line 1   Identifies the location of the Perl interpreter. Note that the .cgi extension was not used with getdb.cgi—it was left off in order to prevent the browser from expecting a file of a different MIME type.

Line 2   Identifies the MIME type of the data returned by getdb.cgi as application/x-javascript. Note that a blank line follows the Content header.

Line 3   Returns the beginning of a JavaScript array definition that is assigned to variable r.

Lines 4–6   Open db.txt for input, initialize the @totals array to 0, and set $num to 0.

Lines 7–15   Loop through db.txt and read each line. $num counts the number of lines read. $totals[6*$i+$n] counts the number of times radio button $n is selected for topic $i.

Lines 16–19   Print the values of $totals to the JavaScript output.

Lines 20–21   Add the number of lines in db.txt as the 25th value of the r array.

Getting back to results.htm, the second script contains two functions, displayResults() and writeResult(). The first of these, display-Results(), performs further processing on the r array to summarize and display the results of the survey. It sets n to r[24], which is the number of lines in db.txt. It then calculates the percentage of favorable responses, the percentage of responses in which the product quality and price were acceptable, and the percentage of respondents who are potential purchasers. These results are then displayed using the writeResult() function.

Listing 7.5: Displaying the Results of the Product Survey (results.htm)

```
<HTML>
<HEAD>
<TITLE>Survey Results</TITLE>
<SCRIPT LANGUAGE="JavaScript"
 SRC="http://www.jaworski.com/cgi-bin/getdb.cgi"><!--
// --></SCRIPT>
<SCRIPT LANGUAGE="JavaScript"><!--
function displayResults() {
 var n=r[24]
 var favorable=(r[0]+r[1])/n
 favorable=Math.round(favorable*100)
 var quality=(r[6]+r[7]+r[8])/n
 quality=Math.round(quality*100)
 var price=(r[14]+r[15]+r[16])/n
 price=Math.round(price*100)
 var purchase=(n-r[22])/n
 purchase=Math.round(purchase*100)
 document.write("<P><B>Number of responses: "+n+"</B></P>")
 writeResult("Favorable responses: ",favorable)
 writeResult("Satisfied with product quality: ",quality)
 writeResult("Satisfied with product price: ",price)
 writeResult("Potential purchasers: ",purchase)
}
function writeResult(s,n) {
 document.write("<P><B>"+s+n+"%</B></P>")
}
// --></SCRIPT>
</HEAD>
```

Part ii

```
<BODY>
<H1 ALIGN="CENTER">Survey Results</H1>
<SCRIPT LANGUAGE="JavaScript"><!--
displayResults()
// --></SCRIPT>
</BODY>
</HTML>
```

Listing 7.6: A CGI Script That Returns Its Results as JavaScript (*getdb.cgi*)

```perl
#!/usr/bin/perl
print "Content-type: application/x-javascript\ n\ n";
print "r= new Array(";
open (INPUT,"db.txt");
@totals=(0,0,0,0,0,0,0,0,0,0,0,0,0,0,0,0,0,0,0,0,0,0,0,0);
$num=0;
while(<INPUT>) {
 $num++;
 chop;
 $line=$_;
 for($i=0;$i<4;$i++){
  $n=substr($line,$i,1);
  $totals[6*$i+$n]++;
 }
}
for($i=0;$i<24;$i++){
 print $totals[$i];
 print ",";
}
print $num;
print ")\ n";
```

SUMMARY

In this chapter, you learned how CGI programs work and saw the types of Web applications in which CGI programs are used. You learned how to interface JavaScript scripts with CGI scripts and how to use CGI programs to generate JavaScript code.

PART iii
Perl & CGI Fundamentals

CHAPTER 8

INTRODUCING PERL AND CGI

The Internet has become—perhaps arguably—the most important communication medium in the world. There is virtually no argument, however, about the World Wide Web. It is the Internet's most important channel of communication. If you want to deal with the Net, pretty soon you'll have to deal with the Web.

Adapted from *Perl CGI Programming: No experience required*, by Erik Strom

ISBN 0-7821-2157-8   447 pages $29.99

You'll learn about one of the most important aspects of the Web in this part. The *Common Gateway Interface* (CGI) and applications written in the Perl programming language give you the tools to create dynamic, informative Web pages, with which you can fashion a Web site that your visitors will find truly useful and worth revisiting.

A good Web site is not just a collection of pretty pictures. It has to *do* something. With Perl and CGI, you can make it do just that.

WHY PERL?

A Web page is a text document that is formatted with a set of commands—a programming language, if you will—called the *Hypertext Markup Language,* or HTML. The name is descriptive: HTML is a "markup" language; that is, it controls the way a document looks. HTML instructions tell a Web browser, such as Netscape's Navigator or Microsoft's Internet Explorer, how it should go about displaying the page on-screen. But HTML all by itself has practically no facilities for making a Web page do things. You have to rely on other means for that.

The Perl programming language is hands-down the most popular method of making a Web page "do" something, mainly because Perl is freely available and will run on every computer platform that can host a Web server. Coupled with the Common Gateway Interface (CGI), Perl is used on the vast majority of Web sites to create Web pages that have to do more than sit there and look pretty.

There are a couple of other tools you can use to create a dynamic Web page:

► Java

► Proprietary languages

The following sections will look at each of them.

Java

Java, which was originally invented by Sun Microsystems to control toasters, is a popular and highly touted method for making interactive Web pages these days. As a programming language, Java is a very rich resource, one that will allow you to do almost anything you desire with your page. However, not all Web browsers support Java, so by including an *applet* written in that language in your page, you are necessarily excluding an entire class of visitors.

TIP

An *applet* in Java is a program that is run by the Web browser, if the browser is capable of running it (many Web browsers aren't).

To work properly, Java depends on the browser software that your visitors use. If the browser supports Java, your applets work. If not, and you are a kind Webmaster, your visitors will get a message telling them essentially to buy another browser. If you are unkind, they will get either a blank screen or some wonderfully obscure HTTP error message that, if nothing else, will ensure that they never return to your Web page again.

Proprietary Languages

Along the same lines as Java are the proprietary packages, notably Visual Basic Script from Microsoft and Netscape's JavaScript.

TIP

Proprietary software packages usually target a specific hardware and/or software platform. They won't work with everything.

Visual Basic Script is, of course, based on Visual Basic, Microsoft's heavily Windows-laden version of the BASIC programming language. JavaScript is an *interpreted* flavor of Java, which means that the Web browser interprets and executes each line in the script. While the intent of both—essentially extending HTML to make the Web page itself more dynamic—probably is laudable, neither will run on any but the newer browsers from both companies, because the older browsers were written before these tools existed.

They're slick, yes. By taking advantage of a specific platform, the proprietary tools can run faster and do more than a generic package that is intended to run on *all* platforms. But they don't allow you to accommodate every visitor to your site because not all visitors will have the hardware or software that the proprietary tools target (see Figure 8.1). Not all visitors will be using Intel-based PCs, nor will all visitors be running a version of Netscape or Internet Explorer, or Windows 95/98 or NT.

Part iii

Some visitors may not even be able to display graphics. But *all* of them need to be considered when setting up a site.

NOTE

The proprietary methods extend HTML by creating programs that run on a visitor's computer, rather than at your site on your Web server. As a result, they depend totally on the computer and software the visitor is using.

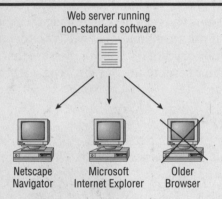

Web server running
non-standard software

Netscape   Microsoft   Older
Navigator   Internet Explorer   Browser

FIGURE 8.1: Proprietary languages can exclude visitors to your Web site.

CGI

Long before Java, there was the Common Gateway Interface, CGI for short. CGI is the most common method for passing information from an HTML document to a program that can process the information. CGI doesn't care what browser you're using; even non-graphical Lynx-type software will work.

Unlike Java and its more proprietary cousins, CGI is not a programming language, nor does it load itself onto the visitor's machine to run. CGI is, as its name spells out, an interface, a set of rules. It resides on the Web-server computer, providing a way for the page to communicate in a rough fashion with the server. CGI allows you to write programs to deal with the page in *any* language—including Perl.

PERL'S ANCIENT HISTORY

There is only one reason that Perl programs—or *scripts*, which is a lexical convention that will be explained shortly—are so universal in World Wide Web programming. The simple fact of the matter is, until the last few years, virtually every Web server in existence was running on a UNIX system and Perl is among the most useful of UNIX tools.

The first *Hypertext Transfer Protocol* (HTTP) servers were written for UNIX, too, and freely distributed among system administrators who wanted to try out the World Wide Web. CGI was developed as a standard of communication on these systems. In a sense, Perl and HTTP and CGI *all* became standards for doing Web work (see Figure 8.2).

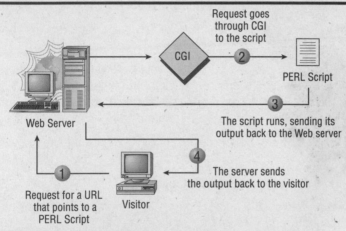

FIGURE 8.2: The HTTP-CGI-Perl connection

The beauty of standards is that they usually transcend the platforms on which they originated. The number of non-UNIX Web servers and Web sites on the Internet increases every day. Yet the HTTP-CGI-Perl connection remains the same because it was lifted intact into the newer platforms.

UNIX is, in a very large sense, an operating system written by and, most importantly, *for* programmers. It really was never intended for humans to use easily, which is why so many people have gone to such extraordinary lengths to make UNIX more friendly, with X Windows and various other graphical interfaces. These interfaces require tremendous amounts of processing power, so in many cases system designers have simply given up and relegated bare-bones UNIX to the background, running it on the system server and hanging Macintoshes or other workstations running Windows on the network for users.

The beauty of UNIX for those who have taken the time to learn it is in the rich set of software tools that it provides. Unadorned UNIX is like a box of wonderful Swiss Army knives; with any one of them, you can carve any masterpiece your imagination can conjure.

Perl is one of the most useful of those Swiss Army knives.

THE UNIX TOOLBOX

Consider some of the more obscure tools you can pull out of UNIX:

grep   Allows you to search through files, directories, or entire disks for words or phrases.

sh, csh, ksh   Some of the UNIX "shells," which are akin to the MS-DOS command line but considerably more powerful. Shell scripts are like DOS batch files with turbochargers attached. You really don't need another programming language.

ed, sed, vi   The UNIX editors that everyone hates...and everyone uses.

whereis   Finds files *anywhere*; actually a shell script.

man   Calls up the **man**ual pages for programs and other utilities, often serving to further confuse the hapless user.

We Owe It All to Larry Wall: A History of Perl

Larry Wall is a linguist-turned-programmer who began working on Perl more than 10 years ago while attempting a sticky project for Unisys.

NOTE

The Perl language grew out of the classic UNIX philosophy: If the system doesn't allow you to do your job easily, then you simply write another tool to solve the problem.

Perl actually is an acronym whose most accepted expanded version is *Practical Extraction and Report Language*, though UNIX wags have come up with many more earthy descriptions, such as "Pathologically Eclectic Rubbish Lister." It was derived in large part from *sed* and *awk*, jackhammers of the UNIX toolbox for those who understand them, utterly unintelligible command programs for those who don't. After all, what can one say about a program whose most famous error message is awk: bailing out near Line 1?

The strengths of sed and awk, and their offspring Perl, lie mainly in their built-in capabilities for processing text through pattern-matching, searching for and replacing phrases—or "strings"—in entire groups of files, and the use of UNIX's obscure yet extremely powerful regular expressions, which are discussed in full in Chapter 12.

REGULAR EXPRESSIONS: BANE *AND* BOON

Regular expressions are among the most useful—and most difficult to master—tools in the UNIX array.

You can think of them as supercharged search-and/or-replace operations. Where most any text editor will let you find phrases and replace them with other phrases throughout a file, regular expressions add a great deal of power to the operation. For example, you can use regular expressions to look for strings at the beginning or end of a line, or in a word, or for a specific number of occurrences.

But it's not easy. A Perl regular expression that swaps the first two words in a line of text looks like this:

```
s/^([^ ]*) *([^ ]*)/$2 $1/;
```

Doesn't make much sense, does it? But that could be a very useful operation, couldn't it?

We'll defer a full explanation of regular expressions until Chapter 12. For now, let's just say that you will find many uses for them.

Part iii

The bedrock of UNIX is the C programming language—most of it is written in C—but C, in its position at the foundation of the operating system, adheres to the minimalist philosophy of UNIX, which means that you often have to write scads of C code to accomplish relatively simple tasks. A trivial search-and-replace operation on a text file, written in C, requires the programmer to at least scan the file character by character and could easily grow from a simple subroutine into an entire application (see Figure 8.3).

But the same operation can be accomplished in a few lines of Perl code (see Figure 8.4).

```
WebPage - [C:\usr\erik\PERL-CGI\ADDGUEST.CPP]
File  Edit  Search  Window  Help

    ZeroMemory (&GuestEntry, sizeof (GUEST_ENTRY));       // Hose out the structure.

    char*   INFO_ARRAY [] =
    {
        GuestEntry.FirstName,
        GuestEntry.LastName,
        GuestEntry.City,
        GuestEntry.State,
        GuestEntry.Country,
        GuestEntry.EMail,
        GuestEntry.Comments,
        NULL
    };

    char*   o;                        // Couple of pointers for string manipulation.
    char*   p = buf;
    int     n = 0;                    // Counter.

    while ((o = strchr (p, '&')) != NULL)
    {
        *o = NULL;                    // End the substring here.
        strcpy (INFO_ARRAY [n++], p); // Copy the data into the correct spot.
        p = ++o;                      // Get the next one.
    }
```

FIGURE 8.3: An example of code written in C++

TIP

Perl is a challenge to learn, but it is infinitely more efficient for the programmer (read: "fewer lines of code") and easier to use than C.

UNIX programmers snapped up Perl as a tool of choice almost immediately for doing tasks ranging from "quick and dirty" to horribly complex. Because you have the ability to call most of the standard UNIX system services from a Perl script, including the internetworking functions, you probably could write an entire operating system in it. It would be very slow, but it would run a computer.

To this day, almost every serious UNIX systems programmer works with Perl almost daily. It's just too useful for programmers to ignore.

```
                @InfoArray = split (/&/, $post_info);

# Go through each element in @InfoArray, split off the
# "variable=" part, then translate pluses into spaces and
# any escaped hex chars back into their real character values.

    for ($n = 0; @InfoArray[$n]; $n++)
        (
        ($dummy, $temp) = split (/=/, @InfoArray[$n]);
        $temp =~ tr/+/ /;
        $temp =~ s/%([\dA-Fa-f][\dA-Fa-f])/pack ("C", hex ($1))/eg;
        @InfoArray [$n] = $temp;
        )

# Now we'll check to see if we have anything to write
# to the guest book.  We need a first or last name, at
# least; otherwise, we'll jump around the routines that
# write this stuff to the guest book file.

    if ((length (@InfoArray[$FirstNameIndex]) != 0)
        || (length (@InfoArray [$LastNameIndex]) != 0))
        (

    # Tack the current time to the end of the array.
```

FIGURE 8.4: An example of code written in Perl

Perl and the World Wide Web

Perl has become popular for Web work because in most of its incarnations it is an *interpreted* language, like the first versions of BASIC, rather than a *compiled* language, such as C or C++. However, this isn't strictly true, because Perl compilers are available from many sources, just as there are many C interpreters to be had. The essential difference between a compiled and interpreted application is that a compiled program has been translated into the machine language of the computer on which it will run by another program called a *compiler*. The translated, or compiled, file will run all by itself. An *interpreted* program, on the other hand, is actually translated and run on the fly by a program called an *interpreter*.

Compiled programs, because they consist of machine-language instructions, generally run faster. But for the same reason, they are not portable from one computer platform to another. Code compiled for a

Sun box or a Macintosh won't run on an Intel-based PC because the different processors that power these machines all speak radically different tongues. Your program would have to be recompiled for the target machine before it would work. It may even have to be rewritten.

There are no such restrictions on interpreted Perl code. All you need is some version of the Perl interpreter—called *perl*—on the target computer. Perl interpreters have been written for every popular computer platform, from Sun to Alpha to Apple to Intel and more, and with very few exceptions your Perl programs should transport unchanged into every environment.

This feature won't sound very important to novice programmers. However, porting C code even between the different flavors of UNIX is an art that not many people have the patience or skill to do full time. It is tedious, difficult, and time-consuming. The capability to develop and test code on one computer and then simply drop it into another, as you can do with Perl, is a boon cherished by all professional programmers.

Perl programs are not compiled, which is why we refer to them as *scripts*. Like shell scripts in UNIX or batch and command files on MS-DOS and Windows NT, Perl programs are just text files that run through an application to process their commands.

However, make no mistake about it: Perl programs are just that— programs, with all the power and versatility the word implies. If you've never written a line of code in your life, Perl will forever spoil you against the more traditional programming languages. If you are a programmer but this is your introduction to Perl, you will find yourself using it more and more as your familiarity with it increases, because it makes things so *easy*.

For the nuts and bolts of Web site processing, administration, and maintenance, tedious system chores that should *always* be hidden from users, in addition to the creation of truly dynamic Web pages, Perl can't be beat.

BUILDING A PERL SCRIPT

Now that you have a little background, you're going to write your first Perl program. It's a simple example that gives you the basic idea of how a Perl script is written and run. All of our subsequent examples will build on this one.

"Hello World" probably seems kind of dumb, but those of us who have been programming for a while have a soft spot for this snippet of code. It's the first programming example given in the monumental *C Programming Language* by Brian Kernighan and Dennis Ritchie, published in 1976. Many programmers cut their teeth on this work; forgive us, please, if we remember it fondly.

USING EXISTING PERL SCRIPTS

Perl scripts are simply text files that you can create using your favorite text editor. Perl is the language of choice for Web developers these days because of its ease of use on UNIX machines. Its popularity, which may be one reason why you bought this book, also has other benefits: for one thing, a huge body of existing code out there in the ether. Most of it is free, which means you can simply drop it into your Web server and run it, regardless of the operating system that powers your computer. Most of that code was written, tested, and debugged by UNIX programmers who had their own Web sites to maintain. You can find lots of stuff in USENET—go to comp.lang.perl. Or try one of the Web search engines such as Yahoo!.

So it makes sense for you to be running Perl on your Web site, if only from the standpoint of the effort you want to put into writing software. If you have a task to perform and someone else has already written the code to perform it—and has no compunctions at all about you using it—then why shouldn't you avoid reinventing wheels?

Part iii

First Things First: Perls before Code

You can't do anything without the Perl language interpreter. Make sure you have a copy of it before you go further or you'll get snotty error messages from whatever operating system you're using.

TIP

You can get Perl for Win32—Windows NT and Windows 95—by pointing your Web browser to http://www.activestate.com. UNIX sources for Perl are numerous and ever-changing; the best way to find them is in the Internet newsgroups at comp.sources.unix. MacPERL for the Macintosh is available at www.iis.ee.ethz.ch/~neeri/macintosh/perl.html.

I'll make very few assumptions about the computer you are using or the operating system that it runs. However, most of the really good Perls that can be obtained are intended to run on Windows NT and Windows 95/98 or UNIX, and most of our examples will emphasize those two platforms.

Installing the Perl interpreter can be as simple as running a setup program or as complicated as extracting the source code and compiling it yourself.

Fortunately, Perl is included in many UNIX distributions these days. If that's the case on your system, obviously you don't have to do anything. The Perl executable for NT and Windows 95/98 can be downloaded for nothing from Microsoft's Web site and several others. It performs flawlessly.

COMPILING YOUR OWN PERL INTERPRETER...

Compiling the Perl source code yourself is the method preferred by UNIX system administrators, who usually have a rather macho attitude about such things. Because the most freely available C code for Perl was written primarily for UNIX systems, it compiles easily most of the time.

Likewise, compiling the code for Windows is possible, but only for the most daring of systems gurus; the process certainly is beyond the scope of this book. The latest versions of the most popular C/C++ development packages available for Windows—Visual C++ from Microsoft and Borland C++ for Windows from Borland International—both contain quirks that prevent a straightforward compilation of the Perl source code. Unless you want to change the functionality of Perl (which is an exercise of dubious logical value in itself) and devote hours to debugging someone else's code, you're much better off simply using whatever executable files you can find for the operating system you're using.

Loading the Interpreter

Regardless of your operating system, once you have the Perl interpreter, you're ready to go. On UNIX, things will be a little easier if you put the Perl interpreter in a subdirectory that is included in your PATH environment string, which is a system variable that maps out where the operating system should look when you type the name of a program at the command line. In other words, if you have loaded PATH by typing **PATH=/usr/bin;/usr/me;/pub/local/etc** at the command line and you then enter **perl**, the operating system will look in each of those directories for Perl before it gives up and complains to you that the command couldn't be found. The same is true in Windows NT and Windows 95.

TIP

The setup program for the Win32 Perl at www.activestate.com will ask you if you want Perl to be added to your PATH. If you answer affirmatively, the change will take place the next time to restart your computer.

As we discussed earlier, Perl scripts are simple text files that you can create using your favorite text editor. To put together your first Perl program, start that text editor now and enter the following lines:

```
#!/usr/bin/perl

    print "Hello World!", "\n";

#           End hello.pl
```

NOTE

The first line in the program begins with Perl's "comment" character (#), and it will be ignored by the interpreter. However, it must contain the path to your Perl interpreter. If your system's Perl interpreter is not in /usr/bin, change the path to the correct subdirectory.

That's fairly easy, isn't it? We'll explain what's going on in the next section; for now, save the file as hello.pl ("hello.pl" in quotes if you're using Notepad on Windows) and close your text editor.

Part iii

Running the "Hello" Example

The hello.pl is about as tiny as programs get, both in the writing and in the execution. It is intended to be run from the *command line*, which means the shell in UNIX, the console command processor in Windows NT, or CMD.EXE or COMMAND.COM in Windows 95/98.

TIP

The term "command line" will be used frequently in this book, so to avoid the confusion of having to refer to both operating system methods, we'll henceforth refer to the UNIX shell and the NT/95 console as the "command line." Also, because Perl adheres to the UNIX convention of specifying path names with the forward slash (/) rather than Microsoft's backslash (\) we will adhere to it, too, in the text of our examples. Remember the difference when you're typing commands in the NT console.

Open a command-line window (a shell in UNIX, a command console or MS-DOS window in Windows 95 and NT). Because Perl is an interpreted language, you won't be running your first Perl program directly. You have to run perl with your Perl program as an argument to it. If, when you installed the Perl software on your system, you did as we suggested and put it somewhere in your PATH, then you can simply type:

```
perl hello.pl
```

Otherwise, you'll have to type in the full path to perl followed by the name of your program. For example, if you installed Perl in /myprogs/perl, and that subdirectory is not in your PATH environment variable, you would have to type:

```
/myprogs/perl hello.pl
```

In any event, when you run the program, the result should look something like Figure 8.5.

Notice that the program prints "Hello, World!" with a line-ender to the screen.

Congratulations! You are now a Perl programmer.

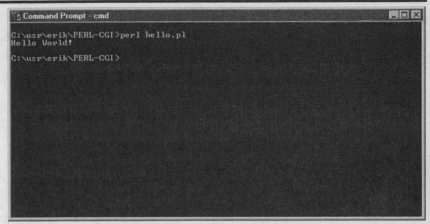

FIGURE 8.5: The results of running your first Perl program

How Perl Programs Run

In a technical sense, the Perl interpreter is a language compiler that doesn't write its translated output to a file on the disk. Its "output file" is the screen, which is called *standard output* or *stdout* in systems parlance.

If a program name is given on the command line, the interpreter first checks the validity of each line, dumping out error messages for incorrect code and stopping if it finds any. If your program passes muster, the interpreter executes each of its lines of code.

One of the convenient aspects of doing it this way is that you find out immediately if your program does something wrong—and programs inevitably do! Most developers work on "windowed" systems, and they run the text editor with their Perl program code in one window and keep the command-line screen in another (see Figure 8.6). It is then quite easy to pop from window to window, writing and fixing code in the text editor and testing the code from the command line. With Perl, you get all your errors at once, and that speeds up the coding process. With a compiled language such as C or C++, you have to write the code, compile it, fix any errors that have cropped up in the compilation, compile it again, link it to the external libraries it needs, then—*whew!*—run it and see what errors occur there. Then you get to start all over again. It's little wonder that Perl has become so popular!

Part iii

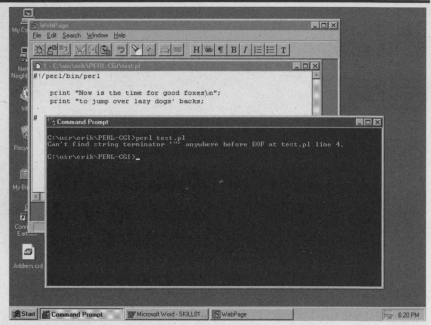

FIGURE 8.6: The two-window debugging process

Dissecting the "Hello" Example

We have briefly covered the first line in the program. We'll now take apart this line, #!/usr/bin/perl, piece by piece:

(pound sign)   This is Perl's "comment" character, which means that anything following it up to the end of the line is ignored by the interpreter. This is where you can document your program, so that others (or *you* after you haven't touched the program in a few months!) can understand what is being accomplished in the code.

! (exclamation point)   This *first* comment line is a special case. UNIX aficionados will read to the exclamation point (!) and recognize it as an instruction to the shell; a command for the command line. Strictly speaking, this tells the shell to run the Perl interpreter with the program code as its input.

NOTE

The first line is required, and it should always contain the full path to your Perl interpreter, which may or may not be in /usr/bin. I used /usr/bin as an example because it is a common place to put it. Oddly, though there is no direct way under Windows 95 or NT to run a command with the ! character, some Win32 Perl interpreters require you to follow this convention. You will get an error message if the path is specified incorrectly.

The Heart of the Program: *print*

We have used only one real Perl function in this short program—print. This function is a real workhorse, especially in Web programming, where you will use Perl to construct HTML pages. print is a function that you very likely will use in every program you write.

How does print work? We'll go into a detailed description later, because print can do a lot. For now, let's look at what it does in hello.pl:

```
print "Hello, World!", "\ n";
```

The unadorned print, as we have used it in the example program, takes a list of *strings* (that is, text enclosed by quotation marks) as its *arguments*, or *parameters*.

TIP

The terms *argument* and *parameter* will be used interchangeably throughout this book in reference to the data you will use with Perl functions.

In this case, we are telling print that we want it to "print" the phrases "Hello World!" and "\n" to the screen. Notice that the two phrases, which are the print function's arguments, are separated by a comma. It is also important that the line ends with a semicolon. *All* code lines in Perl must end with the semicolon; the interpreter will complain bitterly if you forget to do this, and it's usually the first thing you will do wrong. Be forewarned!

Part iii

WARNING

All code lines in Perl must end in a semicolon. Why? The interpreter can't decide for itself where a code statement ends, because it may extend for more than one line. The semicolon tells the interpreter, "This statement ends here."

The Strange \ n

"Hello World!" is easy enough to figure out, but what is this \n? C-language programmers and others who are, by necessity, familiar with UNIX conventions know this as the *newline* character. If you've never seen this before, remember carefully the backslash (\) that precedes the n. This is called an *escape* character because it gives a special meaning to the character that follows it. The \n specifically refers to the line-feed character, with a value of 10 in the ASCII character set.

The line-feed is the standard line ender in UNIX; the MS-DOS convention, which has been retained by Windows 95 and NT, is to end each line with a carriage return *and* a line feed, which in a Perl print command would be set up as \r\n. However, the Perl interpreter knows what operating system it's running on, and it makes certain allowances for these differences. For now, whether you compose your code on UNIX or Windows NT, you can use the simple \n as a line ender.

Table 8.1 lists some other Perl "escaped" characters.

TABLE 8.1: Some of the Perl Special Characters

CHARACTER STRING	DOES THIS
\n	Newline or line-feed
\r	Carriage return
\t	Tab
\f	Form-feed
\b	Backspace
\033	ASCII 27 (Escape) in octal

CONTINUED ➡

TABLE 8.1 continued: Some of the Perl Special Characters

CHARACTER STRING	DOES THIS
\x1B	Same in hexadecimal
\cD	Control-D
\\	Backslash
\"	Double quote
\'	Single quote
\u	Uppercase next character
\U	Uppercase following characters
\l, \L	Same as above, but lowercase
\E	End \U or \L

NOTE
Table 8.1 doesn't list all of the Perl special "escaped" characters. These are just the most common.

The escaped double quote (\") can be somewhat confusing. It is used when you want to actually use the double quote character in a string, rather than using it to *delimit* the string. For example, the following Perl code:

```
print "Hello World!", "\n";
print "\"Hello World\"", "\n";
```

would result in the following output to the screen:

```
Hello, World!
"Hello, World!"
```

Perl also allows a construct to keep you from loading up your strings with backslashes. You may use q/STRING/ and qq/STRING/ too, where *STRING* is the phrase enclosed between the slashes.

Goodbye to "Hello"

We have done just about all we can with this first version of "Hello World!" You should now be familiar with Perl comment lines, with emphasis on the important first line, which actually is an instruction. Additionally, you've gained a passing acquaintance with the workhorse print function and some of the things that you can do with it.

The results of running the new version of the script are illustrated in Figure 8.7.

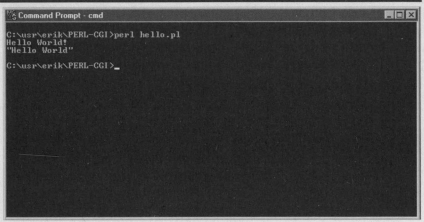

FIGURE 8.7: The new results of running hello.pl

There's one more line in the program, however, and we shouldn't move on without explaining it:

```
#                      End hello.pl
```

This is a comment line, as you have learned, but why? Obviously, it's the end of the program because there's no more program after it.

Yes, it *is* quite obvious in a tiny snippet of code such as we've typed into hello.pl. However, the programs we will work on as your knowledge increases will be much more complicated, much larger, and won't be as clear on where one subroutine starts or another ends.

It is simply good programming practice to document your code well, not just for others but for your own benefit. And good documentation starts with clearly marking the beginning and end of important sections of code.

Variables, Scalars, and Lists in Perl

The code we've written so far is simple. Let's make it a bit more complicated—and therefore useful—by introducing three new concepts:

Variable   Data stored in specific memory location

Scalar   A single variable that defines either numeric or string (character) data

List   A number of scalars stored sequentially in one variable

Perl Variables: What's in a Name

The capability to store data in locations that have specific names lies at the heart of any useful programming language. Moving data to a specific spot in memory and being able to recall them by name (or location) at a later time is known as working with *variables*. Perl is no different in this respect.

If you have done any programming at all, you will be familiar with the concept of variables. However, the conventions used in Perl can be a little weird for the uninitiated, so if you're thinking of skipping this section, please don't!

Storing data in a variable is as straightforward as picking a name and setting it equal to a value. Complex programming languages such as C have lots of complex rules for what types of data can be stored where; for example, in C, integers have to go into `int` variables, and strings of characters are stored as `char` arrays, and so forth. Variables have to be declared and given types before they can be used.

Perl, despite all that it owes to C, plays very fast and loose with those rules. In Perl, you declare a variable merely by using it, which helps to make the Perl development process somewhat quicker and easier than programming in C.

WARNING

The rules of good, structured programming apply to Perl as they do to any other language: make your Perl code readable by using lots of comments. Just because a language allows a fast and loose form of variable declaration is no excuse for writing "spaghetti code."

Introducing Scalars

The most fundamental data in Perl are called *scalars*. The word can be intimidating to beginners because its meaning is not immediately apparent. A scalar is nothing more than a single piece of data. Scalars differ from another fundamental Perl data-type, which is the *list* (defined in the *Perl Lists* section).

Perl regards numeric *and* string data as scalar values, and, in most cases, it's pretty good at telling the difference between the two and acting properly.

NOTE

"Strings" in most programming languages are simply strings of characters. "Now is the time for all good folks to come to the aid of their party" is a string. Notice that it is enclosed in quotes. This is important in Perl.

The important thing to remember about scalar variables is that they always begin with a dollar sign ($). You can call them anything you want, just never forget the dollar sign.

WARNING

Perl is a case-sensitive language, which means that it distinguishes between upper- and lowercase letters in names. Thus, it will regard $VariableName and $variablename as two different scalar variables.

We can create a second version of hello.pl to illustrate the concept of storing data in scalar variables. Type the following lines into your text editor and save the file as hello2.pl:

```
#!/usr/bin/perl

# hello2, a slightly more sophisticated "Hello World"
```

```
$Hello = "Hello, World";        # String variable
$TimeAround = 2;                # Numeric variable

print $Hello, " for the ", $TimeAround, "nd time!",
➥ "\n";

#       End hello2.pl
```

Now run the program as we did the one we created earlier. You'll see this on your screen (see Figure 8.8):

```
Hello, World for the 2nd time!
```

```
C:\usr\erik\PERL-CGI>perl hello2.pl
Hello, World for the 2nd time!

C:\usr\erik\PERL-CGI>_
```

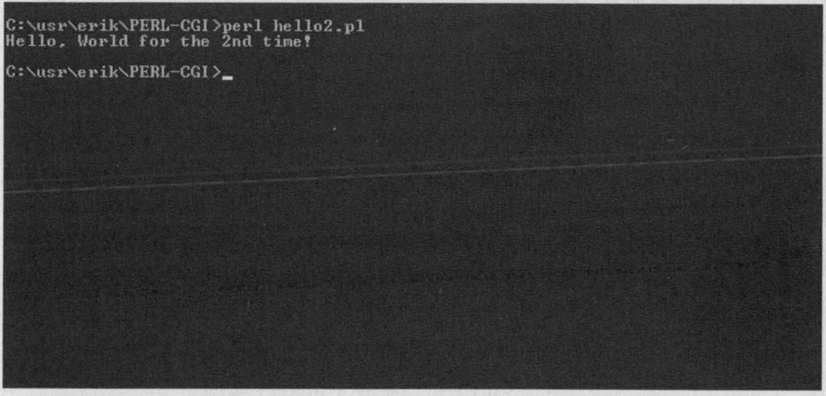

FIGURE 8.8: Using variables in your Perl script

Notice that you were able to set the two variables, $Hello and $TimeAround, to two entirely unrelated types. Yet the print function knew precisely what to do with them and assembled the resulting output string flawlessly. print is even smarter than we've made it appear here; the line could have been written to include the variables in one long string argument, such as the following:

```
print "$Hello for the ${TimeAround} nd time!";
```

The important thing to note here is that TimeAround was enclosed in curly braces to set it off from the nd. But you can see that print has no trouble culling the variables from the other parts of the string and behaving properly.

This "shorthand" capability is one of Perl's great strengths, as you will see when we begin to do more complicated programs. However, brevity in code is not necessarily an ideal to strive for, unless it directly leads to more efficient code. Writing a program that is clear and understandable is much more important.

Perl Lists

You have learned so far that scalar variables handle and store individual pieces of data. But what if you have a collection of related data? It would be convenient to store *all* of them in a variable, wouldn't it?

Perl lists are intended to do just that. Lists are similar to arrays in many other programming languages, where the variable name defines a starting point, index 0, and the members are stored consecutively. You just increase the index and add it to the starting point to arrive at the array member you want.

NOTE

A Perl *list* is the equivalent of an *array* in Visual Basic, C++, and many other languages. The terms will be used interchangeably in this book.

The C language requires that all members of the array are of the same *type*, which really only means that they are all the same size. Perl doesn't care about type at all. Any old thing can go into a list—strings, numbers, characters, anything—and they all happily coexist.

What's in a List?

List notation in Perl is as specific as scalar notation. List names begin with the @ character; after that, you can call them anything you want.

Setting a list equal to something, or loading it with data, is a bit more complex, but we can make it understandable with a few examples.

An array of numbers would be set up like this:

```
@Numbers = (1, 2, 3, 4, 5, 6);
```

We now have an array of six consecutive numbers called @Numbers. In Perl, as in many other languages, arrays start at position 0, so if we were to set a scalar variable to the value of the first member of @Numbers:

```
$OneNumber = $Numbers[0];
```

$OneNumber would be equal to 1.

Notice that the notation changed a little in the last line: We referred to the first element of @Numbers with a dollar sign in front of it. But isn't that how we note a *scalar* value?

Yes, it is. And the notation is correct because just one member of a list *is* a scalar, so you must use the dollar sign in front of it. The *subscript,* which is the part of $Numbers[0] enclosed in brackets, is where you tell Perl which member of the array you want.

STREAMLINED PERL...

Here's a handy Perl shortcut. Because the members of the array are consecutive numbers, you could have initialized it like this:

```
@Numbers = (1..6);
```

It's the same as specifying each of the numbers from 1 to 6, as far as Perl is concerned.

Lists of Strings

When you load strings into an array, they need to be distinguished somehow. The Perl convention departs slightly from what we have learned so far, which is to enclose strings of characters in double quotes. This can be done with lists, but it is considered more correct to delimit lists of strings with single quotes (').

Table 8.2 illustrates some of the things you can do with strings.

TABLE 8.2: Perl List Examples

INITIALIZATION	COMMENT
@list = (4..8);	same as @list = (4,5,6,7,8)
@list1 = ('red', 'green', 'blue');	array of colors
@list2 = (1, 'yellow', @list1);	same as @list2 = (1, 'yellow', 'red', 'green', 'blue');
@list3 = ();	null (empty) list
@list4 = (0,1, @list3, 3);	same as @list4 = (0,1,3);

Perl lists have numerous other features, but we'll save those for when we approach more complex programming topics. For now, you should know what a list is, how to initialize it, and how to access one of its members.

NOTE

Presumably, we're all fully qualified computer nerds here, so we are allowed to use "access" as a verb. Be advised, however, that the practice in common usage drives English-language purists to scowling fidgets.

PERL AND THE COMMON GATEWAY INTERFACE

You've learned a little about the Perl programming language. But how does it fit into the World Wide Web? The Common Gateway Interface (CGI) is the key. CGI has been used for many years as a facility for passing information from a Web page to a program that can process the information.

CGI, despite what many programmers put on their resumes, is not a programming language. It is, as the name states explicitly, an *interface*. It allows you to write a program that will take all of its input from an HTML document, a page on the World Wide Web, and *do something* with that input. You can regard CGI as a kind of pipeline between your Web page and a Perl program (see Figure 8.9): Whatever is entered on the page is available to your program through CGI.

HTML is quite good at describing how a Web page should look in a browser, but the language all by itself has virtually no facilities for processing information or even making rudimentary decisions.

WARNING

Some browsers include extensions written to HTML that support all kinds of fancy interpretation. In the real world, however, you cannot depend on your Web site visitors possessing the latest and greatest browsers with all of their non-standard HTML extensions.

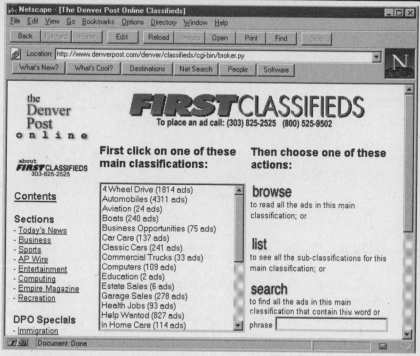

FIGURE 8.9: A search phrase or a list selection entered in this form will be processed by a Perl program through CGI.

When you run a Perl program from the command line, it takes its input, generally, from you, at your keyboard, and it sends its output, generally, back to you, at the screen. CGI reroutes those standard conventions. The Perl program's input comes from the Web page. Most importantly, CGI sends your program's output back to the Web server. If the output happens to be formatted correctly in HTML, the server will put it out as an HTML document to whatever browser is connected to it. In other words, a `print` statement from within your Perl program will be printing to the Web server, not the screen (see Figure 8.10).

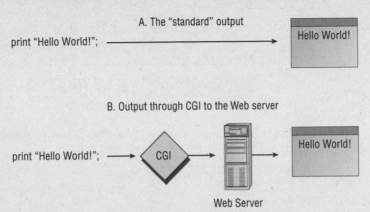

The Difference Between Standard and CGI Output

A. The "standard" output

print "Hello World!"; ⟶ Hello World!

B. Output through CGI to the Web server

print "Hello World!"; ⟶ CGI ⟶ Web Server ⟶ Hello World!

FIGURE 8.10: The difference between "standard" and CGI output

This is a difficult concept for many neophytes to grasp, but it is the foundation of using CGI as a pipeline between Perl and HTML. You can *draw a Web page* from a Perl program. And, because Perl is a fully functional programming language, rather than a markup language such as HTML, you can decide within your program *what to draw* based on what has been entered in the page and sent to you.

Of course, this facility isn't limited to Perl. You can interface with CGI using *any* program written in *any* language (provided, of course, that it will run on your computer!). Indeed, there may be occasions when you need the brute force of C/C++ or some other high-level compiled language to tackle some process that would bring your Web server to its knees if the program were written in Perl. For example, a program that does a lot of heavy number crunching would be much more efficient in C or C++ than in Perl. Those occasions will be rare, however. Most of what you need to do can be accomplished more easily from a Perl script than from a compiled program. Additionally, your Perl program won't have to be rewritten and recompiled if you move to another operating system or computer platform.

What Is CGI, Anyway?

Does *Common Gateway Interface* mean much, if anything, to you? Probably not. However, CGI really is the *raison d'être* for this book. Without it, there would be no reason to talk about Perl and Web pages because there would be no way to link the two.

CGI as a *concept* has been applied to many systems other than links between Web servers and application programs. For example, it would provide a clean and near-universal interface for database servers and their clients without the barriers introduced by proprietary systems. Software manufacturers sometimes seem to worry about making sure that you only do business with them, but a "common gateway" from one system to another provides a standard of sorts to which the manufacturers have to adhere; if they can't deal with it, no one will buy their applications.

For now, anyone who actually knows what you're talking about when you bandy about terms such as *CGI* will assume that you're talking exclusively about World Wide Web applications. In that context, without the Web, there would be no CGI. And without the Internet, there would be no Web.

CGI: The Force Behind the Web

Where HTML gives the World Wide Web its *look*, CGI makes it *functional*. It is what its name implies: A "common gateway" between the Web server and applications that can be useful to the server, but doesn't run as a part of it. CGI is the only way the server can communicate with these other applications, such as a database.

NOTE

Keep in mind that no support exists for CGI outside of HTTP servers. In other words, CGI only works with HTTP servers. Its uses outside that realm have been interesting, but strictly marginal.

Part iii

A Common Gateway

In technical terms, a *gateway* is an interface or an application that allows two systems to pass information between them.

For example, Microsoft's old Mail program and its newer Exchange are limited to sending mail only to other Microsoft Mail users. A separate product provides a Simple Mail Transfer Protocol (SMTP) Gateway so that mail can be sent to and received from the Internet.

Likewise with your Web server. It doesn't know Perl from Adam, but through the mechanism of CGI it can handle requests from "clients," or visitors to your site, and pass the results back.

Because the server is only following a set of rules for passing information, it does not know or care what you use in the background to process what it sends you. The functions are totally independent of one another. Thus, you can write CGI programs in *any* programming language. The only requirement is that the information you send back has to be formatted in a way that the server recognizes.

TIP

You can find a great deal of information on the formal CGI specification at http://hoohoo.ncsa.uiuc.edu/cgi/interface.html.

The CGI Environment

MS-DOS, UNIX, and, to a limited extent, Windows users should be at least a little familiar with the concept of *environment variables.* For example, on both MS-DOS and UNIX, an environment variable called PATH stores the list of directories through which the operating system will search when you type a program name on the command line.

To the operating system, whether it's Windows or UNIX, the *environment* is a block of memory where variable names can be stored as string values, such as PATH=c:/bin;c:/usr/bin;c:/usr/local/bin. Taking this example further, whenever the user refers to %PATH% (on Windows) or $PATH (on UNIX), the operating system substitutes "c:/bin;c:/usr/bin;c:/usr/local/bin".

Programs can get into this block of memory, too. What makes this facility especially useful is that the environment is in *global* memory, which means that anything there is accessible by other programs running at the same time.

The Web server fills in a standard list of environment variables when it runs; it fills in others when requests are made of it. Because the Web server runs all the time, anything it places in the environment can be read by another program, such as your Perl script, if the other program knows the names of the variables to read.

In the simplest sense, this is how CGI gets information between the server and your program (see Figure 8.11).

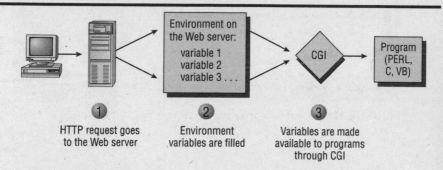

1 HTTP request goes to the Web server

2 Environment variables are filled

3 Variables are made available to programs through CGI

FIGURE 8.11: The Web server, CGI, and the environment

CGI PROGRAMMING LANGUAGES

This book deals with Perl as the preferred programming vehicle for CGI applications. However, as you have learned previously, the HTTP-CGI gateway has no requirements or preferences when it comes to the language in which a CGI application is written. Let's examine briefly the advantages and disadvantages of some of the most widely used languages.

C, C++

C, and more recently, C++, are the most popular languages for application and systems development. Figure 8.12 shows a snippet of code in C++.

```
/*
 *  At this point, all CGI-significant characters have been translated into
 *  something we don't want.  Spaces are designated by '+', for example, and
 *  other characters are flagged by a '%' followed by their two-digit hex
 *  value.  We'll take two passes to translate them.
 */

    for (n = 0; INFO_ARRAY [n] != NULL; ++n)
        {
        p = INFO_ARRAY [n];                    // Set a pointer to the string.

        while ((o = strchr (p, '+')) != NULL)  // Look for '+'.
            {
            *o = ' ';                          // Make it a space.
            p = o + 1;                         // Point to next search area.
            }
        }

    // The hex translation is a bit more complicated.

        char    tmp [3];
        int     i;

        p = INFO_ARRAY [n];
```

FIGURE 8.12: A C++ code snippet—this is very similar to C.

Advantages

These are some of the advantages of C and C++:

▶ When it comes to sheer, raw power, it is very difficult to beat these two compiled languages for either CGI or normal applications. For extremely large and complicated CGI projects, C or C++ probably is a better choice than Perl, especially on a busy Web site where processing speed will be a concern.

▶ In addition, both languages are common on both UNIX and Windows systems, so there are generally few problems porting code between the platforms.

▶ The popularity of C/C++ means that there is a large body of existing code that you can tap into.

Disadvantages

Some of the disadvantages of these two languages are:

- As you learned earlier, there are so many nifty shortcuts built into Perl that you generally can accomplish a lot more in a lot less code than you can in C or C++. Perl's string-manipulation functions, especially, are so much stronger that it's almost ridiculous to try to do the same thing in C/C++.
- Here's something else to keep in mind: It would not be an exaggeration to say that upward of 90 percent of all CGI programs involve heavy string manipulation.

Visual Basic

Visual Basic is Microsoft's workhorse language for simple Windows application development. Figure 8.13 shows some VB code in a Word macro.

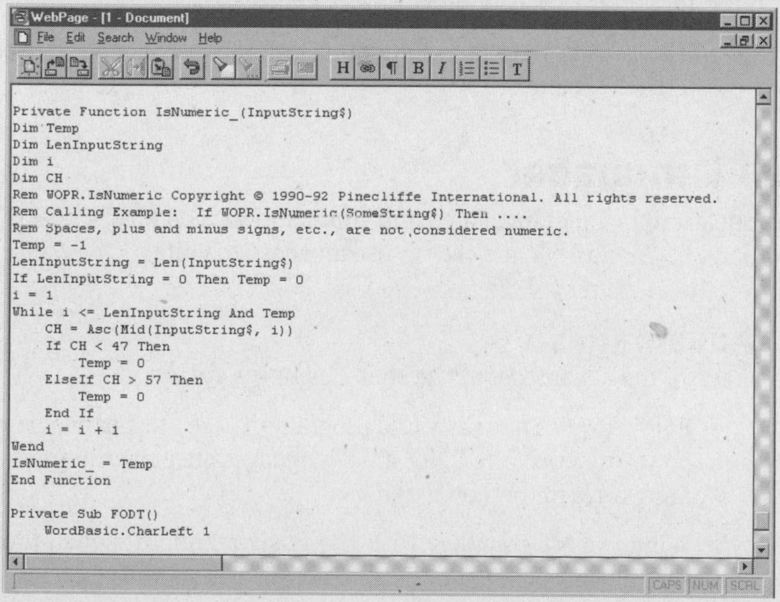
WebPage - [1 - Document]
File Edit Search Window Help
Private Function IsNumeric_(InputString$)
Dim Temp
Dim LenInputString
Dim i
Dim CH
Rem WOPR.IsNumeric Copyright © 1990-92 Pinecliffe International. All rights reserved.
Rem Calling Example: If WOPR.IsNumeric(SomeString$) Then ....
Rem Spaces, plus and minus signs, etc., are not considered numeric.
Temp = -1
LenInputString = Len(InputString$)
If LenInputString = 0 Then Temp = 0
i = 1
While i <= LenInputString And Temp
CH = Asc(Mid(InputString$, i))
If CH < 47 Then
Temp = 0
ElseIf CH > 57 Then
Temp = 0
End If
i = i + 1
Wend
IsNumeric_ = Temp
End Function
Private Sub FODT()
WordBasic.CharLeft 1
CAPS NUM SCRL

FIGURE 8.13: A Visual Basic example in a Microsoft Word macro

Advantages

Some of the advantages of VB in a CGI context are:

▶ VB is Microsoft's version of the BASIC language, which has been around for decades and is familiar to just about anyone who's ever done any programming.

▶ It is easy to learn, easy to use, fast, and popular.

▶ In a totally Microsoft environment, it can work quickly and efficiently for CGI applications.

Disadvantages

Some of VB's disadvantages are:

▶ VB was developed primarily for doing Windows applications, so at least half of its power is wasted on CGI programs, which most often run in the background and depend on sending properly formatted HTML to a Web browser for display.

▶ VB would be extremely difficult, if not impossible, to port over to a UNIX system.

Shell Languages

Shell scripts, including batch and command files on MS-DOS and Windows 95/98 and NT, are easy to use and easy to write.

Advantages

Some of the advantages of the shell languages are:

▶ For very quick and dirty CGI programs, these utilities can be very powerful tools. The UNIX shell languages are powerful programming tools in their own right.

▶ Windows NT complies with the Posix standard, which means that the most common UNIX tools, such as sh, will run on it, too.

▶ Programs written in these languages are small and tight, don't involve the overhead of the Perl interpreter, and easily port from one system to another.

Disadvantages

Some of the disadvantages are:

- ▶ Shell programs don't allow any of the flexibility and powerful control structures that "real" programming languages do.

- ▶ You constantly need to call other utilities such as grep or sed (or even Perl!).

WARNING

Anything of more than a minimum level of complexity should be avoided in the shell languages. They are slow, difficult to maintain, and generally not worth the trouble.

Proprietary CGI Methods

Some of the proprietary CGI methods such as ActiveX from Microsoft and JavaScript from Netscape are worth mentioning. These are very powerful tools, make no mistake about it. Because they take full and specific advantage of the hardware/software platforms on which they run, the proprietary packages are naturally much faster and much more efficient than more "traditional" CGI software.

After all, there's just no comparison between a program that runs according to a strictly imposed set of rules, basically on top of the operating system, and a program that is able to utilize even the most bare-metal of operating system functions.

However, it is not in the spirit of CGI to adhere to a particular hardware or software platform. Like the spirit of the Internet, it is to let as many people as possible, with as many varied machines as possible, become part of the community.

No restrictions—that's the way it's supposed to be.

Part iii

CHAPTER 9

WRITING YOUR FIRST PROGRAM

Introductions are important. You can describe someone with words, but a real introduction should be done in person. This chapter provides a personal introduction to Perl 5. You will meet Perl 5 through two programs. The first program, which shows your system configuration variables, demonstrates the simplicity of Perl 5. The second program illustrates Perl 5's most recent application, which is CGI programming. These two programs represent the minor poles of Perl 5: system administration and Internet programming. One program is five lines long; the other program is more than 75 lines. You'll see that Perl 5 is a programming language for a myriad of uses.

Adapted from *Mastering Perl 5*, by Eric C. Herrmann
ISBN 0-7821-2200-0   958 pages $39.99

This chapter begins with some background on Perl 5 and explains what type of programming language Perl is. It then progresses rapidly through running and editing Perl 5 programs. In the final sections of the chapter, you'll work through a CGI program example. When you're finished with this chapter, you'll have some useful Perl 5 programs and you'll understand how to edit and run Perl 5 programs on your own computer and over the Internet.

INTRODUCING PERL 5

Perl 5 is the most powerful, easy to use, and full-featured programming language available today. That's my opinion, so let me tell you why I think Perl 5 is the best.

Perl was written by a linguist, not a computer scientist, named Larry Wall. Larry built Perl to evolve over time, as a language does. Traditional programming languages evolve slowly and at some point stop changing. Perl, like a spoken language, evolves quickly to meet each new generation's needs.

The Evolution of Perl

Perl stands for Practical Extraction and Report Language. Perl's original purpose was to generate reports that tracked errors and corrections to a software development project that involved multiple types of machines and spanned the United States.

The distribution of Perl 5 has always been freely available on the Internet, and that distribution includes the source code. Distributing a language's source code is a bold and uncommon move. It means anyone can modify the language to meet individual needs and goals.

Perl attracted the attention of Unix system administrators, who needed a language that was easier to use than the C programming language and more powerful than scripting languages such as Bourne and C-shell. Unix system administrators and others contributed to the language, updating it and submitting free scripts that made their jobs easier. Originally, most Perl users were Unix system administrators and other people with similar needs, who used Perl's text-processing power to generate reports and write scripts that aided in the configuration and monitoring of Unix systems.

In 1994, the World Wide Web, through the Netscape browser, became a new and powerful influence on the jobs of Unix system administrators. They turned to Perl as their tool to help them with their new World Wide Web tasks. As they built new tools, they continued their practice of sharing those tools.

When new users of the web wanted to create dynamic web pages through CGI programming, they were generally working on a Unix web server. Perl was freely available on those Unix web servers, and users started using Perl for their CGI applications. Because Perl was built to process text, and much of CGI programming is processing user input and returning HTML text pages, Perl was a natural fit for this new programming environment.

These new users of Perl continued the tradition of sharing their programs freely throughout the Internet. In the middle 1990s, Perl continued to evolve and went through a major maturation stage with revision five, called Perl 5. Much like the difference between Windows 3.1 and Windows 95, Perl 5 is more than just another upgrade of Perl. Perl 5 is a total rewrite of the original Perl, with many new features. Perl 5 is not just Perl any more than C++ is just C.

Perl was always designed to run on any computer, but because it usually ran on a Unix computer, it had (and still has) a decidedly Unix flavor. In the later half of the 1990s, applications and versions of Perl targeted toward Windows programming environments started appearing. Today, Windows versions of Perl 5 are freely available and are distributed with the main Perl 5 distribution. The programs written for *Mastering Perl 5* are first run on a Windows computer and then tested on a Unix computer, if necessary.

This is the state of Perl 5 today. It is the de facto programming language for dynamic HTML web pages. It is easy to use, and there are thousands of free CGI, system administrative, and text processing programs written in Perl available on the Internet. With the addition of references to Perl 5, the language is maturing into the mainstream programming world.

A Perl Program

As I said at the beginning of this chapter, the best way to introduce you to Perl 5 is with some Perl code. Listing 9.1 is a little program that lets you see some information about your computer.

Listing 9.1: Environment Variables

```
1. #!/usr/local/bin/perl
2. foreach $key (keys %ENV){
3. print qq|The value of $key is $ENV{ "$key"} \ n|;
4. }
```

TIP

The program shown in Listing 9.1 is available from *Mastering Perl 5*'s companion web pages on the Sybex web site (go to www.sybex.com, click on Catalog, then perform a search for the book to go to the companion pages), as are all the examples in this book that are drawn from *Mastering Perl 5* chapters. (Note that this chapter was actually Chapter 1 in *Mastering Perl 5*, so you'll need to access the Chapter 1 files—Listing 1.1 in place of Listing 9.1 in this instance, for example.) However, I recommend typing in most of the listings, except for the long ones. Just the act of typing in a program seems to help you remember what you just read about it. It's easy to just go to sleep reading a technical book. So, here's your opportunity to get some Dilbert-type exercise—make those finger muscles humongous!

The output from Listing 9.1 is shown in Figure 9.1. If you have Perl 5 installed on your computer, you can run this program without compiling it and see the environment variables on your computer.

Environment variables are created each time you run a program. An environment variable contains information about the services, hardware, and data available to your program. The environment variables available to your program vary based on where the program is executed. For example, the environment variables available from an MS-DOS window, a Unix command shell, or a CGI program are different. As you can see in Figure 9.1, environment variables include things like your username, your processor's type, and the name of your operating system.

If you don't have Perl 5 installed yet, see Appendix A. If you don't know how to run this program from your computer, don't worry. You'll learn how to run Perl programs in this chapter. If you don't know what I meant when I said you could run this program "without compiling it," let me explain that Perl 5 is an interpreted language, which means it is not compiled to a binary executable. The difference between an interpreted language and a binary executable is important to Perl programmers, so we will explore those concepts in the next section.

```
% Mastering Perl                                               _ □ ✕
D:\sybex\MasteringPerl5>env.pl
The value of USERNAME is eherrmann
The value of PROMPT is $P$G
The value of PROCESSOR_IDENTIFIER is x86 Family 6 Model 1 Stepping 9, GenuineIntel
The value of PROCESSOR_ARCHITECTURE is x86
The value of OS is Windows_NT
The value of HOMEDRIVE is U:
The value of CLASSPATH is C:\Program Files\Plus!\Microsoft Internet\plugins\nplvscrn.dll;c:\U
k1.2beta3\bin;c:\jdk1.2beta3\lib\classes.zip;c:\h\jedi\lib;c:\jce12-ea2-dom\lib\jce12-ea2-dom
The value of SYSTEMROOT is C:\WINNT
The value of COMSPEC is C:\WINNT\system32\cmd.exe
The value of WINDIR is C:\WINNT
The value of PATH is c:\perl5\bin;c:\perl5\bin;D:\jdk1.2beta3\bin;C:\WINNT\system32;C:\WINNT;
ROS~1\Office
The value of PROCESSOR_REVISION is 0109
The value of PERL5DB is BEGIN { require 'C:\Program Files\ActiveState Perl Debugger\PerlDB.pl
The value of NUMBER_OF_PROCESSORS is 1
The value of USERPROFILE is C:\WINNT\Profiles\eherrmann.000
The value of COMPUTERNAME is JUDGE
The value of UXCLASSPATH is C:\Program Files\Plus!\Microsoft Internet\plugins\nplvscrn.dll;c:
jdk1.1.5\bin;c:\jdk1.1.5\lib\classes.zip;c:\h\jedi\lib;
The value of TMP is C:\TEMP
The value of TEMP is C:\TEMP
The value of HOMEPATH is \eherrmann
The value of LOGONSERVER is \\HEMI
The value of USERDOMAIN is AUSTIN.INRI.COM
The value of PROCESSOR_LEVEL is 6
The value of OS2LIBPATH is C:\WINNT\system32\os2\dll;
The value of HOMESHARE is \\HEMI\users
The value of PATHEXT is .COM;.EXE;.BAT;.CMD
The value of SYSTEMDRIVE is C:

D:\sybex\MasteringPerl5>
```

FIGURE 9.1: Running a Perl program to get environment variables

Perl as an Interpreted Language

Perl 5 is an interpreted language. Programs are usually run in one of two forms: as binary executables or as interpreted. *Binary executables* are programs that have been compiled and linked into a format that can run on a computer without the compiler or linker present. *Interpreted programs*, on the other hand, require the interpreter to be installed on the computer they are running on. But this explanation doesn't make much sense without definitions of the terms compiler, linker, and interpreter.

A *compiler* takes the code you type into a file, like the code in Listing 9.1, and converts it into a series of ones and zeros, or binary numbers, that your computer understands. However, the compiled program is only a small piece of an overall binary executable. Modern programs use preexisting library routines to add, subtract, print output, and get input. These library routines are like pieces of a puzzle that need to be linked together with the newly compiled program to create a binary executable. This is the job of the *linker*. A compiled language, such as C, requires you to install a compiler and linker on your computer. You then compile and link your program, which can be a lengthy and painful process. The result of this process, however, produces a binary executable program that runs without the compiler and linker.

A program written in an interpreted language, such as Perl 5, is converted to machine-readable format when the program is run. This means that it does not go through the standard compilation and linking process that binary executables do. Interpreted programs run the code that is in a file just as you see it, as in Listing 9.1. The steps required to run a program—converting the programming language to machine-readable format and then linking in other library routines—still occur. These steps take place when your interpreted program begins execution, and they are handled by the *interpreter*. This means that the interpreter that converts your program must be installed wherever your program runs, which has two main effects.

First, because your program is converted into machine format at the moment it is run, that machine format is more likely to be compatible with the machine it is running on. This is one of the primary features of Perl 5. Your Perl 5 programs are likely to run on any platform without modifications. This is in contrast to binary executable programs. Because binary executables usually contain operating system–specific information, you usually must compile and link a version of your program for every version of each operating system you want your program to run on.

NOTE

Binary executable programs usually need to be run on a computer that has the same operating system and operating system version as the one it was compiled and linked on. Different versions of the same operating system are sometimes compatible, but this is not always the case. MS-DOS, Windows 3.1, Windows 95/98, and Windows NT are versions of the same or similar operating systems that are not compatible. Different operating systems like Unix, Windows, and the Macintosh operating system are seldom compatible.

Second, because your program is converted to machine format when it is executed, most interpreted programs are slower than similar programs that are compiled. It takes time to convert your Perl 5 syntax to machine format. However, since Perl 5 is an extremely optimized and fast interpreted language, it isn't much slower than compiled code. For this small sacrifice in speed, you get a language that is very portable (can be run on different operating systems without modification).

Another benefit of an interpreted language is that the coding and testing process is much easier and faster. With a compiled language, you must write your code, compile it, link it, and then test it. The compiling and linking steps usually take a bit of time and sometimes create additional debugging issues unrelated to the syntax errors in your code. With Perl 5, you just write your code and test it. This process is very quick and leads to a programming paradigm called "code a little; test a little," which is an excellent way to develop programs. (*Paradigm*, by the way, just means a way of doing something; in short, a pattern or a model to follow.)

In summary, every program is eventually converted to a machine-readable format, and supporting libraries are made available for the program's use. Binary executables, such as C programs, are converted to machine format before the program is run. Interpreted programs, such as Perl 5 programs, are converted to machine format when your program starts up or sometimes as the program is run. Binary executables are typically faster than interpreted programs, but Perl 5 code usually performs well in speed performance tests against binary executables. Interpreted code is usually more portable than binary executable code. Finally, the code and test process for Perl 5 programs is easier and quicker than the code, compile, link, and test process necessary for binary executables.

Windows, Unix, and Perl

Perl 5, like the Java programming language, will run on a Unix, Windows, or Macintosh operating system, with little or no change required to the code you've written. This feature is called *portability*. The Java jingle of "Write once, run anywhere" also applies to Perl 5. This portability feature of Perl 5 means the beginning programming skills taught in this chapter must be taught for both the Unix and the Windows operating systems. (I will not be covering the Macintosh operating system.)

The Windows operating system family is currently made up of Windows NT, Windows 98, and Windows 95. I will not be addressing the Windows 3.1 operating system, although I suspect Perl 5 would run just fine on Windows 3.1.

The Unix operating systems brands are too numerous to name. Some of the more widely used Unix operating systems are the HP-UX, Sun Solaris, Linux, and Linux Red Hat. Perl 5 runs on all of these brands of Unix without modification.

DIFFERENCES BETWEEN UNIX AND WINDOWS

The differences between the Unix and Windows operating systems can be traced back to the fundamentally different approaches taken in their development. Here's a comparison:

Windows	Unix
Initially developed by an entrepreneur	Developed by some university grad students
Developed for commercial sale	Though now developed by several vendors for commercial sale, is still available in several free varieties
Developed with one man's vision for its future	Developed by many, many contributors with a variety of visions and goals
Developed for ease of use	Developed for easy access to the operating system

Unix may be powerful, but the user interface is frequently cryptic and unknown. Windows may be weak in many areas, but the user interface is easy to learn and consistent.

As Windows moved away from the DOS interface to support the ease-of-use paradigm, its programming interface became less friendly. Unix has always supported the programming interface, and the tools to support programming have increased over the years. The programming interface is where you will notice the greatest difference between the two operating systems but, of course, that is where you will be working. As you learn to use Perl programs, you will learn the differences between these two operating systems' programmer interface, which is the command line.

RUNNING PERL PROGRAMS

You run Perl 5 programs from either an MS-DOS window (from a Windows 95/98/NT computer) or the Unix command shell (if you're running the Unix operating system). Both are referred to as the *command-line interface*. In this section, you will learn the few commands that are necessary on the Windows and Unix operating systems to run Perl 5 programs (such as the one shown in Listing 9.1).

NOTE

You won't be able to run any Perl 5 programs unless you have Perl 5 installed on your computer. If you don't have Perl 5 installed yet, turn to Appendix A for instructions.

You may be thinking that if you're running Windows, you don't need to read the information about using the Unix command shell. However, if you are writing Perl scripts, some of those scripts are likely to be CGI programs that require installation on a Unix server. You'll learn more about CGI programs later in this chapter. For now, you should read through the Unix command shell section so you will be prepared.

Using the MS-DOS Window

The MS-DOS window is an independent window that allows you to enter MS-DOS commands from the keyboard. You open an MS-DOS window by selecting Start ➢ Programs ➢ Command Prompt (or MS-DOS Prompt), as shown in Figure 9.2.

When you open an MS-DOS window, your cursor is placed at the right of the command prompt (>). The *command prompt* is the keyboard interface for issuing MS-DOS commands. The command prompt, by default, displays the current working directory, as you can see in Figure 9.3.

TIP

On a Windows NT computer, you can modify the starting size, background color, and window fonts of the MS-DOS window by right-clicking on the MS-DOS program icon and selecting the Properties menu option.

There are just a few commands you must know to run Perl programs from the MS-DOS window. You need to know how to view the contents of a directory, change directories, create a directory, and start a program.

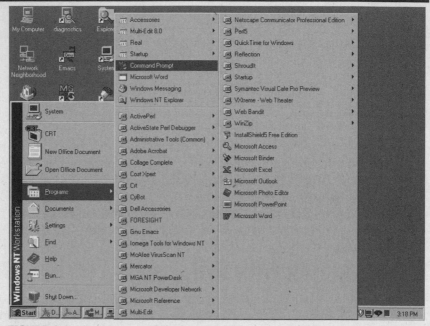

FIGURE 9.2: Opening an MS-DOS window

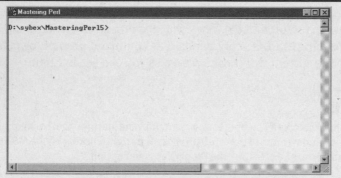

FIGURE 9.3: The command prompt in an MS-DOS window

Working with Directories

To view the contents of a directory, use the `dir` command. This command lists the directory in long format, which shows each file's eight-character filename and extension, size, last modified date, and full name. To see the directory in abbreviated format, use the command `dir/w`.

Abbreviated format shows only the eight-character name and three-character extension of each file in the directory.

To change to a different directory, use the cd command. To tell the command which directory you want to change to, you enter a path name as a command argument. A *path name* is a guide to a location on your computer, including the drive, directory, and subdirectories. A *command argument* is the additional information you supply to the command that specifies how the command should operate or what the command should operate on. The cd command takes either an absolute or relative path name as a command argument. An *absolute* path name starts from the root of the directory tree, represented by a backslash (\), and lists the path all the way to the destination directory. A *relative* path name starts with the current directory and lists the path from there to the one you want.

If you are not starting from the disk drive the absolute path is on, you must change to that particular disk drive. To change disk drives, just type the correct disk drive letter followed by a colon and press Enter (you don't need to type the cd part). For instance, if you want to change to disk drive E, simply type E: and press Enter.

To create a new directory, use the mkdir command. Like the cd command, the mkdir command takes an absolute or relative path name as its command argument.

Now that you know what the commands do, you can follow the steps listed below to create a Test directory for your Perl 5 programs, create an MPListings subdirectory under the Test directory, and copy the Listing 9.1 file into the MPListings subdirectory. Here, I assume that you have installed Perl 5 onto your D drive in the directory Perl5 (that's where I have it installed on my computer). If you have installed Perl 5 on another disk drive and/or directory, substitute those names in the following steps.

PERL INSTALLATION INFORMATION

You can find Perl source code, pre-built binaries, modules and scripts, documentation, and announcements at http://www.cpan.org.

1. Select Start ➢ Programs ➢ Command Prompt (or MS-DOS Prompt) to bring up an MS-DOS window. This should put you at the command prompt in some directory on the C disk drive (such as C:\ WINDOWS >).

2. Move to the D disk drive by typing **D:** and pressing Enter. (You should press Enter after entering each command, so I won't mention it again.)

When you first change to the D disk drive, you should be at the root directory, which is D:\. If you are not, you can change to the root directory by typing **cd **.

3. To create a Test directory with an MPListings subdirectory, type:

```
mkdir \ Perl5\ Test\ MPListings
```

4. Now copy the file that contains Listing 9.1 into the D:\ Perl5\ Test\ MPListings directory. You can use the copy command from the MS-DOS window, like this:

```
copy environmentVariables.pl
     D:\ Perl5\ Test\ MPListings\ environmentVariables.pl
```

Or you can run Windows Explorer and drag-and-drop the environment Variables.pl file into the new directory, which is the method I prefer.

In step 3, we used an absolute path name to create the directory. This command could be executed from anywhere on the D drive. On your Windows computer, you can create a directory node without first creating previous directory nodes. In other words, it is not necessary to create the Test directory before you create the MPListings directory.

NOTE

A *directory node* is another name for any individual directory along a directory path. A *directory tree* is a set of directories that has a beginning node and several nodes that are subdirectories beneath the beginning node. The beginning node of a directory tree is called the root node. When you install Perl 5 into the directory D:\ Perl5, this creates a directory tree. The root node is Perl5. The subdirectories underneath the root node, such as Test, lib, html, and eg, are branches along the Perl5 directory tree.

You could also create the directories using relative path names, which would look like this:

```
>D:
>cd Perl5
>mkdir test
>cd test
>mkdir MPListings
```

Each of these commands uses a relative path name. The path name is relative to the current working directory. Changing directories to the Perl5 directory is relative to the root directory. Creating the Test directory is relative to the Perl5 directory. Changing directories to the Test directory is relative to the Perl5 directory also. Creating the MPListings directory is relative to the Test directory.

Running a Program

Now you're ready to run a Perl program. To run the program shown in Listing 9.1, follow these steps from the MS-DOS window:

1. Change directories to the MPListings directory using an absolute path name by typing:

    cd \ Perl5\ test\ MPListings

2. If you are on a Windows 95/98 computer, run the program by typing:

    perl environmentVariables.pl

If you are on a Windows NT computer, type:

environmentVariables.pl

Now you should see something on your screen similar to Figure 9.1. Getting results without compiling or linking is one of the features I really like about Perl 5.

Using Other MS-DOS Window Commands

There are several other MS-DOS window commands that you might find useful.

If you are on a Windows 95/98 computer, the DOSKEY command will make your life easier. Every time you bring up the MS-DOS window, the first thing you should type is **DOSKEY**. The DOSKEY command tells the MS-DOS window to remember your previously typed-in commands, saving them in a previous command buffer.

With DOSKEY installed, you can use the up arrow key to display your previous commands. You can then press Enter to execute a previous command exactly as you used it last time, or you can modify a previous command to perform a similar but slightly different command. To modify a previous command, press the up or down arrow key until you see the command you want to modify, then use the left and right arrow, Delete, Backspace, and/or regular alphanumeric keys to modify the command to perform the new operation. Once you get used to using the previous command buffer, you'll save a lot of time entering new commands.

The previous command buffer, created by the DOSKEY command on a Windows 95/98 computer, exists by default on a Windows NT computer. In Windows NT, you can access the buffer by pressing the up and down arrow keys or the F7 key. When you press F7 from an MS-DOS window, you get a pop-up window that lets you select the next command to execute.

Another command you might want to use in the MS-DOS window is rmdir, which deletes a directory. The directory must be empty before it can be deleted. Use the rmdir command with relative and absolute path names, in the same way that you use the mkdir and cd commands.

If you want to delete a file, you can use the del command from the MS-DOS window, like this:

```
del fileName.pl
```

Finally, you can get additional help on MS-DOS commands by typing **help** at the MS-DOS command prompt.

Using the Unix Command Shell

Navigating around the Unix command shell isn't a lot different from navigating through the MS-DOS window. However, unlike with the Windows operating system, the Unix command shell is the default interface for the Unix operating system. Some Unix brands, like HP-UX and Sun Solaris, have a more Windows-like environment, but most Unix users start out at the Unix command shell when they log on to a Unix computer.

If you are reading this section, it's probably because you need to install a CGI program on a Unix web server. Your CGI programming interface is likely through a telnet session, which is discussed later in this chapter. The commands you use to run the program in Listing 9.1 on your Unix computer are the same commands that you use to install your CGI program, and they are similar to the MS-DOS commands explained in the previous section.

Working with Unix Directories

The Unix command shell has a command prompt, much like the MS-DOS window. However, the default Unix command prompt is not the current working directory, and it may be something as simple as the right arrow (>). Figure 9.4 shows the Unix command shell. To see the current working directory on a Unix computer, use the pwd (print working directory) command.

To view the contents of the current directory on a Unix computer, use the ls (list) command. The ls command shows the contents of the directory in an abbreviated format, much like the MS-DOS dir/w command. To view more details about the files in the current working directory, add switches to the ls command (a *switch* modifies the basic behavior of a command). To view the contents of the directory in long format, use the ls -lat command. These switches tell the ls command to list the directory contents in long format (1), list all filenames (a), and show the times associated with each file (t).

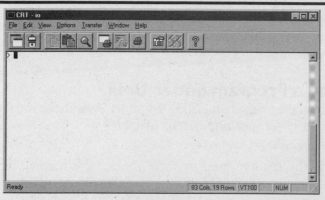

FIGURE 9.4: The Unix command shell

To change directories, use the cd command, using the same syntax as described for the MS-DOS cd command in the previous section. One difference between the two commands is the separator used in the path name. Unix uses a forward slash (/) directory separator rather than the backslash (\) used by MS-DOS. Another difference is that unlike MS-DOS path names and filenames, Unix path names and filenames are case-sensitive. In other words, the directory test is different from the directory Test.

The following steps show you how to create a Perl5 test directory and an MPListings subdirectory, then copy the program shown in Listing 9.1 into that subdirectory. Note that the Unix environment is less forgiving than the MS-DOS environment. You need to explicitly create each directory node separately. Also, unlike with Windows systems, I don't recommend creating your test directory in the Perl5 installation directory. It's a better idea to create the MPListings directory underneath the default login directory on your Unix computer. The default login directory is likely to be a directory named after your login user name. For example, on my web server, my default login directory (or *home directory* as it is often called) is ~yawp.

1. Create the MPListings directory node by using relative directory paths. The beginning relative path will be relative to your home directory. Type this:

    ```
    mkdir Perl5
    mkdir Perl5\ test
    mkdir Perl5\ test\ MPListings
    ```

2. To copy the file that contains Listing 9.1 to the MPListings directory, type (all on one line):

    ```
    cp environmentVariables.pl Perl5\ test\ MPListings\
    ➡ environmentVariables.pl
    ```

Running a Program under Unix

You could run the program in Listing 9.1 under Unix just as you did from the Windows 95/98 operating system, like this:

```
>perl environmentVariables.pl
```

However, this is not the preferred way of running executable programs on a Unix computer. Unlike MS-DOS, which uses file extensions to associate a file type with a program (the file type of .PL is associated with Perl 5 executables when you install Perl 5 on a Windows computer), Unix associates file types with permission modes. *Permission modes* tell the system whether the file is readable, writable, and/or executable.

After the Unix command shell has determined a file is executable, it looks for a line in the file that tells it which program to run with the executable file. Perl 5 programs that run on a Unix computer must include a line that has the path to the Perl 5 installation (as in Listing 9.1), like this:

```
#!/usr/local/bin/perl
```

Unix file permissions are separated into three groups: owner, group, and world. Each group has three privileges that may be turned on or off: read access, write access, and executable access. The Unix chmod command modifies a file-access permission using a three-digit number that assigns a permissions value to the files. The possible permissions values make up a binary number, which is typed in as an octal value. The possible octal numbers and their meanings are shown in Table 9.1.

TABLE 9.1: Unix Permissions

BINARY NUMBER	OCTAL NUMBER	MEANING
000	0	No permissions
001	1	Execute only
010	2	Write only
011	3	Write and execute
100	4	Read only
101	5	Read and execute
110	6	Read and write
111	7	Read, write, and execute

You set the file permissions for each group using a single octal digit to represent each group's permissions. To set the permissions to read, write, and execute for the owner and to read and execute for the group and world, combine the three permission values like this:

owner = 7, group = 5, world = 5

Therefore, to make your Perl program executable from the command line, you must change its permissions mode to executable (755), using the chmod command, like this:

```
>chmod 755 filename.pl
```

CHANGING UNIX FILE PERMISSIONS FOR THE OCTAL IMPAIRED

You can also make the same file permissions change on most Unix systems by typing **chmod u+rwx,g+rx,o+rx** (user = read, write, execute; group = read, execute; other = read, execute).

To run the program shown in Listing 9.1, follow these steps from the Unix command shell:

1. Change directories to the `MPListing` directory by typing:

   `cd \ Perl5\ test\ MPListings`

2. Make the program executable by typing:

   `chmod 755 environmentVariables.pl`

NOTE

Remember that Unix filenames are case-sensitive: `environmentVariables.pl` is not the same file as `EnvironmentVariables.pl`.

3. To run the program, simply type the name of the executable file (just as from a Windows NT computer):

   `environmentVariables.pl`

If this doesn't work for you, try including the current working directory, like this:

   `./environmentVariables.pl`

You should see something similar to Figure 9.1 on your screen. As with the MS-DOS window example, compiling and linking a Perl 5 program is not necessary to run the program file.

Using Other Unix Commands

In the MS-DOS window section, I suggested that you use the DOSKEY command to save your commands in a previous command buffer. Unix has a DOSKEY-like command, called `history`. To make the `history` command active, type **set history=100**. To view the history list, type **history**. To use the last command, type ! !. To use a particular number in the history list, type **!n**. To use the first few unique characters of a previous command, type **!ls**.

The `history` command is fairly complex. If you want to use this command, I suggest learning more about it by reading the man pages. (Unix online help is always available from the man pages.) The command man is short for manual. To see the online manual for the `history` command from the command prompt, type **man history**.

The Unix commands for creating and deleting directories are the same as those used in the MS-DOS window: `mkdir` creates a directory and `rmdir` removes one. The Unix command for deleting a file is `rm`, and the command for copying a file is `cp`.

USING PROGRAMMER'S EDITORS

While you are learning Perl, you should be writing and editing the listings in this book. However, I don't recommend using just any text editor or word processing program. If you are working on a Windows computer and using Notepad or Microsoft Word to edit your programs, you are making your job harder, not easier. If you are working on a Unix computer and using vi as your editor, you are making the same mistake. When you are writing Perl programs, you should be working in an environment that enhances your productivity. You should be using an editor that understands the programming language. These types of editors are called language-sensitive or programmer's editors, and they make your programming job a lot easier.

In this section, I will briefly describe four editors that I recommend for writing and editing Perl programs. Each of these programs is available from the companion pages for this book at the Sybex web site (www.sybex.com), as well as from the individual sites mentioned in the following sections, for you to download and test. All of these editors are free, with the exception of Multi-Edit.

Choosing a Windows Editor

For Windows users, I recommend two editors. One of these is free, and the other is a commercial product.

If you want to save money, I highly recommend NTEmacs, which runs on Windows 95/98 systems (despite its name), as well as on Windows NT systems. As shown in Figure 9.5, NTEmacs has all the features of Xemacs, a powerful Unix editor described in the next section. This is a great editor, so don't let the fact that it is free scare you away. NTEmacs is available at www.cs.washington.edu/hones/voelker/ntemacs or ftp://ftp.sunet.selfpublos/Win32/ntEmacs/docs/ntemacs.html.

The other Windows editor I recommend is called Multi-Edit, which costs between $100 and $130. As shown in Figure 9.6, Multi-Edit has a highly configurable user interface. It's easy to use, so you won't waste a lot of time learning the tool, and it has tons of features. A fully functional demo version (it has a nag screen in the demo) of Multi-Edit is available at www.multiedit.com.

If Multi-Edit doesn't know about a filename extension, like .CGI or .NOTES, you can add extensions and customize existing ones. The keyboard interface is customizable, as is the language-sensitive interface.

Multi-Edit has a fantastic file-compare feature, in-line file numbering, a multiple-window interface, and much too much more to list. It makes my programming editing tasks incredibly easier than using Notepad or Microsoft Word.

```
emacs@JUDGE                                                          _ □ ×
Buffers  Files  Tools  Edit  Search  Help
   #Now create an array    Emacs News      (C-h n)   ind the keyword .
   #Does line begin with   Emacs FAQ       (C-h F)
   while ($continue){      Browse Manuals  (C-h i)
      if ($infile[$i] =~   Describe Mode   (C-h m)
         $continue = 0;    Command Apropos...
      )                    List Keybindings  (C-h b)
      else {               Describe Key...   (C-h k)
         $tempArray[$k++    Describe Function...  (C-h f)
         ▌                 Describe Variable...  (C-h v)
   )                       Man...
                           Emacs Tutorial    (C-h t)
   foreach $letter (@alp   Find Lisp Packages...  (C-h p)
      if ($letter eq $be   Send Bug Report...
         while ($endAlph    Show Version
            $alphaList[$                        );
            if ($i > $#alphaTable){
               $i = 0 ;
               #This is the index into the alphaList when where the first
               #wrapped Alpha exists
               $letterWrap = $k;
            )
         )
         last LETTERLOOP;
      )
      $i++;
   )
sub extractRules($$){
   my ($ruleString,$match) = @_;
   while ( ($type, $segmentNumber)= $ruleString =~ /\+?([REPLC])(\d+)/){
      #save the what remained after the match'
----Emacs:  111 01.pl        (T:Perl)--L9--Top------------------------------
menu-bar buffer
```

FIGURE 9.5: The NTEmacs editor

NOTE

In case you are curious, I am not affiliated with Multi-Edit in any way except that I use Multi-Edit daily on both my Windows 98 and NT computers. When I started working regularly on an NT platform, I needed an editor to replace my first love, Emacs. I learned about Multi-Edit after trying to use Notepad and Word as my editor. Multi-Edit found me when I was most vulnerable—lost and cursing my dadgum NT computer. What a relief to find an editor that worked well on the Windows operating system and understood Perl 5, Java, and C++, my three primary programming languages. However, I don't use Multi-Edit when I'm writing a book, and you shouldn't use Word or Notepad when you're working on a program.

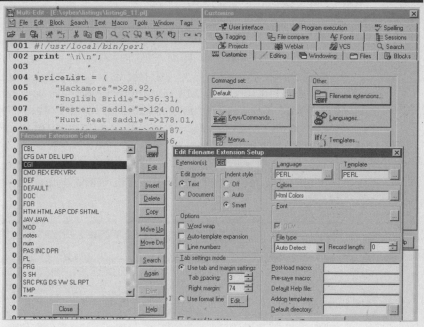

FIGURE 9.6: The Multi-Edit interface

Multi-Edit now includes an HTML editor. Personally, I am not a big fan of most HTML editors because I think they try to do too much. But the Multi-Edit HTML editor gives me just the right amount of source code control.

Choosing a Unix Editor

For the Unix platform, I recommend Xemacs or Nedit. I used Emacs for years in a Unix environment. I was always raving to my peers about this wonderful editor, but they waited until it was converted to the Windows-like Xemacs tool.

Xemacs is a free editor with a Windows-like menu-driven command interface. You can find Xemacs precompiled for a variety of Unix systems, as shown in Figure 9.7. Xemacs is available at www.xemacs.org/ftp-sites.html.

If you don't like the Xemacs interface, you should try Nedit. The Nedit editor also has a Windows-like user interface, as shown in Figure 9.8.

Part_iii

The Nedit editor has most of the power of Xemacs, and many users think it is easier to use and learn than Xemacs. Like Xemacs, Nedit is freeware and available for a variety of Unix platforms, as shown in Figure 9.9. You can get Nedit at `ftp://ftp.fnal.gov/pub/nedit`.

In this and the previous sections, you learned about four different editors (two for Windows and two for Unix) that will increase your programming productivity. Test these editors or search online for other programmer's editors, but do make sure to take advantage of these powerful editing environments and increase your productivity.

In the next section, you'll make a small modification to the program in Listing 9.1, allowing you to test one of the editors and double-check your Perl 5 installation.

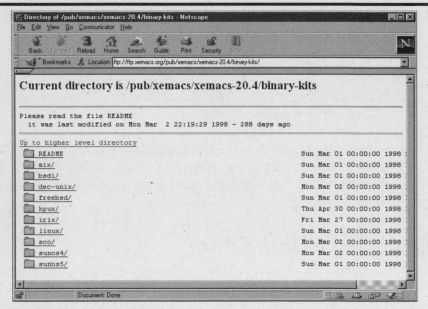

FIGURE 9.7: Xemacs platforms

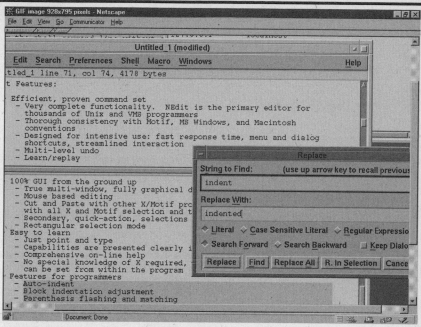

FIGURE 9.8: The Nedit interface

Modifying a Program

The program in Listing 9.1 prints out the environment variables on your Unix or Windows operating system. The environment variables are printed in a seemingly random order. (Actually, the order in which the environment variables are printed is the order in which they are stored in the Perl 5 hash %ENV, which you'll learn about later in the book.) In this section, you are going to modify Listing 9.1 so it prints the environment variables in alphabetical order. This is not a difficult task. The goal of this section is to show you how easy it is to modify and use a Perl 5 program.

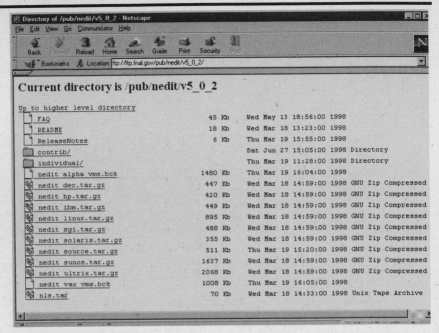

FIGURE 9.9: Nedit platforms

Follow these steps to edit the program:

1. Open Listing 9.1 in your editor of choice.

2. Save Listing 9.1 using a different filename. The filename can be anything, but it should have the extension .PL. I used the filename sortedEnvVars.pl.

3. Modify line 2 by inserting the word **sort** after the opening parenthesis. Make sure you leave a space between the word sort and the word keys, as shown here:

   ```
   foreach $key (sort keys %ENV){
   ```

4. Save your modified file.

5. Open a command-line interface window (either an MS-DOS window or a Unix command shell). At the command prompt, change directories to the same directory where you saved the modified file.

6. Run the modified file. If you are on a Windows 95/98 computer, type:

   ```
   perl sortedEnvVars.pl
   ```

   If you are on a Windows NT computer, type:

   ```
   sortedEnvVars.pl
   ```

   If you are on a Unix computer, type:

   ```
   chmod 755 sortedEnvVars.pl
   sortedEnvVars.pl
   ```

Regardless of which type of computer you are using, you should see the same information that Listing 9.1 printed, but it should now be in alphabetical order, as shown in Figure 9.10.

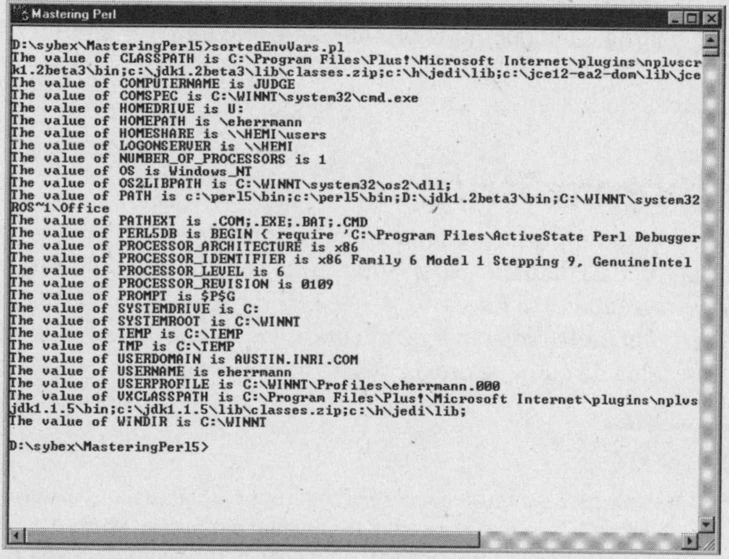

FIGURE 9.10: Sorted environment variables

UNDERSTANDING PERL SYNTAX BASICS

Now that you've run and edited a Perl 5 program, you're ready to learn what Perl expects to see in a program. Here, we'll go over some of the requirements for a program's structure and the components of a Perl 5 program.

All programs do three basic things:

▶ They manipulate data, which involves storing, retrieving, and modifying data.

▶ They perform operations (such as adding and subtracting) that modify the data structures created to receive the results of an operation.

▶ They jump around through branching statements. Branching statements in higher-level languages are called *loop* and *conditional statements*.

A program is made up of many variations on these three basic themes: manipulating data, operating on that data, and jumping around based on testing the contents of a piece of data. The organization of these basic structures makes a program.

Perl Program Structure

Some programming languages require your program to be in a particular format, such as data first, then subroutine declarations, and then the main program. Perl 5 forces very little program structure on you. As you will learn in more detail in later chapters, Perl 5 allows you to declare and define data and subroutines anywhere in your program.

NOTE

A *subroutine* is a reusable piece of code. Subroutines usually are given a name and then referred to as needed throughout a program. When a subroutine is called, your program jumps to the first line of the subroutine. The code in the subroutine runs to completion and then returns control to the calling statement. All subroutines in Perl 5 return a value, which may be saved into a variable. Subroutines that return a value are also called *functions*.

A subroutine or piece of data that is *declared* is named but not assigned any value. A subroutine or data item that is *defined* is assigned a value and may also be declared at the same time.

A data declaration looks like this:

```
my ($time);
```

The keyword my declares a variable. A *variable* is a name used to store data and refer to that data. The variable in this statement is $time. (The parentheses are not required, but they are convenient if you want to create a definition list.)

A data definition looks like this:

```
my ($length) = 10;
```

This data definition stores the value 10 into the variable $length.

In addition to data and subroutine declarations and definitions, a Perl 5 program includes *statements* (both simple and complex), which you will learn about in the next section.

All Perl 5 programs are part of a package. If the package is undeclared, the package name is main.

Perl Program Components

I'm not really sure why every field—computer programmers, as well as doctors, lawyers, truck drivers, and so on—finds it necessary to change the English language when perfectly ordinary words would work just as well. Nevertheless, there are some terms that you must understand in order to build a program. In this section, you will learn the basic terms used to describe components of Perl 5 programs.

Operators and Lvalues

An *operator* performs a function or operation on a piece of data. For example, the addition operator (+) adds two numbers together, then assigns one value to another data object. The assignment operator (=) takes the value on the right side of the equal sign and stores it into the variable (lvalue) on the left side of the equal sign.

The term *lvalue* can be easily translated into left-hand value. It usually refers to the variable on the left side of an assignment operator. An lvalue always refers to some type of modifiable variable. The computer term for modifiable variable is *mutable*. Variables that cannot be modified are called *immutable*. (That's a little bit of geekese you can toss around at parties to awe your friends and attract the fawning attention of the opposite sex, although I must admit that this technique never worked for me.) In Perl 5, the terms *lvalue* and *variable* are interchangeable.

Expressions and Statements

Expression is another one of those computer terms that seems to be used to confuse the uninitiated. Expression in plain English means value. What's unique about an expression is the value is usually the result of some type of operation. An expression may be an operation such as addition, the value returned from a subroutine call, or any other valid Perl 5 operation that returns a value.

A *statement* is made up of an operation and an lvalue. All Perl 5 statements end with a semicolon. (There is an exception to this rule—the semicolon on the last statement of any block, defined in the next section, is optional.) The *syntax* (format) of an assignment statement is:

```
lvalue = expression;
```

For example, you might use this assignment statement:

```
$sum = $subTotal + $tax;
```

This statement adds the values in the variables $subTotal and $tax together and then assigns the result to the variable $sum. Another way to say this is that the lvalue $sum is assigned the value of the expression $subTotal plus $tax.

Blocks

A *block* is a series of related program lines typically used in *control statements*, which are loop and conditional statements used to jump around in programs based on testing the contents of a piece of data. A block begins and ends with opening and closing curly braces. All Perl 5 control statements, such as if and while, must be formed as a block, like this:

```
if (conditional expression) {
    $lvalue = expression;
}
```

The block of statements may be empty, but it is required.

Comments

A *comment* is any text in your program that is ignored by the computer or, rather, by the interpreter. Programmers use comments to document their programs, to make it clear to themselves and to other programmers what is being done by the code. A comment in Perl 5 begins with the pound sign (#), like this:

```
# Determine whether the line from the database matches
# the search criteria
```

The pound sign tells the Perl 5 interpreter to ignore everything on the line following the pound sign. A comment may begin anywhere within a line. Everything following the pound sign on that line will be ignored. A newline character terminates the comment. Comments do not affect your code's execution or correctness in any way, but they are extremely important.

WRITING A CGI PROGRAM

CGI programming is a major application of Perl 5 programming. A CGI program runs on a web server, interfacing with both the web browser and web server. If you've never run a CGI program on your web server, you'll learn how to in this section. Our example uses an HTML registration form and a CGI program that reads registration data to explain the fundamentals of CGI programming.

Before we go into the details of the CGI program, we need to cover some definitions and underlying concepts of CGI programs and the environment in which they work. We'll start with definitions of CGI, client/server model, and HTTP communications. Then we'll get to the web server, HTTP form, and CGI program for the example.

Have you ever started to drink from a water fountain and been squirted in the eye? Prepare yourself to get wet! In fact, the following sections may seem more like trying to take a drink from a fire hose. I have tried to pack in as much information as possible in a limited space.

Defining CGI

CGI programs can create dynamic web pages, which are built in response to a customer profile or query. CGI programs can be obvious, like a complex shopping cart application, or completely hidden, saving or serving data but never creating a line of HTML. CGI stands for Common Gateway Interface, which is the application and interpretation of the HTTP specification. That definition may be complete, but it isn't very informative. Let's see how the terms *Common, Gateway,* and *Interface* actually apply.

The Common Gateway Interface is *common* between the client and the server, which is usually your web browser and your web server. All web servers and web clients communicate using HTTP request and response headers. You'll learn more about HTTP headers later in this chapter.

The Common Gateway Interface acts as a *gateway* between the web client and the web server. The gateway program acts as a bridge between the web client and the web server, interpreting and responding to dynamic and data-driven requests from the web client. Without a gateway program, the web server would respond to a URL request by returning a nondynamic, or static, web page. The gateway program assists the web server in returning dynamic web pages, built on the fly, in response to URL and data requests from the web client.

The Common Gateway Interface acts as an *interface* between the web server and other applications on the server machine. The interface program understands the HTTP interface protocols required by the web server and can act as an interface between other computer applications and the web server.

NOTE

Exporting databases is a common CGI task. The CGI program doesn't perform the actual database tasks, but instead acts as an interface program interpreting the incoming data requests into the correct syntax for Microsoft Access, Microsoft SQL Server, Oracle, and other major database applications. When the database responds to the query, the interface program translates the response into the correct format for transmission through the web server to the web client. Exporting databases and e-mail are the two of the larger interface applications of CGI programming.

To recap, here's how the CGI breaks down:

▶ *Common* stands for the HTTP protocol used between the web client and the web server.

▶ *Gateway* stands for the bridge programming used to communicate between the web client and web server.

▶ *Interface* stands for the programming required to communicate between the web server and large applications such as databases, search engines, and e-mail.

A CGI program is part of the communication between a web client and a web server. This communication is a key element in the client/server interface model, which we will examine next.

Understanding the Client/Server Interface Model

The Internet is the ultimate client/server model. Your web browser, the client, communicates with your server, appropriately called a web server, which is interacting with many other services.

The web browser (client) requests a resource from the web server. The client, your web browser, then waits for the web server to respond. This is the essence of client/server communication.

If you've been around computing at all in the last five years, you've heard the term *client/server model*. This is the paradigm of the Internet (and of the 1990s).

Let's use a restaurant as a client/server analogy. When you go to a busy restaurant and you don't have a reservation, you ask the maitre d' or hostess for a table. At that point, you are the *client* and the maitre d' is the *server*. You have made a request and been placed on a list to be served (seated). When your name pops to the top of the list, you will be served. Your client request has been processed by the server, and the resource you requested has been allocated to you.

Now you are at your table and your waiter (or waitress) is ready to take your order. Your waiter is the server, who takes the order from you, the client. The waiter takes the order to the kitchen and gives the order to the chef. The waiter, your server, has become a client of the chef, and the chef is now the server. The server is always the process that has the resource you, the client, want. In this example, the resource you want is food. However, this resource is not directly available from your server, the waiter. The waiter passes your resource request to another server, which makes the waiter a client to the next server, the chef.

This illustrates the power of the client/server model very well. You need a single-resource dinner. You have a single server—the waiter getting you that resource. That server is specialized, however. The server's only job is to take requests for resources and pass them on to other servers—the chef or bartender in our restaurant analogy. If your server only took care of a single client, you, your server would spend a lot of wasted time waiting for your food to get ready and then for you to eat. Your service from this one server might be very good, but it would be very expensive. Dedicated processes are always more expensive.

Instead of just serving you and wasting time while waiting for something to do, your server serves other clients, and usually stays busier but still takes good care of you. This is the power of the client/server model. The server serves multiple clients, and in a properly balanced system (which isn't necessarily easy to design), the client processes receive the resources they requested in a timely manner.

Obviously, the client and server need to have some way to communicate so that the client can make requests and the server can respond. In the case of the web client and web server, this communication is done using HTTP headers, as explained in the next section.

Understanding HTTP Communications

As you have learned, a client/server communication is usually initiated by the client requesting a service. Figure 9.11 shows a simple client/server HTTP communication. If this communication were initiated from your web browser, you would only see the output shown in Figure 9.12.

To try this yourself, telnet to any World Wide Web site. (For the example shown in Figure 9.11, I used my own virtual domain so I could return a small HTML document, which makes the HTTP headers easier to see.) For example, to telnet to the Yahoo! web site, you would use this command:

```
telnet www.yahoo.com 80
```

You must telnet to port 80, which is the default network port where the web server process listens for client requests. This port is similar to the radio frequency HAM radio operators transmit and listen on. The HAM radio operators can transmit and receive on any frequency, but they are more likely to hear and be heard on a commonly known frequency.

To retrieve a document from the web server, you must send it an HTTP request header. In Figure 9.11, you can see the GET header on the fifth line. To retrieve the default document for the document root on a web server, issue this command:

```
GET/HTTP/1.1
```

Then press Enter twice to end the HTTP request. A blank line terminates all HTTP client/server header transmissions. This is like the HAM radio operators saying, "Over," when they are finished transmitting to tell the receiver that they have switched their radio set to receive and are now listening for messages. The GET method header is the default method when requesting a URL.

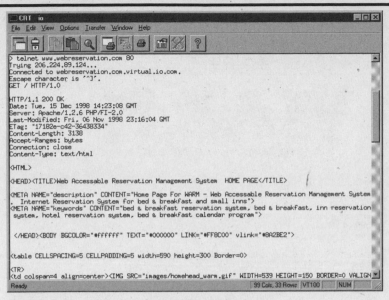

```
CRT io                                                                    _ □ ✕
File  Edit  View  Options  Transfer  Window  Help

  ▯▤  ▮▤  ▤▤  ▯  ▤  ▤▤  ▤  ▥▣  ▤▨  ▯

> telnet www.webreservation.com 80
Trying 206.224.89.124...
Connected to webreservation.com.virtual.io.com.
Escape character is '^]'.
GET / HTTP/1.0

HTTP/1.1 200 OK
Date: Tue, 15 Dec 1998 14:23:08 GMT
Server: Apache/1.2.6 PHP/FI-2.0
Last-Modified: Fri, 06 Nov 1998 23:16:04 GMT
ETag: "17182e-c42-36438334"
Content-Length: 3138
Accept-Ranges: bytes
Connection: close
Content-Type: text/html

<HTML>

<HEAD><TITLE>Web Accessible Reservation Management System   HOME PAGE</TITLE>

<META NAME="description" CONTENT="Home Page For WARM - Web Accessible Reservation Management System
. Internet Reservation System for bed & breakfast and small inns">
<META NAME="keywords" CONTENT="bed & breakfast reservation system, bed & breakfast, inn reservation
system, hotel reservation system, bed & breakfast calendar program">


</HEAD><BODY BGCOLOR="#ffffff" TEXT="#000000" LINK="#FF8C00" vlink="#8A2BE2">

<table CELLSPACING=5 CELLPADDING=5 width=590 height=300 Border=0>

<TR>
<td colspan=4 align=center><IMG SRC="images/homehead_warm.gif" WIDTH=539 HEIGHT=150 BORDER=0 VALIGN ▼
Ready                                          99 Cols, 33 Rows  VT100    NUM
```

FIGURE 9.11: HTTP client/server communication

If you have made a valid HTTP request header, you will receive an HTTP status response header of 200 and further information in response to your HTTP request. You can see this response on the line following the blank line after the GET request in Figure 9.11.

The web server's most common HTTP request header is the method request header. This header indicates the type of request the web client is making. The three most common method header types are GET, POST, and HEAD. The HEAD method type is primarily used by the search-bots of the major search engines like Yahoo!, Excite, Infoseek, and Lycos. Your browser commonly uses the GET and POST method headers when requesting HTML documents. As you just saw, the GET method header is usually used when you are requesting a URL. The POST method is frequently used when transferring data from the client to the server, as you'll see in our CGI program example, coming up shortly.

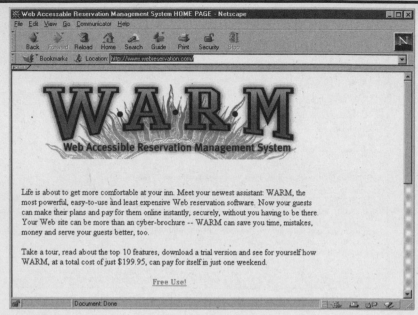

FIGURE 9.12: Web browser client/server communication

NOTE

Data transferred using the HTTP method GET is available to your CGI program in the environment hash, %ENV, using the hash key QUERY_STRING. Data transferred using the HTTP method POST is available to your CGI program in the STDIN input buffer handle. The amount of data in the STDIN input buffer is available to your CGI program in the environment hash (%ENV), using the hash key CONTENT_LENGTH. You'll see examples of retrieving data in CGI programs in later chapters.

The web server always begins an HTTP response to the client's HTTP request with an HTTP status response header. A valid HTTP status code of 200 means that the web server was able to respond correctly to the client's request.

The primary role of a CGI program is to generate and decode HTTP headers. A CGI program contains two main parts:

- ▶ Part one reads any incoming HTTP headers and data from the web client.

- ▶ Part two generates any required response from the web server.

Both parts are optional but are usually present. Each of these parts uses the HTTP headers to communicate between the web client and the web server. Your CGI program typically responds with a Content-Type: text/html HTTP response header, which tells the browser to expect an HTML document.

The elements of client/server interaction you've learned about are used for the web browser and web server communication in our CGI program example. Now we'll look at the web server configuration for CGI.

Configuring the Web Server

As you've learned, a CGI program is part of the communication between a web client and a web server. The CGI program runs on the web server, usually under a directory called cgi-bin. In this section, you will learn about the web server directories and configuration variables that are necessary for installing and running CGI programs.

The HTML page is served up by the web server to the web client from a directory tree called the document root. The *document root* is the directory path on your web server to the beginning of the HTML directory tree. The HTML directory tree is the directory and subdirectories that contain your web site's HTML documents. The web server begins searching for HTML documents by prepending the document root path to the directory path given after the domain portion of the URL address.

A URL address is made up of three parts: the protocol, the domain name, and the file identifier. These parts contain the following information:

▶ The protocol indicates the protocol name. The web server handles protocols of type http://, but URL protocols also may be ftp, wais, gopher, telnet, and other types, which are handled by other server-side applications. The protocol name is not case-sensitive.

▶ The domain name is the machine Internet address your web browser is contacting. The machine Internet address is a unique series of numbers or characters. Like the protocol name, the domain name is not case-sensitive.

▶ The file identifier is the path (absolute or relative) to the file, beginning from the document root. The file may be any valid filename. The filename extension tells the web server what file type headers to return to the web client. The file identifier is case-sensitive.

How your web server interprets filename extensions, searches for documents, handles CGI requests, and performs other functions is determined by your web server's configuration files. These files are usually located in a configuration directory inside the server root directory tree. The server root, like the document root, is a directory path on the web server. The web server usually stores your configuration, log, and error files within the server root directory tree.

Listing 9.2 is an edited copy of a web server configuration file from one of my virtual domains. Lines 8 and 9 of Listing 9.2 show the definition of the server root and document root. On line 12 of Listing 9.2, you can see a handler defined for CGI scripts.

NOTE

A *script* is another name for a program. Scripts are usually short programs, and typically they are written in an interpreted programming language (like Perl 5) rather than a compiled language.

NOTE

The line numbers in code listings are provided for easy reference and, of course, aren't part of the code itself.

Listing 9.2: Web Server Configuration File

```
1.  ##### Apache conf file
2.  ServerType standalone
3.  BindAddress www.practical-inet.com
4.  Port 80
5.  ServerAdmin webmaster@practical-inet.com
6.  ServerName www.practical-inet.com
7.
8.  ServerRoot /virtual/customer/practical-inet.com
9.  DocumentRoot /virtual/customer/practical-inet.com/htdocs
10.
11. DirectoryIndex blocked.html index.html index.htm
➥ index.php index.cgi home.html home.htm welcome.html
➥ welcome.htm
12. AddHandler cgi-script .cgi
13.
14. UserDir disabled
15. FancyIndexing on
16. XBitHack Full
```

```
17.
18. Alias /icons/ /virtual/customer/practical-inet.com/icons/
19. ScriptAlias /cgi-bin/ /virtual/customer/
➥ practical-inet.com/cgi-bin/
20.
21. AddIconByEncoding (CMP,/icons/compressed.gif)
➥ x-compress x-gzip
22. AccessFileName .htaccess
23. DefaultType text/plain
24.
25. AddEncoding x-compress Z
26. AddEncoding x-gzip gz
27.
28. AddType text/html .shtml
29. AddHandler server-parsed .shtml
```

Writing the Registration Form

Using a registration form for gathering information over the Internet is another common CGI application. Figure 9.13 shows the Internet registration form we will use in our example. The source code used to generate this HTML registration form is shown in Listing 9.3.

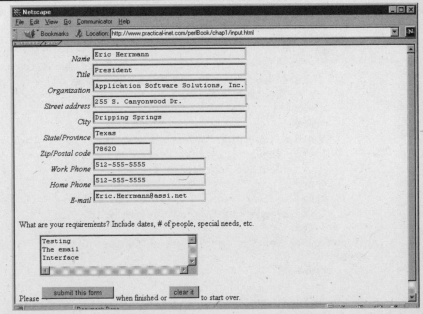

FIGURE 9.13: An HTML registration form

Listing 9.3: HTML Registration Form Source

```html
<html> <head></head>
<body bgcolor="#FFFFFF" link="#808000">
<p align="center"> </p> <div align="left">
<form
action="http://www.practical-inet.com/cgi-bin/perlBook/
chap9/readInput.cgi"
method="POST">
<blockquote>
    <table border="0">
        <tr>
          <td align="right"><em>Name</em></td>
          <td><input type="text" size="35" name=
              "Contact_FullName"> </td>
        </tr>
        <tr>
          <td align="right"><em>Title</em></td>
          <td>
<input type="text" size="35" name="Contact_Title">
</td>
        </tr>
        <tr>
          <td align="right"><em>Organization</em></td>
          <td><input type="text" size="35" name=
              "Contact_Organization"> </td>
        </tr>
        <tr>
          <td align="right"><em>Street address</em></td>
          <td><input type="text" size="35" name=
              "Contact_StreetAddress"> </td>
        </tr>
        <tr>
          <td align="right"><em>Address (cont.)</em></td>
          <td><input type="text" size="35" name=
              "Contact_Address2"> </td>
        </tr>
        <tr>
          <td align="right"><em>City</em></td>
          <td>
<input type="text" size="35" name="Contact_City">
</td>
        </tr>
        <tr>
          <td align="right"><em>State/Province</em></td>
          <td>
<input type="text" size="35" name="Contact_State">
</td>
```

```
      </tr>
      <tr>
        <td align="right"><em>Zip/Postal code</em></td>
        <td>
<input type="text" size="12" maxlength="12" name=
        "Contact_ZipCode"> </td>
      </tr>
      <tr>
        <td align="right"><em>Country</em></td>
        <td><input type="text" size="25" name=
        "Contact_Country"> </td>
      </tr>
      <tr>
        <td align="right"><em>Work Phone</em></td>
        <td>
<input type="text" size="25" maxlength="25" name=
        "Contact_WorkPhone"> </td>
      </tr>
      <tr>
        <td align="right"><em>Home Phone</em></td>
        <td>
<input type="text" size="25" maxlength="25" name=
        "Contact_HomePhone"> </td>
      </tr>
      <tr>
        <td align="right"><em>FAX</em></td>
        <td>
<input type="text" size="25" maxlength="25" name=
        "Contact_FAX"> </td>
      </tr>
      <tr>
        <td align="right"><em>E-mail</em></td>
        <td>
<input type="text" size="25" name="Contact_Email"> </td>
      </tr>
      <tr>
        <td align="right"><em>URL</em></td>
        <td>
<input type="text" size="25" maxlength="25" name=
        "Contact_URL"> </td>
      </tr>
    </table>
  </blockquote>
  <p>What are your requirements? Include dates, # of people,
    special needs, etc.</p>
  <blockquote>
```

```
    <p><textarea name="comments" rows="5" cols="35">
</textarea> <br>
    </p>
    </blockquote>
    <p>Please <input type="submit" value="submit this form">
      when finished or <input
type="reset" value="clear it"> to start over. </p>
</form>
</body>
</html>
```

When submitted, the HTML registration source of Listing 9.3 calls the CGI program readInput.cgi, described next.

NOTE

You will need to modify the fifth line of Listing 9.3, action=http://www .practical-inet.com/cgi-bin/perlBook/chap9/readInput.cgi, to reflect the URL for your web server.

Creating the CGI Program

The CGI program readInput.cgi, shown in Listing 9.4, follows the steps that every CGI program must follow:

- ▶ First, a CGI program must decode any incoming data.

- ▶ Next, a CGI program uses that data to interface with any server-side programs.

- ▶ Finally, a CGI program must return valid HTTP headers.

These three steps are the basics of any web-browser-to-web-server communication. The web browser and the web server create a classic client/server relationship, as explained earlier. The web browser, through the HTML form in Listing 9.3, calls the web server requesting the resource readInput.cgi in Listing 9.4.

NOTE

The program `readInput.cgi` teaches you Perl and CGI programming in the context of their environment instead of a simple made-for-the-book example. This makes your job a little harder at first but more rewarding in the long run. You will need to confront more new concepts at once, but you can rest assured that the skills you learn are practical and relevant to a real-world programming environment.

Listing 9.4: readInput.cgi

```
1.  #!/usr/bin/perl
2.
3.  %postInputs = readPostInput();
4.  $dateCommand = "date";
5.  $time = `$dateCommand`;
6.  open (MAIL, "|/usr/sbin/sendmail -t") || return 0;
7.
8.  select (MAIL);
9.  print << "EOF";
10. To:    YOUR_ADDRESS\ @YOUR_DOMAIN.com
11. From: $postInputs{ 'Contact_Email'}
12. Subject: $postInputs{ 'Organization'}  Information
➥ Requested
13.
14. $time
15. $postInputs{ 'Organization'}  Information Requested
16. Name: $postInputs{ 'Contact_FullName'}
17. Email: $postInputs{ 'Contact_Email'}
18. Street Address: $postInputs{ 'Contact_StreetAddress'}
19. Street Address (cont): $postInputs{ 'Contact_Address2'}
20. City: $postInputs{ 'Contact_City'}
21. State : $postInputs{ 'Contact_State'}
22. Zip: $postInputs{ 'Contact_ZipCode'}
23. Work Phone: $postInputs{ 'Contact_WorkPhone'}
24. Home Phone: $postInputs{ 'Contact_HomePhone'}
25. FAX: $postInputs{ 'Contact_FAX'}
26. Email: $postInputs{ 'Contact_Email'}
27. Comments: $postInputs{ 'comments'}
28.
29.
30. EOF
31.    close(MAIL);
32.    select (STDOUT);
33.    printThankYou();
34.
```

Part iii

```perl
35. sub readPostInput(){
36.    my (%searchField, $buffer, $pair, @pairs);
37.    if ($ENV{ 'REQUEST_METHOD'} eq 'POST'){
38.        read(STDIN, $buffer, $ENV{ 'CONTENT_LENGTH'} );
39.        @pairs = split(/&/, $buffer);
40.        foreach $pair (@pairs){
41.            ($name, $value) = split(/=/, $pair);
42.            $value =~ tr/+/ /;
43.            $value =~ s/%([a-fA-F0-9][a-fA-F0-9])
➡ /pack("C", hex($1))/eg;
44.            $name =~ tr/+/ /;
45.            $name =~ s/%([a-fA-F0-9][a-fA-F0-9])
➡ /pack("C", hex($1))/eg;
46.            $searchField{ $name} = $value;
47.        }
48.    }
49.    return (%searchField);
50. }
51.
52. sub printThankYou(){
53. print << "EOF";
54. Content-Type: text/html
55.
56. <HEAD>
57. <TITLE>THANK YOU FOR FOR YOUR REQUEST</TITLE>
58. </HEAD>
59. <BODY>
60. <TABLE CELLSPACING=2 CELLPADDING=2 border=0 width=600>
61. <TR><th><BR>
62. <center>
63. <FONT SIZE=+3><B>Thank You
➡ $postInputs{ 'Contact_FullName'} </b></font>
64. </center><BR><BR>
65.
66. <CENTER><B><FONT SIZE=+1>
67. <P>For submitting your information.
➡ We will get back with you shortly.
68. </P>
69. </FONT></B><CENTER>
70. </th>
71. </table>
72. </BODY>
73. </HTML>
74.
75. EOF
76. }
```

Before you can test this example, you need to know how the installation of a CGI program works. In the next section, you will learn how and where to install your CGI programs.

Installing CGI Programs

To install the HTML registration form shown in Listing 9.3, you must know the document root and the script alias. The script alias identifies the CGI program's directory tree for the web server. The web server will look only within the CGI program directory tree for CGI programs. In Listing 9.2, the script alias is on line 19:

```
ScriptAlias /cgi-bin/
➡ /virtual/customer/practical-inet.com/cgi-bin/
```

The HTML registration form must be installed into a directory underneath your web server's document root. Each web server's document root is unique. Your web server probably has a FAQ (Frequently Asked Questions) list, telling you where to install HTML files. If it doesn't, you'll need to get this information from your web administrator.

Copy the program in Listing 9.3 to your web server using ftp, placing the file into your document root. (Refer to the note that follows Listing 9.1 for a reminder about how to access copies of this chapter's listings.) Now copy the CGI program shown in Listing 9.4 to your web server's cgi-bin directory.

WARNING

Whenever you copy files from a Windows to a Unix computer, be sure to set the transfer mode to ASCII. Unix and Windows use different characters to determine the end of a line. If you copy a program from Windows to Unix in the default binary mode, your program may not work.

Next, if you are on a Unix web server, you must set the correct file permissions on the files. As explained earlier, file permissions tell the Unix operating system who can read, write, and/or execute a file.

Your HTML file should have its permissions set to owner = 6, group = 4, world = 4. This gives you permission to read and write to the file; the group and world get read access to the file. Use the chmod command like this:

```
chmod 644 register.html
```

Your CGI program should have its permissions set to owner = 7, group = 5, world = 5. This gives you permission to read, write, and execute the file. The group and world get read and execute access to the file. Use the chmod command like this:

```
chmod 755 readInput.html
```

To test the installation of your CGI program, execute it from the command line, as you learned earlier in this chapter, in the "Using the Unix Command Shell" section. If you have problems, see the next chapter for information about debugging your CGI program.

To test your HTML installation, in your web browser, enter the URL of your web server followed by the filename of the installed HTML file as the location, like this:

```
http://www.yourDomain.com/registration.html
```

Now that you have a working CGI program installed on your web server, let's dissect that program and get a better understanding of how Perl 5 and CGI programs work.

Understanding How a CGI Program Works

You've learned about the client/server interface model, and you put together a CGI application. Now it's time to see how the programming code works. As we work through the code, you'll come across many types of Perl 5 constructs that will probably be new to you. Don't worry if all this is not crystal clear (or even vaguely comprehensible) right now. This is just a quick-start example to show you the power of Perl 5 and make you eager to learn all those details you need to know to write your own programs.

First, your web browser requests a resource from the web server. This happens when you click the submit this form button (in the form shown earlier in Figure 9.13), which has the web browser call the CGI program identified by the action attribute of the HTML registration form tag. The web browser then generates an HTTP method request header. The method type for the HTML registration form in Listing 9.3 is POST, which is also an attribute of the HTML form tag. Here is that HTML form tag from Listing 9.3:

```
<form action=www.practical-inet.com/cgi-bin/
➡ perlBook/readInput.cgi" method ="POST">
```

This means the data submitted by the form will be available for your CGI program through Standard Input (also known as the special variable STDIN), just as though you fed the data to your program right from the command prompt except that the data contains special encoding for data submitted through web forms.

Now that the web browser has sent the web server an HTTP request header, the web server will decode and respond to the web client's request. The web server decodes the HTTP request header and determines by looking at the file extension that it must pass the request to a CGI program.

The web server activates the CGI program `readInput.cgi`. The first thing the CGI program does is read the input data sent by the HTML form. This is done on line 3 of Listing 9.3:

```
%postInputs = readPostInput();
```

This is a subroutine call, which means the program jumps to line 35 of Listing 9.3 and continues execution from there:

```
sub readPostInput(){
```

The subroutine `readPostInput` is made up of the block of statements that begins with the opening curly brace on line 35 and continues to the closing curly brace of line 50. The subroutine `readPostInput` verifies that the request header method was POST on line 37 and then reads the data from the HTML form on line 38 into the variable `$buffer`.

```
if ($ENV{ 'REQUEST_METHOD'}  eq 'POST'){
    read(STDIN, $buffer, $ENV{ 'CONTENT_LENGTH'} );
```

The CGI input is passed from the web browser to the web server in URL-encoded name/value pairs. Each name/value pair is directly associated with the HTML form `input` tag. Each HTML form `input` tag has a name and value attribute. The name should be set inside the HTML file. Look back at Listing 9.3 and notice that each HTML form `input` tag contains a `name` attribute that is set to some unique name, as in these two examples:

```
<td><input type="text" size="35" name="Contact_FullName">
<td><input type="text" size="35" name="Contact_Title"> </td>
```

The value is set by the user's input. When the user clicks on the HTML form's submit button, the browser collects all the data associated with the HTML input tags and URL-encodes the data. This URL encoding converts some characters for safe transfer over the Internet and associates each name and value attribute with an equal sign. Each name/value pair is separated from the next name/value pair by an ampersand (&).

Part III

Line 39 of Listing 9.4 separates the name/value pairs into an array named @pairs:

```
@pairs = split(/&/, $buffer);
```

The array is then URL-decoded from lines 42 through 45 and saved into a Perl 5 hash named %searchField.

```
$value =~ tr/+/ /;
$value =~ s/%([a-fA-F0-9][a-fA-F0-9])/pack("C", hex($1))/eg;
$name =~ tr/+/ /;
$name =~ s/%([a-fA-F0-9][a-fA-F0-9])/pack("C", hex($1))/eg;
```

The hash is returned to the calling program on line 49:

```
return (%searchField);
```

HASHES

Associative arrays, or hashes, are common data structures used by Perl programmers. Unlike an array, which is a list of elements defined with a statement like:

```
@myarray = ("a", "b", "c");
```

an associative array is a list of paired elements, defined like this:

```
%myhash = ("a","b","c","d");
```

or this:

```
%myhash = ('a' => "b", 'c' => "d");
```

You can also define an individual hash pair as needed:

```
$myhash{'a'} = "b";
```

Once your CGI program has decoded the incoming data, it can use the data as part of an interface to other programs. On line 6 in Listing 9.4, it creates a connection to the e-mail program sendmail:

```
open (MAIL, "|/usr/sbin/sendmail -t") || return 0;
```

The e-mail message (lines 10 through 29) is sent to the sendmail program via the print statement on line 9:

```
print << "EOF";
```

This print statement, using the heredoc operator (<<), sends everything from lines 10 through 29 to the file handle selected on line 8, which is connected to the sendmail program.

The e-mail message is sent to the e-mail address on line 10:

```
To:   YOUR_ADDRESS\ @YOUR_DOMAIN.com
```

The EOF marker on line 30 ends the data transfer initiated by the `print` statement on line 9. The results of the e-mail message generated between lines 10 through 29 are shown in Figure 9.14. The connection to the `sendmail` program is closed on line 31:

```
close(MAIL);
```

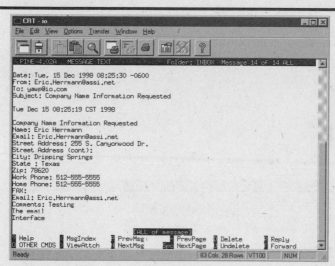

FIGURE 9.14: Registration e-mail

On line 33, the CGI program prepares to respond with a valid HTTP response header by the subroutine call:

```
printThankYou();
```

This subroutine call jumps to line 52:

```
sub printThankYou(){
```

CGI programs are responsible for returning a valid HTTP header. Lines 54 through 56 create the required HTTP response headers:

```
Content-Type: text/html
```

```
<HEAD>
```

The `Content-Type: text/html` HTTP response header tells the web browser that the remaining data returned by the web server will be HTML text. The results are shown in Figure 9.15.

Part III

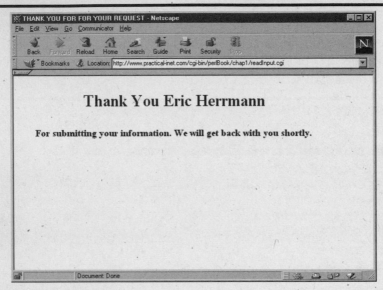

FIGURE 9.15: Registration Thank You response

NOTE

The blank line on line 55 of Listing 9.4, following the Content-Type:text/html response header on line 54, is critical. The blank line tells the web browser (client) this is the last HTTP response header. Any data following the blank line is not part of the HTTP header traffic. Your web browser will decode the Content-Type HTTP response header to determine what type of data follows the last HTTP response header.

This completes the HTML communication between the web browser and web server, which I believe deserves a recap. Here are the steps involved in using our sample CGI program:

1. Your web browser, the client, through the HTML form's action field, submits an HTTP request header method of type POST (the type most frequently used when transferring data from a client to a server).

2. The web server decodes the HTTP request header and calls the CGI program identified in the HTTP request header.

3. The CGI program readInput.cgi decodes the incoming POST data.

4.   The CGI program `readInput.cgi` uses the incoming data to interface with the `sendmail` program and creates an e-mail message.

5.   The CGI program `readInput.cgi` completes the client/server transaction by returning an HTTP response header, which is the Thank You HTML page shown in Figure 9.15.

SUMMARY

This chapter began with an introduction to Perl 5. Because Perl was built to evolve, it is changing faster and faster as its user community grows and contributes to Perl 5. Like a snowball rolling downhill, as Perl 5 picks up new users, it grows in contributions to the language and evolves faster to meet new needs.

Next, the chapter explained some fundamental procedures required to accomplish everyday Perl 5 programming tasks. You learned how to run a Perl 5 program from the command-line interface on both Windows and Unix computers and how to edit a program. This part of the chapter used a simple example of a Perl 5 program that shows your computer's environment variables.

The second example in this chapter was a CGI program. CGI programming is a major application of Perl 5 programming. You learned how your web browser and server communicate using client/server technology and HTTP headers. Then you learned how to install an HTML registration form and the CGI program that reads the form data.

Both of the examples in this chapter are useful, real-world programs. In other chapters drawn from *Mastering Perl 5* for inclusion in this book, this will be the rule, not the exception. Practical examples will be used to introduce, explain, and illustrate each new topic.

In the next chapter, you'll learn how to accomplish another fundamental programming task. This task helps you follow a major programming rule: Just writing the code isn't enough—it also needs to do the right thing. Making your code do the right thing is called *debugging*. Before you get frustrated because your code doesn't work, you're going to learn how to fix and avoid the inevitable bugs (errors) that creep into everyone's programs.

CHAPTER 10

DEBUGGING YOUR PROGRAMS

When you *debug* your code, you look for coding errors and try to fix them. Inevitably, some bugs will creep into your code. You can use the techniques you'll read about in this chapter to speed up the debugging process.

Adapted from *Mastering Perl 5*, by Eric C. Herrmann
ISBN 0-7821-2200-0   958 pages $39.99

Coding errors usually come in two forms: syntax errors and logic errors. When looking for errors in programs that you typed in from this book, you can concentrate on syntax errors. Syntax errors are errors created when you fail to follow the required format of a Perl 5 statement. The first section of this chapter explains how to locate and fix syntax errors quickly and painlessly.

Eliminating errors is, of course, what debugging is all about. In the section on avoiding errors, you'll learn about coding practices and techniques that will help you prevent errors in your code. You'll also learn about some mistakes that are commonly made in Perl 5 programs.

Since every program has bugs, every decent language has a debugger. Perl 5 comes with a fully functional Perl debugger. In addition to the free debugger distributed with Perl 5, the builders of one of the Windows versions of Perl 5 offer a Windows Perl 5 debugger, which is also described in this chapter.

What about your CGI programs? The techniques used for standard debugging don't work as well in the CGI environment. Over the years, I've developed a few techniques to help locate my CGI bugs, which you'll learn about in the final section of this chapter.

If you code, you debug. Learn the rules of debugging, and your Perl 5 coding experience will be a lot less frustrating.

NOTE

Debugging means removing errors from your code. How did the word *bug* get associated with removing errors? Well, back in the early days of programming, computers with less power than your PC took up entire rooms. These computers operated with large servos that opened and closed, defining the bits and bytes of a program. During one of the demonstrations of these ancient dinosaurs, a moth got stuck between one of the servos, causing the computer to malfunction. When the problem was found, someone said "It had a bug in it!" Removing the bugs from your code became and has remained the popular terminology for find and removing coding errors.

HANDLING SYNTAX ERRORS

You will make all kinds of mistakes if you take my advice and type in the programs you're reading about in this book. Don't let those mistakes discourage you from typing in the programs. Not only will that help you learn how to write Perl 5 programs, but it will also help you learn how to debug programs. You know that the examples work, so you only need to concentrate on one kind of coding error—your typing mistakes. Once you become familiar with the typing errors you make, you'll be able to quickly track them down and correct them in your own code.

Let's begin with an example of how Perl 5 reacts when it finds a syntax error. You'll see that Perl 5's diagnostic messages are very helpful, but you need to learn how to interpret them.

Pinpointing Syntax Errors

Figure 10.1 graphically illustrates the effect of just one typo in a program— a missing quotation mark. In Figure 10.1, five different error messages (eight on-screen lines) are printed for a small typing error.

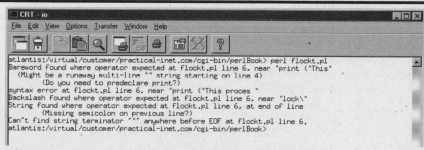

FIGURE 10.1: Perl 5 syntax error messages

What can you learn from Figure 10.1 that will help you become better at debugging your code?

- ▸ One error can create multiple error messages.

- ▸ Those error messages usually have the information you need to locate your problem, so don't ignore them.

The last error message in Figure 10.1 is the best clue to the problem. The Perl 5 interpreter is telling you that there is an unbalanced double quotation mark somewhere in the program. It tells you this with the message "Can't find string terminator '"' anywhere before EOF at flockt.pl line 6." When you see this type of message, you know you forgot to include a closing quotation mark at the end of a string (a *string* is character data surrounded by quotation marks). Then you just need to locate where the missing quotation mark should be inserted. Perl 5's other messages help you pinpoint the error.

NOTE

The program used for Figure 10.1 is small, so the EOF (end of file) in the "Can't find string terminator" message references line 6. If this program had been 100 lines long, with the error created on line 5, Perl 5 would continue looking for the ending quote until it reached the end of the file at line 100. The EOF condition would still occur, but it would be referencing line 100 instead of line 6.

NOTE

The line numbers in code listings are provided for easy reference and, of course, aren't part of the code itself.

Listing 10.1 shows the program that generated the error messages in Figure 10.1.

Listing 10.1: Missing Quote

```
1.  #!/usr/local/bin/perl
2.  use Fcntl ":flock";
3.  open (OUTFILE, ">>flockTest.txt") || warn $!;
4.  # The following line generates the error!
➥ Can you find it?
5.  print ("Requesting Exclusive lock\ n);
6.  flock(OUTFILE, LOCK_EX) || warn $!;
7.  print ("This process now owns the Exclusive lock\ n");
8.  $in = <STDIN>;
9.  flock(OUTFILE, LOCK_UN)|| warn $!;
10. close (OUTFILE);
```

The actual error in this small program is on line 5, where Perl 5 complains about having a bare word where an operator was expected:

```
print ("Requesting Exclusive lock\ n);
```

Bare words are character strings without surrounding quotation marks and that do not begin with $, @, or %, which are the variable designators.

When you begin looking for an error, look for the obvious things first. The messages in Figure 10.1 are generated by a common syntax error made by both experienced and inexperienced programmers. This error is among the most frequently repeated syntax errors, which are listed here:

▶ Keyword misspelled, such as if as fi or elsif as elseif

▶ Semicolon missing

- ▸ Comma missing

- ▸ Parenthesis missing

- ▸ Curly brace (block delineator) missing

- ▸ Quotation mark missing

As you saw in Figure 10.1, a common syntax error (a missing quotation mark) can generate a variety of error messages. Your job as a debugger is to learn to ignore the extraneous information and focus on the important information. For example, the error messages in Figures 10.2 and 10.3 contain important debugging information.

The syntax error messages in both figures give you a good indication of the problem. In Figure 10.2, the error message tells you that you have a syntax error at line 5 near the right parenthesis. In this example, a semicolon was left off the end of the Perl 5 statement on line 4. However, the message identifies line 5. Rarely does the error message identify the correct line when you forgot a semicolon.

In Figure 10.3, the error message tells you that the program is missing a right bracket at line 26. You can believe Perl 5 when it tells you your program is missing a parenthesis or a right bracket, but again, don't believe the line number identification. Perl will match the brackets up out of order until it runs out of brackets.

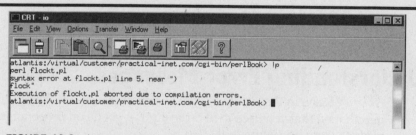

FIGURE 10.2: A syntax error message identifying a program line

The lesson here is that Perl is kind enough to tell you what the problem is, but it is up to you to find the precise location. Fortunately, Perl usually gets you close enough to the real problem that you should be able to figure it out.

Whenever you see an error message that identifies a line number, you know one thing for certain: The error is not on any line after the line identified in the error message. You also know that the error is likely to be on the line identified or on a previous line. Unfortunately, sometimes the previous line may be 100 or more lines back. Messages about syntax errors that fail to complete a Perl 5 statement—such as missing quotes, right brackets, and missing semicolons—rarely identify the correct line. Messages about syntax errors that are wholly contained within a single statement—such as misspelled keywords or improperly formed conditional expressions—usually correctly identify the line number of the error.

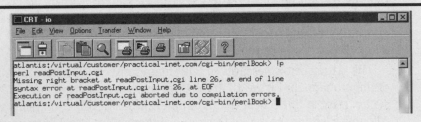

```
atlantis:/virtual/customer/practical-inet.com/cgi-bin/perlBook> !p
perl readPostInput.cgi
Missing right bracket at readPostInput.cgi line 26, at end of line
syntax error at readPostInput.cgi line 26, at EOF
Execution of readPostInput.cgi aborted due to compilation errors.
atlantis:/virtual/customer/practical-inet.com/cgi-bin/perlBook> █
```

FIGURE 10.3: Missing braces

TIP

I hope you like "Where's Waldo?" puzzles, because hunting down bugs in your code is kind of like looking for Waldo in a crowd. Another way to look at debugging is like a treasure hunt to find that missing semicolon or quotation mark. Find the missing operator, and your code magically works. If you take the "it's a game" approach to your debugging, you'll have a lot more success and fun as a programmer.

Understanding Error Messages

As you've seen in the examples, Perl 5 error messages usually contain the information that you need to find the error. A good Perl programmer reads the error messages.

When you see a lot of error messages, realize that usually only the first few messages point to the real error. You should concentrate on the early messages because the later error messages are probably a result of some earlier error. Now, you're probably thinking that I just contradicted myself, since the previous paragraph says that good programmers read the messages, and this one implies that you should ignore the messages at the end of a long list of error messages. The best guideline is a balance of focusing on some of the messages and ignoring others, and achieving this balance comes only with practice.

Perl 5 has almost 500 error messages that you can read at your leisure in the HTML documentation under the filename `perldiag.html`. You can find this file under the documentation directory of your Perl 5 installation or at *Mastering Perl 5*'s companion page at the Sybex web site. (See the note following Listing 9.1 in the preceding chapter for detailed instructions about accessing this information.) You don't need to read the entire list of error messages, but it is a good idea to know about this file in case you run across a message you don't understand. The following sections describe some of the error and warning messages that you are likely to see early in your Perl 5 programming career.

NOTE

Warning messages appear only when you run your program with the warning switch (-w) enabled. This is a good debugging technique, as explained later in this chapter.

Syntax Errors

Syntax error messages are usually generated by the common syntax errors you just learned about. These messages are frequently interrelated and should be interpreted as Perl's best guess. Use these error messages as clues to help identify and locate the error. Syntax error messages include the following:

▶ "Missing semicolon in previous line."

▶ "Can't find terminator before EOF." This message is usually the result of a missing right bracket or quotation mark.

▶ "Might be runaway multi-line string starting on line *n*." This is usually a missing quotation mark.

▶ "Missing right bracket."

Did Not Return a True Value

Every required or used file must return a true value as the last line of the file. This means that whenever you write a program that will be included in another program using the `require` or `use` keyword, the last line of the required file must equal some value other than zero or `null`. Perl 5 interprets zero and `null` values as false. You can write reusable Perl 5 subroutines and include them in your main programs with the `require` or `use` keyword.

To fix this problem, just add the following statement to the end of any file included in other files using the `require` or `use` statement:

```
return 1;
```

Can't Locate Function in @*INC*

The `@INC` array is used by Perl 5 to locate library modules and files when loading subroutines. Frequently, this error occurs because you misspelled a function name. Perl 5 dutifully went looking for the misspelled function and couldn't find it.

Look carefully at the error message. If the function name is wrong, correct it. If the function name is correct, you need to modify the locations Perl is searching for library routines. You can modify the `@INC` array by using the `push` or `unshift` functions to place the correct path into `@INC`.

Panic: Some System Error

When you see an error that starts with "panic," don't panic. This is an error at the system level instead of at your code level. Several possible problems may have created this type of error. Your program may have used up all of your system resources, which happens when your code doesn't release resources when it finishes using them. Perhaps you initialized a variable to a negative number and it was used as an input to a system function before the variable was properly set.

You cannot fix a system error, but it's likely you are using a reference to an invalid location in memory, building an array in an infinite loop, or using some other resource related to the error. First, determine the type of system error by looking at the panic message. Then look at your code and try to locate the sections that might affect the error identified in the panic message. If there are previous errors before the panic error, solve those problems first.

Missing Comma after First Argument

This error message appears when you forget to type the comma after the first argument of a function. For example, here is an error that I make quite often:

```
@names = split(/:/ @nameList,3);
```

You'll learn how to use various Perl 5 functions and their arguments throughout this book.

String @varName Now Must Be Written as \ @varName

You must use the escape character (\) with all literal at signs (@). This error is commonly found in Perl 4 code being upgraded to a Perl 5 installation. In the Perl 4 distribution, you could print e-mail addresses directly in your HTML code. With Perl 5, you will see an error message if you write an e-mail address like this:

```
print "mailto:Recipient@domainName.com";
```

Instead, you must write the e-mail address like this:

```
print "mailto:Recipient\ @domainName.com";
```

Use of Function Is Deprecated

Deprecated means that the function has been replaced with a new function or method. A deprecated function works in the currently released version of Perl 5 but may not be supported in future releases of Perl 5.

You'll see this type of warning message when your code uses a function that has been replaced with a newer function, variable, or syntax. The warning message usually includes information on how to fix the error. For example, one of the deprecated messages in the current build is "Use of implicit split to @_ is deprecated." The diagnostic message tells you to "assign the results of a split() explicitly to an array (or list)."

When the warning message isn't helpful enough, you can look up the deprecated function in the online documentation that was delivered with your Perl distribution. Each deprecated function or variable should have an explanation of the newer replacement function or variable.

WARNING

Don't write new code with deprecated functions. Your code and the deprecated function will work today, but your program may not run under future releases of Perl.

Use of Uninitialized Value

This warning message tells you that an assignment statement uses a variable that has never been explicitly set in your program. See the "Avoiding Misspelled Variable Names" section later in this chapter for more information about problems that can result.

qw Used Commas in List

The qw operator separates bare words in a list with white space characters (blank, tab, newline, and so on). Putting commas in lists built using the qw operator is unnecessary and creates words that include the comma symbol.

You will see this type of warning message when your code has initialized an array like this:

```
@trees = qw|Elm, Birch, Cedar, Oak|;
```

Initializing your array this way creates tree names like Elm, when you really wanted names like Elm (without the comma included as part of the name). You probably meant to initialize the array like this:

```
@trees = qw|Elm Birch Cedar Oak|;
```

Name Only Used Once: Possible Typo

Pay attention to this warning message. This error usually occurs when you misspell a variable name. Debugging misspelled variable names can be frustrating and time consuming. See the "Avoiding Misspelled Variable Names" section later in this chapter for more information about this type of error.

Found = in Conditional, Should Be ==

This is another warning message that could save you hours of debugging time. This message says that a conditional expression included an assignment operator (=) instead of the equal to Boolean operator (==). Most conditional expressions test the contents of data instead of making an assignment statement. Making an assignment in a conditional expression is not an error and usually results in a true value, but it's often not what you meant to code.

AVOIDING ERRORS

If it isn't broken, you don't have to fix it! That's pretty obvious, isn't it? You can make sure it isn't broken by taking some preventative maintenance measures in your code. There are some types of errors that can be avoided by setting the correct Perl command-line switch. Other errors can be avoided by following good coding practices. In this section, you will learn a few things you can do that will limit the number of bugs that creep into your code, and thereby reduce the amount of time you spend debugging your code.

Turning On Warning Messages

The first tip for avoiding bugs in your code doesn't even require a coding change. Whenever you change your code, always run it the first time with Perl 5 warnings enabled, like this:

```
perl -w programName.pl
```

This is likely to print out a lot of warning messages. Don't ignore these messages. Warning messages tell you where to look in your code for potential problems. For example, the following types of messages, which were discussed in the previous section, appear only when you run your program with warnings enabled:

- ▶ Use of function is deprecated
- ▶ Use of uninitialized value
- ▶ qw used commas in list
- ▶ Name only used once: possible typo
- ▶ Found = in conditional, should be ==

Avoiding Misspelled Variable Names

One of the features of Perl 5 is the ability to declare and use variables at any place in your code. Sometimes this feature introduces some hard-to-find bugs. Also, Perl 5 is a case-sensitive language. If you change the case of one character in a variable name, the variables are not the same. For example, the variable names $firstName and $FirstName refer to different storage locations.

If you make a typing mistake in assigning or using a variable name, Perl 5 creates a new variable. Now your code is using the wrong variable name, and either the data you meant to use elsewhere won't be available or the data your code is now using isn't valid. There are two simple steps you can take to avoid this problem (and one of them isn't careful typing). One is to use the warning switch (-w), as described in the previous section.

An alternative to using the warning switch is to use the Perl 5 pragma strict. The pragma strict tells the compiler to generate three types of errors:

- ▶ An error for any variable used before it was declared
- ▶ An error if your code uses symbolic references
- ▶ An error if your code uses bare words

You can use the pragma `strict` to restrict only the use of variable names, excluding the restrictions on symbolic references and bare words, by adding the following line in your code:

```
use strict 'vars';
```

You can put this line anywhere in your code. Then all the variable names that follow this line must be declared using the keywords my or `local`.

You can turn this restriction off by inserting this line:

```
no strict 'vars';
```

If you use the `strict` pragma in your code, you'll never have to debug a variable misspelling because all variables must be declared before they can be used.

WARNING

The `strict` pragma can make it difficult for your code to use other modules and programs that don't follow this rule. If you have a problem using other modules, turn off `strict 'vars'` around the offending module and turn it back on when you need it.

Following Good Coding Practices

Following good coding practices will make it easier for you (and others) to debug your programs. Here are a few tips to get you started.

Comments

Comment your code. My first boss made me comment every single line of code I wrote. That was a bit much, but comments are very important to avoiding and removing bugs. Before you start a new section of code, you should clearly define what you want the new section to do, then write the code the way you described it. You'll see examples throughout this book.

Indentation

Indent your code. This is easy to do if you have a good editor. However, if you aren't using a tool that indents your code for you automatically, you should do it manually. Every time you open a new block of statements with a left curly brace, indent your code some common amount. I like to use three spaces, but the indentation amount doesn't really matter—just be consistent. After you close a block of statements with a right curly brace, outdent a consistent number of spaces.

Meaningful Variable Names

Use meaningful variable names. Don't create variable names of one or two characters. Use variable names that reflect the purpose of the variable. You shouldn't go overboard and make every variable half a line long, but every variable should be understandable when you try to read your own code next week (or next year). If you are not very creative with names, just append the data type onto the end of the variable name. For example, `line:`, `$line`, `@line`, and `%line` become `lineLabel:`, `$lineScalar`, `@lineArray`, and `%lineHash`. The little bit of extra typing is worth the time you'll save debugging.

Testing Loop and Conditional Expressions

The rule here is to build a little; test a little. Test your code as you write it. Don't wait until you're finished writing the entire program to see if it works. Test each piece as you build it. When you build a new `while` loop, run a couple of tests on it to make sure it stops and starts when you expect it to. As you build each new logical block of code, test it.

Beginning or End of Array Tests

Some places in code are particularly error prone. Loop indexes and any conditional expressions that check for the beginning or end of an array should be carefully tested. In your code, let Perl 5 index through your arrays, like this:

```
foreach (@array){ ...}
```

instead of explicitly indexing through the array, like this:

```
for ($index=0; $index<$max; $index++){
    $array[$index]; ...
    }
```

When your code must explicitly use the beginning or last index, make sure you test those cases.

Positive Logic

Another way to avoid errors in conditional expressions is to use positive logic. Don't be negative! That may sound like a philosophy of life, but it should be your programming philosophy also. Every time you write a conditional expression, you have a choice of testing for the existence of some condition or testing for the absence of some condition, like this:

```
while (!red) { …}    #negative
until (red) { …}     #positive
```

Whenever possible, test for the presence of a condition. If you find your conditional logic checks for the negative case, take a moment to look for the positive condition. Every coin has two sides, and every conditional expression has a positive and negative solution. Sometimes the positive condition isn't practical, but that should be the exception in your code. Testing for positive logic makes your code easier to understand, and positive logic usually requires less maintenance.

Special Cases

Along with avoiding negative conditions in your conditional expressions, you should also try to avoid handling special cases. This is called *exception handling*. Code that works for every case except one, two, three, or more cases is very prone to errors. There always seems to be one more exception. Look for the solution that doesn't require exception handling.

For example, if you are writing a program that determines when the chicken should cross the road, you might write something like this: Cross the road except when the light is red or yellow, or when there is a vehicle in the way, or when a bicycle is coming.... As you can see, the exception list can get very long. Instead, write something like this: Cross the road when the light facing you is green and the cross traffic is clear.

Avoiding Common Perl 5 Mistakes

The tips in this section relate directly to Perl 5. They help you avoid common Perl 5 programming mistakes.

String and Numeric Tests

The testing of scalar data is context-based. If you use a string operator, Perl 5 tests the data in string context. New programmers frequently test for equality using the numeric test operator (==) when they should be using the string equality operator (eq). This isn't an error in Perl 5, but it is likely to produce erroneous results. Most Perl 5 operators have numeric and string counterparts. Make sure you use the correct operator for the correct data context.

List and Scalar Context

Perl 5 functions and operators perform different operations when operating in list or scalar context. The file input operator (<>) reads an entire file in list context. The same operator reads only one line in scalar context. An array returns its size when used in scalar context, like this:

```
$size = @array;
```

In list context, an array assignment copies the entire array like this:

```
@arrayCopy = @array;
```

Bare Words

Perl 5, like a natural language, makes a lot of decisions based on context. As explained earlier in the chapter, bare words are character strings that do not begin with $, @, or % characters, or have surrounding quotation marks, like this:

```
@languages = (Perl, C, C++, Fortran, Pascal);
```

Perl 5 must decide whether the bare word is a subroutine call (its first choice), a file handle, a label, or a character string. In previous versions of Perl, the default was to treat the bare word as a quoted string unless context clearly determined an alternative. In Perl 5, the bare word defaults to a subroutine call unless context determines another choice. When Perl 5 finds a bare word in your code that it cannot associate with a subroutine, file handle, or label, Perl 5 will treat the bare word as a double quoted string.

TIP

To avoid conflicts with current and future built-in subroutines, when you name file handles or labels, use only uppercase characters. Perl 5's built-in subroutines and functions are named using lowercase characters.

You should avoid using bare words in your code unless the context is obvious. I like to use bare words in initializing arrays (as shown in the example above), because in those cases the context is obvious.

If you run your code at least once with warnings enabled (using the warning switch, -w, discussed earlier in the chapter), Perl 5 will point out all the bare words in our code. You can then decide if these are errors or features.

Default Variables

Perl 5 provides default choices for many functions and operations. Use the default variables, such as $_ and ARGV, only when it is clear by context and convention that the default variables are being used. The use of the default options can make your code hard to understand, error prone, and difficult to maintain. The defaults for various functions and operators are discussed as each function is introduced throughout this book.

The *my* and *local* Keywords

Use the keyword my to declare your variables. Using the keyword local creates a variable whose scope includes any called subroutines. If you create a variable with the keyword local and then call a subroutine, the subroutine may overwrite the variable or the main routine may overwrite the subroutine's variable, like this:

```
...
local $myTemp = 15;
local $yourTemp = 20
doSomething ();
...
sub doSomething () {
    $yourTemp = True;
    while ($yourTemp){
        $myTemp++;
        if ($myTemp ==10){
            $yourTemp = 0;
        }
    }
}
```

There is absolutely no way to determine what the real intent of this code might have been, but the calling routine has modified the initial value of $myTemp, and the value of $yourTemp was modified in the subroutine. If the declarations in both the calling routine and the subroutine had used my instead of local, the subroutine variables $myTemp and $yourTemp would not have been affected by or would not have interfered with the calling routine's variables.

Global Variables versus Parameters

It seems easier to not pass your variables to your subroutine explicitly. If you don't declare a variable using my, it is global in scope and can be seen by any subroutine you call, as you saw in the example in the previous section.

Using global variables creates code that is hard to modify and has unusual side effects throughout the program. When you call a subroutine, pass the data to the subroutine explicitly, like this:

```
my $myVar=15;
my $yourVar=0;
doSomething($myVar, $yourVar);
...
sub doSomething($$){
   my($myVar, $yourVar)=@_;
...
}
```

Now an action taken in the subroutine affects only the subroutine. Then your subroutine can explicitly return any data it wants to make available to the calling program.

Loop Variable Modification

The foreach statement creates an optional loop variable when processing arrays and lists. The loop variable is a reference to the actual array or list variable. If you modify the loop variable, you are also modifying the actual value. This is a nice feature if you understand it, but it's a big surprise to many programmers who expect the loop variable to be a temporary location.

HANDLING RUNTIME ERRORS

If you try to run your program and Perl tells you your program didn't compile, then you have a syntax error, as discussed earlier in this chapter. When your code runs but produces the wrong results, you have a runtime error. This section focuses on runtime errors, which usually take a little more work to fix than syntax errors.

When you don't have a debugger handy, use print statements or some other type of error message to tell you what went wrong with your code. You'll learn about using debuggers a little later in the chapter. Here, we'll look at some other debugging techniques.

Using the System Error Variable

When you perform any system functions, such as opening a file, a special variable ($!) contains information about any failure conditions. This variable always contains the last system error message, which means you should only check it if the last operation you performed failed.

Perl provides two functions, `die` and `warn`, that work hand in hand with the system error message variable (`$!`). Both the `die` and the `warn` functions will print the filename and line number in the file where the error occurred or the contents of the specified print list (any data that you want printed when your program stops).

The `die` function causes your program to stop executing, or die. The syntax of the `die` function to output the filename and line number is:

```
die print_list;
```

To output only the contents of `print_list`, include a newline character (\ n) at the end of `print_list`, like this:

```
die print_list\ n;
```

The following form uses the `die` function with the system error message variable to output the filename and line number:

```
die "$!";
```

In some cases, you want your program to continue executing but still need an error message printed to the screen. In those cases, use the `warn` function, which has the same syntax as the `die` function.

```
warn print_list;
```

I like to use a combination of the system error message variable and the `die` or `warn` function whenever I call a system function. Listing 10.2 (a program named (errorMessage.pl) demonstrates how to use these functions with system calls, and Figure 10.4 shows the output.

Listing 10.2: The System Error Message

```
1.  #!/usr/local/bin/perl
2.  open (FH,"<t.t") || warn "$!\ n";
3.  open (FH,"<t.t") || warn "$!";
4.  print "after warn\ n";
5.  open (FH,"<t.t") || die "$!";
6.  print "after die";
```

Though Listing 10.2 is a very contrived example, it illustrates the easiest mechanism for calling `die` or `warn`. The OR operator (||) after the open call activates the `die` or `warn` function only if the return value from the open function is false.

Line 1 of Listing 10.2 illustrates the use of the `warn` function with a newline character in the print list. As you can see in Figure 10.4, the first error message does not include any file information. Line 5 of Listing 10.2 illustrates the result of the die function. Line 5 never executes because the die function stops execution of the errorMessage.pl program.

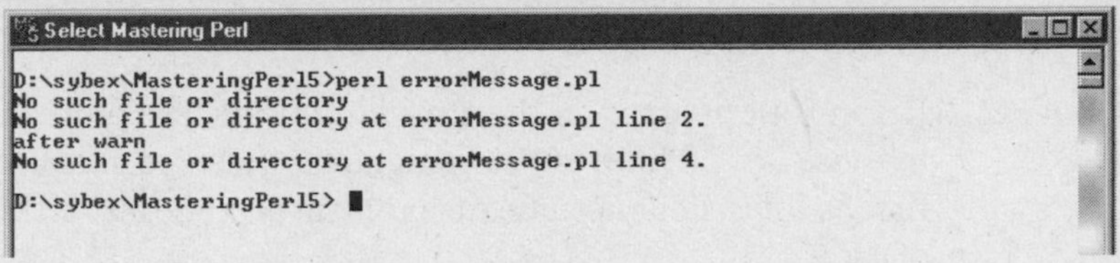

```
 Select Mastering Perl                                               _ □ ×

D:\sybex\MasteringPerl5>perl errorMessage.pl
No such file or directory
No such file or directory at errorMessage.pl line 2.
after warn
No such file or directory at errorMessage.pl line 4.

D:\sybex\MasteringPerl5> ▮
```

FIGURE 10.4: Using the system error message variable

Inserting *print* Statements

One of the most common methods of debugging a program is to insert print statements throughout the program. The print statement can be a simple statement identifying that you reached a particular location in your code. More frequently, however, the print statement includes some variable names that tell you the current state of your program.

I used to insert print statements and then remove them. Then I would need to rewrite the dadgum things all over again the next time a new bug appeared. There is an easier way. Every time you add a debug print statement, use an if $DEBUG clause, like this:

```
print "some Debug Info \ n" if $DEBUG;
```

You must initialize the $DEBUG variable at the front of your program, like this:

```
$DEBUG=1 if $ARGV[0]=~/-D(ebug)?/i;
```

This statement will set the variable $DEBUG to 1 only if the first argument from the command line is –d (uppercase or lowercase), followed by an optional ebug. Now when you need to debug your code, you can add print statements and leave them in your code. The only time they will execute is when you add a -Debug argument after your program name, like this:

```
perl errorMessage.pl –d
```

Searching for Bugs

When you have a large program with a runtime error, just finding where the bug is can be a real pain. When trying to locate bugs in a large program, I use a method called *binary search*. The binary search method

Part iii

looks in only one half of the code at one time. For example, here are the steps for using this method with a 100-line program:

1. Copy the last 50 lines to a temporary file and then delete them from your program. (You may need to leave in closing braces or other required statements.)

2. Rerun your program. If the error disappears, the problem is in those last 50 lines of your program; otherwise, it is in the first 50 lines. Let's assume the problem is in the last 50 lines of code.

3. Take the half of the code with the error in it and return it to the main program. Now your main program has lines 1 through 75 and your temporary program has lines 76 through 100.

4. Rerun your program. If the error is still missing, you now know the error is in the last 25 lines.

5. Add one half of the last 25 lines back in and rerun your program. If the error shows up, you know the problem is between lines 76 and 87.

6. Repeat this process until you have identified the exact line that contains the error. You can find the error because you have a much smaller area in which to look.

The ultimate way to find bugs is with a debugger. In the next section, you'll learn about the Perl 5 debugger and a commercial Windows-based debugger.

USING A DEBUGGER

A *debugger* is a tool that allows you to execute your code one or more lines at a time. Every debugger should allow you to view variables and set breakpoints, which stop execution of your code at predetermined locations. Perl 5 comes delivered with a free debugger, which performs these basic functions and more. Here, we'll look at the Perl 5 debugger, including how to use it with the Emacs editor in an interactive window. Then I'll tell you about the ActiveState Windows debugger, which I use to debug my code.

Running the Perl Debugger

The Perl debugger is available with all Perl 5 distributions at no charge. To start the Perl 5 debugger, you must be at the command prompt. From the command prompt, enter:

```
perl-d filename.pl
```

NOTE

The examples shown in this section use the DOS command window, but these commands also work from the Unix command shell.

The debugger will be invoked on the file regardless of the filename extension (it doesn't need to be .PL). If your program has syntax errors, Perl will exit with an error message (remember that Perl 5 first compiles your program before running it). You will need to use one of the debugging techniques discussed earlier in this chapter to fix the syntax error before starting the debugger.

If your program is syntactically correct, you will see a beginning debugger screen, which should look like the one shown in Figure 10.5. You can see the debug prompt, DB<1>, on the last line of the opening window.

NOTE

Notice in Figure 10.5 that the debugger says "Emacs support available." Many of the commands you will learn here work both from your Emacs editor and the command line. In the next section, I'll explain how to run an interactive Emacs debugging session.

Part iii

```
Mastering Perl - perl -d slices.pl                                    _ □ ×

D:\sybex\MasteringPerl5>perl -d slices.pl

Loading DB routines from perl5db.pl version 1.0401
Emacs support available.

Enter h or 'h h' for help.

main::(slices.pl:1):     @digits = (11..21);
  DB<1>
```

FIGURE 10.5: The Perl 5 debugger window

Getting Help

The second line printed by the Perl debugger tells you how to get help. Because your DOS command window on a Windows 95/98 computer may not have a scroll bar, the first thing you need to be aware of is how to get help on help. If you type in h at the debug prompt, all the help information will rapidly scroll off the screen. To get an abbreviated list of the debugging commands, type in **h h** at the debug prompt. Figure 10.6 shows an example of what you will see.

The help function from the DOS command window provides further help on additional commands. To get help on a particular command, type **h** *command* (where *command* is a help command) at the debug prompt. If you type **h 0**, you get a screen full of information on the various debugger options. Other requests for help just repeat a one-line help statement, which is the same information as shown in Figure 10.6.

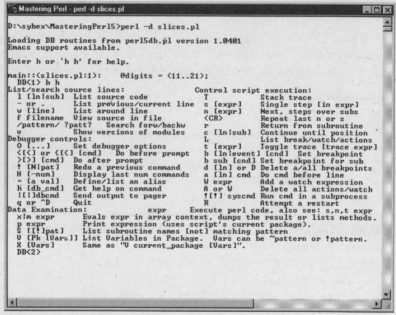

FIGURE 10.6: The Perl 5 debugger's help information

Displaying Source Code

If you're not looking at the help messages, then you probably want to look at your code. The two commands I most frequently use to view my source code in the Perl debugger are list (1) and window (w). These two commands tell the debugger to show you your source code.

As shown in Figure 10.7, you can type 1 from the debug prompt to list the next 10 lines of your program. Each time you enter 1, the next 10 lines of your source code are printed. The 1 command starts displaying from the last displayed line. For example, if line 50 were the last displayed line and you entered 1, lines 51 through 60 would be displayed.

```
Mastering Perl - perl -d slices.pl                                    _ □ ×
D:\sybex\MasteringPerl5>perl -d slices.pl

Loading DB routines from perl5db.pl version 1.0401
Emacs support available.

Enter h or `h h' for help.

main::(slices.pl:1):    @digits = (11..21);
  DB<1> 1
1==>      @digits = (11..21);
2:        @slice[10..20] = (@digits);
3:        printLine();
4:        print "The contents of the array are: @slice\n";
5:        print "The last index of the array is $#slice.\n";
6:        printLine();
7
8:        @09 = (0..9);
9:        @slice[@09] = (@digits);
10:       print "The contents of the array are: @slice\n";
  DB<1> 1
11:       print "The last index of the array is $#slice.\n";
12:       printLine();
13
14:       @slice[1,3,5,7,9] = (2,4,6,8,10);
15:       @evenNumbers = @slice[1,3,5,7,9];
16:       print "The contents of the array are: @evenNumbers\n";
17:       print "The last index of the array is $#evenNumbers.\n";
18:       printLine();
19
20:       @slice[@digits,77,55,33] = (666,241,42,43,44,45,56,66,67,65,66,67,76,77,
  DB<1>
```

FIGURE 10.7: Listing your source code

The 1 command has the following options:

▶ To display a particular line, enter 1 *lineNumber*, like this: 1 8. This command displays only the requested line.

▶ To display a range of lines, use the 1 command with a starting and ending line number. For example, to see lines 21 through 42, enter 1 21-42. Alternatively, you could enter the starting line number, a plus sign, and then the number of additional lines you would like. For example, to see line 15 and the following 20 lines, enter 1 15+20.

▶ To list the contents of a subroutine, type l followed by the sub-routine name: l *subName*.

When I'm debugging, I usually like to see a few lines surrounding the current line. The w command shows a few lines before the current line and a few lines after the current line. The w command also can be used with a line number to show the lines surrounding a particular location. Figure 10.8 shows an example of each of these forms of the command.

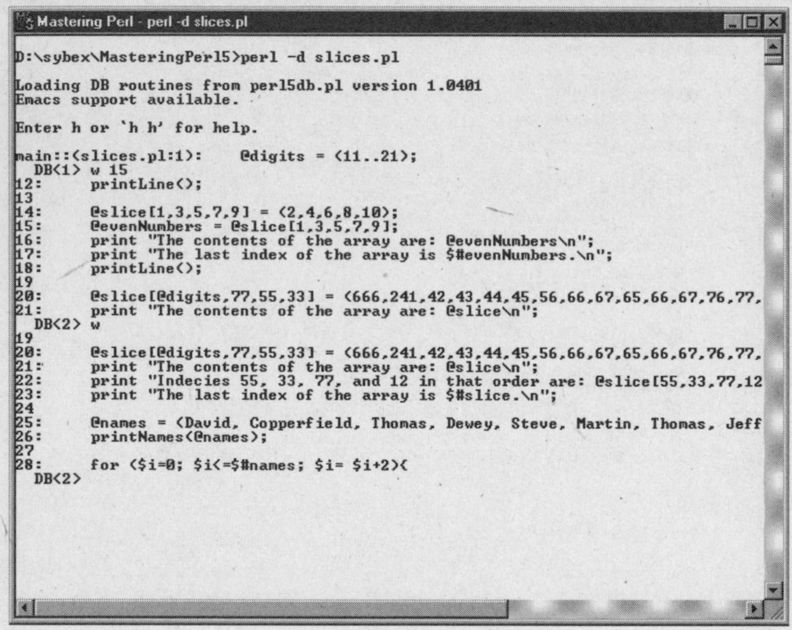

```
Mastering Perl - perl -d slices.pl                              _ □ X

D:\sybex\MasteringPerl5>perl -d slices.pl

Loading DB routines from perl5db.pl version 1.0401
Emacs support available.

Enter h or 'h h' for help.

main::(slices.pl:1):    @digits = (11..21);
  DB<1> w 15
12:     printLine();
13
14:     @slice[1,3,5,7,9] = (2,4,6,8,10);
15:     @evenNumbers = @slice[1,3,5,7,9];
16:     print "The contents of the array are: @evenNumbers\n";
17:     print "The last index of the array is $#evenNumbers.\n";
18:     printLine();
19
20:     @slice[@digits,77,55,33] = (666,241,42,43,44,45,56,66,67,65,66,67,76,77,
21:     print "The contents of the array are: @slice\n";
  DB<2> w
19
20:     @slice[@digits,77,55,33] = (666,241,42,43,44,45,56,66,67,65,66,67,76,77,
21:     print "The contents of the array are: @slice\n";
22:     print "Indecies 55, 33, 77, and 12 in that order are: @slice[55,33,77,12
23:     print "The last index of the array is $#slice.\n";
24
25:     @names = (David, Copperfield, Thomas, Dewey, Steve, Martin, Thomas, Jeff
26:     printNames(@names);
27
28:     for ($i=0; $i<=$#names; $i= $i+2){
  DB<2>
```

FIGURE 10.8: Using the window (w) command

Executing Your Code

The purpose of a debugger is to give you control over the execution of your program. The following are the primary commands for executing your code one or a few lines at a time:

▶ To execute one line of code at a time, use the step (s) command. To execute the next statement in your program, at the debug prompt, type **s** and then press Enter. Then you can just press Enter again to continue stepping through your code. The step command shows you the sequential execution of your code. If your code calls a subroutine, you will step into that subroutine, which you can continue to execute one statement at a time.

▶ To execute the next line of code, stepping over any subroutine calls, use the next (n) command. When you are stepping through your code, you frequently know whether a subroutine works or not. If you want to sequentially execute your code but do not want to enter a subroutine, use the next command.

▶ To execute until the next program interrupt, use the continue (c) command. The continue command tells the debugger to execute your code until it finds a breakpoint. Your code will execute to completion unless you have set breakpoints to interrupt your program. Setting breakpoints is described in the next section.

▶ To execute the remaining statements in the current subroutine, use the return (r) command. If you have stepped into a subroutine to view some specific information, but you don't need to step through each line in the subroutine, use the return command. The return command completes the execution of the subroutine and stops execution of your program on the first Perl 5 statement after the subroutine call.

Setting Breakpoints

Executing your code one line at a time gets old very fast. When your code is several hundred lines long, you need to be able to skip the pieces of your program that you've already tested. The breakpoint (b) command allows you to tell the debugger to execute your program until it reaches a particular line number, subroutine, or loading of an external file.

To set a breakpoint at a particular line, enter b *lineNumber*, like this: b 8. To execute until you reach that line, just type c at the debugger prompt. Your program will execute up to but not including the breakpoint line.

Conditional breakpoints stop execution of your program only when a specific condition is met. The syntax of conditional breakpoints is like this:

```
B lineNumber condition
```

The condition may be any expression. The breakpoint will stop execution of your program only if the condition evaluates to true. Figure 10.9 shows an example of a breakpoint set on line 8 with this conditional statement:

```
($slice[10] == 11)
```

This means to stop execution of the program when the tenth element of the slice array is equal to 11. The breakpoint is set in the middle of Figure 10.9 and looks like this:

```
b 8 $slice[10]==11
```

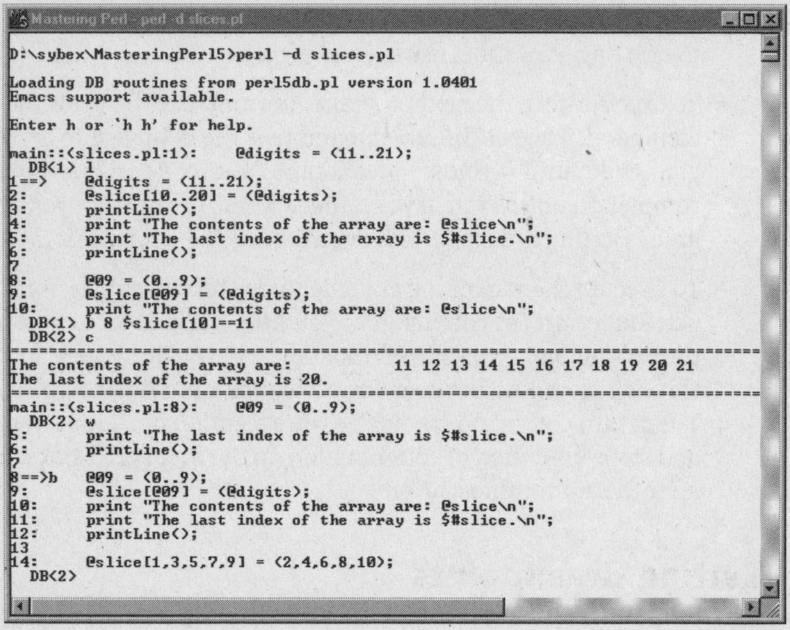

FIGURE 10.9: Setting a conditional breakpoint

To show all the breakpoints you have active in your debugging session, type **L**. To delete all your breakpoints, type **D**. To delete an individual breakpoint, type **d** followed by the line number of the breakpoint, like this: d 8.

I like to include external program files into my code using the require command (the require command includes subroutines into a program from other files on the hard disk). Frequently, I need to set breakpoints in these required files. You cannot set a breakpoint in a required file unless you are currently executing in the required file. The easiest way to stop your code at a required file is with the breakpoint on load command, like this:

```
b load filename
```

For example, if the required filename is `readPostInput.cgi`, the breakpoint on load command looks like this:

```
b load readPostInput.cgi
```

The breakpoint command also accepts a subroutine name as a breakpoint value. When you use the breakpoint command with a subroutine name, your program will stop on the first executable line of the subroutine. Breakpoints on subroutine names may also be conditional, like this:

```
b readPostInput $DEBUG == 1
```

This conditional breakpoint will stop here only if the variable $DEBUG is equal to 1.

Viewing Program Data

Once you've stopped your program using the step or breakpoint commands, you need to be able to look at your program's data to determine what is wrong with your code. The print (p) command prints the contents of a variable or expression. The syntax of the p command is like this:

```
p expression
```

For example, if you want to print the contents of an array, enter the command like this:

```
p @arrayName
```

Figure 10.10 (on the next page) shows several examples of printing the contents of an array. Notice the command with quotation marks around the array name:

```
p "@slice"
```

This form inserts a space character between each array cell.

Quitting the Debugger

You will find your debugging sessions are interactive with your programming sessions. Your programming development cycle will begin to look like this: Build a little, test a little, debug a little, fix a little, build a little.... Quite often, the test-a-little, debug-a-little, and fix-a-little cycles take a lot more time than the build a little portion.

Once you have located your coding error in the debugger, there is usually no reason to continue running your program. You exit the debugger by entering the quit (q) command.

```
Select Mastering Perl - perl -d slices.pl                    _ □ ×

D:\sybex\MasteringPerl5>perl -d slices.pl

Loading DB routines from perl5db.pl version 1.0401
Emacs support available.

Enter h or `h h' for help.

main::(slices.pl:1):     @digits = (11..21);
  DB<1> b 10
  DB<2> c
================================================================
The contents of the array are:    11 12 13 14 15 16 17 18 19 20 21
The last index of the array is 20.
================================================================
main::(slices.pl:10):    print "The contents of the array are: @slice\n";
  DB<2> w
7
8:        @09 = (0..9);
9:        @slice[@09] = (@digits);
10==>b    print "The contents of the array are: @slice\n";
11:       print "The last index of the array is $#slice.\n";
12:       printLine();
13
14:       @slice[1,3,5,7,9] = (2,4,6,8,10);
15:       @evenNumbers = @slice[1,3,5,7,9];
16:       print "The contents of the array are: @evenNumbers\n";
  DB<2> p @slice
1112131415161718192011121314151617181920 21
  DB<3> p "@slice"
11 12 13 14 15 16 17 18 19 20 11 12 13 14 15 16 17 18 19 20 21
  DB<4> p $slice[10]
11
  DB<5> p $digits[0]
11
  DB<6> p $digits[20]

  DB<7> █
```

FIGURE 10.10: Printing the contents of arrays

Once you exit the debugger, you will most likely open your favorite editor and modify your program based on the information gathered during your debugging session. After you have made your changes, test your code to see if you have really fixed the error.

As you get more experienced with programming and debugging, you should explore the debug commands in more detail. The commands you have learned here are the basic ones that you will use with almost every debugging session.

Debugging Using Emacs

With the basic Perl debugger, you must continually list the lines of your program. Using either the Unix or Windows Emacs editor (described in Chapter 9), you can invoke the Perl debugger in an interactive window interface.

To begin debugging a program within the Emacs editor, first start an Emacs session and then enter the Emacs command window by typing *meta* x. On most computers, *meta* is the Escape key (the only way to be sure you have the correct key is experimenting from your keyboard).

Once you are in the command window, type **perldb** and press Enter. You will be prompted for the program you want to debug, as shown in the last line of Figure 10.11.

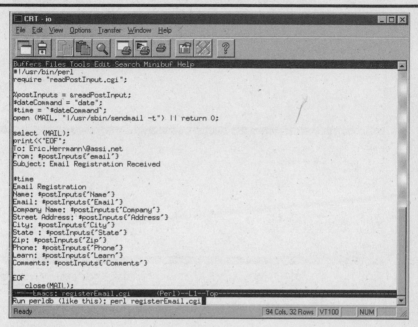

```
#!/usr/bin/perl
require "readPostInput.cgi";

%postInputs = &readPostInput;
$dateCommand = "date";
$time = `$dateCommand`;
open (MAIL, "|/usr/sbin/sendmail -t") || return 0;

select (MAIL);
print<<"EOF";
To: Eric.Herrmann\@assi.net
From: $postInputs{'email'}
Subject: Email Registration Received

$time
Email Registration
Name: $postInputs{'Name'}
Email: $postInputs{'Email'}
Company Name: $postInputs{'Company'}
Street Address: $postInputs{'Address'}
City: $postInputs{'City'}
State : $postInputs{'State'}
Zip: $postInputs{'Zip'}
Phone: $postInputs{'Phone'}
Learn: $postInputs{'Learn'}
Comments: $postInputs{'Comments'}

EOF
    close(MAIL);
```
`----Emacs: registerEmail.cgi     (Perl)--L1--Top----`
`Run perldb (like this): perl registerEmail.cgi`

FIGURE 10.11: Starting an Emacs debugging session

NOTE

Figures 10.11 and 10.12 show an interactive Emacs debugging session run on a Unix computer. The Emacs commands shown for Unix also will work for Windows computers.

Once you tell Emacs which program you wish to debug, you will be presented with a split-window interface, as shown in Figure 10.12. In the top window, you can enter any valid debugging command. In the bottom window, the next line to execute is identified by a right arrow in the left column. The Emacs editor allows you to switch between these two windows. You can enter debugging commands in the top window and switch to the bottom window when you want to scroll through your program. If you change the contents of the bottom window, you are changing the contents of the actual file.

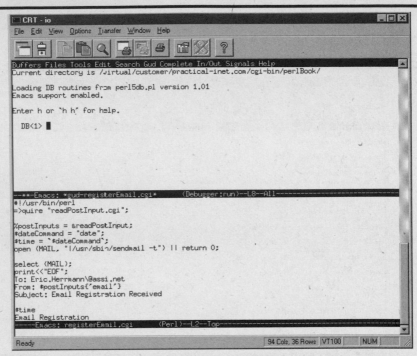

FIGURE 10.12: The split-window Emacs debugging interface

Running the ActiveState Windows Debugger

The Perl debugger has everything you need in a debugger, but it lacks a little in ease of use. Because I spend a good portion of my day writing and debugging code, I use the ActiveState debugger, shown in Figure 10.13. Like the Multi-Edit editor (discussed in Chapter 9), this tool is not free, but it is well worth the cost. This debugger enhances the built-in Perl debugger with an intuitive and easy-to-use interface.

TIP

The ActiveState debugger is available at www.activestate.com. You can run an evaluation copy on your computer at no cost. Instructions for integrating the ActiveState debugger with the Multi-Edit editor are available at the ActiveState Web site.

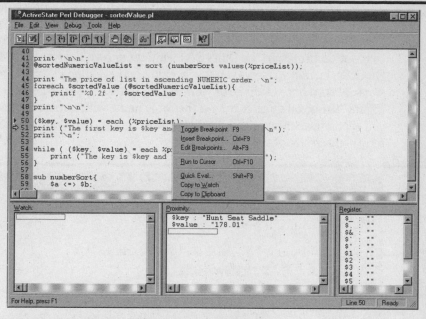

FIGURE 10.13: The ActiveState Windows debugger

The toolbar buttons and menus across the top of the window allow you to manage your debugging session. From left to right, the buttons perform the following operations: continue, quit, show the next statement, step, step over, step out of, run to cursor, insert breakpoint, and delete all breakpoints. As you can see, these operations are similar to (if not the same as) the free Perl 5 debugger operations.

The right three buttons on the top toolbar (excluding the help button) activate the bottom three windows of the ActiveState debugger:

▶ The Watch window shows the values of variables you have explicitly requested.

▶ The Proximity window shows the values of scalar variables surrounding the current execution point of your program. (The current execution point is also called the instruction pointer location.)

▶ The Registry window shows the contents of the Perl 5 special variables that are relevant to the current instruction pointer.

If you right-click with your mouse, you bring up the pop-up menu also shown in Figure 10.13. (This pop-up menu is the interface I most frequently use.) One of the options on this menu is QuickEval. Selecting that option brings up the QuickEval window, shown in Figure 10.14. The QuickEval window allows you to view data and evaluate Perl 5 expressions. Note that to evaluate or view the contents of an array, as shown in Figure 10.14, you must surround the array name with quotation marks. If you evaluate an array without surrounding quotation marks, you are returned the size of the array.

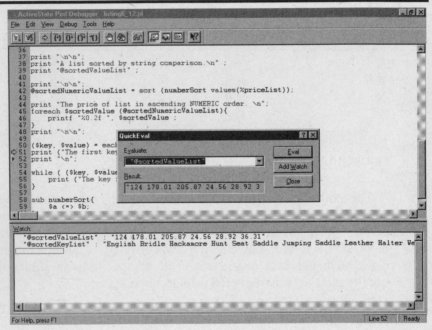

FIGURE 10.14: Evaluating data

Figure 10.14 also shows the Watch window fully expanded at the bottom of the screen. You can add variables to the Watch window through the QuickEval window. Once a variable is added to the Watch window, its current value is displayed throughout your program's execution.

Here, you've learned about just a few of the main features of the ActiveState debugger. The user interface is intuitive, and as you work with it, you will learn about the other capabilities of this debugger.

DEBUGGING CGI PROGRAMS

Debugging CGI programs usually involves creative use of `print` statements. Here are the three basic steps for the CGI programmer:

- ▶ Make sure your code is syntactically correct.

- ▶ Test your code with sample data.

- ▶ Print the data sent to your CGI program using a debugging interface subroutine.

First, make sure that your CGI program compiles without syntax errors before you begin debugging it through your web server. If you are running the program on a Unix computer, make sure that the file permissions are set to 755. Then test the program by running it from the command line.

After you know that your program does not have any syntax errors, you can move on to the next steps. The following sections explain the techniques that I use to debug my CGI programs and include some examples.

Running the Program with Test Data

If the program is free of syntax errors, I run it with special test data. This step is critical because most CGI programs require external data sent via a web page. If this method does not solve the problem, then I modify my CGI program to show the data it is receiving and add `print` statements as necessary, as described in the next section.

To test my CGI program, I first create a file of debug information. This file should contain data already in the format your CGI program expects. The file shown in Listing 10.3 is a debug data file I used to debug an online reservation program. The debug file is then included in your CGI program using the `require` command, an example of which follows the listing.

Listing 10.3: Debug Data

```
%lodgingInfo = (
'ARRIVAL_DATE' => "10/6/98",
'ROOM_PREFERRENCE' => "Red River",
'LENGTH_OF_STAY' => 4,
'PAYMENT_METHOD' => "Credit Card",
```

Part III

```
'NAME' => "Eric C. Herrmann",
'ADDRESS' => "255 S. Canyonwood Dr.",
'CITY' => "Austin",
'STATE' => "Texas",
'ZIP' => "78620",
'TELEPHONE' => "512-442-2991",
'EMAIL' => "yawp\ @io.com",
'OCCASION' => "20th Wedding Anniversary",
'SPECIAL_REQUEST' => "It would be really nice if you would
➡do something very nice and let us take the raft down
➡the creek",
'NUMBER_IN_PARTY' => 2,
'UID' => 62878766310,
'PAYMENT_METHOD' => "onLine",
) ;
$ENV{ 'QUERY_STRING'} ="UID=  14fa7198.49.249.718";
return 1;
```

When I want to test a CGI program I insert a line like this:

```
require "debugConstants.cgi" if $DEBUG:
```

Notice that the last line of Listing 10.3 returns a 1. If the last line of a required file does not return a true value, your program will fail.

This mechanism of testing a CGI program allows you to load and run your program from the command line using your favorite debugger interface.

Adding *print* Statements

If I need to do further debugging of my CGI program, my next step is to modify the program to show the data it is receiving and add print statements as necessary. The first thing I modify the program to do is print the HTTP response header Content-Type: text/html. I also modify the program so that it performs this special debug function only when I send it a unique input variable.

As an example, I modified Listing 9.4 of Chapter 9, modifying line 3 to run the printDebug subroutine when the input form sends the user's name as Debug, as shown in Listing 10.4.

NOTE

The subroutine printDebug may be inserted at any reasonable place into your code. I usually put my subroutines at the end of the file, as shown here.

Listing 10.4: Debugging CGI Programs

```perl
1. #!/usr/bin/perl
2.
# REPLACE LINE 3:
# 3. %postInputs = readPostInput();
# WITH THIS LINE:
3. printDebug() if $postInputs{ 'Contact_FullName'}
➥ =~ /Debug/i;
4. $dateCommand = "date";
5. $time = `$dateCommand`;
6. open (MAIL, "|/usr/sbin/sendmail -t") || return 0;
7.
8. select (MAIL);
9. print<<"EOF";
# ...lines omitted for space purposes

sub printDebug(){
    print "Content-type: text/html\ n\ n";

    foreach $key (sort keys %postInputs){
      print qq|$key ==> $postInputs{ "$key"}  <br>|;
    }
    exit(1);
}
```

As shown in Figure 10.15, this allows you to see your incoming CGI data. If you need to see other data in the program, insert print statements as required.

I recommend that you always print your input CGI data as your first online CGI debugging step. The input data is the most likely source of errors. Notice that the subroutine printDebug in Listing 10.4 calls the exit function after printing the input data. This prevents the remaining portion of the CGI program from running. You should comment out the exit statement if you need other parts of your CGI program to execute after you call the printDebug subroutine.

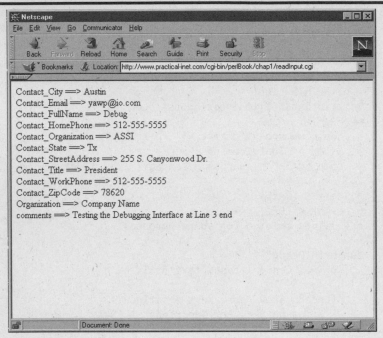

FIGURE 10.15: Viewing incoming CGI POST data

Summary

The goal of this chapter is to reduce your frustration as you work through the details of learning Perl 5. Each section is designed to teach you how to deal with the common coding problems you will encounter as you learn Perl 5. If you code, you will debug.

The first types of errors you will encounter are likely to be syntax related. In the section on syntax and error messages, you learned how to separate erroneous error messages from error messages that help you find your bug. The most common error messages were explained in this section.

Of course, it would be nice if you could prevent errors before they occur. In the section on avoiding errors, you learned about programming techniques that help you prevent bugs before they become a problem. These techniques include good programming practices such as commenting and indenting your code and using meaningful variable names. The section on avoiding errors also included how to avoid common logic errors such as boundary conditions and negative logic.

You also learned about the most common Perl 5 mistakes, such as using numeric instead of string conditional logic. Once you become familiar with the language, you may be tempted to use bare words and default variables. When to use these features and when to avoid them were also discussed in the section. Perl 5 allows the programmer wide latitude in variable declaration and use. This section included a discussion of the misuse of global variables and when to use the keyword my.

Even the best programmer writes code that includes errors. In the section on debugging techniques, you learned that the system error message can be used to help locate an error. This section also explained how to apply a binary search to quickly isolate a difficult bug in a large program.

Every good language has a good debugger. You learned about using the built-in Perl debugger, the Emacs interactive window interface, and a Windows-based debugger.

Finally, this chapter included three basic techniques for debugging CGI programs. First, make sure your code is syntactically correct. Next, test your code with sample data. Finally, print the data sent to your CGI program using a debugging interface subroutine.

If you've never coded with Perl before, you're now prepared to enter the Perl 5 programming world. These last couple of chapters were designed to give you the foundation you need to work though the remainder of the Perl chapters with confidence.

Part iii

CHAPTER 11

USING PERL AND CGI IN THE REAL WORLD

You are fairly well grounded by now in the processes that allow CGI to work with the World Wide Web. You can create a Perl program that draws its own Web page. You are also familiar with the methods used in CGI to pass information between the Web server and a CGI program.

Adapted from *Perl CGI Programming: No experience required*, by Erik Strom

ISBN 0-7821-2157-8   447 pages $29.99

But we haven't done anything really *useful* yet. In this chapter, you'll dive right in, take what you've learned thus far, and put it to work by creating an access counter for your Web site.

THE TASK: COUNTING YOUR VISITORS

A popular feature among Webmasters is a simple *access counter* that keeps track of every visit to the Web site and puts up a little message at the bottom of the home page that displays for the user what number visitor they are, such as: "You are visitor No. 10,001!" See Figure 11.1 for an example of an access counter display.

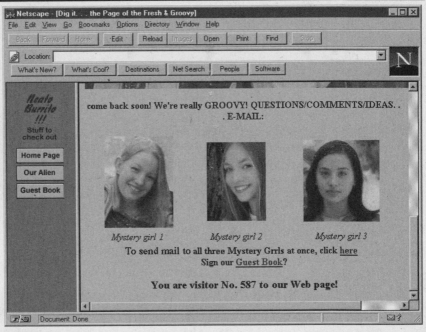

FIGURE 11.1: An example of one of the many access counters on the Web

Such a little thing should be fairly easy to lash together, shouldn't it? Well, yes and no. It is a straightforward task, but it can't be accomplished with HTML alone. You need the power of Perl in the background to do the work for you.

How to Go About It?

Creating an access counter is a programming problem—a system problem—and the best way to go about solving it is to first get up and walk away from your computer. That's right; turn the thing off if you need to. You'll be designing a system, a small and simple one, but a system nevertheless. The computer and the code are the *last* steps in the process of analyzing, designing, and implementing the solution to a problem.

NOTE

In technospeak, a "system" really is nothing but the solution to a problem: It's the analysis, design, and implementation of a tool or set of tools that will do the "thing" you want to do. The "thing" might be as monumental as keeping track of the daily transactions in a stock exchange, or it might be as simple as keeping track of a Web site's visitors. No matter. The beginning steps are the same regardless of the complexity of the ultimate solution.

Think, Don't Code!

Many programmers, especially beginners, just jump right in and start coding, and refine the bugs as they go along.

The problem with this approach is that it ties you inexorably to the computer and the programming tools you have at your disposal. As a result, you will end up with a solution that is entirely dependent on these tools.

It is more logical to approach a problem from a more general perspective. You have something you want to do, so how do you go about it? What, in general, do you need to do to implement a solution? We can distill this "thinking" phase down to three categories:

- ▶ Analysis
- ▶ Design
- ▶ Implementation

Once you have mapped out the steps, you must take to solve the problem, once you have identified a general approach to a solution, *then* you can rummage through your kit of available tools and identify the ones you'll need to solve the problem with what you have at hand.

So, to begin, find a nice, comfortable chair in a dimly lit corner of the den, take a pad and pencil with you, and begin sketching. You need to *think*, not code.

Analysis

The first step in your "sketching" process is analysis. To effectively accomplish your task (or solve your problem) you need to properly identify what needs to be done. For example (as in Figure 11.2), to count the hits on a Web page you need to:

- ▶ Store a number somewhere
- ▶ Be able to read the number
- ▶ Be able to increment it (add 1)
- ▶ Write it out to the Web page
- ▶ Store the number again

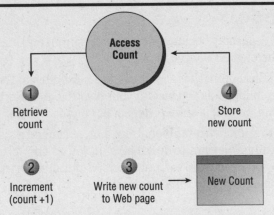

FIGURE 11.2: The requirements of an access counter

Design

Once you have analyzed your problem, you need to start thinking about design. For instance, the number your access counter derives has to be stored in a "permanent" place, where you can get to it any time you need to, change it, and store it again. A file on disk is a logical candidate, because data will stay in files even when your computer is turned off, barring some catastrophe. A disk file is the first choice of most programmers for storing data gathered by a program because it's easy and relatively safe. So decide to store the number in a file.

Having made that decision, we can flesh out the list of requirements from the analysis of the problem. The design of your solution, which is illustrated in Figure 11.3, can proceed step by step:

1. If this is the first time the program runs, create a file, and store the value 1 in it. Proceed to Step 3.

2. Otherwise, open and read the file. Add 1 to the value you have read.

3. Display the new value on the Web page.

4. Write the new value to the file.

5. Close the file.

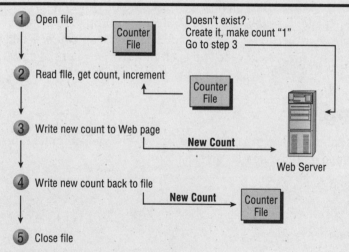

FIGURE 11.3: Opening, reading, writing, and closing the counter file

Implementation

You will implement your solution using Perl, of course, and HTML. However, the requirements of the Web page access counter highlight one concept you haven't covered yet: files.

How Perl Deals with Files

You have analyzed and designed a solution for the task of putting an access counter on your Web page. But the implementation step, according to the design, needs a method to store the counter in a disk file.

A disk is nothing more than a magnetic platter, very similar to a recording tape, that is capable of storing data. The low-level details of how that is accomplished aren't particularly relevant to a discussion of files.

What *is* relevant is the idea that a file is nothing more than a collection of characters. They may not be characters in forms or combinations that are meaningful to humans, as in the case of a program file. But the characters are stored (recorded) in their original sequence on the disk, and that's how you deal with them.

The concept of a "file" on disk was intended originally to make an analogy to paper files in a cabinet full of folders, though the "folder" concept is only now becoming widespread in computer software. When you want to read a file, you have to "open" it first. When you're done with it, you have to "close" it.

Files in Perl

The file-cabinet analogy carries neatly into Perl. The Perl functions that allow you to manipulate files are:

- ▶ open
- ▶ close
- ▶ read
- ▶ print
- ▶ write

It's always best to learn by doing, so rather than wading into a lengthy discussion of these file functions, why don't you write a program to handle the rudimentary requirements of the access counter? Enter the following code, which we will analyze shortly:

```
#!/perl/bin/perl

# access.pl
#
```

```
# First version.  Creates or opens a file with a number
# in it, increments the number, writes it back.
    $CountFile = "counter.dat";    # Name of counter file.

# Open the file and read it.  If it doesn't exist, its
# "contents" will be read into a program variable as "0".

    open (COUNT, $CountFile);
    $Counter = <COUNT>;                # Read the contents.

# Close the file, then reopen it for output.

    close (COUNT);
    open (COUNT, ">$CountFile");

# Increment $Counter, then write it back out.  Put up a
# message with the new value.  Close the file and exit.

    $Counter += 1;
    print COUNT $Counter;
    print "$CountFile has been written to $Counter times.\n";
    close (COUNT);

#                        End access.pl
```

Save this sample code as access.pl and run it a few times from the command line. Figure 11.4 illustrates what you should see.

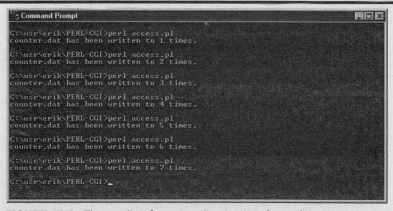

FIGURE 11.4: The results of running the simplest form of the access counter

Opening, Closing, and Writing Files

When you ran `access.pl`, you probably noticed that it uses only two of the new Perl functions listed above: `open` and `close`. They really are all you need to do simple file manipulation.

And, as usual when using new Perl stuff, you saw some strange and unfamiliar operators. Let's dissect this program so you can see what you've done.

The first program line sets a program variable:

```
$CountFile = "counter.dat";    # Name of counter file.
```

The file's name is `counter.dat`. Of course, you can call it anything you want, within the file-naming rules of your operating system. Whatever you do, it is best to do it here, at the top of the program, and *put it in a variable.* You could have referred to `counter.dat` throughout the program, but what if you decided to change it? By putting the name in a variable, you've ensured that it only has to be changed once. Laziness and impatience win the day again!

File Handles

The next two code lines in `access.pl` open the file and read whatever is in it.

```
open (COUNT, $CountFile);
$Counter = <COUNT>;                # Read the contents.
```

The arguments to open take this form

```
open (HANDLE, Expression);
```

where `Expression` usually is a file name or some variable that contains one. But what is this `HANDLE`?

When you open a file, you actually are instructing Perl to perform a rather complex series of steps. Information about the file is stored in the computer's memory, where you can deal with it if you want, and the processes that allow you to read from it and write to it are initialized. Perl then needs a handy way to refer to the file, so it sets up a *handle*, which you can treat as a variable name for the file. Until the file is closed and the handle is put back into circulation, you will perform *all* of your file operations on this handle.

TIP

MS-DOS and Windows mavens may recall an instruction in their `config.sys` files that goes `files=40` or some other number. Technically, the number refers to the maximum file handles that the operating system can have opened at any one time.

The next line of the program shows the handle in action, and it also shows a useful shortcut.

```
$Counter = <COUNT>;               # Read the contents.
```

You can read directly from a file handle by putting brackets (< >) around it, as you did with <COUNT>. Because you can be reasonably certain that `counter.dat` contains either one number or nothing, you can simply set the value of the `$Counter` variable to whatever you read from the file.

But what about the first time the program is run, when `counter.dat` doesn't even exist yet? When you open a nonexistent file name for reading, Perl returns a NULL handle. So, setting a scalar variable to the handle's contents would effectively set the variable to 0.

Input, Output

The next two lines in `access.pl` are liable to be a little confusing to beginners.

```
close (COUNT);
open (COUNT, ">$CountFile");
```

Why do we `close` the file and then instantly re-open it? And why is `$CountFile` in quotes this time with a > character in front of it?

The > operator is the difference between *input* and *output* on a file in Perl. You might remember the > and < symbols as the operators for *redirection* of input and output in MS-DOS. These conventions actually were borrowed from UNIX, so it's no wonder they're used in Perl.

When you put the greater-than sign in front of the file name parameter to open, the file is opened for output, or writing, and it will create the file, if it doesn't exist, or overwrite anything that is in the file. The less-than sign opens the file for input to the program, or reading, but this is so common that Perl regards it as the default if you leave it off. The append symbol (>>) will append anything you write to the file to what already is in the file.

Part iii

You put quotes around the file name variable $CountFile to avoid confusing the Perl interpreter between the output redirection symbol and the $ to indicate a scalar variable.

TIP

Try leaving the quotes out of ">$CountFile" and see what happens when you run the program.

So, the code snippet

```
close (COUNT);
open (COUNT, ">$CountFile");
```

creates counter.dat the first time you run the program, and opens it for overwriting on any subsequent runs.

"REDIRECTING" INPUT AND OUTPUT

UNIX and Windows, as well as the Windows progenitors all the way back to the early versions of MS-DOS, interpret < and > (the greater-than and less-than signs) as special symbols. They are used to *redirect* the channels through which you normally interact with your computer, essentially the screen and the keyboard, into other places, usually files.

Normally, a command-line program expects its *input* to come from the keyboard, and it ships its *output* to the screen. However, if you were to run a program called foo in this manner

```
foo > bar
```

whatever foo is supposed to print to the screen would instead be written into a file called bar, which would be created if it didn't exist already, or overwritten if it did.

Likewise, the line

```
foo < bar
```

would expect the information that the user would normally enter through the keyboard to come from a file called bar.

One more redirection symbol combines two greater-than signs (>>) to create an *append* command. This command will tack any new data to the end of the file to its right, rather than overwriting it.

print Works with Files, Too

The last bit of code from `access.pl` brings up a couple of interesting new Perl concepts.

```
$Counter += 1;
print COUNT $Counter;
print "$CountFile has been written to $Counter times.\n";
close (COUNT);
```

In the first line, `$Counter += 1`, the `+=` is a shortcut borrowed from the C programming language. In this example, it is identical to writing:

```
$Counter = $Counter + 1;
```

Why not simply write `$Counter = $Counter + 1`? Well, for one thing, `$Counter += 1` is shorter and, therefore, follows the twin precepts of laziness and impatience. However, some programmers might insist that the longer form is clearer—that is, that it more clearly states the intention of the code. In the end, it's a matter of taste.

NOTE
Probably the most common criticism of C as a programming language is that its inherent economy encourages programmers to write programs that are too terse. Perl, with its roots deep in the C language, must shoulder this criticism as well.

NOTE
Perl's += operator is one of a family that includes all of the arithmetic operators used in the language. You also can use -= for subtraction, *= for multiplication, and /= for division. The number on the right side of the equation doesn't have to be 1 either but can be any valid number or scalar variable.

The other line worthy of special mention in this code snippet is the second:

```
print COUNT $Counter;
```

This brings up a feature of `print` that we haven't covered yet: The function presumes that its first argument is a file handle. If it's left out, `print` will use the current output file handle, which, unless you have done something special and specific, will be the *standard output*, or the screen.

Part iii

That's why there isn't a comma between COUNT and $Counter in the example. If there were, `print` would treat COUNT as a scalar or list variable and try to write it to the standard output, leading to strange and possibly indecipherable results. In any event, nothing would get into the file to which COUNT refers.

THE *READ* AND *WRITE* FUNCTIONS IN PERL

Perl has just about all the simple functionality you need when you're dealing with the most common manipulations on a file. The best example of this is the one you just finished: You were able to write a program that creates, reads, and writes to a file without once invoking the Perl functions that specifically refer to these actions, `read` and `write`.

Do you need them both? Most definitely, especially `read`.

In `access.pl`, your only responsibility was to read the entire contents of `counter.dat` into a scalar variable. There will be many occasions when you *don't* want to do this. You will instead want to read a chunk from the file, process the chunk, and then get another.

`read` is the tool of choice for such operations. It expects at least three, possibly four, arguments:

```
read (HANDLE, BUFFER, LENGTH, OFFSET);
```

You know HANDLE; it's just a file handle. BUFFER is a scalar variable that will hold the chunk of the file that you read, and LENGTH is the number of characters—or *bytes*—in the chunk. For example,

```
read (COUNT, $Buffer, 256);
```

would read 256 bytes into `$Buffer` from the file referred to by COUNT.

OFFSET is not used that often and is, therefore, optional. It tells `read` to load the bytes into BUFFER at a different starting point than the beginning.

The `write` function is almost never used in normal Perl file processing. `print` is preferable—and, in fact, more correct—in nearly every case you will encounter.

`write` is used to put formatted records into a file. It is intended to be used with reports printed on paper, so its functionality veers toward formatting headings, pages, and such.

We will not use `write` in any program in this book.

WARNING

Putting the comma between the file handle and the first string argument to print is such an easy gaffe to commit that Larry Wall placed it second in the "Common Goofs for Novices" section of his definitive book, *Programming Perl* (O'Reilly & Associates, Inc., 1996).

The remaining lines in access.pl write a nice message to the screen and close the file. Nothing new here, right? Now you're ready to turn the program into a CGI application and bring it to the Web!

BRINGING YOUR COUNTER TO THE WEB

You have the rudiments of a Web page access counter written already. You also should have a fair-to-middling understanding of how files work in Perl. However, access.pl will only work from the command line at this point, and we want it to run on the Web. Let's make this basic program CGI-ready.

You've Been Here Before

You already know which wrappers need to be fit over a Perl program to turn it into a CGI application. Here's a recap of what it needs to do:

- ▶ Send a proper HTTP header to the Web server.
- ▶ print information you want displayed in HTML format.
- ▶ Send a proper HTML ender to the Web server, so it knows when you're finished.
- ▶ Run the program as a URL in a Web browser.

Following these rules, we can fit the wrapper over access.pl. Here's the wrapper code specified in access.pl's require statement:

```
# html.pl

# Contains header and ender subroutines for setting
# up HTML documents from Perl.

# Set up a standard HTML header section with the page title
# passed on the command line.
```

Part III

```perl
sub HTML_Header
{
        # Put up standard HTTP opening line.
    print "Content-type: text/html", "\n\n";
        # Specify HTML document.
    print "<HTML>", "\n\n";
        # Specify header section.
    print "<HEAD>", "\n\n";
        # Put up the title line.
    print "<TITLE>", "@_", "</TITLE>", "\n\n";
        # End header section.
    print "</HEAD>", "\n\n";

}                       #       End HTML_Header.pl.

# Set up a standard HTML footer section.  At this point,
# it simply ends the BODY and HTML sections.

sub HTML_Ender
{
    print "\n", "</BODY>", "\n\n";
    print "</HTML>", "\n\n";

}                           # End HTML_Ender
1;
```

And here's access.pl:

```perl
#!/perl/bin/perl

 # access.pl
 #
 # Second version.  Creates or opens a file with a number
 # in it, increments the number, writes it back, then
 # displays the result in a message on a Web page.

     # Get HTML header, ender.
     require "perl-cgi/html.pl";
     # Name of counter file.
     $CountFile = "counter.dat";
     # Web page title.
     $PageTitle = "Web Page Access Counter";

# Open the file and read it.  If it doesn't exist, its
# "contents" will be read into a program variable as "0".
```

```
    open (COUNT, $CountFile);
    $Counter = <COUNT>;        # Read the contents.

# Close the file, then reopen it for output.

    close (COUNT);
    open (COUNT, ">$CountFile");

# Increment $Counter, then write it back out.
# Put up a message with the new value.  Close the file.

    $Counter += 1;
    print COUNT $Counter;
    close (COUNT);

# Put the result up in a standard HTML document.

    &HTML_Header ($PageTitle);          # HTTP header info.
    print "<BODY>\ n";
    print "<H1>$PageTitle</H1>\ n";   # Big heading.
    print "<HR>\ n";                    # Draw a rule.
    print "<H3>You are visitor #$Counter ";
    print "to our Web page!</H3>\ n";
    &HTML_Ender;

#                        End access.pl
```

Save this as access.pl again, overwriting the old version, and run it, this time as a URL in your Web browser. Figure 11.5 illustrates what you should see.

WARNING

Make sure that the directory in which you have installed access.pl has "write" permission set for users coming in from the World Wide Web, or make the program put counter.dat in some other accessible directory. Otherwise, the file will never be written, and the only number of visitors you'll ever see is 1!

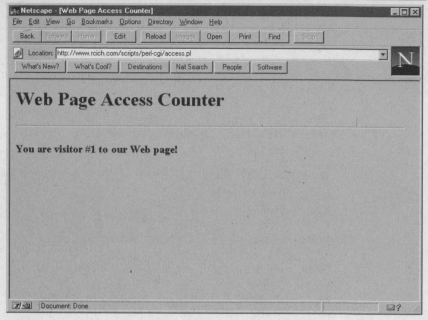

FIGURE 11.5: The access counter moves to the Web.

Refining the Program

Our access.pl program doesn't make a very spiffy home page, but all of the elements are there for you to add this code to your own page.

However, you'll be annoyed to notice very soon that your access count is incremented every time *you* call up the page, too. If you test your Web pages thoroughly—and you certainly should!—the counter can be boosted to quite unrealistic heights in no time at all.

Fortunately, CGI provides a way to get around this problem. One of the environment variables available through CGI contains the IP address of the Web site visitor who initiated the HTTP session. If you can read that address and compare it with your own, it is a simple matter to decide whether or not the count should go up. Perl makes it easy for you to automate the process.

Checking a visitor's IP address also provides the opportunity to introduce a new Perl concept: conditional expressions using the if statement, which we'll discuss in the next section.

To Increment or Not

Recall from Chapters 8 and 9 that the Web server fills its environment with a great deal of information about the computer that has started up an HTTP session. This information is passed along to a Perl program through CGI.

The environment variable that contains a visitor's IP address is called REMOTE_ADDR, and you can get to it by using Perl's @ENV array of environment variables:

```
$VisitorAddress = $ENV{ 'REMOTE_ADDR'} ;
```

$VisitorAddress now will contain an Internet address in the form nnn.nnn.nnn.nnn, where n is some number.

Let's get back into access.pl and add a line near the top to store *your* IP address.

TIP

Your IP address is something you should have at your disposal. If you don't, your Internet Service Provider should be able to get it for you.

Here's the code:

```
# Second version.  Creates or opens a file with a number
# in it, increments the number, writes it back, then
# displays the result in a message on a Web page.

    # Get HTML header, ender.
    require "perl-cgi/html.pl";
    # Name of counter file.
    $CountFile = "counter.dat";
    # Web page title.
    $PageTitle = "Web Page Access Counter";
    # My IP address.
    $HomeBase = "198.66.21.24";
    # Visitor's IP address.
    $VisitorAddress = $ENV{ 'REMOTE_ADDR'} ;
```

Two new variables are initialized in this revision to access.pl, $HomeBase, in which your IP address is stored, and $VisitorAddress, which pulls the visitor's IP out of the environment. As usual, you should replace the string given to $HomeBase with your own IP address.

Part iii

Comparing Conditions

You should now be able to compare the incoming address with your own and decide whether the access count will be incremented or not. How?

if is known as a *conditional* statement. A conditional statement allows you to compare two conditions and essentially go in one direction or another based on the results of the comparison.

In Perl, if begins a code block similar to what you learned about with the while statement. It looks like this:

```
if (This statement is true)
    {
    Execute;
    this block;
    of code;
    }
```

The truthfulness or falseness of the statement in parentheses usually is determined by the result of an *equality*. In other words, in the statement if (1 > 2), the comparison in parentheses is false (1 is not greater than 2, at least not in this dimension), so the code block would not be executed.

Because scalar variables can contain either string or numeric information, Perl needs to know what kind of comparison is being made. As a result, two sets of operators are used to differentiate between the two types of data. Table 11.1 summarizes these *relational operators*.

TABLE 11.1: Perl Relational Operators

NUMERIC	STRING	MEANS
==	eq	Is equal to
!=	ne	Is not equal to
>	gt	Is greater than
<	lt	Is less than
>=	ge	Is greater than or equal to
<=	le	Is less than or equal to
<=>	cmp	Not equal, signed result

IP addresses are numeric, but not in the form passed back to you in REMOTE_ADDR. You should use the string comparison operator, eq, to determine whether they match.

NOTE

IP addresses in the form nnn.nnn.nnn.nnn are set up as a convenience for humans. The address goes through a complex transformation to become a real number that then is passed out to the Internet.

Change the line in access.pl that increments $Counter

```
$Counter += 1;
```

to say this:

```
if ($VisitorAddress ne $HomeBase)
    {
    $Counter += 1;
    }
```

Can you see how it works? If the visitor's address is *not equal* to your address, *then* add 1 to the counter.

NOTE

Why not say if ($VisitorAddress eq $HomeBase)? Because the only time an action is required is if the two addresses are not equal. If the visitor's address is the same as yours, you don't increment the counter—you don't do anything.

Now you won't be artificially boosting the number of visits recorded to your Web page.

RUNNING THE COUNTER

You have run access.pl so far by typing a URL into your Web browser and having it tell the Web server to execute the code. Eventually, however, you will want to add this feature to your own Web page, which visitors visit by typing *its* URL into *their* browsers. How do you get access.pl to run automatically?

Unfortunately, standard HTML doesn't provide a straightforward way of doing this. The only HTML method for jumping to a URL is through a hyperlink, and those usually have to be clicked, or otherwise specifically requested, by a user.

Getting around HTML

The quick and dirty way around this limitation would be to change the name of your Web site from, say, `www.MySite.com` to `www.MySite.com/scripts/access.pl`.

That's ugly. You don't want to do that.

Some Webmasters point their site URLs to an HTML document that is just a *facing page*, which puts up a "Welcome!" message and advises the visitor to click on a hyperlink to enter the site. Figure 11.6 is an example of a facing page. The "Click here to enter!" message is the hyperlink.

FIGURE 11.6: A Web site facing page with a hyperlink to the real thing

The hyperlink is a URL to a Perl script that runs the access counter and also draws the entire home page. This is not a bad solution, though it requires a somewhat inelegant extra step.

Sadly, the only other solutions are based on proprietary extensions to HTML or equally proprietary graphics packages. This is such a perplexing problem that a small industry has sprung up around it—you can actually rent space on Web sites that do nothing more than keep track of your visitors and draw the count on your home page!

You will learn about some of the HTML extensions in. However, one extension, frames, is interesting enough to discuss here.

Using Frames to Automate a URL

A few versions back, Netscape developers came up with the idea of including *frames* in the HTML that their Navigator browser would understand. This gave the browser, and the HTML developer writing Web pages for Navigator, the ability to break a Web page up into different "windows," each operating independently of the others. At the time, it only worked with Netscape's software, which is why you still see a lot of Web pages that give you a choice between "frame-capable" displays and regular HTML.

Microsoft included the ability to recognize and deal with frames in its Internet Explorer browser, so the two most popular Web packages on the market today will do frames. As a result, it is not absolutely imperative to make provisions for "frame-damaged" browsers any more, which definitely was *not* the case even a few years ago. These days, the chances are extremely good that you can depend on your visitors having the capability to display frames.

Figure 11.7 illustrates a home page constructed with frames.

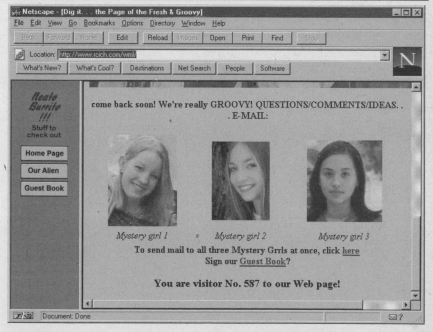

FIGURE 11.7: This is a Web page that uses Netscape frames.

Interestingly, Figure 11.7 also illustrates a home page with a built-in access counter. Its creator used a feature of the frame extensions that Netscape tacked on to HTML.

On a frame-capable Web site, you generally make the home-page HTML document the one that sets up the frames. It then calls in the actual HTML documents that comprise the home page. The beauty of this setup, for our purposes, is that each frame declaration needs to know what HTML document it should call in, but the declaration effectively is in the form of a URL. The result is that you can put *any* valid URL in a frame declaration, including the path to a Perl script that will generate a number showing the "hits" on the Web site *and* draw the home page for you.

Figure 11.8 shows the HTML document that draws the page in Figure 11.7. Notice that the source for the frame named Main, which is the window on the right in Figure 11.7, is a URL pointing to access.pl. The remaining information is a list of arguments to access.pl. It specifies the HTML document to draw as the home page and the location of the file in which the access count is stored.

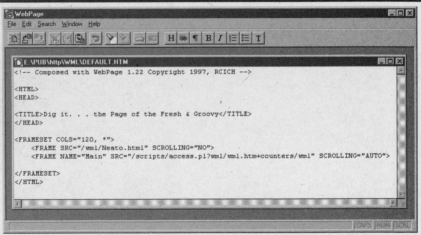

FIGURE 11.8: This HTML code produces the Web page shown in Figure 11.7.

TIP

Rather than generating HTML documents directly through strings that are printed out to the Web server, it is cleaner to make your Perl program read and print each line of an actual HTML file. This keeps the two types of code separate, and it's quite a bit easier to maintain. You'll learn more about this in Chapter 12.

Moving On

HTML forms are the most heavily used interactive construct on the World Wide Web. In the next chapter, you'll learn how to gather and process information sent to you through CGI from a form.

CHAPTER 12

CREATING REAL-WORLD HTML FORMS WITH PERL AND CGI

Forms in HTML are what make the World Wide Web interactive; they make it something more than a collection of good-looking graphics. Forms are what your Web site visitors will use to communicate with you, the Webmaster.

Adapted from *Perl CGI Programming: No experience required,* by Erik Strom
ISBN 0-7821-2157-8   447 pages $29.99

CGI is the heart of the communication; Perl is the brain. With these two tools, you will make your Web site *useful*—both for your visitors and you.

BUILDING AN HTML FORM

The concept of a form in the Hypertext Markup Language (HTML) is really quite simple. It gives the user the capability to *enter* information, rather than just *display* it. This feature alone is what allows two-way communication over the World Wide Web (see Figure 12.1).

But HTML can't do anything with the information in a form all by itself. What it *can* do is send the information to something that knows how to deal with it.

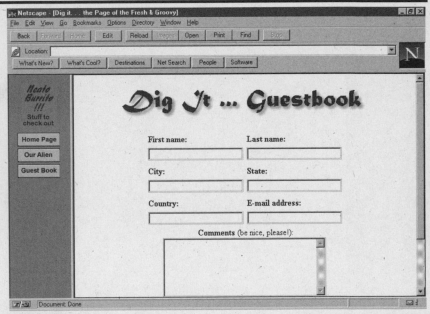

FIGURE 12.1: Two-way communication on the Web is accomplished with forms.

Through CGI, a Perl script can process the data a visitor deposits on your Web site and proceed according to your plan (see Figure 12.2).

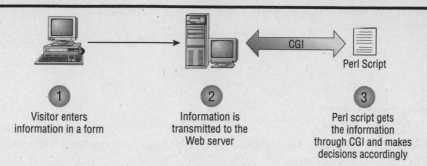

1 Visitor enters information in a form

2 Information is transmitted to the Web server

3 Perl script gets the information through CGI and makes decisions accordingly

FIGURE 12.2: Processing visitor information through CGI and Perl

This is important. Your intelligently written Perl script is capable of making decisions about how information should be digested and what to send back to the visitor as a result. Without the interaction that HTML forms allow, you would have no way of learning anything about your visitors.

You'd be working in the dark.

A Simple Form

Forms in HTML are used for two purposes: collecting information and creating interactivity between the visitor and the Web server. As an example of the former, you can create a small visitor information form with the following HTML code:

```
<HTML>
<HEAD>
<TITLE>Visitor Information Form</TITLE>
</HEAD>
<BODY>
<H1 ALIGN="LEFT">Visitor Information Form</H1>
<HR>
<FORM ACTION="perl.bat" METHOD="GET">
<B>
Last name: <INPUT TYPE="text" NAME="LastName" SIZE=16>
First Name: <INPUT TYPE="text" NAME="FirstName" SIZE=16>
<BR><BR>
Address: <INPUT TYPE="text" NAME="Address" SIZE=32>
City: <INPUT TYPE="text" NAME="City" SIZE=32>
<BR><BR>
State: <INPUT TYPE="text" NAME="State" SIZE=2>
<BR><BR>
<CENTER>
<INPUT TYPE="submit" VALUE="Send Information">
```

CGI

Perl Script

Part iii

```
<INPUT TYPE="reset" VALUE="Clear Form Fields">
</B>

</FORM>
</BODY>
</HTML>
```

NOTE

An "interactive" Web site is one that can tailor an individual response to a visitor's input.

If you save this as `form1.html`, you can run it in your Web browser by telling it to open the file in whatever location you've stored it. The result should look similar to Figure 12.3.

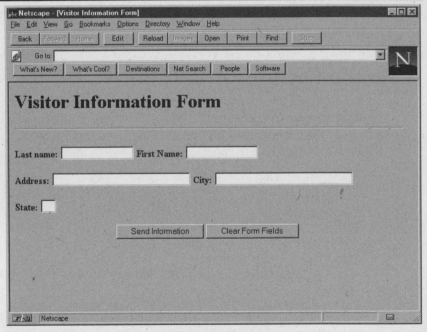

FIGURE 12.3: The first version of the visitor information form

HTML FORMS REDUX

A form is kicked off in HTML with the <FORM> statement, of course, but there is a bit more to it than that. Here's a brief review of the form tools used in the example.

ACTION The "action" the form should take when the user presses the button given a "submit" INPUT TYPE. More often than not, this is a URL to a CGI program.

INPUT TYPE Indicates that some kind of interaction with the user, or some "input," is expected here. The type can be checkbox, hidden, image, password, radio, reset, submit, or text.

METHOD Usually GET or POST, though the default is GET if no method is given. The method determines how the form data will be sent out to a CGI application. (Details on this later in the chapter.)

NAME Essentially a variable name; this string is sent to the CGI application along with the information in the field it names in the form name = value.

Table 12.1 lists the various input types, with details on what they do.

TABLE 12.1: HTML Input Types

TYPE	DESCRIPTION
checkbox	An on/off checked box that is used to indicate that a certain choice has been selected.
hidden	A field hidden from the user. It can be used to pass information between the browser and the Web server, and then to the CGI program.
image	An inline image (such as a GIF or JPEG file) with its URL indicated by SRC=. Clicking on the image will submit the form data along with the x-y coordinates of where it was clicked (measured from the top-left corner of the image).
password	A one-line text field in which typed text is displayed as asterisks or some other character. Used for passwords, obviously.

CONTINUED ➞

TABLE 12.1 continued: HTML Input Types

Type	Description
radio	A radio button. Similar to a check box, but radio buttons usually are set up in groups with the same name given to each button. Only one button in the group can be "on"; clicking one turns off any others.
reset	A special button that resets (clears) the form. Its VALUE parameter determines what is displayed on the button.
submit	Another special button. This one submits the form data to the URL specified in the form's ACTION parameter. Its VALUE parameter determines what is displayed on the button.
text	A one-line field for entering text, with its width on the screen determined by the SIZE parameter.

Submitting the Form

form1.html uses very few of HTML's tricks, just a few text input types and the submit and reset buttons. Your purpose here is not to see how great-looking forms are put together, but to learn what happens when you or one of your visitors clicks that submit button.

There are two *methods* that can be used to send out the form's data—the information that has been entered in its fields—and these are specified in the METHOD parameter to the HTML FORM command. You have used GET in this example; the other choice is POST. The difference between them is in how they send the data. As you will see, your choice in methods will be determined by the amount of data in the form; *very* generally, GET is used for small amounts and "POST" for large amounts or when you want to hide the information from the user.

You used GET in the example for two reasons: First, it's short. Second, without even loading it on a Web site, you can get a visual idea of how the data are sent when you submit the form.

Create something to fool the browser. On Windows NT or Windows 95, if Perl is in your path (and it should be!), you can create a little file called perl.bat that has nothing in it but the word perl. A shell script on UNIX would accomplish the same thing.

Save it in the same directory in which you put `form1.html`, then crank up your Web browser of choice and open the file.

TIP

Netscape Navigator has an option on its File menu to Open File in Browser. Microsoft Internet Explorer brings up an Open File dialog box when you choose the Open option in its File menu.

Fill out the form with anything that fits. Figure 12.4 illustrates some suggested bogus data.

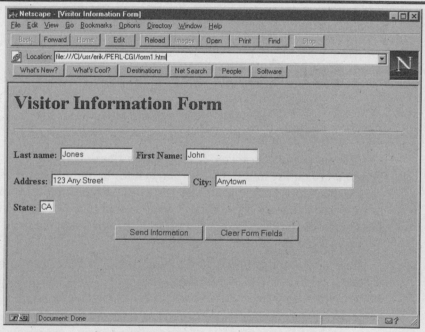

FIGURE 12.4: The form is filled out and ready to submit.

Now, submit the form by clicking the Send Information button.

Figure 12.5 illustrates what appears in Netscape Navigator's Location field when you ship this form. The "CGI" program you specified in the form's ACTION field doesn't do anything, of course, but you can see what would be shipped to it.

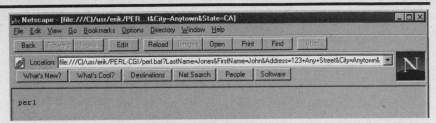

FIGURE 12.5: The URL sent by the form in Figure 12.4

This *query string* is set up by the browser as a URL. You don't have to worry about how it's done; any browser will do it automatically. However, you *do* have to interpret it in your CGI program, so you'd better know how it's put together.

URLs AND CGI

You have seen how an HTML form is built and the functions it uses to send information to the Web server. The form the information takes is important, because your Perl program has to be able to interpret it.

URLs, or *Uniform Resource Locators*, were developed as a way to specify resources on the Internet with a single line of *printable* ASCII text. Notice the emphasis on "printable"—this will become important to you as you learn to decode the special characters sent in a URL. In its simplest and most familiar form, a URL simply gives the domain name of a Web site, for example, www.rcich.com.

URLs aren't limited to the World Wide Web. All of the major Internet protocols, such as FTP, Gopher, WAIS, and HTTP, can read and understand a URL. They are set up in a very specific way, containing:

- ▶ The protocol of the URL's server (Gopher, WAIS, HTTP, etc.)
- ▶ The server's domain name
- ▶ The server's TCP/IP port number, which, if omitted, will default to the well-known port for the service—again, Gopher, WAIS, HTTP, etc.
- ▶ The location of the resource on the server

The URL that was constructed by your browser in submitting form1.html is set up in this fashion, with file// as the protocol, and the domain name, port, and resource location all addressed in the path to perl.bat. Figure 12.6 illustrates a full URL pointing over the Internet to the same location.

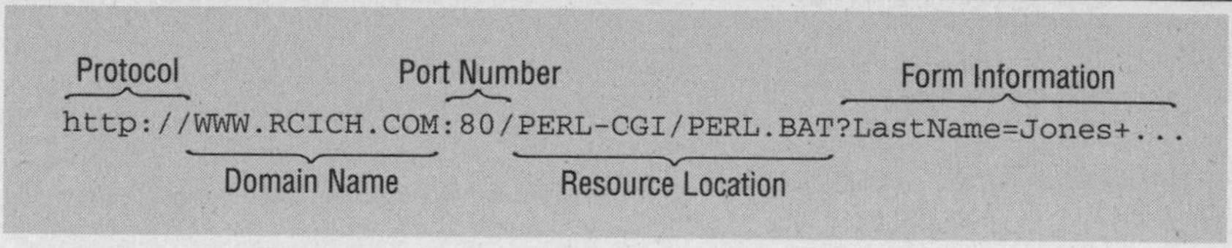

Protocol   Port Number   Form Information

`http://WWW.RCICH.COM:80/PERL-CGI/PERL.BAT?LastName=Jones+...`

Domain Name   Resource Location

FIGURE 12.6: The anatomy of a URL

"Printable" Characters

Like most other Internet protocols, URLs were originally designed to ensure that they could be sent via e-mail. Most older mail systems were capable of recognizing only 7-bit characters, so the characters used in a URL must conform to that.

However, even some of these characters have a special meaning in a URL. For example, the ampersand (&) is used to separate the parameters in the query string. But you will encounter many occasions when you *have* to send ampersands and plus signs and equal signs and even 8-bit, non-ASCII characters in a URL. How can it be done?

The solution in the URL scheme of things is to *encode* these special characters in the form

%nn

where the percent sign (%) indicates that the next two characters are the *hexadecimal value* of the actual, encoded character. A good example of this is the question mark (?) that begins the query string in our example:

```
perl.bat?LastName=Jones&FirstName=John&
➥Address=123+Any+Street . . .
```

Again, this character has a special meaning in the URL because it indicates that perl.bat should be run with the arguments that follow it. If a *literal* question mark is included in any of the arguments, it is encoded as

%26

because 26 is the hexadecimal code for a question mark in the ASCII table.

Table 12.2 shows the other printable ASCII characters that have a special meaning in a URL and, therefore, will be encoded by the browser.

TABLE 12.2: Printable Characters Encoded in URLs

CHARACTER	"HEX" VALUE
Tab	09
Space	20
"	22
<	3C
>	3E
[	5B
\	5C
]	5D
^	5E
`	60
{	7B
|	7C
}	7D
~	7E

Any control characters that wind up in a URL will be encoded, too.

Because you, as the CGI programmer, are sitting at the other end of this scheme, you don't have to deal with *encoding* characters. The rule for you will be simple: Any time you encounter a percent sign in a query string, you may assume that the next two characters are the hexadecimal code of the character that is really intended to be there.

TIP

If you're worried about getting literal percent signs in a URL, don't be. They will be encoded too.

You don't have to be too concerned with the actual ASCII values of the characters, although every programmer usually has an ASCII table handy for reference. Perl has a number of handy tricks for turning hexadecimal values into characters, as you'll soon see.

What you'll have to do at your end is recognize an encoded character, strip off the percent sign, and send the remaining number to a Perl function that will translate it for you.

HEXADECIMAL NUMBERING: A LITTLE MATH LESSON

The *hexadecimal*, or base-16, number system is meat and potatoes to people who program for a living. This is primarily because it is a convenient way to represent the *binary*, or base-2, numbers that are meat and potatoes to computers.

Computers deal with data in *bits*, or 1s and 0s, that indicate an *on* or *off* state. So the binary numbering system is especially important, because binary numbers are the only kind that computers can process at the lowest level. However, this is a system in which there are only two allowable digits: 1 and 0. The *decimal* number 5 in this system would be 101 because it consists of 1 of 2^0 (1), 0 of 2^1 (0), and 1 of 2^2 (4): $1 + 0 + 4 = 5$.

In the hexadecimal numbering system, "hex" for short, there are 16 allowable digits. In decimal, 0 through 9 are the numbers you would expect. The decimal numbers 10 through 15 are represented by the characters A through F. The hex number FF would be 255 in decimal because it consists of F of 16^0 (15) and F of 16^1 (16 x 15, or 240): $15 + 240 = 255$.

Because of its binary, on-off architecture, *everything* on a computer at some point boils down to a power of two. When you hear technicians talking about a 32-bit microprocessor, which is what powers most PCs these days, they are referring to a processor that handles data in chunks of 32 bits. That's a maximum number of one less than 2^{32}, or a binary number consisting of 32 1s:

11111111111111111111111111111111

CONTINUED ➡

This number is not any less intimidating in decimal: 4294967295.

The beauty of hex numbering is that each digit represents exactly four binary bits. You can't say that about decimal, where 32 bits comes out to that awful 4-billion-something. Broken down to 4 bits per digit, the hex value of $2^{32} - 1$ is rather elegant:

```
1111 1111 1111 1111 1111 1111 1111 1111
  F    F    F    F    F    F    F    F
```

Plus, FFFFFFFF certainly is easier to keep track of than a number consisting of 32 ones.

URL Encoding with GET

The QUERY_STRING environment variable is the method of storage for the information passed from an HTML form to a CGI program through GET. When you use the GET method to pass the information, it is just tacked on to the end of the URL:

```
perl.bat?LastName=Jones&FirstName=John&
➥Address=123+Any+Street . . .
```

The arguments to the CGI application are separated from the application name by a question mark (?) and the URL is built in name=value pairs, with each pair separated from the others by an ampersand (&). Notice, too, that all of the spaces in the URL have been replaced with plus signs (+).

These three characters, plus the percent sign that will flag any encoded characters and the equal sign that separates the name=value pairs, are what you'll need to deal with in your Perl-CGI script.

To get a little practice with these concepts and to learn some new concepts in Perl, you'll write a program to read the QUERY_STRING, decode it, and print all of its names and values in an HTML document.

Here's the program:

```
#!/perl/bin/perl

# geturl.pl
#
# A little Perl script to read, decode and print the names
# and values passed to it from an HTML form through CGI.
```

```
    # Get HTML header, ender, define the page title.

        require "/pub/scripts/perl-cgi/html.pl";  # Full path.
        $Title = "Get Information From A URL";

    # Get the query string.

        $QueryString = $ENV{ 'QUERY_STRING'} ;

    # Use split to make an array of name-value pairs broken at
    # the ampersand character.

        @NameValuePairs = split (/&/, $QueryString);

    # Put up an HTML header, page title and a rule.


        &HTML_Header ($Title);
        print "<BODY>\ n";
        print "<H1>$Title</H1>\ n";
        print "<HR>\ n";

    # Split each of the name-value pairs and print them
    # on the page.

        foreach $NameValue (@NameValuePairs)
            {
            ($Name, $Value) = split (/=/, $NameValue);
            print "Name = $Name, value = $Value<BR>\ n";
            }

    # End the HTML document.

        &HTML_Ender;

    #                      End geturl.pl
```

Store it as `geturl.pl` in a directory from which you can run Perl scripts over the Web server. Now, change the ACTION= string in `form1.html` to the correct path to `geturl.pl`. Also, move `form1.html` into a directory on your Web server. You'll be calling it up through your Web site this time, rather than as a simple file in the browser.

Start your browser and connect with the Web site with the correct URL to `form1.html`. Fill in the form with information similar to what has been entered in Figure 12.7. But this time use some characters that will be encoded by the browser when they're shipped through CGI.

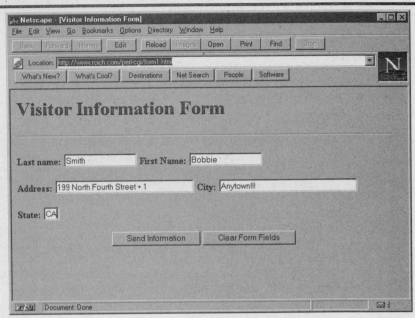

FIGURE 12.7: An information form with some special characters

When you click the Send Information button, the result should be similar to what is illustrated in Figure 12.8.

Decoding a Query String

You no doubt noticed that the information displayed by geturl.pl is full of strange encodings and separators. You'll take care of those shortly. For now, let's examine how you broke a single URL into series of *name* and *value* pairs.

The hero in this program is split, another workhorse Perl function that you will use again and again in your applications. split is specified in this way:

```
split (/PATTERN/, STRING, LIMIT);
```

where PATTERN is some delimiter or point of separation, STRING is the string to split and the optional LIMIT tells split to do no more than LIMIT separations.

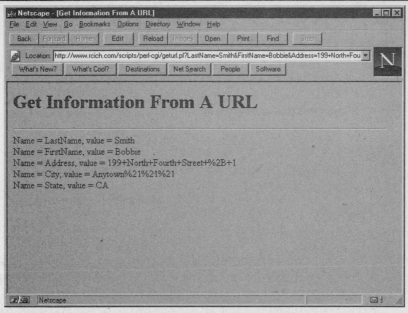

FIGURE 12.8: What the Perl script gets from the information form

split returns an array of strings broken apart at the PATTERN, which is eliminated in the array. PATTERN is *always* put between the forward slash (/) characters, but it can be left out. This call to split

```
@Array = split (//, $String);
```

would fill @Array with the contents of $String broken out at any instance of *white space*, which is spaces, tabs, and line-enders.

PATTERN also can be a regular expression, which we'll cover shortly.

Other than split, there is very little in geturl.pl that you haven't seen before. You used the QUERY_STRING environment variable to obtain the URL submitted by form1.html; you broke the query string into individual name=value pairs by using split to separate it on the ampersand character; and you split up the pairs into their component parts by specifying the equal sign as the PATTERN.

However, the strings still have all of those URL-encoded characters in them, and it looks as if it will be a tedious job to take them out, doesn't it?

Well, let's see.

The Power of Regular Expressions

Change the foreach loop in geturl.pl to read this way:

```
# Split, decode each of the name-value pairs and print
# them on the page.

foreach $NameValue (@NameValuePairs)
    {
    ($Name, $Value) = split (/=/, $NameValue);
        $Value = ~ tr/+/ /;
        $Value = ~ s/%([\ dA-Fa-f][\ dA-Fa-f])/
    pack ("C", hex ($1))/eg;
    print "Name = $Name, value = $Value<BR>\ n";
    }
```

If you've never worked with regular expressions, the two new lines in geturl.pl probably are among the weirdest things you've ever seen. However, install the new program, fill out form1.html in your Web browser, and submit it, using all the bizarre characters you want. Your result will be what you typed in, as illustrated in Figure 12.9.

Where did all the garbage go?

If you had any doubts about the power of Perl, this little trick should dispel them. If you have been intimidated by the perplexing and strange conventions of regular expressions, you now should feel inspired to learn them. You have accomplished *in two lines of code* what probably would have taken an entire program to do in C or C++. In Perl, you just have to learn the lingo.

They're easy to avoid, these Perl regular expressions. They generally look like something only Martians would understand.

However, you now have seen what you can do with a simple, though quite turgid, regular expression. You simply have no choice but to learn more about them!

Let's begin by examining the two new lines in geturl.pl.

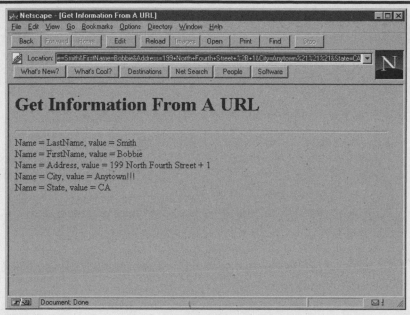

FIGURE 12.9: All of the encoded characters are translated.

Translations, Substitutions

The first new line is fairly simple, though utterly meaningless to the untrained eye:

```
$Value = ~ tr/+/ /;
```

A couple of new Perl concepts surface in this line:

▶ In the expression `"$String = ~ /PATTERN/"`, the `= ~` operator, the match operator, is true if `$String` contains `/PATTERN/`.

▶ `tr`, the translate function, turns all characters found between the first two forward-slash characters following it into the characters between the second two slashes.

You will use the `= ~` operator frequently—always, in fact, when you want to change characters in a string into other characters. The specification for `tr` is

```
tr /SEARCH_LIST/REPLACE_LIST/
```

where SEARCH_LIST is the characters for which you want to search, and REPLACE_LIST is what their new values will be.

Part iii

NOTE

There are three optional parameters to `tr` that go after the last slash: c, d, and s. We don't need them at this point, so we won't discuss them. (For the particular among you readers, they stand for complement, delete, and squeeze.)

The line from `geturl.pl` that utilizes `tr`:

```
$Value =~ tr/+/ /;
```

has the + character as its SEARCH_LIST and a space as its REPLACE_LIST. Therefore, it will go through the $Value string and replace every occurrence of the plus character (+) with a space. This is handy in URLs, where all spaces are designated by plus signs.

The second new line in `geturl.pl` is trickier to understand.

```
$Value = ~ s/%([\ dA-Fa-f][\ dA-Fa-f])/
➥ pack ("C", hex ($1))/eg;
```

It's a little easier to understand if it is explained in the sequence of events that it kicks off.

First of all, what does this code do? This is the program line that turns URL-encoded characters back into *printable* characters. Remember the %nn convention, in which special characters are encoded with a percent sign followed by their hexadecimal ASCII values? This is where the encoded values revert to real characters. Let's step through the program line:

- ► s is the Perl substitute function. Like `tr`, it takes everything it finds in $Value that matches the string between the first two forward slashes and replaces it with what is between the second two slashes.

- ► In this example, s has been told to look for % followed by two characters that are either digits, designated by \ d, or the characters A through F (or a through f), which are the valid hexadecimal numbers.

- ► The expression `pack ("C", hex ($1))`, which is specified as the REPLACE_LIST for s, is best understood if it is taken apart from the inside out. hex is a Perl function that expects its argument to be a hexadecimal number, and it returns a decimal number. $1 is the value found by the expression in the first set of parentheses in SEARCH_LIST, minus the percent sign. pack is a function that takes its second argument and "packs" it into a binary value or structure based on the template that is its first argument. In our example, the template is C, which tells pack to stuff the value in the second argument into a character.

- The e at the end of the line indicates to s that REPLACE_LIST is an expression rather than a string. Without it, every %nn string in $Value would be literally replaced with pack ("C", hex ($1)). e tells s to do the replacement with the result of the expression.

- The g following e tells s to do a global substitution; in other words, replace every instance of SEARCH_LIST in $Value with what is calculated in REPLACE_LIST. If you left this parameter off, s would do the operation on the first occurrence and then quit.

Here's a recap of the Perl regular-expression functions we've covered so far with their formal parameters:

- tr /SEARCH_LIST/REPLACE_LIST/ Translates a regular expression in SEARCH_LIST to the characters or expression in REPLACE_LIST.

- hex (EXPRESSION) Interprets EXPRESSION as a hexadecimal number and returns the decimal value. For example, hex (10) would return 16.

- pack (TEMPLATE, EXPRESSION) Packs EXPRESSION into a binary structure based on TEMPLATE.

YOU'RE RIGHT: REGULAR EXPRESSIONS *ARE* HARD

One of Perl's biggest strengths over bare-metal programming languages such as C and C++ comes from its ability to format text so easily. However, it uses regular expressions heavily to accomplish the formatting. Make no mistake about it, regular expressions are difficult.

But another of Perl's strengths is that you can write a workable, useful program in it without knowing *every detail* of the language, something you've already demonstrated in the examples we've built so far. As you gain more proficiency with Perl, your programs will utilize the knowledge you've gained, too.

You will learn about some hairy details of regular expressions in this chapter, but don't be too concerned if you don't get it right away. With practice, it'll come to you.

Meanwhile, it's helpful to think of regular expressions as nothing more than a search-and-replace function on steroids.

Part iii

Regular Expressions in Detail

A regular expression is used to match a pattern in a string and, possibly, replace it with another pattern. The string can match any of the alternatives of the regular expression; alternatives are separated with a vertical bar (|), are evaluated from left to right, and always stop on the first match.

The building blocks of a regular expression are the characters used to represent events or other characters.

- ▶ ^ stands for the beginning of a string.
- ▶ $ stands for the end of the string.
- ▶ \ B is a non-word boundary.
- ▶ \ b is a single word boundary (see \ w and \ W).

Regular expressions may include *quantifiers,* which tell how many times an event or string must occur.

- ▶ { bottom, top} where bottom and top are numbers that mean the event must occur bottom times and no more than top times.
- ▶ { number, } means it has to happen at least number times.
- ▶ { number} *exactly* number times.
- ▶ * is the same as { 0, }.
- ▶ + is the same as { 1, }.
- ▶ ? is the same as { 0,1}.

The period character, or *dot* (.), is an often-used tool because it matches *any* character except the newline. For specific characters, you may include them in lists enclosed by square brackets; ranges are indicated with a hyphen as in A-Z.

The backslash (\) before a character gives it a special meaning. Table 12.3 illustrates the backslashed special characters.

TABLE 12.3: Special Characters in Regular Expressions

CHARACTER	DOES
\ n	Newline
\ r	Carriage return

CONTINUED ➡

TABLE 12.3 continued: Special Characters in Regular Expressions

CHARACTER	DOES
\ t	Tab
\ f	Form feed
\ d	A digit, or single number
\ D	A non-digit
\ s	White space, such as space, tab, or newline
\ S	Non-white space
\ w	An alphanumeric character
\ W	Non-alphanumeric
\ xnn	Where *nn* is a hex value, the character having that value
\ 0nn	Same as above, using octal (base 8) numbers

Another convention you'll see often in regular expressions is the use of $1, $2, $3, etc. These scalar variables correspond, left to right, to the expressions in *parentheses* in SEARCH_LIST. What makes them especially valuable is that they maintain their value outside of the regular expression. For example, the string 19 May 1997 could be split into its parts with this code snippet:

```
$string = ~ /(...) (..) (....)/;
$day = $1;
$month = $2;
$year = $3;
```

WARNING

$1, $2, $3, etc. are equivalent to \1, \2, \3, etc. in regular expressions. Keep this in mind if you mistakenly try to interpret a number literally by "escaping" it and the results aren't what you expect.

EXERCISE: THE SAMBAR SERVER: BUILDING YOUR WEB SITE

You've done some simple forms in this chapter. You can prepare yourself for the next chapter by expanding on them. After all, HTML forms aren't difficult to set up. It's processing the information in the forms that presents the knotty problems. Try the following:

▶ Just as an experiment, create some more complex forms that use all of the available HTML controls. Use radio buttons, check boxes, and the rest—it doesn't matter if you know what they'll return. Play with them and *see* what comes back in the resulting URLs.

▶ Analyze the URLs that are created with each of the forms you create. Look at what appears on the Go To line of your Web browser. Your familiarity with these conventions will be invaluable later.

Moving On

This is enough about regular expressions for now. You'll learn more about them as you become comfortable with what you've been exposed to so far.

In the next chapter, you'll use Perl to perform some more complicated tasks: creating a guest book and a quiz form for your Web site.

PART iv

BUILDING WEB APPLICATIONS WITH PERL

CHAPTER 13

CREATING A GUEST BOOK FOR YOUR WEB SITE

O ne of the wonderful capabilities of the World Wide Web is that it can be used as a repository. Information stored anywhere can be retrieved—from anywhere—so long as it's accessible to and from the Web. Research avenues have been blown wide open by the Web.

Adapted from *Perl CGI Programming: No Eexperience required,* by Erik Strom

ISBN 0-7821-2157-8   447 pages $29.99

So far, the Perl-CGI programs you've written have provided *instant feedback* for your visitors. But once the information has been entered and displayed, it's gone; it can't be retrieved again, because it was never stored anywhere.

In this chapter you'll design a "guest book" Web page that will allow visitors to enter pertinent details about themselves. You'll write CGI programs in Perl to get a guest book entry for a single visitor, store the entry in a disk file, and display the entire roster of visitors. You'll also learn the basics of Web site security and what you can do in your CGI programs to prevent visitors from inadvertently or maliciously entering data that could damage your site or your system.

DESIGNING THE GUEST BOOK

A good guest book design is simple, but not too much so. You want a visitor to provide enough information to benefit you and anyone who calls up the list. Conversely, most visitors *won't* take the time to write their autobiographies, so don't expect them to. You'll take several steps to ensure that they don't, in fact, because you don't want visitors unnecessarily eating up disk space on your Web site. Figure 13.1 illustrates a Web site with a guest book. If it looks familiar, it's because we used it as an example in Chapter 12.

Let's take a look at the HTML source for a page similar to the one illustrated in Figure 13.1. You can call it `guestbook.html`.

```
<HTML>
<HEAD>
<TITLE>Perl-CGI Guest Book</TITLE>
</HEAD>

<BODY>
<CENTER>
<H1 ALIGN="CENTER">Perl-CGI Guest Book</H1>
<HR>

<FORM ACTION="/scripts/perl-cgi/addguest.pl" METHOD="POST">

<TABLE WIDTH="50%">

<TR>
```

```
<TD><STRONG>First name: </STRONG></TD> <TD><STRONG>
➥ Last name: </STRONG></TD>
</TR>
<TR>
<TD> <INPUT TYPE="text" NAME="first_name" SIZE="24"
➥ MAXLENGTH="30"> </TD>
<TD> <INPUT TYPE="text" NAME="last_name" SIZE="24"
➥ MAXLENGTH="30"> </TD>
</TR>
</TABLE>

<TABLE WIDTH="50%">

<TR>
<TD><STRONG>City: </STRONG></TD> <TD><STRONG>
➥ State: </STRONG></TD>
</TR>
<TR>
<TD> <INPUT TYPE="text" NAME="city" SIZE="24"
➥ MAXLENGTH="30"> </TD>
<TD> <INPUT TYPE="text" NAME="state" SIZE="24"
➥ MAXLENGTH="30"> </TD>
</TR>
</TABLE>
<TABLE WIDTH="50%">

<TR>
<TD><STRONG>Country: </STRONG></TD> <TD><STRONG>
➥ E-mail address: </STRONG></TD>
</TR>
<TR>
<TD> <INPUT TYPE="text" NAME="country" SIZE="24"
➥ MAXLENGTH="30"> </TD>
<TD> <INPUT TYPE="text" NAME="email" SIZE="24"
➥ MAXLENGTH="72"> </TD>
</TR>
</TABLE>

<STRONG>Comments</STRONG><BR>
<TEXTAREA NAME="comments" COLS="36" ROWS="6"
➥ WRAP="virtual"></TEXTAREA>

<BR>
<P>
<INPUT TYPE="submit" VALUE="Add your name">
```

```
<INPUT TYPE="reset" VALUE="Clear form">
</P>
</FORM>
</CENTER>

</BODY>
</HTML>
```

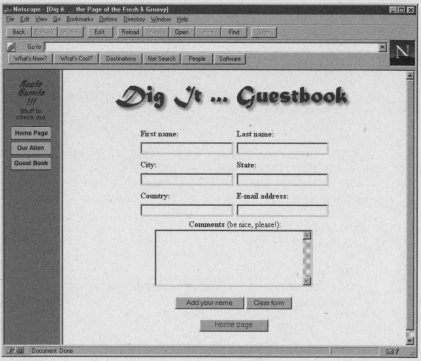

FIGURE 13.1: An example of a guest book Web page

Called up in your Web browser, the guest book form should look similar to what is shown in Figure 13.2.

This page is a pretty good example of how tables are constructed in HTML. Notice the table declaration at the top:

```
<TABLE WIDTH="50%">

<TR>
<TD><STRONG>First name: </STRONG></TD> <TD><STRONG>
Last name: </STRONG></TD>
</TR>
```

```
<TR>
<TD> <INPUT TYPE="text" NAME="first_name" SIZE="24"
➡ MAXLENGTH="30"> </TD>
<TD> <INPUT TYPE="text" NAME="last_name" SIZE="24"
➡ MAXLENGTH="30"> </TD>
</TR>
</TABLE>
```

This code sets the width of the table to 50 percent of the screen width and then formats the rows and columns for the first block of text fields, in this case for the visitor's first and last names.

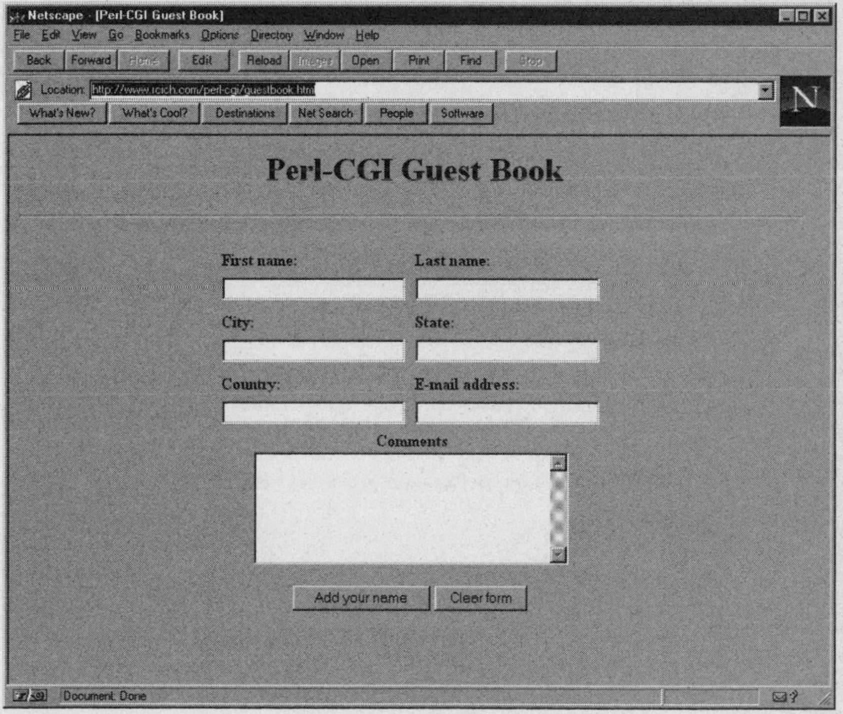

FIGURE 13.2: The entry page for your guest book

TIP
It's a good idea to use percentages rather than fixed values for setting the width of a table. Your visitors will have a variety of screens, each running at different resolutions. An HTML table that has its width set to a certain number of pixels will be larger or smaller, depending on the display resolution — in extreme cases, it might not even fit on the screen. Using the percentage width ensures that your tables will be sized to fit the screen proportionally, regardless of the visitor's equipment.

The text fields have been given MAXLENGTH values, too, which helps to prevent a user from entering too much data in a field.

Notice, too, that each block of the form is set up in its own table. It makes the page neat and tidy, and it's easier to make additions or subtractions later on when the tables are laid out this way.

ADDING GUEST BOOK ENTRIES

Gathering and filing an entry from the guest book form is a straightforward job in Perl. Let's create a program called addguest.pl.

```perl
#!/perl/bin/perl

    require ("d:/pub/scripts/perl-cgi/GuestBook.pm") ||
        die ("Can't find GuestBook header file: $!\ n");

# Get the POSTed information from STDIN and put it in
# $post_info.

    read (STDIN, $post_info, $ENV { 'CONTENT_LENGTH'} );

# Split off the fields, which are delimited with '&',
# and put them in @InfoArray.

    @InfoArray = split (/&/, $post_info);

# Go through each element in @InfoArray, split off the
# "variable=" part, then translate pluses into spaces and
# any escaped hex chars back into their real character
values.

    for ($n = 0; @InfoArray[$n]; $n++)
        {
        ($dummy, $temp) = split (/=/, @InfoArray[$n]);
        $temp = ~ tr/+/ /;
```

```
        $temp = ~ s/%([\ dA-Fa-f][\ dA-Fa-f])/
➡ pack ("C", hex ($1))/eg;
        @InfoArray [$n] = $temp;
        }

# Now we'll check to see if we have anything to write
# to the guest book. We need a first or last name, at
# least; otherwise, we'll jump around the routines that
# write this stuff to the guest book file.

    if ((length (@InfoArray[$FirstNameIndex]) != 0)
            || (length (@InfoArray [$LastNameIndex]) != 0))
        {

    # Tack the current time to the end of the array.

        # Get the current time.
        $time = time ();
        # Put it in the array.
        @InfoArray[$NumEntryTime] = $time;

    # Pack the data into a binary structure, open the guest
    # book file for appending, and write it all out to disk.

        $GuestEntry = pack ($GuestEntryStruct, @InfoArray);
        open (GUEST_LOG, ">>$GuestBookPath")
            || die "Can't open guest book: $!";
        print GUEST_LOG $GuestEntry;
        close (GUEST_LOG);
        }                       # End if ((length...)

# Finally, we put up a cute little HTML document announcing
# that everything's done, with a link to the guest book
# viewer.

    &HTML_Header ("All done!");
    print "<BODY>\ n";
    print "<CENTER>\ n";
    print "<H1>Thanks for taking the time to ";
    print "sign our guest book...</H1>\ n";
    print "<HR>\ n";
    print "Click <A HREF=\
➡ "/scripts/perl-cgi/guestbook.pl\ "> here</A> ";
    print "to view the guest book.<BR>\ n";
    &HTML_Ender ();

#                       End addguest.pl
```

You probably noticed a new `require` statement at the top of the program. Put this code in another file in the same directory as `addguest.pl`.

```
# GuestBook.pm
#
# Header file for the routines to add data to and read it
# back from the Web page Guest Book.
#

    require ("d:/pub/scripts/perl-cgi/html.pm")
        || die ("Can't find header file\ n");

# Some useful constants.

    # Format for pack ()
    $GuestEntryStruct    = "a30a30a30a30a30a30a2561";
    # Path to guest book file
    $GuestBookPath       = "/pub/http/perl-cgi/ngbook.dat";

# Indexes of elements in the packed structure.

    $FirstName           = 0;
    $LastName            = 1;
    $City                = 2;
    $State               = 3;
    $Country             = 4;
    $EMail               = 5;
    $Comments            = 6;
    $NumEntryTime        = 7;
    $NumElements         = 8;    # Number of elements in
 structure.
    $RecordSize          = 440;  # All the sizes added up.


    #                    End GuestBook.pm
```

Save this file as `guestbook.pm` (note the pm). Rename `html.pl` to give it a `.pm` extension. Now connect with your Web server and `guestbook.html`. Fill out the form, as shown in Figure 13.3.

Now submit the form. You'll see a page similar to the one shown in Figure 13.4.

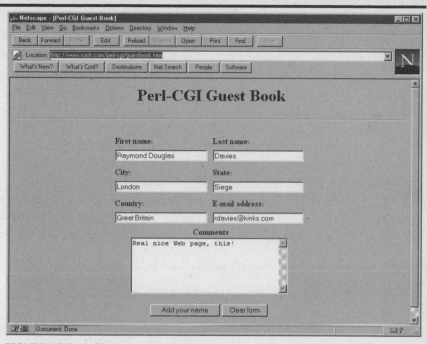

FIGURE 13.3: A filled-out guest book entry in Netscape Navigator

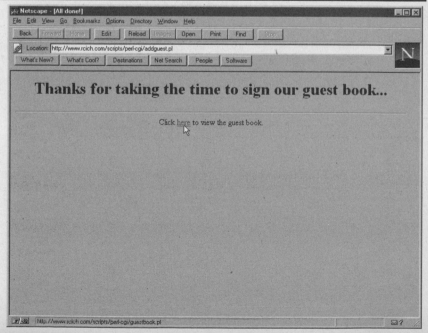

FIGURE 13.4: The guest book entry has been filed.

Dissecting the Code

You've gone through so many new concepts in the last two files that your head may be treading water by now. You have a working guest book entry form and CGI back-end, so let's slow down a little and take the program apart.

The `required` file at the top (`guestbook.pm`) itself contains the `require` that brings in the familiar subroutines of `html.pl`, which itself is `html.pm` now. The `pm` extension for the file is a convention you'll begin following now for Perl *header* files that can be used over and over by many programs. It's the extension used for Perl *packages*.

The scalar variables defined in `guestbook.pm` are not used only in `addguest.pl`. You'll need these variables to list the guest book entries, too. Rather than duplicate them in two programs, it's easier to include all of them in one file.

Note the `require` line:

```
require ("d:/pub/scripts/perl-cgi/html.pm")
        || die ("Can't find header file\ n");
```

What's this `die` function, and why does it follow a logical OR symbol?

This is another of Perl's many handy shortcuts. `die` amounts to a "bail out now!" instruction, allowing you to print an explanatory message along with it. It is used when errors are encountered—errors so bad that the program cannot continue.

Many Perl functions can be tied to `die` with the logical OR (| |) symbol. Used in this fashion, it means "do this; if it doesn't work, call `die` and terminate the program." In other words, if `require` can't find the file that is its argument, control goes to `die`, the message is printed, and the program exits.

TIP

The Perl global variable $! always contains the value of the last system error. `die` understands this. If you put $! in its message string, it will print a semi-explanatory message all by itself. (Sometimes you may not find them too helpful!)

NOTE

die is probably used most often with open; if the file can't be opened, die prints a message explaining why and exits. die's less-fanatical little brother is warn, which operates the same way with the same argument but doesn't terminate the program.

There is one unfamiliar exception: The $GuestEntryStruct appears to be a string of nonsense, but its comment line says it is a format for pack (). What could that be?

Reading and Writing "Structured" Data

pack and its Perl complement unpack are ubiquitous in programs that read and write binary data to and from disk files. They are necessary because Perl would like to believe that everything it deals with is in the form of a string. Oh, it can convert pretty easily between numbers and strings on an individual basis, but it falls apart when things get too complicated.

In the real world, programmers run into situations all the time in which they have to manipulate pieces of information that are structured in records, each of which has a fixed length and each member of which has its own fixed length. For example, if you were putting an employee-information database together, you would fashion each employee entry with a certain size for each bit of information: The name would be 32 characters, the address might be 64, the employee's age and salary would be two numeric fields, each taking 4-byte integers, etc. The entire entry would be a record with a length equal to the combined maximum sizes of each field. Each record would fit into the same amount of space in a disk file; each record could be called into another program and manipulated, then written back to the disk.

The file into which all these records go is called a *database*. You have created a small one, in fact, with addguest.pl. Here's how pack works to make it possible.

pack and Its Many Formats

The specification for pack couldn't be simpler:

```
pack (TEMPLATE, LIST);
```

It turns LIST into a scalar value based on what is contained in TEMPLATE. However, the template is where things get hairy.

The template tells pack the *type* of the data in the list and its *length*. Table 13.1 shows a list of the pack template formats.

TABLE 13.1: The pack Formats

CHARACTER	DESCRIPTION
A	ASCII string that will be padded with spaces
a	ASCII string, no space padding
B	Bit string, high- to low-order
b	Bit string, low- to high-order
C	An unsigned character
c	A signed character
d	Double-precision floating-point number
f	Single-precision floating-point number
H	Hexadecimal string, high nybble (4 bits) first
h	Hex string, low nybble first
I	Unsigned integer
i	Signed integer
L	Unsigned long integer
l	Signed long integer
N	Long integer in "network" order
n	Short integer in "network" order
p	Pointer to string
X	Back up a byte
x	NULL byte

CONTINUED ➡

TABLE 13.1 continued: The pack Formats

CHARACTER	DESCRIPTION
u	Uuencoded string
@	Fill with NULLs to absolute position

While these formats may look strange and intimidating, you generally will use only a few of them—until you reach the point where they don't look so strange and intimidating any more.

It would be useful for you to review the use of pack in Chapter 12, where you learned how to decode URL-encoded characters. The same translation code is in addguest.pl, so you don't have to go very far to refresh your memory.

```
$temp = ~ s/%([\ dA-Fa-f][\ dA-Fa-f])/
➡ pack ("C", hex ($1))/eg;
```

Recall that the pack function in this line of code takes the number calculated by hex and turns it into a character. The "C" template is what tells pack to do it; it isn't followed by a number, so it does just one. The line

```
$string = pack ("C4", 48, 49, 50, 51);
```

yields 0123 because "C4" says to do four characters, and 48 through 51 are the decimal ASCII values of the characters (*not* numbers!) "0" through "3".

addguest.pl deals mainly with strings, so it uses the "a" template format heavily. "an", where *n* is some number, sets aside the space required by the number, runs in its corresponding string from the list, and fills whatever is left with NULL characters. The line

```
$string = pack ("a8", "Now is");
```

yields "Now is\0\0" (remember "\0" is a NULL byte?) because "Now is" only contains six characters; the remainder is padded.

TIP

The "A" template format, as shown in Table 13.1, uses space characters to do the padding. This is not usually what you want to do with strings stored in a binary structure because the spaces count as part of the string and its length. A NULL ends the string right where it stands.

Inversely, a format that is too short will *truncate* the string passed to it.

```
$string = pack ("a2", "Now is");
```

will result in `"No"`.

Now, let's take a look at the format string in `addguest.pl` (actually, the string passed in from `guestbook.pm`).

```
$GuestEntryStruct = "a30a30a30a30a30a30a256l";
```

You should be able to decode it yourself now; it will set up six 30-byte strings, followed by one of 256 bytes, and end with a signed long integer. These happen to correspond with the:

First name

Last name

City

State

Country

E-mail address

Comments

coming from the guest book form. The last field is reserved for the time of the visit, which is calculated in `addguest.pl`.

We mentioned pack's companion function, unpack, at the beginning of this section. It takes the same arguments as pack but works in reverse. In other words,

```
$string = pack ("a30a30a30a30a30a30a256l",
                $first, $last, $city, $state, $country,
                $email, $comments, $time);
```

stuffs all of those variables into `$string` in a form that is suitable for writing into a 440-byte record in a disk file (long integers are 4 bytes long). When you read it back into a program with

```
read (FILEHANDLE, $string, 440);
```

you can then invoke unpack

```
($first, $last, $city, $state, $country, $email, $comments,
$time) =
    unpack ("a30a30a30a30a30a30a256l", $string);
```

to bring all of the data back.

The only other unfamiliar part of addguest.pl is the function that fills the last element of the record with the time of the visit.

The Perl function time returns the current time as a 4-byte-long integer measured in seconds from midnight, January 1, 1970, according to the UNIX convention. This makes time—and the values it calculates—completely portable between UNIX and Microsoft-powered systems.

TIP

Microsoft operating systems keep track of time based on other epochs—and it can get fairly weird. Some Win32 API time functions, for example, measure time in 8-byte integers consisting of seconds dating back to the 1600s! But, again, Perl works the same no matter what system it's running on.

Before you move on to writing a Perl program to display the entries in your new guest book, take note of one feature of addguest.pl. The conditional expression

```
if ((length (@InfoArray[$FirstNameIndex]) != 0)
            || (length (@InfoArray [$LastNameIndex]) != 0))
```

tests the first- and last-name fields to ensure that they contain something. If they don't, the form information is *not* written into the guest book file, and the program proceeds directly to the last display page, from which you can get the entire list of entries.

That's how to get the list without adding to it: Just submit a blank form.

DISPLAYING THE GUEST BOOK

Listing the entries in your guest book file is less challenging than getting them into the file to begin with. You just do everything in reverse.

Still, there are some perplexing details you'll need to deal with. The steps are straightforward:

1. Set up variables to hold the information you'll read from the file. Obviously, you need to know how the variables are structured, but you took care of that in addguest.pl.

2. Open the guest book file for reading.

3. Read one record. You need to know its length, but you've taken care of that, too.

4. Format the data to your liking in HTML.

5. print it out to the Web server.

6. If there are any more records in the file, go back to Step 3.

7. If not, close the file.

You're finished.

Displaying the Guest Book with Perl

Save the following Perl code as guestbook.pl in a directory accessible to your CGI pipeline.

```perl
#!perl/bin/perl

# guestbook.pl
#
# Reads records from the guest book file specified in
# guestbook.pm, formats them in HTML and sends them
# to a Web page.

# Get the header file; scream loudly and exit if it can't be
# found. Otherwise, define the title string.

    require ("d:/pub/scripts/perl-cgi/GuestBook.pm") ||
        die ("Can't find GuestBook header file: $!\ n");

    $Title = "Perl-CGI Guest Book Entries";

# Attempt to open the guest book file.  Again, this is
# a fatal error if it doesn't succeed.

    open (GUEST_LOG, $GuestBookPath) ||
        die "Can't open guest book: $!";

# Set up the HTML document.

    &HTML_Header ($Title);
    print "<BODY>\ n";
    print "<H1 ALIGN=\ "CENTER\ ">$Title</H1>\ n";
    print "<HR>\ n";
```

```
# Read records and display them in a while loop. The test
# at the top of the while block fails when all the records
# have been read.

   while (read (GUEST_LOG, $buffer, $GuestEntrySize))
      {

   # Use unpack to load the record into an array of fields
   # based on the same template we used with pack to format
   # them for the file.

      @InfoArray = unpack ($GuestEntryStruct, $buffer);

   # Loop through the elements of the array and remove any
   # NULL padding from the strings, in case this is being
   # run on a browser that prints spaces for NULLs.

      for ($n = 0; $n < ($NumElements - 1); $n++)
         {
         $InfoArray[$n] = ~ s/\ 0//g;
         }

   # Load separate variables with the elements in
   # @InfoArray.

      ($FirstName, $LastName, $City, $State, $Country,
         $Email, $Comments, $NumAccessTime) = @InfoArray;

      print "<STRONG>Name:</STRONG><BR>\ n";
      printf ("%s %s<BR>\ n", $FirstName, $LastName);
      print "<STRONG>E-mail address:</STRONG><BR>\ n";
      print $Email, "<BR>\ n";
      print "<STRONG>From:</STRONG><BR>\ n";
      print $City, " ", $State, " ", $Country, "<BR>\ n";
      print "<STRONG>On:</STRONG><BR>\ n";

   # Set up a string time description after running the
   # 4-byte time value through localtime ().

      ($sec, $min, $hour, $mday, $mon,
         $year, $wday, $yday, $isdst)
         = localtime ($NumAccessTime);
```

```
          print "$WeekDay[$wday], $Month[$mon] $mday, ",
➥ $year + 1900;
          print " at $hour:";
          if ($min < 10)
             {
             print "0";
             }
          print "$min:";
          if ($sec < 10)
             {
             print "0";
             }
          print "$sec <BR>\ n";
          print "<STRONG>Comments:</STRONG><BR>\ n";
          print $Comments, "<BR>\ n";
          print "<HR>\ n";
          }

     close (GUEST_LOG);
     &HTML_Footer ();

  #                    End GuestBook.pl
```

Now add the following two arrays to the bottom of guestbook.pm:

```
# Days of the week.

    @WeekDay = ("Sunday", "Monday", "Tuesday",
                "Wednesday", "Thursday", "Friday",
                "Saturday");


# Months of the year.

    @Month = ("January", "February", "March", "April",
              "May", "June", "July", "August",
              "September", "October", "November",
              "December");


  #                    End GuestBook.pm
```

Start up your Web browser and connect with guestbook.html. Fill in the form a few times with bogus or real entries. You should see something similar to what is illustrated in Figure 13.5.

TIP

If you click your browser's Back button after submitting the form, you will go back to the form page. Click Clear Form to get a blank one up and do it again.

Finally, click the link on your Thank-you page that invokes the display script (that's guestbook.pl). You'll see something similar to the illustration in Figure 13.6 (on the next page).

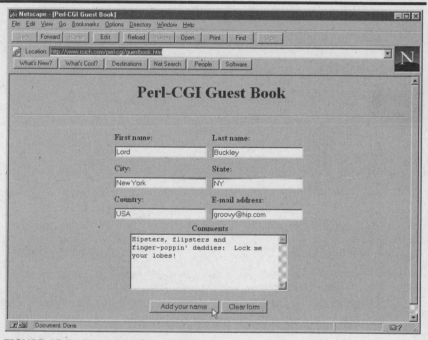

FIGURE 13.5: Fill out the form again.

Dissecting the Display Program

It's exhilarating to get something to work, isn't it? Now comes the sticky part: What have you done?

Actually, there isn't much in guestbook.pl that you haven't already done. The Perl read function that gets the records from the file is set up in a while loop that terminates when read reaches the end of the file.

```
# Read records and display them in a while loop. The test
# at the top of the while block fails when all the records
```

```
# have been read.

    while (read (GUEST_LOG, $buffer, $GuestEntrySize))
        {
    .
    .
    .
```

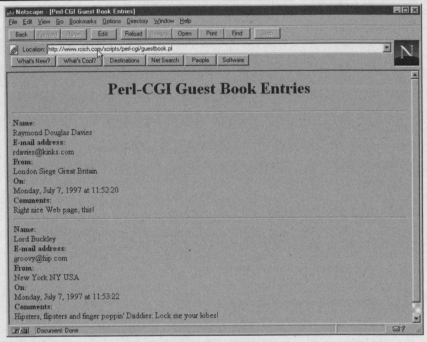

FIGURE 13.6: Running out the guest book entries

Notice that read's LENGTH parameter uses $GuestEntrySize instead of a hard-coded number; this is another example of the wisdom of placing *constant*—that is, non-variable—values in one place, where they can be changed easily.

Each record read from the file is unpacked into an array, as you learned previously.

for Loops, NULLs

The code block that follows the call to unpack introduces the Perl for statement. for is similar to foreach in that it sets up a loop. But where foreach is ideal for pulling elements out of arrays until they are empty, for provides a great deal more control over many more data structures than foreach.

for uses a counter variable, $n in this example, and a *terminating condition* to decide when it's finished. The for specification looks like this:

```
for (starting count; terminating condition;
➡ do something with count)
    {
    Do this code block;
    }
```

for is especially good for stepping through subscripted arrays, as you do in the for block in guestbook.pl.

The purpose in this example is to go through each of the string members of @InfoArray and strip out the trailing NULL characters that were used to pad them when they went through pack.

NOTE

It is not strictly necessary to strip the NULLs out of formatted strings. However, some Web browsers regard NULLs as spaces and print them out in an HTML document. It is safer—and quite easy, as you will see—to simply get rid of them.

The for starts the counter, $n, at 0. It will terminate when $n equals $NumElements - 1, which is all of the elements in the array except for the last one (the long-integer value denoting the time the guest book entry was made). Each time through the loop, $n++ is executed, which increments it.

The elements go through a regular expression substitution in the body of the loop.

```
$InfoArray[$n] = ~ s/\0//g;
```

The substitution operator in this case searches *globally* (note the g at the end) for all occurrences of \0, the NULL character, and replaces them with nothing, which effectively removes the NULLs from the string.

Keeping Time

The last bit of new stuff in guestbook.pl is the Perl function localtime. Four-byte integers denoting *billions* of seconds from some epoch may be quite meaningful to the computer as a way of telling time, but humans can't do much with them. Perl provides `localtime` to break the huge time values down into something you can use in your programs.

`localtime`'s spécification looks like this:

```
($sec, $min, $hour, $mday, $mon, $year, $wday, $yday, $isdst)
    = localtime (time);
```

where

- ► `$sec` is the number of seconds past the minute
- ► `$min` is the number of minutes past the hour
- ► `$hour` is the hours past midnight
- ► `$mday` is the day of the month, starting from 0, *not* 1
- ► `$mon` is the numeric month, again starting from 0
- ► `$year` is the number of years from 1900, such as 97 for 1997
- ► `$wday` is the numeric day of the week, starting from 0
- ► `$yday` is the numeric day of the year
- ► `$isdst` is a flag indicating whether it's daylight saving time
- ► `time` is the 4-byte integer

`localtime`'s return values are the impetus for the two arrays you added to `guestbook.pm`. You can use the numeric values from `localtime` as subscripts into these arrays to pull out the real names of days of the week and months, as in `guestbook.pl`:

```
print "$WeekDay[$wday], $Month[$mon] $mday, ", $year + 1900;
print " at $hour:";
if ($min < 10)
    {
    print "0";
    }
print "$min:";
if ($sec < 10)
    {
    print "0";
    }
print "$sec <BR>\ n";
```

The conditionals testing `$min` and `$sec` for values less than 10 are intended to pad them out with 0s so you don't print times such as 11:6:5.

WHAT'S IN A FORM: SECURITY ISSUES

HTML text input types and TEXTAREA fields allow a visitor to type in just about anything. This makes the HTML text types quite useful in terms of gathering information. However, they are your largest window of vulnerability to attack by malicious or clumsy visitors, too.

There isn't much you can do about obscene or libelous entries in a guest book, unless you write your Perl script to filter out the "seven dirty words" or some such thing. Putting a table of obscenities together might be a fascinating exercise, but, in the end, it would be a waste of time.

The list is probably somewhat longer since George Carlin first drew it up anyway!

But little troglodytes who spray-paint nasty words in your guest book are merely an annoyance.

A bigger worry for you should be the *amount* of text a visitor can enter in one field. For example, it would be relatively simple for a visitor from the Dark Side to crank up a file transfer and dump a few megabytes of garbage into the First Name: field of your form. If you hadn't planned for that possibility, the garbage would hopelessly clog up the CGI program that you've hooked up to the HTML document. Assuming it made it through the Perl script without crashing it—and your Web server—it would needlessly hog disk space in the guest book file.

Perhaps the worst part would be when other visitors wanted to look at the guest book and got page after page of strange hieroglyphs instead, maybe even crashing *their* browsers.

A good start at limiting this sort of nonsense can be found in the text declarations in guestbook.html.

```
<TD> <INPUT TYPE="text" NAME="first_name" SIZE="24"
➥ MAXLENGTH="30"> </TD>
```

The MAXLENGTH tag tells the browser to accept a *maximum* number of characters in the field. Note that we have made it slightly larger than the width of the field itself, in case someone really does have a long first_name. But there's a great deal of difference between 30 and 30 million bytes.

Unfortunately, HTML's TEXTAREA tag, which allows the user to type in more than one line of text, has no provision for limiting the amount that goes into it. You'll fall back on a second line of defense for that: the Perl-CGI script itself.

Part iv

NOTE

The WRAP="virtual" parameter in guestbook.html's TEXTAREA tag is a non-standard HTML command that "wraps" text in the window. In other words, when the user types to the edge of the window, the text automatically word-wraps down to the next line. The WRAP parameter was added by Netscape, but it's supported by Microsoft's Internet Explorer. Other values for WRAP are "off" (the default case), in which the user must press the ⏎ key to bring the cursor to the next line; and "physical", which has the same behavior as "virtual" but actually places new line characters into the text at the end of each line.

A Last Word on Security

It's possible to enter system commands and HTML code into an HTML text field such as the ones you used in the guest book programs. Sometimes this can actually damage your system if your Perl code takes any of the text and executes it as a system command.

It's also possible to enter a URL into one of the text fields. For example, a visitor could drop the path to a picture file into the Comments field of the guest book, as illustrated in Figure 13.7.

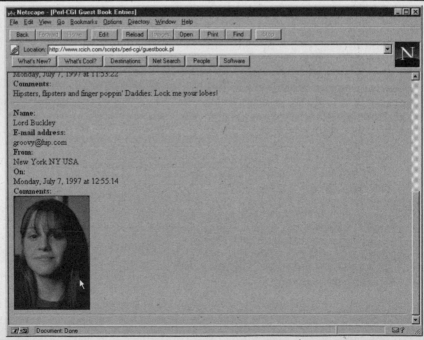

FIGURE 13.7: A picture gets into the guest book

Figure 13.8 illustrates how easy it is.

The picture in Figure 13.7 certainly is not going to harm anything, but it *could* have been something not so nice. In any event, it isn't what you intended to have in the guest book, is it?

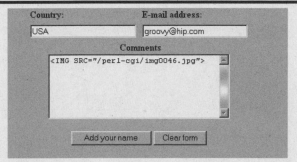

FIGURE 13.8: A URL in a form text field

The easiest way to guard against such intrusions is to filter out characters that obviously go into HTML code, shell commands, or URLs.

Adding one small code block to addguest.pl will provide the filter:

```
# Go through each element in @InfoArray, split off the
# "variable=" part, then translate pluses into spaces and
# any escaped hex chars back into their real character
➥ values.

    for ($n = 0; @InfoArray[$n]; $n++)
        {
        ($dummy, $temp) = split (/=/, @InfoArray[$n]);
        $temp = ~ tr/+/ /;
        $temp =~ s/%([\ dA-Fa-f][\ dA-Fa-f])/
➥ pack ("C", hex ($1))/eg;
        e if ($temp = ~ /[;<>&\ *`|]/)
            {
            print "Illegal entry!!\ n";
            exit;
            }
        @InfoArray [$n] = $temp;
        }
```

Calling exit to just drop the program is merely a suggestion; you can proceed in any way you want. The point is this: There is no reason for *any* of the characters in the test to be in a guest book entry, and there is *every* reason for any of them to be in something you don't want.

This is just one more line in your defenses.

CHAPTER 14

MONITORING WEB SITE ACTIVITY

Web server software is written to connect with the whole wide world. Such grand ambition may not be completely fulfilled at your Web site, though you certainly can give it a try. But whether large or small, heavily visited or not, your Web server generates a nearly breathtaking amount of information about itself and what your visitors do when they connect with your site.

Adapted from *Perl CGI Programming: No experience required,* by Erik Strom
ISBN 0-7821-2157-8   447 pages $29.99

As a beginning Webmaster, you may not have looked at the logs created by your server or even know where the log files are. However, after completing this chapter, you certainly will be able to find the logs—and use them to your distinct advantage.

Using Log Files and Simple Reports

The logs maintained by your Web server contain a voluminous amount of information, which you can use in any way you like. Using a Perl script as your template, it isn't difficult to extract simple information from the log files and fashion the information into a report.

The benefits of keeping track of people who visit your Web site may not be immediately apparent. Also, when you consider that the standard server log records not just every visit to the site but *every transaction* made during the connection, you may begin to wonder what you're going to do with all of that information.

The benefits depend entirely on how you plan to use your Web site. When the World Wide Web began to become popular, most non-corporate Webmasters who could afford to hang a server on the Internet were running what could be termed "vanity" Web sites—"Hi, welcome to my Web site, here's some pictures of the kids." Increasingly, however, the Web is being regarded as a vehicle for commercial enterprises. Web sites are actually selling advertising space to businesses, which can then pop their messages up in your browser when you visit the sites. Most of them are set up as links to the advertisers' own Web sites.

Whether advertising on the Web will become as profitable a venture as advertising elsewhere may be arguable. But you can't argue with numbers, and most of the statistics you need to put a marketing profile together are available in your server logs. Because every transaction is recorded, you can see where the visitor came from and what stuff on your site was actually visited. You can take these two statistics and do anything you like with them, wrong or right. Your analyses may be *way* off the mark—that's up to you. But think about the advantage this gives you over other advertisers: Newspapers and other more traditional advertising media have to depend on surveys and polls to develop profiles of the type of person who reads a particular ad. They have to depend on the honesty of the people participating in the surveys and polls to determine who even looks at the ads.

On a Web site, you have no such vagaries to contend with. The information is there, always at your fingertips. All you have to do is take advantage of it.

Decoding a Log File

To the uninitiated, a Web server log file looks just plain weird. You'll learn in this section what each of the log entries means, and how to decode an entry.

The log files are text files—you can even edit them if you like, though this is *not* a recommended practice. There are a couple of formats and several log file locations to deal with, depending on the server.

TIP

Internet Information Server stores its log files in winnt\system32\logfiles with a different file for each day. The NCSA server puts its logging information in a file called access_log, which can be found where the HTTPD server was installed. The Sambar server puts its log files in a logs directory in its main installation location. Sambar logs several other aspects of a Web connection, including the types of software—browsers, mostly—that are used to connect with it and the local error messages from the server. It keeps its logging files in access.log.

Getting Information from IIS Logs

One of Internet Information Server's log files, opened with Notepad, is illustrated in Figure 14.1.

As you can see in Figure 14.1, it's not pretty. But all of it means something. Let's start by taking one line apart:

```
152.163.195.39, -, 6/13/97, 21:37:00, W3SVC, OWSLEY,
207.77.84.202, 328, 60, 29, 304, 0, GET,
/wml/homepage.gif, -,
```

Normally, log entries span only one line; the example is broken because that's the only way it will fit on the page.

Notice that each of the 15 entries is separated from the others with a comma. This is how you distinguish them, and this will also be Perl's hint for breaking out entries when you run the log information into a report.

Part iv

The entries in IIS's log file are broken down in this way:

- IP address of the client
- Client's username, which is always empty (-) in IIS

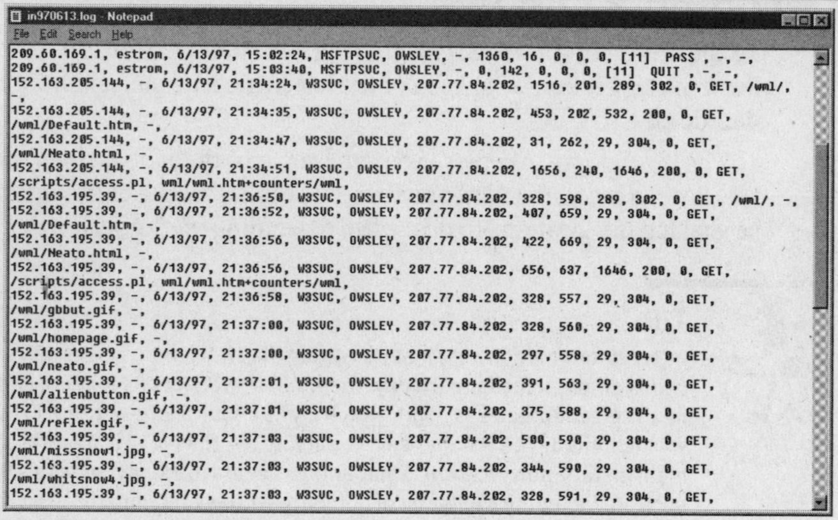

```
in970613.log - Notepad
File Edit Search Help
209.60.169.1, estrom, 6/13/97, 15:02:24, MSFTPSVC, OWSLEY, -, 1360, 16, 0, 0, 0, [11]  PASS , -, -,
209.60.169.1, estrom, 6/13/97, 15:03:40, MSFTPSVC, OWSLEY, -, 0, 142, 0, 0, 0, [11]  QUIT , -, -,
152.163.205.144, -, 6/13/97, 21:34:24, W3SVC, OWSLEY, 207.77.84.202, 1516, 201, 289, 302, 0, GET, /wml/,
-,
152.163.205.144, -, 6/13/97, 21:34:35, W3SVC, OWSLEY, 207.77.84.202, 453, 202, 532, 200, 0, GET,
/wml/Default.htm, -,
152.163.205.144, -, 6/13/97, 21:34:47, W3SVC, OWSLEY, 207.77.84.202, 31, 262, 29, 304, 0, GET,
/wml/Neato.html, -,
152.163.205.144, -, 6/13/97, 21:34:51, W3SVC, OWSLEY, 207.77.84.202, 1656, 240, 1646, 200, 0, GET,
/scripts/access.pl, wml/wml.htm+counters/wml,
152.163.195.39, -, 6/13/97, 21:36:50, W3SVC, OWSLEY, 207.77.84.202, 328, 598, 289, 302, 0, GET, /wml/, -,
152.163.195.39, -, 6/13/97, 21:36:52, W3SVC, OWSLEY, 207.77.84.202, 407, 659, 29, 304, 0, GET,
/wml/Default.htm, -,
152.163.195.39, -, 6/13/97, 21:36:56, W3SVC, OWSLEY, 207.77.84.202, 422, 669, 29, 304, 0, GET,
/wml/Neato.html, -,
152.163.195.39, -, 6/13/97, 21:36:56, W3SVC, OWSLEY, 207.77.84.202, 656, 637, 1646, 200, 0, GET,
/scripts/access.pl, wml/wml.htm+counters/wml,
152.163.195.39, -, 6/13/97, 21:36:58, W3SVC, OWSLEY, 207.77.84.202, 328, 557, 29, 304, 0, GET,
/wml/gbbut.gif, -,
152.163.195.39, -, 6/13/97, 21:37:00, W3SVC, OWSLEY, 207.77.84.202, 328, 560, 29, 304, 0, GET,
/wml/homepage.gif, -,
152.163.195.39, -, 6/13/97, 21:37:00, W3SVC, OWSLEY, 207.77.84.202, 297, 558, 29, 304, 0, GET,
/wml/neato.gif, -,
152.163.195.39, -, 6/13/97, 21:37:01, W3SVC, OWSLEY, 207.77.84.202, 391, 563, 29, 304, 0, GET,
/wml/alienbutton.gif, -,
152.163.195.39, -, 6/13/97, 21:37:01, W3SVC, OWSLEY, 207.77.84.202, 375, 588, 29, 304, 0, GET,
/wml/reflex.gif, -,
152.163.195.39, -, 6/13/97, 21:37:03, W3SVC, OWSLEY, 207.77.84.202, 500, 590, 29, 304, 0, GET,
/wml/misssnow1.jpg, -,
152.163.195.39, -, 6/13/97, 21:37:03, W3SVC, OWSLEY, 207.77.84.202, 344, 590, 29, 304, 0, GET,
/wml/whitsnow4.jpg, -,
152.163.195.39, -, 6/13/97, 21:37:03, W3SVC, OWSLEY, 207.77.84.202, 328, 591, 29, 304, 0, GET,
```

FIGURE 14.1: The raw information in an IIS log file

- Date of request
- Time of request
- Service name (always W3SVC in IIS)
- Web server's name (computer name)
- Server IP address
- Elapsed CPU time (in milliseconds) of the operation
- Number of bytes received
- Number of bytes sent
- Service status code
- Windows NT status code
- Operation requested
- Target of the operation
- Ender (always -)

As illustrated in Figure 14.2, each of the entries in our list is strung out in a line of text in the log file.

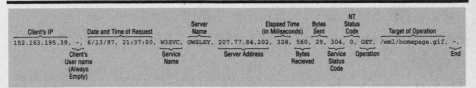

FIGURE 14.2: The format of an IIS log file entry

Setting the "Standard": The UNIX Logging Format

The log format used by IIS is considered "non-standard"; in other words, it's something new. The "old" standard is known as the UNIX Common Log Format, and it's used on the NCSA and CERN servers.

Here's an example log entry in the Common Log Format:

```
website.com 140.172.165.58 admin
➥ [27/Apr/1997:20:47:43 -0700]
➥ "GET session\ adminlogin HTTP/1.0" 200 160
```

Again, this entry normally appears in one line but is broken up here to fit on the page.

NOTE

The format used by the Sambar server in its access.log file is almost identical to the UNIX Common Log Format. The difference is that Sambar doesn't attempt to decode the client IP address unless you tell it to, which isn't recommended by Sambar because of all the processing time it takes. A Sambar entry starts with the IP. It also logs a Windows NT result code for each operation and inserts it between the server result code and the number of bytes sent.

The entries in the Common Log Format log file are broken down in this way:

- ▶ Client's domain name (not used by Sambar server)
- ▶ Client's IP address
- ▶ Date and time of request
- ▶ Operation requested, plus the target of the operation and the HTTP version being used

- ▶ Result code from the server
- ▶ Number of bytes transferred

Figure 14.3 breaks out the components of a Common Log Format entry.

NOTE

UNIX Web servers have access to more built-in Internet software than Windows-based servers. This is why the UNIX CGI environment and the server log files contain client domain names as well as IP addresses. The only information the client sends, in most cases, is its IP address; the address is resolved into a name by the server. However, it isn't too difficult to include the capability to resolve IP addresses into names on a Windows system.

```
Client Name
(Not Used by                  Username                    Time Zone                                    HTTP
Sambar Server)                                                                                      Result Code
website.com 140.172.165.58 admin [27/Apr/1997:20:47:43 -0700] "GET \session\adminlogin HTTP/1.0" 200 160
           Client IP Address            Date and Time                        Operation and Target            Bytes
                                        of Request                           Requested, plus             Transferred
                                                                             HTTP Version
```

FIGURE 14.3: The UNIX Common Log Format broken down

NOTE

Note the format of the date and time stamp: [27/Apr/1997:20:47:43 -0700]. The date and time are easily picked out, but you may not be familiar with the −0700 that ends the string. This is a time zone value, indicating the number of hours that were added to Greenwich Mean Time (GMT) to obtain the correct local time, which is displayed in the string. In this example, −0700 says to subtract seven hours (note the − in front of it) from GMT. If you know your time zones, you'll know that Mountain Standard Time is seven hours behind GMT. If you don't know your time zones, it's pretty easy to look them up somewhere, load them all into a table, and use it to calculate the correct zone with a Perl program. Also, all of the operating systems covered by *Perl CGI Programming* are capable of correcting for daylight saving time, and the date and time stamp in the log file will reflect this correction.

Making IIS Compatible with UNIX

If you're using the Internet Information Server on your Web site but you decide that you like the UNIX Common Log Format better than Microsoft's format, it is easy to make IIS conform to your wishes.

The configuration program for the IIS Web server is found in the Internet Service Manager, which can be found on NT's Start menu by choosing Programs ➤ Microsoft Internet Server. When you click Internet Service Manager, you'll see a window containing a list of all the Internet services running on your computer. Click the line that shows WWW under Service, then click Properties ➤ Service Properties.

You will see a Logging tab on the property sheet that appears. Click it and it moves to the front. A window similar to the illustration in Figure 14.4 will be displayed.

FIGURE 14.4: The Logging options for Internet Information Server

Notice the Log Format list box under Log to File. If you click it, you will see two choices: Standard Format and NCSA Format. Microsoft, of course, considers *its* format to be the standard, so it refers to the UNIX format as "NCSA," a nod to the popular UNIX Web server. If you choose NCSA Format, IIS will then start logging entries in the Common Log Format.

NOTE

Any changes made to the IIS Web server configuration won't take effect until you stop the server and restart it. You can do this from Internet Service manager, too, by clicking the Stop Service button on the toolbar, then clicking the Start Service button.

The Logging property sheet in Internet Service manager is also where you tell IIS how to structure logging in general. The default installation sets up a directory of log files, one file for each day. The files are named in the format *SVCYYMMDD.log*, where *SVC* refers to either IIS or NCSA log formats and *YY, MM,* and *DD* are the year, month, and date, respectively. In IIS format, the server log for August 23, 1997, would be named in970823.log. The in is replaced with nc in NCSA format.

You have several other choices if you don't like this daily logging scheme. A new log file can also be created every week, every month, or when the file reaches a size that you specify in megabytes. Just click the radio button of your choice and IIS will follow the new scheme.

TIP

If you change the IIS logging scheme, notice that the file-naming format changes, too. The current format is shown under Log file name: at the bottom of the Logging property sheet.

EXTRACTING LOG FILE INFORMATION

You have learned about the formats for Web server log files and where they are kept by the various servers. Now, what can you *do* with all of the information in the logs?

Perl is especially adept at handling projects that involve processing "formatted" text, much more so than a higher-level compiled language such as C or C++ is. Let's see how it's done.

Using Perl to Decode a Server Log

Perl has so many facilities built into it for dealing with text—especially if the text is set up in a consistent way—that there is very little reason to even attempt to take a Web server log file apart in any other language.

First of all, if you know what the format of the log file is (and you certainly should, on your own server!), you can break a line of log entries into individual fields and store them in *one line* of Perl code. Let's use the example in the previous section from the Internet Information Server logs:

```
   152.163.195.39, -, 6/13/97, 21:37:00, W3SVC, OWSLEY,
➡ 207.77.84.202, 328, 60, 29, 304, 0,
➡ GET, /wml/homepage.gif, -,
```

Because the entries are separated by commas, we can use Perl's `split` function to put each entry in its own variable.

Remember from the previous section that the entries are:

- ► IP address of the client
- ► Client's user name, which is always empty (-) in IIS
- ► Date of request
- ► Time of request
- ► Service name (always W3SVC in IIS)
- ► Web server's name (computer name)
- ► Server IP address
- ► Elapsed CPU time (in milliseconds) of the operation
- ► Number of bytes received
- ► Number of bytes sent
- ► Service status code
- ► Windows NT status code
- ► Operation requested
- ► Target of the operation
- ► Ender (always -)

The most difficult task in creating a Perl program to extract these fields is thinking up variable names for all of them. The critical thing to remember is that the *order* of the variables in the call to `split` must match the order of entries in the log file line. These lines of Perl code will do it:

```
($ClientIP, $Dummy, $DateTime, $SvcName, $SrvrName,
        $SrvrIP, $CPUTime, $BytesRecv, $BytesSent,
        $SvcStatus, $NTStatus, $Operation,
        $Target, $Dummy) = split (/,/, $LogLine);
```

Remember that `split` parses the string passed to it for the pattern between the slash characters (//) in its first argument and uses the pattern as a way to break the string down into components separated by the pattern. In this example, we're looking for the comma as a delimiter in the `$LogLine` string. Any time that `split` encounters a comma, it will load the text it has read previously into the next variable in the list on the left side of the equation.

Let's turn the example into a snippet of executable code by:

1. Loading the example log file line into a local variable.

2. Processing the variable with `split`, extracting each field into its own variable.

3. Printing the individual values to the screen.

Enter the following code into your text editor:

```
#!perl/bin/perl

# Hard-code an example log line into a local variable.

    $LogLine = "152.163.195.39, -, 6/13/97, 21:37:00, W3SVC"
              ", OWSLEY, 207.77.84.202, 328, 60, 29, 304, 0"
              ", GET, /wml/homepage.gif, -";

# Extract the components using split()

    ($ClientIP, $Dummy, $Date, $Time, $SvcName,
        $SrvrName, $SrvrIP, $CPUTime, $BytesRecv,
        $BytesSent, $SvcStatus, $NTStatus,
        $Operation, $Target, $Dummy) =
    split (/,/, $LogLine);

# Print the values to the screen.
    print "Client's IP address = $ClientIP\n";
    print "Date of request = $Date\n";
```

```
print "Time of request = $Time\n";
print "Service name = $SvcName\n";
print "Server name = $SrvrName\n";
print "Server's IP address = $SrvrIP\n";
print "Processing time = $CPUTime\n";
print "Received $BytesRecv bytes of data\n";
print "Sent $BytesSent bytes of data\n";
print "Server returned status of $SvcStatus\n";
print "Windows NT returned status code $NTStatus\n";
print "Operation requested = $Operation\n";
print "Target of operation = $Target\n";

#                          End logs.pl
```

Save this script as logs.pl and run it from the command line. Your output should look similar to Figure 14.5.

FIGURE 14.5: An example of a simple extraction from a log file line

Dissecting the Example Code

You probably noticed one aspect of our rudimentary log entry extraction program immediately: it's ugly, at least in the way it prints the information. Don't worry: You'll learn how to pretty it up shortly.

Meanwhile, let's discuss the program we have so far.

In the code line that calls split, notice that two variables are called $Dummy:

```
# Extract the components using split()
```

Part iv

```
($ClientIP, $Dummy, $Date, $Time, $SvcName,
    $SrvrName, $SrvrIP, $CPUTime, $BytesRecv,
    $BytesSent, $SvcStatus, $NTStatus,
    $Operation, $Target, $Dummy) =
split (/,/, $LogLine);
```

Recall from the definition of an IIS log file entry line in the previous section that two fields are always empty and, therefore, designated with hyphens: the client's user name and the last entry in the line. The variable $Dummy is actually being filled twice, which means that after split is finished $Dummy will contain the value of the *last* field put in it. It really doesn't matter, because we intend to ignore whatever the variable contains. That's why it's called $Dummy.

TIP

Because of the way split works, the second declaration of $Dummy in the list could have been left out entirely. The processing of the $LogLine string would have simply stopped when split ran out of variables in which to place the extracted fields.

The logs.pl script introduces another new Perl concept, too: the *concatenation* operator, or dot (.). Notice the line in which $LogFile is given a string value:

```
# Hard-code an example log line into a local variable.

$LogLine = "152.163.195.39, -, 6/13/97, 21:37:00, W3SVC"
         ."," OWSLEY, 207.77.84.202, 328, 60, 29, 304, 0"
         ."," GET, /wml/homepage.gif, -";
```

The $LogLine string is being set in the program rather than actually read from a log file, and it's rather long. You could have typed the whole string on one line, but it would have stretched far past the right margin of the screen. It would have looked ugly.

Perl's string concatenation operator joins two (or more) strings. It is similar to the addition operator (+) in an arithmetic equation. In other words, given two strings:

```
$Str1 = "Now is the time ";
$Str2 = "for all brown foxes";
```

you can combine—or *concatenate*—them into one with the dot:

```
$Str3 = $Str1.$Str2;
```

If you print $Str3, you'll see

```
Now is the time for all brown foxes
```

In the example, we needed to break $LogLine up into parts of a manageable length. Using the dot operator in the declaration, the parts reassembled themselves.

TIP

You can join as many strings as you like with the concatenation operator. What would be the result of $Str1. $Str2. $Str3? Give up? Here's a hint: It's "Now is the time for all brown foxes" times 2.

Reading Data from a Real Log File

The example in the previous section was just that: an example, using log data that you hard-coded into the Perl script. However, it isn't too big a job to modify the logs.pl script to read lines from a real log file.

Let's broaden your logging experience a bit by using the Sambar server's log file in this example. Remember that the Sambar log format is almost identical to the UNIX Common Log Format:

- Client's IP address

- Date and time of request

- Operation requested, plus the target of the operation and the HTTP version being used

- Result code from the server

- Result code from Windows NT or Windows 95 (not used in standard Common Log Format)

- Number of bytes transferred

Decoding a Common Log Format log entry line is not nearly as straightforward as with IIS. Let's take another look at the previous example, refined somewhat to conform to the Sambar format:

```
140.172.165.58 - admin [27/Apr/1997:20:47:43 -0700]
"GET session\ adminlogin HTTP/1.0" 200 0 160
```

You know enough about the individual entries by now to be able to pick them out visually. But your task at the moment is to feed them into a Perl program. Notice that entries are separated with spaces, but two of the entries—the date/time string and the operation string—have spaces in them. What can you do about that?

You *could* hack together a Perl regular expression string that would extract each field intact. But the regular expression would be totally unintelligible to anyone but an expert in regular expressions. Why bother when you know which fields are which to begin with?

The date/time string

```
[27/Apr/1997:20:47:43 -0700]
```

contains a single space, separating the date/time and the time zone value. The operation string

```
"GET session\ adminlogin  HTTP/1.0"
```

has one space after the operation requested and two spaces after the operation target. According to the log format, these spaces will always be in the same place, so you can still use split with a simple pattern argument to split up the string. Besides, it probably isn't a bad idea to be able to get to these "extra" fields individually anyway.

Your original Perl script, logs.pl, will need a complete rewrite, so crank up the text editor and enter the following code:

```perl
#!perl/bin/perl

# logs1.pl
#
# A Perl script to read, extract, and print a log file from
# the Sambar Web server.
#

# Put the log file name into a local variable -- full path.

    $LogFile = "c:/sambar/logs/access.log";

# Open the file; die if that's not possible.

    open (LOG, $LogFile) ||
➡ die "Can't open $LogFile: $!\n";

# Read, extract, and print each line from the log file.

    while (<LOG>)
        {
        $LogLine = $_;              # Store the line locally

    # Strip out the characters we don't need.

        $LogLine = ~ s/\ [|\ ]|\ "//g;
```

```
        chop ($LogLine);

   .# Extract the components using split()
        ($ClientIP, $Dummy, $UserName, $DateTime, $TimeZone,
         $Operation,$Target, $HTTPVers, $SrvrStatus,
         $NTStatus,$BytesXfer) = split (/[ ]+/, $LogLine);

   # Print the values to the screen.
        print "Client's IP address = $ClientIP\n";
        print "Name of user on client = $UserName\n";
        print "Date and time of request = $DateTime\n";
        print "Operation requested = $Operation\n";
        print "Operation target = $Target\n";
        print "Server returned status of $SrvrStatus\n";
        print "Windows NT returned status code $NTStatus\n";
        print "Transferred $BytesXfer bytes of data\n\n";
        }            # End while (<LOG>)

   close (LOG);      # Close the log file.

#                    End logs1.pl
```

Save the script as logs1.pl and run it from the command line. Stop it from time to time (Ctrl+S works on both UNIX and Windows systems) to see what the output looks like—if the log file has many entries in it, it will roll off the screen in no time. The output should look similar to what is illustrated in Figure 14.6.

FIGURE 14.6: Data extracted from the Sambar log file

Part iv

Breaking Down the New Code Sample

The new Perl script, `logs1.pl`, mainly deals with a new format in log files. However, there are a couple of new Perl goodies that should be explained.

Notice first of all the code at the beginning of the program:

```
# Put the log file name into a local variable -- full path.

$LogFile = "c:/sambar/logs/access.log";

# Open the file; die if that's not possible.

open (LOG, $LogFile) || die "Can't open $LogFile: $!\n";
```

We store the full path to the Sambar log file in a variable; this makes it easier to deal with and change, you'll remember from previous chapters. The file is opened for reading (or the script dies trying) with the file handle LOG.

Next, we set up a loop that reads the log file line by line:

```
# Read, extract and print each line from the log file.

while (<LOG>)
    {
    $LogLine = $_;                    # Store the line locally.
```

The `while` statement refers to the LOG file handle enclosed in less-than and greater-than signs, which will read a line at a time into the Perl variable $_ until nothing is left in the file. The first line in the loop stores the line in the local variable $LogLine.

TIP

The incoming log line could be left in $_ without putting it in a local variable. It seems a little clearer, especially in subsequent references in the program, to put the value in a descriptive variable. However, as usual in Perl, it's a matter of taste. The implementation is ultimately up to you.

In the next couple of code lines, we do some simple formatting to $LogLine.

```
# Strip out the characters we don't need.

$LogLine = ~ s/\ [|\ ]|\ "//g;
chop ($LogLine);
```

The string contains three characters—[,], and "—that we don't need. The substitution in the first line strips them out. If you look closely at the regular expression in the substitution, it begins to make sense: You can pick out the three characters to be stripped. All of them have special meaning in a regular expression, so they're escaped with the backslash (\); and, finally, each substitution is separated from the others with the Perl OR operator (|).

The next line calls a function that you haven't seen before: chop. It's one of those handy little utilities that doesn't do much, but you find yourself using it a lot. The function does nothing but chop the last character off of a string. It's usually used to get rid of the newline (\n) character at the end of a line, and that's how we've used chop here. The last line of interest in logs1.pl is the one that calls split.

```
# Extract the components using split()
        ($ClientIP, $Dummy, $UserName, $DateTime, $TimeZone,
            $Operation,$Target, $HTTPVers, $SrvrStatus,
            $NTStatus,$BytesXfer) = split (/[ ]+/, $LogLine);
```

Notice that some new variables had to be declared to match the format of a Sambar log file entry. The pattern specified for split has changed, too. It looks a little strange, but, like the substitution done on $LogLine, it begins to make sense if you examine it closely. We want to break out the fields in the log entry separated by spaces. However, there are *two* spaces between the operation target and the HTTP version, as in the example that was used to start this section:

```
"GET session\ adminlogin  HTTP/1.0"
```

The regular expression [ ] will match on a space, but two spaces will constitute two matches and will thereby throw off the count of variables. Remember that split will go through the list of variables on the left side of the equation sequentially, throwing values into variables as it encounters matches for its pattern. Putting a plus sign after the brackets ([ ]+) will match on one *or more* spaces, thus ensuring that all white space is ignored and the proper values go to the proper variables.

Part iv

MONITORING ACTIVITY FROM A WEB PAGE

Your experience with Web server log files now includes negotiating the formats for Microsoft's Internet Information Server and the Sambar server, which produces logs in a format very similar to the UNIX Common Log Format. You may be wondering: What can you do with all of that information?

Well, this is another of those situations in which you are limited only by your imagination. You have the information; you have the tools to manipulate the information; and you have the tools to display the information in really any way you like.

A good place to start is a Web page. You already know quite a bit about using Perl scripts to create HTML documents that can be displayed on your Web site through CGI. Why not use some of that knowledge to create a statistical Web page that uses the information in your server log files?

Who Gets In and How Often?

With a little manipulation, you can determine the sources of "hits" on your Web site and how often they connect.

You'll use the IIS log files for this example. Recall from the previous section that the default IIS log file scheme is to create a new file for each day. This scheme results in a directory full of log files, each of which you will have to step through to get the information for a particular day.

Here's what you'll do with the log information for each day:

- ▶ Identify the various IP addresses from which your Web site has been contacted.

- ▶ Count the number of IPs.

- ▶ Count the number of hits from each IP.

- ▶ Format the resulting data in an HTML document and display it in a browser.

Let's start with one file, then build up to the entire directory. The output will go to the screen for now.

Enter the following code in your text editor, ensuring that the file and path names defined at the top match valid names on your system:

```perl
#!perl/bin/perl

# hitcnt.pl
#

# First version. Goes through a single IIS log file,
# tallying the hits and IP addresses from which they came.
# Command-line version -- output to screen.

# Define path to a single log file.
    $LogDir = "c:/winnt/system32/logfiles/";
    $LogFile = "in970502.log";
    $LogPath = $LogDir.$LogFile;

# Attempt to open the log file; die if it doesn't happen.

    open (LOG, $LogPath) || die "Can't open $LogPath: $!\n";

# Loop through the log file a line at a time and extract
# the entry information.

    $n = 0;                 # Initialize a counter.

    while (<LOG>)
        {
    ($ClientIP, $Dummy, $Date, $Time, $SvcName,
        $SrvrName, $SrvrIP, $CPUTime, $BytesRecv,
        $BytesSent, $SvcStatus, $NTStatus,
        $Operation, $Target, $Dummy) =
      split (/,/);

      # Store the client IP address, increment counter.

        $IPArray[$n] = $ClientIP;
        $n++;
        }                       # end while (<LOG>)

    close (LOG);            # Close the log file.

# Store the total hits, then initialize two arrays for
# the IPs and the number of hits for each.

    $TotalHits = $n;
    @IPHits = ();
```

```
@NumHits = ();
$HitCount = 0;

# Loop through @IPArray and sort out the IPs that match,
# incrementing that IPs hit count for each match.

for ($n = 0, $i = 0; $n < $TotalHits; $n++)
    {
    for ($p = 0; $p < $HitCount; $p++)
        {
        if ($IPArray[$n] eq $IPHits[$p])
            {
            $NumHits[$p]++;
            last;                # Same as break in C
            }
        }

    # If $p == $HitCount, no matches were found. This is a
    # new IP address, so add it to the list.

    if ($p == $HitCount)
        {
        $IPHits[$HitCount] = $IPArray[$n];
        $NumHits[$HitCount]++;
        $HitCount++;
        }
    }            # end for ($n = 0...)

# Print out the results.

print "On 05/02/97:\n\n";

for ($n = 0; $n < $HitCount; $n++)
    {
    print "$IPHits[$n] registered $NumHits[$n] hits\n";
    }

#                    End hitcnt.pl
```

Save this Perl script as hitcnt.pl and run it from the command line. Output similar to that illustrated in Figure 14.7 will be written to the screen.

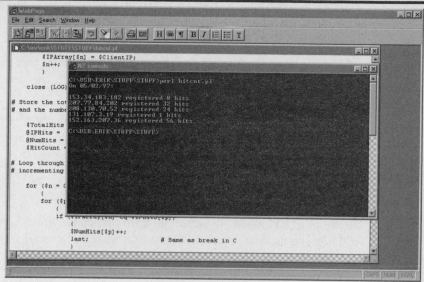

FIGURE 14.7: The hits on the Web site are tallied and written to the screen.

Analyzing the First Hit Counter

The first version of `hitcnt.pl` is ugly in its output—as are most command-line applications—but you have built the foundation for something much bigger.

TIP

Sambar server users need to make only two small changes to get `hitcnt.pl` to work with their log files. First, of course, change the log file locations defined at the top of the program. Then change the line that calls Perl's `split` function to the same call in `logs1.pl`, the script you wrote in the previous section.

The only new Perl construct presented in `hitcnt.pl` is the `last` statement, which will be covered shortly. The script presents some slightly knotty logical concepts, though, and they might be easier to understand if we step through the logic in English:

1. Pick up the IP address from every entry in the log file. Store all of them in an array.

2. Define two empty arrays: one to hold individual IP addresses and the other to hold the number of times a particular IP appeared in the log file.

3. Set up two loops: one to go through the first array of IPs from the log file entries and another to go through the second array of individual IPs.

4. Check each IP in the first array against the members of the second. If the two match, increment the hit count for that member of the second array. If no matches occur, this is a new IP—add it to the second array.

5. Print them out.

The client IP addresses are picked up from the log file in the same way you did it in the previous section. Notice that we didn't change the call to split:

```
while (<LOG>)
    {
    ($ClientIP, $Dummy, $Date, $Time, $SvcName,
        $SrvrName, $SrvrIP, $CPUTime, $BytesRecv,
        $BytesSent, $SvcStatus, $NTStatus,
        $Operation, $Target, $Dummy) =
    split (/,/);
```

There is one exception, however. Rather than storing the input line in a local variable, we have allowed split to take its data directly from the standard input, defined in Perl, you'll recall, as $_. This is why split has only its search pattern as a parameter.

NOTE

There is no reason to call split with the full list of variables for an entire log file entry, because only the first variable is used in hitcnt.pl. However, you probably will want more than just an IP address in future versions of the script, so you might as well leave the rest of the variables there.

The next code section stores the total number of entries in the log file and initializes a couple of empty arrays:

```
# Store the total hits, then initialize two arrays for the
# IPs and the number of hits for each.
    $TotalHits = $n;
    @IPHits = ();
```

```
@NumHits = ();
$HitCount = 0;
```

The variable $HitCount will be used to store the number of *individual* IP addresses—that is, unique IPs—that will be picked out of the full array of entries.

Now the two loops are set up to pick out the individual IPs and keep track of the number of times they've hit.

```
# Loop through @IPArray and sort out the IPs that match,
# incrementing that IPs hit count for each match.

for ($n = 0; $n < $TotalHits; $n++)
   {
   for ($p = 0; $p < $HitCount; $p++)
      {
      if ($IPArray[$n] eq $IPHits[$p])
         {
         $NumHits[$p]++;
         last;                   # Same as break in C
         }
      }

   # If $p == $HitCount, no matches were found.  This is a
   # new IP address, so add it to the list.

   if ($p == $HitCount)
      {
      $IPHits[$HitCount] = $IPArray[$n];
      $NumHits[$HitCount]++;
      $HitCount++;
      }
   }           # end for ($n = 0...)
```

There are two for loops in this block of code, an *inner* and *outer* loop. The outer loop:

```
for ($n = 0; $n < $TotalHits; $n++)
   {
```

is intended to step through @IPArray, which is the list of IP addresses taken directly from the log file. Many of them are duplicates, because an entry is created in the log every time a client makes a request of the Web server. We want to distill this list down to individual IPs and count the number of requests that each of them makes.

The inner loop takes care of the distillation:

```
for ($p = 0; $p < $HitCount; $p++)
    {
    if ($IPArray[$n] eq $IPHits[$p])
        {
        $NumHits[$p]++;
        last;              # Same as break in C
        }
    }
```

Remember that the variable $HitCount stores the number of individual IPs. This for loop steps through the second array checking for an IP address in $IPArray[$n] that matches the one in $IPHits[$p]. If a match is found, the @NumHits array member at *the same index*, which is the value in $p, is incremented. This allows us to associate an IP address with a hit count; the IP address in one array and the hit count in another both have the same index numbers.

This is the point at which a new Perl statement, last, is called. Sometimes you need a way to break out of a loop before it's finished (in fact, the identical statement in the C and C++ languages is break). In this example, we have satisfied the test in the if conditional code block, so we don't want to continue through until the loop completes. By calling last at this point, the loop ends.

The last part of the outer loop:

```
# If $p == $HitCount, no matches were found. This is a new
# IP address, so add it to the list.

        if ($p == $HitCount)
            {
            $IPHits[$HitCount] = $IPArray[$n];
            $NumHits[$HitCount]++;
            $HitCount++;
            }
```

checks the value in $p against that in $HitCount. If they are equal, it means the inner loop completed without finding a match, which means that this is another unique IP address and we can add it to the list. Notice that the two counters are incremented, too.

Counting Hits on the Entire Log Directory

You have gone through one IIS log file and extracted enough information from it to determine the number of hits from individual IP addresses in that file. With an extension to `hitcnt.pl`, you can extend your reach to the whole directory of IIS log files.

Perl, as usual, provides the method in a very straightforward fashion. Perl is able to handle directories in much the same way that it handles files: by opening, reading, and closing them. The main difference is that you have to use a new set of Perl functions to do the job:

- `opendir`, which returns a handle to the directory
- `readdir`, which returns the list of files in the directory
- `closedir`, which closes the directory handle

The specification for `opendir` is

```
opendir (HANDLE, PATH);
```

where HANDLE is the handle that you will use in subsequent references to the directory and PATH is the full path to the directory.

To read the directory entries, use

```
readdir (HANDLE);
```

which can fill a list variable with the contents of the directory as in

```
@FileList = readdir (HANDLE);
```

WARNING

UNIX and Windows directories always contain two special files designated by dots. The current directory is named "`.`" and the parent directory is "`..`". You will find very few uses for these special files if you just want a list of file names from a particular directory. You need to explicitly bypass them if you don't want to use them.

THE PERL-C-UNIX DIRECTORY FUNCTIONS

The directory functions in Perl are directly descended from—in fact, are virtually copies of—the *dirent* functions in the C standard library, which, of course, is descended from UNIX. Perl doesn't give

CONTINUED ➡

Part iv

you access to all of the information you can obtain with the C library functions, but the functions are called in the same way.

In addition to opendir, readdir, and closedir, there are three other Perl functions for manipulating directories:

▶ rewinddir, specified as rewinddir (HANDLE), which "rewinds" a directory handle back to its first entry.

▶ seekdir, specified as seekdir (HANDLE, POSITION), where POSITION is a place in the directory where the next readdir will take place (at the fifth or sixth file name, for example).

▶ telldir, specified as telldir (HANDLE), which returns the *current* position in the directory.

To change htcnt.pl to read and process a whole directory, you will:

1. Get a handle for the log file directory with opendir.

2. Read all of the files into an array with readdir.

3. Process the files one at a time as you did in the previous section.

The difference is that you will have more than just one file to process, so the bulk of the code in hitcnt.pl can go into a foreach loop that pulls the filenames out of the array. The new program looks like this:

```perl
#!perl/bin/perl

# hitcnt1.pl
#
# Second version. Goes through the entire IIS log file
# directory.
# Extracts the hits and IP addresses from which they came.
# Command-line version -- output to screen.

# Define path to a log directory.

    $LogDir = "c:/winnt/system32/logfiles";

# Open the directory; die if it's not possible.

    opendir (LOGD, $LogDir) || die "Can't open $LogDir:
$!\n";

# Get the list of log files into an array.
```

```
    @LogFiles = readdir (LOGD);

# Loop through the list, avoiding the . and .. entries.

    foreach $LogFile (@LogFiles)
        {
        if (($LogFile eq ".") || ($LogFile eq ".."))
            {
            next;
            }

    # Attempt to open the log file; die if it doesn't
    # happen.

        $LogPath = $LogDir."/".$LogFile;
        open (LOG, $LogPath) || die "Can't open $LogPath:
➥ $!\n";

    # Loop through the log file a line at a time and extract
    # the entry information.

        $n = 0;                    # Initialize a counter.

        while (<LOG>)
            {
            ($ClientIP, $Dummy, $Date, $Time, $SvcName,
                $SrvrName, $SrvrIP, $CPUTime, $BytesRecv,
                $BytesSent, $SvcStatus, $NTStatus,
                $Operation, $Target, $Dummy) = split (/,/);

        # Store the client IP address, increment counter.

            $IPArray[$n] = $ClientIP;
            $n++;
            }                         # end while (<LOG>)

        close (LOG);              # Close the log file.

    # Store the total hits, then initialize two arrays for
    # the IPs and the number of hits for each.
        $TotalHits = $n;
        @IPHits = ();
        @NumHits = ();
        $HitCount = 0;

    # Loop through @IPArray and sort out the IPs that match,
```

Part iv

```
            # incrementing that IPs hit count for each match.

        for ($n = 0, $i = 0; $n < $TotalHits; $n++)
            {
            for ($p = 0; $p < $HitCount; $p++)
                {
                if ($IPArray[$n] eq $IPHits[$p])
                    {
                    $NumHits[$p]++;
                    last;                    # Same as break in C
                    }
                }

        # If $p == $HitCount, no matches were found. This is a
        # new IP address, so add it to the list.

            if ($p == $HitCount)
                {
                $IPHits[$HitCount] = $IPArray[$n];
                $NumHits[$HitCount]++;
                $HitCount++;
                }
            }                          # end for ($n = 0...)

        # Print out the results after formatting date from
        # file name.

            if ($LogFile = ~ /(..)(..)(..)(..)/)
                {
                $year = $2;
                $month = $3;
                $day = $4;
                }

            print "On $month/$day/$year:\n\n";

            for ($n = 0; $n < $HitCount; $n++)
                {
                print "$IPHits[$n] registered $NumHits[$n]
➥ hits\n";
                }

            print "\n";          # Extra line.

        }                              # end foreach $LogFile...

    # Close the directory.
```

```
              closedir (LOGDIR);
```

```
    #                              End hitcnt1.pl
```

Save this script as `hitcnt1.pl` and, again, run it from the command line. Stop the output from time to time with Ctrl+S; you should see something similar to what's illustrated in Figure 14.8.

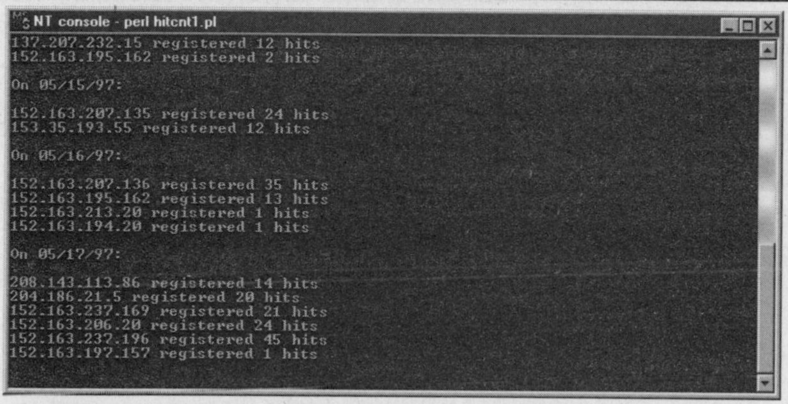

FIGURE 14.8: Counting the hits in an entire directory of log files

Analyzing the Whole-Directory Hit Counter

Despite what looks like an intimidating new program, you have only added two new features to your original `hitcnt.pl`. You have used Perl's directory functions to get a handle to the log file directory, and you put the code that processes the IP addresses and counts hits into a `foreach` loop.

The changes at the top of the program are minimal:

```
$LogDir = "c:/winnt/system32/logfiles";
opendir (LOGD, $LogDir) || die "Can't open $LogDir: $!\n";
@LogFiles = readdir (LOGD);
```

Notice that the only string constant you need to define now is the path to the log directory. The string, $LogDir,.is the argument to `opendir`, which returns the `LOGD` handle. The handle is used by `readdir` to put all of the directory's files into `@LogFiles`.

There are two items of special interest at the top of the `foreach` loop. The first:

```
foreach $LogFile (@LogFiles)
        {
```

```
if (($LogFile eq ".") || ($LogFile eq ".."))
    {
    next;
    }
```

tests for the two special files present in every Windows and UNIX directory. The file name "." refers to the current directory, and ".." is the parent; we don't need them in this example, so they are ignored.

How? By using the Perl next statement, which is essentially the opposite of the last statement you learned about in the previous section. Where last breaks *out* of the loop, next makes it loop again without executing any more of the subsequent code. In this example, if $LogFile has the value of either of the special file names, we don't want to do anything but get the next file name.

The next code section prevents a common mistake in working with directory handles.

```
$LogPath = $LogDir."/".$LogFile;
open (LOG, $LogPath) || die "Can't open $LogPath: $!\n";
```

Notice that an entire path to the file is built into $LogPath by combining the directory name and the file name. Why? Because $LogFile will work all by itself to open the file only if you happen to have the log directory set as your current directory, too. The chances of this being true every time you run hitcnt1.pl are quite slim—it's wisest to specify the full path to the file.

The last new feature in hitcnt1.pl makes a date out of an IIS log file name.

```
if ($LogFile = ~ /(..)(..)(..)(..)/)
    {
    $year = $2;
    $month = $3;
    $day = $4;
    }
```

```
print "On $month/$day/$year:\n\n";
```

Remember how daily IIS log names are formatted? The first two characters are in followed by the two-digit year, month, and day. In other words, the log file for August 24, 1997, would be named in970824.log. The regular expression /(..)(..)(..)(..)/ matches each of the first four pairs of characters in the file name in order. Therefore, we can pull the year out of $2, the month out of $3, and the day out of $4, ignoring $1 altogether.

Taking the Hit Counter to the Web

You now know how to navigate through an entire directory of IIS log files and calculate and display the number of hits on each day from every IP address that has connected to your Web site. The last step—putting the whole thing on a Web page—is the easiest.

You've already done all the hard work in reading the log files and manipulating the data. The only changes that need to be made are in the print statement at the bottom of hitcnt1.pl. They'll need to put out HTML-formatted code now.

The HTML conversion requires a few lines of additional code. First, call in your HTML header and ender code near the top:

```
# Bring in HTML header and ender stuff.

require "d:/pub/scripts/perl-cgi/html.pl";

# Define path to a single log file and a page title.

$LogDir = "c:/winnt/system32/logfiles";
$Title = "Counting Web page hits from various IPs";
```

Then, set up the header and titles for an HTML document in the program just after reading all of the files in the log directory into the list:

```
# Get the list of log files into an array.

@LogFiles = readdir (LOGD);

# Crank up a Web page.
    HTML_Header ($Title);
    print "<BODY>\n";
    print "<H1 ALIGN=\ "CENTER\ ">$Title</H1>\n";
    print "<HR>\n";
```

Last, the portion of the script that prints the data needs a near-total rewrite:

```
if ($LogFile = ~ /(..)(..)(..)(..)/)
    {
    $year = $2;
    $month = $3;
    $day = $4;
    }

print "<H3>Date: $month/$day/$year:</H3>\n<HR>\n";
print "<TABLE WIDTH=50%>\n";
```

```
for ($n = 0; $n < $HitCount; $n++)
{
print "<TR>\n<TD>$IPHits[$n]</TD> <TD>$NumHits[$n]
➡ accesses</TD>\n";
print "</TR>\n";
}

print "</TABLE>\n<HR>\n";
```

Notice that the print statements format the data in HTML tables. They look better that way.

Make these changes, then save the file as webhit.pl in a directory accessible to your Web server through CGI. Then invoke it as a URL from your Web browser. You'll see something similar to what is illustrated in Figure 14.9.

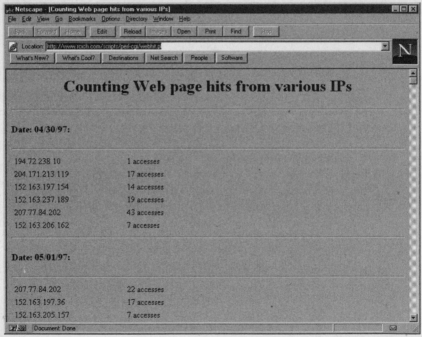

FIGURE 14.9: The hit counter moves to the World Wide Web.

Congratulations! You've moved your hit counter to the World Wide Web.

Moving On

You've undertaken a lot in this chapter. You have built, from the ground up, the capability to analyze your Web server logs in a simple fashion. You have built a foundation for a full statistical analysis of your Web site.

CHAPTER 15

E-MAIL SOLUTIONS

Despite the popularity of the World Wide Web, e-mail is still the most commonly used application on the Internet. The SMTP protocol and the Unix `sendmail` program are well-established tools for transferring e-mail messages. The Windows mail interface has been problematic over the years, but there are now several options that you can use.

Adapted from *Mastering Perl 5*, by Eric C. Herrmann
ISBN 0-7821-2200-0   958 pages $39.99

In this chapter, you will learn how to apply some e-mail solutions for both Unix and Windows computers. The first two examples you'll work through require you to have a connection to a Unix sendmail process. I connected to my local ISP via a telnet connection to build these examples. In the second part of this chapter, you'll learn about two Windows e-mail solutions: the Blat program and the Sender.pm module. The Blat application is a Windows-only solution. The Sender.pm module runs on any system with a connection to an SMTP server, which you have if you can receive e-mail on your computer.

AN INTRODUCTION TO E-MAIL PROGRAMS AND PROTOCOLS

SMTP (Simple Mail Transport Protocol) is the protocol used to transmit e-mail messages across the Internet. The most popular implementation of SMTP is the sendmail program. The sendmail program is the e-mail backbone of the Internet. SMTP and sendmail have been around since the 1980s. If you have an e-mail account, you use an SMTP server.

TIP

The full definition of the SMTP protocol can be found in RFC821. RFC stands for Request For Comments. RFCs are used as a means to document new and emerging Internet protocols. You can learn more about RFCs at http://www.faqs.org/rfcs/.

To communicate with an SMTP server, you must follow an exacting protocol. Doesn't that sound ominous—an exacting protocol? In practice, it is not difficult to make SMTP connections. The SMTP server will reject your e-mail request if you don't talk to it correctly, but if you know the secret handshake, you can talk to any SMTP server.

The following sections provide an overview of the sendmail program and SMTP servers. You'll learn how to use these in Unix and Windows programs later in the chapter.

The *sendmail* Program

The sendmail program sends messages to one or more recipients, routing the messages over whatever networks are necessary. If sendmail is invoked without a switch, it can be used to send mail from a file. In this mode, sendmail reads to the end-of-file marker or a single line that contains the period character (.) in the leftmost column.

The following are the most common switches used with sendmail:

▶ With the −bd switch (sendmail −bd), the sendmail program is started as a daemon; this is usually done by the system administrator. (A *daemon* is a process that runs in the background, performing its task without human intervention.) The sendmail daemon listens on port 25 for incoming SMTP connections, routing messages appropriately.

▶ With the −t switch, sendmail scans the message for recipient addresses. Each line that contains a To:, Cc:, or Bcc: will be searched for e-mail addresses. The Bcc: line, which is used as a recipient address, is deleted before the message is actually sent.

▶ With the -bv switch, sendmail will verify e-mail names but not try to collect or deliver a message. This is a convenient tool for managers of mailing lists.

▶ With the −f switch and the correct privileges, you can use sendmail to set the From: line in an e-mail header. You need normal privileges to set the From: value the same as your user name or superuser, or root privileges to set the From: value to an address that is different from the user name.

The sendmail program returns a status code when it exits. The status codes are shown in Table 15.1.

TABLE 15.1: The sendmail Program Status Codes

STATUS CODE	MEANING
EX_OK	Successful completion on all addresses
EX_NOUSER	User name not recognized
EX_UNAVAILABLE	Necessary resources were not available
EX_SYNTAX	Syntax error in address
EX_SOFTWARE	Internal software error, including bad arguments

CONTINUED ➡

Part iv

TABLE 15.1 continued: The sendmail Program Status Codes

Status Code	Meaning
EX_OSERR	Temporary operating system error, such as "cannot fork"
EX_NOHOST	Host name not recognized
EX_TEMPFAIL	Message could not be sent immediately but was queued

SMTP Servers

An SMTP server is an instance of a mail program like sendmail that operates as a daemon listening for incoming e-mail on port 25. When operating as an SMTP server, sendmail (or any other SMTP server program) listens for incoming e-mail messages. When a message is received, the SMTP server determines the correct routing for the e-mail message by examining the e-mail headers. Local e-mail messages are delivered to their mailboxes, and remote messages are forwarded to the next SMTP server along the route to the final destination.

The SMTP server only requires that you communicate with it in a formatted manner. You don't need a special e-mail tool to talk to your SMTP server. You can use telnet to connect to your SMTP server and send an e-mail message directly from the command line. However, using telnet to send an e-mail message does present one minor problem. This problem is apparent in Figures 15.1 and 15.2.

Figure 15.1 is the telnet session I used to produce the e-mail message shown in Figure 15.2. Unfortunately, one of the things you may notice in Figure 15.1 is that only the response from the SMTP server is visible. The input to the SMTP server during the telnet session is not echoed to the terminal. This means that you cannot see what you are typing, opening the door for typos and other errors. Sending an e-mail message via telnet is a little impractical, but you might want to use this method in an emergency.

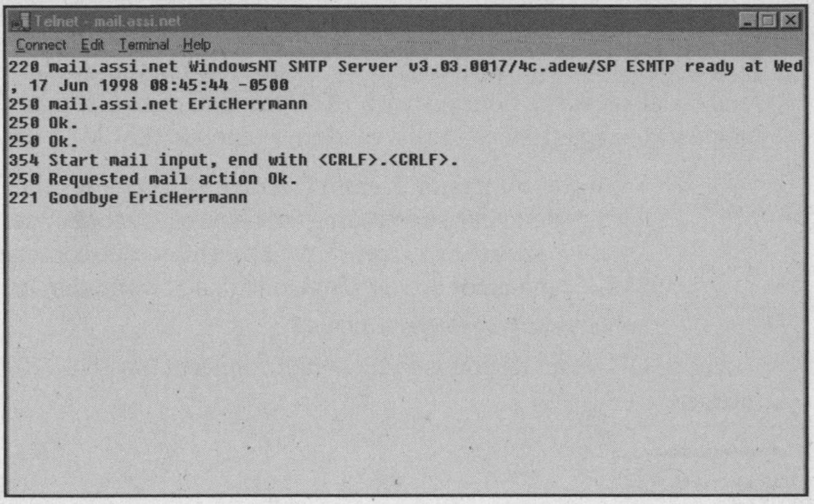

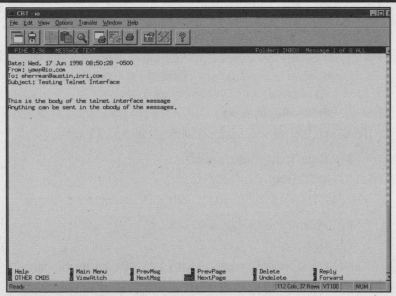

FIGURE 15.1: A telnet session to produce an e-mail message

FIGURE 15.2: A telnet e-mail message

The following steps show the procedure for using a telnet session to send an e-mail message. The messages and their sequence are the same, whether you are connected to port 25 via telnet or through a programmatic socket interface. After you issue each SMTP command, the SMTP server will respond with the appropriate status message, as shown in Figure 15.1. By following the steps outlined below in your program, you can successfully send e-mail messages from anywhere. The only difference is that in your program you replace step 1 with a valid connection to the SMTP server.

1. From the command prompt (DOS or Unix), enter the following command, substituting the name of your SMTP server for *mail.somewhere.com*. (Press Enter after each command; SMTP commands are terminated with a newline character.)

    `telnet `*mail.somewhere.com*` 25`

The SMTP server responds to the telnet connection with a 220 status message.

NOTE

Not all SMTP servers are named `mail`. You must know the name of the SMTP server to which you wish to connect. The SMTP server is the same name your e-mail client uses for receiving and sending e-mail. Look in the definition of the outgoing and incoming e-mail server in your favorite e-mail program. You can use that name as your SMTP server name.

2. Type the following command, substituting a computer name or something else (any character string will be accepted as an identity) for *YourIdentity*.

    `Helo `*YourIdentity*

The SMTP server will respond with a 250 status message.

3. Type in the From: header:

    `mail from:`

The SMTP server will respond with a 250 Ok status message.

4. Type in the To: header.

    `rcpt to:`

The SMTP server will respond with a 250 Ok status message.

5. Tell the SMTP server you are ready to send the e-mail message by entering the following command:

    `data`

The SMTP server will respond with a 354 status message.

6. Type in additional To:, From:, Bcc:, Cc:, Reply-To:, Subject:, and other headers you want to send. When you're finished with the e-mail headers, enter a blank line. The SMTP server will not respond.

7. Type in the body of the message. When you are finished entering the body of the message, type in a dot (.) in the left-hand column on a line by itself, then press Enter. The SMTP server responds with a `250 Requested mail action Ok` message.

8. Disconnect from the SMTP server by typing:

   `quit`

The SMTP server responds with a `221 Goodbye` message.

Later in the chapter, you'll learn how to configure a Windows program, Blat, which uses the steps you just used to communicate with the `sendmail` SMTP server to send e-mail messages. The next section shows how to use the `sendmail` program from a Unix machine.

UNIX E-MAIL SOLUTIONS

From a Unix platform, you can use the `sendmail` program directly, without going through an e-mail client program such as Netscape mail or Eudora. The examples presented here include two common e-mail applications: one for sending and responding to an HTML registration form and one for sending personalized e-mail messages to a list of contact names.

A Registration Application

Let's begin with one of the more common uses for e-mail—transferring registration forms. This type of application includes a little HTML and CGI programming. Using an e-mail message is one of the easiest ways to process HTML form data and to notify yourself or your users of the new information.

The HTML E-mail Form

Figure 15.3 (on page 472) shows an example of a registration form made up of text boxes, a pull-down menu, a text area box, and Register and Reset buttons. The form is generated by the HTML shown in Listing 15.1.

Part iv

Listing 15.1: An HTML E-mail Form

```
1.    <HTML>
2.     <HEAD>
3.       <TITLE>Email Registration Form</TITLE>
4.     </HEAD>
5.     <BODY>
6.        <H1>Registration Form</H1>
7.        <form method=post
➥ action=http://www.practical-inet.com/
➥ cgi-bin/perlBook/registerEmail.cgi>
8.        <TABLE>
9.           <TR>
10.            <TH width=10% Align=left>Name</TH>
11.            <TD colspan=5><INPUT ALIGN=Left NAME="Name"
12.             SIZE=60 TYPE=Text></TD>
13.          </TR>
14.          <TR>
15.            <TH width=10% Align=left>Company</TH>
16.            <TD colspan=5><INPUT ALIGN=Left NAME="Company"
17.             SIZE=60 TYPE=Text></TD>
18.          </TR>
19.          <TR>
20.            <TH width=10% Align=left>Title</TH>
21.            <TD colspan=5><INPUT ALIGN=Left NAME="Title"
22.             SIZE=60 TYPE=Text></TD>
23.          </TR>
24.          <TR>
25.            <TH width=10% Align=left>Address</TH>
26.            <TD colspan=5><INPUT ALIGN=Left NAME="Address"
27.             SIZE=60 TYPE=Text></TD>
28.          </TR>
29.          <TR>
30.            <TH width=10% Align=left>City</TH>
31.            <TD width=20%><INPUT ALIGN=Left SIZE=20
32.                           TYPE=Text Name=City></TD>
33.            <TH width=10% Align=left>State</TH>
34.            <TD width=20%><INPUT ALIGN=Left SIZE=10
35.                           TYPE=Text Name=State></TD>
36.            <TH width=10% Align=left>Zip</TH>
37.            <TD width=20%><INPUT ALIGN=Left SIZE=15
38.                           TYPE=Text Name=Zip></TD>
39.          </TR>
40.          <TR>
41.            <TH width=10% Align=left>Phone</TH>
42.            <TD width=20% ><INPUT ALIGN=Left SIZE=20
43.                           TYPE=Text Name=Phone></TD>
```

```
44.        <TH width=10% Align=left>Email</TH>
45.        <TD width=20% colspan=3>
46.        <INPUT ALIGN=Left SIZE=20
47.        TYPE=Text Name=Email></TD>
48.      </TR>
49.      <TR>
50.      <TH colspan=2 align=left>How did you learn about
51.                             us?</TH>
52.        <TD>
53.          <select name="Learn">
54.             <option value="radio">Radio</option>
55.             <option value="Television">Television
➥ </option>
56.             <option value="Lycos">Lycos </option>
57.             <option value="Yahoo">Yahoo </option>
58.             <option value="InfoSeek">Infoseek</option>
59.             <option value="other">Other</option>
60.          </select>
61.        </TD>
62.      </TR>
63.      <TR>
64.      <TH colspan=6>Comments</TH>
65.      </TR>
66.    </TABLE>
67.    <center>
68.       <TextArea rows=5 cols=60 name="Comments" >
➥ </textarea>
69.      </center>
70.      <TABLE>
71.        <TR>
72.         <TD><INPUT NAME="EmailRegister"
73.              TYPE=Submit VALUE="Register"></TD>
74.         <TD><INPUT TYPE=Reset></TD>
75.        </TR>
76.      </TABLE>
77.    </form>
78.  </BODY>
79. </HTML>
```

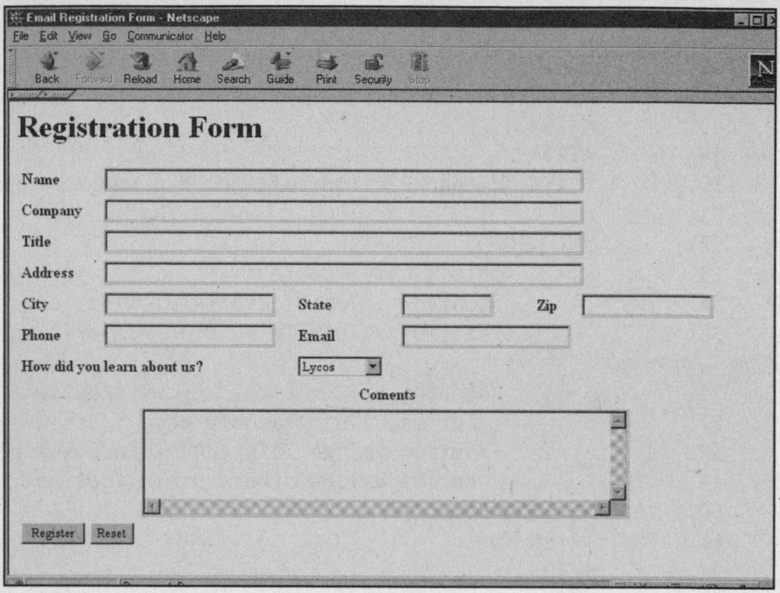

FIGURE 15.3: An e-mail registration form

Your CGI program doesn't care how the data is entered on your HTML form. All data generated from your HTML form and sent via the HTTP POST method header is translated the same way. Each HTML input tag, text area, text box, radio button, or option list is converted into URL-encoded name/value pairs, which your CGI program must decode. The address of the CGI program to receive and decode the data is on line 7 of Listing 15.1:

```
<form method=post action=http://www.practical-inet.com/
➥ cgi-bin/perlBook/registerEmail.cgi>
```

TIP

I prefer to use an absolute URL in the action field when identifying the program the form should send the data to. That way, regardless of how the server is configured, I'm sure the server has the correct address for calling my CGI program.

When your web client selects the Register button (refer to lines 72 and 73 of Listing 15.1), the browser generates the correct HTTP request headers, URL-encodes the data, and ships it to the web server identified in the action field of the HTML form tag.

One other thing to notice about Listing 15.1 is the handling of the HTML table formats and text areas. On line 66, the first table with all the input fields is terminated with the closing </TABLE> tag. On line 70, a new table begins just for the Register and Reset buttons. I created two tables because the extra TextArea tag doesn't work well inside a table format. The TextArea tag spans multiple columns and rows, and that conflicts with the table row tag <TR> and the column tags <TD> and <TH>. It's possible to make the TextArea tag work with the table tags by setting the table rows and colspan fields precisely; however, it's easier to work with the TextArea tag outside the HTML table format.

The CGI Program to Respond to the HTML Form

Listing 15.2 processes the input received from the HTML registration form in Listing 15.1 and returns the page shown in Figure 15.4. The returning of a "Thank You" page is more than just a courtesy to your web client—your CGI program must respond to every HTTP request with a valid HTTP response. The simplest HTTP response is another HTML web page.

Listing 15.2: An E-mail HTTP Response

```
1.   #!/usr/bin/perl
2.   require "readPostInput.cgi";
3.
4.   %postInputs = readPostInput();
5.   $dateCommand = "date";
6.   $time = `$dateCommand`;
7.   open (MAIL, "|/usr/sbin/sendmail -t") || return 0;
8.
9.   select (MAIL);
10.  print<<"EOF";
11.  To: Eric.Herrmann\ @assi.net
12.  From: $postInputs{ 'email'}
13.  Subject: Email Registration Received
14.
15.  $time
16.  Email Registration
17.  Name: $postInputs{ 'Name'}
18.  Email: $postInputs{ 'Email'}
19.  Company Name: $postInputs{ 'Company'}
20.  Street Address: $postInputs{ 'Address'}
21.  City: $postInputs{ 'City'}
22.  State : $postInputs{ 'State'}
```

```
23. Zip: $postInputs{ 'Zip'}
24. Phone: $postInputs{ 'Phone'}
25. Learn: $postInputs{ 'Learn'}
26. Comments: $postInputs{ 'Comments'}
27.
28. EOF
29.    close(MAIL);
30.    select (STDOUT);
31.    printThankYou();
32.
33. sub printThankYou(){
34. print<<"EOF";
35. Content-Type: text/html
36.
37. <HEAD>
38. <TITLE>THANK YOU FOR REGISTERING!</TITLE>
39. <META HTTP-EQUIV="Content-Type" CONTENT="document">
40. </HEAD>
41. <BODY>
42. <TABLE CELLSPACING=2 CELLPADDING=2 border=0 width=600>
43. <TR>
44. <BR>
45. <CENTER>
46. <FONT SIZE=+3><B>Thank You</b></font></center><BR><BR>
47. <CENTER><B><FONT SIZE=+1>
48. <P>Thank you $postInputs{ 'Name'}  for registering <BR>
49. </FONT></B><CENTER>
50. </TD>
51. </TR>
52. </TABLE>
53.
54. </BODY>
55. </HTML>
56.
57. EOF
58. }
```

Listing 15.2 communicates with the Unix sendmail program, which you learned about at the beginning of this chapter. Line 4 of Listing 15.2 reads the HTML POST input into the hash %postInputs:

```
%postInputs = readPostInput();
```

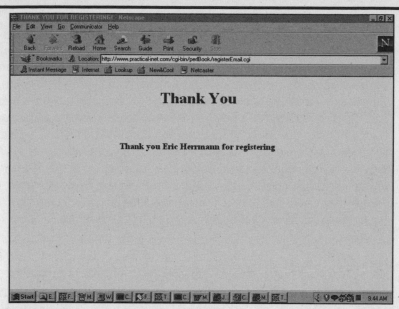

FIGURE 15.4: E-mail Thank You web page

NOTE

The readPostInputs subroutine was first introduced in Chapter 9. This subroutine uses a standard algorithm for decoding the URL-encoded data. You should include this standard algorithm in your CGI programs, via one of the standard CGI modules or libraries, such as CGI.pm or cgi-lib.pl.

The interface with the sendmail program begins on line 7:

```
open (MAIL, "|/usr/sbin/sendmail -t") || return 0;
```

Line 7 links the file handle with the sendmail program. As you learned in Chapter 14, if you want to communicate with a program, open a pipe to it using the open function with the pipe symbol (|) instead of the file-input operator (<>). Line 9 selects the MAIL file handle as the default output device:

```
select (MAIL);
```

The sendmail program requires the standard format, or e-mail headers, you see at the top of most e-mail messages. This format requires the To: and From: lines; the Subject: line is optional. The e-mail headers end with a blank line, which is then followed with the optional body of the e-mail message. You can send any information you want inside the body of the e-mail message. When the file handle `MAIL` is closed on line 29, your mail is sent via the `sendmail` program.

The `printThankYou` subroutine that returns the user response in Figure 15.4 isn't sent until your communication with `sendmail` is completed. This can create a time delay between when the Register button is pressed and the HTML Thank You page is received. You could write a CGI program that eliminates this delay by first sending the HTML Thank You page and then sending the e-mail message. However, based on a web server's configuration, a CGI program is considered to be operating improperly if it continues to process after responding to the HTML request. Since you rarely have control over where the final CGI program will be hosted, I recommend finishing your e-mail work before returning the HTTP response headers.

Listing 15.2 generates the e-mail message shown in Figure 15.5. As you can see, no special formatting or processing of the HTML form hash `%postInputs` is required to interface with the `sendmail` program.

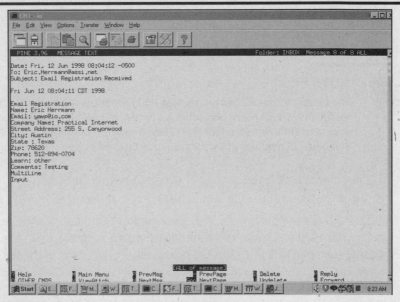

FIGURE 15.5: The e-mail message received

A Mailing List Application

Many text editors, such as Microsoft Word, offer a mail merge feature that allows you to generate multiple personalized letters using a single letter template. You can write one form letter and send it to different people, with each person's name used in strategic places in your letter.

These days, many of us prefer to communicate via e-mail. Rather than producing multiple personalized letters, you can send e-mail to a lot of friends, relatives, or business clients by using the program in Listing 15.3.

Listing 15.3: Personalized E-mail to a Contact List

```perl
1.  #!/usr/bin/perl
2.  if ($#ARGV < 1){
3.     print "contact file first letter file 2nd\n";
4.     exit 1;
5.     }
6.  $contactFile = $ARGV[0];
7.  $letterFile = $ARGV[1];
8.
9.  open (CONTACTLIST, "<$contactFile") || die "Can't open
                                    $contactFile\n";
10. open (LETTER, "<$letterFile") ||
    die "Can't open $letterFile\n";
11. @contactList = <CONTACTLIST>;
12. @letter = <LETTER>;
13. close (CONTACTLIST);
14. close (LETTER);
15. $count = 0;
16. for $line (@contactList){
17.
18.    if ($line =~ /@/){
19.        $count++;
20.        open (MAIL, "|/usr/sbin/sendmail -t") ||
           die "Can't openpipe to sendmail \n";
21.        ($companyName, $emailAddress, $FLName) =
           split(/,/,$line);
22.        $emailAddress =~ s/\ t//g;
23.        $FLName =~ /\ s*(\ w+)\ s*(\ w+)/;
24.        $firstName= $1;   $lastName = $2;
25.        chomp $lastName;
26.        select (MAIL);
27.        $subjectLine = $letter[0];
28.        chop $subjectLine ;
29.        $subjectLine = "$companyName";
```

```
30.          $returnAddress = "Eric.Herrmann\ @assi.net";
31.          print<<"EOF";
32. To: $emailAddress
33. From: $returnAddress
34. Subject: $subjectLine
35.
36. EOF
37.          for $index (0 .. $#letter){
38.              $letterLine = $letter[$index];
39.              chop $letterLine;
40.              if ($letterLine =~ /companyName/) {
41.                  $letterLine =~ s/companyName/$companyName/g;
42.              }
43.              if ($letterLine =~ /firstName/) {
44.                  $letterLine =~ s/firstName/$firstName/g;
45.              }
46.              if ($letterLine =~ /lastName/) {
47.                  $letterLine =~ s/lastName/$lastName/g;
48.              }
49.              print "$letterLine\n";
50.          } #end for loop
51.      close (MAIL);
52.      } #end if
53. }
54.
55. print STDOUT "\ nYou sent $count emails\n";
```

Listing 15.3 uses a contact list and a form letter to send personalized e-mail messages to a list of e-mail address and names. The program gets both filenames—for the contact list and the form letter files—from the command line. This is a Unix interface, but later in this chapter you'll learn how to use the Sender.pm module, which allows you to create a Perl e-mail interface on both a Unix and Windows computer.

The contact list read in on line 9 of Listing 15.3 is formatted so that each line is made up of an e-mail address and the recipient's name separated by a space. The contact list is read into an array and then processed one line at a time. Because the file can include blank lines and comment lines, line 18 specifies that only lines that have the e-mail at sign (@) in them are processed:

```
if ($line =~ /@/){
```

A pipe to the sendmail program is opened on line 20, then the e-mail address and contact name are extracted on line 21:

```
open (MAIL, "|/usr/sbin/sendmail -t") ||
die "Can't open pipe to sendmail \n";
($companyName, $emailAddress, $FLName) = split(/,/,$line);
```

Each time a new e-mail message is sent, a new connection is made to the sendmail program. Making a connection to a program always requires some extra processing time. Usually, it is faster to open a connection and keep it open as long as you are communicating with the other program. In the case of Listing 15.3, opening and closing a pipe to sendmail is slower than opening a connection and sending multiple e-mail messages through that one connection. If it is slow and I know it is slow, why do I do it this way? I open and close a pipe to sendmail for two important reasons:

▶ You can start the program in Listing 15.3 and leave it running. You don't need to be concerned with whether it takes ten minutes or ten hours to run. It's not slowing your machine or your work. The time involved in running the program revolves around making a single connection to sendmail to send a single letter.

▶ Each mailing is an individual e-mail delivery, which keeps the e-mail message as personal as possible, considering it is a form letter. The letter may read like a form letter (depending on the author's writing skill), but it will look like an individual e-mail message because it is sent individually.

One alternative to this method of sending e-mail involves opening a connection to sendmail and sending a blast of e-mail messages with a lot of CC: or BCC: lines. But how personal would the e-mail message seem when its recipients see a lengthy CC: list?

The message is personalized on lines 29 through 34 of Listing 15.3:

```
        $subjectLine = "$companyName";
        $returnAddress = "Eric.Herrmann\ @assi.net";
        print<<"EOF";
To: $emailAddress
From: $returnAddress
Subject: $subjectLine
```

The subject line of each e-mail includes the recipient's name. (If your recipients are like me, they will probably toss any e-mail that looks like a spam that has nothing to do with them.)

Lines 37 through 50 process each line of the letter, looking for the unique characters, companyName, firstName, and lastName. Each time one of these character strings is matched, all occurrences of those characters are replaced with the actual company name, first name, or last name, which was retrieved from the contact list:

```
for $index (0 .. $#letter){
$letterLine = $letter[$index];
```

```
chop $letterLine;
if ($letterLine =~ /companyName/) {
$letterLine =~ s/companyName/$companyName/g;
}
if ($letterLine =~ /firstName/) {
$letterLine =~ s/firstName/$firstName/g;
}
if ($letterLine =~ /lastName/) {
$letterLine =~ s/lastName/$lastName/g;
}
print "$letterLine\ n";
} #end for loop
```

TIP

If you're going to send form letters, take the time to personalize them. Your recipients will appreciate the extra time, and they are more likely to read the letter.

WINDOWS E-MAIL SOLUTIONS

Sending e-mail from a Perl program running on a Windows computer can be a pain in the neck if you don't have some type of interface to an SMTP server. As explained earlier in this chapter, opening up a telnet session on port 25 to your Internet service provider's SMTP server is possible but not very practical. Here, you'll learn about two interfaces to SMTP servers. One is a freeware program, and the other is a module that provides a direct Perl–to–e-mail interface.

Blat: A Windows E-mail Program

Originally intended as only a command-line interface, Blat became popular as a programming interface because it is the cheapest game in town. Blat is freeware. The authors of Blat are Mark Neal (mjn@aber.ac.uk) and Pedro Mendes (prm@aber.ac.uk).

Blat is available in the public domain for you to use and/or modify. As is the case with all types of public domain programs, many people have helped to make Blat a useful and easy-to-install SMTP interface. The following sections explain how to install and use Blat.

Blat Installation

To install Blat on your Windows computer, you need to copy two DLLs (dynamic link libraries) to your `WinNT/System32` directory and tell Blat how to communicate with your SMTP server. The two DLLs are `gqinsock.dll` and `cw3215.dll`. You can get these files from `http://gepasi.dbs.aber.ac.uk/softw/blat.html`.

Next, run the Blat installation program, which takes two parameters: your SMTP server name and your e-mail address. Enter the following command:

```
blat -install
```

If you don't know your SMTP server's name, look in your existing mail program's configuration setup. For example, my Internet service provider's SMTP server is located at `mail.io.com`.

After you install Blat this way, when you send mail from the command line using Blat, it will try to connect to an SMTP server at *mail .yourDomain.com* and will identify all e-mail messages as from *yourName @yourDomain.com*.

Blat in Action

Blat is designed as a command-line program for sending the contents of a file as the body of an e-mail message. You can also use Blat from within Perl programs.

To send a file as an e-mail message, use this syntax:

```
blat filename.txt -t yourName@yourDomain.com
```

This sends the contents of the specified filename to the specified e-mail address.

Blat version 1.7 (the current release at the time of this writing) has several command-line options that allow you to send binary files, send the same message multiple times, and read input from `STDIN`. These options are listed in Table 15.2.

TABLE 15.2: Blat Options

OPTION	PARAMETER	DESCRIPTION
-	None	For console input, end input with Ctrl+Z
-attach	<file>	Attach a binary file to the message (may be repeated)

CONTINUED ➡

TABLE 15.2 continued: Blat Options

Option	Parameter	Description
-c	<recipient>	Carbon-copy recipient list (comma-separated)
-b	<recipient>	Blind carbon-copy recipient list (comma-separated)
-base64	None	MIME Base64 content transfer encoding
-f	<sender>	Override the default sender address (the new address must be known to server)
-h	None	Display help
-i	<address>	A From: address, not necessarily known to the SMTP server (<sender> is included in the message header's Reply-to: and Sender: fields)
-mime	None	MIME quoted printable content transfer encoding
-o	<organization>	Set Organization: to appear in the header fields
-p	<profile>	Use stored profile for -server, -sender, -try, and -port options
-port	None	Override the default port on the server
-q	None	Suppress all output
-s	<subject>	Subject line (if you do not include a subject line, the subject "contents of console input" will be sent)
-server	<address>	Override the default SMTP server to be used
-t	<recipient>	Recipient list (comma-separated)
-try	None	Set how many times Blat should try to send a message

The -q (suppress all output) and the - (console input) options are important from a programmer's viewpoint. The -q option means your program doesn't have to worry about output from Blat interrupting your web server or any other program. The - option means your program can send data directly to the Blat program.

The programmer's interface to Blat can be downright finicky. Blat works flawlessly from the command line, but a misplaced switch or quote character stops the program without any helpful error messages. If you use Blat in your code, I suggest using one of the two subroutines in Listing 15.4.

Listing 15.4: The Blat Interface

```
1.   $msg = "Testing the Blat Interface\ n";
2.   blatSTDIN("Eric.Herrmann\ @assi.net",
     "dummy\ @noWhere.com", "test blat", $msg);
3.   sub blatSTDIN ($$$$){
4.      my ($toName, $fromName, $subject, $message) = @_;
5.      $blat = "c:\ \ Winnt\ \ system32\
⇒ \ blat.exe - -t $toName  -s
                \ "$subject\ " -q";
6.      open (MAIL, "| $blat -f \ "$fromName\ " ") || die $!;
7.      print MAIL $msg;
8.      print MAIL "TESTING BLAT STDIN\ n";
9.      close MAIL;
10.     }
11.
12. blatFILE("Eric.Herrmann\ @assi.net",
    "dummy\ @noWhere.com", "test blat", $msg);
13. sub blatFILE ($$$$){
14.     my ($toName, $fromName, $subject, $message) = @_;
15.     open (OUTFILE, ">$$");
16.     print OUTFILE $msg;
17.     print OUTFILE "Testing FILE interface\ n";
18.     close (OUTFILE);
19.     `c:\ \ Winnt\ \ system32\
⇒ \ blat.exe $$ -t $toName  -s
                \ "$subject\ " -q`;
20.     unlink ($$);
21.     }
```

On line 5, the subroutine blatSTDIN uses the - (console input) option to force Blat to get its input from STDIN, or, in this case, from the open MAIL file handle. It also uses the -q (suppress all output) option:

```
$blat = "c:\ \ Winnt\ \ system32\ \ blat.exe -
⇒ -t $toName  -s \ "$subject\ " -q";
```

The `blatSTDIN` subroutine produces the mail message shown in Figure 15.6.

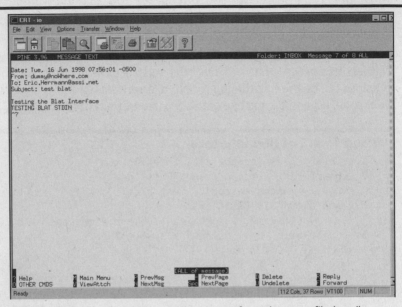

FIGURE 15.6: Sending a Blat mail message from the open file handle

You might notice that Figure 15.6 uses a spoofed e-mail address (hiding the original address). Obviously, dummy@noWhere.com did not send this message. Blat allows you to change the From: e-mail address, but it always includes the registered e-mail address of the login process executing the Blat program in the Reply-to: headers.

When you test Blat on your computer, expand the headers to show the entire path. You'll see the name of the SMTP server that Blat connects to, the name of the computer that connected to the SMTP server, and the e-mail address of the person logged in to the computer that executed the Blat program. Blat is not a good tool if you are trying to hide the original sender's address.

NOTE

Blat uses an SMTP feature called server relay. This feature is often used to spoof e-mail addresses, hiding the original sender of the e-mail. My primary Internet service provider does not allow this type of e-mail routing. It compares the address of the original message with the address of the sender. If the address did not originate on my Internet service provider's domain, it does not relay the message. However, most SMTP servers allow this type of relay traffic.

The ^? characters that you see at the bottom of the e-mail message in Figure 15.6 are the result of a bug in release 1.7 of Blat. The ^? characters are always sent when a message uses the - option. The subroutine blatFILE, on lines 13 through 21 of Listing 15.4, solve this problem by writing the message to a temporary file.

Line 15 creates an output file handle to a file named as the current process ID of the script:

```
open (OUTFILE, ">$$");
```

The process ID is guaranteed to be unique among all the processes currently executing, thereby creating a unique temporary filename.

Lines 16 and 17 write your message to the file:

```
print OUTFILE $msg;
print OUTFILE "Testing FILE interface\ n";
```

Before you send your message, you must close your temporary file. This makes sure the output buffers are flushed and any system file locks are released.

Line 19 uses the command-line interface of Blat to send the temporary file as an e-mail message:

```
`c:\ \ Winnt\ \ system32\ \ blat.exe $$ -t
➥ $toName  -s \ "$subject\ " -q`;
```

As shown in Figure 15.7, those pesky extra ^? characters are no longer included in the e-mail message.

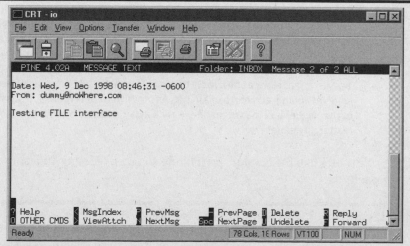

FIGURE 15.7: Sending a Blat mail message from a file

Line 20 cleans up the temporary file, deleting it from your computer.

```
unlink ($$);
```

The two subroutines of Listing 15.4 make Blat a useful e-mail tool for Windows programmers.

Sender.pm: A Perl E-mail Interface

In this section, you'll learn about `Sender.pm`, a Perl module that provides a direct Perl interface to the SMTP server. The `Sender.pm` module can be used on any platform that has a connection to an SMTP server. If you can send and receive e-mail, you probably can use `Sender.pm`. The CPAN site includes an older module called `Net::SMTP`, which can also be used as a programmer's e-mail interface. However, I think `Sender.pm` is easier to use. To send an e-mail, you only need to create a `Sender` object and call the `MailMsg` method. That's it!

In this section, you'll learn how easy it is to use `Sender.pm`, and then you will progressively step into the methods that perform the actual connections to the SMTP server. This way, when you are finished with this chapter, you'll know how to use `Sender.pm` and why and how `Sender.pm` works. If you should decide to extend `Sender.pm` or implement your own SMTP interface, you'll know how to proceed.

TIP

The `Sender.pm` module was written by Jan Krynicky (`Jenda@Krynicky.cz`). She says that this is her first module, and she has only been writing Perl code for 1.5 years (as of the writing of this chapter). Congratulations are certainly in order. Her code makes the interface to an SMTP server easier to understand. `Sender.pm` and other modules by Jan are available from `http://Jenda.Krynicky.cz`. Jan tells me she lives in the Czech Republic, which is east of Germany, south of Poland, and north of Austria. As far as I am concerned, Jan is at the end of the next e-mail message, only a click away. Country boundaries just don't matter any more!

Why do I like the `Sender.pm` module so much? Listing 15.5 shows the reason.

Listing 15.5: The *Sender.pm* Module

```
1.  use Mail::Sender;
2.  $sender = new Mail::Sender({ from => 'yawp@io.com',
3.                              smtp => 'mail.assi.net'} );
```

```
4.
5.  if (!(ref $sender) =~ /Sender/i){
6.    die $Mail::Sender::Error;
7.  }
8.
9.  $sender->MailMsg({ to =>'Eric.Herrmann@assi.net',
10.                    subject => 'Testing Sender',
11.                    msg => "An easy email interface?"} );
12.
13. if ( ($sender->{ 'error'} ) < 0) {
14.    print "ERROR: $Mail::Sender::Error\ n";
15. }
16. else {
17.    print "Msg Sent Ok\ n";
18. }
```

What could be easier than that? There are only two real lines of functional code in Listing 15.5. The rest of it is error-checking code. All that is required to send a mail message using Sender.pm is initializing the $sender object with a From: address and a valid SMTP server to connect to. This is done on lines 2 and 3, which actually contain just one Perl statement:

```
$sender = new Mail::Sender({ from => 'yawp@io.com',
                             smtp => 'mail.assi.net'} );
```

Then all you need to do is call MailMsg method with your instance of a Sender object providing the recipient address, subject line, and a message. This is done on lines 9 through 11, which again contain only a single Perl statement:

```
$sender->MailMsg({ to =>'Eric.Herrmann@assi.net',
                   subject => 'Testing Sender',
                   msg => "An easy email interface?"} );
```

If you want to send a longer message, create a variable—either a scalar or an array of strings—and send the variable in the message field. If you want to send a file or several files, just use the MailFile syntax, as explained in the section about Sender methods, coming up soon.

Listing 15.5 uses several groups of Sender methods that work together to send an e-mail message. You'll learn more about using the Sender methods shortly. First, you'll see how to use the lower-level and more direct methods of this module, which better illustrate the steps involved in communicating with the SMTP server.

Part iv

Sender.pm Communication with an SMTP Server

Rather than the code in Listing 15.5, you can use the more direct methods shown in Listing 15.6 to send an e-mail message. This example, which sends a binary file as an e-mail attachment, illustrates each of the steps you learned in the section on using an SMTP server through a telnet connection. Listing 15.5 is more practical for everyday use, but it doesn't demonstrate the SMTP interface through Sender.pm as well as Listing 15.6.

Listing 15.6: *Sender.pm* Module Lower-Level Methods

```
1.    use Mail::Sender;
2.    $sender = new Mail::Sender({ from => 'yawp@io.com',
3.                                 smtp => 'mail.assi.net'} );
4.
5.    if (!(ref $sender) =~ /Sender/i){
6.      die $Mail::Sender::Error;
7.    }
8.
9.    $sender->OpenMultipart(
   { to =>'eherrmann@austin.inri.com',
10.                    subject =>
   'Testing Sender Direct I/F'} );
11.   $sender->Body;
12.   $sender->SendLine("Attached is a our
   new Logo jpg file\ n");
13.   $sender->SendFile({ description => 'Chapter 15 image 2',
14.                  ctype => 'Image Tif type',
15.                  encoding => 'Base64',
16.                  disposition =>
   'attachment; filename="f0602.tif";
                     type="tiff image"',
17.                  file => 'f0602.tif'} );
18.   $sender->Close;
19.
20. if ( ($sender->{ 'error'} ) ) < 0) {
21.     print "ERROR: $Mail::Sender::Error\ n";
22. }
23. else {
24.     print "Msg Sent Ok\ n";
25. }
```

Listing 15.6 shows the steps required when communicating with the SMTP server. The SMTP communication works in the following order:

1. Connect.

2. Say hello.

3. Tell the server who is sending the e-mail.

4. Tell the server whom you are sending e-mail to.

5. Tell the SMTP server you are sending it data.

6. Send the mail headers.

7. Complete the OpenMultipart message headers line on line 11 by sending the body.

The remaining lines separate the message from the file attachment and then disconnect from the SMTP server.

The following section describes the syntax and use of the various methods. After you learn the complete syntax of the main methods of Sender.pm, you'll step through the lower-level code that makes the actual connection to the SMTP server.

Sender.pm Method Syntax

The Sender.pm module uses object-oriented syntax. The new method of Sender.pm initializes the Sender object so that the Sender methods listed in Table 15.3 can use the default values. Table 15.4 lists the default Sender method parameters. Each of the default parameters may be overridden by explicitly passing the value in the appropriate method.

TABLE 15.3: Sender.pm Methods

METHOD	DESCRIPTION
Body	Send the head of the multipart message body. You can specify the character set and the encoding. The default is "US-ASCII", "7BIT".
Cancel	Cancel an opened message.
Close	Close and send the mail.
MailMsg(msg)	Send a message.

CONTINUED ➡

Part iv

TABLE 15.3 continued: Sender.pm Methods

METHOD	DESCRIPTION
MailFile(msg, file)	Send one or more files by mail.
New	Prepare a Sender.
Open	Open a new message.
OpenMultipart	Open a multipart message.
Part	Print a part header for the multipart message. The undef or empty variables are ignored.
Send(@strings)	Print the strings to the socket. Doesn't add any end-of-line characters. Use \r\n as the end-of-line characters.
SendEnc(@strings)	Print the strings to the socket. Doesn't add any end-of-line characters. Use \r\n as the end-of-line characters. Encodes the text using the selected encoding (Base64/Quoted-printable).
SendEx(@strings)	Print the strings to the socket. Doesn't add any end-of-line characters but changes all end-of-line characters to \r\n.
SendLine(@strings)	Print the strings to the socket. Adds the end-of-line character at the end.
SendLineEnc(@strings)	Print the strings to the socket. Adds the end-of-line character at the end. Encodes the text using the selected encoding (Base64/Quoted-printable).
SendLineEx(@strings)	Print the strings to the socket. Doesn't add any end-of-line characters, but changes all end-of-line characters to \r\n.
SendFile(file)	In multipart mode, send a file as a separate part of the mail message.

WARNING

Do not mix up SendEx and SendEnc or SendLineEx and SendLineEnc! SendEnc and SendLIneEnc do some buffering necessary for correct Base64 encoding, and the Send method, which does the actual sending of the message, is not aware of that. Usage of SendLine and SendLineEx in non–7-bit parts is not recommended. In particular, if you use SendLine or SendLineEx to send several lines, eventually creating a single message, the data is likely to become corrupted.

TABLE 15.4: Default Sender Method Parameters

PARAMETER	DESCRIPTION
From	The address of the sender of the e-mail message
Replyto	The address the e-mail message should be replied to
To	The recipient's e-mail address
Smtp	The IP or domain address of the SMTP being connected to
Subject	The subject line of the e-mail message
Headers	Any additional headers sent before the body of the message
Boundary	The message boundary

The Sender.pm methods return detailed failure information as shown in Table 15.5. The method Mail::Sender::Error contains a textual description of the last error.

TABLE 15.5: Sender.pm Method Failure Codes

CODE	MEANING
-1	SMTP host unknown
-2	Socket failed
-3	Connect failed

CONTINUED ➡

TABLE 15.5 continued: Sender.pm Method Failure Codes

CODE	MEANING
-4	Service not available
-5	Unspecified communication error
-6	Local user $to unknown on host $smtp
-7	Transmission of message failed
-8	Argument $to empty
-9	No message specified in call to MailMsg or MailFile
-10	No filename specified in call to SendFile or MailFile
-11	File not found
-12	Not available in single-part mode

Most of the methods of Sender.pm are straightforward and don't require a special explanation. The following are some of the more important methods or those that do not follow the default syntax.

new   This method is used to initialize a Sender object and must be called before any other Sender method. It initializes the default parameters listed in Table 15.4. You can set smtp, from, and other parameters here and then use the information in all messages.

The new method does not open a connection to the SMTP server. You must use $Sender->Open or $Sender->OpenMultipart to start talking to the server. The parameters passed to the new method are used in subsequent calls to $Sender->Open and $Sender->OpenMultipart. Each call to a method with new default parameters, such as the to or from address, changes the variables initialized by the new method. If the new method is successful, it returns a reference variable to a Mail::Sender object. If a mail message in $sender is opened, it is closed and a new mail message is created and sent. $sender is then closed. The file parameter may be a filename, a list of filenames (separated by commas), or a reference to a list of filenames.

Close   Although this method does not require any parameters, it is important to note that the mail message being sent to the server is not processed until the `Sender` object is closed. The `Close` method should be called automatically when destroying the object, but you should call it yourself just to be sure—and you should do it as soon as possible to close the connection and free the socket.

Part   This method prints a part header for the multipart message. It accepts the following special parameters:

ctype   defines the content type (MIME type) of this part. This parameter defaults to `"application/octet-stream"`.

encoding   defines the encoding used for this part of message. This parameter defaults to `"7BIT"`.

disposition   defines the type of e-mail as a message or an attachment. This parameter defaults to `"attachment"`.

SendFile   This method sends a file as a separate part of the mail message and operates only in multipart mode. `SendFile` accepts the same parameters as the `part` method and, in addition, accepts the `file` parameter. The `file` parameter identifies the name of the file to send, a list of filenames, or a reference to a list of filenames. Each file will be sent as a separate part.

MailFile   This method lets you send a file or several files. For example, using the `MailFile` method, you can replace lines 9 through 18 of Listing 15.6 with this one simple call:

```
MailFile ({ msg=> "msg",
            file => 'f06022.tif'} );
```

MailMsg   This method sends the message. If a mail message in `$sender` is already open, it is closed, which sends the message, and a new mail message is then created and sent. `$sender` is then closed. The `MailMsg` method shows the exact sequence and syntax necessary for your program to communicate with the SMTP server. If you want to build your own interface to the SMTP server, you should study this method. You'll do that in the next section.

Part iv

SMTP Server Communication Revisited

The SMTP server communicates in an asynchronous handshaking mode. Commands do not need to follow each other in a strict time frame. Commands can sometimes be minuted apart; however, the SMTP server will timeout eventually. What is required is to follow a strict sequencing of commands. Therefore, as you examine Listing 15.7, take note of the communication sequence over the socket connection. The socket connection is the connection to the SMTP server. If you decide to further investigate Sender.pm, you will see the same sequence of communication regardless of the type of e-mail message being sent.

Listing 15.7: The SMTP Server Connection

```
1.   sub MailMsg {
2.     my $self = shift;
3.     my $msg;
4.     if (ref $_[0] eq 'HASH') {
5.       my $hash=$_[0];
6.       $msg=$hash->{ msg} ;
7.       delete $hash->{ msg}
8.     } else {
9.       $msg = pop;
10.    }
11.    return $self->{ 'error'} =NOMSG unless $msg;
12.
13.    $self->Open(@_);
14.    $self->SendEx($msg);
15.    $self->Close;
16.    return $self;
17. }
```

Listing 15.7 does not include the constructor or initialization routines of Sender.pm. The constructor saves the SMTP information, but the communication to the SMTP server isn't started until one of the Open methods is called.

The MailMsg subroutine, which begins on line 1 of Listing 15.7, establishes the sequence of events for communication with an SMTP server. Lines 13 through 16 open communications with the SMTP server (this involves some initial handshaking and header transfer), send the body of the message, and then close communication:

```
$self->Open(@_);
$self->SendEx($msg);
$self->Close;
return $self;
```

Let's examine the steps involved. Knowing how they work will help you to understand how to design and build your own module.

As implemented in the Sender.pm module, the Open method is where all the action occurs. With this design, the Open method connects to the SMTP server and then tells the SMTP server whom the message is coming from, where it is going, and that the data is about to be sent. From that point, the SMTP server will accept almost any data you send it. Listing 15.8 steps through the initial communication sequence with the SMTP server.

Listing 15.8: SMTP Connection Initialization

```
1.   sub Open {
2.    my $self = shift;
3.    if ($self->{ 'socket'} ) {
4.     if ($self->{ 'error'} ) {
5.       $self->Cancel;
6.     } else {
7.       $self->Close;
8.     }
9.    }
10.   delete $self->{ 'error'} ;
11.   my %changed;
12.   $self->{ multipart} =0;
13.
14.   if (ref $_[0] eq 'HASH') {
15.    my $key;
16.    my $hash=$_[0];
17.    foreach $key (keys %$hash) {
18.     $self->{ lc $key} =$hash->{ $key} ;
19.     $changed{ $key} =1;
20.    }
21.   } else {
22.    my ($from, $reply, $to,
        $smtp, $subject, $headers ) = @_;
23.
24.    if ($from) { $self->{ 'from'} =$from;
        $changed{ 'from'} =1;}
25.    if ($reply) { $self->{ 'reply'} =$reply;
        $changed{ 'reply'} =1;}
26.    if ($to) { $self->{ 'to'} =$to;$changed{ 'to'} =1;}
27.    if ($smtp) { $self->{ 'smtp'} =$smtp;
        $changed{ 'smtp'} =1;}
28.    if ($subject) { $self->{ 'subject'} =$subject;$changed
                                  { 'subject'} =1;}
```

```
29.   if ($headers) { $self->{ 'headers'} =$headers;$changed
                                            { 'headers'} =1;}
30.   }
31.
32.   $self->{ 'to'} =~ s/[ \ t]+/, /g if ($changed{ to} );
33.   $self->{ 'to'} =~ s/,,/,/g if ($changed{ to} );
34.   $self->{ 'boundary'} =~ tr/=/-/
➡ if $changed{ boundary} ;
35.
36.   if ($changed{ from} ) {
37.   $self->{ 'fromaddr'} = $self->{ 'from'} ;
38.   $self->{ 'fromaddr'} =~ s/.*<([^\ s]*?)>/$1/;
➡ #get from address
39.   }
40.
41.   if ($changed{ reply} ) {
42.   $self->{ 'replyaddr'} = $self->{ 'reply'} ;
43.   $self->{ 'replyaddr'} =~ s/.*<([^\ s]*?)>/$1/;
➡ #get reply address
44.   $self->{ 'replyaddr'} =~ s/^([^\ s]+).*/$1/;
➡ #use first address
45.   }
46.
47.   if ($changed{ smtp} ) {
48.   $self->{ 'smtp'} =~ s/^\ s+//g;
➡ #remove spaces around $smtp
49.   $self->{ 'smtp'} =~ s/\ s+$//g;
50.   $self->{ 'smtpaddr'} = ($self->{ 'smtp'} =~
51.   /^(\d{ 1,3} )\ .(\d{ 1,3} )\ .
➡ .(\d{ 1,3} )\ .(\d{ 1,3} )$/)
52.   ? pack('C4',$1,$2,$3,$4)
53.   : (gethostbyname($self->{ 'smtp'} ))[4];
54.   }
55.
56.   if (!$self->{ 'to'} )
➡ { return $self->{ 'error'} =TOEMPTY; }
57.
58.   if (!defined($self->{ 'smtpaddr'} )) {   return
         $self->{ 'error'} =HOSTNOTFOUND($self->{ smtp} ); }
59.
60.   my $s = &FileHandle::new(FileHandle);
61.   $self->{ 'socket'} = $s;
62.
63.   if (!socket($s, AF_INET, SOCK_STREAM,
➡ $self->{ 'proto'} )) {
64.   return $self->{ 'error'} =SOCKFAILED; }
```

```
65.
66.  if (!connect($s, pack('Sna4x8',
➥ AF_INET, $self->{ 'port'} ,
          $self->{ 'smtpaddr'} ))) {
67.    return $self->{ 'error'} =CONNFAILED; }
68.
69.  my($oldfh) = select($s); $| = 1; select($oldfh);
70.
71.  $_ = <$s>; if (/^[45]/) {  close $s; return
          $self->{ 'error'} =SERVNOTAVAIL; }
72.
73.  print $s "helo localhost\r\n";
74.  $_ = <$s>; if (/^[45]/) {  close $s; return
          $self->{ 'error'} =COMMERROR; }
75.
76.  print $s "mail from: <$self->{ 'fromaddr'} >\r\n";
77.  $_ = <$s>; if (/^[45]/) {  close $s; return
          $self->{ 'error'} =COMMERROR; }
78.
79.  foreach (split(/, /, $self->{ 'to'} )) {
80.    print $s "rcpt to: <$_>\r\n";
81.    $_ = <$s>; if (/^[45]/) {  close $s; return
            $self->{ 'error'} =USERUNKNOWN($self->{ to} ,
➥ $self->{ smtp} ); }
82.    }
83.
84.  print $s "data\r\n";
85.  $_ = <$s>; if (/^[45]/) {  close $s; return
          $self->{ 'error'} =COMMERROR; }
86.
87.  print $s "To: $self->{ 'to'} \r\n";
88.  print $s "From: $self->{ 'from'} \r\n";
89.  print $s "Reply-to: $self->{ 'replyaddr'} \r\n"
                if $self->{ 'replyaddr'} ;
90.  print $s "X-Mailer: Perl Mail::Sender Version
            $Mail::Sender::ver Jan Krynicky
➥ <Jan\ @chipnet.cz>
            Czech Republic\r\n";
91.  if ($self->{ 'headers'} )
➥ { print $s $self->{ 'headers'} ,"\r\n"} ;
92.  print $s "Subject: $self->{ 'subject'} \r\n\r\n";
93.
94.  return $self;
95. }
```

Lines 3 through 9 of Listing 15.8 clean up after any previous communication:

```
if ($self->{ 'socket'} ) {
    if ($self->{ 'error'} ) {
        $self->Cancel;
    } else {
        $self->Close;
    }
}
```

Each call to the Open method closes any previously opened sockets, completing any communication currently in progress.

Lines 14 through 30 are involved in reading the incoming parameter list and determining if any of the initialized parameters have changed. Lines 32 through 54 make sure e-mail and SMTP addresses are in the correct format. The network communication begins on line 60. The protocol used in establishing the initial socket on line 63 is a standard Internet socket protocol.

The actual communication with the SMTP server begins on line 66, which establishes the initial connection with the SMTP server on the public port 25:

```
if (!connect($s, pack('Sna4x8', AF_INET, $self->{ 'port'} ,
➡ $self->{ 'smtpaddr'} ))) {
```

After the initial connection on line 66, the server responds on the socket with a 220 status message, briefly describing itself. If the response status code is a 400 or 500 series message, the message sequence has failed in some manner and communication must be reestablished. The server response is read off the socket on line 71, followed by the if check to verify a valid status response code:

```
$_ = <$s>; if (/^[45]/) { close $s; return
➡ $self->{ 'error'} = SERVNOTAVAIL; }
```

This is part of the handshaking process. You must use the correct sequence of commands to the SMTP server, but you must also read, and thereby clear, each response communication from the SMTP server.

NOTE

Reading the response from the SMTP server is critical, and it is called completing the handshake. A *handshake* is a two-step communication. One side initiates a message, and the other side acknowledges the receipt of the message. If the receipt of the message is not acknowledged, then the message sender never knows if the message is received. By reading the SMTP server's response message, you are actually removing the message from the connection, called a *socket*. By removing the message, you have acknowledged the message, which completes the handshake.

After successfully connecting to the SMTP server, it's polite to say hello and identify yourself. In fact, it's required to say `helo` and identify yourself, which is done on line 73:

```
print $s "helo localhost\r\n";
```

The identity value can be any value. The `Sender.pm` module uses a hard-coded `localhost` value. It would be more polite to get your actual local host name and send that value. The SMTP server's response to the `helo` message is a 250 status message, echoing back the SMTP server name and your identity.

Next, on line 76, you must tell the SMTP server who the mail is from:

```
print $s "mail from: <$self->{ 'fromaddr'} >\r\n";
```

The response should be a 250 Ok status message. Then on line 80, each recipient's name is sent to the SMTP server:

```
print $s "rcpt to: <$_>\r\n";
```

The server responds with a 250 Ok status message for each recipient.

At this point, you've completed the initial communication exchange. Your next step, on line 84, is to tell the SMTP server that you're going to send it some real data:

```
print $s "data\r\n";
```

The SMTP server responds with a 354 status message telling you it is ready to receive mail input.

Now you're ready to send the actual e-mail headers. In this implementation, the To:, From:, Reply-to:, X-mailer:, Subject:, and any other e-mail headers are sent to the SMTP server in the Open method. From this point forward, the SMTP server will not respond with a new status message until you have completed sending the e-mail message. The headers are sent between lines 87 through 92:

```
print $s "To: $self->{ 'to'} \r\n";
```

```
    print $s "From: $self->{ 'from'} \r\n";
    print $s "Reply-to: $self->{ 'replyaddr'}
➥ \r\n" if $self->{ 'replyaddr'} ;
    print $s "X-Mailer: Perl Mail::Sender Version $Mail::Sender
➥ ::ver Jan Krynicky  <Jan\ @chipnet.cz>
➥ Czech Republic\r\n";
    if ($self->{ 'headers'} ) { print $s
➥ $self->{ 'headers'} ,"\r\n"} ;
    print $s "Subject: $self->{ 'subject'} \r\n\r\n";
```

You can put any value in the X-mailer: header. This header is essentially used as a comment line to let the programmer identify the tool used to send the e-mail message. Also, you can change the From: address, but this will not hide the actual Sender. The protocol requires the SMTP server to identify the originating computer, the hops made through the SMTP chain, and the original login username. When you send the message, these additional headers show up when your e-mail receiver clicks on the option to show all headers. Finally, notice that all communication with the SMTP server ends with \r\n. You must send a carriage return character (\r) in addition to the newline character (\n) to the SMTP server.

NOTE

I'm not sure I agree that the headers sent from lines 87 through 92 of Listing 15.8 should be in an Open method. The e-mail headers are part of the e-mail message and are not required as part of the initial communication sequence.

The rest of the SMTP communication is anticlimactic. Listing 15.9 shows how the body of the message is sent to the SMTP server using the SendEx method.

Listing 15.9: The E-mail Body

```
1.  sub SendEx {
2.    my $self = shift;
3.    my $s;
4.    $s = $self->{ 'socket'} ;
5.    my $str;
6.    foreach $str (@_) {
7.      $str =~ s/\n/\r\n/;
8.    }
9.    print $s @_;
10.   return 1;
11. }
```

As you can see from Listing 15.9, sending the body of the message only involves writing to the SMTP socket after the standard newline character (\n) has been replaced with the carriage return/linefeed character (\r\n).

The SMTP server has nothing to say until you complete the e-mail message, which is done in Listing 15.10.

Listing 15.10: E-mail Message Completion

```
1.  sub Close {
2.    my $self = shift;
3.    my $s;#=new FileHandle;
4.    $s = $self->{ 'socket'} ;
5.    if ($self->{ buffer} ) {
6.      my $code = $self->{ code} ;
7.      print $s (&$code($self->{ buffer} ));
8.      delete $self->{ buffer} ;
9.    }
10.   if ($self->{ 'multipart'} ) { print $s "\r\n-",
➥ $self->{ 'boundary'} , "-\r\n";}
11.   print $s "\r\n.\r\n";
12.
13.   $_ = <$s>; if (/^[45]/) { close $s;
➥ return $self->{ 'error'} = TRANSFAILED;}
14.
15.   print $s "quit\r\n";
16.   $_ = <$s>;
17.
18.   close $s;
19.   delete $self->{ 'socket'} ;
20.   return 1;
21. }
```

Line 11 of Listing 15.10 actually completes the sending of one e-mail message. The SMTP server responds on line 13 with a 250 Requested mail action 0k message. At this point, if you wanted to send multiple e-mail messages, you could begin the data sequence again.

Sender.pm chooses to only send one e-mail per SMTP connection. Line 15 of Listing 15.10 closes the connection to the SMTP server with a quit command. The SMTP server responds with a polite "Goodbye" response. Your communication with the SMTP server is now complete.

This communication process is basically the same, regardless of the type of e-mail being sent. A multipart e-mail message with a file attachment only requires a boundary header separating the different parts of the e-mail message. The file itself should be binary encoded using a protocol like Base64. This process is fully covered in the Sender.pm module's MailFile method. If you examine that method, you'll see that you can easily use MailFile to send any type of attachment, or you can build your own method or module.

TIP

The functions for binary encoding a file are available in the Mime::Base64 and the MIME modules. These modules are freely available from the CPAN web site, www.perl.com/CPAN.

SUMMARY

What happens when you learn how to program in Perl 5? You get to use and write some really cool applications. In this chapter, you learned about coding Perl applications that use one of the earliest and most widely used tools of the Internet—e-mail. You can use the examples presented in this chapter as a starting point for your own HTML and e-mail programs.

Most e-mail programs on the Internet communicate through the sendmail daemon. The sendmail program, when run as a daemon, is frequently referred to as your SMTP server. The STMP server is responsible for routing e-mail messages from domain to domain, across the network.

Although it's more convenient to use an interface program to talk with your SMTP server, in this chapter you also learned the commands necessary to communicate with an SMTP server using a telnet session.

After you learned about the sendmail program and SMTP servers, you saw an example of one of the more common CGI applications—reading an HTML registration form and sending an e-mail response. Then you learned more about the sendmail program through a Perl 5 interface program that sends form letters to a mailing list.

There is a growing demand for e-mail applications that run on a Windows computer. In this chapter, you learned about a Windows freeware program called Blat. Blat is an interface program to your SMTP server. To avoid problems with the Blat interface, you can use the two subroutines that were included in this section. The blatSTDIN subroutine sends e-mail messages directly through your program. The blatFILE subroutine uses a file interface to send e-mail messages.

Finally, you learned about the Sender.pm module. Perl 5 comes delivered with an SMTP interface module called Net::SMTP, but I think Sender.pm is easier to use. The module Sender.pm is an e-mail interface built by a Perl 5 user. With fewer than 20 lines of code and this module, you can send e-mail messages and attached files.

CHAPTER 16

DATABASES AND THE WEB

Business applications all seem to have one thing in common: a lot of data. Whether your program deals with sales figures, inventory, employee salary, or any other common business information, the data is made up of rows and columns of names and numbers that need to be sorted, extracted, entered, updated, and manipulated. Once a program collects information, people want to see that data in a variety of forms.

Adapted from *Mastering Perl 5*, by Eric C. Herrmann
ISBN 0-7821-2200-0   958 pages $39.99

Quite often, you may be tempted to write all the code yourself to sort, track, and store your program's information. You usually end up wishing you had an easy way to meet the growing demands for reports, sorts, and more. The solution is to transfer most of the data manipulation to a database. In this chapter, you will step through the process of importing a growing list of data into a new database.

Ultimately, the Internet is extending into all forms of programming and business applications, and database programming is no exception. Once you have learned how to build and manipulate your database, you'll learn how to export it to the web.

An Introduction to Databases

The data you collect (about your business, your family, your hobbies, and so on) and the medium used to store and organize that data is called a *database*. That means the shoe box of receipts you pull out for the auditor is a database. As your business grows, you may decide you need something more than a shoe box—perhaps a ledger. Later, you may decide to copy the data into a file on your computer. Each of the previous storage mediums represents a database. The problem with those types of databases is that they don't provide any built-in means of automatically sorting, printing, or managing the data. You need a database management system to do these things.

A database management system is a set of tools for managing data in a particular format. You could create your own tool set, or you could buy an existing one. One thing all database management systems include is a database engine. A *database engine* is the application, such as Microsoft Access or Oracle, that manipulates the data in your database. The database engine is the heart of your database management system, and it will usually be either an object-oriented or relational database engine. The object-oriented system, which is gaining in popularity, is still not available on the average desktop PC.

NOTE

The examples in this chapter use Microsoft Access, one of the more popular database engines, but the process applies to all the major database programs available today.

If you have a copy of Microsoft Access on your desktop PC, you have a copy of an inexpensive relational database management system. A relational database is made up of *tables*. Each table contains rows of information about each object stored in the table. A *row* contains data about one object of information, such as an e-mail contact. A row is made up of columns of information that describe an individual object. In an e-mail table, an e-mail contact object would include columns about the e-mail address, the name of the e-mail contact, and other information. In a database table for car data, the car object row would include columns about the make and model of the car, specific options, and other information. Each database file may contain multiple tables, and each table may contain multiple columns.

A single table or multiple tables may also be accessed via a *view*. A view is a logical subset of a table or a combination of tables. The view defines a different way to access, or see, the table's data, but it does not contain data itself. The view allows you to create further logical relationships between tables without creating a second copy of the data. You might create a single view from the relationships between several different contact tables, such as an e-mail contact table, a business contact table, and a party guest contact table.

THE ODBC CONNECTION

Are you familiar with Esperanto? Well neither am I, and that's probably because it didn't have the support of every major government in the world. Esperanto was supposed to be the common language of our globe. Are you familiar with ODBC and SQL? If you are a database programmer, the answer is almost certainly yes. That's because ODBC and SQL have the support of every major software company in the world, including Microsoft, Sun, and IBM.

ODBC stands for Open DataBase Connectivity. You can think of it as a universal connector. In this section, you'll learn how to connect your program to your database. SQL (pronounced "sequel"), which stands for Structured Query Language, is the common language that all major databases understand. It will be explained after you are connected to your database.

We'll be using two applications to accomplish this first step: Microsoft Access and Win32::ODBC. The module Win32::ODBC has become a standard for connecting Win32 applications to various database programs. Its interface to your database engine will be a common thread throughout this chapter.

Creating a DSN

The `Win32::ODBC` module and other ODBC applications connect to your Access database through a Data Source Name (DSN). For ODBC to work across many different database engines, it requires a standard way to communicate with all databases. The DSN contains a common set of information that all databases must supply. You must create the DSN on your computer before you can begin connecting your program to your database.

The DSN supplies the following information:

▶ The locations of the database

▶ The type of database driver (Microsoft Access in our example)

▶ Username and password information

There are two primary types of DSNs:

▶ A User DSN is accessible by only the account that created it. If you are creating a DSN for your own use, you should create a User DSN.

▶ A System DSN is accessible by any account. If you are creating a DSN that will be used by multiple users, you should create a System DSN.

The DSN created for this example will eventually be accessed through a web server, so it should be a System DSN.

You can create a DSN through the Windows Control Panel or by using the `Win32::ODBC` module. As a programmer, I prefer the `Win32::ODBC` programmatic method to the GUI interface of the Control Panel, because I can handle the whole process easily through my code. However, I think understanding both the GUI and programmatic interface to a DSN gives you a better concept of the entire process and the links involved. The following sections describe both methods.

Using the Control Panel

To create a DSN for your Access database, open your Control Panel and click on the ODBC icon. In Figure 16.1, the ODBC icon is in the middle of the first line of icons.

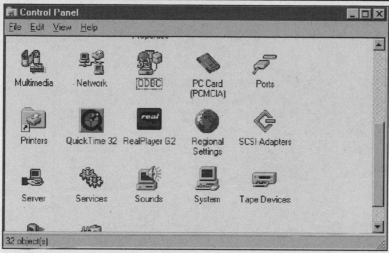

FIGURE 16.1: The 32-bit ODBC icon in the Control Panel

Clicking on the ODBC icon brings up the ODBC Data Source Administrator, which is used to define and configure DSN entries. Select the System DSN tab, and then click on the Add button to bring up the Create New Data Source dialog box. In this dialog box, select the specific driver used for your database engine. I have selected the Microsoft Access Driver, as shown in Figure 16.2.

Selecting the Access driver brings up the ODBC Microsoft Access 97 Setup dialog box. Here, you enter the name of your DSN, which is the same name you will use in your program to reference the DSN. You also can enter a brief description of the DSN. Then select the Database radio button in the System Database portion of the dialog box (for a System DSN) and click on the System Database button. The Select System Database dialog box appears, as shown in Figure 16.3. Navigate to the directory that contains your database and select it.

FIGURE 16.2: Selecting a data source driver

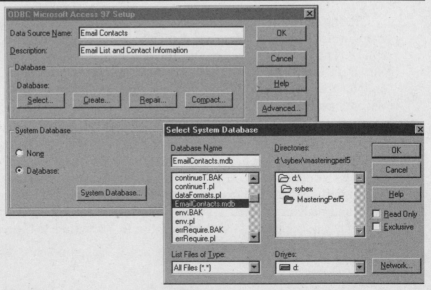

FIGURE 16.3: Selecting the database

Using the *Win32::ODBC* Module

To create a DSN via a program, you first need to know what drivers are on your computer. Listing 16.1 uses the Win32::ODBC module to collect a list of all the ODBC drivers on your computer and print them to your computer monitor. Figure 16.4 shows the list for my computer.

NOTE

The line numbers in code listings are provided for easy reference and, of course, aren't part of the code itself.

Listing 16.1: Getting the ODBC Drivers

```
1.  use Win32::ODBC;
2.  #Get the available drivers
3.  %drivers = Win32::ODBC::Drivers();
4.  #I want to print the driver attributes comma separated
5.  #Load the dynamic copy of array
    #separator with a new separator
6.  local $" = ", ";
7.  foreach $driver (sort keys %drivers){
8.      @attributes = split (/;/,$drivers{ $driver} );
9.      print "Driver = $driver\n";
10.     print "@attributes\n\n";
11. }
```

```
Mastering Perl                                                    _ 8 X
Driver = INTERSOLV 2.11 32-bit Oracle ?
APILevel=1, ConnectFunctions=YYY, DriverODBCVer=02.10, FileUsage=0, smProcessPerConnect=N, SQLLeve

Driver = INTERSOLV 2.11 32-bit SQLBase
APILevel=1, ConnectFunctions=YYY, DriverODBCVer=02.10, FileUsage=0, smProcessPerConnect=Y, SQLLeve

Driver = INTERSOLV 2.11 32-bit SQLServer
APILevel=1, ConnectFunctions=YYY, DriverODBCVer=02.10, FileUsage=0, smProcessPerConnect=Y, SQLLeve

Driver = INTERSOLV 2.11 32-bit Sybase System 10
APILevel=1, ConnectFunctions=YYY, DriverODBCVer=02.10, FileUsage=0, smProcessPerConnect=Y, SQLLeve

Driver = INTERSOLV 2.11 32-bit Textfile (*.*)
APILevel=1, ConnectFunctions=YYN, DriverODBCVer=02.10, FileUsage=1, smProcessPerConnect=N, SQLLeve

Driver = INTERSOLV 2.11 32-bit dBASEFile (*.dbf)
APILevel=1, ConnectFunctions=YYN, DriverODBCVer=02.10, FileExtns=*.dbf, FileUsage=1, smProcessPerC

Driver = Microsoft Access Driver (*.mdb)
UsageCount=8, APILevel=1, ConnectFunctions=YYN, DriverODBCVer=02.50, FileUsage=2, FileExtns=*.mdb,

Driver = Microsoft Excel Driver (*.xls)
UsageCount=3, APILevel=1, ConnectFunctions=YYN, DriverODBCVer=02.50, FileUsage=1, FileExtns=*.xls,

Driver = Microsoft FoxPro Driver (*.dbf)
UsageCount=4, APILevel=1, ConnectFunctions=YYN, DriverODBCVer=02.50, FileUsage=1, FileExtns=*.dbf,
Level=0

Driver = Microsoft ODBC Driver for Oracle
UsageCount=2, SQLLevel=1, DriverODBCVer=02.50, ConnectFunctions=YYY, APILevel=1

Driver = Microsoft Paradox Driver (*.db )
UsageCount=1, APILevel=1, ConnectFunctions=YYN, DriverODBCVer=02.50, FileUsage=1, FileExtns=*.db,

Driver = Microsoft Text Driver (*.txt; *.csv)
UsageCount=2, APILevel=1, ConnectFunctions=YYN, DriverODBCVer=02.50, FileUsage=1, FileExtns=*.,*.a
.csv, SQLLevel=0

Driver = Microsoft dBase Driver (*.dbf)
UsageCount=4, APILevel=1, ConnectFunctions=YYN, DriverODBCVer=02.50, FileUsage=1, FileExtns=*.dbf,
0, J^=, *=, Jg=

Driver = SQL Server
DSNConverted=F, UsageCount=7, SQLLevel=1, FileUsage=0, DriverODBCVer=02.50, ConnectFunctions=YYY,
srv32.dll, .01=, s=YYN, FileExtns=Null
```

FIGURE 16.4: Listing the ODBC drivers

Part iv

Although Listing 16.1 prints the driver types to screen, I recommend sending the output to file for later reference. When configuring the DSN driver, you must use the exact format of the driver definition. If you created a file of your driver types from Listing 16.1, use the same format captured in the file. I used the driver format returned by Listing 16.1 in the program shown in Listing 16.2 to configure the DSN driver type. Listing 16.2 creates and configures the DSN.

Listing 16.2: Creating a Data Source Name (DSN)

```
1.  use Cwd;
2.  use Win32::ODBC;
3.  #Define the driver type for this database
4.  $DriverType = "Microsoft Access Driver (*.mdb)";
5.  #Define the Data Source Name
6.  $DSN = "Email Contacts";
7.  #Describe the Data Source Name
8.  #The format is required
9.  $Description = "Description=Email List and
10. Contact Information";
11. #The filename of the database.
12. #This must be created before you can connect to the DSN
13. $DataBase = "EmailContacts.mdb";
14. #Set the directory to current directory
15. $dir = cwd();
16. #Configure the DSN
17. if (Win32::ODBC::ConfigDSN(ODBC_ADD_DSN,
18.                            $DriverType,
19.                            ("DSN=$DSN",
20.                            $Description,
21.                            "DBQ=$dir\ \ $DataBase",
22.                            "DEFAULTDIR=$dir",
23.                            "UID=", "PWD="))){
24.   print "Successful configuration of $DSN!\n";
25. }
26. else{
27.   print "Error Creating $DSN\n";
28.   #Always use the DumpError routine.
29.   #It tells you what is going on
30.   Win32::ODBC::DumpError();
31.   die;
32. }
33.
34. #Create a Win32::ODBC object
35. #Lots of Perl programmers use this notation:
36. #$myDBConnection = new Win32::ODBC($DSN);
```

```
37. #But I prefer this syntax
38. my $myDb = Win32::ODBC->new($DSN);
39. #Create a lexical that will be accessible
40. #outside the else block
41. my $connection;
42. #Verify the connection is valid
43. if (! $myDb){
44.    print "Failed to Connect $DSN\n";
45.    Win32::ODBC::DumpError();
46.    #You can't do anything without a
47.    #connection so die here
48.    die;
49. }
50. else {
51.    $connection = $myDb->Connection();
52.    print "Successful Connection $connection, $DSN\n";
53. }
54. #Always close the database connection
55. $myDb->Close();
```

Line 4 of Listing 16.2 assigns the driver type, which was retrieved by Listing 16.1, for connecting to the Access database.

```
$DriverType = "Microsoft Access Driver (*.mdb)";
```

The DSN is created on lines 17 through 23:

```
if (Win32::ODBC::ConfigDSN(ODBC_ADD_DSN,
                           $DriverType,
                           ("DSN=$DSN",
                           $Description,
                           "DBQ=$dir\ \ $DataBase",
                           "DEFAULTDIR=$dir",
                           "UID=", "PWD="))){
```

This uses the common ODBC API (Application Program Interface), ODBC_ADD_ DSN. The parameters, driver type, and DSN definition are common across ODBC modules. The parameters define the DSN name, description, the location of the database file, the default directory, and the username and password assigned to the DSN. The default directory will be used as a location for writing temporary working files by Access. Access must have privileges to write into the default directory.

The database file (emailContacts.mdb in this example) must be created through Access before a connection to the file can be made. The only way I know to do this is by creating a blank database in Access and then saving it to a file. The name of the file is the database parameter to the Win32::ODBC ConfigDSN method, as you can see on lines 13 and 21:

```
$DataBase = "EmailContacts.mdb";
"DBQ=$dir\ \ $DataBase",
```

Lines 27 through 31 perform error processing for an invalid DSN configuration:

```
print "Error Creating $DSN\n";
#Always use the DumpError routine.
#It tells you what is going on
Win32::ODBC::DumpError();
die;
```

It's relatively easy to corrupt a database. Error processing, which is sometimes overlooked in other applications, should never be ignored. The DumpError routine prints to the selected file handle the error number, text of the error message, and current connection information. I like to include one additional line, such as line 27, which prints a message that tells me what the code was doing when the error occurred.

Once you have created the DSN, you can connect to your new database. Connecting to the database is accomplished on line 38:

```
my $myDb = Win32::ODBC->new($DSN);
```

This line calls the class constructor, which initializes the connection to the Access database.

The last thing this program does is close the connection to the database. This is extremely important with all database applications. An open database is likely to become corrupted. The Win32::ODBC class contains a destructor that disconnects from the database and clears the class's error codes.

The Win32::ODBC module will be used throughout this chapter to connect and manipulate a database. The primary functions of the Win32::ODBC module are explained in the next section. After that, you will learn how to create rows and columns in a database and then insert new data into that database.

The *Win32::ODBC* Module

Win32::ODBC, written by Dave Roth, is a module extension to Win32 Perl. Dave Roth has created a wonderful set of methods that make connecting to your Win32 database a portable and simple task. Using Win32::ODBC methods, you can connect to your database, create tables, insert data, and retrieve data. Here, you will learn about the more frequently used methods of Win32::ODBC. There are many more methods in the Win32::ODBC class, and I recommend that you read the online documentation.

TIP

You can download the Win32::ODBC module and find further documentation at www.roth.net. Installing the module on your computer is a relatively easy process. Win32::ODBC expects two files to be in the Win32 and odbc subdirectories. Beneath your Perl 5 installation, you have a lib directory. Copy ODBC.pm to C:\ Perl5\ lib\win32 and copy ODBC.pll to C:\ Per5\ lib\ auto\win32\ odbc. If the Win32 and auto\win32\ odbc subdirectories do not exist below the lib directory, create them. Both of these files and detailed installation instructions are available at ftp://ftp.roth.net/pub/ntperl and http://www.perl.com/CPAN/ authors/ Dave_Roth.

The *close* Method

The close method disconnects your program from the database engine. You should always close your database connection. Do not depend on Perl 5 to close the open file handle. Your database engine is likely to have opened working files, which may not be properly closed when your program exits.

The close method requires an object reference as its first and only parameter.

```
$myDb->close();
```

The *Data* Method

The Data method accesses a data structure internal to the Win32::ODBC module to retrieve the column values of an individual row. The Data method has meaning only after your program has retrieved data from your database through a SQL statement. The Data method retrieves the columns from the current row; use the FetchRow method to get the next row of data.

You can retrieve all the columns of a row in unspecified order like this:

```
lvalue = $myDb->Data();
```

You can retrieve an ordered list of the columns in a row by specifying which columns you wish to retrieve, as in this example:

```
lvalue = $myDb->Data(lastName, firstName, emailAddress);
```

The data will be returned in the same order as requested. If the lvalue is a scalar, the Data method returns the column values in one concatenated string. If the lvalue is a list, the data is returned in list context, where each item in the list is a column value.

```
while ($myDb->FetchRow()){
    ($lastName, $firstName, $emailAddress =
$myDb->Data(lastName, firstName, emailAddress);
    sendLetter($emailAddress, $lastName, $firstName);
}
```

The *DataHash* Method

The DataHash method accesses an internal data structure to retrieve the column values of an individual row. The DataHash method only has meaning after your program has retrieved data from your database through a SQL statement. The DataHash method retrieves the columns from the current row; use the FetchRow method to get the next row of data.

The DataHash method returns a hash containing the column name and column values of the current row. You can retrieve specific columns by providing the column names, like this:

```
%columnData = $myDb->DataHash(Model, Year, Price);
```

The DataHash method is usually used to retrieve an entire row of data, like this:

```
%columnData = $myDb->DataHash();
```

There is usually very little time and space penalty for retrieving the entire contents of a row using the DataHash method. Because the Data-Hash method retrieves both the column name and the column value, you can get the entire contents of a row and still access only the columns you need. Later, if you need to change your program to access more or fewer values from the column, you will have the data available without needing to modify your program:

```
while ($myDb->FetchRow()){
    %model = $myDb->DataHash();
    print<<"EOF";
    <tr>
        <td Align=left>$model{ model}
        <td Align=left>$model{ year}
        <td Align=left>$model{ price}
        <td Align=left width=70%>$model{ comments}
    </tr>
EOF
}
```

The *DumpError* Method

Though you don't really want to see the response from the DumpError method (because it means your program has a bug), it should be liberally sprinkled throughout your code. Use the DumpError method to verify the successful completion of every call to your database engine.

The DumpError method prints a formatted output, showing which database connection produced the error, the error number, and the text of the error message, returned by the database engine. The DumpError method prints error information about the last error condition, which may not be instance-specific. The DumpError method prints only the last error message. Usually, that message is related to the last error your object created. If the error your object created did not cause a new error message, the message printed will be the last error message created, even though it may not be relevant to the error your object created. You can use the DumpError method with an object reference or class notation, like this:

```
#class notation calling syntax
Win32::ODBC::DumpError();
#object reference calling syntax
$myDb->DumpError();
```

The DumpError method tells you information about the type of error, but it doesn't tell you where the error occurred in your program. Listing 16.3 illustrates a method of calling the DumpError method that tracks when your program was running and what your code was doing at the time the error occurred. Listing 16.4 shows the output when an error occurred from running Listing 16.3.

Listing 16.3: Calling *DumpError*

```
1.  #Log the errors to file for later review
2.  #The filename will be unique because the Process ID is
3.  #appended using the special variable $$
4.  open (ERRORFILE, ">errorList$$.txt") || die ;
5.  (@times) = localtime(time);
6.  #Date the file
7.  $time = $times[2] . ':' . $times[1] . ':' . $times[0];
8.  select ERRORFILE;
9.  print  "$time\n";
10.
11. $SQLStatment = qq|Create Table $make
➥(ad_ID char(20) NOT NULL,
12.      model char(20) NOT NULL,
```

```
13.        year Integer,
14.        price Integer,
15.        phone char(10),
16.        comments char(80))|;
17. if ($myDb->Sql($SQLStatment)){
18.    print "error creating table $make\n";
19.    $myDb->DumpError();
20. }
```

Listing 16.4: Output from Calling *DumpError*

```
15:52:15
error creating table Buick
----- Error Report: -----
Errors for "16" on connection 1:
Connection Number: 1
Error number: -1303
Error message: "[Microsoft][ODBC Microsoft Access 97 Driver]
➡Table 'Buick' already exists."
-------------------
```

The *FetchRow* Method

The FetchRow method retrieves the next row of data from the latest SQL query of your database. The FetchRow method must be used with an object reference, which points to a valid ODBC connection:

```
my $myDb = Win32::ODBC->new($DSN);
$myDb->FetchRow();
```

The FetchRow method populates an internal data structure. After calling the FetchRow method, you must call either the Data or DataHash method to retrieve the column values of a row. The FetchRow method returns undef if there is an error or no more data to retrieve, which makes it suitable for use in a while loop, like this:

```
while ($myDb->FetchRow()){
    %model = $myDb->DataHash();
```

The *new* Method

The new method is the Win32::ODBC class constructor. The new method takes one parameter, a valid DSN, and returns an ODBC object reference:

```
my $myDb = Win32::ODBC->new("Auto Ads");
```

The ODBC object reference is then used to communicate further ODBC commands to the connected database

If the new method fails, it returns undef. Always check the result returned by the new method. If an invalid result is returned, your best solution is to print or log the error message and exit your program:

```
my $myDb = Win32::ODBC->new($DSN);
#Verify the connection is valid
if (! $myDb){
    print "Failed to Connect $DSN\n";
    Win32::ODBC::DumpError();
    #You can't do anything without a connection so die here
    die;
}
else {
    print "Connected to $DSN\n";
}
```

The *RowCount* Method

Sometimes you just want to count the number of rows in a table. The quickest method to accomplish this task is the RowCount method. The RowCount method returns the number of rows that were traversed by the last SQL command:

```
$myDb->Sql($SQL)
$numberOfRows = $myDb->RowCount();
```

NOTE

The RowCount method is an ODBC extension and may not work for all database engines.

The *Sql* Method

The Sql method is the real workhorse of the Win32::ODBC class, but it really isn't an ODBC command. The Sql method makes a call to ODBCExecute, which passes the SQL statement to the database:

```
$SQL = "Select model, year, price,
➡ comments From $cars{ Make}  ";
if ($myDb->Sql($SQL)){
        $prevFH = select(ERRORFILE);
        print "Error selecting car make.\n";
        Win32::ODBC::DumpError();
        select ($prevFH);
}
```

The Sql method returns undef on success. This means your error-checking syntax is reversed. Instead of checking for a positive response to indicate success, you check for a positive response to indicate failure. In the example above, the error-handling code will be called when anything other than undef is returned by the Sql method.

EXISTING DATA

I can type, but it is an error-prone operation that takes way too much time. If you already have your database information in some type of electronic media, manually entering it into a database table should be one of your last options. With Perl 5, Win32::ODBC, and a little SQL, you can import your data into a new database in a matter of moments.

Creating a Database Table

A database makes it easy to keep track of all sorts of information. For example, I used to keep my e-mail contact list in Netscape Messenger. My data in Netscape Messenger was simple—just an e-mail address and a name for each contact. However, once I had a database, I decided to put my list there and track several additional items.

Listing 16.5 creates an e-mail contact table in the emailContact.mdb Access database.

Listing 16.5: Creating a Database Table

```
1.  use Win32::ODBC;
2.
3.  #Define the Data Source Name
4.  $DSN = "Email Contacts";
5.
6.  #Create a Win32::ODBC object
7.  #Lots of Perl programmers use this notation:
8.  #$myDBConnection = new Win32::ODBC($DSN);
9.  #But I prefer this syntax
10. my $myDb = Win32::ODBC->new($DSN);
11. #Verify the connection is valid
12. if (! $myDb){
13.     print "Failed to Connect $DSN\n";
14.     Win32::ODBC::DumpError();
15.     #You can't do anything without
16.     #a connection so die here
17.     die;
18. }
19.
```

```
20. #Create the table rows and columns
21. #This statement should be run only
22.  #once during initialization
23. $SQLStatment = qq|Create Table emailContacts
➡ (address char(40) NOT NULL,
24.                                    lastName char(20),
25.                                    firstName char(10),
26.                                    MI char (2))|;
27.
28. if ($myDb->Sql($SQLStatment)){
29.    print "Error creating the initial Table\n";
30.    Win32::ODBC->DumpError();
31. }
32.
33. #Always close the database connection
34. $myDb->Close();
```

Lines 23 through 26 illustrate how to create a SQL statement for the Win32::ODBC Sql method:

```
$SQLStatment = qq|Create Table
➡ emailContacts(address char(40) NOT NULL,
                lastName char(20),
                firstName char(10),
                MI char (2))|;
```

I prefer to use the quote operators, which allow me the freedom to define the SQL statement on several lines. (The SQL Create command and other SQL commands will be explained in the next section.)

Importing Text Data

Listing 16.6 imports a text file into the table created in Listing 16.5. You'll learn how to add columns to database tables later, so it doesn't matter if this table doesn't have all the items you might want in a normal contact list.

Listing 16.6: Importing Text Data

```
1.  use Win32::ODBC;
2.  if ($#ARGV < 0){
3.     die "You must enter the contact list
➡ file name as the first argument";
4.  }
5.  #Define the Data Source Name
6.  $DSN = "Email Contacts";
7.
```

```
8.   #Create a Win32::ODBC object
9.   #Lots of Perl programmers use this notation:
10.  #$myDBConnection = new Win32::ODBC($DSN);
11.  #But I prefer this syntax
12.  my $myDb = Win32::ODBC->new($DSN);
13.  #Verify the connection is valid
14.  if (! $myDb){
15.      print "Failed to Connect $DSN\n";
16.      Win32::ODBC::DumpError();
17.      #You can't do anything without a
18.      #connection so die here
19.      die;
20.  }
21.
22.  #Read the contact data in and add it to the new table
23.  open (CONTACTS, "<$ARGV[0]") ||
24.          die "Invalid file name specified: $ARGV[0]";
25.  @contacts = <CONTACTS>;
26.  close (CONTACTS);
27.  #Log the errors to file for later review
28.  #The filename will be unique because the process ID is
29.  #appended using the special variable $$
30.  open (ERRORFILE, ">errorList$$.txt") || die;
31.  (@times) = localtime(time);
32.  #Date the file
33.  $time = $times[2] . ':' . $times[1] . ':' . $times[0];
34.  print ERRORFILE "$time\n";
35.
36.  #Read each line of the contact list
37.  #and add it to the database
38.  foreach $contact (@contacts){
39.      ($firstName, $MI, $lastName, $emailAddress) =
40.      split(/:/,$contact);
41.      chomp $emailAddress;
42.      #Insert the contact list into the emailContacts
43.  table
44.      $SQL = qq|Insert Into emailContacts ( address,
45.          firstName,  MI, lastName)
46.                              Values ('$emailAddress',
47.                                  '$firstName',
48.                                  '$MI',
49.                                  '$lastName')|;
50.      if ($myDb->Sql($SQL)){
51.          #Force the output from DumpError
52.          #into the error file
53.          $prevFH = select(ERRORFILE);
```

```
54.        print "Error Creating emailContacts\n";
55.        Win32::ODBC::DumpError();
56.        select ($prevFH);
57.    }
58. }
59.
60. close (ERRORFILE);
61.
62. #Always close the database connection
63. $myDb->Close();
```

Lines 23 and 24 of Listing 16.6 read from the command line the name of the file that contains the e-mail contact information:

```
open (CONTACTS, "<$ARGV[0]") ||
die "Invalid file name specified: $ARGV[0]";
```

Because you may be importing a large amount of data, this program creates a file for collecting errors. The file is initialized with a time stamp on line 34, so you can distinguish between import runs. The time stamp uses the `localtime` function (on line 31). This function returns an array of information based on the current time, which is returned by the `time` function:

```
(@times) = localtime(time);
```

The array that is returned by the `localtime` function is time formatted in the order shown here:

► The seconds from 0 to 60

► The minutes from 0 to 60

► The hour of the day from 1 to 12

► The day of the month from 1 to 31

► The month of the year from 0 to 11

► The year in four-digit format

► The day of the week from 0 to 6

► The day of the year from 1 to 365

► Whether or not it is daylight saving time (1 indicates true)

This time is formatted into an hours, minutes, seconds format on line 33:

```
$time = $times[2] . ':' . $times[1] . ':' . $times[0];
```

Each error file is also given a unique name by appending the special variable $$, which contains the process ID, to the filename (on line 30):

```
open (ERRORFILE, ">errorList$$.txt") || die;
```

This program then connects to the DSN and begins adding data to the e-mail contacts database on lines 44 through 50:

```
$SQL = qq|Insert Into emailContacts (address,
            firstName,  MI, lastName)
                    Values ('$emailAddress',
                            '$firstName',
                            '$MI',
                            '$lastName')|;

if ($myDb->Sql($SQL)){
```

Lines 44 through 49 take the data retrieved from the contact list file and create a SQL statement from the data. You may notice that the column names listed first are not in the same order as they are stored in the database. If you list the names of the columns first in a SQL `Insert` statement, the values will be inserted into the table in the correct order. Running Listing 16.6 imports from a file into the `emailContacts` table, as shown in Figure 16.5.

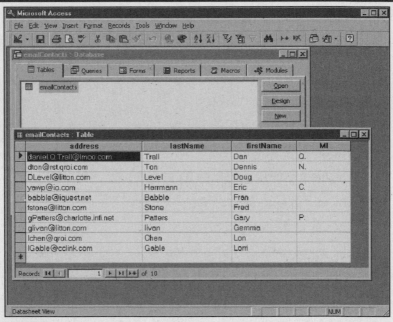

FIGURE 16.5: Imported Microsoft Access data

SQL is a large part of interacting with any database. The next section provides an introduction to SQL.

SQL — The Database Language

SQL is a programming language designed specifically for database operations, and it is a common language among many database engines.

WARNING

You can do almost any database task with SQL, but sometimes it can be a little cumbersome. To make SQL easier to use, most database engines extend SQL. These SQL extensions create unique dialects of SQL that are no longer portable between the various database engines. The ability to use the same queries between different database engines is the entire purpose of SQL, so I urge you to avoid SQL extensions whenever possible.

The common form of SQL is called ANSI-SQL. Like every other programming language, SQL has data types, keywords, and operators. Table 16.1 shows the subset of the ANSI-SQL data types that are compatible with the Microsoft Access database engine. The data types are used to define the columns of data that make up a table.

TABLE 16.1: ANSI-SQL and Access Compatible Data Types

ANSI SQL	ACCESS SQL EQUIVALENT	DESCRIPTION
BIT, BIT VARYING	BINARY	A Boolean data type (True/False)
DATE, TIME, TIMESTAMP	DATETIME	A data type for date-specific operations
REAL	SINGLE	A single-precision real number
DOUBLE PRECISION, FLOAT DOUBLE	FLOAT, FLOAT8	A double-precision real number
SMALLINT	SHORT	A small integer, usually two bytes
INTEGER	LONG	A long integer, usually two words
CHARACTER, CHARACTER VARYING	TEXT	Character strings

Part iv

The following sections provide a brief overview of using SQL to create tables and to manipulate tables and the data that they contain.

TIP

The file that contains the 1993 definition of ANSI-SQL is more than 3000 lines long, without comments. Here, you will spend only a few pages learning about the most common SQL commands. If you want to learn more about SQL, I recommend three resources: the Internet, your local bookstore, and the help function of Microsoft Access or the database engine of your choice.

Creating a Table

You create a table using the `Create Table` SQL statement. The syntax of the `Create Table` statement is:

```
Create Table tableName (columnNameList)
```

The table name should be a single string of alphanumeric characters. The column name list is a comma-separated list that defines the column names, their data types, and constraints on the column. Column names may include spaces; if the name has spaces, surround it with single quotes. The valid constraints on a column are listed in Table 16.2.

TABLE 16.2: Column Constraints

CONSTRAINT	DESCRIPTION	EXAMPLE
Check	Before the column's data is added, it is validated. If the data does not pass validation, it is not added to the row.	`Price Integer Check (Price > 1000)`
Default	When a new object is added to the table, any columns that are not filled in will be assigned their default value.	`Salary Real Default = 28000.42`
Foreign Key	Declares this column as a foreign key. A foreign key creates a relationship between two or more tables.	`ad_id char (20) Foreign Key References UsedCars`
NOT NULL	Generates an error if the column data is not assigned a value. (NULL is also a constraint, but it is the default for all columns.)	`Year Integer Not Null`

CONTINUED ➡

TABLE 16.2 continued: Column Constraints

CONSTRAINT	DESCRIPTION	EXAMPLE
Primary Key	Declares this column as the table's primary key. A primary key must be a unique value	emailAddress char (60) Primary Key
Unique	Prevents the same column in two rows from containing the same value.	nickName char(20) Unique

As an example, Listing 16.7 creates a set of tables for the headings in the transportation section of a newspaper's classified ads. When I ran this program against my local newspaper online classified section, it produced the tables shown in Figure 16.6.

Listing 16.7: Creating Transportation Tables

```
1.  use Win32::ODBC;
2.
3.  #Define the Data Source Name
4.  $DSN = "Auto Ads";
5.
6.  #Create a Win32::ODBC object
7.  #Lots of Perl programmers use this notation:
8.  #$myDBConnection = new Win32::ODBC($DSN);
9.  #But I prefer this syntax
10. my $myDb = Win32::ODBC->new($DSN);
11.
12. #Verify the connection is valid
13. if (! $myDb){
14.     print "Failed to Connect $DSN\n";
15.     Win32::ODBC::DumpError();
16.     #You can't do anything without
17.     #a connection so die here
18.     die;
19. }
20. else {
21.     print "Connected to $DSN\n";
22. }
23.
24. #Read the classified section
25. open (ADS, "<$ARGV[0]") ||
26. die "Invalid file as first param $ARGV[0], $!";
```

```
27. @ads = <ADS>;
28. close ADS;
29.
30. #Log the errors to file for later review
31. #The filename will be unique because the process ID is
32. #appended using the special variable $$
33. open (ERRORFILE, ">errorList$$.txt") || die;
34. (@times) = localtime(time);
35. #Date the file
36. $time = $times[2] . ':' . $times[1] . ':' . $times[0];
37. print ERRORFILE "$time\n";
38. select ERRORFILE;
39. for ($i=0; $i<=$#ads; $i++){
40.     #Match the transportation line
41.     #Classified file has unique header
42.     #before each car info line
43.     if ($ads[$i] =~ /^\d+\s+-\s+(.*)<\ /a>/){
44.         $make = $1;
45.         #Remove commas and spaces
46.         $make =~ s/[,\s]//g;
47.         #Create the table rows and columns
48.         #This statement should be run
49.         #only once during initialization
50.         #If the table already exists, it's okay
51.         #Creating the table will fail
52.         #but processing can continue
53.         $SQLStatment = qq|Create Table
➥ $make(ad_ID char(20) NOT NULL,
54.                     model char(20) NOT NULL,
55.                     year Integer,
56.                     price Integer,
57.                     phone char(10),
58.                     comments char(80))|;
59.     if ($myDb->Sql($SQLStatment)){
60.         print ERRORFILE "error creating table $make\n";
61.         $myDb->DumpError();
62.     }
63.     }
64. }
65. close ERRORFILE;
66. $myDb->Close();
```

Lines 53 through 58 create the tables shown in Figure 16.6:

```
$SQLStatment = qq|Create Table
➥ $make (ad_ID char(20) NOT NULL,
                    model char(20) NOT NULL,
                    year Integer,
```

```
price Integer,
phone char(10),
comments char(80))|;
```

Each table will contain information about a specific transportation heading.

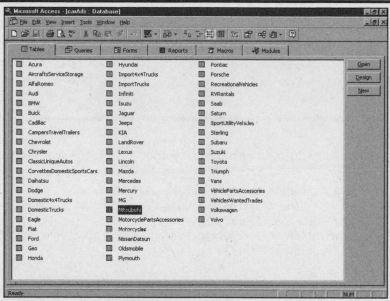

FIGURE 16.6: Transportation tables

Modifying a Table

Once you create a table, its column definitions can be modified, deleted, and added to with the `Alter Table` statement. Only one column definition may be changed per `Alter Table` statement. The syntax of the `Alter Table` statement is:

```
Alter Table tableName modifyType columnDefinition
```

The table name must already exist in the database. The modify type can be one of three values shown in Table 16.3. The column definition follows the same rules as defined in the previous section.

TABLE 16.3: Alter Table Modify Types

TYPE	DESCRIPTION	EXAMPLE
Add	Adds a new column to the table	`Alter Table emailContacts Add ('Last Contact' Date)`
Drop	Deletes a column from an existing table	`Alter Table emailContacts Drop (MI)`
Modify	Modifies the column definition	`Alter Table emailContacts Modify (emailAddress char (80))`

The following code adds the last contact date to the emailContacts database:

```
$SQLStatment = qq|Alter Table emailContacts
        Add (lastContact Date Default = LastUpdated)|;
if ($myDb->Sql($SQLStatment)){
    print ERRORFILE "error adding Column lastContact\n";
    $myDb->DumpError();
}
```

NOTE

The LastUpdated function used in the Default statement may not be available in all database engines.

Inserting Data into a Table

A database, no matter how well defined, is useless without data. To add data to your database table, use the Insert Into statement. This statement has the following syntax:

```
Insert Into tableName (columnNameList) Values (valueList)
```

The column name list is an optional parameter that allows you to insert the values in a row in any order. The column name list is an unordered list of the names of the columns in the named table. The values in the value list will be inserted into the table in a one-to-one correspondence with the column order defined in the column name list. The column name list does not need to name all of the columns in a table; any missing column names will be filled in with their default values.

For example, suppose that you created a table with First, Middle, and Last Name columns (in that order), but you have data on only the first and last names. You could use the `Insert Into` statement to add the data like this:

```
$SQL = qq|Insert Into emailContacts (Last, First)
            Values ('$lastName', '$firstName')|;
```

The single quotes are required in the value list when using the `Insert Into` statement with `Win32::ODBC` and Microsoft Access. Single quotes are only used on text column data, however.

Deleting Data from a Table

Most databases will grow to unmanageable sizes if they don't receive regular maintenance. To delete rows from a database, use the `Delete From` statement. Its syntax is:

```
Delete From tableName Where selectionCriteriaList
```

The selection criteria list is a list of column names and relational operators that define the matching criteria used to select a row for deletion. The selection criteria may be several expressions connected by the logical operators. Table 16.4 lists the relational and logical operators.

TABLE 16.4: Relational and Logical Operators

OPERATOR	MEANING
=	Equality
>	Greater than
<	Less than
>=	Greater than or equal to
<=	Less than or equal to
!=	Not equal
And	Logical AND
Not	Logical NOT
Or	Logical OR

Part iv

As an example, Listing 16.8 deletes all of the rows in the tables of the Auto Ads DSN whose date is 10 days old or older or whose sold column is True.

Listing 16.8: Deleting the Sold and the Old

```
1.  use Win32::ODBC;
2.  open (OUTFILE, ">searchCars.htm");
3.  select (OUTFILE);
4.  #Define the Data Source Name
5.  $DSN = "Auto Ads";
6.
7.  #Create a Win32::ODBC object
8.  my $myDb = Win32::ODBC->new($DSN);
9.
10. #Verify the connection is valid
11. if (! $myDb){
12.     print "Failed to Connect $DSN\n";
13.     Win32::ODBC::DumpError();
14.     #You can't do anything without
15.     #a connection so die here
16.     die;
17. }
18. @makes = $myDb->TableList;
19. (@times) = localtime(time);
20. #Date is stored in the tables as a day of year and year
21. $oldDay = $times[7] - 10;
22. $year = $times[5];
23. #If we are in a new year, back up to the previous year
24. if ($oldDay < 1){
25.     $oldDay += 365;
26.     $year-;
27. }
28. foreach $make (@makes){
29.     $SQL = qq|Delete From $make Where (
30.             (Day <= $oldDay AND Year = $year)
31.             OR Sold = True)|;
32.     if ($myDb->Sql($SQL)){
33.         print "Error deleting from $make,
34.         $oldDay, $year\n";
35.         $myDb->DumpError();
36.     }
37. }
38. $myDb->Close();
```

Lines 29 through 31 of Listing 16.8 delete the items:

```
$SQL = qq|Delete From $make Where (
            (Day <= $oldDay AND Year = $year)
            OR Sold = True)|;
```

Note that comparisons are made to the columns Day and Year, which are integer in format. If you are comparing character data, be sure to place single quotes around the actual data values.

Updating Data in a Table

To update a column in a table, you use the Update statement. The Update statement requires that you define which column you are going to modify and the new value to place in the column. You may also define selection criteria to select a particular column for updating. If you do not define selection criteria, all the columns in the table will be updated. The syntax of the Update statement is:

```
Update tableName Set columnNameValueList
➡ Where selectionCriteria
```

The column-name value list is a comma-separated list of column names and the new value. A single column-name value pair looks like this:

```
columnName=value
```

For example, suppose that you just sent an e-mail message to all of the recipients on your contact list and you want to update the last contact date. You could use this program fragment, which updates all of the rows in the emailContacts table to the current year and current day of the year:

```
(@times) = localtime(time);
#Date is stored in the tables as a day of year and year
$day = $times[7] ;
$year = $times[5];
$SQL = qq|Update emailContacts Set
➡ Day = $day, Year = $year|;
```

Selecting Data from a Table

Now that you've created your table and filled it with useful data, you need some way to retrieve all that information. The SQL statement for retrieving data is the Select statement. The basic syntax of the Select statement is:

```
Select (columnList) From (tableList) selectionCriteria
```

You can use functions, selection criteria, predicates, and more in the column list. The table list may be one or more tables or views. The selection criteria are used to determine which rows of the table the Select statement will return. The selection criteria may be a combination of one or more of the criteria clauses listed in Table 16.5.

TABLE 16.5: Selection Criteria Clauses

Keyword	Syntax	Description
Group By	Group By *columns*	Combines rows with the same values in the Group By *columns* into a single row.
Having	Having *conditionalExpression*	Used with the Group By criteria, returns only the records that meet the Having conditional expression.
Like	Like *partialString%*	Used in the Where clause as a wildcard to select all strings that match the partial string value. You may use multiple percent signs and multiple partial strings to create a pattern.
Order By	Order By *columnName* ASC|DESC	Returns the selected data in ascending or descending order, ordered by the data in the named column. The default is ascending.
Where	Where *conditionalExpression*	Returns the data that meets the criteria in the conditional expression.

For example, to select all the models in a table ordered by model, year, and price, you would use the following Select statement:

```
$SQL = qq| Select model, year, price,
➥ comments From $cars{ Make}
                Order By Model, Year, Make|;
```

NOTE

There are many variations on the basic Select statement. For more information on this and other SQL statements, you can refer to the resources mentioned earlier—the Internet, a book devoted to SQL, or the help function for your database engine.

YOUR DATABASE AND THE INTERNET

In this section, you will create an Internet connection to the transportation database created in Listing 16.7. You will step through each phase of this project, importing the data, querying for data from the web, and displaying the data on the Internet. The database is a live connection to a Microsoft Access database engine through the Internet Information Server (IIS) 3.0.

This application uses the standard ODBC APIs and ANSI-SQL. Because we use these standards, changing to another database engine such as FoxPro or a low-cost Unix solution like MiniSQL will require only a few changes in the program. Your computer requires a little setup to deal with the idiosyncrasies of the Microsoft Access database, so you will begin by taking care of that setup.

Setting Up for Access and the Web

If you plan on displaying or updating your data through Microsoft's IIS, make sure you give it read and write access to the directories and subdirectories where your database is located. The Microsoft Access database engine needs to write working files out to your disk when you access and update your database. Access must have the privileges necessary to create and delete these temporary files. When your program is accessed from the web, Access will be running under the privileges of your web server, which will be named something like IUSR_MAIN. You must explicitly add read and write access through the Properties window for the Web Server User.

NOTE
This code was tested with the Microsoft IIS server, which runs on Windows NT.

To explicitly set the permissions for a directory, first select the directory in Windows Explorer, then select the Properties option from the File menu, as shown in Figure 16.7.

From the Properties dialog box, select the Security tab and click on the Permissions button. This brings up the Directory Permissions dialog box. Check the Replace Permissions on Subdirectories and Replace Permission on Existing Files check boxes at the top of the dialog box, as shown in Figure 16.8. Then click on the Add button at the bottom of the dialog box to display the Add Users and Groups dialog box, as shown in Figure 16.9.

Search through the list until you find your web server. You may need to change the List Names From selection (use the drop-down list box). You also may need to click on the Show Users button in the middle of the window. Give the web server (named something like IUSR_MAIN) full control over the directory in which your database file is located. Because you are giving open access to this directory, I recommend separating this directory from your regular directory tree.

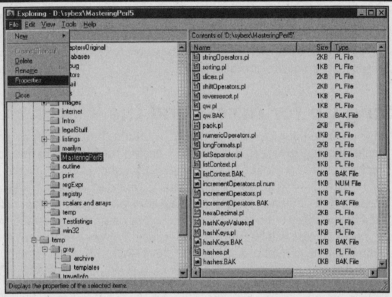

FIGURE 16.7: Selecting directory properties

Once you click on OK from the Add Users and Groups dialog box, you should select OK and continue to answer Yes at each of the several confirmation dialog boxes.

In the following examples, Access is executed through a web server. Access writes temporary working files and then later deletes them from the directory where your database file is located. This means the web server must have full control of the directory (and subdirectories) that contains your Access database files, which you have just set up.

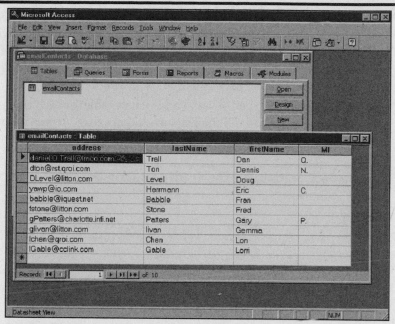

FIGURE 16.8: Setting directory permissions

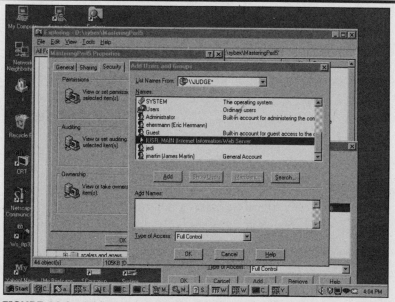

FIGURE 16.9: Adding users

Part iv

Initializing the Transportation Database

The first step after design is creating the DSN and the tables that will be populated with your database's data. For this example, I accessed the classified section of my local online newspaper and downloaded a transportation list. I used this list as an input to Listing 16.9.

Listing 16.9 creates the DSN and adds a new table for each transportation entry in the input file. If the DSN or a table exists, Access returns an error, but processing on other tables continues.

Listing 16.9: Initializing the Transportation Database

```
1.  use Cwd;
2.  use Win32::ODBC;
3.  #Define the driver type for this database
4.  $DriverType = "Microsoft Access Driver (*.mdb)";
5.  #Define the Data Source Name
6.  $DSN = "Auto Ads";
7.  #Describe the Data Source Name
8.  #The format is required
9.  $Description = "Description=Transportation Classifieds";
10. #The filename of the database.
11. #This must be created before you can connect to the DSN
12. $DataBase = "carAds.mdb";
13. #Set the directory to current directory
14. $dir = cwd();
15. #Configure the DSN
16. if (Win32::ODBC::ConfigDSN(ODBC_ADD_DSN,
17.                            $DriverType,
18.                            ("DSN=$DSN",
19.                            $Description,
20.                            "DBQ=$dir\ \ $DataBase",
21.                            "DEFAULTDIR=$dir",
22.                            "UID=", "PWD="))){
23.     print "Successful configuration of $DSN!\n";
24. }
25. else{
26.     print "Error Creating $DSN\n";
27.     #Always use the DumpError routine.
28.     #It tells you what is going on
29.     Win32::ODBC::DumpError();
30.     die;
31. }
32.
33. #Create a Win32::ODBC object
```

```
34. my $myDb = Win32::ODBC->new($DSN);
35. #Verify the connection is valid
36. if (! $myDb){
37.     print "Failed to Connect $DSN\n";
38.     Win32::ODBC::DumpError();
39.     #You can't do anything without
40.     #a connection so die here
41.     die;
42. }
43. else {
44.     #I like giving myself confirmation
45.     #that things are going well
46.     print "Connected to $DSN\n";
47. }
48.
49. #Read the classified section
50. open (ADS, "<$ARGV[0]") ||
51. die "Invalid file as first param $ARGV[0], $!";
52. @ads = <ADS>;
53. close ADS;
54.
55. #Log the errors to file for later review
56. #The filename will be unique because the process ID is
57. #appended using the special variable $$
58. open (ERRORFILE, ">errorList$$.txt") || die ;
59. (@times) = localtime(time);
60. #Date the file
61. $time = $times[2] . ':' . $times[1] . ':' . $times[0];
62. print ERRORFILE "$time\n";
63. select ERRORFILE;
64.
65. for ($i=0; $i<=$#ads; $i++){
66.     #Match the transportation line
67.     #Classified file has unique header
68.     #before each car info line
69.     if ($ads[$i] =~ /^\d+\s+-\s+(.*)<\ /a>/){
70.         my $make = $1;
71.         #Remove commas and spaces
72.         $make =~ s/[,\s]//g;
73.         #Create the table rows and columns
74.         #This statement should be run only
75.         #once during initialization
76.         #if the table already exists, it's okay
77.         #Creating the table will fail
78.         #but processing can continue
79.         $SQLStatment = qq|Create Table
```

```
➥ make (ad_ID char(20) NOT NULL,
80.                      model char(20) NOT NULL,
81.                      year Integer,
82.                      price Integer,
83.                      phone char(10),
84.                      comments char(80))|;
85.      if ($myDb->Sql($SQLStatment)){
86.        print ERRORFILE "error creating table $make\n";
87.        $myDb->DumpError();
88.      }
89.    }
90. }
91. close ERRORFILE;
92. $myDb->Close();
```

This program expects to be run in the same directory as the Access database and will fail if this is not true. The directory is explicitly set using the cwd() method of the Cwd class on line 14:

```
$dir = cwd();
```

The DSN is created beginning on lines 16 through 22:

```
if (Win32::ODBC::ConfigDSN(ODBC_ADD_DSN,
                           $DriverType,
                           ("DSN=$DSN",
                           $Description,
                           "DBQ=$dir\ \ $DataBase",
                           "DEFAULTDIR=$dir",
                           "UID=", "PWD="))){
```

Once the DSN is created, the transportation list is read into memory on lines 50 and 51:

```
open (ADS, "<$ARGV[0]") ||
die "Invalid file as first param $ARGV[0], $!";
@ads = <ADS>;
close ADS;
```

Each transportation table is created between lines 66 through 84. The transportation file has a unique header format that looks like this:

```
1930 - Aircrafts, Service, Storage</a>
```

which is matched by the regular expression on line 69:

```
if ($ads[$i] =~ /^\d+\s+-\s+(.*)<\ /a>/){
```

The type of transportation item is saved in a back reference variable, which is stored into a lexical variable on line 70:

```
my $make = $1;
```

A database table name in Access should not contain spaces or commas, so these offending characters are removed on line 72:

```
$make =~ s/[,\s]//g;
```

Once the data is formatted correctly, the SQL statement to create each new table is generated on lines 79 through 84:

```
$SQLStatment = qq|Create Table
➥ $make (ad_ID char(20) NOT NULL,
      model char(20) NOT NULL, year Integer, price Integer,
      phone char(10), comments char(80))|;
```

Line 85 executes the SQL statement through the Win32::ODBC Sql method:

```
if ($myDb->Sql($SQLStatment)){
```

If an error occurs, it is logged but processing continues:

```
    print ERRORFILE "error creating table $make\n";
    $myDb->DumpError();
}
```

Now that the tables have been created for our transportation database, we need to import the data into each transportation table, which is accomplished in the next section.

Importing Data into the Transportation Database

You will populate the database tables with today's classified ads. To load the tables, I downloaded the transportation listings and then ran the files through Listing 16.10, which uses the Insert Into SQL statement to load each transportation table with data. When I ran Listing 16.10 on the Mitsubishi classified listings, it produced the table shown in Figure 16.10.

Listing 16.10: Importing the Transportation Data

```
1.  use Win32::ODBC;
2.  #Define the Data Source Name
3.  $DSN = "Auto Ads";
4.  #Create a Win32::ODBC object
5.  my $myDb = Win32::ODBC->new($DSN);
6.  #Verify the connection is valid
7.  if (! $myDb){
8.      print "Failed to Connect $DSN\n";
9.      Win32::ODBC::DumpError();
10.     #You can't do anything without
11.     #a connection so die here
```

```
12.   die;
13. }
14.
15. #Read the classified section
16. open (ADS, "<$ARGV[0]") ||
17. die "Invalid file as first param $ARGV[0], $!";
18. @ads = <ADS>;
19. close ADS;
20.
21. #Log the errors to file for later review
22. #The filename will be unique because the process ID is
23. #appended using the special variable $$
24. open (ERRORFILE, ">errorList$$.txt") || die;
25. (@times) = localtime(time);
26. #Date the file
27. $time = $times[2] . ':' . $times[1] . ':' . $times[0];
28. print ERRORFILE "$time\n";
29.
30. for ($i=0; $i<=$#ads; $i++){
31.     #Match the transportation line
32.     #Classified file has unique header
33.     #before each car info line
34.     if ($ads[$i] =~ /TRANSPORTATION\s+-\s+(\w+)H/){
35.         my $make = $1;
36.         #Get the next line that has the car data
37.         my $carLine = $ads[++$i];
38.         #This regular expression pulls
39.         #the relevant info from an ad
40.         #All the ads list the year
41.         #model price and phone number
42.         #If an ad doesn't have this
43.         #info, it will be ignored
44.         ($year,$model,$comments1, $price,
45.          $comments2, $phone) =
46.         ($carLine =~ /.*?(\d+)\s*(\w+)\s*(.*)
➥ \$(\d+,?\d*)\s*(.*)
47.                     (\d{ 3} -\d{ 4} )/);
48.         #This creates a 2030 bug but we'll live with it
49.         if (length ($year) <= 2){
50.             if ($year > 30){
51.                 $year = "19" . $year;
52.             }
53.             else{
54.                 $year = "20" . $year;
55.             }
56.         }
57.         #The price has to match a comma
58.         #that occurs sometimes
```

```
59.            #so remove it to keep all the
60.            #prices in the same format
61.            $price =~ s/,//;
62.            #Create a unique table ID
63.            $ad_ID = $i . "_" . time;
64.            #Put all the extra stuff into one scalar
65.            $comments = $comments1 . $comments2;
66.          #Insert the car data into the model table
67.          $SQL = qq|Insert Into $make (ad_ID, model, year,
68.                  phone, comments, price)
69.                  Values ('$ad_ID', '$model', '$year',
70.                  '$phone','$comments', '$price')|;
71.        if ($myDb->Sql($SQL)){
72.            $prevFH = select(ERRORFILE);
73.            print "Error Creating $make\n";
74.            Win32::ODBC::DumpError();
75.            select ($prevFH);
76.        }
77.    }
78. }
79.
80. close ERRORFILE;
81.
82. #Always close the database connection
83. $myDb->Close();
```

ad_ID	model	year	price	phone	comments
89_910460649	3000	1991	10500	358-4064	GTSL; gold ext.; charcoal int. Lthr. 70K miles. AT; fully loa
123_910460649	3000	1995	16995	546-6807	GT RED HOT, Auto, Sunroof, Tint, Black/Grey cloth int.
119_910460649	3000GT	1994	11500	867-2086	, 5 speed, 56K miles. Black/black lthr seats. Sunroof. Full
105_910460649	DIAMANTE	1992	6750	789-4567	LS Pearl, leather, loaded, very clean, 108K miles. OBO. M
121_910460649	DIAMANTE	1994	8200	607-0204	, automatic, cold AC, loaded, excellent condition, 71k mile
85_910460649	ECLIPSE	1990	5500	862-0182	GS - Turbo, 16dohc, red, 5spd, tint, alarm, CD, 103K. Exc
91_910460649	ECLIPSE	1991	3400	894-1358	GS. 5spd, PW, PL, AC, alarm, CD, tint. New clutch. Good
87_910460649	Eclipse	1991	3995	395-3027	. Red, AT, cass, tint, 86K, Many new parts: timing belt, fue
97_910460649	ECLIPSE	1992	5500	239-8736	GS, silver, all power, sunroof, excellent condition.
115_910460649	Eclipse	1993	4250	999-9459	; 87K mi; 4 cyl., 5 spd; red; AM-FM cass; new tires; alarm
113_910460649	ECLIPSE	1993	5975	939-0133	, 1 owner, 5spd, A/C, CD player, new brakes and tires, ver
127_910460649	ECLIPSE	1995	8990	459-9489	Auto., Emerald, 1 Owner, Must See! AUSTIN INFINITI
141_910460649	ECLIPSE	1997	11900	629-5117	GS - black, custom exhaust, 19K, very clean, , 248-8967
145_910460649	ECLIPSE	1997	16200	869-6833	GS. White, auto, sunroof, exc. cond. . 930-4848 days, 512
139_910460649	ECLIPSE	1997	17900	839-0845	SPYDER CONV. Black, tan top & leather, 5spd, 30K mi. .
143_910460649	ECLIPSE	1997	19990	459-9489	Spyder, Conv, Turbo, AT, Black/Lea, 30K, 1 Owner AUSTII
83_910460649	GALANT	1986	1400	839-0375	Runs good. /OBO. Call
111_910460649	GALANT	1992	3450	919-6706	. 5spd. Black. Excellent condition. Very strong. . 371-9993
109_910460649	MIRAGE	1992	3700	569-2730	LS, AT, A/C, stereo, nice condition, 46K miles, .
117_910460649	MIRAGE	1993	2850	241-7692	S 2DR COUPE 5spd, cold AC, 105k miles, 1 owner, runs
95_910460649	MISTUBISHI	1991	1295	456-1131	4DR, 4cyl automatic, AC, runs/drives excellent, 80k miles,
125_910460649	MITS	1995	14990	329-2837	DIAMANTE LS, AT, Burgundy/Lea,Full Pwr, Was$15,990 I
93_910460649	MITSUBISHI	1991	3800	457-9235	GALANT • White, 4dr, auto, PW, PL, AC, tint. . Call
103_910460649	MITSUBISHI	1992	4200	352-0207	ECLIPSE, 5spd, 115K mi, maroon, cold AC, orig. owner, ru
99_910460649	MITSUBISHI	1992	5200	281-9658	ECLIPSE GS, A/C, new tires, 86K mi, runs great, Must se
107_910460649	Mitsubishi	1992	7995	388-2419	Diamante LS, 4DR, Fully Equipped, Alloy Wheels, 88K Mi

FIGURE 16.10: The Mitsubishi table

Lines 30 through 65 prepare the input data for the SQL statement that begins on line 67. Each classified entry is actually made up of two lines in the transportation file. Each line of the ad's file must be processed, looking for a line that identifies itself as a classified information. A typical classified ad looks like this:

```
<!-H#TRANSPORTATION - MitsubishiH#->
'91 3000 GTSL; gold ext.; charcoal int. Lthr. 70K miles.
➥ AT; fully loaded. 1 owner. Exc. cond. Must sell;
➥ $10,500. Marble Falls area. 915-388-4064. <HR>
```

These two lines of data must be processed together. The first line, which is identified by line 34 of Listing 16.10, always occurs before the actual classified data, so this line is used to mark the beginning of a new ad:

```
if ($ads[$i] =~ /TRANSPORTATION\s+-\s+(\w+)H/){
```

If this line is not found, the `for` loop increments the index variable and we continue processing with the next line. If this line is found, we save the next line into the lexical `$carLine` at the same time the index to the next line of data is incremented. This is one way to process two lines at a time, where the first line is used to identify that the next line has significance to the program:

```
my $carLine = $ads[++$i];
```

Now that we have identified a line for importing into the database, a decision must be made on the minimum set of required data. The regular expression on lines 44 and 46 requires that a classified ad contain the year, model, price, and phone number. If this data is not included in the ad, the regular expression will fail and the data will not be added to the database:

```
($year, $model, $comments1, $price, $comments2, $phone) =
($carLine =~ /.*?(\d+)\s*(\w+)\s*(.*)\$
➥ (\d+,?\d*)\s*(.*)(\d{ 3} -\d{ 4} )/);
```

The regular expression, which looks rather daunting, is really quite straightforward when you break it into pieces. Here is a breakdown of this regular expression:

`.*?(\d+)`	The year is preceded by an arbitrary amount of data until the first digit is located. Then all consecutive digits are saved into the first back reference variable.
`\s*(\w+)`	The next part of the regular expression matches the first word to follow the model year; the model may be preceded by zero or more space characters.

`\s*(.*)`	After the model name, everything goes into a comments variable until we find a price.
`\$(\d+,?\d*)`	The price is always preceded by a dollar sign and then a series of digits that are saved into the fourth back reference variable. Some prices contain commas, and some don't, so the price regular expression looks for a series of digits followed by zero or one commas, which is followed by zero or more digits.
`\s*(.*)`	After the price is another set of freeform characters that are followed by a phone number.
`(\d{ 3} -\d{ 4} )`	The phone number must be three digits followed by a dash followed by four digits, which means we will match only local phone numbers.

Each regular expression that is surrounded by parentheses is saved into a back reference variable and, in this example, into the lvalue list on the left of the assignment operator.

Lines 48 through 65 make sure the data is all in the same format. Each piece of data will eventually be queried, and invalid comparisons will occur if prices include commas or two-digit years versus four-digit years are included in the data. As a database programmer, it is your responsibility to make sure the data is properly formatted before it is inserted into the database.

The creation of the SQL statement used to make the actual insertion of the data begins on line 67:

```
$SQL = qq|Insert Into $make (ad_ID, model, year,
                      phone, comments, price)
          Values ('$ad_ID', '$model', '$year',
                  '$phone','$comments', '$price')|;
```

This SQL statement uses the column list and values format to insert data into each transportation table. You should use this format whenever possible, because it allows you to modify the column order and add new columns within your database without changing your import code. Each of the values in the value list is surrounded by single quotes, a requirement of the Access database engine.

Searching for Cars on the Web

Now that you've got something to display on the web, you need to create a means for people to query your classified ads database. I don't think the average user wants to enter SQL queries, so it's up to you to make the query request intuitive to the user. A reasonable goal is to come up with something simple that will satisfy 80 percent of most users' queries. An example of this type of search page is shown in Figure 16.11 (on page 566), which is generated by Listing 16.11.

Listing 16.11: Searching for Transportation

```
1.  use Win32::ODBC;
2.  #Define the Data Source Name
3.  $DSN = "Auto Ads";
4.
5.  #Create a Win32::ODBC object
6.. #Lots of Perl programmers use this notation:
7.  #$myDBConnection = new Win32::ODBC($DSN);
8.  #But I prefer this syntax
9.  my $myDb = Win32::ODBC->new($DSN);
10.
11. #Verify the connection is valid
12. if (! $myDb){
13.     print "Failed to Connect $DSN\n";
14.     Win32::ODBC::DumpError();
15.     #You can't do anything without
16.     #a connection so die here
17.     die;
18. }
19. @makes = $myDb->TableList;
20. #Remember whenever you return an HTML page
21. #from a CGI program you must include a valid HTTP header
22. #followed by at least one blank line
23. print<<"EOF";
24. Content-Type: text/html
25.
26. <html>
27. <body>
28. <form method=POST
29. action="cgi-bin/classifiedCarSearch.cgi">
30. <center>
31. <h1>Search Our Transportation<br>
32. Classified ADS</h1>
33. <table>
34.     <tr>
```

```
35.         <th width=20%>Select a Make </th>
36.         <th Align=Left> Order By: </th>
37.     </tr>
38.     <tr>
39.         <td><select name="Make">
40. EOF
41. #This foreach loop creates option list values that
42. #are part of the previous select HTML statement
43. #The value is returned as a part of the CGI data
44. #The $make outside the Option tag is what the user sees.
45. #The newline is for convenience if debugging is required
46. foreach $make (@makes){
47.     print  qq|<Option value="$make"> $make\n|;
48. }
49. #After the option list is created we just need to
50. #list the order that they want to see their cars
51. print<<"EOF";
52.         </select>
53.       </td>
54.       <td witdh=80%>
55.         <table>
56.           <tr>
57.             <td>
  <input type=checkbox name="Price"> Price </td>
58.             <td>
  <input type=checkbox name="Model"> Model </td>
59.             <td>
  <input type=checkbox name="Year"> Year </td>
60.           </tr>
61.         </table>
62.       </td>
63.     </tr>
64. </table>
65. <input type=submit Value="Get Search Results">
66. <input type=reset>
67. </form>
68. </center>
69. </body>
70. </html>
71. EOF
```

When the CGI program in Listing 16.11 is called, it makes a connection to the database, as you have seen in almost all of the examples in this chapter. In fact, the initial CGI program is no different from any other database program. Line 19 uses the Win32::ODBC method TableList to get all of the tables of the transportation database:

```
@makes = $myDb->TableList;
```

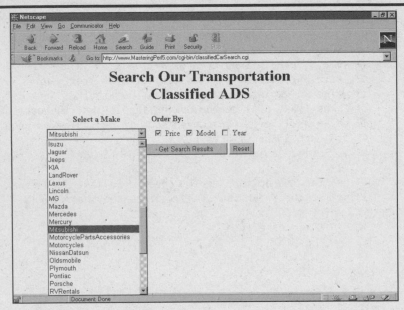

FIGURE 16.11: Searching online

Lines 23 through 25 fulfill the basic requirement of a CGI program, which is returning a valid HTTP header followed by a blank line. (The blank line signifies the end of the HTTP headers.) You can have as many HTTP headers as needed, but a blank line must follow the last HTTP header:

```
print<<"EOF";
Content-Type: text/html
<html>
<body>
```

The selection list shown in Figure 16.11 is created by the foreach loop on lines 46 through 48, which processes the table list created on line 19. Each table is presented to the user as part of the option list:

```
foreach $make (@makes){
    print  qq|<Option value="$make"> $make\n|;
}
```

The check boxes that print (lines 57 through 60) have a unique characteristic that you will see in the classifiedCarSearch.cgi program in the next section. The classifiedCarSearch.cgi program is called when the user selects the Get Search Results button, which is created on line 65:

```
<input type=submit Value="Get Search Results">
```

The submit button knows which program to call based on the action field in the HTML form tag beginning on line 28:

```
<form method=POST action="cgi-bin/classifiedCarSearch.cgi">
```

In the next section, you'll complete your online database project by returning the request made in Figure 16.11.

Displaying the Online Search Results

The CGI program in Listing 16.11 calls the CGI program in Listing 16.12, which reads the transportation database and generates the HTML page shown in Figure 16.12 (on page 566).

Listing 16.12: Classified Ads Online

```
1.    use Win32::ODBC;
2.    require "readPostInput.cgi";
3.    %cars = readPostInput();
4.    #Define the Data Source Name
5.    $DSN = "Auto Ads";
6.    #Create a Win32::ODBC object
7.    my $myDb = Win32::ODBC->new($DSN);
8.    #Verify the connection is valid
9.    if (! $myDb){
10.       print "Failed to Connect $DSN\n";
11.       Win32::ODBC::DumpError();
12.       #You can't do anything without
13.       #a connection so die here
14.       die;
15.    }
16.    #Using the data read by readPostInput in the cars hash,
17.    #create the SQL statement
18.    $SQL = "Select model, year,
➡ price, comments From $cars{ Make} ";
19.    #Checkboxes are only returned
20.    #if they are checked. We can
21.    #use this to our advantage to
22.    #determine if the user wants
23.    #an ordered search result
24.    if ((defined ($cars{ Model}  || defined ($cars{ Year} )
25.       || defined $cars{ Price} ))){
26.       $SQL .= " Order By ";
```

```
27.      my $count = 0;
28.      #At least one type of ordered search was requested.
29.      #The foreach processes only those
30.      #list items that are defined
31.      foreach $order (  $cars{ Model} ,
   $cars{ Year} , $cars{ Price} ){
32.          #Each time through the loop at
33.          #the order request to
34.          #the SQL statement
35.          $orderList .= " $order,;
36.          #If count is greater than zero we know we have an
37.          #ordered search
38.          $count++;
39.      }
40.      if ($count){
41.          #Get rid of the trailing comma
42.          chop $orderList;
43.          $SQL .= $orderList ;
44.      }
45.  }
46.
47.  if ($myDb->Sql($SQL)){
48.      print "Error getting Make info for $car{ Make} \n";
49.      $myDb->DumpError();
50.  }
51.
52.  print<<"EOF";
53.  Content-Type: text/html
54.
55.
56.  <html>
57.  <title> $cars{ Make}  Classifieds </title>
58.  <body>
59.  <center>
60.  <h1> You Searched for $cars{ Make}  </h1>
61.  EOF
62.  #If there is any data in orderlist
63.  #then tell the user the
64.  #type of order requested
65.  if ($orderList){
66.      @orderRequested = split(/,/,$orderList);
67.      #Save the list separator's previous value
68.      $prevSeparator = $";
69.      #This will print out , AND between
70.      #each element of the array
71.      local $" = ", AND";
```

```
72.       print "<h2> Ordered by  @orderRequested </h2>\n";
73.       #Return the list separator to its previous value
74.       $" = $prevSeparator;
75.  }
76.
77.  #The cell padding puts some space
78.  #around the data in the table cell
79.  #The 70% width forces the last cell
80.  #to take up most of the screen
81.  print<<"EOF";
82.  <table border=1 cellpadding=5>
83.     <tr>
84.         <th Align=left>Model
85.         <th Align=left>Year
86.         <th Align=left>Price
87.         <th Align=left width=70%>Additional Information
88.     </tr>
89.  EOF
90.  while ($myDb->FetchRow()){
91.     %model = $myDb->DataHash;
92.  print<<"EOF";
93.     <tr>
94.         <td Align=left>$model{ model}
95.         <td Align=left>$model{ year}
96.         <td Align=left>$model{ price}
97.         <td Align=left width=70%>$model{ comments}
98.     </tr>
99.  EOF
100. }
102.
102. print<<"EOF";
103. </table>
104. </center>
105. </body>
106. </html>
107. EOF
```

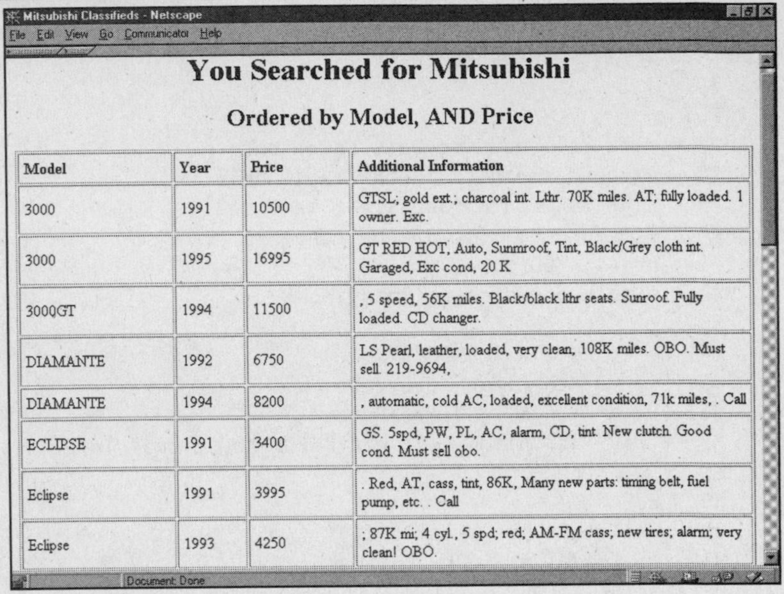

FIGURE 16.12: Displaying classified ads online

Listing 16.12 reads the data sent to it via the POST method into the %cars hash on line 3:

```
%cars = readPostInput();
```

The %cars hash contains each of the name/value pairs of the input items generated from the HTML form in Listing 16.11. The first thing this program uses from the %cars hash is the name of the table it will be querying. The data is available via the hash key Make ($car{ Make}), which was created in the option list generated in Listing 16.11. This name/value pair is retrieved on line 18, which initializes the SQL query statement:

```
$SQL = "Select model, year, price,
➥ comments From $cars{ Make} ";
```

At this point, the program must check the input values from the Order By check boxes to determine if the SQL query statement is complete.

Unlike other HTML form input tags, the check box name/value pair is sent only when the check box is selected. Lines 24 and 25 determine if any name/value pairs from the Order By check boxes were selected:

```
if ((defined ($cars{ Model}   ||
defined ($cars{ Year} ) ||defined $cars{ Price} ))){
```

If at least one of the check boxes was selected, the SQL query will use the Order By constraint clause. The Order By portion of the SQL query is added on line 26:

```
$SQL .= " Order By ";
```

Lines 31 through 39 check to see which check boxes were actually selected. The foreach loop contains a list of each of the check boxes, one list item for each check box name. The foreach loop processes only defined elements of a list, however, so the $order variable will be set only to check box values that were selected. As the loop is processed, the $orderList is built, one check box item at a time:

```
foreach $order ($cars{ Model} ,
➥ $cars{ Year} , $cars{ Price} ){
        #Each time through the loop at the order request to
        #rhe SQL statement
        $orderList .= " $order,";
        #If count is greater than zero we know we have an
        #ordered search.
        $count++;
}
```

Once the $orderList is complete, a trailing comma must be removed, which is accomplished by the chop function on line 42:

```
chop $orderList;
```

The $orderList variable is appended to the formatted $SQL variable on line 43, and the actual SQL query is made on line 47:

```
$SQL .= $orderList;
if ($myDb->Sql($SQL)){
```

If the user made a request for an ordered search, the type of request is echoed back to the user on lines 65 through 75:

```
if ($orderList){
    @orderRequested = split(/,/,$orderList);
    #Save the list separator's previous value
    $prevSeparator = $";
    #This will print out , AND between
    #each element of the array
    local $" = ", AND";
    print "<h2> Ordered by  @orderRequested </h2>\n";
    #Return the list separator to its previous value
    $" = $prevSeparator;
}
```

Line 71 takes advantage of the list separator variable to produce the formatted output:

Ordered By Model, AND Price (shown in Figure 16.12).

Each row returned by the SQL query is displayed in HTML format in the `while` loop from lines 90 through 100. The row of the query result is fetched on line 90, and then the data is retrieved through the `Win32::ODBC` method `DataHash`:

```
while ($myDb->FetchRow()){
    %model = $myDb->DataHash;
```

This creates the hash data used to display each row of the table data between lines 94 and 97:

```
print<<"EOF";
    <tr>
        <td Align=left>$model{ model}
        <td Align=left>$model{ year}
        <td Align=left>$model{ price}
        <td Align=left width=70%>$model{ comments}
    </tr>
EOF
```

As with most programming projects, producing the final result is a matter of taking one step at a time and then stringing those steps together until the project is completed. Here, you stepped through each of the processes required to create an online database. You can now apply this simple solution to your more complex problems.

SUMMARY

In this chapter, you first learned about the requirements for database applications. ODBC is a commonly agreed upon standard for connecting to the major database engines of the world. To connect to a database, you must create a Data Source Name (DSN), which defines the location of the database, the type of database, and the username and password of a database.

You can create a Microsoft Access Database DSN through the Windows interface or via the `Win32::ODBC` method `ConfigDSN`. The `Win32::ODBC` class contains a set of methods (written by Dave Roth) that provides an ODBC interface to your `Win32::ODBC` compliant database engines.

Next, the chapter covered `Win32::ODBC` and SQL statements. The `Win32::ODBC` methods allow you to create a DSN and connect and close your database. They also include several debugging routines to help you interpret the errors returned from your database engine. SQL is used after you connect to your database to manipulate tables and the data contained by those tables.

Using the `Win32::ODBC` APIs, you can send SQL statements to your database and retrieve the results:

▶ To create tables, use the `Create Table` statement.

▶ To modify the columns defined in the table, use the `Alter Table` statement.

▶ To add data to a table, use the `Insert Into` command.

▶ To delete from a table, use the `Delete From` statement.

▶ To modify data in a table, use the `Update` statement.

▶ To retrieve data from a table, use the SQL `Select` statement.

At the end of this chapter, you stepped through the complete process of creating an online database. First, you set permissions on your directories so the web server and Microsoft Access would have the correct privileges to read and write from your database directory. Then you created a new DSN and more than 50 tables in a transportation database. Once the database was defined, you imported data into the database through a Perl 5 program. With your database populated, you then built a CGI program to query your transportation database. The last step was displaying the results of an online query in HTML format to the user.

PART V
JavaScript and Perl References

Appendix A

JavaScript Object Reference

This appendix provides an object reference manual for the JavaScript and Jscript languages. It covers Navigator objects up to JavaScript 1.3 and Internet Explorer objects up to Jscript 5. It identifies the properties, methods, and events of Navigator *and* Internet Explorer objects, making it easier to select objects, properties, methods, and events that support cross-browser scripting.

Each object is presented in alphabetical order and includes a brief description and a listing of its properties, methods, and events. Properties and methods that are supported by both Navigator and Internet Explorer are described. The earliest browser version that supports a particular property, method, and event is identified.

A (Anchor)

Browser Support: Navigator 2, Internet Explorer 3

The Anchor object is referred to as the A object in Microsoft's documentation and is combined with the Netscape Link object.

The Anchor object represents a document-internal target of a hypertext link. An Anchor object is created for each A tag in the document that specifies a NAME attribute. These objects may be accessed from the anchors property of the document object.

Under Navigator, an Anchor object may also be a Link object if the A tag specifies the HREF attribute in addition to the NAME attribute.

Properties

Properties Supported by Both Navigator and Internet Explorer

name (Navigator 4, Internet Explorer 4)

The anchor's NAME attribute.

Other Properties

accessKey (Internet Explorer 4), className (Internet Explorer 4), dataFld (Internet Explorer 4), dataSrc (Internet Explorer 4), document (Internet Explorer 4), hash (Internet Explorer 4), host (Internet Explorer 4), hostname (Internet Explorer 4), href (Internet Explorer 4), id (Internet Explorer 4), innerHTML (Internet Explorer 4), innerText (Internet Explorer 4), isTextEdit (Internet Explorer 4), lang (Internet Explorer 4), language (Internet Explorer 4), Methods (Internet Explorer 4), offsetHeight (Internet Explorer 4), offsetLeft (Internet Explorer 4), offsetParent (Internet Explorer 4), offsetTop (Internet Explorer 4), offsetWidth (Internet Explorer 4), outerHTML (Internet Explorer 4), outerText (Internet Explorer 4), parentElement (Internet Explorer 4), parentTextEdit (Internet Explorer 4), pathname (Internet Explorer 4), port (Internet Explorer 4), protocol (Internet Explorer 4), recordNumber (Internet Explorer 4), rel (Internet Explorer 4), rev (Internet Explorer 4), search (Internet Explorer 4), sourceIndex (Internet Explorer 4), style (Internet Explorer 4), tabIndex (Internet Explorer 4), tagName (Internet Explorer 4), target (Internet Explorer 4), text (Navigator 4), title (Internet Explorer 4), urn (Internet Explorer 4), x (Navigator 4), y (Navigator 4)

Methods

Methods Supported by Both Navigator and Internet Explorer
None.

Other Methods
blur (Internet Explorer 4), click (Internet Explorer 4), contains (Internet Explorer 4), focus (Internet Explorer 4), getAttribute (Internet Explorer 4), insertAdjacentHTML (Internet Explorer 4), insertAdjacentext (Internet Explorer 4), removeAttribute (Internet Explorer 4), scrollIntoView (Internet Explorer 4), setAttribute (Internet Explorer 4)

Events

ondblclick (Navigator 4, Internet Explorer 4), onmouseout (Navigator 3, Internet Explorer 4), onmouseover (Navigator 22, Internet Explorer 3), onblur (Internet Explorer 4), onclick (Internet Explorer 4), ondragstart (Internet Explorer 4), onerrorupdate (Internet Explorer 4), onfilterchange (Internet Explorer 4), onfocus (Internet Explorer 4), onhelp (Internet Explorer 4), onkeydown (Internet Explorer 4), onkeypress (Internet Explorer 4), onkeyup (Internet Explorer 4), onmousedown (Internet Explorer 4), onmousemove (Internet Explorer 4), onmouseup (Internet Explorer 4), onselectstart (Internet Explorer 4)

ACRONYM

Browser Support: Internet Explorer 4
Provides access to the HTML ACRONYM tag.

Properties

Properties Supported by Both Navigator and Internet Explorer
None.

Other Properties
className (Internet Explorer 4), document (Internet Explorer 4), id (Internet Explorer 4), innerHTML (Internet Explorer 4), innerText (Internet Explorer 4), isTextEdit (Internet Explorer 4),

lang (Internet Explorer 4), language (Internet Explorer 4), offsetHeight
(Internet Explorer 4), offsetLeft (Internet Explorer 4), offset-
Parent (Internet Explorer 4), offsetTop (Internet Explorer 4), offset-
Width (Internet Explorer 4), outerHTML (Internet Explorer 4), outerText
(Internet Explorer 4), parentElement (Internet Explorer 4), parentText-
Edit (Internet Explorer 4), sourceIndex (Internet Explorer 4), style
(Internet Explorer 4), tagName (Internet Explorer 4), title (Internet
Explorer 4)

Methods

Methods Supported by Both Navigator and Internet Explorer
None.

Other Methods
click (Internet Explorer 4), contains (Internet Explorer 4), get-
Attribute (Internet Explorer 4), insertAdjacentHTML (Internet
Explorer 4), insertAdjacentText (Internet Explorer 4), remove-
Attribute (Internet Explorer 4), scrollIntoView (Internet Explorer 4),
setAttribute (Internet Explorer 4)

Events

onclick (Internet Explorer 4), ondblclick (Internet Explorer 4), ondragstart (Internet Explorer 4), onfilterchange (Internet Explorer 4),
onhelp (Internet Explorer 4), onkeydown (Internet Explorer 4), onkeypress (Internet Explorer 4), onkeyup (Internet Explorer 4), onmousedown (Internet Explorer 4), onmousemove (Internet Explorer 4),
onmouseout (Internet Explorer 4), onmouseover (Internet Explorer 4),
onmouseup (Internet Explorer 4)

ActiveXObject

Browser Support: Internet Explorer 4

Provides access to ActiveX objects via JavaScript.

Constructors

```
var newObject = new ActiveXObject("servername.typename"[,
"location"])
```

Creates the ActiveXObject of the specified type from the specified server. The location can be used to specify the location of a remote server.

Properties

This object does not define any properties.

Methods

This object does not define any methods.

Events

This object does not define any events.

ADDRESS

Browser Support: Internet Explorer 4

Provides access to the HTML **ADDRESS** tag.

Properties

Properties Supported by Both Navigator and Internet Explorer
None.

Other Properties
className (Internet Explorer 4), document (Internet Explorer 4), id (Internet Explorer 4), innerHTML (Internet Explorer 4), inner-Text (Internet Explorer 4), isTextEdit (Internet Explorer 4), lang (Internet Explorer 4), language (Internet Explorer 4), offset-Height (Internet Explorer 4), offsetLeft (Internet Explorer 4), off-setParent (Internet Explorer 4), offsetTop (Internet Explorer 4), offsetWidth (Internet Explorer 4), outerHTML (Internet Explorer 4), outerText (Internet Explorer 4), parentElement (Internet Explorer 4), parentTextEdit (Internet Explorer 4), sourceIndex (Internet

Explorer 4), `style` (Internet Explorer 4), `tagName` (Internet Explorer 4), `title` (Internet Explorer 4)

Methods

Methods Supported by Both Navigator and Internet Explorer
None.

Other Methods
`click` (Internet Explorer 4), `contains` (Internet Explorer 4), `getAttribute` (Internet Explorer 4), `insertAdjacentHTML` (Internet Explorer 4), `insertAdjacentText` (Internet Explorer 4), `removeAttribute` (Internet Explorer 4), `scrollIntoView` (Internet Explorer 4), `setAttribute` (Internet Explorer 4)

Events

`onclick` (Internet Explorer 4), `ondblclick` (Internet Explorer 4), `ondragstart` (Internet Explorer 4), `onhelp` (Internet Explorer 4), `onkeydown` (Internet Explorer 4), `onkeypress` (Internet Explorer 4), `onkeyup` (Internet Explorer 4), `onmousedown` (Internet Explorer 4), `onmousemove` (Internet Explorer 4), `onmouseout` (Internet Explorer 4), `onmouseover` (Internet Explorer 4), `onmouseup` (Internet Explorer 4), `onselectstart` (Internet Explorer 4)

Applet

Browser Support: Navigator 3, Internet Explorer 4

The `Applet` object represents a Java applet that is loaded with a document. The `applets` property of the document object provides access to an enumeration of the `Applet` objects that are associated with the document. An applet is accessible to JavaScript only if the `MAYSCRIPT` attribute is supplied in the applet's `APPLET` tag.

For example, the following `APPLET` tag loads an applet that is accessible from JavaScript:

```
<APPLET CODE="myClassFile" MAYSCRIPT></APPLET>
```

Because the following APPLET tag does not include the MAYSCRIPT attribute, it cannot be accessed from JavaScript:

```
<APPLET CODE="myClassFile></APPLET>
```

The Applet object inherits all of the public properties and methods of the applet.

Properties

Properties Supported by Both Navigator and Internet Explorer
None.

Other Properties
accessKey (Internet Explorer 4), align (Internet Explorer 4), altHTML (Internet Explorer 4), className (Internet Explorer 4), code (Internet Explorer 4), codeBase (Internet Explorer 4), dataFld (Internet Explorer 4), dataSrc (Internet Explorer 4), document (Internet Explorer 4), height (Internet Explorer 4), hspace (Internet Explorer 4), id (Internet Explorer 4), isTextEdit (Internet Explorer 4), lang (Internet Explorer 4), language (Internet Explorer 4), name (Internet Explorer 4), offsetHeight (Internet Explorer 4), offsetLeft (Internet Explorer 4), offsetParent (Internet Explorer 4), offsetTop (Internet Explorer 4), offsetWidth (Internet Explorer 4), outerHTML (Internet Explorer 4), outerText (Internet Explorer 4), parentElement (Internet Explorer 4), parentTextEdit (Internet Explorer 4), sourceIndex (Internet Explorer 4), src (Internet Explorer 4), style (Internet Explorer 4), tagName (Internet Explorer 4), title (Internet Explorer 4), vspace (Internet Explorer 4)

Methods

Methods Supported by Both Navigator and Internet Explorer
None.

Other Methods
blur (Internet Explorer 4), click (Internet Explorer 4), contains (Internet Explorer 4), focus (Internet Explorer 4), getAttribute (Internet Explorer 4), insertAdjacentHTML (Internet Explorer 4), insertAdjacentText (Internet Explorer 4), removeAttribute (Internet

Explorer 4), `scrollIntoView` (Internet Explorer 4), `setAttribute` (Internet Explorer 4)

Events

`onafterupdate` (Internet Explorer 4), `onbeforeupdate` (Internet Explorer 4), `onblur` (Internet Explorer 4), `onclick` (Internet Explorer 4), `ondataavailable` (Internet Explorer 4), `ondatasetchanged` (Internet Explorer 4), `ondatasetcomplete` (Internet Explorer 4), `ondblclick` (Internet Explorer 4), `onerrorupdate` (Internet Explorer 4), `onfocus` (Internet Explorer 4), `onhelp` (Internet Explorer 4), `onkeydown` (Internet Explorer 4), `onkeypress` (Internet Explorer 4), `onkeyup` (Internet Explorer 4), `onload` (Internet Explorer 4), `onmousedown` (Internet Explorer 4), `onmousemove` (Internet Explorer 4), `onmouseout` (Internet Explorer 4), `onmouseover` (Internet Explorer 4), `onmouseup` (Internet Explorer 4), `onreadystatechange` (Internet Explorer 4), `onresize` (Internet Explorer 4), `onrowenter` (Internet Explorer 4), `onrowexit` (Internet Explorer 4)

Area

Browser Support: Navigator 3, Internet Explorer 4

The Area object defines an area of an image map. It is like a `Link` object in that it is associated with a URL. This URL is loaded when a user clicks on the area of the image map represented by the `Area` object.

Properties

Properties Supported by Both Navigator and Internet Explorer

`hash` (Navigator 2.02, Internet Explorer 3)

The name of an anchor in the URL.

`host` (Navigator 2.02, Internet Explorer 3)

A host name or IP address that represents the URL's host value.

`hostname` (Navigator 2.02, Internet Explorer 3)

The `host:port` portion of the URL.

`href` (Navigator 2.02, Internet Explorer 3)

The text of the entire URL.

pathname (Navigator 2.02, Internet Explorer 3)

The path name portion of the URL.

port (Navigator 2.02, Internet Explorer 3)

The port value of the URL.

protocol (Navigator 2, Internet Explorer 3.03)

The URL's protocol type.

search (Navigator 2, Internet Explorer 3.03)

The value of any query string that is included in the URL.

target (Navigator 2, Internet Explorer 3.03)

The value of the URL's TARGET attribute.

Other Properties

alt (Internet Explorer 4), className (Internet Explorer 4), coords (Internet Explorer 4), document (Internet Explorer 4), id (Internet Explorer 4), isTextEdit (Internet Explorer 4), lang (Internet Explorer 4), language (Internet Explorer 4), noHref (Internet Explorer 4), offsetHeight (Internet Explorer 4), offsetLeft (Internet Explorer 4), offsetParent (Internet Explorer 4), offsetTop (Internet Explorer 4), offsetWidth (Internet Explorer 4), outerHTML (Internet Explorer 4), outerText (Internet Explorer 4), parentElement (Internet Explorer 4), parentTextEdit (Internet Explorer 4), sourceIndex (Internet Explorer 4), style (Internet Explorer 4), tabIndex (Internet Explorer 4), tagName (Internet Explorer 4), text (Navigator 4), title (Internet Explorer 4), x (Navigator 4), y (Navigator 4)

Methods

Methods Supported by Both Navigator and Internet Explorer

None.

Other Methods

blur (Internet Explorer 4), click (Internet Explorer 4), contains (Internet Explorer 4), focus (Internet Explorer 4), getAttribute (Internet Explorer 4), handleEvent (Navigator 4), insertAdjacentHTML (Internet Explorer 4), insertAdjacentText (Internet Explorer 4), removeAttribute (Internet Explorer 4), scrollIntoView (Internet Explorer 4), setAttribute (Internet Explorer 4)

Events

ondblclick (Navigator 2, Internet Explorer 3), onmouseout (Navigator 3, Internet Explorer 4), onmouseover (Navigator 2, Internet Explorer 3), onblur (Internet Explorer 4), onclick (Internet Explorer 4), ondragstart (Internet Explorer 4), onfilterchange (Internet Explorer 4), onfocus (Internet Explorer 4), onhelp (Internet Explorer 4), onkeydown (Internet Explorer 4), onkeypress (Internet Explorer 4), onkeyup (Internet Explorer 4), onmousedown (Internet Explorer 4), onmousemove (Internet Explorer 4), onmouseup (Internet Explorer 4), onselectstart (Internet Explorer 4)

Array

Browser Support: Navigator 3, Internet Explorer 4

The Array object was introduced in JavaScript 1.1, but it was modified in JavaScript 1.3 to ensure ECMA 262 compliance. It is supported in JScript 3 and later.

The Array object represents a JavaScript array.

Constructors

Arrays can be constructed in the following ways:

```
myArray = new Array(10) // new Array(length)
myArray = new Array(100, 20, 40) // new Array(element_1, ...,
➥ element_n)
myArray = [2, 4, 6, 8] // Assignment of array literal
[These are 3 distinct examples which need to be on separate
➥ lines]
```

In the first form, an array of length 10 is created. Its elements are initially undefined. In the second form, an array of length 3 is created. This array consists of the elements 100, 20, and 40. In the third form, the myArray variable is assigned an array literal that represents a four-element array consisting of the values 2, 4, 6, and 8.

If the constructor, new Array(n), where n is a positive integer, is used with Navigator 4 or later and the script's LANGUAGE attribute is set to JavaScript1.2, then the constructor creates a one-element array consisting of the value *n*. This is a quirk that was designed into JavaScript 1.2 by Netscape. This problem does not occur with Internet Explorer or

with Navigator when the LANGUAGE attribute is not set to
JavaScript1.2.

Properties

Properties Supported by Both Navigator and Internet Explorer
constructor (Navigator 3, Internet Explorer 4)

   A reference to the object's constructor.

length (Navigator 3, Internet Explorer 4)

   The number of elements.

prototype (Navigator 3, Internet Explorer 4)

   Used to define additional properties.

Other Properties
index (Navigator 4), input (Navigator 4)

Methods

Methods Supported by Both Navigator and Internet Explorer
concat(array1, array2, ..., array3) (Navigator 4, Internet
Explorer 4)

   Returns a new Array object that is the original array concatenated
with the arrays identified as the method's arguments.

join(separator) (Navigator 3, Internet Explorer 4)

   Joins the elements of the array together as a string. The separator is
placed between the joined elements.

reverse() (Navigator 3, Internet Explorer 4)

   Reverses the elements of the array.

slice(begin[,end]) (Navigator 4, Internet Explorer 4)

   Extracts and returns the array slice from begin (inclusive) to end
(exclusive). If end is not supplied, then the slice continues to the end of
the array.

sort(compareFunction) (Navigator 3, Internet Explorer 4)

Sorts the elements of the array using the specified compare function. If the compare function is omitted, then the elements are sorted in dictionary order. This method was updated to achieve ECMA 262 compliance in JavaScript 1.2.

toString() (Navigator 3, Internet Explorer 4)

Returns a string representation of the array. This method is compatible with toSource().

valueOf() (Navigator 3, Internet Explorer 4)

Returns the primitive value of the array. For Boolean arrays, a Boolean value is returned. For number and data arrays, a number value is returned. For all other arrays, a string value is returned.

Other Methods

pop (Navigator 4), push (Navigator 4), shift (Navigator 4), splice (Navigator 4), toSource (Navigator 4.06), unshift (Navigator 4)

Events

No events are defined for the Array object.

Attribute

Browser Support: Internet Explorer 5

Encapsulates an attribute of an HTML element as an object.

Properties

Properties Supported by Both Navigator and Internet Explorer

None.

Other Properties

nodeName (Internet Explorer 5), nodeType (Internet Explorer 5), nodeValue (Internet Explorer 5), specified (Internet Explorer 5)

Methods

This object does not define any methods.

Events

This object does not define any events.

B

Browser Support: Internet Explorer 4

Provides access to the HTML B tag.

Properties

Properties Supported by Both Navigator and Internet Explorer
None.

Other Properties

className (Internet Explorer 4), document (Internet Explorer 4), id (Internet Explorer 4), innerHTML (Internet Explorer 4), innerText (Internet Explorer 4), isTextEdit (Internet Explorer 4), lang (Internet Explorer 4), language (Internet Explorer 4), offsetHeight (Internet Explorer 4), offsetLeft (Internet Explorer 4), offsetParent (Internet Explorer 4), offsetTop (Internet Explorer 4), offsetWidth (Internet Explorer 4), outerHTML (Internet Explorer 4), outerText (Internet Explorer 4), parentElement (Internet Explorer 4), parentTextEdit (Internet Explorer 4), sourceIndex (Internet Explorer 4), style (Internet Explorer 4), tagName (Internet Explorer 4), title (Internet Explorer 4)

Methods

Methods Supported by Both Navigator and Internet Explorer
None.

Other Methods

click (Internet Explorer 4), contains (Internet Explorer 4), getAttribute (Internet Explorer 4), insertAdjacentHTML (Internet

Explorer 4), `insertAdjacentText` (Internet Explorer 4), `remove-Attribute` (Internet Explorer 4), `scrollIntoView` (Internet Explorer 4), `setAttribute` (Internet Explorer 4)

Events

`onclick` (Internet Explorer 4), `ondblclick` (Internet Explorer 4), `ondragstart` (Internet Explorer 4), `onfilterchange` (Internet Explorer 4), `onhelp` (Internet Explorer 4), `onkeydown` (Internet Explorer 4), `onkeypress` (Internet Explorer 4), `onkeyup` (Internet Explorer 4), `onmousedown` (Internet Explorer 4), `onmousemove` (Internet Explorer 4), `onmouseout` (Internet Explorer 4), `onmouseover` (Internet Explorer 4), `onmouseup` (Internet Explorer 4), `onselectstart` (Internet Explorer 4)

BASE

Browser Support: Internet Explorer 4

Provides access to the HTML BASE tag.

Properties

Properties Supported by Both Navigator and Internet Explorer

None.

Other Properties

`className` (Internet Explorer 4), `document` (Internet Explorer 4), `href` (Internet Explorer 4), `id` (Internet Explorer 4), `isTextEdit` (Internet Explorer 4), `lang` (Internet Explorer 4), `outerHTML` (Internet Explorer 4), `outerText` (Internet Explorer 4), `parentElement` (Internet Explorer 4), `parentTextEdit` (Internet Explorer 4), `sourceIndex` (Internet Explorer 4), `tagName` (Internet Explorer 4), `target` (Internet Explorer 4), `title` (Internet Explorer 4)

Methods

Methods Supported by Both Navigator and Internet Explorer

None.

Other Methods

contains (Internet Explorer 4), getAttribute (Internet Explorer 4), removeAttribute (Internet Explorer 4), setAttribute (Internet Explorer 4)

Events

This object does not define any events.

BASEFONT

Browser Support: Internet Explorer 4

Provides access to the HTML BASEFONT tag.

Properties

Properties Supported by Both Navigator and Internet Explorer

None.

Other Properties

className (Internet Explorer 4), color (Internet Explorer 4), document (Internet Explorer 4), face (Internet Explorer 4), id (Internet Explorer 4), isTextEdit (Internet Explorer 4), outerHTML (Internet Explorer 4), outerText (Internet Explorer 4), parentElement (Internet Explorer 4), parentTextEdit (Internet Explorer 4), size (Internet Explorer 4), sourceIndex (Internet Explorer 4), tagName (Internet Explorer 4)

Methods

Methods Supported by Both Navigator and Internet Explorer

None.

Other Methods

contains (Internet Explorer 4), getAttribute (Internet Explorer 4), removeAttribute (Internet Explorer 4), setAttribute (Internet Explorer 4)

Events

This object does not define any events.

BDO

Browser Support: Internet Explorer 5

Provides the capability to control the reading order of a block of text.

Properties

Properties Supported by Both Navigator and Internet Explorer

None.

Other Properties

accessKey (Internet Explorer 5), canHaveChildren (Internet Explorer 5), canHaveHTML (Internet Explorer 5), className (Internet Explorer 5), clientHeight (Internet Explorer 5), clientLeft (Internet Explorer 5), clientTop (Internet Explorer 5), clientWidth (Internet Explorer 5), contentEditable (Internet Explorer 5), currentStyle (Internet Explorer 5), dir (Internet Explorer 5), disabled (Internet Explorer 5), firstChild (Internet Explorer 5), hasLayout (Internet Explorer 5), hideFocus (Internet Explorer 5), id (Internet Explorer 5), innerHTML (Internet Explorer 5), innerText (Internet Explorer 5), isContentEditable (Internet Explorer 5), isDisabled (Internet Explorer 5), isTextEdit (Internet Explorer 5), lang (Internet Explorer 5), language (Internet Explorer 5), lastChild (Internet Explorer 5), nextSibling (Internet Explorer 5), nodeName (Internet Explorer 5), nodeType (Internet Explorer 5), nodeValue (Internet Explorer 5), offsetHeight (Internet Explorer 5), offsetLeft (Internet Explorer 5), offsetParent (Internet Explorer 5), offsetTop (Internet Explorer 5), offsetWidth (Internet Explorer 5), outerHTML (Internet Explorer 5), outerText (Internet Explorer 5), parentElement (Internet Explorer 5), parentNode (Internet Explorer 5), parentTextEdit (Internet Explorer 5), previousSibling (Internet Explorer 5), readyState (Internet Explorer 5), scopeName (Internet Explorer 5), scrollHeight (Internet Explorer 5), scrollLeft (Internet Explorer 5), scrollTop (Internet Explorer 5), scrollWidth (Internet Explorer 5), sourceIndex (Internet Explorer 5), tabIndex (Internet Explorer 5), tagName (Internet Explorer 5), tagUrn (Internet Explorer 5), title (Internet Explorer 5)

Methods

Methods Supported by Both Navigator and Internet Explorer
None.

Other Methods

appendChild (Internet Explorer 5), applyElement (Internet Explorer 5), blur (Internet Explorer 5), clearAttributes (Internet Explorer 5), cloneNode (Internet Explorer 5), componentFromPoint (Internet Explorer 5), fireEvent (Internet Explorer 5), focus (Internet Explorer 5), getAdjacentText (Internet Explorer 5), getElementsByTagName (Internet Explorer 5), getExpression (Internet Explorer 5), hasChildNodes (Internet Explorer 5), insertAdjacentElement (Internet Explorer 5), insertBefore (Internet Explorer 5), mergeAttributes (Internet Explorer 5), removeChild (Internet Explorer 5), removeExpression (Internet Explorer 5), removeNode (Internet Explorer 5), replaceAdjacentText (Internet Explorer 5), replaceChild (Internet Explorer 5), replaceNode (Internet Explorer 5), setActive (Internet Explorer 5), setExpression (Internet Explorer 5), swapNode (Internet Explorer 5)

Events

onafterupdate (Internet Explorer 5), onbeforecopy (Internet Explorer 5), onbeforecut (Internet Explorer 5), onbeforefocusenter (Internet Explorer 5), onbeforefocusleave (Internet Explorer 5), onbeforepaste (Internet Explorer 5), onbeforeupdate (Internet Explorer 5), onblur (Internet Explorer 5), oncellchange (Internet Explorer 5), onclick (Internet Explorer 5), oncontextmenu (Internet Explorer 5), oncontrolselect (Internet Explorer 5), oncopy (Internet Explorer 5), oncut (Internet Explorer 5), ondblclick (Internet Explorer 5), ondrag (Internet Explorer 5), ondragend (Internet Explorer 5), ondragenter (Internet Explorer 5), ondragleave (Internet Explorer 5), ondragover (Internet Explorer 5), ondragstart (Internet Explorer 5), ondrop (Internet Explorer 5), onerrorupdate (Internet Explorer 5), onfilterchange (Internet Explorer 5), onfocus (Internet Explorer 5), onfocusenter (Internet Explorer 5), onfocusleave (Internet Explorer 5), onhelp (Internet Explorer 5), onkeydown (Internet Explorer 5), onkeypress (Internet Explorer 5), onkeyup (Internet Explorer 5), onlosecapture (Internet Explorer 5), onmousedown (Internet Explorer 5), onmouseenter (Internet Explorer 5), onmouseleave (Internet Explorer 5), onmousemove (Internet Explorer 5), onmouseout (Internet Explorer 5), onmouseover (Internet Explorer 5), onmouseup (Internet Explorer 5), onpaste (Internet Explorer 5), onpropertychange (Internet Explorer 5), onreadystatechange (Internet Explorer 5), onresizeend (Internet Explorer 5), onresizestart (Internet Explorer 5), onscroll (Internet Explorer 5), onselectstart (Internet Explorer 5)

BGSOUND

Browser Support: Internet Explorer 4

Provides access to the HTML BGSOUND tag.

Properties

Properties Supported by Both Navigator and Internet Explorer
None.

Other Properties
balance (Internet Explorer 4), className (Internet Explorer 4), document (Internet Explorer 4), id (Internet Explorer 4), isTextEdit (Internet Explorer 4), loop (Internet Explorer 4), offsetHeight (Internet Explorer 4), offsetLeft (Internet Explorer 4), offsetParent (Internet Explorer 4), offsetTop (Internet Explorer 4), offsetWidth (Internet Explorer 4), outerHTML (Internet Explorer 4), outerText (Internet Explorer 4), parentElement (Internet Explorer 4), parentTextEdit (Internet Explorer 4), sourceIndex (Internet Explorer 4), src (Internet Explorer 4), style (Internet Explorer 4), tagName (Internet Explorer 4), title (Internet Explorer 4), volume (Internet Explorer 4)

Methods

Methods Supported by Both Navigator and Internet Explorer
None.

Other Methods

contains (Internet Explorer 4), getAttribute (Internet Explorer 4), removeAttribute (Internet Explorer 4), setAttribute (Internet Explorer 4)

Events

This object does not define any events.

BIG

Browser Support: Internet Explorer 4

Provides access to the HTML BIG tag.

Properties

Properties Supported by Both Navigator and Internet Explorer
None.

Other Properties

className (Internet Explorer 4), document (Internet Explorer 4), id (Internet Explorer 4), innerHTML (Internet Explorer 4), innerText (Internet Explorer 4), isTextEdit (Internet Explorer 4), lang (Internet Explorer 4), language (Internet Explorer 4), offsetHeight (Internet Explorer 4), offsetLeft (Internet Explorer 4), offsetParent (Internet Explorer 4), offsetTop (Internet Explorer 4), offsetWidth (Internet Explorer 4), outerHTML (Internet Explorer 4), outerText (Internet Explorer 4), parentElement (Internet Explorer 4), parentTextEdit (Internet Explorer 4), sourceIndex (Internet Explorer 4), style (Internet Explorer 4), tagName (Internet Explorer 4), title (Internet Explorer 4)

Methods

Methods Supported by Both Navigator and Internet Explorer
None.

Other Methods

click (Internet Explorer 4), contains (Internet Explorer 4), get-Attribute (Internet Explorer 4), insertAdjacentHTML (Internet Explorer 4), insertAdjacentText (Internet Explorer 4), remove-Attribute (Internet Explorer 4), scrollIntoView (Internet Explorer 4), setAttribute (Internet Explorer 4)

Events

onclick (Internet Explorer 4), ondblclick (Internet Explorer 4), ondragstart (Internet Explorer 4), onfilterchange (Internet Explorer 4), onhelp (Internet Explorer 4), onkeydown (Internet Explorer 4), onkeypress (Internet Explorer 4), onkeyup (Internet Explorer 4), onmousedown (Internet Explorer 4), onmousemove (Internet Explorer 4), onmouseout (Internet Explorer 4), onmouseover (Internet Explorer 4), onmouseup (Internet Explorer 4), onselectstart (Internet Explorer 4)

BLOCKQUOTE

Browser Support: Internet Explorer 4

Provides access to the HTML BLOCKQUOTE tag.

Properties

Properties Supported by Both Navigator and Internet Explorer

None.

Other Properties

className (Internet Explorer 4), document (Internet Explorer 4), id (Internet Explorer 4), innerHTML (Internet Explorer 4), innerText (Internet Explorer 4), isTextEdit (Internet Explorer 4), lang (Internet Explorer 4), language (Internet Explorer 4), offsetHeight (Internet Explorer 4), offsetLeft (Internet Explorer 4), offsetParent (Internet Explorer 4), offsetTop (Internet Explorer 4), offsetWidth (Internet Explorer 4), outerHTML (Internet Explorer 4), outerText (Internet Explorer 4), parentElement (Internet Explorer 4), parentTextEdit (Internet Explorer 4), sourceIndex (Internet Explorer 4), style (Internet Explorer 4), tagName (Internet Explorer 4), title (Internet Explorer 4)

Methods

Methods Supported by Both Navigator and Internet Explorer
None.

Other Methods
click (Internet Explorer 4), contains (Internet Explorer 4), getAttribute (Internet Explorer 4), insertAdjacentHTML (Internet Explorer 4), insertAdjacentText (Internet Explorer 4), removeAttribute (Internet Explorer 4), scrollIntoView (Internet Explorer 4), setAttribute (Internet Explorer 4)

Events

onclick (Internet Explorer 4), ondblclick (Internet Explorer 4), ondragstart (Internet Explorer 4), onfilterchange (Internet Explorer 4), onhelp (Internet Explorer 4), onkeydown (Internet Explorer 4), onkeypress (Internet Explorer 4), onkeyup (Internet Explorer 4), onmousedown (Internet Explorer 4), onmousemove (Internet Explorer 4), onmouseout (Internet Explorer 4), onmouseover (Internet Explorer 4), onmouseup (Internet Explorer 4), onselectstart (Internet Explorer 4)

BODY

Browser Support: Internet Explorer 4

Provides access to the HTML BODY tag.

Properties

Properties Supported by Both Navigator and Internet Explorer
None.

Other Properties
accessKey (Internet Explorer 4), aLink (Internet Explorer 4), background (Internet Explorer 4), bgColor (Internet Explorer 4), bgProperties (Internet Explorer 4), bottomMargin (Internet Explorer 4), className (Internet Explorer 4), clientHeight (Internet Explorer 4), clientLeft (Internet Explorer 4), clientTop (Internet Explorer 4),

clientWidth (Internet Explorer 4), document (Internet Explorer 4), filter (Internet Explorer 4), id (Internet Explorer 4), innerHTML (Internet Explorer 4), innerText (Internet Explorer 4), isTextEdit (Internet Explorer 4), lang (Internet Explorer 4), language (Internet Explorer 4), leftMargin (Internet Explorer 4), link (Internet Explorer 4), noWrap (Internet Explorer 4), offsetHeight (Internet Explorer 4), offsetLeft (Internet Explorer 4), offsetParent (Internet Explorer 4), offsetTop (Internet Explorer 4), offsetWidth (Internet Explorer 4), outerHTML (Internet Explorer 4), outerText (Internet Explorer 4), parentElement (Internet Explorer 4), parentTextEdit (Internet Explorer 4), recordNumber (Internet Explorer 4), rightMargin (Internet Explorer 4), scroll (Internet Explorer 4), scrollHeight (Internet Explorer 4), scrollLeft (Internet Explorer 4), scrollTop (Internet Explorer 4), scrollWidth (Internet Explorer 4), sourceIndex (Internet Explorer 4), style (Internet Explorer 4), tabIndex (Internet Explorer 4), tagName (Internet Explorer 4), text (Internet Explorer 4), title (Internet Explorer 4), topMargin vLink (Internet Explorer 4)

Methods

Methods Supported by Both Navigator and Internet Explorer

None.

Other Methods

click (Internet Explorer 4), contains (Internet Explorer 4), createTextRange (Internet Explorer 4), getAttribute (Internet Explorer 4), insertAdjacentHTML (Internet Explorer 4), insertAdjacentText (Internet Explorer 4), removeAttribute (Internet Explorer 4), setAttribute (Internet Explorer 4)

Events

onafterupdate (Internet Explorer 4), onbeforeunload (Internet Explorer 4), onbeforeupdate (Internet Explorer 4), onchange (Internet Explorer 4), onclick (Internet Explorer 4), ondataavailable (Internet Explorer 4), ondatasetchanged (Internet Explorer 4), ondatasetcomplete (Internet Explorer 4), ondblclick (Internet Explorer 4), ondragstart (Internet Explorer 4), onerrorupdate (Internet Explorer 4), onfilterchange (Internet Explorer 4), onhelp (Internet

Explorer 4), onkeydown (Internet Explorer 4), onkeypress (Internet Explorer 4), onkeyup (Internet Explorer 4), onload (Internet Explorer 4), onmousedown (Internet Explorer 4), onmousemove (Internet Explorer 4), onmouseout (Internet Explorer 4), onmouseover (Internet Explorer 4), onmouseup (Internet Explorer 4), onrowenter (Internet Explorer 4), onrowexit (Internet Explorer 4), onscroll (Internet Explorer 4), onselectstart (Internet Explorer 4), onunload (Internet Explorer 4)

Boolean

Browser Support: Navigator 3, Internet Explorer 4

The Boolean object was introduced in JavaScript 1.1, but it was modified in JavaScript 1.3 to ensure ECMA 262 compliance. It is supported in JScript 3 and later.

The Boolean object provides an object representation of the primitive Boolean true and false values. Do not confuse Boolean objects with Boolean primitive values. Boolean objects always evaluate to true when used in place of a Boolean primitive value.

Constructors

The Boolean constructor takes the following form:

```
new Boolean(value)
```

The *value* used in the constructor creates an object that represents false if *value* is false, 0, "", NaN, null, or undefined, or if *value* is omitted. For any other *value*, an object is created that represents true.

Properties

Properties Supported by Both Navigator and Internet Explorer

constructor (Navigator 3, Internet Explorer 4)

A reference to the object's constructor.

prototype (Navigator 3, Internet Explorer 4)

Used to define additional properties.

Methods

Methods Supported by Both Navigator and Internet Explorer

toString() (Navigator 3, Internet Explorer 4)

Returns a string value of the object that is compatible with toSource().

valueOf() (Navigator 3, Internet Explorer 4)

Returns the object's primitive value.

Other Methods

toSource (Navigator 4.06)

Events

No events are associated with this object.

BR

Browser Support: Internet Explorer 4

Provides access to the HTML BR tag.

Properties

Properties Supported by Both Navigator and Internet Explorer

None.

Other Properties

className (Internet Explorer 4), clear (Internet Explorer 4), document (Internet Explorer 4), id (Internet Explorer 4), isTextEdit (Internet Explorer 4), language (Internet Explorer 4), offsetHeight (Internet Explorer 4), offsetLeft (Internet Explorer 4), offsetParent (Internet Explorer 4), offsetTop (Internet Explorer 4), offsetWidth (Internet Explorer 4), outerHTML (Internet Explorer 4), outerText (Internet Explorer 4), parentElement (Internet Explorer 4), parentTextEdit (Internet Explorer 4), sourceIndex (Internet Explorer 4), style (Internet Explorer 4), tagName (Internet Explorer 4), title (Internet Explorer 4)

Methods

Methods Supported by Both Navigator and Internet Explorer
None.

Other Methods
contains (Internet Explorer 4), getAttribute (Internet Explorer 4), insertAdjacentHTML (Internet Explorer 4), insertAdjacentText (Internet Explorer 4), removeAttribute (Internet Explorer 4), scrollIntoView (Internet Explorer 4), setAttribute (Internet Explorer 4)

Events

This object does not define any events.

Button

Browser Support: Navigator 2, Internet Explorer 3

The basic Button object was introduced in JavaScript 1. It has been updated with JavaScript 1.1 and 1.2.

The Button object provides access to the buttons of an HTML form.

Properties

Properties Supported by Both Navigator and Internet Explorer
form (Navigator 2, Internet Explorer 3)

Provides a reference to the form object that contains the button.

name (Navigator 2, Internet Explorer 3)

The value of the button's NAME attribute.

type (Navigator 3, Internet Explorer 4)

The value of the button's TYPE attribute.

value (Navigator 2, Internet Explorer 3)

The value of the button's VALUE attribute.

Other Properties

accessKey (Internet Explorer 4), className (Internet Explorer 4),
dataFld (Internet Explorer 4), dataFormatAs (Internet Explorer 4),
dataSrc (Internet Explorer 4), disabled (Internet Explorer 4), document (Internet Explorer 4), id (Internet Explorer 4), isTextEdit (Internet Explorer 4), lang (Internet Explorer 4), language (Internet Explorer 4),
offsetHeight (Internet Explorer 4), offsetLeft (Internet Explorer 4),
offsetParent (Internet Explorer 4), offsetTop (Internet Explorer 4),
offsetWidth (Internet Explorer 4), outerHTML (Internet Explorer 4),
outerText (Internet Explorer 4), parentElement (Internet Explorer 4),
parentTextEdit (Internet Explorer 4), readOnly (Internet Explorer 4),
recordNumber (Internet Explorer 4), sourceIndex (Internet Explorer 4),
style (Internet Explorer 4), tabIndex (Internet Explorer 4), tagName
(Internet Explorer 4), title (Internet Explorer 4)

Methods

Methods Supported by Both Navigator and Internet Explorer

blur() (Navigator 2, Internet Explorer 3)

 Removes input focus from the button.

click() (Navigator 2, Internet Explorer 3)

 Simulates clicking of the button.

focus() (Navigator 2, Internet Explorer 3)

 Moves input focus to the button.

Other Methods

contains (Internet Explorer 4), createTextRange (Internet Explorer 4),
getAttribute (Internet Explorer 4), handleEvent (Navigator 4),
insertAdjacentHTML (Internet Explorer 4), insertAdjacentText
(Internet Explorer 4), removeAttribute (Internet Explorer 4),
scrollIntoView (Internet Explorer 4), select (Internet Explorer 4),
setAttribute (Internet Explorer 4)

Events

onblur (Navigator 3, Internet Explorer 4), onclick (Navigator 2, Internet Explorer 3), onfocus (Navigator 3, Internet Explorer 4), onmousedown (Navigator 2, Internet Explorer 3), onmouseup (Navigator 2, Internet

Explorer 3), ondblclick (Internet Explorer 4), onhelp (Internet Explorer 4), onkeydown (Internet Explorer 4), onkeypress (Internet Explorer 4), onkeyup (Internet Explorer 4), onmousemove (Internet Explorer 4), onmouseout (Internet Explorer 4), onmouseover (Internet Explorer 4), onresize (Internet Explorer 4), onselect (Internet Explorer 4)

BUTTON

Browser Support: Internet Explorer 4

Provides the capability to access buttons that contain HTML.

Properties

Properties Supported by Both Navigator and Internet Explorer

None.

Other Properties

accessKey (Internet Explorer 4), className (Internet Explorer 4), dataFld (Internet Explorer 4), dataFormatAs (Internet Explorer 4), dataSrc (Internet Explorer 4), disabled (Internet Explorer 4), document (Internet Explorer 4), form (Internet Explorer 4), id (Internet Explorer 4), innerHTML (Internet Explorer 4), innerText (Internet Explorer 4), isTextEdit (Internet Explorer 4), lang (Internet Explorer 4), language (Internet Explorer 4), name (Internet Explorer 4), offsetHeight (Internet Explorer 4), offsetLeft (Internet Explorer 4), offsetParent (Internet Explorer 4), offsetTop (Internet Explorer 4), offsetWidth (Internet Explorer 4), outerHTML (Internet Explorer 4), outerText (Internet Explorer 4), parentElement (Internet Explorer 4), parentTextEdit (Internet Explorer 4), sourceIndex (Internet Explorer 4), status (Internet Explorer 4), style (Internet Explorer 4), tagName (Internet Explorer 4), title (Internet Explorer 4), type (Internet Explorer 4), value (Internet Explorer 4)

Methods

Methods Supported by Both Navigator and Internet Explorer

None.

Other Methods

blur (Internet Explorer 4), click (Internet Explorer 4), contains (Internet Explorer 4), createTextRange (Internet Explorer 4), focus (Internet Explorer 4), getAttribute (Internet Explorer 4), insert-AdjacentHTML (Internet Explorer 4), insertAdjacentText (Internet Explorer 4), removeAttribute (Internet Explorer 4), scrollIntoView (Internet Explorer 4), setAttribute (Internet Explorer 4)

Events

onafterupdate (Internet Explorer 4), onbeforeupdate (Internet Explorer 4), onblur (Internet Explorer 4), onclick (Internet Explorer 4), ondblclick (Internet Explorer 4), ondragstart (Internet Explorer 4), onfilterchange (Internet Explorer 4), onfocus (Internet Explorer 4), onhelp (Internet Explorer 4), onkeydown (Internet Explorer 4), onkeypress (Internet Explorer 4), onkeyup (Internet Explorer 4), onmousedown (Internet Explorer 4), onmousemove (Internet Explorer 4), onmouseout (Internet Explorer 4), onmouseover (Internet Explorer 4), onmouseup (Internet Explorer 4), onresize (Internet Explorer 4), onrowenter (Internet Explorer 4), onrowexit (Internet Explorer 4), onselectstart (Internet Explorer 4)

CAPTION

Browser Support: Internet Explorer 4

Provides access to the HTML CAPTION tag.

Properties

Properties Supported by Both Navigator and Internet Explorer

None.

Other Properties

align (Internet Explorer 4), className (Internet Explorer 4), clientHeight (Internet Explorer 4), clientLeft (Internet Explorer 4), clientTop (Internet Explorer 4), clientWidth (Internet Explorer 4), document (Internet Explorer 4), id (Internet Explorer 4), innerText (Internet Explorer 4), isTextEdit (Internet Explorer 4), lang (Internet Explorer 4), language (Internet Explorer 4), offsetHeight (Internet

Explorer 4), offsetLeft (Internet Explorer 4), offsetParent (Internet Explorer 4), offsetTop (Internet Explorer 4), offsetWidth (Internet Explorer 4), outerText (Internet Explorer 4), parentElement (Internet Explorer 4), parentTextEdit (Internet Explorer 4), sourceIndex (Internet Explorer 4), style (Internet Explorer 4), tagName (Internet Explorer 4), title (Internet Explorer 4), vAlign (Internet Explorer 4)

Methods

Methods Supported by Both Navigator and Internet Explorer
None.

Other Methods
blur (Internet Explorer 4), click (Internet Explorer 4), contains (Internet Explorer 4), focus (Internet Explorer 4), getAttribute (Internet Explorer 4), insertAdjacentHTML (Internet Explorer 4), insertAdjacentText (Internet Explorer 4), removeAttribute (Internet Explorer 4), scrollIntoView (Internet Explorer 4), setAttribute (Internet Explorer 4)

Events

onafterupdate (Internet Explorer 4), onbeforeupdate (Internet Explorer 4), onblur (Internet Explorer 4), onchange (Internet Explorer 4), onclick (Internet Explorer 4), ondblclick (Internet Explorer 4), ondragstart (Internet Explorer 4), onfilterchange (Internet Explorer 4), onfocus (Internet Explorer 4), onhelp (Internet Explorer 4), onkeydown (Internet Explorer 4), onkeypress (Internet Explorer 4), onkeyup (Internet Explorer 4), onmousedown (Internet Explorer 4), onmousemove (Internet Explorer 4), onmouseout (Internet Explorer 4), onmouseover (Internet Explorer 4), onmouseup (Internet Explorer 4), onresize (Internet Explorer 4), onrowenter (Internet Explorer 4), onrowexit (Internet Explorer 4), onscroll (Internet Explorer 4), onselect (Internet Explorer 4), onselectstart (Internet Explorer 4)

CENTER

Browser Support: Internet Explorer 4

Provides access to the HTML CENTER tag.

Properties

Properties Supported by Both Navigator and Internet Explorer
None.

Other Properties
className (Internet Explorer 4), document (Internet Explorer 4), id (Internet Explorer 4), innerHTML (Internet Explorer 4), innerText (Internet Explorer 4), isTextEdit (Internet Explorer 4), lang (Internet Explorer 4), language (Internet Explorer 4), offsetHeight (Internet Explorer 4), offsetLeft (Internet Explorer 4), offsetParent (Internet Explorer 4), offsetTop (Internet Explorer 4), offsetWidth (Internet Explorer 4), outerHTML (Internet Explorer 4), outerText (Internet Explorer 4), parentElement (Internet Explorer 4), parentTextEdit (Internet Explorer 4), sourceIndex (Internet Explorer 4), style (Internet Explorer 4), tagName (Internet Explorer 4), title (Internet Explorer 4)

Methods

Methods Supported by Both Navigator and Internet Explorer
None.

Other Methods
click (Internet Explorer 4), contains (Internet Explorer 4), getAttribute (Internet Explorer 4), insertAdjacentHTML (Internet Explorer 4), insertAdjacentText (Internet Explorer 4), removeAttribute (Internet Explorer 4), scrollIntoView (Internet Explorer 4), setAttribute (Internet Explorer 4)

Events

onclick (Internet Explorer 4), ondblclick (Internet Explorer 4), ondragstart (Internet Explorer 4), onfilterchange (Internet Explorer 4), onhelp (Internet Explorer 4), onkeydown (Internet Explorer 4), onkeypress (Internet Explorer 4), onkeyup (Internet Explorer 4), onmousedown (Internet Explorer 4), onmousemove (Internet Explorer 4), onmouseout (Internet Explorer 4), onmouseover (Internet Explorer 4), onmouseup (Internet Explorer 4), onselectstart (Internet Explorer 4)

Checkbox

Browser Support: Navigator 2, Internet Explorer 3

The basic Checkbox object was introduced in JavaScript 1. It has been updated with JavaScript 1.1 and 1.2.

The Checkbox object provides access to the checkboxes of an HTML form.

Properties

Properties Supported by Both Navigator and Internet Explorer

checked (Navigator 2, Internet Explorer 3)

Provides the Boolean value of the checkbox's selection state.

defaultChecked (Navigator 2, Internet Explorer 3)

The value of the checkbox's CHECKED attribute.

form (Navigator 2, Internet Explorer 3)

Provides a reference to the form object that contains the checkbox.

name (Navigator 2, Internet Explorer 3)

The value of the checkbox's NAME attribute.

type (Navigator 3, Internet Explorer 4)

The value of the checkbox's TYPE attribute.

value (Navigator 2, Internet Explorer 3)

The value of the checkbox's VALUE attribute.

Other Properties

accessKey (Internet Explorer 4), className (Internet Explorer 4), dataFld (Internet Explorer 4), dataSrc (Internet Explorer 4), disabled (Internet Explorer 4), document (Internet Explorer 4), id (Internet Explorer 4), indeterminate (Internet Explorer 4), isTextEdit (Internet Explorer 4), lang (Internet Explorer 4), language (Internet Explorer 4), offsetHeight (Internet Explorer 4), offsetLeft (Internet Explorer 4), offsetParent (Internet Explorer 4), offsetTop (Internet Explorer 4), offsetWidth (Internet Explorer 4), outerText (Internet Explorer 4), parentElement (Internet Explorer 4), parentTextEdit (Internet Explorer 4), recordNumber (Internet Explorer 4), size (Internet Explorer 4), sourceIndex (Internet Explorer 4), status (Internet Explorer 4), style

(Internet Explorer 4), `tabIndex` (Internet Explorer 4), `tagName` (Internet Explorer 4), `title` (Internet Explorer 4)

Methods

Methods Supported by Both Navigator and Internet Explorer

`blur()` (Navigator 2, Internet Explorer 3)

Removes input focus from the checkbox.

`click()` (Navigator 2, Internet Explorer 3)

Simulates clicking of the checkbox.

`focus()` (Navigator 2, Internet Explorer 3)

Moves input focus to the checkbox.

Other Methods

`contains` (Internet Explorer 4), `getAttribute` (Internet Explorer 4), `handleEvent` (Navigator 4), `insertAdjacentHTML` (Internet Explorer 4), `insertAdjacentText` (Internet Explorer 4), `removeAttribute` (Internet Explorer 4), `scrollIntoView` (Internet Explorer 4), `select` (Internet Explorer 4), `setAttribute` (Internet Explorer 4)

Events

`onblur` (Navigator 3, Internet Explorer 4), `onclick` (Navigator 2, Internet Explorer 3), `onfocus` (Navigator 3, Internet Explorer 4), `onafterupdate` (Internet Explorer 4), `onbeforeupdate` (Internet Explorer 4), `onchange` (Internet Explorer 4), `ondblclick` (Internet Explorer 4), `onerrorupdate` (Internet Explorer 4), `onfilterchange` (Internet Explorer 4), `onhelp` (Internet Explorer 4), `onkeydown` (Internet Explorer 4), `onkeypress` (Internet Explorer 4), `onkeyup` (Internet Explorer 4), `onmousedown` (Internet Explorer 4), `onmousemove` (Internet Explorer 4), `onmouseout` (Internet Explorer 4), `onmouseover` (Internet Explorer 4), `onmouseup` (Internet Explorer 4), `onresize` (Internet Explorer 4), `onselect` (Internet Explorer 4)

CITE

Browser Support: Internet Explorer 4

Provides access to the HTML `CITE` tag.

Properties

Properties Supported by Both Navigator and Internet Explorer
None.

Other Properties
className (Internet Explorer 4), document (Internet Explorer 4), id (Internet Explorer 4), innerHTML (Internet Explorer 4), innerText (Internet Explorer 4), isTextEdit (Internet Explorer 4), lang (Internet Explorer 4), language (Internet Explorer 4), offsetHeight (Internet Explorer 4), offsetLeft (Internet Explorer 4), offsetParent (Internet Explorer 4), offsetTop (Internet Explorer 4), offsetWidth (Internet Explorer 4), outerHTML (Internet Explorer 4), outerText (Internet Explorer 4), parentElement (Internet Explorer 4), parentTextEdit (Internet Explorer 4), sourceIndex (Internet Explorer 4), style (Internet Explorer 4), tagName (Internet Explorer 4), title (Internet Explorer 4)

Methods

Methods Supported by Both Navigator and Internet Explorer
None.

Other Methods
click (Internet Explorer 4), contains (Internet Explorer 4), getAttribute (Internet Explorer 4), insertAdjacentHTML (Internet Explorer 4), insertAdjacentText (Internet Explorer 4), removeAttribute (Internet Explorer 4), scrollIntoView (Internet Explorer 4), setAttribute (Internet Explorer 4)

Events

onclick (Internet Explorer 4), ondblclick (Internet Explorer 4), ondragstart (Internet Explorer 4), onfilterchange (Internet Explorer 4), onhelp (Internet Explorer 4), onkeydown (Internet Explorer 4), onkeypress (Internet Explorer 4), onkeyup (Internet Explorer 4), onmousedown (Internet Explorer 4), onmousemove (Internet Explorer 4), onmouseout (Internet Explorer 4), onmouseover (Internet Explorer 4), onmouseup (Internet Explorer 4), onselectstart (Internet Explorer 4)

clientInformation

Browser Support: Internet Explorer 5

Provides properties and methods that describe the browser that executes a script.

Properties

Properties Supported by Both Navigator and Internet Explorer
None.

Other Properties
appCodeName (Internet Explorer 5), appMinorVersion (Internet Explorer 5), appName (Internet Explorer 5), appVersion (Internet Explorer 5), browserLanguage (Internet Explorer 5), cookieEnabled (Internet Explorer 5), cpuClass (Internet Explorer 5), onLine (Internet Explorer 5), platform (Internet Explorer 5), systemLanguage (Internet Explorer 5), userAgent (Internet Explorer 5), userLanguage (Internet Explorer 5), userProfile (Internet Explorer 5)

Methods

Methods Supported by Both Navigator and Internet Explorer
None.

Other Methods
javaEnabled (Internet Explorer 5), taintEnabled (Internet Explorer 5)

Events

This object does not define any events.

clipboardData

Browser Support: Internet Explorer 5

Properties

This object does not define any properties.

Methods

Methods Supported by Both Navigator and Internet Explorer
None.

Other Methods
clearData (Internet Explorer 5), getData (Internet Explorer 5), set-Data (Internet Explorer 5)

Events

This object does not define any events.

CODE

Browser Support: Internet Explorer 4

Provides access to the HTML CODE tag.

Properties

Properties Supported by Both Navigator and Internet Explorer
None.

Other Properties
className (Internet Explorer 4), document (Internet Explorer 4), id (Internet Explorer 4), innerHTML (Internet Explorer 4), innerText (Internet Explorer 4), isTextEdit (Internet Explorer 4), lang (Internet Explorer 4), language (Internet Explorer 4), offsetHeight (Internet Explorer 4), offsetLeft (Internet Explorer 4), offsetParent (Internet Explorer 4), offsetTop (Internet Explorer 4), offsetWidth (Internet Explorer 4), outerHTML (Internet Explorer 4), outerText (Internet Explorer 4), parentElement (Internet Explorer 4), parentTextEdit (Internet Explorer 4), sourceIndex (Internet Explorer 4), style (Internet Explorer 4), tagName (Internet Explorer 4), title (Internet Explorer 4)

Methods

Methods Supported by Both Navigator and Internet Explorer

None.

Other Methods

click (Internet Explorer 4), contains (Internet Explorer 4), get-Attribute (Internet Explorer 4), insertAdjacentHTML (Internet Explorer 4), insertAdjacentText (Internet Explorer 4), remove-Attribute (Internet Explorer 4), scrollIntoView (Internet Explorer 4), setAttribute (Internet Explorer 4)

Events

onclick (Internet Explorer 4), ondblclick (Internet Explorer 4), ondragstart (Internet Explorer 4), onfilterchange (Internet Explorer 4), onhelp (Internet Explorer 4), onkeydown (Internet Explorer 4), onkeypress (Internet Explorer 4), onkeyup (Internet Explorer 4), onmousedown (Internet Explorer 4), onmousemove (Internet Explorer 4), onmouseout (Internet Explorer 4), onmouseover (Internet Explorer 4), onmouseup (Internet Explorer 4), onselectstart (Internet Explorer 4)

COL

Browser Support: Internet Explorer 4

Provides access to the HTML COL tag.

Properties

Properties Supported by Both Navigator and Internet Explorer

None.

Other Properties

align (Internet Explorer 4), className (Internet Explorer 4), document (Internet Explorer 4), id (Internet Explorer 4), isTextEdit (Internet Explorer 4), parentElement (Internet Explorer 4), parentTextEdit (Internet Explorer 4), span (Internet Explorer 4), style (Internet

Explorer 4), tagName (Internet Explorer 4), title (Internet Explorer 4), vAlign (Internet Explorer 4), width (Internet Explorer 4)

Methods

Methods Supported by Both Navigator and Internet Explorer
None.

Other Methods
contains (Internet Explorer 4), getAttribute (Internet Explorer 4), removeAttribute (Internet Explorer 4), setAttribute (Internet Explorer 4)

Events

This object does not define any events.

COLGROUP

Browser Support: Internet Explorer 4

Provides access to the HTML COLGROUP tag.

Properties

Properties Supported by Both Navigator and Internet Explorer
None.

Other Properties
align (Internet Explorer 4), className (Internet Explorer 4), document (Internet Explorer 4), id (Internet Explorer 4), isTextEdit (Internet Explorer 4), parentElement (Internet Explorer 4), parentTextEdit (Internet Explorer 4), span (Internet Explorer 4), style (Internet Explorer 4), tagName (Internet Explorer 4), title (Internet Explorer 4), vAlign (Internet Explorer 4), width (Internet Explorer 4)

Methods

Methods Supported by Both Navigator and Internet Explorer
None.

Other Methods
contains (Internet Explorer 4), getAttribute (Internet Explorer 4), removeAttribute (Internet Explorer 4), setAttribute (Internet Explorer 4)

Events

This object does not define any events.

COMMENT

Browser Support: Internet Explorer 4

Provides access to the HTML COMMENT tag.

Properties

Properties Supported by Both Navigator and Internet Explorer
None.

Other Properties
className (Internet Explorer 4), document (Internet Explorer 4), id (Internet Explorer 4), isTextEdit (Internet Explorer 4), lang (Internet Explorer 4), parentElement (Internet Explorer 4), parentTextEdit (Internet Explorer 4), sourceIndex (Internet Explorer 4), tagName (Internet Explorer 4), title (Internet Explorer 4)

Methods

Methods Supported by Both Navigator and Internet Explorer
None.

Other Methods

`contains` (Internet Explorer 4), `getAttribute` (Internet Explorer 4), `removeAttribute` (Internet Explorer 4), `setAttribute` (Internet Explorer 4)

Events

This object does not define any events.

currentStyle

Browser Support: Internet Explorer 5

Provides access to the current CSS style (Cascading Style Sheets) of an object.

Properties

Properties Supported by Both Navigator and Internet Explorer
None.

Other Properties

`backgroundAttachment` (Internet Explorer 5), `backgroundColor` (Internet Explorer 5), `backgroundImage` (Internet Explorer 5), `backgroundPositionX` (Internet Explorer 5), `backgroundPositionY` (Internet Explorer 5), `backgroundRepeat` (Internet Explorer 5), `borderBottomColor` (Internet Explorer 5), `borderBottomStyle` (Internet Explorer 5), `borderBottomWidth` (Internet Explorer 5), `borderColor` (Internet Explorer 5), `borderLeftColor` (Internet Explorer 5), `borderLeftStyle` (Internet Explorer 5), `borderLeftWidth` (Internet Explorer 5), `borderRightColor` (Internet Explorer 5), `borderRightStyle` (Internet Explorer 5), `borderRightWidth` (Internet Explorer 5), `borderStyle` (Internet Explorer 5), `borderTopColor` (Internet Explorer 5), `borderTopStyle` (Internet Explorer 5), `borderTopWidth` (Internet Explorer 5), `borderWidth` (Internet Explorer 5), `bottom` (Internet Explorer 5), `clear` (Internet Explorer 5), `clipBottom` (Internet Explorer 5), `clipLeft` (Internet Explorer 5), `clipRight` (Internet Explorer 5), `clipTop` (Internet Explorer 5), `color` (Internet Explorer 5), `cursor` (Internet Explorer 5), `direction` (Internet Explorer 5), `fontFamily` (Internet Explorer 5), `fontSize` (Internet Explorer 5), `fontStyle` (Internet Explorer 5), fontVariant (Internet Explorer 5), fontWeight (Internet Explorer 5), hasLayout (Internet Explorer 5), height (Internet Explorer 5), layoutFlow (Internet Explorer 5), layoutGridChar (Internet Explorer 5), layoutGridCharSpacing (Internet Explorer 5), layoutGridLine (Internet Explorer 5), layoutGridMode (Internet Explorer 5), layoutGridType (Internet Explorer 5), left (Internet Explorer 5), letterSpacing (Internet Explorer 5), lineHeight (Internet Explorer 5), listStyleImage (Internet Explorer 5), listStylePosition (Internet Explorer 5), listStyleType (Internet Explorer 5), margin (Internet Explorer 5), marginBottom (Internet Explorer 5), marginLeft (Internet Explorer 5), marginRight (Internet Explorer 5), marginTop (Internet Explorer 5), overflow (Internet Explorer 5), overflowX (Internet Explorer 5), overflowY (Internet Explorer 5), pageBreakAfter (Internet Explorer 5), pageBreakBefore (Internet Explorer 5), rectangular (Internet Explorer 5), right (Internet Explorer 5), scrollbar3dLightColor (Internet Explorer 5), scrollbarArrowColor (Internet Explorer 5), scrollbarBaseColor (Internet Explorer 5), scrollbarDarkShadowColor (Internet Explorer 5), scrollbarFaceColor (Internet Explorer 5), scrollbarHighlightColor (Internet Explorer 5), scrollbarShadowColor (Internet Explorer 5), styleFloat (Internet Explorer 5), tableLayout (Internet Explorer 5), textAlign (Internet Explorer 5), textDecoration (Internet Explorer 5), textIndent (Internet Explorer 5), textTransform (Internet Explorer 5), textUnderlinePosition (Internet Explorer 5), top (Internet Explorer 5), unicodeBidi (Internet Explorer 5), verticalAlign (Internet Explorer 5), visibility (Internet Explorer 5), width (Internet Explorer 5), wordWrap (Internet Explorer 5), writingMode (Internet Explorer 5), zIndex (Internet Explorer 5), zoom (Internet Explorer 5)

Methods

This object does not define any methods.

Events

This object does not define any events.

custom

Browser Support: Internet Explorer 5

Provides access to custom HTML tags.

Properties

Properties Supported by Both Navigator and Internet Explorer
None.

Other Properties

accessKey (Internet Explorer 5), canHaveChildren (Internet Explorer 5), canHaveHTML (Internet Explorer 5), className (Internet Explorer 5), clientHeight (Internet Explorer 5), clientLeft (Internet Explorer 5), clientTop (Internet Explorer 5), clientWidth (Internet Explorer 5), contentEditable (Internet Explorer 5), currentStyle (Internet Explorer 5), dir (Internet Explorer 5), disabled (Internet Explorer 5), document (Internet Explorer 5), hasLayout (Internet Explorer 5), hideFocus (Internet Explorer 5), id (Internet Explorer 5), innerHTML (Internet Explorer 5), innerText (Internet Explorer 5), isContentEditable (Internet Explorer 5), isDisabled (Internet Explorer 5), isTextEdit (Internet Explorer 5), lang (Internet Explorer 5), language (Internet Explorer 5), offsetHeight (Internet Explorer 5), offsetLeft (Internet Explorer 5), offsetParent (Internet Explorer 5), offsetTop (Internet Explorer 5), offsetWidth (Internet Explorer 5), outerHTML (Internet Explorer 5), outerText (Internet Explorer 5), parentElement (Internet Explorer 5), parentTextEdit (Internet Explorer 5), readyState (Internet Explorer 5), recordNumber (Internet Explorer 5), runtimeStyle (Internet Explorer 5), scopeName (Internet Explorer 5), scrollHeight (Internet Explorer 5), scrollLeft (Internet Explorer 5), scrollTop (Internet Explorer 5), scrollWidth (Internet Explorer 5), sourceIndex (Internet Explorer 5), style (Internet Explorer 5), tabIndex (Internet Explorer 5), tagName (Internet Explorer 5), tagUrn (Internet Explorer 5), title (Internet Explorer 5)

Methods

Methods Supported by Both Navigator and Internet Explorer
None.

Other Methods

addBehavior (Internet Explorer 5), applyElement (Internet Explorer 5), attachEvent (Internet Explorer 5), blur (Internet Explorer 5), clearAttributes (Internet Explorer 5), click (Internet Explorer 5), componentFromPoint (Internet Explorer 5), contains (Internet Explorer 5), detachEvent (Internet Explorer 5), doScroll (Internet Explorer 5), fireEvent (Internet Explorer 5), focus (Internet Explorer 5), getAdjacentText (Internet Explorer 5), getAttribute (Internet Explorer 5), getBoundingClientRect (Internet Explorer 5), getClientRects (Internet Explorer 5), getElementsByTagName (Internet Explorer 5), getExpression (Internet Explorer 5), insertAdjacentHTML (Internet Explorer 5), insertAdjacentText (Internet Explorer 5), mergeAttributes (Internet Explorer 5), releaseCapture (Internet Explorer 5), removeAttribute (Internet Explorer 5), removeBehavior (Internet Explorer 5), removeExpression (Internet Explorer 5), replaceAdjacentText (Internet Explorer 5), scrollIntoView (Internet Explorer 5), setActive (Internet Explorer 5), setAttribute (Internet Explorer 5), setCapture (Internet Explorer 5), setExpression (Internet Explorer 5)

Events

onafterupdate (Internet Explorer 5), onbeforecopy (Internet Explorer 5), onbeforecut (Internet Explorer 5), onbeforeeditfocus (Internet Explorer 5), onbeforefocusenter (Internet Explorer 5), onbeforefocusleave (Internet Explorer 5), onbeforepaste (Internet Explorer 5), onbeforeupdate (Internet Explorer 5), onblur (Internet Explorer 5), onclick (Internet Explorer 5), oncontextmenu (Internet Explorer 5), oncontrolselect (Internet Explorer 5), oncopy (Internet Explorer 5), oncut (Internet Explorer 5), ondblclick (Internet Explorer 5), ondrag (Internet Explorer 5), ondragend (Internet Explorer 5), ondragenter (Internet Explorer 5), ondragleave (Internet Explorer 5), ondragover (Internet Explorer 5), ondragstart (Internet Explorer 5), ondrop (Internet Explorer 5), onerrorupdate (Internet Explorer 5), onfilterchange (Internet Explorer 5), onfocus (Internet Explorer 5), onfocusenter (Internet Explorer 5), onfocusleave (Internet Explorer 5), onhelp (Internet Explorer 5), onkeydown (Internet Explorer 5), onkeypress (Internet Explorer 5), onkeyup (Internet Explorer 5), onlosecapture (Internet Explorer 5), onmousedown (Internet Explorer 5), onmouseenter (Internet Explorer 5), onmouseleave (Internet Explorer 5), onmousemove (Internet Explorer 5), onmouseout (Internet Explorer 5), onmouseover (Internet Explorer 5), onmouseup (Internet Explorer 5), onpaste (Internet Explorer 5), onpropertychange (Internet Explorer 5), onreadystatechange (Internet Explorer 5), onresize (Internet Explorer 5), onresizeend (Internet Explorer 5), onresizestart (Internet Explorer 5), onscroll (Internet Explorer 5), onselectstart (Internet Explorer 5)

dataTransfer

Browser Support: Internet Explorer 5

Provides clipboard support for drag-and-drop.

Properties

Properties Supported by Both Navigator and Internet Explorer
None.

Other Properties

dropEffect (Internet Explorer 5), effectAllowed (Internet Explorer 5)

Methods

Methods Supported by Both Navigator and Internet Explorer
None.

Other Methods

clearData (Internet Explorer 5), getData (Internet Explorer 5), set-Data (Internet Explorer 5)

Events

This object does not define any events.

Date

Browser Support: Navigator 2, Internet Explorer 3

The basic Date object was introduced in JavaScript 1. It has been updated with JavaScript 1.1 and 1.3. It is supported in JScript 1 and later.

The Date object provides access to basic date and time services. It is a core object that has been standardized in ECMAS 262.

Constructors

```
new Date()
```

Creates a Date object that represents the current (local) date and time.

```
new Date(milliseconds)
```

Creates a Date object that represents the time specified by the number of milliseconds since 12am 1 January 1970.

```
new Date(dateString)
```

Creates a Date object based on the date specified by dateString. The string should have a value that is recognized by the parse method of Date.

```
new Date(year, month, day[, hour, minute, second,
 ➡ millisecond])
```

Creates a Date object with the specified year, month (0–11), day (1–31), hour (0–23), minute (0–59), second (0–59), and millisecond (0–999) values.

Properties

Properties Supported by Both Navigator and Internet Explorer

constructor (Navigator 3, Internet Explorer 4)

A reference to the object's constructor.

prototype (Navigator 3, Internet Explorer 4)

Used to define additional properties.

Methods

Methods Supported by Both Navigator and Internet Explorer

getDate() (Navigator 2, Internet Explorer 3)

Returns the day of the month as an integer between 1 and 31.

getDay() (Navigator 2, Internet Explorer 3)

Returns the day of the week as an integer between 0 (Sunday) and 6 (Saturday).

getFullYear() (Navigator 4.06, Internet Explorer 4)

Returns the full value of a year.

getHours() (Navigator 2, Internet Explorer 3)

Returns the current hours (local time) between 0 and 23.

getMilliseconds() (Navigator 4.06, Internet Explorer 4)

Returns the current milliseconds (local time) between 0 and 999.

getMinutes() (Navigator 2, Internet Explorer 3)

Returns the current minutes (local time) between 0 and 59.

getMonth() (Navigator 2, Internet Explorer 3)

Returns the current month (local time) between 0 and 11.

getSeconds() (Navigator 2, Internet Explorer 3)

Returns the current seconds (local time) between 0 and 59.

getTime() (Navigator 2, Internet Explorer 3)

Returns the number of milliseconds since 1 January 1970 00:00:00.

getTimezoneOffset() (Navigator 2, Internet Explorer 3)

Returns the current timezone offset in minutes between local time and Greenwich Mean Time (GMT).

getUTCDate() (Navigator 4.06, Internet Explorer 4)

Returns the current day of the month in Universal Coordinated Time.

getUTCDay() (Navigator 4.06, Internet Explorer 4)

Returns the current day of the week in Universal Coordinated Time.

getUTCFullYear() (Navigator 4.06, Internet Explorer 4)

Returns the current year in Universal Coordinated Time.

getUTCHours() (Navigator 4.06, Internet Explorer 4)

Returns the current hours in Universal Coordinated Time.

getUTCMilliseconds() (Navigator 4.06, Internet Explorer 4)

Returns the current milliseconds in Universal Coordinated Time.

getUTCMinutes() (Navigator 4.06, Internet Explorer 4)

Returns the current minutes in Universal Coordinated Time.

getUTCMonth() (Navigator 4.06, Internet Explorer 4)

Returns the current month in Universal Coordinated Time.

getUTCSeconds() (Navigator 4.06, Internet Explorer 4)

Returns the current seconds in Universal Coordinated Time.

getYear() (Navigator 2, Internet Explorer 3)

Returns the current year minus 1900.

parse(dateString) (Navigator 2, Internet Explorer 3)

Returns the number of milliseconds in a date string since 12am January 1, 1970.

setDate(dayOfMonth) (Navigator 2, Internet Explorer 3)

Sets the day of the month (local time).

setFullYear(year[,month, day]) (Navigator 4.06, Internet Explorer 4)

Sets the current year (local time).

setHours(hour[,minutes, seconds, milliseconds]) (Navigator 2, Internet Explorer 3)

Sets hours (local time).

setMilliseconds(milliseconds) (Navigator 4.06, Internet Explorer 4)

Sets the number of milliseconds (local time).

setMinutes(minutes[,seconds,milliseconds]) (Navigator 2, Internet Explorer 3)

Sets the minutes (local time).

setMonth(month[,day]) (Navigator 2, Internet Explorer 3)

Sets the month (local time).

setSeconds(seconds[,milliseconds]) (Navigator 2, Internet Explorer 3)

Sets the seconds (local time).

setTime(milliseconds) (Navigator 2, Internet Explorer 3)

Sets the date/time as the number of milliseconds since 12am January 1, 1970 local time).

setUTCDate(dayOfMonth) (Navigator 4.06, Internet Explorer 4)

Sets the day of the month (in Universal Coordinated Time).

setUTCFullYear(year[,month,day]) (Navigator 4.06, Internet Explorer 4)

Sets the current year (in Universal Coordinated Time).

setUTCHours(hours[,minutes,seconds,milliseconds]) (Navigator 4.06, Internet Explorer 4)

Sets the current hours (in Universal Coordinated Time).

setUTCMilliseconds(milliseconds) (Navigator 4.06, Internet Explorer 4)

Sets the number of milleseconds (in Universal Coordinated Time).

setUTCMinutes(minutes[,seconds,milliseconds]) (Navigator 4.06, Internet Explorer 4)

Sets the number of minutes (in Universal Coordinated Time).

setUTCMonth(month[,day]) (Navigator 4.06, Internet Explorer 4)

Sets the current month (in Universal Coordinated Time).

setUTCSeconds(seconds[,milliseconds]) (Navigator 4.06, Internet Explorer 4)

Sets the seconds value (in Universal Coordinated Time).

setYear(year) (Navigator 2, Internet Explorer 3)

Sets the current year based on a year value between 0 and 99.

toGMTString() (Navigator 2, Internet Explorer 3)

Converts a date to a string formatted according to GMT conventions used on the Internet.

toLocaleString() (Navigator 2, Internet Explorer 3)

Converts the date to a string using locale conventions.

toString() (Navigator 3, Internet Explorer 4)

Converts the date to a string in local time.

toUTCString() (Navigator 4.06, Internet Explorer 4)

Converts the date to a string in UTC (Universal Coordinated Time)

UTC(year, month, day[, hours, minutes, seconds, milliseconds]) (Navigator 2, Internet Explorer 3)

Returns the number of milliseconds elapsed since 12am January 1, 1970 for the date specified by year through milliseconds. The milliseconds value was added in JavaScript 1.3.

valueOf() (Navigator 3, Internet Explorer 4)

Returns the primitive value of the Date object, which is the number of milliseconds elapsed since 12am January 1, 1970.

Other Methods

getVarDate (Internet Explorer 4), toSource (Navigator 4.06)

Events

This object defines no events.

DD

Browser Support: Internet Explorer 4

Provides access to the HTML DD tag.

Properties

Properties Supported by Both Navigator and Internet Explorer
None.

Other Properties
className (Internet Explorer 4), document (Internet Explorer 4), id (Internet Explorer 4), innerHTML (Internet Explorer 4), innerText (Internet Explorer 4), isTextEdit (Internet Explorer 4), lang (Internet Explorer 4), language (Internet Explorer 4), offsetHeight (Internet Explorer 4), offsetLeft (Internet Explorer 4), offsetParent (Internet Explorer 4), offsetTop (Internet Explorer 4), offsetWidth (Internet Explorer 4), outerHTML (Internet Explorer 4), outerText (Internet Explorer 4), parentElement (Internet Explorer 4), parentTextEdit (Internet Explorer 4), sourceIndex (Internet Explorer 4), tagName (Internet Explorer 4), title (Internet Explorer 4)

Methods

Methods Supported by Both Navigator and Internet Explorer
None.

Other Methods
click (Internet Explorer 4), contains (Internet Explorer 4), getAttribute (Internet Explorer 4), insertAdjacentHTML (Internet Explorer 4), insertAdjacentText (Internet Explorer 4), removeAttribute (Internet Explorer 4), scrollIntoView (Internet Explorer 4), setAttribute (Internet Explorer 4)

Events
onclick (Internet Explorer 4), ondblclick (Internet Explorer 4), ondragstart (Internet Explorer 4), onfilterchange (Internet Explorer 4),

onhelp (Internet Explorer 4), onkeydown (Internet Explorer 4), onkey-press (Internet Explorer 4), onkeyup (Internet Explorer 4), onmouse-down (Internet Explorer 4), onmousemove (Internet Explorer 4), onmouseout (Internet Explorer 4), onmouseover (Internet Explorer 4), onmouseup (Internet Explorer 4), onselectstart (Internet Explorer 4)

DEL

Browser Support: Internet Explorer 4

Provides access to the HTML DEL tag.

Properties

Properties Supported by Both Navigator and Internet Explorer

None.

Other Properties

className (Internet Explorer 4), document (Internet Explorer 4), id (Internet Explorer 4), innerHTML (Internet Explorer 4), innerText (Internet Explorer 4), isTextEdit (Internet Explorer 4), lang (Internet Explorer 4), language (Internet Explorer 4), offsetHeight (Internet Explorer 4), offsetLeft (Internet Explorer 4), offsetParent (Internet Explorer 4), offsetTop (Internet Explorer 4), offsetWidth (Internet Explorer 4), outerHTML (Internet Explorer 4), outerText (Internet Explorer 4), parentElement (Internet Explorer 4), parentTextEdit (Internet Explorer 4), sourceIndex (Internet Explorer 4), style (Internet Explorer 4), tagName (Internet Explorer 4), title (Internet Explorer 4)

Methods

Methods Supported by Both Navigator and Internet Explorer

None.

Other Methods

click (Internet Explorer 4), contains (Internet Explorer 4), get-Attribute (Internet Explorer 4), insertAdjacentHTML (Internet Explorer 4), insertAdjacentText (Internet Explorer 4), remove-

Attribute (Internet Explorer 4), scrollIntoView (Internet Explorer 4), setAttribute (Internet Explorer 4)

Events

onclick (Internet Explorer 4), ondblclick (Internet Explorer 4), ondragstart (Internet Explorer 4), onfilterchange (Internet Explorer 4), onhelp (Internet Explorer 4), onkeydown (Internet Explorer 4), onkeypress (Internet Explorer 4), onkeyup (Internet Explorer 4), onmousedown (Internet Explorer 4), onmousemove (Internet Explorer 4), onmouseout (Internet Explorer 4), onmouseover (Internet Explorer 4), onmouseup (Internet Explorer 4)

DFN

Browser Support: Internet Explorer 4

Provides access to the HTML DFN tag.

Properties

Properties Supported by Both Navigator and Internet Explorer

None.

Other Properties

className (Internet Explorer 4), document (Internet Explorer 4), id (Internet Explorer 4), innerHTML (Internet Explorer 4), innerText (Internet Explorer 4), isTextEdit (Internet Explorer 4), lang (Internet Explorer 4), language (Internet Explorer 4), offsetHeight (Internet Explorer 4), offsetLeft (Internet Explorer 4), offsetParent (Internet Explorer 4), offsetTop (Internet Explorer 4), offsetWidth (Internet Explorer 4), outerHTML (Internet Explorer 4), outerText (Internet Explorer 4), parentElement (Internet Explorer 4), parentTextEdit (Internet Explorer 4), sourceIndex (Internet Explorer 4), style (Internet Explorer 4), tagName (Internet Explorer 4), title (Internet Explorer 4)

Methods

Methods Supported by Both Navigator and Internet Explorer
None.

Other Methods
click (Internet Explorer 4), contains (Internet Explorer 4), get-Attribute (Internet Explorer 4), insertAdjacentHTML (Internet Explorer 4), insertAdjacentText (Internet Explorer 4), remove-Attribute (Internet Explorer 4), scrollIntoView (Internet Explorer 4), setAttribute (Internet Explorer 4)

Events

onclick (Internet Explorer 4), ondblclick (Internet Explorer 4), ondragstart (Internet Explorer 4), onhelp (Internet Explorer 4), onkeydown (Internet Explorer 4), onkeypress (Internet Explorer 4), onkeyup (Internet Explorer 4), onmousedown (Internet Explorer 4), onmousemove (Internet Explorer 4), onmouseout (Internet Explorer 4), onmouseover (Internet Explorer 4), onmouseup (Internet Explorer 4), onselectstart (Internet Explorer 4)

DIR

Browser Support: Internet Explorer 4

Provides access to the HTML DIR tag.

Properties

Properties Supported by Both Navigator and Internet Explorer
None.

Other Properties
className (Internet Explorer 4), document (Internet Explorer 4), id (Internet Explorer 4), innerHTML (Internet Explorer 4), innerText (Internet Explorer 4), isTextEdit (Internet Explorer 4), lang (Internet Explorer 4), language (Internet Explorer 4), offsetHeight (Internet

Explorer 4), offsetLeft (Internet Explorer 4), offsetParent (Internet Explorer 4), offsetTop (Internet Explorer 4), offsetWidth (Internet Explorer 4), outerHTML (Internet Explorer 4), outerText (Internet Explorer 4), parentElement (Internet Explorer 4), parentTextEdit (Internet Explorer 4), sourceIndex (Internet Explorer 4), style (Internet Explorer 4), tagName (Internet Explorer 4), title (Internet Explorer 4)

Methods

Methods Supported by Both Navigator and Internet Explorer
None.

Other Methods
click (Internet Explorer 4), contains (Internet Explorer 4), getAttribute (Internet Explorer 4), insertAdjacentHTML (Internet Explorer 4), insertAdjacentText (Internet Explorer 4), removeAttribute (Internet Explorer 4), scrollIntoView (Internet Explorer 4), setAttribute (Internet Explorer 4)

Events

onclick (Internet Explorer 4), ondblclick (Internet Explorer 4), ondragstart (Internet Explorer 4), onfilterchange (Internet Explorer 4), onhelp (Internet Explorer 4), onkeydown (Internet Explorer 4), onkeypress (Internet Explorer 4), onkeyup (Internet Explorer 4), onmousedown (Internet Explorer 4), onmousemove (Internet Explorer 4), onmouseout (Internet Explorer 4), onmouseover (Internet Explorer 4), onmouseup (Internet Explorer 4), onselectstart (Internet Explorer 4)

DIV

Browser Support: Internet Explorer 4

Provides access to the HTML DIV tag.

Properties

Properties Supported by Both Navigator and Internet Explorer
None.

Other Properties

align (Internet Explorer 4), className (Internet Explorer 4), client-
Height (Internet Explorer 4), clientWidth (Internet Explorer 4),
dataFld (Internet Explorer 4), dataFormatAs (Internet Explorer 4),
dataSrc (Internet Explorer 4), document (Internet Explorer 4), id (Internet Explorer 4), innerText (Internet Explorer 4), isTextEdit (Internet
Explorer 4), lang (Internet Explorer 4), language (Internet Explorer 4),
offsetHeight (Internet Explorer 4), offsetLeft (Internet Explorer 4),
offsetParent (Internet Explorer 4), offsetTop (Internet Explorer 4),
offsetWidth (Internet Explorer 4), outerText (Internet Explorer 4),
parentElement (Internet Explorer 4), parentTextEdit (Internet Explorer 4),
scrollHeight (Internet Explorer 4), scrollLeft (Internet Explorer 4),
scrollTop (Internet Explorer 4), scrollWidth (Internet Explorer 4),
sourceIndex (Internet Explorer 4), style (Internet Explorer 4), tagName
(Internet Explorer 4), title (Internet Explorer 4)

Methods

Methods Supported by Both Navigator and Internet Explorer

None.

Other Methods

blur (Internet Explorer 4), click (Internet Explorer 4), contains (Internet Explorer 4), focus (Internet Explorer 4), getAttribute (Internet
Explorer 4), insertAdjacentHTML (Internet Explorer 4), insertAdjacentText (Internet Explorer 4), removeAttribute (Internet Explorer 4),
scrollIntoView (Internet Explorer 4), setAttribute (Internet
Explorer 4)

Events

onafterupdate (Internet Explorer 4), onbeforeupdate (Internet
Explorer 4), onblur (Internet Explorer 4), onclick (Internet Explorer 4),
ondblclick (Internet Explorer 4), ondragstart (Internet Explorer 4),
onfocus (Internet Explorer 4), onhelp (Internet Explorer 4), onkeydown
(Internet Explorer 4), onkeypress (Internet Explorer 4), onkeyup (Internet Explorer 4), onmousedown (Internet Explorer 4), onmousemove (Internet Explorer 4), onmouseout (Internet Explorer 4), onmouseover

(Internet Explorer 4), onmouseup (Internet Explorer 4), onresize (Internet Explorer 4), onrowenter (Internet Explorer 4), onrowexit (Internet Explorer 4), onscroll (Internet Explorer 4), onselectstart (Internet Explorer 4)

DL

Browser Support: Internet Explorer 4

Provides access to the HTML DL tag.

Properties

Properties Supported by Both Navigator and Internet Explorer

None.

Other Properties

className (Internet Explorer 4), compact (Internet Explorer 4), document (Internet Explorer 4), id (Internet Explorer 4), innerHTML (Internet Explorer 4), innerText (Internet Explorer 4), isTextEdit (Internet Explorer 4), lang (Internet Explorer 4), language (Internet Explorer 4), offsetHeight (Internet Explorer 4), offsetLeft (Internet Explorer 4), offsetParent (Internet Explorer 4), offsetTop (Internet Explorer 4), offsetWidth (Internet Explorer 4), outerHTML (Internet Explorer 4), outerText (Internet Explorer 4), parentElement (Internet Explorer 4), parentTextEdit (Internet Explorer 4), sourceIndex (Internet Explorer 4), style (Internet Explorer 4), tagName (Internet Explorer 4), title (Internet Explorer 4)

Methods

Methods Supported by Both Navigator and Internet Explorer

None.

Other Methods

click (Internet Explorer 4), contains (Internet Explorer 4), getAttribute (Internet Explorer 4), insertAdjacentHTML (Internet

Explorer 4), `insertAdjacentText` (Internet Explorer 4), `remove-Attribute` (Internet Explorer 4), `scrollIntoView` (Internet Explorer 4), `setAttribute` (Internet Explorer 4)

Events

`onclick` (Internet Explorer 4), `ondblclick` (Internet Explorer 4), `ondragstart` (Internet Explorer 4), `onfilterchange` (Internet Explorer 4), `onhelp` (Internet Explorer 4), `onkeydown` (Internet Explorer 4), `onkeypress` (Internet Explorer 4), `onkeyup` (Internet Explorer 4), `onmousedown` (Internet Explorer 4), `onmousemove` (Internet Explorer 4), `onmouseout` (Internet Explorer 4), `onmouseover` (Internet Explorer 4), `onmouseup` (Internet Explorer 4), `onselectstart` (Internet Explorer 4)

document

Browser Support: Navigator 2, Internet Explorer 3

The basic document object was introduced in JavaScript 1. It has been updated with JavaScript 1.1 and 1.2.

The document object is a fundamental object of client-side JavaScript. It provides access to a Web page that is displayed in a browser window. It also provides properties and methods for accessing the objects that comprise the document.

Properties

Properties Supported by Both Navigator and Internet Explorer

`alinkColor` (Navigator 2, Internet Explorer 3)

Specifies the color of an active link—a link that has been clicked on (mouse down) before the mouse is released (mouse up).

`anchors` (Navigator 2, Internet Explorer 3)

Provides access to the document's Anchor objects as an array. The array's elements are ordered according to how the objects appear in the document.

`applets` (Navigator 3, Internet Explorer 4)

`bgColor` (Navigator 2, Internet Explorer 3)

Provides access to the document's background color.

cookie (Navigator 2, Internet Explorer 3)

Provides access to the HTTP cookies that are associated with the document.

embeds (Navigator 3, Internet Explorer 4)

fgColor (Navigator 2, Internet Explorer 3)

Provides access to the document's foreground color.

forms (Navigator 3, Internet Explorer 4)

Provides access to the document's Form objects as an array. The array's elements are ordered according to how the objects appear in the document.

images (Navigator 3, Internet Explorer 4)

lastModified (Navigator 2, Internet Explorer 3)

Identifies when the document was last modified based on information provided in its HTTP header.

linkColor (Navigator 2, Internet Explorer 3)

Specifies the normal color of all links contained in the document.

links (Navigator 2, Internet Explorer 3)

Provides access to the document's Link objects as an array. The array's elements are ordered according to how the objects appear in the document.

plugins (Navigator 3, Internet Explorer 4)

Provides access to the document's Plugin objects as an array. The array's elements are ordered according to how the objects appear in the document.

referrer (Navigator 2, Internet Explorer 3)

Identifies the URL of the document (if any) that provided the link to this document.

title (Navigator 2, Internet Explorer 3)

Provides access to the document's title.

URL (Navigator 2, Internet Explorer 3)

Provides access to the URL from which the document was loaded.

vlinkColor (Navigator 2, Internet Explorer 3)

Specifies the color of visited links.

Other Properties

activeElement (Internet Explorer 4), body (Internet Explorer 4), charset (Internet Explorer 4), classes (Navigator 4), defaultCharset

(Internet Explorer 4), domain (Navigator 3), domain (Internet Explorer 4), expando (Internet Explorer 4), height (Navigator 4), ids (Navigator 4), layers (Navigator 4), linkColor (Internet Explorer 4), location (Internet Explorer 4), parentWindow (Internet Explorer 4), readyState (Internet Explorer 4), selection (Internet Explorer 4), tags (Navigator 4), width (Navigator 4)

Methods

Methods Supported by Both Navigator and Internet Explorer

close() (Navigator 2, Internet Explorer 3)

Closes output to the document object.

open([mimeType,[replace]]) (Navigator 2, Internet Explorer 3)

Creates and opens a new document of the specified MIME type. The replace argument specifies that the new document is to reuse the history entry of the previous document.

write(expr1[, ...,exprN]) (Navigator 2, Internet Explorer 3)

Writes the HTML expressions to the current document object.

writeln(expr1[, ...,exprN]) (Navigator 2, Internet Explorer 3)

Writes the HTML expressions to the current document object. A newline character is appended to the last expression.

Other Methods

captureEvents (Navigator 4), clear (Internet Explorer 4), contextual (Navigator 4), createElement (Internet Explorer 4), createStyleSheet (Internet Explorer 4), elementFromPoint (Internet Explorer 4), exec-Command (Internet Explorer 4), getSelection (Navigator 4), handle-Event (Navigator 4), queryCommandEnabled (Internet Explorer 4), queryCommandIndeterm (Internet Explorer 4), queryCommandState (Internet Explorer 4), queryCommandSupported (Internet Explorer 4), queryCommandText (Internet Explorer 4), queryCommandValue (Internet Explorer 4), releaseEvents (Navigator 4), routeEvent (Navigator 4), ShowHelp (Internet Explorer 4)

Events

onclick (Navigator 2, Internet Explorer 3), ondblclick (Navigator 4, Internet Explorer 4), onkeydown (Navigator 4, Internet Explorer 4), onkeypress (Navigator 4, Internet Explorer 4), onkeyup (Navigator 4, Internet Explorer 4), onmousedown (Navigator 4, Internet Explorer 4), onmouseup (Navigator 4, Internet Explorer 4), onafterupdate (Internet Explorer 4), onbeforeupdate (Internet Explorer 4), ondragstart (Internet Explorer 4), onerrorupdate (Internet Explorer 4), onhelp (Internet Explorer 4), onmousemove (Internet Explorer 4), onmouseout (Internet Explorer 4), onmouseover (Internet Explorer 4), onreadystate-change (Internet Explorer 4), onrowenter (Internet Explorer 4), onrowexit (Internet Explorer 4), onselectstart (Internet Explorer 4)

DT

Browser Support: Internet Explorer 4

Provides access to the HTML DT tag.

Properties

Properties Supported by Both Navigator and Internet Explorer
None.

Other Properties
className (Internet Explorer 4), document (Internet Explorer 4), id (Internet Explorer 4), innerHTML (Internet Explorer 4), innerText (Internet Explorer 4), isTextEdit (Internet Explorer 4), lang (Internet Explorer 4), language (Internet Explorer 4), offsetHeight (Internet Explorer 4), offsetLeft (Internet Explorer 4), offsetParent (Internet Explorer 4), offsetTop (Internet Explorer 4), offsetWidth (Internet Explorer 4), outerHTML (Internet Explorer 4), outerText (Internet Explorer 4), parentElement (Internet Explorer 4), parentTextEdit (Internet Explorer 4), sourceIndex (Internet Explorer 4), style (Internet Explorer 4), tagName (Internet Explorer 4), title (Internet Explorer 4)

Methods

Methods Supported by Both Navigator and Internet Explorer
None.

Other Methods

click (Internet Explorer 4), contains (Internet Explorer 4), get-Attribute (Internet Explorer 4), insertAdjacentHTML (Internet Explorer 4), insertAdjacentText (Internet Explorer 4), remove-Attribute (Internet Explorer 4), scrollIntoView (Internet Explorer 4), setAttribute (Internet Explorer 4)

Events

onclick (Internet Explorer 4), ondblclick (Internet Explorer 4), ondragstart (Internet Explorer 4), onfilterchange (Internet Explorer 4), onhelp (Internet Explorer 4), onkeydown (Internet Explorer 4), onkeypress (Internet Explorer 4), onkeyup (Internet Explorer 4), onmousedown (Internet Explorer 4), onmousemove (Internet Explorer 4), onmouseout (Internet Explorer 4), onmouseover (Internet Explorer 4), onselectstart (Internet Explorer 4)

EM

Browser Support: Internet Explorer 4

Provides access to the HTML EM tag.

Properties

Properties Supported by Both Navigator and Internet Explorer

None.

Other Properties

className (Internet Explorer 4), document (Internet Explorer 4), id (Internet Explorer 4), innerHTML (Internet Explorer 4), innerText (Internet Explorer 4), isTextEdit (Internet Explorer 4), lang (Internet Explorer 4), language (Internet Explorer 4), offsetHeight (Internet Explorer 4), offsetLeft (Internet Explorer 4), offsetParent (Internet Explorer 4), offsetTop (Internet Explorer 4), offsetWidth (Internet Explorer 4), outerHTML (Internet Explorer 4), outerText (Internet Explorer 4), parentElement (Internet Explorer 4), parentTextEdit (Internet Explorer 4), sourceIndex (Internet Explorer 4), style (Internet Explorer 4), tagName (Internet Explorer 4), title (Internet Explorer 4)

Methods

Methods Supported by Both Navigator and Internet Explorer
None.

Other Methods
click (Internet Explorer 4), contains (Internet Explorer 4), get-Attribute (Internet Explorer 4), insertAdjacentHTML (Internet Explorer 4), insertAdjacentText (Internet Explorer 4), remove-Attribute (Internet Explorer 4), scrollIntoView (Internet Explorer 4), setAttribute (Internet Explorer 4)

Events

onclick (Internet Explorer 4), ondblclick (Internet Explorer 4), ondragstart (Internet Explorer 4), onfilterchange (Internet Explorer 4), onhelp (Internet Explorer 4), onkeydown (Internet Explorer 4), onkeypress (Internet Explorer 4), onkeyup (Internet Explorer 4), onmousedown (Internet Explorer 4), onmousemove (Internet Explorer 4), onmouseout (Internet Explorer 4), onmouseover (Internet Explorer 4), onselectstart (Internet Explorer 4)

EMBED

Browser Support: Internet Explorer 4

Provides access to the HTML EMBED tag.

Properties

Properties Supported by Both Navigator and Internet Explorer
None.

Other Properties
accessKey (Internet Explorer 4), align (Internet Explorer 4), className (Internet Explorer 4), document (Internet Explorer 4), height (Internet Explorer 4), Hidden (Internet Explorer 4), id (Internet Explorer 4), isTextEdit (Internet Explorer 4), lang (Internet Explorer 4), language (Internet Explorer 4), offsetHeight (Internet Explorer 4),

offsetLeft (Internet Explorer 4), offsetParent (Internet Explorer 4),
offsetTop (Internet Explorer 4), offsetWidth (Internet Explorer 4),
outerHTML (Internet Explorer 4), outerText (Internet Explorer 4),
palette (Internet Explorer 4), parentElement (Internet Explorer 4),
parentTextEdit (Internet Explorer 4), pluginspage (Internet Explorer 4),
sourceIndex (Internet Explorer 4), src (Internet Explorer 4), style
(Internet Explorer 4), tagName (Internet Explorer 4), title (Internet
Explorer 4), units (Internet Explorer 4), width (Internet Explorer 4)

Methods

Methods Supported by Both Navigator and Internet Explorer
None.

Other Methods
blur (Internet Explorer 4), contains (Internet Explorer 4), focus (Internet Explorer 4), getAttribute (Internet Explorer 4), insertAdjacent-
HTML (Internet Explorer 4), insertAdjacentText (Internet Explorer 4),
removeAttribute (Internet Explorer 4), scrollIntoView (Internet
Explorer 4), setAttribute (Internet Explorer 4)

Events

onblur (Internet Explorer 4), onfocus (Internet Explorer 4)

Enumerator

Browser Support: Internet Explorer 4

The Enumerator object is an Internet Explorer object that is used to
iterate through a collection of objects.

Constructors

```
new Enumerator(collection)
```

Creates an Enumerator object from the collection argument.

Properties

This object does not define any properties.

Methods

Methods Supported by Both Navigator and Internet Explorer

None.

Other Methods

atEnd (Internet Explorer 4), item (Internet Explorer 4), moveFirst (Internet Explorer 4), moveNext (Internet Explorer 4)

Events

This object does not define any events.

Error

Browser Support: Internet Explorer 5

Provides information about errors that occur during the execution of a script.

Constructors

```
new Error()
```

Creates a new Error object with no error number or description.

```
new Error(number)
```

Creates a new Error object with the specified error number but no description.

```
new Error(number, description)
```

Creates a new Error object with the specified error number and description.

Properties

Properties Supported by Both Navigator and Internet Explorer
None.

Other Properties
`description` (Internet Explorer 5), `number` (Internet Explorer 5)

Methods

This object does not define any methods.

Events

This object does not define any events.

event

Browser Support: Navigator 4, Internet Explorer 4

The event object is used to encapsulate all events that can be handled by JavaScript. It is passed as an argument to an event handler and contains properties that describe the event.

Properties

Properties Supported by Both Navigator and Internet Explorer

`screenX` (Navigator 4, Internet Explorer 4)

Identifies the cursor's horizontal position (in pixels) relative to the screen.

`screenY` (Navigator 4, Internet Explorer 4)

Identifies the cursor's vertical position (in pixels) relative to the screen.

`x` (Navigator 4, Internet Explorer 4)

Equivalent to the `layerX` property.

`y` (Navigator 4, Internet Explorer 4)

Equivalent to the `layerY` property.

Other Properties

altKey (Internet Explorer 4), button (Internet Explorer 4), cancelBubble (Internet Explorer 4), clientX (Internet Explorer 4), clientY (Internet Explorer 4), ctrlKey (Internet Explorer 4), data (Navigator 4), fromElement (Internet Explorer 4), height (Navigator 4), keyCode (Internet Explorer 4), layerX (Navigator 4), layerY (Navigator 4), modifiers (Navigator 4), offsetX (Internet Explorer 4), offsetY (Internet Explorer 4), pageX (Navigator 4), pageY (Navigator 4), reason (Internet Explorer 4), returnValue (Internet Explorer 4), shiftKey (Internet Explorer 4), srcElement (Internet Explorer 4), srcFilter (Internet Explorer 4), target (Navigator 4), toElement (Internet Explorer 4), type (Navigator 4), type (Internet Explorer 4), which (Navigator 4), width (Navigator 4)

Methods

The event object does not define any methods of its own.

Events

Event handlers are defined for each event by type.

external

Browser Support: Internet Explorer 4

Provides access to an external object model.

Properties

This object does not define any properties of its own.

Methods

Methods Supported by Both Navigator and Internet Explorer

None.

Other Methods

addChannel (Internet Explorer 4), isSubscribed (Internet Explorer 4)

Events

This object does not define any events.

FIELDSET

Browser Support: Internet Explorer 4

Provides access to the HTML FIELDSET tag.

Properties

Properties Supported by Both Navigator and Internet Explorer

None.

Other Properties

accessKey (Internet Explorer 4), align (Internet Explorer 4), class-
Name (Internet Explorer 4), clientHeight (Internet Explorer 4),
clientWidth (Internet Explorer 4), document (Internet Explorer 4),
id (Internet Explorer 4), innerHTML (Internet Explorer 4), innerText
(Internet Explorer 4), isTextEdit (Internet Explorer 4), lang (Internet
Explorer 4), language (Internet Explorer 4), margin (Internet Explorer 4),
offsetHeight (Internet Explorer 4), offsetLeft (Internet Explorer 4),
offsetParent (Internet Explorer 4), offsetTop (Internet Explorer 4),
offsetWidth (Internet Explorer 4), outerHTML (Internet Explorer 4),
outerText (Internet Explorer 4), padding (Internet Explorer 4), parent-
Element (Internet Explorer 4), parentTextEdit (Internet Explorer 4),
recordNumber (Internet Explorer 4), scrollHeight (Internet Explorer 4),
scrollLeft (Internet Explorer 4), scrollTop (Internet Explorer 4),
scrollWidth (Internet Explorer 4), sourceIndex (Internet Explorer 4),
style (Internet Explorer 4), tabIndex (Internet Explorer 4), tagName
(Internet Explorer 4), title (Internet Explorer 4)

Methods

Methods Supported by Both Navigator and Internet Explorer

None.

Other Methods

blur (Internet Explorer 4), click (Internet Explorer 4), contains (Internet Explorer 4), focus (Internet Explorer 4), getAttribute (Internet Explorer 4), insertAdjacentHTML (Internet Explorer 4), insertAdjacentText (Internet Explorer 4), removeAttribute (Internet Explorer 4), scrollIntoView (Internet Explorer 4), setAttribute (Internet Explorer 4)

Events

onafterupdate (Internet Explorer 4), onbeforeupdate (Internet Explorer 4), onblur (Internet Explorer 4), onclick (Internet Explorer 4), onchange (Internet Explorer 4), ondblclick (Internet Explorer 4), ondragstart (Internet Explorer 4), onerrorupdate (Internet Explorer 4), onfilterchange (Internet Explorer 4), onfocus (Internet Explorer 4), onhelp (Internet Explorer 4), onkeydown (Internet Explorer 4), onkeypress (Internet Explorer 4), onkeyup (Internet Explorer 4), onmousedown (Internet Explorer 4), onmousemove (Internet Explorer 4), onmouseout (Internet Explorer 4), onmouseover (Internet Explorer 4), onmouseup (Internet Explorer 4), onresize (Internet Explorer 4), onrowenter (Internet Explorer 4), onrowexit (Internet Explorer 4), onscroll (Internet Explorer 4), onselect (Internet Explorer 4), onselectstart (Internet Explorer 4)

file (FileUpload)

Browser Support: Navigator 2, Internet Explorer 4

The basic FileUpload object was introduced in JavaScript 1. It has been updated with JavaScript 1.1 and 1.2. It is also referred to as a file object in the Internet Explorer 4 documentation.

The FileUpload object provides access to the file upload objects of an HTML form. These objects are INPUT tags with their TYPE attribute set to FILE. They provide the user with the capability to upload a file to your Web site.

Properties

Properties Supported by Both Navigator and Internet Explorer

form (Navigator 2, Internet Explorer 3)

Provides a reference to the form object that contains the file upload element.

name (Navigator 2, Internet Explorer 3)

The value of the file upload's NAME attribute.

type (Navigator 3, Internet Explorer 4)

The value of the file upload's TYPE attribute.

value (Navigator 2, Internet Explorer 3)

The name of the file selected by the user.

Other Properties

accessKey (Internet Explorer 4), className (Internet Explorer 4), defaultValue (Internet Explorer 4), disabled (Internet Explorer 4), document (Internet Explorer 4), id (Internet Explorer 4), isTextEdit (Internet Explorer 4), lang (Internet Explorer 4), language (Internet Explorer 4), offsetHeight (Internet Explorer 4), offsetLeft (Internet Explorer 4), offsetParent (Internet Explorer 4), offsetTop (Internet Explorer 4), offsetWidth (Internet Explorer 4), outerText (Internet Explorer 4), parentElement (Internet Explorer 4), parentTextEdit (Internet Explorer 4), readOnly (Internet Explorer 4), recordNumber (Internet Explorer 4), sourceIndex (Internet Explorer 4), style (Internet Explorer 4), tabIndex (Internet Explorer 4), tagName (Internet Explorer 4), title (Internet Explorer 4)

Methods

Methods Supported by Both Navigator and Internet Explorer

blur() (Navigator 2, Internet Explorer 3)

Removes input focus from the file upload element.

focus() (Navigator 2, Internet Explorer 3)

Moves input focus to the file upload element.

select() (Navigator 2, Internet Explorer 3)

Selects (highlights) the input area of the file upload element.

Other Methods

click (Internet Explorer 4), contains (Internet Explorer 4), getAttribute (Internet Explorer 4), handleEvent (Navigator 4), insertAdjacentHTML (Internet Explorer 4), insertAdjacentText (Internet Explorer 4), removeAttribute (Internet Explorer 4), scrollIntoView (Internet Explorer 4), setAttribute (Internet Explorer 4)

Events

onblur (Navigator 3, Internet Explorer 4), onChange (Navigator 3, Internet Explorer 4), onfocus (Navigator 3, Internet Explorer 4), onclick (Internet Explorer 4), ondblclick (Internet Explorer 4), onfilterchange (Internet Explorer 4), onhelp (Internet Explorer 4), onkeydown (Internet Explorer 4), onkeypress (Internet Explorer 4), onkeyup (Internet Explorer 4), onmousedown (Internet Explorer 4), onmousemove (Internet Explorer 4), onmouseout (Internet Explorer 4), onmouseover (Internet Explorer 4), onmouseup (Internet Explorer 4), onresize (Internet Explorer 4), onselect (Internet Explorer 4)

FONT

Browser Support: Internet Explorer 4

Provides access to the HTML FONT tag.

Properties

Properties Supported by Both Navigator and Internet Explorer

None.

Other Properties

className (Internet Explorer 4), color (Internet Explorer 4), document (Internet Explorer 4), face (Internet Explorer 4), id (Internet Explorer 4), innerHTML (Internet Explorer 4), innerText (Internet Explorer 4), isTextEdit (Internet Explorer 4), lang (Internet Explorer 4), language (Internet Explorer 4), offsetHeight (Internet Explorer 4), offsetLeft (Internet Explorer 4), offsetParent (Internet Explorer 4), offsetTop (Internet Explorer 4), offsetWidth (Internet Explorer 4), outerHTML (Internet Explorer 4), outerText (Internet Explorer 4), parentElement (Internet Explorer 4), parentTextEdit (Internet

Explorer 4), size (Internet Explorer 4), sourceIndex (Internet Explorer 4), style (Internet Explorer 4), tagName (Internet Explorer 4), title (Internet Explorer 4)

Methods

Methods Supported by Both Navigator and Internet Explorer
None.

Other Methods
click (Internet Explorer 4), contains (Internet Explorer 4), getAttribute (Internet Explorer 4), insertAdjacentHTML (Internet Explorer 4), insertAdjacentText (Internet Explorer 4), removeAttribute (Internet Explorer 4), scrollIntoView (Internet Explorer 4), setAttribute (Internet Explorer 4)

Events

onclick (Internet Explorer 4), ondblclick (Internet Explorer 4), ondragstart (Internet Explorer 4), onfilterchange (Internet Explorer 4), onhelp (Internet Explorer 4), onkeydown (Internet Explorer 4), onkeypress (Internet Explorer 4), onkeyup (Internet Explorer 4), onmousedown (Internet Explorer 4), onmousemove (Internet Explorer 4), onmouseout (Internet Explorer 4), onmouseover (Internet Explorer 4), onmouseup (Internet Explorer 4), onselectstart (Internet Explorer 4)

Form

Browser Support: Navigator 2, Internet Explorer 3

The basic Form object was introduced in JavaScript 1. It has been updated with JavaScript 1.1 and 1.2.

The Form object encapsulates an HTML form and provides access to the elements contained in a form. It is used to handle user interactions with form elements and to perform form data validation prior to submission of form data to a Web server.

Properties

Properties Supported by Both Navigator and Internet Explorer

action (Navigator 2, Internet Explorer 3)

Identifies the form's ACTION attribute.

elements (Navigator 2, Internet Explorer 3)

An array containing all of the form's input elements in the order that they appear in the form.

encoding (Navigator 2, Internet Explorer 3)

Identifies the form's ENCTYPE attribute.

length (Navigator 2, Internet Explorer 3)

Identifies the number of elements contained in the form (the length of the elements array).

method (Navigator 2, Internet Explorer 3)

Identifies the form's METHOD attribute.

name (Navigator 2, Internet Explorer 3)

Identifies the form's NAME attribute.

target (Navigator 2, Internet Explorer 3)

Identifies the form's TARGET attribute.

Other Properties

className (Internet Explorer 4), document (Internet Explorer 4), id (Internet Explorer 4), innerHTML (Internet Explorer 4), innerText (Internet Explorer 4), isTextEdit (Internet Explorer 4), lang (Internet Explorer 4), language (Internet Explorer 4), offsetHeight (Internet Explorer 4), offsetLeft (Internet Explorer 4), offsetParent (Internet Explorer 4), offsetTop (Internet Explorer 4), offsetWidth (Internet Explorer 4), outerHTML (Internet Explorer 4), outerText (Internet Explorer 4), parentElement (Internet Explorer 4), parentTextEdit (Internet Explorer 4), sourceIndex (Internet Explorer 4), style (Internet Explorer 4), tagName (Internet Explorer 4), title (Internet Explorer 4)

Methods

Methods Supported by Both Navigator and Internet Explorer
submit() (Navigator 2, Internet Explorer 3)
Submits the form's data.

Other Methods
click (Internet Explorer 4), contains (Internet Explorer 4), get-Attribute (Internet Explorer 4), handleEvent (Navigator 4), insert-AdjacentHTML (Internet Explorer 4), insertAdjacentText (Internet Explorer 4), removeAttribute (Internet Explorer 4), reset (Navigator 3), scrollIntoView (Internet Explorer 4), setAttribute (Internet Explorer 4)

Events

onReset (Navigator 3, Internet Explorer 4), onSubmit (Navigator 2, Internet Explorer 3), onclick (Internet Explorer 4), ondblclick (Internet Explorer 4), ondragstart (Internet Explorer 4), onfilterchange (Internet Explorer 4), onhelp (Internet Explorer 4), onkeydown (Internet Explorer 4), onkeypress (Internet Explorer 4), onkeyup (Internet Explorer 4), onmousedown (Internet Explorer 4), onmousemove (Internet Explorer 4), onmouseout (Internet Explorer 4), onmouseover (Internet Explorer 4), onmouseup (Internet Explorer 4), onselectstart (Internet Explorer 4)

Frame

Browser Support: Navigator 2, Internet Explorer 3

Updated in JavaScript 1.1.

The Frame object provides access to an HTML frame. It is equivalent to a window object. Refer to the window object for a description of frame.

FRAMESET

Browser Support: Internet Explorer 4

Provides access to the HTML FRAMESET tag.

Properties

Properties Supported by Both Navigator and Internet Explorer
None.

Other Properties
border (Internet Explorer 4), borderColor (Internet Explorer 4), className (Internet Explorer 4), cols (Internet Explorer 4), document (Internet Explorer 4), frameBorder (Internet Explorer 4), frameSpacing (Internet Explorer 4), id (Internet Explorer 4), isTextEdit (Internet Explorer 4), lang (Internet Explorer 4), language (Internet Explorer 4), parentElement (Internet Explorer 4), parentTextEdit (Internet Explorer 4), rows (Internet Explorer 4), sourceIndex (Internet Explorer 4), style (Internet Explorer 4), tagName (Internet Explorer 4), title (Internet Explorer 4)

Methods

Methods Supported by Both Navigator and Internet Explorer
None.

Other Methods
contains (Internet Explorer 4), getAttribute (Internet Explorer 4), removeAttribute (Internet Explorer 4), setAttribute (Internet Explorer 4)

Events

onbeforeunload (Internet Explorer 4), onload (Internet Explorer 4), onresize (Internet Explorer 4), onunload (Internet Explorer 4)

Function

Browser Support: Navigator 3, Internet Explorer 4

Updated in JavaScript 1.2 and 1.3.

The Function object provides access to JavaScript functions as objects.

Constructors

The following constructor is supported by the `Function` object:

```
new Function ([arg1[, arg2[, ... argN]],] functionBody)
```

This constructor creates a function that accepts arguments 1 through *N* with the specified function body (expressed as a string).

Properties

Properties Supported by Both Navigator and Internet Explorer

`arguments` (Navigator 3, Internet Explorer 4)

Identifies the arguments that are passed to a function.

`arguments.length` (Navigator 3, Internet Explorer 4)

Identifies the number of arguments passed to the function.

`constructor` (Navigator 3, Internet Explorer 4)

Identifies the object's constructor.

`prototype` (Navigator 3, Internet Explorer 4)

Provides the capability to add new properties to the object.

Other Properties

`arguments.callee` (Navigator 4), `arguments.caller` (Navigator 3), `arity` (Navigator 4), `caller` (Internet Explorer 4), `length` (Navigator 3)

Methods

Methods Supported by Both Navigator and Internet Explorer

`toString()` (Navigator 3, Internet Explorer 4)

Returns a string representing the source code of the function.

`valueOf()` (Navigator 3, Internet Explorer 4)

Returns a string representing the source code of the function.

Other Methods

`apply` (Navigator 4.06), `call` (Navigator 4.06), `toSource` (Navigator 4.06)

Events

The Function object does not define any events.

Global

Browser Support: Navigator 2, Internet Explorer 4

This object is identified in ECMAScript 1 as the Global object. It has been supported in Navigator and Internet Explorer since JavaScript 1 via "top-level" properties and methods. Additional properties and methods have been defined since JavaScript 1. In JavaScript 1.3, ECMA compliance was achieved in Navigator.

Properties

Properties Supported by Both Navigator and Internet Explorer

Infinity (Navigator 4.06, Internet Explorer 4)

A value that represents infinity.

NaN (Navigator 4.06, Internet Explorer 4)

Represents the value *Not-A-Number*.

Other Properties

undefined (Navigator 4.06)

Methods

Methods Supported by Both Navigator and Internet Explorer

escape(string) (Navigator 2, Internet Explorer 3)

Returns the URL-encoding of string.

eval(string) (Navigator 2, Internet Explorer 3)

Evaluates the string as JavaScript code.

isFinite(number) (Navigator 4.06, Internet Explorer 4)

Returns a Boolean value indicating whether or not number is finite.

isNaN(value) (Navigator 2, Internet Explorer 3)

Returns a Boolean value indicating whether or not number is *Not-A-Number*.

parseFloat(string) (Navigator 2, Internet Explorer 3)

Converts a string to a floating-point number.

parseInt(string[, radix]) (Navigator 2, Internet Explorer 3)

Converts a string to an integer.

unescape(string) (Navigator 2, Internet Explorer 3)

Converts the URL-encoded string to its value before encoding.

Other Methods

Number (Navigator 4), String (Navigator 4), taint (Navigator 3), untaint (Navigator 3)

Events

The Global object doesn't define any event handlers.

H1

Browser Support: Internet Explorer 4

Provides access to the HTML H1 tag.

Properties

Properties Supported by Both Navigator and Internet Explorer

None.

Other Properties

align (Internet Explorer 4), className (Internet Explorer 4), document (Internet Explorer 4), id (Internet Explorer 4), innerHTML (Internet Explorer 4), innerText (Internet Explorer 4), isTextEdit (Internet Explorer 4), lang (Internet Explorer 4), language (Internet Explorer 4), offsetHeight (Internet Explorer 4), offsetLeft (Internet Explorer 4), offsetParent (Internet Explorer 4), offsetTop (Internet Explorer 4), offsetWidth (Internet Explorer 4), outerHTML (Internet Explorer 4), outerText (Internet Explorer 4), parentElement (Internet Explorer 4), parentTextEdit (Internet Explorer 4), sourceIndex (Internet Explorer 4), style (Internet Explorer 4), tagName (Internet Explorer 4), title (Internet Explorer 4)

Methods

Methods Supported by Both Navigator and Internet Explorer
None.

Other Methods
click (Internet Explorer 4), contains (Internet Explorer 4), get-
Attribute (Internet Explorer 4), insertAdjacentHTML (Internet
Explorer 4), insertAdjacentText (Internet Explorer 4), removeAttribute (Internet Explorer 4), scrollIntoView (Internet Explorer 4),
setAttribute (Internet Explorer 4)

Events

onclick (Internet Explorer 4), ondblclick (Internet Explorer 4),
ondragstart (Internet Explorer 4), onfilterchange (Internet Explorer 4),
onhelp (Internet Explorer 4), onkeydown (Internet Explorer 4), onkeypress (Internet Explorer 4), onkeyup (Internet Explorer 4), onmousedown (Internet Explorer 4), onmousemove (Internet Explorer 4),
onmouseout (Internet Explorer 4), onmouseover (Internet Explorer 4),
onmouseup (Internet Explorer 4), onselectstart (Internet Explorer 4)

H2

Browser Support: Internet Explorer 4

Provides access to the HTML H2 tag.

Properties

Properties Supported by Both Navigator and Internet Explorer
None.

Other Properties
align (Internet Explorer 4), className (Internet Explorer 4), docu
ment (Internet Explorer 4), id (Internet Explorer 4), innerHTML (Internet Explorer 4), innerText (Internet Explorer 4), isTextEdit (Internet
Explorer 4), lang (Internet Explorer 4), language (Internet Explorer 4),
offsetHeight (Internet Explorer 4), offsetLeft (Internet Explorer 4),

offsetParent (Internet Explorer 4), offsetTop (Internet Explorer 4), offsetWidth (Internet Explorer 4), outerHTML (Internet Explorer 4), outerText (Internet Explorer 4), parentElement (Internet Explorer 4), parentTextEdit (Internet Explorer 4), sourceIndex (Internet Explorer 4), style (Internet Explorer 4), tagName (Internet Explorer 4), title (Internet Explorer 4)

Methods

Methods Supported by Both Navigator and Internet Explorer
None.

Other Methods
click (Internet Explorer 4), contains (Internet Explorer 4), getAttribute (Internet Explorer 4), insertAdjacentHTML (Internet Explorer 4), insertAdjacentText (Internet Explorer 4), removeAttribute (Internet Explorer 4), scrollIntoView (Internet Explorer 4), setAttribute (Internet Explorer 4)

Events

onclick (Internet Explorer 4), ondblclick (Internet Explorer 4), ondragstart (Internet Explorer 4), onfilterchange (Internet Explorer 4), onhelp (Internet Explorer 4), onkeydown (Internet Explorer 4), onkeypress (Internet Explorer 4), onkeyup (Internet Explorer 4), onmousedown (Internet Explorer 4), onmousemove (Internet Explorer 4), onmouseout (Internet Explorer 4), onmouseover (Internet Explorer 4), onmouseup (Internet Explorer 4), onselectstart (Internet Explorer 4)

H3

Browser Support: Internet Explorer 4

Provides access to the HTML H3 tag.

Properties

Properties Supported by Both Navigator and Internet Explorer
None.

Other Properties

align (Internet Explorer 4), className (Internet Explorer 4), document (Internet Explorer 4), id (Internet Explorer 4), innerHTML (Internet Explorer 4), innerText (Internet Explorer 4), isTextEdit (Internet Explorer 4), lang (Internet Explorer 4), language (Internet Explorer 4), offsetHeight (Internet Explorer 4), offsetLeft (Internet Explorer 4), offsetParent (Internet Explorer 4), offsetTop (Internet Explorer 4), offsetWidth (Internet Explorer 4), outerHTML (Internet Explorer 4), outerText (Internet Explorer 4), parentElement (Internet Explorer 4), parentTextEdit (Internet Explorer 4), sourceIndex (Internet Explorer 4), style (Internet Explorer 4), tagName (Internet Explorer 4), title (Internet Explorer 4)

Methods

Methods Supported by Both Navigator and Internet Explorer

None.

Other Methods

click (Internet Explorer 4), contains (Internet Explorer 4), getAttribute (Internet Explorer 4), insertAdjacentHTML (Internet Explorer 4), insertAdjacentText (Internet Explorer 4), removeAttribute (Internet Explorer 4), scrollIntoView (Internet Explorer 4), setAttribute (Internet Explorer 4)

Events

onclick (Internet Explorer 4), ondblclick (Internet Explorer 4), ondragstart (Internet Explorer 4), onfilterchange (Internet Explorer 4), onhelp (Internet Explorer 4), onkeydown (Internet Explorer 4), onkeypress (Internet Explorer 4), onkeyup (Internet Explorer 4), onmousedown (Internet Explorer 4), onmousemove (Internet Explorer 4), onmouseout (Internet Explorer 4), onmouseover (Internet Explorer 4), onmouseup (Internet Explorer 4), onselectstart (Internet Explorer 4)

H4

Browser Support: Internet Explorer 4

Provides access to the HTML H4 tag.

Properties

Properties Supported by Both Navigator and Internet Explorer
None.

Other Properties
align (Internet Explorer 4), className (Internet Explorer 4), document (Internet Explorer 4), id (Internet Explorer 4), innerHTML (Internet Explorer 4), innerText (Internet Explorer 4), isTextEdit (Internet Explorer 4), lang (Internet Explorer 4), language (Internet Explorer 4), offsetHeight (Internet Explorer 4), offsetLeft (Internet Explorer 4), offsetParent (Internet Explorer 4), offsetTop (Internet Explorer 4), offsetWidth (Internet Explorer 4), outerHTML (Internet Explorer 4), outerText (Internet Explorer 4), parentElement (Internet Explorer 4), parentTextEdit (Internet Explorer 4), sourceIndex (Internet Explorer 4), style (Internet Explorer 4), tagName (Internet Explorer 4), title (Internet Explorer 4)

Methods

Methods Supported by Both Navigator and Internet Explorer
None.

Other Methods
click (Internet Explorer 4), contains (Internet Explorer 4), getAttribute (Internet Explorer 4), insertAdjacentHTML (Internet Explorer 4), insertAdjacentText (Internet Explorer 4), removeAttribute (Internet Explorer 4), scrollIntoView (Internet Explorer 4), setAttribute (Internet Explorer 4)

Events

onclick (Internet Explorer 4), ondblclick (Internet Explorer 4), ondragstart (Internet Explorer 4), onfilterchange (Internet Explorer 4), onhelp (Internet Explorer 4), onkeydown (Internet Explorer 4), onkeypress (Internet Explorer 4), onkeyup (Internet Explorer 4), onmousedown (Internet Explorer 4), onmousemove (Internet Explorer 4), onmouseout (Internet Explorer 4), onmouseover (Internet Explorer 4), onmouseup (Internet Explorer 4), onselectstart (Internet Explorer 4)

H5

Browser Support: Internet Explorer 4

Provides access to the HTML H5 tag.

Properties

Properties Supported by Both Navigator and Internet Explorer
None.

Other Properties
align (Internet Explorer 4), className (Internet Explorer 4), document (Internet Explorer 4), id (Internet Explorer 4), innerHTML (Internet Explorer 4), innerText (Internet Explorer 4), isTextEdit (Internet Explorer 4), lang (Internet Explorer 4), language (Internet Explorer 4), offsetHeight (Internet Explorer 4), offsetLeft (Internet Explorer 4), offsetParent (Internet Explorer 4), offsetTop (Internet Explorer 4), offsetWidth (Internet Explorer 4), outerHTML (Internet Explorer 4), outerText (Internet Explorer 4), parentElement (Internet Explorer 4), parentTextEdit (Internet Explorer 4), sourceIndex (Internet Explorer 4), style (Internet Explorer 4), tagName (Internet Explorer 4), title (Internet Explorer 4)

Methods

Methods Supported by Both Navigator and Internet Explorer
None.

Other Methods
click (Internet Explorer 4), contains (Internet Explorer 4), getAttribute (Internet Explorer 4), insertAdjacentHTML (Internet Explorer 4), insertAdjacentText (Internet Explorer 4), removeAttribute (Internet Explorer 4), scrollIntoView (Internet Explorer 4), setAttribute (Internet Explorer 4)

Events

onclick (Internet Explorer 4), ondblclick (Internet Explorer 4), ondragstart (Internet Explorer 4), onfilterchange (Internet Explorer 4), onhelp (Internet Explorer 4), onkeydown (Internet Explorer 4), onkeypress (Internet Explorer 4), onkeyup (Internet Explorer 4), onmousedown (Internet Explorer 4), onmousemove (Internet Explorer 4), onmouseout (Internet Explorer 4), onmouseover (Internet Explorer 4), onmouseup (Internet Explorer 4), onselectstart (Internet Explorer 4)

H6

Browser Support: Internet Explorer 4

Provides access to the HTML H6 tag.

Properties

Properties Supported by Both Navigator and Internet Explorer

None.

Other Properties

align (Internet Explorer 4), className (Internet Explorer 4), document (Internet Explorer 4), id (Internet Explorer 4), innerHTML (Internet Explorer 4), innerText (Internet Explorer 4), isTextEdit (Internet Explorer 4), lang (Internet Explorer 4), language (Internet Explorer 4), offsetHeight (Internet Explorer 4), offsetLeft (Internet Explorer 4), offsetParent (Internet Explorer 4), offsetTop (Internet Explorer 4), offsetWidth (Internet Explorer 4), outerHTML (Internet Explorer 4), outerText (Internet Explorer 4), parentElement (Internet Explorer 4), parentTextEdit (Internet Explorer 4), sourceIndex (Internet Explorer 4), style (Internet Explorer 4), tagName (Internet Explorer 4), title (Internet Explorer 4)

Methods

Methods Supported by Both Navigator and Internet Explorer

None.

Other Methods

click (Internet Explorer 4), contains (Internet Explorer 4), get-Attribute (Internet Explorer 4), insertAdjacentHTML (Internet Explorer 4), insertAdjacentText (Internet Explorer 4), remove-Attribute (Internet Explorer 4), scrollIntoView (Internet Explorer 4), setAttribute (Internet Explorer 4)

Events

onclick (Internet Explorer 4), ondblclick (Internet Explorer 4), ondragstart (Internet Explorer 4), onfilterchange (Internet Explorer 4), onhelp (Internet Explorer 4), onkeydown (Internet Explorer 4), onkeypress (Internet Explorer 4), onkeyup (Internet Explorer 4), onmousedown (Internet Explorer 4), onmousemove (Internet Explorer 4), onmouseout (Internet Explorer 4), onmouseover (Internet Explorer 4), onmouseup (Internet Explorer 4), onselectstart (Internet Explorer 4)

HEAD

Browser Support: Internet Explorer 4

Provides access to the HTML HEAD tag.

Properties

Properties Supported by Both Navigator and Internet Explorer

None.

Other Properties

className (Internet Explorer 4), document (Internet Explorer 4), id (Internet Explorer 4), isTextEdit (Internet Explorer 4), parent-Element (Internet Explorer 4), sourceIndex (Internet Explorer 4), tagName (Internet Explorer 4), title (Internet Explorer 4)

Methods

Methods Supported by Both Navigator and Internet Explorer

None.

Other Methods

contains (Internet Explorer 4), getAttribute (Internet Explorer 4),
removeAttribute (Internet Explorer 4), setAttribute (Internet
Explorer 4)

Events

This object does not define any events.

Hidden

Browser Support: Navigator 2, Internet Explorer 3

Updated in JavaScript 1.1.

Represents a hidden form field. Hidden form fields are INPUT tags
with their TYPE attribute set to HIDDEN. They are used to store state information in forms.

Properties

Properties Supported by Both Navigator and Internet Explorer

form (Navigator 2, Internet Explorer 3)

Provides a reference to the form object that contains the hidden field.

name (Navigator 2, Internet Explorer 3)

The value of the hidden field's NAME attribute.

type (Navigator 3, Internet Explorer 4)

The value of the hidden field's TYPE attribute.

value (Navigator 2, Internet Explorer 3)

The value stored in the hidden field.

Other Properties

className (Internet Explorer 4), dataFld (Internet Explorer 4),
dataSrc (Internet Explorer 4), disabled (Internet Explorer 4), document (Internet Explorer 4), id (Internet Explorer 4), isTextEdit (Internet Explorer 4), language (Internet Explorer 4), parentElement
(Internet Explorer 4), parentTextEdit (Internet Explorer 4), source-
Index (Internet Explorer 4), style (Internet Explorer 4), tagName (Internet Explorer 4)

Methods

Methods Supported by Both Navigator and Internet Explorer
None.

Other Methods
contains (Internet Explorer 4), getAttribute (Internet Explorer 4), removeAttribute (Internet Explorer 4), setAttribute (Internet Explorer 4)

Events

onafterupdate (Internet Explorer 4), onbeforeupdate (Internet Explorer 4), onerrorupdate (Internet Explorer 4)

History

Browser Support: Navigator 2, Internet Explorer 3

Updated in JavaScript 1.1.

The History object maintains information on the URLs that the client has visited for a particular window.

Properties

Properties Supported by Both Navigator and Internet Explorer
length (Navigator 2, Internet Explorer 3)
Identifies the length of the history list.

Other Properties
current (Navigator 3), next (Navigator 3), previous (Navigator 3)

Methods

Methods Supported by Both Navigator and Internet Explorer
back() (Navigator 2, Internet Explorer 3)
Loads the previous URL in the history list.

forward() (Navigator 2, Internet Explorer 3)

Loads the next URL in the history list.

go(delta) (Navigator 2, Internet Explorer 3)

Loads a URL from the relative position in the history list specified by delta.

go(location) (Navigator 2, Internet Explorer 3)

Loads a URL based on the partial URL specified by location by matching it with other URLs in the history list.

Events

The History object does not define any events.

HR

Browser Support: Internet Explorer 4

Provides access to the HTML HR tag.

Properties

Properties Supported by Both Navigator and Internet Explorer

None.

Other Properties

align (Internet Explorer 4), className (Internet Explorer 4), color (Internet Explorer 4), document (Internet Explorer 4), id (Internet Explorer 4), isTextEdit (Internet Explorer 4), lang (Internet Explorer 4), language (Internet Explorer 4), noShade (Internet Explorer 4), offsetHeight (Internet Explorer 4), offsetLeft (Internet Explorer 4), offsetParent (Internet Explorer 4), offsetTop (Internet Explorer 4), offsetWidth (Internet Explorer 4), outerHTML (Internet Explorer 4), outerText (Internet Explorer 4), parentElement (Internet Explorer 4), parentTextEdit (Internet Explorer 4), size (Internet Explorer 4), sourceIndex (Internet Explorer 4), style (Internet Explorer 4), tagName (Internet Explorer 4), title (Internet Explorer 4), width (Internet Explorer 4)

Methods

Methods Supported by Both Navigator and Internet Explorer
None.

Other Methods
blur (Internet Explorer 4), click (Internet Explorer 4), contains (Internet Explorer 4), focus (Internet Explorer 4), getAttribute (Internet Explorer 4), insertAdjacentHTML (Internet Explorer 4), insertAdjacentText (Internet Explorer 4), removeAttribute (Internet Explorer 4), scrollIntoView (Internet Explorer 4), setAttribute (Internet Explorer 4)

Events

onbeforeupdate (Internet Explorer 4), onblur (Internet Explorer 4), onclick (Internet Explorer 4), ondblclick (Internet Explorer 4), ondragstart (Internet Explorer 4), onfilterchange (Internet Explorer 4), onfocus (Internet Explorer 4), onhelp (Internet Explorer 4), onkeydown (Internet Explorer 4), onkeypress (Internet Explorer 4), onkeyup (Internet Explorer 4), onmousedown (Internet Explorer 4), onmousemove (Internet Explorer 4), onmouseout (Internet Explorer 4), onmouseover (Internet Explorer 4), onmouseup (Internet Explorer 4), onresize (Internet Explorer 4), onrowenter (Internet Explorer 4), onrowexit (Internet Explorer 4), onselectstart (Internet Explorer 4)

HTML

Browser Support: Internet Explorer 4

Provides access to the HTML HTML tag.

Properties

Properties Supported by Both Navigator and Internet Explorer
None.

Other Properties

className (Internet Explorer 4), document (Internet Explorer 4),
id (Internet Explorer 4), isTextEdit (Internet Explorer 4), language
(Internet Explorer 4), parentElement (Internet Explorer 4), source-
Index (Internet Explorer 4), style (Internet Explorer 4), tagName (Internet Explorer 4), title (Internet Explorer 4)

Methods

Methods Supported by Both Navigator and Internet Explorer
None.

Other Methods

contains (Internet Explorer 4), getAttribute (Internet Explorer 4),
removeAttribute (Internet Explorer 4), setAttribute (Internet
Explorer 4)

Events

This object does not define any events.

I

Browser Support: Internet Explorer 4
Provides access to the HTML I tag.

Properties

Properties Supported by Both Navigator and Internet Explorer
None.

Other Properties

className (Internet Explorer 4), document (Internet Explorer 4),
id (Internet Explorer 4), innerHTML (Internet Explorer 4), innerText
(Internet Explorer 4), isTextEdit (Internet Explorer 4), lang (Internet Explorer 4), language (Internet Explorer 4), offsetHeight (Internet

Explorer 4), `offsetLeft` (Internet Explorer 4), `offsetParent` (Internet Explorer 4), `offsetTop` (Internet Explorer 4), `offsetWidth` (Internet Explorer 4), `outerHTML` (Internet Explorer 4), `outerText` (Internet Explorer 4), `parentElement` (Internet Explorer 4), `parentTextEdit` (Internet Explorer 4), `sourceIndex` (Internet Explorer 4), `style` (Internet Explorer 4), `tagName` (Internet Explorer 4), `title` (Internet Explorer 4)

Methods

Methods Supported by Both Navigator and Internet Explorer
None.

Other Methods
`click` (Internet Explorer 4), `contains` (Internet Explorer 4), `getAttribute` (Internet Explorer 4), `insertAdjacentHTML` (Internet Explorer 4), `insertAdjacentText` (Internet Explorer 4), `removeAttribute` (Internet Explorer 4), `scrollIntoView` (Internet Explorer 4), `setAttribute` (Internet Explorer 4)

Events

`onclick` (Internet Explorer 4), `ondblclick` (Internet Explorer 4), `ondragstart` (Internet Explorer 4), `onfilterchange` (Internet Explorer 4), `onhelp` (Internet Explorer 4), `onkeydown` (Internet Explorer 4), `onkeypress` (Internet Explorer 4), `onkeyup` (Internet Explorer 4), `onmousedown` (Internet Explorer 4), `onmousemove` (Internet Explorer 4), `onmouseout` (Internet Explorer 4), `onmouseover` (Internet Explorer 4), `onmouseup` (Internet Explorer 4), `onselectstart` (Internet Explorer 4)

IFRAME

Browser Support: Internet Explorer 4

Provides access to the HTML `IFRAME` tag.

Properties

Properties Supported by Both Navigator and Internet Explorer
None.

Other Properties

align (Internet Explorer 4), className (Internet Explorer 4), dataFld (Internet Explorer 4), dataSrc (Internet Explorer 4), document (Internet Explorer 4), frameBorder (Internet Explorer 4), frameSpacing (Internet Explorer 4), hspace (Internet Explorer 4), id (Internet Explorer 4), innerHTML (Internet Explorer 4), innerText (Internet Explorer 4), isTextEdit (Internet Explorer 4), lang (Internet Explorer 4), language (Internet Explorer 4), marginHeight (Internet Explorer 4), margin-Width (Internet Explorer 4), offsetHeight (Internet Explorer 4), offsetLeft (Internet Explorer 4), offsetParent (Internet Explorer 4), offsetTop (Internet Explorer 4), offsetWidth (Internet Explorer 4), outerHTML (Internet Explorer 4), outerText (Internet Explorer 4), parentElement (Internet Explorer 4), parentTextEdit (Internet Explorer 4), scrolling (Internet Explorer 4), sourceIndex (Internet Explorer 4), src (Internet Explorer 4), style (Internet Explorer 4), tagName (Internet Explorer 4), title (Internet Explorer 4), vspace (Internet Explorer 4)

Methods

Methods Supported by Both Navigator and Internet Explorer

None.

Other Methods

contains (Internet Explorer 4), getAttribute (Internet Explorer 4), insertAdjacentHTML (Internet Explorer 4), insertAdjacentText (Internet Explorer 4), removeAttribute (Internet Explorer 4), scrollIntoView (Internet Explorer 4), setAttribute (Internet Explorer 4)

Events

This object does not define any events.

image

Browser Support: Internet Explorer 4

This object is a form element that enables an image to be clicked to submit a form. It is not the same as the Image object that is supported by both Navigator and Internet Explorer.

Properties

Properties Supported by Both Navigator and Internet Explorer

None.

Other Properties

accessKey align (Internet Explorer 4), alt (Internet Explorer 4), border (Internet Explorer 4), className (Internet Explorer 4), complete (Internet Explorer 4), disabled (Internet Explorer 4), document (Internet Explorer 4), dynsrc (Internet Explorer 4), filter (Internet Explorer 4), form (Internet Explorer 4), height (Internet Explorer 4), hspace (Internet Explorer 4), id (Internet Explorer 4), innerHTML (Internet Explorer 4), isTextEdit (Internet Explorer 4), language (Internet Explorer 4), loop (Internet Explorer 4), lowsrc (Internet Explorer 4), name (Internet Explorer 4), offsetHeight (Internet Explorer 4), offsetLeft (Internet Explorer 4), offsetParent (Internet Explorer 4), offsetTop (Internet Explorer 4), offsetWidth (Internet Explorer 4), outerHTML (Internet Explorer 4), outerText (Internet Explorer 4), parentElement (Internet Explorer 4), parentTextEdit (Internet Explorer 4), readyState (Internet Explorer 4), recordNumber (Internet Explorer 4), sourceIndex (Internet Explorer 4), src (Internet Explorer 4), start (Internet Explorer 4), style (Internet Explorer 4), tabIndex (Internet Explorer 4), tagName (Internet Explorer 4), title (Internet Explorer 4), type vspace (Internet Explorer 4), width (Internet Explorer 4)

Methods

Methods Supported by Both Navigator and Internet Explorer

None.

Other Methods

blur (Internet Explorer 4), click (Internet Explorer 4), contains (Internet Explorer 4), focus (Internet Explorer 4), getAttribute (Internet Explorer 4), insertAdjacentHTML (Internet Explorer 4), insertAdjacentText (Internet Explorer 4), removeAttribute (Internet Explorer 4), scrollIntoView (Internet Explorer 4), select (Internet Explorer 4), setAttribute (Internet Explorer 4)

Events

onabort (Internet Explorer 4), onafterupdate (Internet Explorer 4), onbeforeupdate (Internet Explorer 4), onblur (Internet Explorer 4), onchange (Internet Explorer 4), onclick (Internet Explorer 4), ondataavailable (Internet Explorer 4), ondatasetchanged (Internet Explorer 4), ondatasetcomplete (Internet Explorer 4), ondblclick (Internet Explorer 4), onerror (Internet Explorer 4), onerrorupdate (Internet Explorer 4), onfocus (Internet Explorer 4), onhelp (Internet Explorer 4), onkeydown (Internet Explorer 4), onkeypress (Internet Explorer 4), onkeyup (Internet Explorer 4), onload (Internet Explorer 4), onmousedown (Internet Explorer 4), onmousemove (Internet Explorer 4), onmouseout (Internet Explorer 4), onmouseover (Internet Explorer 4), onmouseup (Internet Explorer 4), onresize (Internet Explorer 4), onrowenter (Internet Explorer 4), onrowexit (Internet Explorer 4), onselect (Internet Explorer 4)

IMG (Image)

Browser Support: Navigator 3, Internet Explorer 4

Updated in JavaScript 1.2. The Image object is also referred to as the IMG object in Microsoft's documentation.

Represents an image that is loaded for the current document. The images property of the document object contains an array of all images loaded for that document.

Properties

Properties Supported by Both Navigator and Internet Explorer

border (Navigator 3, Internet Explorer 4)

Identifies the value of the BORDER attribute.

complete (Navigator 3, Internet Explorer 4)

Identifies whether or not the image's loading has been completed.

height (Navigator 3, Internet Explorer 4)

Identifies the value of the HEIGHT attribute.

hspace (Navigator 3, Internet Explorer 4)

Identifies the value of the HSPACE attribute.

lowsrc (Navigator 3, Internet Explorer 4)

Identifies the value of the LOWSRC attribute.

name (Navigator 3, Internet Explorer 4)

Identifies the value of the NAME attribute.

src (Navigator 3, Internet Explorer 4)

Identifies the value of the SRC attribute.

vspace (Navigator 3, Internet Explorer 4)

Identifies the value of the VSPACE attribute.

width (Navigator 3, Internet Explorer 4)

Identifies the value of the WIDTH attribute.

Other Properties

accesKey (Internet Explorer 4), align (Internet Explorer 4), alt (Internet Explorer 4), className (Internet Explorer 4), dataFld (Internet Explorer 4), dataFormatAs (Internet Explorer 4), dataSrc (Internet Explorer 4), document (Internet Explorer 4), dynsrc (Internet Explorer 4), fileCreatedDate (Internet Explorer 4), fileModifiedDate (Internet Explorer 4), fileSize (Internet Explorer 4), fileUpdateDate (Internet Explorer 4), filter (Internet Explorer 4), href (Internet Explorer 4), id (Internet Explorer 4), innerHTML (Internet Explorer 4), innerText (Internet Explorer 4), isMap (Internet Explorer 4), isTextEdit (Internet Explorer 4), lang (Internet Explorer 4), language (Internet Explorer 4), loop (Internet Explorer 4), mimeTypes (Internet Explorer 4), offsetHeight (Internet Explorer 4), offsetLeft (Internet Explorer 4), offsetParent (Internet Explorer 4), offsetTop (Internet Explorer 4), offsetWidth (Internet Explorer 4), outerHTML (Internet Explorer 4), outerText (Internet Explorer 4), parentElement (Internet Explorer 4), parentTextEdit (Internet Explorer 4), protocol (Internet Explorer 4), readyState (Internet Explorer 4), scrollHeight (Internet Explorer 4), scrollLeft (Internet Explorer 4), scrollTop (Internet Explorer 4), scrollWidth (Internet Explorer 4), sourceIndex (Internet Explorer 4), start (Internet Explorer 4), style (Internet Explorer 4), tabIndex (Internet Explorer 4), tagName (Internet Explorer 4), title (Internet Explorer 4), useMap (Internet Explorer 4)

Methods

Methods Supported by Both Navigator and Internet Explorer
None.

Other Methods
blur (Internet Explorer 4), click (Internet Explorer 4), contains (Internet Explorer 4), focus (Internet Explorer 4), getAttribute (Internet Explorer 4), handleEvent (Navigator 4), insertAdjacentHTML (Internet Explorer 4), insertAdjacentText (Internet Explorer 4), removeAttribute (Internet Explorer 4), scrollIntoView (Internet Explorer 4), setAttribute (Internet Explorer 4)

Events

onAbort (Navigator 3, Internet Explorer 4), onError (Navigator 3, Internet Explorer 4), onkeydown (Navigator 4, Internet Explorer 4), onkeypress (Navigator 4, Internet Explorer 4), onkeyup (Navigator 4, Internet Explorer 4), onLoad (Navigator 3, Internet Explorer 4), onafterupdate (Internet Explorer 4), onbeforeupdate (Internet Explorer 4), onblur (Internet Explorer 4), onclick (Internet Explorer 4), ondataavailable (Internet Explorer 4), ondatasetchanged (Internet Explorer 4), ondatasetcomplete (Internet Explorer 4), ondblclick (Internet Explorer 4), ondragstart (Internet Explorer 4), onfilterchange (Internet Explorer 4), onfocus (Internet Explorer 4), onhelp (Internet Explorer 4), onmousedown (Internet Explorer 4), onmousemove (Internet Explorer 4), onmouseout (Internet Explorer 4), onmouseover (Internet Explorer 4), onmouseup (Internet Explorer 4), onresize (Internet Explorer 4), onrowenter (Internet Explorer 4), onrowexit (Internet Explorer 4), onscroll (Internet Explorer 4), onselectstart (Internet Explorer 4)

INPUT

Browser Support: Internet Explorer 4
Provides access to the HTML INPUT tag.

Properties

This object does not define any properties.

Methods

This object does not define any methods.

Events

This object does not define any events of its own.

INS

Browser Support: Internet Explorer 4

Provides access to the HTML INS tag.

Properties

Properties Supported by Both Navigator and Internet Explorer

None.

Other Properties

className (Internet Explorer 4), document (Internet Explorer 4), id (Internet Explorer 4), innerHTML (Internet Explorer 4), innerText (Internet Explorer 4), isTextEdit (Internet Explorer 4), lang (Internet Explorer 4), language (Internet Explorer 4), offsetHeight (Internet Explorer 4), offsetLeft (Internet Explorer 4), offsetParent (Internet Explorer 4), offsetTop (Internet Explorer 4), offsetWidth (Internet Explorer 4), outerHTML (Internet Explorer 4), outerText (Internet Explorer 4), parentElement (Internet Explorer 4), parentTextEdit (Internet Explorer 4), sourceIndex (Internet Explorer 4), style (Internet Explorer 4), tagName (Internet Explorer 4), title (Internet Explorer 4)

Methods

Methods Supported by Both Navigator and Internet Explorer

None.

Other Methods

click (Internet Explorer 4), contains (Internet Explorer 4), getAttribute (Internet Explorer 4), insertAdjacentHTML (Internet

Explorer 4), `insertAdjacentText` (Internet Explorer 4), `remove-Attribute` (Internet Explorer 4), `scrollIntoView` (Internet Explorer 4), `setAttribute` (Internet Explorer 4)

Events

`onclick` (Internet Explorer 4), `ondblclick` (Internet Explorer 4), `ondragstart` (Internet Explorer 4), `onfilterchange` (Internet Explorer 4), `onhelp` (Internet Explorer 4), `onkeydown` (Internet Explorer 4), `onkeypress` (Internet Explorer 4), `onkeyup` (Internet Explorer 4), `onmousedown` (Internet Explorer 4), `onmousemove` (Internet Explorer 4), `onmouseout` (Internet Explorer 4), `onmouseover` (Internet Explorer 4), `onmouseup` (Internet Explorer 4), `onselectstart` (Internet Explorer 4)

ISINDEX

Browser Support: Internet Explorer 5

Provides access to the HTML ISINDEX tag.

Properties

Properties Supported by Both Navigator and Internet Explorer

None.

Other Properties

`accessKey` (Internet Explorer 5), `canHaveHTML` (Internet Explorer 5), `className` (Internet Explorer 5), `clientHeight` (Internet Explorer 5), `clientLeft` (Internet Explorer 5), `clientTop` (Internet Explorer 5), `clientWidth` (Internet Explorer 5), `contentEditable` (Internet Explorer 5), `currentStyle` (Internet Explorer 5), `disabled` (Internet Explorer 5), `hasLayout` (Internet Explorer 5), `hideFocus` (Internet Explorer 5), `id` (Internet Explorer 5), `isContentEditable` (Internet Explorer 5), `isDisabled` (Internet Explorer 5), `lang` (Internet Explorer 5), `language` (Internet Explorer 5), `parentElement` (Internet Explorer 5), `readyState` (Internet Explorer 5), `scopeName` (Internet Explorer 5), `scrollHeight` (Internet Explorer 5), `scrollLeft` (Internet Explorer 5), `scrollTop` (Internet Explorer 5), `scrollWidth` (Internet Explorer 5), `tabIndex` (Internet Explorer 5), `tagUrn` (Internet Explorer 5)

Methods

Methods Supported by Both Navigator and Internet Explorer
None.

Other Methods
onbeforefocusenter (Internet Explorer 5), onbeforefocusleave (Internet Explorer 5), onblur (Internet Explorer 5), oncontrolselect (Internet Explorer 5), onfocus (Internet Explorer 5), onfocusenter (Internet Explorer 5), onfocusleave (Internet Explorer 5), onreadystatechange (Internet Explorer 5), onresize (Internet Explorer 5), onresizeend (Internet Explorer 5), onresizestart (Internet Explorer 5)

Events

onbeforefocusenter (Internet Explorer 5), onbeforefocusleave (Internet Explorer 5), onblur (Internet Explorer 5), oncontrolselect (Internet Explorer 5), onfocus (Internet Explorer 5), onfocusenter (Internet Explorer 5), onfocusleave (Internet Explorer 5), onreadystatechange (Internet Explorer 5), onresize (Internet Explorer 5), onresizeend (Internet Explorer 5), onresizestart (Internet Explorer 5)

java

Browser Support: Navigator 3

The java object provides access to objects in the java.* packages. The java object is equivalent to Packages.java.

Properties

The java object does not define any properties of its own. It may be used to access the public properties of Java objects.

Methods

The java object does not define any methods of its own. It may be used to access the public methods of Java objects.

Events

The java object does not define any events.

JavaArray

Browser Support: Navigator 3

Provides access to Java arrays.

Properties

Properties Supported by Both Navigator and Internet Explorer

None.

Other Properties

length (Navigator 3)

Methods

Methods Supported by Both Navigator and Internet Explorer

None.

Other Methods

toString (Navigator 3)

Events

The JavaArray object does not define any events.

JavaClass

Browser Support: Navigator 3

The JavaClass object provides access to a Java class.

Properties

The static properties of the Java class being accessed.

Methods

The static methods of the Java class being accessed.

Events

This object does not define any events.

JavaObject

Browser Support: Navigator 3

A JavaObject object is an instance of a Java class that is created in or passed to JavaScript.

Properties

Provides access to the public properties of the Java object being referenced.

Methods

Provides access to the public methods of the Java object being referenced.

Events

This object does not define any events.

JavaPackage

Browser Support: Navigator 3

The JavaPackage object provides access to a Java package.

Properties

Provides access to the elements of the package as properties.

Methods

This object defines no methods.

Events

This object does not define any events.

KBD

Browser Support: Internet Explorer 4

Provides access to the HTML KBD tag.

Properties

Properties Supported by Both Navigator and Internet Explorer

None.

Other Properties

className (Internet Explorer 4), document (Internet Explorer 4), id (Internet Explorer 4), innerHTML (Internet Explorer 4), innerText (Internet Explorer 4), isTextEdit (Internet Explorer 4), lang (Internet Explorer 4), language (Internet Explorer 4), offsetHeight (Internet Explorer 4), offsetLeft (Internet Explorer 4), offsetParent (Internet Explorer 4), offsetTop (Internet Explorer 4), offsetWidth (Internet Explorer 4), outerHTML (Internet Explorer 4), outerText (Internet Explorer 4), parentElement (Internet Explorer 4), parentTextEdit (Internet Explorer 4), sourceIndex (Internet Explorer 4), style (Internet Explorer 4), tagName (Internet Explorer 4), title (Internet Explorer 4)

Methods

Methods Supported by Both Navigator and Internet Explorer

None.

Other Methods

click (Internet Explorer 4), contains (Internet Explorer 4), getAttribute (Internet Explorer 4), insertAdjacentHTML (Internet Explorer 4), insertAdjacentText (Internet Explorer 4), removeAttribute (Internet Explorer 4), scrollIntoView (Internet Explorer 4), setAttribute (Internet Explorer 4)

Events

onclick (Internet Explorer 4), ondblclick (Internet Explorer 4), ondragstart (Internet Explorer 4), onfilterchange (Internet Explorer 4), onhelp (Internet Explorer 4), onkeydown (Internet Explorer 4), onkeypress (Internet Explorer 4), onkeyup (Internet Explorer 4), onmousedown (Internet Explorer 4), onmousemove (Internet Explorer 4), onmouseout (Internet Explorer 4), onmouseover (Internet Explorer 4), onmouseup (Internet Explorer 4), onselectstart (Internet Explorer 4)

LABEL

Browser Support: Internet Explorer 4

Provides access to the HTML LABEL tag.

Properties

Properties Supported by Both Navigator and Internet Explorer

None.

Other Properties

accessKey (Internet Explorer 4), className (Internet Explorer 4), document (Internet Explorer 4), htmlFor (Internet Explorer 4), id (Internet Explorer 4), innerHTML (Internet Explorer 4), innerText (Internet Explorer 4), isTextEdit (Internet Explorer 4), lang (Internet Explorer 4), language (Internet Explorer 4), offsetHeight (Internet Explorer 4), offsetLeft (Internet Explorer 4), offsetParent (Internet Explorer 4), offsetTop (Internet Explorer 4), offsetWidth (Internet Explorer 4), outerHTML (Internet Explorer 4), outerText (Internet Explorer 4), parentElement (Internet Explorer 4), parentTextEdit (Internet Explorer 4), sourceIndex (Internet Explorer 4), style (Internet Explorer 4), tagName (Internet Explorer 4), title (Internet Explorer 4)

Methods

Methods Supported by Both Navigator and Internet Explorer

None.

Other Methods

click (Internet Explorer 4), contains (Internet Explorer 4), get-
Attribute (Internet Explorer 4), insertAdjacentHTML (Internet
Explorer 4), insertAdjacentText (Internet Explorer 4), remove-
Attribute (Internet Explorer 4), scrollIntoView (Internet
Explorer 4), setAttribute (Internet Explorer 4)

Events

onclick (Internet Explorer 4), ondblclick (Internet Explorer 4),
ondragstart (Internet Explorer 4), onfilterchange (Internet Explorer 4),
onhelp (Internet Explorer 4), onkeydown (Internet Explorer 4), onkeypress (Internet Explorer 4), onkeyup (Internet Explorer 4), onmousedown (Internet Explorer 4), onmousemove (Internet Explorer 4),
onmouseout (Internet Explorer 4), onmouseover (Internet Explorer 4),
onmouseup (Internet Explorer 4), onselectstart (Internet Explorer 4)

Layer

Browser Support: Navigator 4

The Layer object provides access to a layer of an HTML page. It is an
object that is unique to Navigator and supports Navigator-specific
DHTML (Dynamic HTML). Layer objects may also be created using the
HTML DIV tag.

Properties

Properties Supported by Both Navigator and Internet Explorer

None.

Other Properties

above (Navigator 4), background (Navigator 4), below (Navigator 4),
bgColor (Navigator 4), clip.bottom (Navigator 4), clip.height (Navigator 4), clip.left (Navigator 4), clip.right (Navigator 4), clip.top
(Navigator 4), clip.width (Navigator 4), document (Navigator 4),
left (Navigator 4), name (Navigator 4), pageX (Navigator 4), pageY (Naviga-
tor 4), parentLayer (Navigator 4), siblingAbove (Navigator 4), sibling-
Below (Navigator 4), src (Navigator 4), top (Navigator 4), visibility

(Navigator 4), window (Navigator 4), x (Navigator 4), y (Navigator 4), zIndex (Navigator 4)

Methods

Methods Supported by Both Navigator and Internet Explorer
None.

Other Methods
captureEvents (Navigator 4), handleEvent (Navigator 4), load (Navigator 4), moveAbove (Navigator 4), moveBelow (Navigator 4), moveBy (Navigator 4), moveTo (Navigator 4), moveToAbsolute (Navigator 4), releaseEvents (Navigator 4), resizeBy (Navigator 4), resizeTo (Navigator 4), routeEvent (Navigator 4)

Events

onmouseover (Navigator 4), onmouseout (Navigator 4), onLoad (Navigator 4), onfocus (Navigator 4), onblur (Navigator 4)

LEGEND

Browser Support: Internet Explorer 4

Provides access to the HTML LEGEND tag.

Properties

Properties Supported by Both Navigator and Internet Explorer
None.

Other Properties
accessKey (Internet Explorer 4), align (Internet Explorer 4), class-Name (Internet Explorer 4), clientHeight (Internet Explorer 4), clientWidth (Internet Explorer 4), document (Internet Explorer 4), id (Internet Explorer 4), innerHTML (Internet Explorer 4), innerText (Internet Explorer 4), isTextEdit (Internet Explorer 4), lang (Internet Explorer 4), language (Internet Explorer 4), margin offsetHeight (Internet Explorer 4), offsetLeft (Internet Explorer 4), offsetParent

(Internet Explorer 4), `offsetTop` (Internet Explorer 4), `offset-Width` (Internet Explorer 4), `outerHTML` (Internet Explorer 4), `outer-Text` (Internet Explorer 4), `padding` (Internet Explorer 4), `parent-Element` (Internet Explorer 4), `parentTextEdit` (Internet Explorer 4), `recordNumber` (Internet Explorer 4), `scrollHeight` (Internet Explorer 4), `scrollLeft` (Internet Explorer 4), `scrollTop` (Internet Explorer 4), `scrollWidth` (Internet Explorer 4), `sourceIndex` (Internet Explorer 4), `style` (Internet Explorer 4), `tabIndex` (Internet Explorer 4), `tagName` (Internet Explorer 4), `title` (Internet Explorer 4)

Methods

Methods Supported by Both Navigator and Internet Explorer
None.

Other Methods
`blur` (Internet Explorer 4), `click` (Internet Explorer 4), `contains` (Internet Explorer 4), `focus` (Internet Explorer 4), `getAttribute` (Internet Explorer 4), `insertAdjacentHTML` (Internet Explorer 4), `insertAdjacentText` (Internet Explorer 4), `removeAttribute` (Internet Explorer 4), `scrollIntoView` (Internet Explorer 4), `setAttribute` (Internet Explorer 4)

Events

`onafterupdate` (Internet Explorer 4), `onbeforeupdate` (Internet Explorer 4), `onblur` (Internet Explorer 4), `onclick` (Internet Explorer 4), `ondblclick` (Internet Explorer 4), `ondragstart` (Internet Explorer 4), `onerrorupdate` (Internet Explorer 4), `onfocus` (Internet Explorer 4), `onhelp` (Internet Explorer 4), `onkeydown` (Internet Explorer 4), `onkeypress` (Internet Explorer 4), `onkeyup` (Internet Explorer 4), `onmousedown` (Internet Explorer 4), `onmousemove` (Internet Explorer 4), `onmouseout` (Internet Explorer 4), `onmouseover` (Internet Explorer 4), `onmouseup` (Internet Explorer 4), `onresize` (Internet Explorer 4), `onrowenter` (Internet Explorer 4), `onrowexit` (Internet Explorer 4), `onscroll` (Internet Explorer 4), `onselectstart` (Internet Explorer 4)

LI

Browser Support: Internet Explorer 4

Provides access to the HTML LI tag.

Properties

Properties Supported by Both Navigator and Internet Explorer

None.

Other Properties

className (Internet Explorer 4), document (Internet Explorer 4), id (Internet Explorer 4), innerHTML (Internet Explorer 4), innerText (Internet Explorer 4), isTextEdit (Internet Explorer 4), lang (Internet Explorer 4), language (Internet Explorer 4), offsetHeight (Internet Explorer 4), offsetLeft (Internet Explorer 4), offsetParent (Internet Explorer 4), offsetTop (Internet Explorer 4), offsetWidth (Internet Explorer 4), outerHTML (Internet Explorer 4), outerText (Internet Explorer 4), parentElement (Internet Explorer 4), parentTextEdit (Internet Explorer 4), sourceIndex (Internet Explorer 4), style (Internet Explorer 4), tagName (Internet Explorer 4), title (Internet Explorer 4), type (Internet Explorer 4), value (Internet Explorer 4)

Methods

Methods Supported by Both Navigator and Internet Explorer

None.

Other Methods

click (Internet Explorer 4), contains (Internet Explorer 4), getAttribute (Internet Explorer 4), insertAdjacentHTML (Internet Explorer 4), insertAdjacentText (Internet Explorer 4), removeAttribute (Internet Explorer 4), scrollIntoView (Internet Explorer 4), setAttribute (Internet Explorer 4)

Events

onclick (Internet Explorer 4), ondblclick (Internet Explorer 4), ondragstart (Internet Explorer 4), onfilterchange (Internet Explorer 4), onhelp (Internet Explorer 4), onkeydown (Internet Explorer 4), onkeypress (Internet Explorer 4), onkeyup (Internet Explorer 4), onmousedown (Internet Explorer 4), onmousemove (Internet Explorer 4), onmouseout (Internet Explorer 4), onmouseover (Internet Explorer 4), onmouseup (Internet Explorer 4), onselectstart (Internet Explorer 4)

LINK

Browser Support: Internet Explorer 4

Provides access to the HTML LINK tag.

Properties

Properties Supported by Both Navigator and Internet Explorer

None.

Other Properties

className (Internet Explorer 4), disabled (Internet Explorer 4), document (Internet Explorer 4), href (Internet Explorer 4), id (Internet Explorer 4), parentElement (Internet Explorer 4), readyState (Internet Explorer 4), rel (Internet Explorer 4), sourceIndex (Internet Explorer 4), tagName (Internet Explorer 4), title (Internet Explorer 4)

Methods

Methods Supported by Both Navigator and Internet Explorer

None.

Other Methods

contains (Internet Explorer 4), getAttribute (Internet Explorer 4), removeAttribute (Internet Explorer 4), setAttribute (Internet Explorer 4)

Events

This object does not define any events.

Link (A)

Browser Support: Navigator 2, Internet Explorer 3

The basic Link object was introduced in JavaScript 1. It has been updated with JavaScript 1.1 and 1.2. It is referred to as the A object in Microsoft's documentation.

The Link tag represents a hypertext link. A Link object is created for each A tag in the document that specifies an HREF attribute. These objects may be accessed from the links property of the document object.

Under Navigator, a Link object may also be an Anchor object if the A tag specifies the NAME attribute in addition to the HREF attribute.

Properties

Properties Supported by Both Navigator and Internet Explorer

hash (Navigator 2, Internet Explorer 3)

The name of an anchor in the URL.

host (Navigator 2, Internet Explorer 3)

A host name or IP address that represents the URL's host value.

hostname (Navigator 2, Internet Explorer 3)

The host:port portion of the URL.

href (Navigator 2, Internet Explorer 3)

The text of the entire URL.

pathname (Navigator 2, Internet Explorer 3)

The path name portion of the URL.

port (Navigator 2, Internet Explorer 3)

The port value of the URL.

protocol (Navigator 2, Internet Explorer 3)

The URL's protocol type.

search (Navigator 2, Internet Explorer 3)

   The value of any query string that is included in the URL.

target (Navigator 2, Internet Explorer 3)

   The value of the URL's TARGET attribute.

Other Properties

accessKey (Internet Explorer 4), className (Internet Explorer 4),
dataFld (Internet Explorer 4), dataSrc (Internet Explorer 4), document
(Internet Explorer 4), id (Internet Explorer 4), innerHTML (Internet
Explorer 4), innerText (Internet Explorer 4), isTextEdit (Internet Explorer 4), lang (Internet Explorer 4), language (Internet Explorer 4),
Methods (Internet Explorer 4), offsetHeight (Internet Explorer 4),
offsetLeft (Internet Explorer 4), offsetParent (Internet Explorer 4),
offsetTop (Internet Explorer 4), offsetWidth (Internet Explorer 4),
outerHTML (Internet Explorer 4), outerText (Internet Explorer 4),
parentElement (Internet Explorer 4), parentTextEdit (Internet
Explorer 4), recordNumber (Internet Explorer 4), rel (Internet Explorer 4),
rev (Internet Explorer 4), sourceIndex (Internet Explorer 4), style
(Internet Explorer 4), tabIndex (Internet Explorer 4), tagName (Internet
Explorer 4), text (Navigator 4), title (Internet Explorer 4), urn (Internet Explorer 4), x (Navigator 4), y (Navigator 4)

Methods

Methods Supported by Both Navigator and Internet Explorer
None.

Other Methods

blur (Internet Explorer 4), click (Internet Explorer 4), contains (Internet
Explorer 4), focus (Internet Explorer 4), getAttribute (Internet Explorer 4),
handleEvent (Navigator 4), insertAdjacentHTML (Internet Explorer 4),
insertAdjacentText (Internet Explorer 4), removeAttribute (Internet
Explorer 4), scrollIntoView (Internet Explorer 4), setAttribute (Internet Explorer 4)

Events

onclick (Navigator 2, Internet Explorer 3), ondblclick (Navigator 4, Internet Explorer 4), onkeydown (Navigator 4, Internet Explorer 4), onkeypress (Navigator 4, Internet Explorer 4), onkeyup (Navigator 4, Internet Explorer 4), onmousedown (Navigator 4, Internet Explorer 4), onmouseout (Navigator 3, Internet Explorer 4), onmouseover (Navigator 2, Internet Explorer 3), onmouseup (Navigator 4, Internet Explorer 4), onblur (Internet Explorer 4), ondragstart (Internet Explorer 4), onerrorupdate (Internet Explorer 4), onfilterchange (Internet Explorer 4), onfocus (Internet Explorer 4), onhelp (Internet Explorer 4), onmousemove (Internet Explorer 4), onselectstart (Internet Explorer 4)

LISTING

Browser Support: Internet Explorer 4

Provides access to the HTML LISTING tag.

Properties

Properties Supported by Both Navigator and Internet Explorer

None.

Other Properties

className (Internet Explorer 4), document (Internet Explorer 4), id (Internet Explorer 4), innerHTML (Internet Explorer 4), innerText (Internet Explorer 4), isTextEdit (Internet Explorer 4), lang (Internet Explorer 4), language (Internet Explorer 4), offsetHeight (Internet Explorer 4), offsetLeft (Internet Explorer 4), offsetParent (Internet Explorer 4), offsetTop (Internet Explorer 4), offsetWidth (Internet Explorer 4), outerHTML (Internet Explorer 4), outerText (Internet Explorer 4), parentElement (Internet Explorer 4), parentTextEdit (Internet Explorer 4), sourceIndex (Internet Explorer 4), style (Internet Explorer 4), tagName (Internet Explorer 4), title (Internet Explorer 4)

Methods

Methods Supported by Both Navigator and Internet Explorer
None.

Other Methods
click (Internet Explorer 4), contains (Internet Explorer 4), getAttribute (Internet Explorer 4), insertAdjacentHTML (Internet Explorer 4), insertAdjacentText (Internet Explorer 4), removeAttribute (Internet Explorer 4), scrollIntoView (Internet Explorer 4), setAttribute (Internet Explorer 4)

Events

onclick (Internet Explorer 4), ondblclick (Internet Explorer 4), ondragstart (Internet Explorer 4), onfilterchange (Internet Explorer 4), onhelp (Internet Explorer 4), onkeydown (Internet Explorer 4), onkeypress (Internet Explorer 4), onkeyup (Internet Explorer 4), onmousedown (Internet Explorer 4), onmousemove (Internet Explorer 4), onmouseout (Internet Explorer 4), onmouseover (Internet Explorer 4), onmouseup (Internet Explorer 4), onselectstart (Internet Explorer 4)

Location

Browser Support: Navigator 2, Internet Explorer 3

Updated in JavaScript 1.1.

A Location object represents the URL of the document loaded into a window. The location property of the window object provides access to the window's Location object.

Properties

Properties Supported by Both Navigator and Internet Explorer
hash (Navigator 2, Internet Explorer 3)

The name of an anchor in the URL.

host (Navigator 2, Internet Explorer 3)

A host name or IP address that represents the URL's host value.

hostname (Navigator 2, Internet Explorer 3)

>The host:port portion of the URL.

href (Navigator 2, Internet Explorer 3)

>The text of the entire URL.

pathname (Navigator 2, Internet Explorer 3)

>The path name portion of the URL.

port (Navigator 2, Internet Explorer 3)

>The port value of the URL.

protocol (Navigator 2, Internet Explorer 3)

>The URL's protocol type.

search (Navigator 2, Internet Explorer 3)

>The value of any query string that is included in the URL.

Methods

Methods Supported by Both Navigator and Internet Explorer

reload([force]) (Navigator 3, Internet Explorer 4)

>Reloads the current document. If the force argument is true, then an HTTP GET is forced by the browser causing the document to be reloaded from the server instead of the browser's cache.

replace(url) (Navigator 3, Internet Explorer 4)

>Loads the specified URL over the current document.

Other Methods

assign (Internet Explorer 4)

Events

No events are defined for this object.

MAP

Browser Support: Internet Explorer 4

>Provides access to the HTML MAP tag.

Properties

Properties Supported by Both Navigator and Internet Explorer
None.

Other Properties
className (Internet Explorer 4), document (Internet Explorer 4), filter (Internet Explorer 4), id (Internet Explorer 4), innerHTML (Internet Explorer 4), innerText (Internet Explorer 4), isTextEdit (Internet Explorer 4), lang (Internet Explorer 4), language (Internet Explorer 4), name offsetHeight (Internet Explorer 4), offsetLeft (Internet Explorer 4), offsetParent (Internet Explorer 4), offsetTop (Internet Explorer 4), offsetWidth (Internet Explorer 4), outerHTML (Internet Explorer 4), outerText (Internet Explorer 4), parentElement (Internet Explorer 4), parentTextEdit (Internet Explorer 4), recordNumber (Internet Explorer 4), sourceIndex (Internet Explorer 4), style (Internet Explorer 4), tagName (Internet Explorer 4), title (Internet Explorer 4)

Methods

Methods Supported by Both Navigator and Internet Explorer
None.

Other Methods
click (Internet Explorer 4), contains (Internet Explorer 4), getAttribute (Internet Explorer 4), removeAttribute (Internet Explorer 4), scrollIntoView (Internet Explorer 4), setAttribute (Internet Explorer 4)

Events

onafterupdate (Internet Explorer 4), onbeforeupdate (Internet Explorer 4), onclick (Internet Explorer 4), ondataavailable (Internet Explorer 4), ondatasetchanged (Internet Explorer 4), ondatasetcomplete (Internet Explorer 4), ondblclick (Internet Explorer 4), ondragstart (Internet Explorer 4), onerrorupdate (Internet Explorer 4), onfilterchange (Internet Explorer 4), onhelp (Internet Explorer 4), onkeydown (Internet Explorer 4), onkeypress (Internet Explorer 4), onkeyup (Internet

Explorer 4), onmousedown (Internet Explorer 4), onmousemove (Internet Explorer 4), onmouseout (Internet Explorer 4), onmouseover (Internet Explorer 4), onmouseup (Internet Explorer 4), onrowenter (Internet Explorer 4), onrowexit (Internet Explorer 4), onselectstart (Internet Explorer 4)

MARQUEE

Browser Support: Internet Explorer 4

Provides access to the HTML MARQUEE tag.

Properties

Properties Supported by Both Navigator and Internet Explorer

None.

Other Properties

accessKey (Internet Explorer 4), behavior (Internet Explorer 4), bgColor (Internet Explorer 4), className (Internet Explorer 4), clientHeight (Internet Explorer 4), clientWidth (Internet Explorer 4), dataFld (Internet Explorer 4), dataFormatAs (Internet Explorer 4), dataSrc (Internet Explorer 4), direction (Internet Explorer 4), document (Internet Explorer 4), height (Internet Explorer 4), hspace (Internet Explorer 4), id (Internet Explorer 4), innerHTML (Internet Explorer 4), innerText (Internet Explorer 4), isTextEdit (Internet Explorer 4), lang (Internet Explorer 4), language (Internet Explorer 4), loop (Internet Explorer 4), offsetHeight (Internet Explorer 4), offsetLeft (Internet Explorer 4), offsetParent (Internet Explorer 4), offsetTop (Internet Explorer 4), offsetWidth (Internet Explorer 4), outerHTML (Internet Explorer 4), outerText (Internet Explorer 4), parentElement (Internet Explorer 4), parentTextEdit (Internet Explorer 4), scrollAmount (Internet Explorer 4), scrollDelay (Internet Explorer 4), scrollHeight (Internet Explorer 4), scrollLeft (Internet Explorer 4), scrollTop (Internet Explorer 4), scrollWidth (Internet Explorer 4), sourceIndex (Internet Explorer 4), style (Internet Explorer 4), tagName (Internet Explorer 4), title (Internet Explorer 4), trueSpeed (Internet Explorer 4), vspace (Internet Explorer 4), width (Internet Explorer 4)

Methods

Methods Supported by Both Navigator and Internet Explorer
None.

Other Methods
blur (Internet Explorer 4), click (Internet Explorer 4), contains (Internet Explorer 4), focus (Internet Explorer 4), getAttribute (Internet Explorer 4), insertAdjacentHTML (Internet Explorer 4), insertAdjacentText (Internet Explorer 4), removeAttribute (Internet Explorer 4), scrollIntoView (Internet Explorer 4), setAttribute (Internet Explorer 4), start (Internet Explorer 4), stop (Internet Explorer 4)

Events

onafterupdate (Internet Explorer 4), onblur (Internet Explorer 4), onbounce (Internet Explorer 4), onclick (Internet Explorer 4), ondblclick (Internet Explorer 4), ondragstart (Internet Explorer 4), onfinish (Internet Explorer 4), onfocus (Internet Explorer 4), onhelp (Internet Explorer 4), onkeydown (Internet Explorer 4), onkeypress (Internet Explorer 4), onkeyup (Internet Explorer 4), onmousedown (Internet Explorer 4), onmousemove (Internet Explorer 4), onmouseout (Internet Explorer 4), onmouseover (Internet Explorer 4), onmouseup (Internet Explorer 4), onresize (Internet Explorer 4), onrowenter (Internet Explorer 4), onrowexit (Internet Explorer 4), onscroll (Internet Explorer 4), onselectstart (Internet Explorer 4), onstart (Internet Explorer 4)

Math

Browser Support: Navigator 2, Internet Explorer 3

Supported in IE 3 and later.

The Math object is a core object that provides a set of static mathematical constants and functions.

Properties

Properties Supported by Both Navigator and Internet Explorer

E (Navigator 2, Internet Explorer 3)

    Euler's constant.

LN10 (Navigator 2, Internet Explorer 3)

    The natural log of 10.

LN2 (Navigator 2, Internet Explorer 3)

    The natural log of 2.

LOG10E (Navigator 2, Internet Explorer 3)

    The base 10 log of e.

LOG2E (Navigator 2, Internet Explorer 3)

    The base 2 log of e.

PI (Navigator 2, Internet Explorer 3)

    The mathematical symbol pi.

SQRT1_2 (Navigator 2, Internet Explorer 3)

    The square root of 1/2.

SQRT2 (Navigator 2, Internet Explorer 3)

    The square root of 2.

Methods

Methods Supported by Both Navigator and Internet Explorer

abs(x) (Navigator 2, Internet Explorer 3)

    Returns the absolute value of x.

acos(x) (Navigator 2, Internet Explorer 3)

    Returns the arc cosine of x.

asin(x) (Navigator 2, Internet Explorer 3)

    Returns the arc sine of x.

atan(x) (Navigator 2, Internet Explorer 3)

    Returns the arc tangent of x.

atan2(y,x) (Navigator 2, Internet Explorer 3)

    Returns the arc tangent of y/x.

`ceil(x)` (Navigator 2, Internet Explorer 3)

Returns the smallest integer that is greater than or equal to x.

`cos(x)` (Navigator 2, Internet Explorer 3)

Returns the cosine of x.

`exp(x)` (Navigator 2, Internet Explorer 3)

Returns e raised to the x power.

`floor(x)` (Navigator 2, Internet Explorer 3)

Returns the largest integer that is less than or equal to x.

`log(x)` (Navigator 2, Internet Explorer 3)

Returns the natural logarithm of x.

`max(x,y)` (Navigator 2, Internet Explorer 3)

Returns the greater of x and y.

`min(x,y)` (Navigator 2, Internet Explorer 3)

Returns the lesser of x and y.

`pow(x,y)` (Navigator 2, Internet Explorer 3)

Returns x raised to the y power.

`random()` (Navigator 2, Internet Explorer 3)

Returns a random floating-point number between 0 and 1.

`round(x)` (Navigator 2, Internet Explorer 3)

Returns the value of x rounded to the nearest integer.

`sin(x)` (Navigator 2, Internet Explorer 3)

Returns the sine of x.

`sqrt(x)` (Navigator 2, Internet Explorer 3)

Returns the square root of x.

`tan(x)` (Navigator 2, Internet Explorer 3)

Returns the tangent of x.

Events

No events are defined for this object.

MENU

Browser Support: Internet Explorer 4

Provides access to the HTML MENU tag.

Properties

Properties Supported by Both Navigator and Internet Explorer
None.

Other Properties
className (Internet Explorer 4), document (Internet Explorer 4), id (Internet Explorer 4), innerHTML (Internet Explorer 4), innerText (Internet Explorer 4), isTextEdit (Internet Explorer 4), lang (Internet Explorer 4), language (Internet Explorer 4), offsetHeight (Internet Explorer 4), offsetLeft (Internet Explorer 4), offsetParent (Internet Explorer 4), offsetTop (Internet Explorer 4), offsetWidth (Internet Explorer 4), outerHTML (Internet Explorer 4), outerText (Internet Explorer 4), parentElement (Internet Explorer 4), parentTextEdit (Internet Explorer 4), sourceIndex (Internet Explorer 4), style (Internet Explorer 4), tagName (Internet Explorer 4), title (Internet Explorer 4)

Methods

Methods Supported by Both Navigator and Internet Explorer
None.

Other Methods
click (Internet Explorer 4), contains (Internet Explorer 4), getAttribute (Internet Explorer 4), insertAdjacentHTML (Internet Explorer 4), insertAdjacentText (Internet Explorer 4), removeAttribute (Internet Explorer 4), scrollIntoView (Internet Explorer 4), setAttribute (Internet Explorer 4)

Events

onclick (Internet Explorer 4), ondblclick (Internet Explorer 4), ondragstart (Internet Explorer 4), onfilterchange (Internet Explorer 4), onhelp (Internet Explorer 4), onkeydown (Internet Explorer 4), onkeypress (Internet Explorer 4), onkeyup (Internet Explorer 4), onmousedown (Internet Explorer 4), onmousemove (Internet Explorer 4), onmouseout (Internet Explorer 4), onmouseover (Internet Explorer 4), onmouseup (Internet Explorer 4), onselectstart (Internet Explorer 4)

META

Browser Support: Internet Explorer 4

Provides access to the HTML META tag.

Properties

Properties Supported by Both Navigator and Internet Explorer
None.

Other Properties

charset (Internet Explorer 4), className (Internet Explorer 4), content (Internet Explorer 4), document (Internet Explorer 4), httpEquiv (Internet Explorer 4), id (Internet Explorer 4), isTextEdit (Internet Explorer 4), lang (Internet Explorer 4), name (Internet Explorer 4), parentElement (Internet Explorer 4), parentTextEdit (Internet Explorer 4), sourceIndex (Internet Explorer 4), tagName (Internet Explorer 4), title (Internet Explorer 4), url (Internet Explorer 4)

Methods

Methods Supported by Both Navigator and Internet Explorer
None.

Other Methods

contains (Internet Explorer 4), getAttribute (Internet Explorer 4), removeAttribute (Internet Explorer 4), setAttribute (Internet Explorer 4)

Events

This object does not define any events.

MimeType

Browser Support: Navigator 3

Represents a MIME type as handled by the browser. MIME types are used to define the type of information contained in a file or data stream.

Properties

Properties Supported by Both Navigator and Internet Explorer
None.

Other Properties
description (Navigator 3), enabledPlugin (Navigator 3), suffixes (Navigator 3), type (Navigator 3)

Methods

This object does not define any methods.

Events

This object does not define any event handlers.

navigator

Browser Support: Navigator 2, Internet Explorer 3

The basic navigator object was introduced in JavaScript 1. It has been updated with JavaScript 1.1 and 1.2.

The navigator object provides access to basic information about the browser that is executing the script.

Properties

Properties Supported by Both Navigator and Internet Explorer
appCodeName (Navigator 2, Internet Explorer 3)

The browser's code name.

appName (Navigator 2, Internet Explorer 3)

The browser's name.

appVersion (Navigator 2, Internet Explorer 3)

The browser's version number.

mimeTypes (Navigator 3, Internet Explorer 4)

An array of MimeType objects supported by the browser.

plugins (Navigator 3, Internet Explorer 4)

An array of all Plugin objects supported by the browser.

userAgent (Navigator 2, Internet Explorer 3)

The user-agent header sent in the HTTP protocol by the browser to a Web server.

Other Properties

appMinorVersion (Internet Explorer 4), browserLanguage (Internet Explorer 4), connectionSpeed (Internet Explorer 4), cookieEnabled (Internet Explorer 4), cpuClass (Internet Explorer 4), language (Navigator 4), onLine (Internet Explorer 4), platform (Navigator 4), systemLanguage (Internet Explorer 4), userProfile (Internet Explorer 4)

Methods

Methods Supported by Both Navigator and Internet Explorer

javaEnabled() (Navigator 3, Internet Explorer 4)

Returns True if Java is enabled by the browser.

taintEnabled() (Navigator 3, Internet Explorer 4)

Returns True if tainting is enabled.

Other Methods

plugins.refresh (Navigator 3), preference (Navigator 4), savePreferences (Navigator 4)

Events

This object does not define any events.

netscape

Browser Support: Navigator 3

Provides access to Java classes in the package netscape.*. It is equivalent to the netscape property of the Packages object.

NEXTID

Browser Support: Internet Explorer 4

Provides access to the HTML NEXTID tag.

Properties

Properties Supported by Both Navigator and Internet Explorer
None.

Other Properties
className (Internet Explorer 4), document (Internet Explorer 4), id (Internet Explorer 4), isTextEdit (Internet Explorer 4), language (Internet Explorer 4), parentElement (Internet Explorer 4), parent-TextEdit (Internet Explorer 4), sourceIndex (Internet Explorer 4), tagName (Internet Explorer 4), title (Internet Explorer 4)

Methods

Methods Supported by Both Navigator and Internet Explorer
None.

Other Methods
contains (Internet Explorer 4), getAttribute (Internet Explorer 4), removeAttribute (Internet Explorer 4), setAttribute (Internet Explorer 4)

Events

This object does not define any events.

NOBR

Browser Support: Internet Explorer 5

Provides access to the HTML NOBR tag.

Properties

Properties Supported by Both Navigator and Internet Explorer
None.

Other Properties

canHaveHTML (Internet Explorer 5), className (Internet Explorer 5), clientHeight (Internet Explorer 5), clientLeft (Internet Explorer 5), clientTop (Internet Explorer 5), clientWidth (Internet Explorer 5), contentEditable (Internet Explorer 5), currentStyle (Internet Explorer 5), dir (Internet Explorer 5), disabled (Internet Explorer 5), hasLayout (Internet Explorer 5), id (Internet Explorer 5), innerHTML (Internet Explorer 5), innerText (Internet Explorer 5), isContentEditable (Internet Explorer 5), isDisabled (Internet Explorer 5), isTextEdit (Internet Explorer 5), lang (Internet Explorer 5), language (Internet Explorer 5), offsetHeight (Internet Explorer 5), offsetLeft (Internet Explorer 5), offsetParent (Internet Explorer 5), offsetTop (Internet Explorer 5), offsetWidth (Internet Explorer 5), outerHTML (Internet Explorer 5), outerText (Internet Explorer 5), parentElement (Internet Explorer 5), parentTextEdit (Internet Explorer 5), readyState (Internet Explorer 5), recordNumber (Internet Explorer 5), runtimeStyle (Internet Explorer 5), scopeName (Internet Explorer 5), scrollHeight (Internet Explorer 5), scrollLeft (Internet Explorer 5), scrollTop (Internet Explorer 5), scrollWidth (Internet Explorer 5), sourceIndex (Internet Explorer 5), style (Internet Explorer 5), tagName (Internet Explorer 5), tagUrn (Internet Explorer 5), uniqueID (Internet Explorer 5)

Methods

Methods Supported by Both Navigator and Internet Explorer
None.

Other Methods

addBehavior (Internet Explorer 5), attachEvent (Internet Explorer 5), click (Internet Explorer 5), componentFromPoint (Internet Explorer 5), contains (Internet Explorer 5), detachEvent (Internet Explorer 5), fireEvent (Internet Explorer 5), getAttribute (Internet Explorer 5), getBoundingClientRect (Internet Explorer 5), getClientRects (Internet Explorer 5), getExpression (Internet Explorer 5), insertAdjacentHTML (Internet Explorer 5), insertAdjacentText (Internet Explorer 5), releaseCapture (Internet Explorer 5), removeAttribute (Internet Explorer 5), removeBehavior (Internet Explorer 5), removeExpression (Internet Explorer 5), scrollIntoView (Internet Explorer 5), setAttribute (Internet Explorer 5), setCapture (Internet Explorer 5), setExpression (Internet Explorer 5)

Events

onbeforecopy (Internet Explorer 5), onbeforecut (Internet Explorer 5), onbeforepaste (Internet Explorer 5), onclick (Internet Explorer 5), oncontextmenu (Internet Explorer 5), oncopy (Internet Explorer 5), oncut (Internet Explorer 5), ondblclick (Internet Explorer 5), ondrag (Internet Explorer 5), ondragend (Internet Explorer 5), ondragenter (Internet Explorer 5), ondragleave (Internet Explorer 5), ondragover (Internet Explorer 5), ondragstart (Internet Explorer 5), ondrop (Internet Explorer 5), onhelp (Internet Explorer 5), onkeydown (Internet Explorer 5), onkeypress (Internet Explorer 5), onkeyup (Internet Explorer 5), onlosecapture (Internet Explorer 5), onmouseenter (Internet Explorer 5), onmouseleave (Internet Explorer 5), onmousemove (Internet Explorer 5), onmouseover (Internet Explorer 5), onmouseup (Internet Explorer 5), onpaste (Internet Explorer 5), onpropertychange (Internet Explorer 5), onreadystatechange (Internet Explorer 5), onselectstart (Internet Explorer 5)

NOFRAMES

Browser Support: Internet Explorer 5

Provides access to the HTML NOFRAMES tag.

Properties

Properties Supported by Both Navigator and Internet Explorer
None.

Other Properties

canHaveHTML (Internet Explorer 5), contentEditable (Internet Explorer 5), disabled (Internet Explorer 5), id (Internet Explorer 5), isContent-Editable (Internet Explorer 5), isDisabled (Internet Explorer 5), parentElement (Internet Explorer 5), readyState (Internet Explorer 5), scopeName (Internet Explorer 5), tagUrn (Internet Explorer 5)

Methods

Methods Supported by Both Navigator and Internet Explorer

None.

Other Methods

addBehavior (Internet Explorer 5), componentFromPoint (Internet Explorer 5), fireEvent (Internet Explorer 5), removeBehavior (Internet Explorer 5)

Events

onreadystatechange (Internet Explorer 5)

NOSCRIPT

Browser Support: Internet Explorer 5

Provides access to the HTML NOSCRIPT tag.

Properties

Properties Supported by Both Navigator and Internet Explorer

None.

Other Properties

canHaveHTML (Internet Explorer 5), contentEditable (Internet Explorer 5), disabled (Internet Explorer 5), id (Internet Explorer 5), isContentEditable (Internet Explorer 5), isDisabled (Internet Explorer 5), parentElement (Internet Explorer 5), readyState (Internet Explorer 5), scopeName (Internet Explorer 5), tagUrn (Internet Explorer 5)

Methods

Methods Supported by Both Navigator and Internet Explorer
None.

Other Methods
addBehavior (Internet Explorer 5), componentFromPoint (Internet Explorer 5), fireEvent (Internet Explorer 5), removeBehavior (Internet Explorer 5)

Events

onreadystatechange (Internet Explorer 5)

Number

Browser Support: Navigator 3, Internet Explorer 4

The Number object was introduced in JavaScript 1.1. It has been updated with JavaScript 1.2 and 1.3.

A core JavaScript object that is an object wrapper for number values.

Constructors

new Number(value)

Creates a number object with the specified value.

Properties

Properties Supported by Both Navigator and Internet Explorer
constructor (Navigator 3, Internet Explorer 4)

Identifies the object's constructor.

MAX_VALUE (Navigator 3, Internet Explorer 4)

Identifies the largest number.

MIN_VALUE (Navigator 3, Internet Explorer 4)

Identifies the smallest number.

NaN (Navigator 3, Internet Explorer 4)

Used to identify values that are not a number.

NEGATIVE_INFINITY (Navigator 3, Internet Explorer 4)

Represents negative infinity

POSITIVE_INFINITY (Navigator 3, Internet Explorer 4)

Represents positive infinity.

prototype (Navigator 3, Internet Explorer 4)

Provides the capability to define additional properties.

Methods

Methods Supported by Both Navigator and Internet Explorer

toString() (Navigator 3, Internet Explorer 4)

Returns a string representation of the number.

valueOf() (Navigator 3, Internet Explorer 4)

Returns the primitive value corresponding to the Number object.

Other Methods

toSource (Navigator 4.06)

Events

This object does not define any events.

Object

Browser Support: Navigator 2, Internet Explorer 4

The Object object was introduced in JavaScript 1. It has been updated with JavaScript 1.1, 1.2, and 1.3.

The core JavaScript object that defines properties and methods that are inherited by all other objects.

Properties

Properties Supported by Both Navigator and Internet Explorer

constructor (Navigator 3, Internet Explorer 4)

Refers to the object's constructor.

prototype (Navigator 3, Internet Explorer 4)

Provides the capability to define additional properties.

Methods

Methods Supported by Both Navigator and Internet Explorer

toString() (Navigator 2, Internet Explorer 4)

Returns the string representation of the object.

valueOf() (Navigator 3, Internet Explorer 4)

Returns the primitive value that is associated with the object.

Other Methods

eval (Navigator 3), toSource (Navigator 4.06), unwatch (Navigator 4), watch (Navigator 4)

Events

This object does not define any events.

OBJECT

Browser Support: Internet Explorer 4

Provides access to the HTML OBJECT tag.

Properties

Properties Supported by Both Navigator and Internet Explorer

None.

Other Properties

accessKey (Internet Explorer 4), align (Internet Explorer 4), altHTML (Internet Explorer 4), classid (Internet Explorer 4), className (Internet Explorer 4), code (Internet Explorer 4), codeBase (Internet Explorer 4), codeType (Internet Explorer 4), data (Internet Explorer 4), dataFld (Internet Explorer 4), dataFormatAs (Internet Explorer 4), dataSrc (Internet Explorer 4), document (Internet Explorer 4), height (Internet Explorer 4), hspace (Internet Explorer 4), id (Internet Explorer 4), isTextEdit (Internet Explorer 4), lang (Internet Explorer 4), language (Internet Explorer 4), name (Internet Explorer 4), object (Internet Explorer 4), offsetHeight (Internet Explorer 4), offsetLeft (Internet Explorer 4), offsetParent (Internet Explorer 4), offsetTop (Internet Explorer 4), offsetWidth (Internet Explorer 4), outerHTML (Internet Explorer 4), outerText (Internet Explorer 4), parentElement (Internet Explorer 4), parentTextEdit (Internet Explorer 4), readyState (Internet Explorer 4), sourceIndex (Internet Explorer 4), style (Internet Explorer 4), tabIndex (Internet Explorer 4), tagName (Internet Explorer 4), title (Internet Explorer 4), type (Internet Explorer 4), vspace (Internet Explorer 4), width (Internet Explorer 4)

Methods

Methods Supported by Both Navigator and Internet Explorer

None.

Other Methods

blur (Internet Explorer 4), click (Internet Explorer 4), contains (Internet Explorer 4), focus (Internet Explorer 4), getAttribute (Internet Explorer 4), removeAttribute (Internet Explorer 4), scrollIntoView (Internet Explorer 4), setAttribute (Internet Explorer 4)

Events

onafterupdate (Internet Explorer 4), onbeforeupdate (Internet Explorer 4), onblur (Internet Explorer 4), onclick (Internet Explorer 4), ondataavailable (Internet Explorer 4), ondatasetchanged (Internet Explorer 4), ondatasetcomplete (Internet Explorer 4), ondblclick (Internet Explorer 4), ondragstart (Internet Explorer 4), onerror (Internet Explorer 4), onerrorupdate (Internet Explorer 4), onfilterchange

(Internet Explorer 4), onfocus (Internet Explorer 4), onreadystate-change (Internet Explorer 4), onrowenter (Internet Explorer 4), onrowexit (Internet Explorer 4), onselectstart (Internet Explorer 4)

OL

Browser Support: Internet Explorer 4

Provides access to the HTML OL tag.

Properties

Properties Supported by Both Navigator and Internet Explorer
None.

Other Properties

className (Internet Explorer 4), document (Internet Explorer 4), id (Internet Explorer 4), innerHTML (Internet Explorer 4), innerText (Internet Explorer 4), isTextEdit (Internet Explorer 4), lang (Internet Explorer 4), language (Internet Explorer 4), offsetHeight (Internet Explorer 4), offsetLeft (Internet Explorer 4), offsetParent (Internet Explorer 4), offsetTop (Internet Explorer 4), offsetWidth (Internet Explorer 4), outerHTML (Internet Explorer 4), outerText (Internet Explorer 4), parentElement (Internet Explorer 4), parentTextEdit (Internet Explorer 4), sourceIndex (Internet Explorer 4), start (Internet Explorer 4), style (Internet Explorer 4), tagName (Internet Explorer 4), title (Internet Explorer 4), type (Internet Explorer 4)

Methods

Methods Supported by Both Navigator and Internet Explorer
None.

Other Methods

click (Internet Explorer 4), contains (Internet Explorer 4), get-Attribute (Internet Explorer 4), insertAdjacentHTML (Internet Explorer 4), insertAdjacentText (Internet Explorer 4), remove-Attribute (Internet Explorer 4), scrollIntoView (Internet Explorer 4), setAttribute (Internet Explorer 4)

Events

onclick (Internet Explorer 4), ondblclick (Internet Explorer 4), ondragstart (Internet Explorer 4), onfilterchange (Internet Explorer 4), onhelp (Internet Explorer 4), onkeydown (Internet Explorer 4), onkeypress (Internet Explorer 4), onkeyup (Internet Explorer 4), onmousedown (Internet Explorer 4), onmousemove (Internet Explorer 4), onmouseout (Internet Explorer 4), onmouseover (Internet Explorer 4), onmouseup (Internet Explorer 4), onselectstart (Internet Explorer 4)

Option

Browser Support: Navigator 2, Internet Explorer 3

The Option object was introduced in JavaScript 1. It has been updated with JavaScript 1.1.

The Option object represents an option in the select field of a form.

Constructors

```
new Option([text[, value[, defaultSelected[, selected]]]])
```

Creates a new Option object with the specified text and (optionally) value. If the default selected argument is supplied, then its value (Boolean) sets the default selection state of the option. If the selected argument is supplied, it determines the object's current selection state.

Properties

Properties Supported by Both Navigator and Internet Explorer

index (Navigator 2, Internet Explorer 3)

Identifies the index of the option in the options array of the corresponding Select object.

length (Navigator 2, Internet Explorer 3)

Identifies the length of the options array of the corresponding Select object.

selected (Navigator 2, Internet Explorer 3)

Identifies the option's current selection state.

text (Navigator 2, Internet Explorer 3)
   Identifies the option's text.
value (Navigator 2, Internet Explorer 3)
   Identifies the option's value.

Other Properties
defaultSelected (Navigator 3)

Methods

Methods Supported by Both Navigator and Internet Explorer
None.

Other Methods
contains (Internet Explorer 4), getAttribute (Internet Explorer 4), removeAttribute (Internet Explorer 4), scrollIntoView (Internet Explorer 4), setAttribute (Internet Explorer 4)

Events

This object does not define any events.

P

Browser Support: Internet Explorer 4
   Provides access to the HTML P tag.

Properties

Properties Supported by Both Navigator and Internet Explorer
None.

Other Properties
className (Internet Explorer 4), document (Internet Explorer 4), id (Internet Explorer 4), innerHTML (Internet Explorer 4), innerText (Internet Explorer 4), isTextEdit (Internet Explorer 4), lang (Internet Explorer 4), language (Internet Explorer 4), offsetHeight (Internet

Explorer 4), offsetLeft (Internet Explorer 4), offsetParent (Internet Explorer 4), offsetTop (Internet Explorer 4), offsetWidth (Internet Explorer 4), outerHTML (Internet Explorer 4), outerText (Internet Explorer 4), parentElement (Internet Explorer 4), parentTextEdit (Internet Explorer 4), sourceIndex (Internet Explorer 4), style (Internet Explorer 4), tagName (Internet Explorer 4), title (Internet Explorer 4)

Methods

Methods Supported by Both Navigator and Internet Explorer

None.

Other Methods

click (Internet Explorer 4), contains (Internet Explorer 4), getAttribute (Internet Explorer 4), insertAdjacentHTML (Internet Explorer 4), insertAdjacentText (Internet Explorer 4), removeAttribute (Internet Explorer 4), scrollIntoView (Internet Explorer 4), setAttribute (Internet Explorer 4)

Events

onclick (Internet Explorer 4), ondblclick (Internet Explorer 4), ondragstart (Internet Explorer 4), onfilterchange (Internet Explorer 4), onhelp (Internet Explorer 4), onkeydown (Internet Explorer 4), onkeypress (Internet Explorer 4), onkeyup (Internet Explorer 4), onmousedown (Internet Explorer 4), onmousemove (Internet Explorer 4), onmouseout (Internet Explorer 4), onmouseover (Internet Explorer 4), onmouseup (Internet Explorer 4), onselectstart (Internet Explorer 4)

Packages

Browser Support: Navigator 3

Provides access to Java packages from within JavaScript.

Properties

Properties Supported by Both Navigator and Internet Explorer

None.

Other Properties

className (Navigator 3), java (Navigator 3), netscape (Navigator 3), sun (Navigator 3)

Methods

This object does not define any methods.

Events

This object does not define any events.

Password

Browser Support: Navigator 2, Internet Explorer 3

The basic Password object was introduced in JavaScript 1. It has been updated with JavaScript 1.1 and 1.2.

A Password object represents a password field of an HTML form. Password fields are represented by INPUT tags with their TYPE attribute set to PASSWORD. Password objects allow a user to type a password without its contents being displayed. However, the password values are not encrypted and are transmitted in the clear from the user's browser to a Web server via HTTP.

Properties

Properties Supported by Both Navigator and Internet Explorer

defaultValue (Navigator 2, Internet Explorer 3)

The default value of the password field.

form (Navigator 2, Internet Explorer 3)

Provides a reference to the form object that contains the password field.

name (Navigator 2, Internet Explorer 3)

The value of the password field's NAME attribute.

type (Navigator 3, Internet Explorer 4)

The value of the password field's TYPE attribute.

value (Navigator 2, Internet Explorer 3)

The value entered by the user in the password field.

Other Properties

accessKey (Internet Explorer 4), align (Internet Explorer 4), class-Name (Internet Explorer 4), dataFld (Internet Explorer 4), dataSrc (Internet Explorer 4), disabled (Internet Explorer 4), document (Internet Explorer 4), id (Internet Explorer 4), isTextEdit (Internet Explorer 4), lang (Internet Explorer 4), language (Internet Explorer 4), maxLength (Internet Explorer 4), offsetHeight (Internet Explorer 4), offsetLeft (Internet Explorer 4), offsetParent (Internet Explorer 4), offsetTop (Internet Explorer 4), offsetWidth (Internet Explorer 4), outerHTML (Internet Explorer 4), outerText (Internet Explorer 4), parentElement (Internet Explorer 4), parentTextEdit (Internet Explorer 4), readOnly (Internet Explorer 4), size (Internet Explorer 4), sourceIndex (Internet Explorer 4), style (Internet Explorer 4), tabIndex (Internet Explorer 4), tagName (Internet Explorer 4), title (Internet Explorer 4)

Methods

Methods Supported by Both Navigator and Internet Explorer

blur() (Navigator 2, Internet Explorer 3)

Removes input focus from the password field.

focus() (Navigator 2, Internet Explorer 3)

Moves input focus to the password field.

select() (Navigator 2, Internet Explorer 3)

Selects (highlights) the input area of the password field.

Other Methods

click (Internet Explorer 4), contains (Internet Explorer 4), getAttribute (Internet Explorer 4), handleEvent (Navigator 4), insertAdjacentHTML (Internet Explorer 4), insertAdjacentText (Internet Explorer 4), removeAttribute (Internet Explorer 4), scrollIntoView (Internet Explorer 4), setAttribute (Internet Explorer 4)

Events

onblur (Navigator 3, Internet Explorer 4), onfocus (Navigator 3, Internet Explorer 4), onchange (Internet Explorer 4), onclick (Internet Explorer 4), ondblclick (Internet Explorer 4), onhelp (Internet Explorer 4), onkeydown (Internet Explorer 4), onkeypress (Internet Explorer 4), onkeyup (Internet Explorer 4), onmousedown (Internet Explorer 4), onmousemove (Internet Explorer 4), onmouseout (Internet Explorer 4), onmouseover (Internet Explorer 4), onmouseup (Internet Explorer 4), onresize (Internet Explorer 4), onselect (Internet Explorer 4)

PLAINTEXT

Browser Support: Internet Explorer 4

Provides access to the HTML PLAINTEXT tag.

Properties

Properties Supported by Both Navigator and Internet Explorer

None.

Other Properties

className (Internet Explorer 4), document (Internet Explorer 4), id (Internet Explorer 4), innerHTML (Internet Explorer 4), innerText (Internet Explorer 4), isTextEdit (Internet Explorer 4), lang (Internet Explorer 4), language (Internet Explorer 4), offsetHeight (Internet Explorer 4), offsetLeft (Internet Explorer 4), offsetParent (Internet Explorer 4), offsetTop (Internet Explorer 4), offsetWidth (Internet Explorer 4), outerHTML (Internet Explorer 4), outerText (Internet Explorer 4), parentElement (Internet Explorer 4), parentTextEdit (Internet Explorer 4), sourceIndex (Internet Explorer 4), style (Internet Explorer 4), tagName (Internet Explorer 4), title (Internet Explorer 4)

Methods

Methods Supported by Both Navigator and Internet Explorer

None.

Other Methods

click (Internet Explorer 4), contains (Internet Explorer 4), get-
Attribute (Internet Explorer 4), insertAdjacentHTML (Internet
Explorer 4), removeAttribute (Internet Explorer 4), scrollIntoView
(Internet Explorer 4), setAttribute (Internet Explorer 4)

Event

onclick (Internet Explorer 4), ondblclick (Internet Explorer 4),
ondragstart (Internet Explorer 4), onfilterchange (Internet Explorer 4),
onhelp (Internet Explorer 4), onkeydown (Internet Explorer 4), onkeypress (Internet Explorer 4), onkeyup (Internet Explorer 4), onmousedown (Internet Explorer 4), onmousemove (Internet Explorer 4),
onmouseout (Internet Explorer 4), onmouseover (Internet Explorer 4),
onmouseup (Internet Explorer 4), onselectstart (Internet Explorer 4)

Plugin

Browser Support: Navigator 3

The Plugin object represents a browser plugin. Plugin objects are
accessed via the plugins property of the navigator object.

Properties

Properties Supported by Both Navigator and Internet Explorer
None.

Other Properties
description (Navigator 3), filename (Navigator 3), length (Navigator 3),
name (Navigator 3)

Methods

This object does not define any methods.

Events

This object does not define any events.

PRE

Browser Support: Internet Explorer 4

Provides access to the HTML PRE tag.

Properties

Properties Supported by Both Navigator and Internet Explorer
None.

Other Properties

className (Internet Explorer 4), document (Internet Explorer 4), id (Internet Explorer 4), innerHTML (Internet Explorer 4), innerText (Internet Explorer 4), isTextEdit (Internet Explorer 4), lang (Internet Explorer 4), language (Internet Explorer 4), offsetHeight (Internet Explorer 4), offsetLeft (Internet Explorer 4), offsetParent (Internet Explorer 4), offsetTop (Internet Explorer 4), offsetWidth (Internet Explorer 4), outerHTML (Internet Explorer 4), outerText (Internet Explorer 4), parentElement (Internet Explorer 4), parentTextEdit (Internet Explorer 4), sourceIndex (Internet Explorer 4), style (Internet Explorer 4), tagName (Internet Explorer 4), title (Internet Explorer 4)

Methods

Methods Supported by Both Navigator and Internet Explorer
None.

Other Methods

click (Internet Explorer 4), contains (Internet Explorer 4), getAttribute (Internet Explorer 4), insertAdjacentHTML (Internet Explorer 4), insertAdjacentText (Internet Explorer 4), removeAttribute (Internet Explorer 4), scrollIntoView (Internet Explorer 4), setAttribute (Internet Explorer 4)

Events

onclick (Internet Explorer 4), ondblclick (Internet Explorer 4), ondragstart (Internet Explorer 4), onfilterchange (Internet Explorer 4),

onhelp (Internet Explorer 4), onkeydown (Internet Explorer 4), onkey-press (Internet Explorer 4), onkeyup (Internet Explorer 4), onmouse-down (Internet Explorer 4), onmousemove (Internet Explorer 4), onmouseout (Internet Explorer 4), onmouseover (Internet Explorer 4), onmouseup (Internet Explorer 4), onselectstart (Internet Explorer 4)

Q

Browser Support: Internet Explorer 4

Provides access to the HTML Q tag.

Properties

Properties Supported by Both Navigator and Internet Explorer
None.

Other Properties
className (Internet Explorer 4), document (Internet Explorer 4), id (Internet Explorer 4), innerHTML (Internet Explorer 4), innerText (Internet Explorer 4), isTextEdit (Internet Explorer 4), lang (Internet Explorer 4), language (Internet Explorer 4), offsetHeight (Internet Explorer 4), offsetLeft (Internet Explorer 4), offsetParent (Internet Explorer 4), offsetTop (Internet Explorer 4), offsetWidth (Internet Explorer 4), outerHTML (Internet Explorer 4), outerText (Internet Explorer 4), parentElement (Internet Explorer 4), parentTextEdit (Internet Explorer 4), sourceIndex (Internet Explorer 4), style (Internet Explorer 4), tagName (Internet Explorer 4), title (Internet Explorer 4)

Methods

Methods Supported by Both Navigator and Internet Explorer
None.

Other Methods
click (Internet Explorer 4), contains (Internet Explorer 4), get-Attribute (Internet Explorer 4), insertAdjacentHTML (Internet Explorer 4), insertAdjacentText (Internet Explorer 4), remove-Attribute (Internet Explorer 4), scrollIntoView (Internet Explorer 4), setAttribute (Internet Explorer 4)

Events

onclick (Internet Explorer 4), ondblclick (Internet Explorer 4), ondragstart (Internet Explorer 4), onfilterchange (Internet Explorer 4), onhelp (Internet Explorer 4), onkeydown (Internet Explorer 4), onkeypress (Internet Explorer 4), onkeyup (Internet Explorer 4), onmousedown (Internet Explorer 4), onmousemove (Internet Explorer 4), onmouseout (Internet Explorer 4), onmouseover (Internet Explorer 4), onmouseup (Internet Explorer 4), onselectstart (Internet Explorer 4)

Radio

Browser Support: Navigator 2, Internet Explorer 3

The basic Radio object was introduced in JavaScript 1. It has been updated with JavaScript 1.1 and 1.2.

Radio buttons are form fields that support the selection of exactly one choice from a set of one or more choices. They are INPUT elements that have their TYPE attribute set to RADIO. Radio buttons are grouped by setting their NAME attributes to the same values.

Properties

Properties Supported by Both Navigator and Internet Explorer

checked (Navigator 2, Internet Explorer 3)

Identifies via a Boolean value whether the radio button is checked or unchecked.

defaultChecked (Navigator 2, Internet Explorer 3)

The value of the button's CHECKED attribute.

form (Navigator 2, Internet Explorer 3)

Provides a reference to the form object that contains the button.

name (Navigator 2, Internet Explorer 3)

The value of the button's NAME attribute.

type (Navigator 3, Internet Explorer 4)

The value of the button's TYPE attribute.

value (Navigator 2, Internet Explorer 3)

The value of the button's VALUE attribute.

Other Properties

accessKey (Internet Explorer 4), className (Internet Explorer 4), dataFld (Internet Explorer 4), dataSrc (Internet Explorer 4), disabled (Internet Explorer 4), document (Internet Explorer 4), id (Internet Explorer 4), isTextEdit (Internet Explorer 4), lang (Internet Explorer 4), language (Internet Explorer 4), offsetHeight (Internet Explorer 4), offsetLeft (Internet Explorer 4), offsetParent (Internet Explorer 4), offsetTop (Internet Explorer 4), offsetWidth (Internet Explorer 4), outerText (Internet Explorer 4), parentElement (Internet Explorer 4), parentTextEdit (Internet Explorer 4), recordNumber (Internet Explorer 4), size (Internet Explorer 4), sourceIndex (Internet Explorer 4), style (Internet Explorer 4), tabIndex (Internet Explorer 4), tagName (Internet Explorer 4), title (Internet Explorer 4)

Methods

Methods Supported by Both Navigator and Internet Explorer

blur() (Navigator 2, Internet Explorer 3)

Removes input focus from the button.

click() (Navigator 2, Internet Explorer 3)

Simulates clicking of the button.

focus() (Navigator 2, Internet Explorer 3)

Moves input focus to the button.

Other Methods

contains (Internet Explorer 4), getAttribute (Internet Explorer 4), handleEvent (Navigator 4), insertAdjacentHTML (Internet Explorer 4), insertAdjacentText (Internet Explorer 4), removeAttribute (Internet Explorer 4), scrollIntoView (Internet Explorer 4), select (Internet Explorer 4), setAttribute (Internet Explorer 4)

Events

onblur (Navigator 3, Internet Explorer 4), onclick (Navigator 2, Internet Explorer 3), onfocus (Navigator 3, Internet Explorer 4), onafterupdate (Internet Explorer 4), onbeforeupdate (Internet Explorer 4), onchange (Internet Explorer 4), ondblclick (Internet Explorer 4), onerrorupdate (Internet Explorer 4), onhelp (Internet Explorer 4),

onkeydown (Internet Explorer 4), onkeypress (Internet Explorer 4),
onkeyup (Internet Explorer 4), onmousedown (Internet Explorer 4),
onmousemove (Internet Explorer 4), onmouseout (Internet Explorer 4),
onmouseover (Internet Explorer 4), onmouseup (Internet Explorer 4),
onresize (Internet Explorer 4), onselect (Internet Explorer 4)

RegExp (Regular Expression)

Browser Support: Navigator 4, Internet Explorer 4

The basic RegExp object was updated with JavaScript 1.3.

A core object that encapsulates a regular expression and provides
properties and methods for accessing the regular expression. Navigator
recognizes a single RegExp object for all regular expressions. Internet
Explorer documents the RegExp object and a separate *Regular Expression*
object that is created via the /pattern/flags constructor.

Constructors

/pattern/flags (Navigator 4)

Creates a RegExp object using the specified pattern and flags.

new RegExp("pattern"[, "flags"]) (Navigator 4)

Creates a RegExp object using the specified pattern and flags.

Properties

Properties Supported by Both Navigator and Internet Explorer

$1 through $9 (Navigator 4, Internet Explorer 4)

Parenthesized substring matches.

input (Navigator 4, Internet Explorer 4)

The string against which a regular expression is matched.

lastIndex (Navigator 4, Internet Explorer 4)

The index at which to start the next match.

source (Navigator 4, Internet Explorer 4)

The pattern to be matched.

Other Properties

$ (Navigator 4), $ (Navigator 4), $' (Navigator 4), $* (Navigator 4), $_ (Navigator 4), $` (Navigator 4), constructor (Navigator 4), global (Navigator 4), ignoreCase (Navigator 4), index (Internet Explorer 4), lastMatch (Navigator 4), lastParen (Navigator 4), leftContext (Navigator 4), multiline (Navigator 4), prototype (Navigator 4), rightContext (Navigator 4)

Methods

Methods Supported by Both Navigator and Internet Explorer

compile(pattern[, flags]) (Navigator 4, Internet Explorer 4)

Compiles the regular expression.

exec([string]) (Navigator 4, Internet Explorer 4)

Executes the regular expression with the specified string.

test([string]) (Navigator 4, Internet Explorer 4)

Tests the regular expression with the specified string.

Other Methods

toSource (Navigator 4.06), toString (Navigator 4), valueOf (Navigator 4)

Events

This object does not define any events.

Reset

Browser Support: Navigator 2, Internet Explorer 3

The basic Reset object was introduced in JavaScript 1. It has been updated with JavaScript 1.1 and 1.2.

Reset buttons are form fields that reset form fields back to their original values. They are INPUT elements that have their TYPE attribute set to RESET.

Properties

Properties Supported by Both Navigator and Internet Explorer

form (Navigator 2, Internet Explorer 3)

Provides a reference to the form object that contains the button.

name (Navigator 2, Internet Explorer 3)

The value of the button's NAME attribute.

type (Navigator 3, Internet Explorer 4)

The value of the button's TYPE attribute.

value (Navigator 2, Internet Explorer 3)

The value of the button's VALUE attribute.

Other Properties

accessKey (Internet Explorer 4), className (Internet Explorer 4), disabled (Internet Explorer 4), document (Internet Explorer 4), id (Internet Explorer 4), isTextEdit (Internet Explorer 4), lang (Internet Explorer 4), language (Internet Explorer 4), offsetHeight (Internet Explorer 4), offsetLeft (Internet Explorer 4), offsetParent (Internet Explorer 4), offsetTop (Internet Explorer 4), offsetWidth (Internet Explorer 4), outerHTML (Internet Explorer 4), outerText (Internet Explorer 4), parentElement (Internet Explorer 4), parentTextEdit (Internet Explorer 4), recordNumber (Internet Explorer 4), sourceIndex (Internet Explorer 4), style (Internet Explorer 4), tabIndex (Internet Explorer 4), tagName (Internet Explorer 4), title (Internet Explorer 4)

Methods

Methods Supported by Both Navigator and Internet Explorer

blur() (Navigator 2, Internet Explorer 3)

Removes input focus from the button.

click() (Navigator 2, Internet Explorer 3)

Simulates clicking of the button.

focus() (Navigator 2, Internet Explorer 3)

Moves input focus to the button.

Other Methods

contains (Internet Explorer 4), getAttribute (Internet Explorer 4), handleEvent (Navigator 4), insertAdjacentHTML (Internet Explorer 4), insertAdjacentText (Internet Explorer 4), removeAttribute (Internet Explorer 4), scrollIntoView (Internet Explorer 4), select (Internet Explorer 4), setAttribute (Internet Explorer 4)

Events

onblur (Navigator 3, Internet Explorer 4), onclick (Navigator 2, Internet Explorer 3), onfocus (Navigator 3, Internet Explorer 4), ondblclick (Internet Explorer 4), onfilterchange (Internet Explorer 4), onhelp (Internet Explorer 4), onkeydown (Internet Explorer 4), onkeypress (Internet Explorer 4), onkeyup (Internet Explorer 4), onmousedown (Internet Explorer 4), onmousemove (Internet Explorer 4), onmouseout (Internet Explorer 4), onmouseover (Internet Explorer 4), onmouseup (Internet Explorer 4), onresize (Internet Explorer 4), onselect (Internet Explorer 4)

RT

Browser Support: Internet Explorer 5

Provides access to the Microsoft RT tag.

Properties

Properties Supported by Both Navigator and Internet Explorer

None.

Other Properties

accessKey (Internet Explorer 5), canHaveHTML (Internet Explorer 5), className (Internet Explorer 5), contentEditable (Internet Explorer 5), dir (Internet Explorer 5), disabled (Internet Explorer 5), hideFocus (Internet Explorer 5), id (Internet Explorer 5), innerHTML (Internet Explorer 5), innerText (Internet Explorer 5), isContentEditable (Internet Explorer 5), isDisabled (Internet Explorer 5), lang (Internet Explorer 5), language (Internet Explorer 5), name (Internet Explorer 5), offsetHeight (Internet Explorer 5), offsetLeft (Internet Explorer 5), offsetParent (Internet Explorer 5), offsetTop (Internet Explorer 5), offsetWidth (Internet Explorer 5), outerHTML (Internet Explorer 5), outerText (Internet Explorer 5), parentElement (Internet Explorer 5), readyState (Internet Explorer 5), scopeName (Internet Explorer 5), tabIndex (Internet Explorer 5), tagName (Internet Explorer 5), tagUrn (Internet Explorer 5), title (Internet Explorer 5)

Methods

Methods Supported by Both Navigator and Internet Explorer
None.

Other Methods
addBehavior (Internet Explorer 5), blur (Internet Explorer 5), componentFromPoint (Internet Explorer 5), fireEvent (Internet Explorer 5), focus (Internet Explorer 5), getExpression (Internet Explorer 5), removeBehavior (Internet Explorer 5), removeExpression (Internet Explorer 5), setActive (Internet Explorer 5), setExpression (Internet Explorer 5)

Events

onafterupdate (Internet Explorer 5), onbeforecut (Internet Explorer 5), onbeforefocusenter (Internet Explorer 5), onbeforefocusleave (Internet Explorer 5), onbeforepaste (Internet Explorer 5), onbeforeupdate (Internet Explorer 5), onblur (Internet Explorer 5), onclick (Internet Explorer 5), oncontextmenu (Internet Explorer 5), oncontrolselect (Internet Explorer 5), oncut (Internet Explorer 5), onblclick (Internet Explorer 5), ondragstart (Internet Explorer 5), onerrorupdate (Internet Explorer 5), onfilterchange (Internet Explorer 5), onfocus (Internet Explorer 5), onfocusenter (Internet Explorer 5), onfocusleave (Internet Explorer 5), onhelp (Internet Explorer 5), onkeydown (Internet Explorer 5), onkeypress (Internet Explorer 5), onkeyup (Internet Explorer 5), onmousedown (Internet Explorer 5), onmouseenter (Internet Explorer 5), onmouseleave (Internet Explorer 5), onmousemove (Internet Explorer 5), onmouseout (Internet Explorer 5), onmouseover (Internet Explorer 5), onmouseup (Internet Explorer 5), onpaste (Internet Explorer 5), onreadystatechange (Internet Explorer 5), onresizeend (Internet Explorer 5), onresizestart (Internet Explorer 5), onselectstart (Internet Explorer 5)

RUBY

Browser Support: Internet Explorer 5

Provides access to the Microsoft RUBY tag.

Properties

Properties Supported by Both Navigator and Internet Explorer

None.

Other Properties

accessKey (Internet Explorer 5), canHaveHTML (Internet Explorer 5), className (Internet Explorer 5), contentEditable (Internet Explorer 5), dir (Internet Explorer 5), disabled (Internet Explorer 5), hideFocus (Internet Explorer 5), id (Internet Explorer 5), innerHTML (Internet Explorer 5), innerText (Internet Explorer 5), isContentEditable (Internet Explorer 5), isDisabled (Internet Explorer 5), lang (Internet Explorer 5), language (Internet Explorer 5), name (Internet Explorer 5), offsetHeight (Internet Explorer 5), offsetLeft (Internet Explorer 5), offsetParent (Internet Explorer 5), offsetTop (Internet Explorer 5), offsetWidth (Internet Explorer 5), outerHTML (Internet Explorer 5), outerText (Internet Explorer 5), parentElement (Internet Explorer 5), readyState (Internet Explorer 5), recordNumber (Internet Explorer 5), scopeName (Internet Explorer 5), tabIndex (Internet Explorer 5), tagName (Internet Explorer 5), tagUrn (Internet Explorer 5), title (Internet Explorer 5)

Methods

Methods Supported by Both Navigator and Internet Explorer

None.

Other Methods

addBehavior (Internet Explorer 5), blur (Internet Explorer 5), componentFromPoint (Internet Explorer 5), fireEvent (Internet Explorer 5),

focus (Internet Explorer 5), getExpression (Internet Explorer 5),
removeBehavior (Internet Explorer 5), removeExpression (Internet
Explorer 5), setActive (Internet Explorer 5), setExpression (Internet Explorer 5)

Events

onafterupdate (Internet Explorer 5), onbeforecut (Internet Explorer 5),
onbeforefocusenter (Internet Explorer 5), onbeforefocusleave
(Internet Explorer 5), onbeforepaste (Internet Explorer 5), onbeforeupdate (Internet Explorer 5), onblur (Internet Explorer 5), onclick
(Internet Explorer 5), oncontextmenu (Internet Explorer 5), oncontrolselect (Internet Explorer 5), oncut (Internet Explorer 5), ondblclick
(Internet Explorer 5), ondragstart (Internet Explorer 5), onerrorupdate (Internet Explorer 5), onfilterchange (Internet Explorer 5),
onfocus (Internet Explorer 5), onfocusenter (Internet Explorer 5),
onfocusleave (Internet Explorer 5), onhelp (Internet Explorer 5),
onkeydown (Internet Explorer 5), onkeypress (Internet Explorer 5),
onkeyup (Internet Explorer 5), onmousedown (Internet Explorer 5),
onmouseenter (Internet Explorer 5), onmouseleave (Internet Explorer 5),
onmousemove (Internet Explorer 5), onmouseout (Internet Explorer 5),
onmouseover (Internet Explorer 5), onmouseup (Internet Explorer 5),
onpaste (Internet Explorer 5), onreadystatechange (Internet Explorer 5),
onresizeend (Internet Explorer 5), onresizestart (Internet Explorer 5),
onselectstart (Internet Explorer 5)

rule

Browser Support: Internet Explorer 5

Provides access to rules that apply CSS attributes, styles that get
applied to an HTML page, to HTML elements.

Properties

Properties Supported by Both Navigator and Internet Explorer
None.

Other Properties

readOnly (Internet Explorer 5), runtimeStyle (Internet Explorer 5), selectorText (Internet Explorer 5), style (Internet Explorer 5)

Methods

This object does not define any methods.

Events

This object does not define any events.

runtimeStyle

Browser Support: Internet Explorer 5

Provides access to CSS styles (Cascading Style Sheets) that override global styles.

Properties

Properties Supported by Both Navigator and Internet Explorer

None.

Other Properties

background (Internet Explorer 5), backgroundAttachment (Internet Explorer 5), backgroundColor (Internet Explorer 5), backgroundImage (Internet Explorer 5), backgroundPosition (Internet Explorer 5), backgroundPositionX (Internet Explorer 5), backgroundPositionY (Internet Explorer 5), backgroundRepeat (Internet Explorer 5), border (Internet Explorer 5), borderBottom (Internet Explorer 5), borderBottomColor (Internet Explorer 5), borderBottomStyle (Internet Explorer 5), borderBottomWidth (Internet Explorer 5), borderColor (Internet Explorer 5), borderLeft (Internet Explorer 5), borderLeftColor (Internet Explorer 5), borderLeftStyle (Internet Explorer 5), borderLeftWidth (Internet Explorer 5), borderRight (Internet Explorer 5), borderRightColor (Internet Explorer 5), borderRightStyle (Internet Explorer 5), borderRightWidth (Internet Explorer 5), borderStyle (Internet Explorer 5), borderTop (Internet Explorer 5), borderTopColor (Internet Explorer 5), borderTopStyle (Internet

Explorer 5), borderTopWidth (Internet Explorer 5), borderWidth (Internet Explorer 5), bottom (Internet Explorer 5), clear (Internet Explorer 5), clip (Internet Explorer 5), color (Internet Explorer 5), cssText (Internet Explorer 5), cursor (Internet Explorer 5), direction (Internet Explorer 5), filter (Internet Explorer 5), font (Internet Explorer 5), fontFamily (Internet Explorer 5), fontSize (Internet Explorer 5), fontStyle (Internet Explorer 5), fontVariant (Internet Explorer 5), fontWeight (Internet Explorer 5), height (Internet Explorer 5), layoutFlow (Internet Explorer 5), layoutGrid (Internet Explorer 5), layoutGridChar (Internet Explorer 5), layoutGridCharSpacing (Internet Explorer 5), layoutGridLine (Internet Explorer 5), layoutGridMode (Internet Explorer 5), layoutGridType (Internet Explorer 5), left (Internet Explorer 5), letterSpacing (Internet Explorer 5), lineHeight (Internet Explorer 5), listStyle (Internet Explorer 5), listStyleImage (Internet Explorer 5), listStylePosition (Internet Explorer 5), listStyleType (Internet Explorer 5), margin (Internet Explorer 5), marginBottom (Internet Explorer 5), marginLeft (Internet Explorer 5), marginRight (Internet Explorer 5), marginTop (Internet Explorer 5), overflow (Internet Explorer 5), overflowX (Internet Explorer 5), overflowY (Internet Explorer 5), pageBreakAfter (Internet Explorer 5), pageBreakBefore (Internet Explorer 5), pixelBottom (Internet Explorer 5), pixelHeight (Internet Explorer 5), pixelLeft (Internet Explorer 5), pixelRight (Internet Explorer 5), pixelTop (Internet Explorer 5), pixelWidth (Internet Explorer 5), posBottom (Internet Explorer 5), posHeight (Internet Explorer 5), position (Internet Explorer 5), posLeft (Internet Explorer 5), posRight (Internet Explorer 5), posTop (Internet Explorer 5), posWidth (Internet Explorer 5), rectangular (Internet Explorer 5), right (Internet Explorer 5), scrollbar3dLightColor (Internet Explorer 5), scrollbarArrowColor (Internet Explorer 5), scrollbarBaseColor (Internet Explorer 5), scrollbarDarkShadowColor (Internet Explorer 5), scrollbarFaceColor (Internet Explorer 5), scrollbarHighlightColor (Internet Explorer 5), scrollbarShadowColor (Internet Explorer 5), styleFloat (Internet Explorer 5), tableLayout (Internet Explorer 5), textAlign (Internet Explorer 5), textDecoration (Internet Explorer 5), textDecorationLineThrough (Internet Explorer 5), textDecorationNone (Internet Explorer 5), textDecorationOverline (Internet Explorer 5), textDecorationUnderline (Internet Explorer 5), textIndent (Internet Explorer 5), textTransform (Internet Explorer 5), textUnderlinePosition (Internet Explorer 5), top (Internet Explorer 5), unicodeBidi (Internet Explorer 5), verticalAlign (Internet Explorer 5), visibility (Internet Explorer 5), width (Internet Explorer 5), word-Wrap (Internet Explorer 5), writingMode (Internet Explorer 5), zIndex (Internet Explorer 5), zoom (Internet Explorer 5)

Methods

This object does not define any methods.

Events

This object does not define any events.

S

Browser Support: Internet Explorer 4

Provides access to the HTML S tag.

Properties

Properties Supported by Both Navigator and Internet Explorer

None.

Other Properties

className (Internet Explorer 4), document (Internet Explorer 4), id (Internet Explorer 4), innerHTML (Internet Explorer 4), innerText (Internet Explorer 4), isTextEdit (Internet Explorer 4), lang (Internet Explorer 4), language (Internet Explorer 4), offsetHeight (Internet Explorer 4), offsetLeft (Internet Explorer 4), offsetParent (Internet Explorer 4), offsetTop (Internet Explorer 4), offsetWidth (Internet Explorer 4), outerHTML (Internet Explorer 4), outerText (Internet Explorer 4), parentElement (Internet Explorer 4), parentTextEdit (Internet Explorer 4), sourceIndex (Internet Explorer 4), style (Internet Explorer 4), tagName (Internet Explorer 4), title (Internet Explorer 4)

Methods

Methods Supported by Both Navigator and Internet Explorer

None.

Other Methods

click (Internet Explorer 4), contains (Internet Explorer 4), get-Attribute (Internet Explorer 4), insertAdjacentHTML (Internet Explorer 4), insertAdjacentText (Internet Explorer 4), remove-Attribute (Internet Explorer 4), scrollIntoView (Internet Explorer 4), setAttribute (Internet Explorer 4)

Events

onclick (Internet Explorer 4), ondblclick (Internet Explorer 4), ondragstart (Internet Explorer 4), onfilterchange (Internet Explorer 4), onhelp (Internet Explorer 4), onkeydown (Internet Explorer 4), onkeypress (Internet Explorer 4), onkeyup (Internet Explorer 4), onmousedown (Internet Explorer 4), onmousemove (Internet Explorer 4), onmouseout (Internet Explorer 4), onmouseover (Internet Explorer 4), onmouseup (Internet Explorer 4), onselectstart (Internet Explorer 4)

SAMP

Browser Support: Internet Explorer 4

Provides access to the HTML SAMP tag.

Properties

Properties Supported by Both Navigator and Internet Explorer

None.

Other Properties

className (Internet Explorer 4), document (Internet Explorer 4), id (Internet Explorer 4), innerHTML (Internet Explorer 4), innerText (Internet Explorer 4), isTextEdit (Internet Explorer 4), lang (Internet Explorer 4), language (Internet Explorer 4), offsetHeight (Internet Explorer 4), offsetLeft (Internet Explorer 4), offsetParent (Internet Explorer 4), offsetTop (Internet Explorer 4), offsetWidth (Internet Explorer 4), outerHTML (Internet Explorer 4), outerText (Internet Explorer 4), parentElement (Internet Explorer 4), parentTextEdit (Internet Explorer 4), sourceIndex (Internet Explorer 4), style (Internet Explorer 4), tagName (Internet Explorer 4), title (Internet Explorer 4)

Methods

Methods Supported by Both Navigator and Internet Explorer
None.

Other Methods
click (Internet Explorer 4), contains (Internet Explorer 4), getAttribute (Internet Explorer 4), insertAdjacentHTML (Internet Explorer 4), insertAdjacentText (Internet Explorer 4), removeAttribute (Internet Explorer 4), scrollIntoView (Internet Explorer 4), setAttribute (Internet Explorer 4)

Events

onclick (Internet Explorer 4), ondblclick (Internet Explorer 4), ondragstart (Internet Explorer 4), onfilterchange (Internet Explorer 4), onhelp (Internet Explorer 4), onkeydown (Internet Explorer 4), onkeypress (Internet Explorer 4), onkeyup (Internet Explorer 4), onmousedown (Internet Explorer 4), onmousemove (Internet Explorer 4), onmouseout (Internet Explorer 4), onmouseover (Internet Explorer 4), onmouseup (Internet Explorer 4), onselectstart (Internet Explorer 4)

screen

Browser Support: Navigator 4, Internet Explorer 4

Provides access to the parameters of the user's display monitor.

Properties

Properties Supported by Both Navigator and Internet Explorer
colorDepth (Navigator 4, Internet Explorer 4)

The number of colors supported by the current color palette.

height (Navigator 4, Internet Explorer 4)

The height of the screen.

width (Navigator 4, Internet Explorer 4)

The width of the screen.

Other Properties

availHeight (Navigator 4), availLeft (Navigator 4), availTop (Navigator 4), availWidth (Navigator 4), bufferDepth (Internet Explorer 4), pixelDepth (Navigator 4), updateInterval (Internet Explorer 4)

Methods

This object does not define any methods.

Events

This object does not define any events.

SCRIPT

Browser Support: Internet Explorer 4

Provides access to the HTML SCRIPT tag.

Properties

Properties Supported by Both Navigator and Internet Explorer

None.

Other Properties

className (Internet Explorer 4), defer (Internet Explorer 4), document (Internet Explorer 4), event (Internet Explorer 4), htmlFor (Internet Explorer 4), id (Internet Explorer 4), innerHTML (Internet Explorer 4), innerText (Internet Explorer 4), isTextEdit (Internet Explorer 4), language (Internet Explorer 4), parentElement (Internet Explorer 4), parentTextEdit (Internet Explorer 4), readyState (Internet Explorer 4), sourceIndex (Internet Explorer 4), src (Internet Explorer 4), style (Internet Explorer 4), tagName (Internet Explorer 4), text (Internet Explorer 4), title (Internet Explorer 4), type (Internet Explorer 4)

Methods

Methods Supported by Both Navigator and Internet Explorer
None.

Other Methods
contains (Internet Explorer 4), getAttribute (Internet Explorer 4),
insertAdjacentHTML (Internet Explorer 4), insertAdjacentText
(Internet Explorer 4), removeAttribute (Internet Explorer 4), setAttribute (Internet Explorer 4)

Events

onerror (Internet Explorer 4), onload (Internet Explorer 4), onreadystatechange (Internet Explorer 4)

Select

Browser Support: Navigator 2, Internet Explorer 3

The basic Select object was introduced in JavaScript 1. It has been
updated with JavaScript 1.1 and 1.2.

A select field provides an HTML menu of choices to users. The SELECT
tags enclose zero or more OPTION tags. The OPTION tags specify the menu
choices and are represented by OPTION objects in JavaScript.

Properties

Properties Supported by Both Navigator and Internet Explorer
form (Navigator 2, Internet Explorer 3)

Provides a reference to the form object that contains the select field.
length (Navigator 2, Internet Explorer 3)

Identifies the number of options.
name (Navigator 2, Internet Explorer 3)

The value of the select field's NAME attribute.
options (Navigator 2, Internet Explorer 3)

An array that identifies the Option objects of the select element.
The objects appear in the same order that they do in the source HTML.

selectedIndex (Navigator 2, Internet Explorer 3)

Identifies (by index) the first selected option in the select element. This property is set to −1 if no options are selected.

type (Navigator 3, Internet Explorer 4)

If the select field's MULTIPLE attribute is set, then type has the value *select-multiple*. Otherwise, it is set to *select-one*.

Other Properties

accessKey (Internet Explorer 4), className (Internet Explorer 4), dataFld (Internet Explorer 4), dataSrc (Internet Explorer 4), disabled (Internet Explorer 4), document (Internet Explorer 4), id (Internet Explorer 4), isTextEdit (Internet Explorer 4), lang (Internet Explorer 4), language (Internet Explorer 4), multiple (Internet Explorer 4), offsetHeight (Internet Explorer 4), offsetLeft (Internet Explorer 4), offsetParent (Internet Explorer 4), offsetTop (Internet Explorer 4), offsetWidth (Internet Explorer 4), outerHTML (Internet Explorer 4), outerText (Internet Explorer 4), parentElement (Internet Explorer 4), parentTextEdit (Internet Explorer 4), recordNumber (Internet Explorer 4), size (Internet Explorer 4), sourceIndex (Internet Explorer 4), style (Internet Explorer 4), tabIndex (Internet Explorer 4), tagName (Internet Explorer 4), value (Internet Explorer 4)

Methods

Methods Supported by Both Navigator and Internet Explorer

blur() (Navigator 2, Internet Explorer 3)

Removes input focus from the button.

focus() (Navigator 2, Internet Explorer 3)

Moves input focus to the button.

Other Methods

add (Internet Explorer 4), click (Internet Explorer 4), contains (Internet Explorer 4), getAttribute (Internet Explorer 4), handleEvent (Navigator 4), insertAdjacentHTML (Internet Explorer 4), insertAdjacentText (Internet Explorer 4), item (Internet Explorer 4), remove (Internet Explorer 4), removeAttribute (Internet Explorer 4), scrollIntoView (Internet Explorer 4), setAttribute (Internet Explorer 4), tags (Internet Explorer 4)

Events

onblur (Navigator 2, Internet Explorer 3), onChange (Navigator 2, Internet Explorer 3), onfocus (Navigator 2, Internet Explorer 3), onafterupdate (Internet Explorer 4), onbeforeupdate (Internet Explorer 4), onclick (Internet Explorer 4), ondblclick (Internet Explorer 4), ondragstart (Internet Explorer 4), onerrorupdate (Internet Explorer 4), onfilterchange (Internet Explorer 4), onhelp (Internet Explorer 4), onkeydown (Internet Explorer 4), onkeypress (Internet Explorer 4), onkeyup (Internet Explorer 4), onmousedown (Internet Explorer 4), onmousemove (Internet Explorer 4), onmouseout (Internet Explorer 4), onmouseover (Internet Explorer 4), onmouseup (Internet Explorer 4), onresize (Internet Explorer 4), onrowenter (Internet Explorer 4), onrowexit (Internet Explorer 4), onselectstart (Internet Explorer 4)

selection

Browser Support: Internet Explorer 4

Provides access to text that is currently selected by the user.

Properties

Properties Supported by Both Navigator and Internet Explorer

None.

Other Properties

type (Internet Explorer 4)

Methods

Methods Supported by Both Navigator and Internet Explorer

None.

Other Methods

clear (Internet Explorer 4), createRange (Internet Explorer 4), empty (Internet Explorer 4)

Events

This object does not define any events.

SMALL

Browser Support: Internet Explorer 4

Provides access to the HTML SMALL tag.

Properties

Properties Supported by Both Navigator and Internet Explorer

None.

Other Properties

className (Internet Explorer 4), document (Internet Explorer 4), id (Internet Explorer 4), innerHTML (Internet Explorer 4), innerText (Internet Explorer 4), isTextEdit (Internet Explorer 4), lang (Internet Explorer 4), language (Internet Explorer 4), offsetHeight (Internet Explorer 4), offsetLeft (Internet Explorer 4), offsetParent (Internet Explorer 4), offsetTop (Internet Explorer 4), offsetWidth (Internet Explorer 4), outerHTML (Internet Explorer 4), outerText (Internet Explorer 4), parentElement (Internet Explorer 4), parentTextEdit (Internet Explorer 4), sourceIndex (Internet Explorer 4), style (Internet Explorer 4), tagName (Internet Explorer 4), title (Internet Explorer 4)

Methods

Methods Supported by Both Navigator and Internet Explorer

None.

Other Methods

click (Internet Explorer 4), contains (Internet Explorer 4), getAttribute (Internet Explorer 4), insertAdjacentHTML (Internet Explorer 4), insertAdjacentText (Internet Explorer 4), removeAttribute (Internet Explorer 4), scrollIntoView (Internet Explorer 4), setAttribute (Internet Explorer 4)

Events

onclick (Internet Explorer 4), ondblclick (Internet Explorer 4), ondragstart (Internet Explorer 4), onfilterchange (Internet Explorer 4), onhelp (Internet Explorer 4), onkeydown (Internet Explorer 4), onkeypress (Internet Explorer 4), onkeyup (Internet Explorer 4), onmousedown (Internet Explorer 4), onmousemove (Internet Explorer 4), onmouseout (Internet Explorer 4), onmouseover (Internet Explorer 4), onmouseup (Internet Explorer 4), onselectstart (Internet Explorer 4)

SPAN

Browser Support: Internet Explorer 4

Provides access to the HTML SPAN tag.

Properties

Properties Supported by Both Navigator and Internet Explorer

None.

Other Properties

className (Internet Explorer 4), dataFld (Internet Explorer 4), dataFormatAs (Internet Explorer 4), dataSrc (Internet Explorer 4), document (Internet Explorer 4), id (Internet Explorer 4), innerText (Internet Explorer 4), isTextEdit (Internet Explorer 4), lang (Internet Explorer 4), language (Internet Explorer 4), offsetHeight (Internet Explorer 4), offsetLeft (Internet Explorer 4), offsetParent (Internet Explorer 4), offsetTop (Internet Explorer 4), offsetWidth (Internet Explorer 4), outerText (Internet Explorer 4), parentElement (Internet Explorer 4), parentTextEdit (Internet Explorer 4), scrollHeight (Internet Explorer 4), scrollLeft (Internet Explorer 4), scrollTop (Internet Explorer 4), scrollWidth (Internet Explorer 4), sourceIndex (Internet Explorer 4), style (Internet Explorer 4), tagName (Internet Explorer 4), title (Internet Explorer 4)

Methods

Methods Supported by Both Navigator and Internet Explorer
None.

Other Methods
blur (Internet Explorer 4), click (Internet Explorer 4), contains (Internet Explorer 4), focus (Internet Explorer 4), getAttribute (Internet Explorer 4), insertAdjacentHTML (Internet Explorer 4), insertAdjacentText (Internet Explorer 4), removeAttribute (Internet Explorer 4), scrollIntoView (Internet Explorer 4), setAttribute (Internet Explorer 4)

Events

onblur (Internet Explorer 4), onclick (Internet Explorer 4), ondblclick (Internet Explorer 4), ondragstart (Internet Explorer 4), onfilterchange (Internet Explorer 4), onfocus (Internet Explorer 4), onhelp (Internet Explorer 4), onkeydown (Internet Explorer 4), onkeypress (Internet Explorer 4), onkeyup (Internet Explorer 4), onmousedown (Internet Explorer 4), onmousemove (Internet Explorer 4), onmouseout (Internet Explorer 4), onmouseover (Internet Explorer 4), onmouseup (Internet Explorer 4), onscroll (Internet Explorer 4), onselectstart (Internet Explorer 4)

STRIKE

Browser Support: Internet Explorer 4

Provides access to the HTML STRIKE tag.

Properties

Properties Supported by Both Navigator and Internet Explorer
None.

Other Properties
className (Internet Explorer 4), document (Internet Explorer 4), id (Internet Explorer 4), innerHTML (Internet Explorer 4), innerText

(Internet Explorer 4), isTextEdit (Internet Explorer 4), lang (Internet Explorer 4), language (Internet Explorer 4), offsetHeight (Internet Explorer 4), offsetLeft (Internet Explorer 4), offsetParent (Internet Explorer 4), offsetTop (Internet Explorer 4), offsetWidth (Internet Explorer 4), outerHTML (Internet Explorer 4), outerText (Internet Explorer 4), parentElement (Internet Explorer 4), parentTextEdit (Internet Explorer 4), sourceIndex (Internet Explorer 4), style (Internet Explorer 4), tagName (Internet Explorer 4), title (Internet Explorer 4)

Methods

Methods Supported by Both Navigator and Internet Explorer

None.

Other Methods

click (Internet Explorer 4), contains (Internet Explorer 4), getAttribute (Internet Explorer 4), insertAdjacentHTML (Internet Explorer 4), insertAdjacentText (Internet Explorer 4), removeAttribute (Internet Explorer 4), scrollIntoView (Internet Explorer 4), setAttribute (Internet Explorer 4)

Events

onclick (Internet Explorer 4), ondblclick (Internet Explorer 4), ondragstart (Internet Explorer 4), onfilterchange (Internet Explorer 4), onhelp (Internet Explorer 4), onkeydown (Internet Explorer 4), onkeypress (Internet Explorer 4), onkeyup (Internet Explorer 4), onmousedown (Internet Explorer 4), onmousemove (Internet Explorer 4), onmouseout (Internet Explorer 4), onmouseover (Internet Explorer 4), onmouseup (Internet Explorer 4), onselectstart (Internet Explorer 4)

String

Browser Support: Navigator 2, Internet Explorer 3

The basic String object was introduced in JavaScript 1. It has been updated with JavaScript 1.1, 1.2, and 1.3.

The String object is a core object that provides an object wrapper for string values.

Constructors

```
new String(string)
```

Constructs a `String` object from the string value.

Properties

Properties Supported by Both Navigator and Internet Explorer

`constructor` (Navigator 3, Internet Explorer 4)

References the constructor used to create the object.

`length` (Navigator 2, Internet Explorer 3)

Identifies the length of the associated string.

`prototype` (Navigator 2, Internet Explorer 4)

Provides the capability to define additional properties.

Methods

Methods Supported by Both Navigator and Internet Explorer

`anchor(attribute)` (Navigator 2, Internet Explorer 3)

Creates an HTML anchor with the specified name attribute.

`big()` (Navigator 2, Internet Explorer 3)

Renders a string using the `BIG` tags.

`blink()` (Navigator 2, Internet Explorer 3)

Renders a string using the `BLINK` tags.

`bold()` (Navigator 2, Internet Explorer 3)

Renders a string using the `BOLD` tags.

`charAt(index)` (Navigator 2, Internet Explorer 3)

Returns the character at the specified index.

`charCodeAt([index])` (Navigator 4, Internet Explorer 4)

Returns a number corresponding to the Unicode character at the specified index.

`concat(string1[,...,stringN])` (Navigator 4, Internet Explorer 4)

Concatenates strings 1 through N to the current string.

fixed() (Navigator 2, Internet Explorer 3)

Renders a string using the TT tags.

fontcolor(color) (Navigator 2, Internet Explorer 3)

Displays the string with the specified color.

fontsize(size) (Navigator 2, Internet Explorer 3)

Displays the string with the specified font size.

fromCharCode(num1,...,numN) (Navigator 4, Internet Explorer 4)

Returns a string created from the Unicode value sequence.

indexOf(searchValue[,index]) (Navigator 2, Internet Explorer 3)

Returns the index of the first occurrence of the search value.

italics() (Navigator 2, Internet Explorer 3)

Renders a string using the I tags.

lastIndexOf(searchValue[,index]) (Navigator 2, Internet Explorer 3)

Returns the index of the last occurrence of the search value.

link(attribute) (Navigator 2, Internet Explorer 3)

Creates a hypertext link with the specified HREF attribute.

match(regexp) (Navigator 4, Internet Explorer 4)

Matches the regular expression against the string.

replace(regexp, newSubstring) (Navigator 4, Internet Explorer 4)

Matches the regular expression and replaces the matches with the new string.

search(regexp) (Navigator 4, Internet Explorer 4)

Searches the string for the regular expression.

slice(beginslice[, endSlice]) (Navigator 2, Internet Explorer 3)

Returns a slice of the string.

small() (Navigator 2, Internet Explorer 3)

Renders a string using the SMALL tags.

split([separator][, limit]) (Navigator 3, Internet Explorer 4)

Splits the string into an array of strings based on the specified separator.

strike() (Navigator 2, Internet Explorer 3)

Renders a string using the STRIKE tags.

sub() (Navigator 2, Internet Explorer 3)

Renders a string using the SUB tags.

substr(start[, length]) (Navigator 2, Internet Explorer 3)
   Returns a substring of the string.
substring(indexA, indexB) (Navigator 2, Internet Explorer 3)
   Returns a substring of the string.
sup() (Navigator 2, Internet Explorer 3)
   Renders a string using the SUP tags.
toLowerCase() (Navigator 2, Internet Explorer 3)
   Returns a lowercase version of the string.
toString() (Navigator 3, Internet Explorer 4)
   Returns a string version of the object.
toUpperCase() (Navigator 2, Internet Explorer 3)
   Returns an uppercase version of the string.
valueOf() (Navigator 3, Internet Explorer 4)
   Returns the primitive value corresponding to the object.

Other Methods

replace (Navigator 4.06), toSource (Navigator 4.06)

Events

No events are defined for this object.

STRONG

Browser Support: Internet Explorer 4
   Provides access to the HTML STRONG tag.

Properties

Properties Supported by Both Navigator and Internet Explorer
None.

Other Properties

className (Internet Explorer 4), document (Internet Explorer 4),
id (Internet Explorer 4), innerHTML (Internet Explorer 4), innerText
(Internet Explorer 4), isTextEdit (Internet Explorer 4), lang (Inter-

net Explorer 4), `language` (Internet Explorer 4), `offsetHeight` (Internet Explorer 4), `offsetLeft` (Internet Explorer 4), `offsetParent` (Internet Explorer 4), `offsetTop` (Internet Explorer 4), `offsetWidth` (Internet Explorer 4), `outerHTML` (Internet Explorer 4), `outerText` (Internet Explorer 4), `parentElement` (Internet Explorer 4), `parentTextEdit` (Internet Explorer 4), `sourceIndex` (Internet Explorer 4), `style` (Internet Explorer 4), `tagName` (Internet Explorer 4), `title` (Internet Explorer 4)

Methods

Methods Supported by Both Navigator and Internet Explorer
None.

Other Methods
`click` (Internet Explorer 4), `contains` (Internet Explorer 4), `getAttribute` (Internet Explorer 4), `insertAdjacentHTML` (Internet Explorer 4), `insertAdjacentText` (Internet Explorer 4), `removeAttribute` (Internet Explorer 4), `scrollIntoView` (Internet Explorer 4), `setAttribute` (Internet Explorer 4)

Events

`onclick` (Internet Explorer 4), `ondblclick` (Internet Explorer 4), `ondragstart` (Internet Explorer 4), `onfilterchange` (Internet Explorer 4), `onhelp` (Internet Explorer 4), `onkeydown` (Internet Explorer 4), `onkeypress` (Internet Explorer 4), `onkeyup` (Internet Explorer 4), `onmousedown` (Internet Explorer 4), `onmousemove` (Internet Explorer 4), `onmouseout` (Internet Explorer 4), `onmouseover` (Internet Explorer 4), `onmouseup` (Internet Explorer 4), `onselectstart` (Internet Explorer 4)

style

Browser Support: Internet Explorer 4

Provides access to the inline style of an HTML element.

Properties

Properties Supported by Both Navigator and Internet Explorer

None.

Other Properties

background (Internet Explorer 4), backgroundAttachment (Internet Explorer 4), backgroundColor (Internet Explorer 4), backgroundImage (Internet Explorer 4), backgroundPosition (Internet Explorer 4), backgroundPositionX (Internet Explorer 4), backgroundPositionY (Internet Explorer 4), backgroundRepeat (Internet Explorer 4), border (Internet Explorer 4), borderBottom (Internet Explorer 4), borderBottomColor (Internet Explorer 4), borderBottomStyle (Internet Explorer 4), borderBottomWidth (Internet Explorer 4), borderColor (Internet Explorer 4), borderLeft (Internet Explorer 4), borderLeftColor (Internet Explorer 4), borderLeftStyle (Internet Explorer 4), borderLeftWidth (Internet Explorer 4), borderRight (Internet Explorer 4), borderRightColor (Internet Explorer 4), borderRightStyle (Internet Explorer 4), borderRightWidth (Internet Explorer 4), borderStyle (Internet Explorer 4), borderTop (Internet Explorer 4), borderTopColor (Internet Explorer 4), borderTopStyle (Internet Explorer 4), borderTopWidth (Internet Explorer 4), borderWidth (Internet Explorer 4), clear (Internet Explorer 4), clip (Internet Explorer 4), color (Internet Explorer 4), cssText (Internet Explorer 4), cursor (Internet Explorer 4), display (Internet Explorer 4), filter (Internet Explorer 4), font (Internet Explorer 4), fontFamily (Internet Explorer 4), fontSize (Internet Explorer 4), fontStyle (Internet Explorer 4), fontVariant (Internet Explorer 4), fontWeight (Internet Explorer 4), height (Internet Explorer 4), left (Internet Explorer 4), letterSpacing (Internet Explorer 4), lineHeight (Internet Explorer 4), listStyle (Internet Explorer 4), listStyleImage (Internet Explorer 4), listStylePosition (Internet Explorer 4), listStyleType (Internet Explorer 4), margin (Internet Explorer 4), marginBottom (Internet Explorer 4), marginLeft (Internet Explorer 4), marginRight (Internet Explorer 4), marginTop (Internet Explorer 4), overflow (Internet Explorer 4), paddingBottom (Internet Explorer 4), paddingLeft (Internet Explorer 4), paddingRight (Internet Explorer 4), paddingTop (Internet Explorer 4), pageBreakAfter (Internet Explorer 4), pageBreakBefore (Internet Explorer 4), pixelHeight (Internet Explorer 4), pixelLeft (Internet Explorer 4), pixelTop (Internet Explorer 4),

pixelWidth (Internet Explorer 4), posHeight (Internet Explorer 4),
position (Internet Explorer 4), posLeft (Internet Explorer 4),
posTop (Internet Explorer 4), posWidth (Internet Explorer 4), style-
Float (Internet Explorer 4), textAlign (Internet Explorer 4), text-
Decoration (Internet Explorer 4), textDecorationBlink (Internet
Explorer 4), textDecorationLineThrough (Internet Explorer 4),
textDecorationNone (Internet Explorer 4), textDecorationOverline
(Internet Explorer 4), textDecorationUnderline (Internet Explorer 4),
textIndent (Internet Explorer 4), textTransform (Internet Explorer 4),
top (Internet Explorer 4), verticalAlign (Internet Explorer 4), visibility (Internet Explorer 4), width (Internet Explorer 4), zIndex (Internet Explorer 4)

Methods

Methods Supported by Both Navigator and Internet Explorer
None.

Other Methods
getAttribute (Internet Explorer 4), removeAttribute (Internet
Explorer 4), setAttribute (Internet Explorer 4)

Events

This object does not define any events.

STYLE

Browser Support: Internet Explorer 4

Allows a CSS style sheet to be specified for the current document.

Properties

Properties Supported by Both Navigator and Internet Explorer
None.

Other Properties

className (Internet Explorer 4), disabled (Internet Explorer 4), document (Internet Explorer 4), id (Internet Explorer 4), isTextEdit (Internet Explorer 4), offsetHeight (Internet Explorer 4), offsetLeft (Internet Explorer 4), offsetParent (Internet Explorer 4), offsetTop (Internet Explorer 4), offsetWidth (Internet Explorer 4), parentElement (Internet Explorer 4), parentTextEdit (Internet Explorer 4), readyState (Internet Explorer 4), sourceIndex (Internet Explorer 4), style (Internet Explorer 4), tagName (Internet Explorer 4), type (Internet Explorer 4)

Methods

Methods Supported by Both Navigator and Internet Explorer

None.

Other Methods

click (Internet Explorer 4), contains (Internet Explorer 4), getAttribute (Internet Explorer 4), insertAdjacentHTML (Internet Explorer 4), insertAdjacentText (Internet Explorer 4), scrollIntoView (Internet Explorer 4), setAttribute (Internet Explorer 4)

Events

onerror (Internet Explorer 4), onload (Internet Explorer 4), onreadystatechange (Internet Explorer 4)

Style

Browser Support: Navigator 4

The Style object forms the basis for Navigator's support of DHTML styles.

Properties

Properties Supported by Both Navigator and Internet Explorer

None.

Other Properties

`align` (Navigator 4), `backgroundColor` (Navigator 4), `backgroundImage` (Navigator 4), `borderBottomWidth` (Navigator 4), `borderColor` (Navigator 4), `borderLeftWidth` (Navigator 4), `borderRightWidth` (Navigator 4), `borderStyle` (Navigator 4), `borderTopWidth` (Navigator 4), `clear` (Navigator 4), `color` (Navigator 4), `display` (Navigator 4), `fontFamily` (Navigator 4), `fontSize` (Navigator 4), `fontStyle` (Navigator 4), `fontWeight` (Navigator 4), `lineHeight` (Navigator 4), `listStyleType` (Navigator 4), `marginBottom` (Navigator 4), `marginLeft` (Navigator 4), `marginRight` (Navigator 4), `marginTop` (Navigator 4), `paddingBottom` (Navigator 4), `paddingLeft` (Navigator 4), `paddingRight` (Navigator 4), `paddingTop` (Navigator 4), `textAlign` (Navigator 4), `textDecoration` (Navigator 4), `textIndent` (Navigator 4), `textTransform` (Navigator 4), `whiteSpace` (Navigator 4), `width` (Navigator 4)

Methods

Methods Supported by Both Navigator and Internet Explorer

None.

Other Methods

`borderWidths` (Navigator 4), `margins` (Navigator 4), `paddings` (Navigator 4)

Events

This object does not define any events.

styleSheet

Browser Support: Internet Explorer 4

Provides access to a CSS style sheet.

Properties

Properties Supported by Both Navigator and Internet Explorer

None.

Other Properties

disabled (Internet Explorer 4), href (Internet Explorer 4), id (Internet Explorer 4), owningElement (Internet Explorer 4), parentStyleSheet (Internet Explorer 4), readOnly (Internet Explorer 4), type (Internet Explorer 4)

Methods

Methods Supported by Both Navigator and Internet Explorer

None.

Other Methods

addImport (Internet Explorer 4), addRule (Internet Explorer 4)

Events

This object does not define any events.

SUB

Browser Support: Internet Explorer 4

Provides access to the HTML SUB tag.

Properties

Properties Supported by Both Navigator and Internet Explorer

None.

Other Properties

className (Internet Explorer 4), document (Internet Explorer 4), id (Internet Explorer 4), innerHTML (Internet Explorer 4), innerText (Internet Explorer 4), isTextEdit (Internet Explorer 4), lang (Internet Explorer 4), language (Internet Explorer 4), offsetHeight (Internet Explorer 4), offsetLeft (Internet Explorer 4), offsetParent (Internet Explorer 4), offsetTop (Internet Explorer 4), offsetWidth (Internet Explorer 4), outerHTML (Internet Explorer 4), outerText (Internet Explorer 4), parentElement (Internet Explorer 4), parentTextEdit (Internet Explorer 4), sourceIndex (Internet Explorer 4), style (Internet Explorer 4), tagName (Internet Explorer 4), title (Internet Explorer 4)

Methods

Methods Supported by Both Navigator and Internet Explorer
None.

Other Methods
click (Internet Explorer 4), contains (Internet Explorer 4), get-Attribute (Internet Explorer 4), insertAdjacentHTML (Internet Explorer 4), insertAdjacentText (Internet Explorer 4), remove-Attribute (Internet Explorer 4), scrollIntoView (Internet Explorer 4), setAttribute (Internet Explorer 4)

Events

onclick (Internet Explorer 4), ondblclick (Internet Explorer 4), ondragstart (Internet Explorer 4), onfilterchange (Internet Explorer 4), onhelp (Internet Explorer 4), onkeydown (Internet Explorer 4), onkeypress (Internet Explorer 4), onkeyup (Internet Explorer 4), onmousedown (Internet Explorer 4), onmousemove (Internet Explorer 4), onmouseout (Internet Explorer 4), onmouseover (Internet Explorer 4), onmouseup (Internet Explorer 4), onselectstart (Internet Explorer 4)

Submit

Browser Support: Navigator 2, Internet Explorer 3

The basic Submit object was introduced in JavaScript 1. It has been updated with JavaScript 1.1 and 1.2.

A submit button is a form field that is used to submit form values to a Web server for processing. A submit button is an INPUT element that has its TYPE attribute set to SUBMIT.

Properties

Properties Supported by Both Navigator and Internet Explorer

form (Navigator 2, Internet Explorer 3)

Provides a reference to the form object that contains the button.

name (Navigator 2, Internet Explorer 3)

The value of the button's NAME attribute.

type (Navigator 3, Internet Explorer 4)

The value of the button's TYPE attribute.

value (Navigator 2, Internet Explorer 3)

The value of the button's VALUE attribute.

Other Properties

accessKey (Internet Explorer 4), className (Internet Explorer 4), disabled (Internet Explorer 4), document (Internet Explorer 4), id (Internet Explorer 4), isTextEdit (Internet Explorer 4), lang (Internet Explorer 4), language (Internet Explorer 4), offsetHeight (Internet Explorer 4), offsetLeft (Internet Explorer 4), offsetParent (Internet Explorer 4), offsetTop (Internet Explorer 4), offsetWidth (Internet Explorer 4), outerHTML (Internet Explorer 4), outerText (Internet Explorer 4), parentElement (Internet Explorer 4), parentTextEdit (Internet Explorer 4), recordNumber (Internet Explorer 4), sourceIndex (Internet Explorer 4), style (Internet Explorer 4), tabIndex (Internet Explorer 4), tagName (Internet Explorer 4), title (Internet Explorer 4)

Methods

Methods Supported by Both Navigator and Internet Explorer

blur() (Navigator 2, Internet Explorer 3)

Removes input focus from the button.

click() (Navigator 2, Internet Explorer 3)

Simulates clicking of the button.

focus() (Navigator 2, Internet Explorer 3)

Moves input focus to the button.

Other Methods

contains (Internet Explorer 4), getAttribute (Internet Explorer 4), handleEvent (Navigator 4), insertAdjacentHTML (Internet Explorer 4), insertAdjacentText (Internet Explorer 4), removeAttribute (Internet Explorer 4), scrollIntoView (Internet Explorer 4), select (Internet Explorer 4), setAttribute (Internet Explorer 4)

Events

onblur (Navigator 3, Internet Explorer 4), onclick (Navigator 2, Internet Explorer 3), onfocus (Navigator 3, Internet Explorer 4), ondblclick (Internet Explorer 4), onfilterchange (Internet Explorer 4), onhelp (Internet Explorer 4), onkeydown (Internet Explorer 4), onkeypress (Internet Explorer 4), onkeyup (Internet Explorer 4), onmousedown (Internet Explorer 4), onmousemove (Internet Explorer 4), onmouseout (Internet Explorer 4), onmouseover (Internet Explorer 4), onmouseup (Internet Explorer 4), onresize (Internet Explorer 4), onselect (Internet Explorer 4)

sun

Browser Support: Navigator 3

The sun object is a shorthand equivalent to the sun property of the Packages object.

SUP

Browser Support: Internet Explorer 4

Provides access to the HTML SUP tag.

Properties

Properties Supported by Both Navigator and Internet Explorer

None.

Other Properties

className (Internet Explorer 4), document (Internet Explorer 4), id (Internet Explorer 4), innerHTML (Internet Explorer 4), innerText

(Internet Explorer 4), isTextEdit (Internet Explorer 4), lang (Internet Explorer 4), offsetHeight (Internet Explorer 4), offsetLeft (Internet Explorer 4), offsetParent (Internet Explorer 4), offsetTop (Internet Explorer 4), offsetWidth (Internet Explorer 4), outerHTML (Internet Explorer 4), outerText (Internet Explorer 4), parentElement (Internet Explorer 4), parentTextEdit (Internet Explorer 4), sourceIndex (Internet Explorer 4), style (Internet Explorer 4), tagName (Internet Explorer 4), title (Internet Explorer 4)

Methods

Methods Supported by Both Navigator and Internet Explorer

None.

Other Methods

click (Internet Explorer 4), contains (Internet Explorer 4), getAttribute (Internet Explorer 4), insertAdjacentHTML (Internet Explorer 4), insertAdjacentText (Internet Explorer 4), removeAttribute (Internet Explorer 4), scrollIntoView (Internet Explorer 4), setAttribute (Internet Explorer 4)

Events

onclick (Internet Explorer 4), ondblclick (Internet Explorer 4), ondragstart (Internet Explorer 4), onfilterchange (Internet Explorer 4), onhelp (Internet Explorer 4), onkeydown (Internet Explorer 4), onkeypress (Internet Explorer 4), onkeyup (Internet Explorer 4), onmousedown (Internet Explorer 4), onmousemove (Internet Explorer 4), onmouseout (Internet Explorer 4), onmouseover (Internet Explorer 4), onmouseup (Internet Explorer 4), onselectstart (Internet Explorer 4)

TABLE

Browser Support: Internet Explorer 4

Provides access to the HTML TABLE tag.

Properties

Properties Supported by Both Navigator and Internet Explorer
None.

Other Properties
align (Internet Explorer 4), background (Internet Explorer 4), bgColor (Internet Explorer 4), border (Internet Explorer 4), borderColor (Internet Explorer 4), borderColorDark (Internet Explorer 4), borderColorLight (Internet Explorer 4), cellPadding (Internet Explorer 4), cellSpacing (Internet Explorer 4), className (Internet Explorer 4), clientHeight (Internet Explorer 4), clientWidth (Internet Explorer 4), cols (Internet Explorer 4), dataFld (Internet Explorer 4), dataPageSize (Internet Explorer 4), dataSrc (Internet Explorer 4), document (Internet Explorer 4), frame (Internet Explorer 4), height (Internet Explorer 4), id (Internet Explorer 4), innerText (Internet Explorer 4), isTextEdit (Internet Explorer 4), lang (Internet Explorer 4), language (Internet Explorer 4), offsetHeight (Internet Explorer 4), offsetLeft (Internet Explorer 4), offsetParent (Internet Explorer 4), offsetTop (Internet Explorer 4), offsetWidth (Internet Explorer 4), outerText (Internet Explorer 4), parentElement (Internet Explorer 4), parentTextEdit (Internet Explorer 4), rules (Internet Explorer 4), scrollHeight (Internet Explorer 4), scrollLeft (Internet Explorer 4), scrollTop (Internet Explorer 4), scrollWidth (Internet Explorer 4), sourceIndex (Internet Explorer 4), style (Internet Explorer 4), tagName (Internet Explorer 4), title (Internet Explorer 4), width (Internet Explorer 4)

Methods

Methods Supported by Both Navigator and Internet Explorer
None.

Other Methods
blur (Internet Explorer 4), click (Internet Explorer 4), contains (Internet Explorer 4), focus (Internet Explorer 4), getAttribute (Internet Explorer 4), insertAdjacentHTML (Internet Explorer 4), insertAdjacentText (Internet Explorer 4), nextPage (Internet Explorer 4),

previousPage (Internet Explorer 4), refresh (Internet Explorer 4), removeAttribute (Internet Explorer 4), scrollIntoView (Internet Explorer 4), setAttribute (Internet Explorer 4)

Events

onafterupdate (Internet Explorer 4), onbeforeupdate (Internet Explorer 4), onblur (Internet Explorer 4), onclick (Internet Explorer 4), ondblclick (Internet Explorer 4), ondragstart (Internet Explorer 4), onfocus (Internet Explorer 4), onhelp (Internet Explorer 4), onkeydown (Internet Explorer 4), onkeypress (Internet Explorer 4), onkeyup (Internet Explorer 4), onmousedown (Internet Explorer 4), onmousemove (Internet Explorer 4), onmouseout (Internet Explorer 4), onmouseover (Internet Explorer 4), onmouseup (Internet Explorer 4), onresize (Internet Explorer 4), onrowenter (Internet Explorer 4), onrowexit (Internet Explorer 4), onscroll (Internet Explorer 4), onselectstart (Internet Explorer 4)

TBODY

Browser Support: Internet Explorer 4

Provides access to the HTML TBODY tag.

Properties

Properties Supported by Both Navigator and Internet Explorer

None.

Other Properties

align (Internet Explorer 4), bgColor (Internet Explorer 4), className (Internet Explorer 4), document (Internet Explorer 4), id (Internet Explorer 4), isTextEdit (Internet Explorer 4), lang (Internet Explorer 4), language (Internet Explorer 4), offsetHeight (Internet Explorer 4), offsetLeft (Internet Explorer 4), offsetParent (Internet Explorer 4), offsetTop (Internet Explorer 4), offsetWidth (Internet Explorer 4), parentElement (Internet Explorer 4), parentTextEdit (Internet Explorer 4), sourceIndex (Internet Explorer 4), style (Internet Explorer 4), tagName (Internet Explorer 4), title (Internet Explorer 4), vAlign (Internet Explorer 4)

Methods

Methods Supported by Both Navigator and Internet Explorer
None.

Other Methods
click (Internet Explorer 4), contains (Internet Explorer 4), getAttribute (Internet Explorer 4), removeAttribute (Internet Explorer 4), scrollIntoView (Internet Explorer 4), setAttribute (Internet Explorer 4)

Events

onclick (Internet Explorer 4), ondblclick (Internet Explorer 4), ondragstart (Internet Explorer 4), onfilterchange (Internet Explorer 4), onhelp (Internet Explorer 4), onkeydown (Internet Explorer 4), onkeypress (Internet Explorer 4), onkeyup (Internet Explorer 4), onmousedown (Internet Explorer 4), onmousemove (Internet Explorer 4), onmouseout (Internet Explorer 4), onmouseover (Internet Explorer 4), onmouseup (Internet Explorer 4), onselectstart (Internet Explorer 4)

TD

Browser Support: Internet Explorer 4

Provides access to the HTML TD tag.

Properties

Properties Supported by Both Navigator and Internet Explorer
None.

Other Properties
align (Internet Explorer 4), background (Internet Explorer 4), bgColor (Internet Explorer 4), borderColor (Internet Explorer 4), borderColorDark (Internet Explorer 4), borderColorLight (Internet Explorer 4), className (Internet Explorer 4), clientHeight (Internet Explorer 4), clientWidth (Internet Explorer 4), colSpan (Internet Explorer 4), document (Internet Explorer 4), height (Internet Explorer 4), id (Internet

Explorer 4), isTextEdit (Internet Explorer 4), lang (Internet Explorer 4), language (Internet Explorer 4), noWrap (Internet Explorer 4), offsetHeight (Internet Explorer 4), offsetLeft (Internet Explorer 4), offsetParent (Internet Explorer 4), offsetTop (Internet Explorer 4), offsetWidth (Internet Explorer 4), parentElement (Internet Explorer 4), parentTextEdit (Internet Explorer 4), rowSpan (Internet Explorer 4), sourceIndex (Internet Explorer 4), style (Internet Explorer 4), tagName (Internet Explorer 4), title (Internet Explorer 4), vAlign (Internet Explorer 4), width (Internet Explorer 4)

Methods

Methods Supported by Both Navigator and Internet Explorer
None.

Other Methods
blur (Internet Explorer 4), click (Internet Explorer 4), contains (Internet Explorer 4), focus (Internet Explorer 4), getAttribute (Internet Explorer 4), insertAdjacentHTML (Internet Explorer 4), insertAdjacentText (Internet Explorer 4), removeAttribute (Internet Explorer 4), scrollIntoView (Internet Explorer 4), setAttribute (Internet Explorer 4)

Events

onafterupdate (Internet Explorer 4), onbeforeupdate (Internet Explorer 4), onblur (Internet Explorer 4), onclick (Internet Explorer 4), ondblclick (Internet Explorer 4), ondragstart (Internet Explorer 4), onfilterchange (Internet Explorer 4), onfocus (Internet Explorer 4), onhelp (Internet Explorer 4), onkeydown (Internet Explorer 4), onkeypress (Internet Explorer 4), onkeyup (Internet Explorer 4), onmousedown (Internet Explorer 4), onmousemove (Internet Explorer 4), onmouseout (Internet Explorer 4), onmouseover (Internet Explorer 4), onmouseup (Internet Explorer 4), onresize (Internet Explorer 4), onrowenter (Internet Explorer 4), onrowexit (Internet Explorer 4), onselectstart (Internet Explorer 4)

Text

Browser Support: Navigator 2, Internet Explorer 3

The basic Text object was introduced in JavaScript 1. It has been updated with JavaScript 1.1 and 1.2.

A text field is a form field that is used to obtain a single line of text from the user. A text field is an INPUT elements that has its TYPE attribute set to TEXT.

Properties

Properties Supported by Both Navigator and Internet Explorer

defaultValue (Navigator 2, Internet Explorer 3)

The value of the field's VALUE attribute.

form (Navigator 2, Internet Explorer 3)

Provides a reference to the form object that contains the field.

name (Navigator 2, Internet Explorer 3)

The value of the field's NAME attribute.

type (Navigator 3, Internet Explorer 4)

The value of the field's TYPE attribute.

value (Navigator 2, Internet Explorer 3)

The text string value currently contained in the field.

Other Properties

accessKey (Internet Explorer 4), align (Internet Explorer 4), class-Name (Internet Explorer 4), dataFld (Internet Explorer 4), dataSrc (Internet Explorer 4), disabled (Internet Explorer 4), document (Internet Explorer 4), id (Internet Explorer 4), innerHTML (Internet Explorer 4), isTextEdit (Internet Explorer 4), lang (Internet Explorer 4), language (Internet Explorer 4), maxLength (Internet Explorer 4), offsetHeight (Internet Explorer 4), offsetLeft (Internet Explorer 4), offsetParent (Internet Explorer 4), offsetTop (Internet Explorer 4), offsetWidth (Internet Explorer 4), outerHTML (Internet Explorer 4), outerText (Internet Explorer 4), parentElement (Internet Explorer 4), parentTextEdit (Internet Explorer 4), readOnly (Internet Explorer 4), recordNumber (Internet Explorer 4), size (Internet Explorer 4), sourceIndex (Internet Explorer 4), style (Internet Explorer 4), tabIndex

(Internet Explorer 4), tagName (Internet Explorer 4), title (Internet Explorer 4)

Methods

Methods Supported by Both Navigator and Internet Explorer

blur() (Navigator 2, Internet Explorer 3)

Removes input focus from the button.

focus() (Navigator 2, Internet Explorer 3)

Moves input focus to the button.

select() (Navigator 2, Internet Explorer 3)

Selects (highlights) the value of the text field.

Other Methods

click (Internet Explorer 4), contains (Internet Explorer 4), createTextRange (Internet Explorer 4), getAttribute (Internet Explorer 4), handleEvent (Navigator 4), insertAdjacentHTML (Internet Explorer 4), insertAdjacentText (Internet Explorer 4), removeAttribute (Internet Explorer 4), scrollIntoView (Internet Explorer 4), setAttribute (Internet Explorer 4)

Events

onblur (Navigator 2, Internet Explorer 3), onchange (Navigator 2, Internet Explorer 3), onfocus (Navigator 2, Internet Explorer 3), onselect (Navigator 2, Internet Explorer 3), onafterupdate (Internet Explorer 4), onbeforeupdate (Internet Explorer 4), onclick (Internet Explorer 4), ondblclick (Internet Explorer 4), onerrorupdate (Internet Explorer 4), onfilterchange (Internet Explorer 4), onhelp (Internet Explorer 4), onkeydown (Internet Explorer 4), onkeypress (Internet Explorer 4), onkeyup (Internet Explorer 4), onmousedown (Internet Explorer 4), onmousemove (Internet Explorer 4), onmouseout (Internet Explorer 4), onmouseover (Internet Explorer 4), onmouseup (Internet Explorer 4), onresize (Internet Explorer 4)

Textarea

Browser Support: Navigator 2, Internet Explorer 3

The basic Textarea object was introduced in JavaScript 1. It has been updated with JavaScript 1.1 and 1.2.

A text area field is a form field that is used to obtain multiple lines of text from the user. A text area field uses the TEXTAREA tags to surround lines of default text to be placed in the field.

Properties

Properties Supported by Both Navigator and Internet Explorer

defaultValue (Navigator 2, Internet Explorer 3)

Identifies the default value of the text area field.

form (Navigator 2, Internet Explorer 3)

Provides a reference to the form object that contains the field.

name (Navigator 2, Internet Explorer 3)

The value of the field's NAME attribute.

type (Navigator 3, Internet Explorer 4)

The value of the field's TYPE attribute.

value (Navigator 2, Internet Explorer 3)

The text string value currently contained in the field.

Other Properties

accessKey (Internet Explorer 4), className (Internet Explorer 4), clientHeight (Internet Explorer 4), clientWidth (Internet Explorer 4), cols (Internet Explorer 4), dataFld (Internet Explorer 4), dataSrc (Internet Explorer 4), disabled (Internet Explorer 4), document (Internet Explorer 4), id (Internet Explorer 4), innerText (Internet Explorer 4), isTextEdit (Internet Explorer 4), lang (Internet Explorer 4), language (Internet Explorer 4), offsetHeight (Internet Explorer 4), offsetLeft (Internet Explorer 4), offsetParent (Internet Explorer 4), offsetTop (Internet Explorer 4), offsetWidth (Internet Explorer 4), outerText (Internet Explorer 4), parentElement (Internet Explorer 4), parentTextEdit (Internet Explorer 4), readOnly (Internet Explorer 4), rows (Internet Explorer 4), scrollHeight (Internet Explorer 4), scrollLeft (Internet Explorer 4), scrollTop (Internet Explorer 4), scrollWidth (Internet Explorer 4), sourceIndex (Internet Explorer 4), status (Internet Explorer 4), style (Internet Explorer 4), tabIndex (Internet Explorer 4), tagName (Internet Explorer 4), title (Internet Explorer 4), wrap (Internet Explorer 4)

Methods

Methods Supported by Both Navigator and Internet Explorer

blur() (Navigator 2, Internet Explorer 3)

Removes input focus from the button.

focus() (Navigator 2, Internet Explorer 3)

Moves input focus to the button.

select() (Navigator 2, Internet Explorer 3)

Selects (highlights) the value of the text field.

Other Methods

click (Internet Explorer 4), contains (Internet Explorer 4), create-TextRange (Internet Explorer 4), getAttribute (Internet Explorer 4), handleEvent (Navigator 4), insertAdjacentHTML (Internet Explorer 4), insertAdjacentText (Internet Explorer 4), removeAttribute (Internet Explorer 4), scrollIntoView (Internet Explorer 4), setAttribute (Internet Explorer 4)

Events

onblur (Navigator 2, Internet Explorer 3), onchange (Navigator 2, Internet Explorer 3), onfocus (Navigator 2, Internet Explorer 3), onkeydown (Navigator 4, Internet Explorer 4), onkeypress (Navigator 4, Internet Explorer 4), onkeyup (Navigator 4, Internet Explorer 4), onselect (Navigator 2, Internet Explorer 3), onafterupdate (Internet Explorer 4), onbeforeupdate (Internet Explorer 4), onclick (Internet Explorer 4), ondblclick (Internet Explorer 4), ondragstart (Internet Explorer 4), onerrorupdate (Internet Explorer 4), onfilterchange (Internet Explorer 4), onhelp (Internet Explorer 4), onmousedown (Internet Explorer 4), onmousemove (Internet Explorer 4), onmouseout (Internet Explorer 4), onmouseover (Internet Explorer 4), onmouseup (Internet Explorer 4), onresize (Internet Explorer 4), onrowenter (Internet Explorer 4), onrowexit (Internet Explorer 4), onscroll (Internet Explorer 4), onse-lectstart (Internet Explorer 4)

TextNode

Browser Support: Internet Explorer 5

Provides access to a text node in a document object hierarchy (XML or HTML).

Properties

Properties Supported by Both Navigator and Internet Explorer

None.

Other Properties

data (Internet Explorer 5), length (Internet Explorer 5), nextSibling (Internet Explorer 5), nodeName (Internet Explorer 5), nodeType (Internet Explorer 5), nodeValue (Internet Explorer 5), previousSibling (Internet Explorer 5)

Methods

This object does not define any methods.

Events

This object does not define any events.

TextRange

Browser Support: Internet Explorer 4

Provides access to text that is contained in an HTML or XML element.

Properties

Properties Supported by Both Navigator and Internet Explorer

None.

Other Properties

htmlText (Internet Explorer 4), text (Internet Explorer 4)

Methods

Methods Supported by Both Navigator and Internet Explorer
None.

Other Methods

collapse (Internet Explorer 4), compareEndPoints (Internet Explorer 4), duplicate (Internet Explorer 4), execCommand (Internet Explorer 4), expand (Internet Explorer 4), findText (Internet Explorer 4), getBookmark (Internet Explorer 4), inRange (Internet Explorer 4), isEqual (Internet Explorer 4), move (Internet Explorer 4), moveEnd (Internet Explorer 4), moveStart (Internet Explorer 4), moveToBookmark (Internet Explorer 4), moveToElementText (Internet Explorer 4), moveToPoint (Internet Explorer 4), parentElement (Internet Explorer 4), pasteHTML (Internet Explorer 4), queryCommandEnabled (Internet Explorer 4), queryCommandIndeterm (Internet Explorer 4), queryCommandState (Internet Explorer 4), queryCommandSupported (Internet Explorer 4), queryCommandValue (Internet Explorer 4), scrollIntoView (Internet Explorer 4), select (Internet Explorer 4), setEndPoint (Internet Explorer 4)

Events

This object does not define any events.

TextRectangle

Browser Support: Internet Explorer 5

Provides access to a rectangular strip of text that is contained in a document element.

Properties

Properties Supported by Both Navigator and Internet Explorer
None.

Other Properties

bottom (Internet Explorer 5), left (Internet Explorer 5), right (Internet Explorer 5), top (Internet Explorer 5)

Methods

This object does not define any methods.

Events

This object does not define any events.

TFOOT

Browser Support: Internet Explorer 4

Provides access to the HTML TFOOT tag.

Properties

Properties Supported by Both Navigator and Internet Explorer

None.

Other Properties

align (Internet Explorer 4), bgColor (Internet Explorer 4), className (Internet Explorer 4), document (Internet Explorer 4), id (Internet Explorer 4), isTextEdit (Internet Explorer 4), lang (Internet Explorer 4), language (Internet Explorer 4), offsetHeight (Internet Explorer 4), offsetLeft (Internet Explorer 4), offsetParent (Internet Explorer 4), offsetTop (Internet Explorer 4), offsetWidth (Internet Explorer 4), parentElement (Internet Explorer 4), parentTextEdit (Internet Explorer 4), sourceIndex (Internet Explorer 4), style (Internet Explorer 4), tagName (Internet Explorer 4), title (Internet Explorer 4), vAlign (Internet Explorer 4)

Methods

Methods Supported by Both Navigator and Internet Explorer
None.

Other Methods
click (Internet Explorer 4), contains (Internet Explorer 4), getAttribute (Internet Explorer 4), removeAttribute (Internet Explorer 4), scrollIntoView (Internet Explorer 4), setAttribute (Internet Explorer 4)

Events

onclick (Internet Explorer 4), ondblclick (Internet Explorer 4), ondragstart (Internet Explorer 4), onfilterchange (Internet Explorer 4), onhelp (Internet Explorer 4), onkeydown (Internet Explorer 4), onkeypress (Internet Explorer 4), onkeyup (Internet Explorer 4), onmousedown (Internet Explorer 4), onmousemove (Internet Explorer 4), onmouseout (Internet Explorer 4), onmouseover (Internet Explorer 4), onmouseup (Internet Explorer 4), onselectstart (Internet Explorer 4)

TH

Browser Support: Internet Explorer 4

Provides access to the HTML TH tag.

Properties

Properties Supported by Both Navigator and Internet Explorer
None.

Other Properties
align (Internet Explorer 4), background (Internet Explorer 4), bgColor (Internet Explorer 4), borderColor (Internet Explorer 4), borderColorDark (Internet Explorer 4), borderColorLight (Internet Explorer 4), className (Internet Explorer 4), colSpan (Internet Explorer 4), document (Internet Explorer 4), id (Internet Explorer 4), isTextEdit (Internet Explorer 4), lang (Internet Explorer 4), language (Internet Explorer 4),

noWrap (Internet Explorer 4), offsetHeight (Internet Explorer 4), off-setLeft (Internet Explorer 4), offsetParent (Internet Explorer 4), offsetTop (Internet Explorer 4), offsetWidth (Internet Explorer 4), parentElement (Internet Explorer 4), parentTextEdit (Internet Explorer 4), rowSpan (Internet Explorer 4), sourceIndex (Internet Explorer 4), style (Internet Explorer 4), tagName (Internet Explorer 4), title (Internet Explorer 4), vAlign (Internet Explorer 4)

Methods

Methods Supported by Both Navigator and Internet Explorer
None.

Other Methods
click (Internet Explorer 4), contains (Internet Explorer 4), getAttribute (Internet Explorer 4), removeAttribute (Internet Explorer 4), scrollIntoView (Internet Explorer 4), setAttribute (Internet Explorer 4)

Events

onclick (Internet Explorer 4), ondblclick (Internet Explorer 4), ondragstart (Internet Explorer 4), onhelp (Internet Explorer 4), onkeydown (Internet Explorer 4), onkeypress (Internet Explorer 4), onkeyup (Internet Explorer 4), onmousedown (Internet Explorer 4), onmousemove (Internet Explorer 4), onmouseout (Internet Explorer 4), onmouseover (Internet Explorer 4), onmouseup (Internet Explorer 4), onselectstart (Internet Explorer 4)

THEAD

Browser Support: Internet Explorer 4

Provides access to the HTML THEAD tag.

Properties

Properties Supported by Both Navigator and Internet Explorer
None.

Other Properties

align (Internet Explorer 4), bgColor (Internet Explorer 4), className (Internet Explorer 4), document (Internet Explorer 4), id (Internet Explorer 4), isTextEdit (Internet Explorer 4), lang (Internet Explorer 4), language (Internet Explorer 4), offsetHeight (Internet Explorer 4), offsetLeft (Internet Explorer 4), offsetParent (Internet Explorer 4), offsetTop (Internet Explorer 4), offsetWidth (Internet Explorer 4), parentElement (Internet Explorer 4), parentTextEdit (Internet Explorer 4), sourceIndex (Internet Explorer 4), style (Internet Explorer 4), tagName (Internet Explorer 4), title (Internet Explorer 4), vAlign (Internet Explorer 4)

Methods

Methods Supported by Both Navigator and Internet Explorer

None.

Other Methods

click (Internet Explorer 4), contains (Internet Explorer 4), getAttribute (Internet Explorer 4), removeAttribute (Internet Explorer 4), scrollIntoView (Internet Explorer 4), setAttribute (Internet Explorer 4)

Events

onclick (Internet Explorer 4), ondblclick (Internet Explorer 4), ondragstart (Internet Explorer 4), onfilterchange (Internet Explorer 4), onhelp (Internet Explorer 4), onkeydown (Internet Explorer 4), onkeypress (Internet Explorer 4), onkeyup (Internet Explorer 4), onmousedown (Internet Explorer 4), onmousemove (Internet Explorer 4), onmouseout (Internet Explorer 4), onmouseover (Internet Explorer 4), onmouseup (Internet Explorer 4), onselectstart (Internet Explorer 4)

TITLE

Browser Support: Internet Explorer 4

Provides access to the HTML TITLE tag.

Properties

Properties Supported by Both Navigator and Internet Explorer
None.

Other Properties
className (Internet Explorer 4), document (Internet Explorer 4), id (Internet Explorer 4), isTextEdit (Internet Explorer 4), lang parent-Element (Internet Explorer 4), parentTextEdit (Internet Explorer 4), sourceIndex (Internet Explorer 4), tagName (Internet Explorer 4), text (Internet Explorer 4), title (Internet Explorer 4)

Methods

Methods Supported by Both Navigator and Internet Explorer
None.

Other Methods
contains (Internet Explorer 4), getAttribute (Internet Explorer 4), removeAttribute (Internet Explorer 4), setAttribute (Internet Explorer 4)

Events

This object does not define any events.

TR

Browser Support: Internet Explorer 4
Provides access to the HTML TR tag.

Properties

Properties Supported by Both Navigator and Internet Explorer
None.

Other Properties

align (Internet Explorer 4), bgColor (Internet Explorer 4), border-
Color (Internet Explorer 4), borderColorDark (Internet Explorer 4),
borderColorLight (Internet Explorer 4), className (Internet Explorer 4),
document (Internet Explorer 4), id (Internet Explorer 4), isTextEdit
(Internet Explorer 4), lang (Internet Explorer 4), language (Internet
Explorer 4), offsetHeight (Internet Explorer 4), offsetLeft (Inter-
net Explorer 4), offsetParent (Internet Explorer 4), offsetTop
(Internet Explorer 4), offsetWidth (Internet Explorer 4), parent-
Element (Internet Explorer 4), parentTextEdit (Internet Explorer 4),
sourceIndex (Internet Explorer 4), style (Internet Explorer 4), tag-
Name (Internet Explorer 4), title (Internet Explorer 4), vAlign (Inter-
net Explorer 4)

Methods

Methods Supported by Both Navigator and Internet Explorer

None.

Other Methods

blur (Internet Explorer 4), click (Internet Explorer 4), contains (Inter-
net Explorer 4), focus (Internet Explorer 4), getAttribute (Internet
Explorer 4), removeAttribute (Internet Explorer 4), scrollIntoView
(Internet Explorer 4), setAttribute (Internet Explorer 4)

Events

onafterupdate (Internet Explorer 4), onbeforeupdate (Internet
Explorer 4), onblur (Internet Explorer 4), onclick (Internet Explorer 4),
ondblclick (Internet Explorer 4), ondragstart (Internet Explorer 4),
onfilterchange (Internet Explorer 4), onfocus (Internet Explorer 4),
onhelp (Internet Explorer 4), onkeydown (Internet Explorer 4), onkeypress (Internet Explorer 4), onkeyup (Internet Explorer 4), onmousedown (Internet Explorer 4), onmousemove (Internet Explorer 4),
onmouseout (Internet Explorer 4), onmouseover (Internet Explorer 4),
onmouseup (Internet Explorer 4), onresize (Internet Explorer 4),
onrowenter (Internet Explorer 4), onrowexit (Internet Explorer 4),
onselectstart (Internet Explorer 4)

TT

Browser Support: Internet Explorer 4

Provides access to the HTML TT tag.

Properties

Properties Supported by Both Navigator and Internet Explorer

None.

Other Properties

className (Internet Explorer 4), document (Internet Explorer 4), id (Internet Explorer 4), innerHTML (Internet Explorer 4), innerText (Internet Explorer 4), isTextEdit (Internet Explorer 4), lang (Internet Explorer 4), language (Internet Explorer 4), offsetHeight (Internet Explorer 4), offsetLeft (Internet Explorer 4), offsetParent (Internet Explorer 4), offsetTop (Internet Explorer 4), offsetWidth (Internet Explorer 4), outerHTML (Internet Explorer 4), outerText (Internet Explorer 4), parentElement (Internet Explorer 4), parentTextEdit (Internet Explorer 4), sourceIndex (Internet Explorer 4), style (Internet Explorer 4), tagName (Internet Explorer 4), title (Internet Explorer 4)

Methods

Methods Supported by Both Navigator and Internet Explorer

None.

Other Methods

click (Internet Explorer 4), contains (Internet Explorer 4), getAttribute (Internet Explorer 4), insertAdjacentHTML (Internet Explorer 4), insertAdjacentText (Internet Explorer 4), removeAttribute (Internet Explorer 4), scrollIntoView (Internet Explorer 4), setAttribute (Internet Explorer 4)

Events

onclick (Internet Explorer 4), ondblclick (Internet Explorer 4), ondragstart (Internet Explorer 4), onfilterchange (Internet Explorer 4),

onhelp (Internet Explorer 4), onkeydown (Internet Explorer 4), onkey-press (Internet Explorer 4), onkeyup (Internet Explorer 4), onmouse-down (Internet Explorer 4), onmousemove (Internet Explorer 4), onmouseout (Internet Explorer 4), onmouseover (Internet Explorer 4), onmouseup (Internet Explorer 4), onselectstart (Internet Explorer 4)

U

Browser Support: Internet Explorer 4

Provides access to the HTML U tag.

Properties

Properties Supported by Both Navigator and Internet Explorer

None.

Other Properties

className (Internet Explorer 4), document (Internet Explorer 4), id (Internet Explorer 4), innerHTML (Internet Explorer 4), innerText (Internet Explorer 4), isTextEdit (Internet Explorer 4), lang (Internet Explorer 4), language (Internet Explorer 4), offsetHeight (Internet Explorer 4), offsetLeft (Internet Explorer 4), offsetParent (Internet Explorer 4), offsetTop (Internet Explorer 4), offsetWidth (Internet Explorer 4), outerHTML (Internet Explorer 4), outerText (Internet Explorer 4), parentElement (Internet Explorer 4), parentTextEdit (Internet Explorer 4), sourceIndex (Internet Explorer 4), style (Internet Explorer 4), tagName (Internet Explorer 4), title (Internet Explorer 4)

Methods

Methods Supported by Both Navigator and Internet Explorer

None.

Other Methods

click (Internet Explorer 4), contains (Internet Explorer 4), get-Attribute (Internet Explorer 4), insertAdjacentHTML (Internet

Explorer 4), `insertAdjacentText` (Internet Explorer 4), `remove-Attribute` (Internet Explorer 4), `scrollIntoView` (Internet Explorer 4), `setAttribute` (Internet Explorer 4)

Events

`onclick` (Internet Explorer 4), `ondblclick` (Internet Explorer 4), `ondragstart` (Internet Explorer 4), `onfilterchange` (Internet Explorer 4), `onhelp` (Internet Explorer 4), `onkeydown` (Internet Explorer 4), `onkeypress` (Internet Explorer 4), `onkeyup` (Internet Explorer 4), `onmousedown` (Internet Explorer 4), `onmousemove` (Internet Explorer 4), `onmouseout` (Internet Explorer 4), `onmouseover` (Internet Explorer 4), `onmouseup` (Internet Explorer 4), `onselectstart` (Internet Explorer 4)

UL

Browser Support: Internet Explorer 4

Provides access to the HTML UL tag.

Properties

Properties Supported by Both Navigator and Internet Explorer
None.

Other Properties

`className` (Internet Explorer 4), `document` (Internet Explorer 4), `id` (Internet Explorer 4), `innerHTML` (Internet Explorer 4), `innerText` (Internet Explorer 4), `isTextEdit` (Internet Explorer 4), `lang` (Internet Explorer 4), `language` (Internet Explorer 4), `offsetHeight` (Internet Explorer 4), `offsetLeft` (Internet Explorer 4), `offsetParent` (Internet Explorer 4), `offsetTop` (Internet Explorer 4), `offsetWidth` (Internet Explorer 4), `outerHTML` (Internet Explorer 4), `outerText` (Internet Explorer 4), `parentElement` (Internet Explorer 4), `parentTextEdit` (Internet Explorer 4), `sourceIndex` (Internet Explorer 4), `style` (Internet Explorer 4), `tagName` (Internet Explorer 4), `title` (Internet Explorer 4), `type` (Internet Explorer 4)

Methods

Methods Supported by Both Navigator and Internet Explorer
None.

Other Methods
click (Internet Explorer 4), contains (Internet Explorer 4), get-
Attribute (Internet Explorer 4), insertAdjacentHTML (Internet
Explorer 4), insertAdjacentText (Internet Explorer 4), remove-
Attribute (Internet Explorer 4), scrollIntoView (Internet
Explorer 4), setAttribute (Internet Explorer 4)

Events

onclick (Internet Explorer 4), ondblclick (Internet Explorer 4),
ondragstart (Internet Explorer 4), onfilterchange (Internet Explorer 4),
onhelp (Internet Explorer 4), onkeydown (Internet Explorer 4), onkeypress (Internet Explorer 4), onkeyup (Internet Explorer 4), onmousedown (Internet Explorer 4), onmousemove (Internet Explorer 4),
onmouseout (Internet Explorer 4), onmouseover (Internet Explorer 4),
onmouseup (Internet Explorer 4), onselectstart (Internet Explorer 4)

userProfile

Browser Support: Internet Explorer 4
Provides access to user profile information.

Properties

This object does not define any properties.

Methods

Methods Supported by Both Navigator and Internet Explorer
None.

Other Methods

addReadRequest (Internet Explorer 4), clearRequest (Internet Explorer 4), doReadRequest (Internet Explorer 4), getAttribute (Internet Explorer 4)

Events

This object does not define any events.

VAR

Browser Support: Internet Explorer 4

Provides access to the HTML VAR tag.

Properties

Properties Supported by Both Navigator and Internet Explorer

None.

Other Properties

className (Internet Explorer 4), document (Internet Explorer 4), id (Internet Explorer 4), innerHTML (Internet Explorer 4), innerText (Internet Explorer 4), isTextEdit (Internet Explorer 4), lang (Internet Explorer 4), language (Internet Explorer 4), offsetHeight (Internet Explorer 4), offsetLeft (Internet Explorer 4), offsetParent (Internet Explorer 4), offsetTop (Internet Explorer 4), offsetWidth (Internet Explorer 4), outerHTML (Internet Explorer 4), outerText (Internet Explorer 4), parentElement (Internet Explorer 4), parentTextEdit (Internet Explorer 4), sourceIndex (Internet Explorer 4), style (Internet Explorer 4), tagName (Internet Explorer 4), title (Internet Explorer 4)

Methods

Methods Supported by Both Navigator and Internet Explorer

None.

Other Methods

click (Internet Explorer 4), contains (Internet Explorer 4), get-Attribute (Internet Explorer 4), insertAdjacentHTML (Internet Explorer 4), insertAdjacentText (Internet Explorer 4), remove-Attribute (Internet Explorer 4), scrollIntoView (Internet xplorer 4), setAttribute (Internet Explorer 4)

Events

onclick (Internet Explorer 4), ondblclick (Internet Explorer 4), ondragstart (Internet Explorer 4), onfilterchange (Internet Explorer 4), onhelp (Internet Explorer 4), onkeydown (Internet Explorer 4), onkey-press (Internet Explorer 4), onkeyup (Internet Explorer 4), onmouse-down (Internet Explorer 4), onmousemove (Internet Explorer 4), onmouseout (Internet Explorer 4), onmouseover (Internet Explorer 4), onmouseup (Internet Explorer 4), onselectstart (Internet Explorer 4)

VBArray

Browser Support: Internet Explorer 4

Provides access to Visual Basic safe array.

Constructors

```
new VBArray(safeArray)
```

Creates a VBArray object from a safe array retrieved from an ActiveX object.

Properties

This object does not define any properties.

Methods

Methods Supported by Both Navigator and Internet Explorer

None.

Other Methods

dimensions (Internet Explorer 4), getItem (Internet Explorer 4), lbound (Internet Explorer 4), toArray (Internet Explorer 4), ubound (Internet Explorer 4)

Events

This object does not define any events.

WBR

Browser Support: Internet Explorer 5

Provides access to the HTML WBR tag.

Properties

Properties Supported by Both Navigator and Internet Explorer

None.

Other Properties

canHaveHTML (Internet Explorer 5), contentEditable (Internet Explorer 5), currentStyle (Internet Explorer 5), disabled (Internet Explorer 5), hasLayout (Internet Explorer 5), id (Internet Explorer 5), isContentEditable (Internet Explorer 5), isDisabled (Internet Explorer 5), outerHTML (Internet Explorer 5), outerText (Internet Explorer 5), parentElement (Internet Explorer 5), scopeName (Internet Explorer 5), tagUrn (Internet Explorer 5)

Methods

Methods Supported by Both Navigator and Internet Explorer

None.

Other Methods

addBehavior (Internet Explorer 5), componentFromPoint (Internet Explorer 5), fireEvent (Internet Explorer 5), getAttribute (Internet Explorer 5), removeAttribute (Internet Explorer 5), removeBehavior (Internet Explorer 5), scrollIntoView (Internet Explorer 5), setAttribute (Internet Explorer 5)

Events

This object does not define any events.

window

Browser Support: Navigator 2, Internet Explorer 3

The basic window object was introduced in JavaScript 1. It has been updated with JavaScript 1.1 and 1.2.

The window object encapsulates a browser window and provides access to the objects that are contained in the window.

Properties

Properties Supported by Both Navigator and Internet Explorer

closed (Navigator 3, Internet Explorer 4)

Identified whether the window is closed.

defaultStatus (Navigator 2, Internet Explorer 3)

The default status displayed in the bottom of the window.

document (Navigator 2, Internet Explorer 3)

The document that is loaded in the window.

frames (Navigator 2, Internet Explorer 3)

An array of frames that are contained in the current window.

history (Navigator 3, Internet Explorer 4).

Provides access to the History object associated with the window.

length (Navigator 2, Internet Explorer 3)

Identifies the length of the frames array property.

location (Navigator 2, Internet Explorer 3)

Provides access to the Location object associated with the window.

name (Navigator 2, Internet Explorer 3)

Identifies the window's name.

offscreenBuffering (Navigator 4, Internet Explorer 4)

Identifies whether offscreen buffering is turned on.

opener (Navigator 3, Internet Explorer 4)

Identifies the window object that caused the current window object to be opened.

parent (Navigator 2, Internet Explorer 3)

Identifies the window's parent window.

self (Navigator 2, Internet Explorer 3)

Refers to the current window.

status (Navigator 2, Internet Explorer 3)

Provides access to the window's status display area.

top (Navigator 2, Internet Explorer 3)

Provides access to the topmost browser window.

window (Navigator 2, Internet Explorer 3)

Refers to the current window.

Other Properties

clientInformation (Internet Explorer 4), crypto (Navigator 4), dialogArguments (Internet Explorer 4), dialogHeight (Internet Explorer 4), dialogLeft (Internet Explorer 4), dialogTop (Internet Explorer 4), dialogWidth (Internet Explorer 4), event (Internet Explorer 4), innerHeight (Navigator 4), innerWidth (Navigator 4), locationbar (Navigator 4), menubar (Navigator 4), navigator (Internet Explorer 4), outerHeight (Navigator 4), outerWidth (Navigator 4), pageXOffset (Navigator 4), pageYOffset (Navigator 4), personalbar (Navigator 4), returnValue (Internet Explorer 4), screen (Internet Explorer 4), screenX (Navigator 4), screenY (Navigator 4), scrollbars (Navigator 4), statusbar (Navigator 4), toolbar (Navigator 4)

Methods

Methods Supported by Both Navigator and Internet Explorer

alert(message) (Navigator 2, Internet Explorer 3)

Displays the alert message.

`blur()` (Navigator 2, Internet Explorer 3)

Removes focus from the window.

`clearInterval(interval)` (Navigator 4, Internet Explorer 4)

Clears the specified interval timer.

`clearTimeout(timeout)` (Navigator 2, Internet Explorer 3)

Clears the specified timeout.

`close()` (Navigator 2, Internet Explorer 3)

Closes the window.

`confirm(string)` (Navigator 2, Internet Explorer 3)

Displays a confirmation message.

`focus()` (Navigator 3, Internet Explorer 4)

Brings focus to the window.

`open(url, name[, features])` (Navigator 2, Internet Explorer 3)

Opens a window with the specified name and features.

`prompt(string[,default])` (Navigator 2, Internet Explorer 3)

Displays a prompt to the user.

`scroll(x,y)` (Navigator 3, Internet Explorer 4)

Scrolls the window to the specified coordinate.

`setInterval(expression, milliseconds)` (Navigator 4, Internet Explorer 4)

Sets an interval timer.

`setInterval(function, milliseconds[, arg1[, ..., argN]])` (Navigator 4, Internet Explorer 4)

Sets an interval timer.

`setTimeout(expression, milliseconds)` (Navigator 2, Internet Explorer 3)

Sets a timeout.

Other Methods

`atob` (Navigator 4), `back` (Navigator 4), `btoa` (Navigator 4), `captureEvents` (Navigator 4), `crypto.random` (Navigator 4), `crypto.signText` (Navigator 4), `disableExternalCapture` (Navigator 4), `enableExternalCapture` (Navigator 4), `execScript` (Internet Explorer 4), `find` (Navigator 4), `forward` (Navigator 4), `handleEvent` (Navigator 4), `home` (Navigator 4), `moveBy` (Navigator 4), `moveTo` (Navigator 4), `navi-`

gate (Internet Explorer 4), print (Navigator 4), releaseEvents (Navigator 4), resizeBy (Navigator 4), resizeTo (Navigator 4), routeEvent (Navigator 4), scrollBy (Navigator 4), scrollTo (Navigator 4), setHotKeys (Navigator 4), setResizable (Navigator 4), setTimeout (Navigator 4), setZOptions (Navigator 4), showHelp (Internet Explorer 4), showModalDialog (Internet Explorer 4), stop (Navigator 4)

Events

onblur (Navigator 3, Internet Explorer 4), ondragdrop (Navigator 4), onerror (Navigator 3, Internet Explorer 4), onfocus (Navigator 3, Internet Explorer 4), onload (Navigator 2, Internet Explorer 3), onmove (Navigator 4), onresize (Navigator 4, Internet Explorer 4), onunload (Navigator 2, Internet Explorer 3), onbeforeunload (Internet Explorer 4), onhelp (Internet Explorer 4), onscroll (Internet Explorer 4)

XML

Browser Support: Internet Explorer 5

Provides access to an XML data island.

Properties

Properties Supported by Both Navigator and Internet Explorer

None.

Other Properties

canHaveHTML (Internet Explorer 5), contentEditable (Internet Explorer 5), disabled (Internet Explorer 5), id (Internet Explorer 5), isContentEditable (Internet Explorer 5), isDisabled (Internet Explorer 5), parentElement (Internet Explorer 5), readyState (Internet Explorer 5), recordset (Internet Explorer 5), scopeName (Internet Explorer 5), src (Internet Explorer 5), tagUrn (Internet Explorer 5), XMLDocument (Internet Explorer 5)

Methods

Methods Supported by Both Navigator and Internet Explorer
None.

Other Methods
addBehavior (Internet Explorer 5), componentFromPoint (Internet Explorer 5), fireEvent (Internet Explorer 5), removeBehavior (Internet Explorer 5)

Events

ondataavailable (Internet Explorer 5), ondatasetchanged (Internet Explorer 5), ondatasetcomplete (Internet Explorer 5), onreadystatechange (Internet Explorer 5), onrowenter (Internet Explorer 5), onrowexit (Internet Explorer 5), onrowsdelete (Internet Explorer 5), onrowsinserted (Internet Explorer 5)

XMP

Browser Support: Internet Explorer 4

Provides access to the HTML XMP tag.

Properties

Properties Supported by Both Navigator and Internet Explorer
None.

Other Properties
className (Internet Explorer 4), document (Internet Explorer 4), id (Internet Explorer 4), innerText (Internet Explorer 4), isTextEdit (Internet Explorer 4), lang (Internet Explorer 4), language (Internet Explorer 4), offsetHeight (Internet Explorer 4), offsetLeft (Internet Explorer 4), offsetParent (Internet Explorer 4), offsetTop (Internet Explorer 4), offsetWidth (Internet Explorer 4), outerHTML (Internet Explorer 4), outerText (Internet Explorer 4), parentElement

(Internet Explorer 4), parentTextEdit (Internet Explorer 4), source-
Index (Internet Explorer 4), style (Internet Explorer 4), tagName (Internet Explorer 4), title (Internet Explorer 4)

Methods

Methods Supported by Both Navigator and Internet Explorer
None.

Other Methods
click (Internet Explorer 4), contains (Internet Explorer 4), get-
Attribute (Internet Explorer 4), insertAdjacentHTML (Internet
Explorer 4), removeAttribute (Internet Explorer 4), scrollIntoView
(Internet Explorer 4), setAttribute (Internet Explorer 4)

Events

onclick (Internet Explorer 4), ondblclick (Internet Explorer 4),
ondragstart (Internet Explorer 4), onfilterchange (Internet Explorer 4),
onhelp (Internet Explorer 4), onkeydown (Internet Explorer 4), onkeypress (Internet Explorer 4), onkeyup (Internet Explorer 4), onmousedown (Internet Explorer 4), onmousemove (Internet Explorer 4),
onmouseout (Internet Explorer 4), onmouseover (Internet Explorer 4),
onmouseup (Internet Explorer 4), onselectstart (Internet Explorer 4)

Appendix B

PERL FUNCTIONS

The following functions, listed alphabetically by function name, are available in the standard installation of Perl (as of version 5.005). When using Perl on OS platforms other than UNIX, some of the functions may operate partially—or not at all. Platform-dependent behavior is noted in an individual function's description.

abs $value

Returns the absolute value of its numeric argument. If $value is non-numeric, a value of 0 is returned.

```
$value = -4;
print abs($value); # prints '4'
```

accept $new_socket, $old_socket

Analogous to the UNIX accept() system call. Accepts a network connection, returning the packed address if successful or returning False if unsuccessful.

alarm $seconds

Sets a timer to have a SIGALRM delivered to this process after the approximate number of seconds have elapsed. There is a single global counter for alarm; if you call alarm a second time before the first call's timer has elapsed, the timer is reset to the $seconds specified in the last call, and the number of seconds that were remaining on the first call are returned. You can cancel the timer by calling with $seconds set to 0.

NOTE

You should not use alarm and sleep in the same block of code, because their timer data structures can interact in undefined ways. The accuracy of the timer is effectively plus or minus one second.

atan2 $y, $x

Returns the arctangent of $y/$x in the range −PI to PI (radians).

Use the following function to obtain the tangent of $x:

```
$tangent = ( sin($x) / cos($x) );
```

bind $socket, $name

Binds a network address to a socket. Analogous to the bind() UNIX system call. Returns True if successful; returns False if not. The $name should be a packed address of the appropriate type for the socket specified in $socket. *See* accept() for an example of usage.

binmode FILEHANDLE

Forces the file to be read or written in binary mode. Effective only on operating systems that distinguish between binary and text files. Binmode has no effect on many operating systems (notably UNIX and MacOS); however, in MS-DOS and Windows, it is essential to prevent file corruption on writes. The FILEHANDLE can be an expression, in which case the value is taken as the name of the filehandle.

bless $reference, $classname
bless $reference

This function causes the object referenced by $reference to be an object in the $classname package. If $classname is omitted, the current package is used. Use the two-argument version if the function doing the blessing might be inherited by a derived class, otherwise the wrong class may be used.

caller

Useful for debugging and profiling, caller() returns information about the current call stack. If the current block of code has been called as a function by some other block of code, the following line can be used:

```
($package, $filename, $line) = caller;
```

If the current block hasn't been called from elsewhere (the stack is empty), $package, $filename, and $line are set to undefined.

chdir $new_directory

Changes the working directory to $new_directory, if possible. If $new_directory is omitted, changes to the user's home directory (this in particular may be undefined on non-UNIX systems). Returns True if successful; returns False if not. You should always check the result, and you may want to use die() or warn() to print the error message if False is returned.

chmod $mode, @filelist

Sets the permissions on a list of files. The $mode should always be numeric; using a string will probably have unintended results. The value returned is the number of files successfully changed.

```
# the following line sets filename.dat to be owner
➡ readable/writeable, and
# readable by everyone else
$mode = 0644;    chmod $mode, 'filename.dat';
# this does the same thing... the string-to-octal
➡ conversion is necessary
$mode = '0644'; chmod oct($mode), 'filename.dat';
# sets mode to -w--r-T, which is probably not what you want
$mode = '0644'; chmod $mode, 'filename.dat';
```

chomp $variable
chomp @list
chomp

Removes the trailing string if it corresponds to the current value of $/ (which will probably be "\n" unless you've set it to something else), and returns the total number of characters removed from all its arguments. Often used to remove the newline from the end of an input record. If $variable and @list are not used, it chomps $_.

For example:

```
while (<MYFILE>) {
    chomp;  # remove last \n from current value in $_
    @array = split(/:/);
    # now the last item in @array doesn't end with a \n
}
```

If you chomp a list, each element is chomped, and the total number of characters removed is returned.

chop $variable
chop @list
chop

Removes the last character of a string and returns the character chopped. Used primarily to remove the newline from the end of an input record, but it is much more efficient than s/\n$// because it doesn't scan or copy the string. If $variable is omitted, it chops '$_'.

If you chop a list, each element is chopped. Only the value of the last chop() is returned.

chown $uid, $gid, @list_of_files

Changes the owner (and group) of a list of files. Returns the number of files successfully changed. Both $uid and $gid must be numeric, or they must evaluate to numbers. Depending on your operating system and its configuration, you may not be able to change $uid; so if you use a value other than the one the file is currently set to, the call will fail.

chr $number
chr

Returns the ASCII character corresponding to $number in the character set. If $number is omitted, the current value of $_ is used. To find the number corresponding to an ASCII character, use ord().

For example:

```
$char = chr(65);
print $char; # prints 'A'
```

chroot $directory
chroot

Works similarly to the chroot() UNIX system call. It makes the directory the new root directory for path names that begin with a "/". The current working directory is unaffected (use chdir() for that). For security reasons, chroot is restricted to the superuser. If $directory is omitted, the current value of $_ is used.

close FILEHANDLE
close

Closes the file or pipe associated with the file handle, returning True if the system call to close the file, pipe, or socket succeeds. Closes the currently selected filehandle if the argument is omitted.

NOTE
You don't need to close FILEHANDLE if you are immediately going to do another open() on it, because open() will close it for you. However, using close() on an input file does reset the line counter $., and using the implicit close performed by open() does not.

closedir DIRHANDLE

Closes a directory opened by opendir() and returns the result code of that system call.

connect $socket, $name

Analogous to the connect()UNIX system call. Attempts to connect to a remote network socket. Returns True if successful, returns False if not. The $name should be a packed address of the appropriate type for the socket. *See* the accept() function for an example of usage.

cos $radians

Returns the cosine of $radians (a numeric value expressed in radians). If $radians is omitted, the value of $_ is used.

For the inverse cosine operation, you can use the following:

```
$acos = atan2( sqrt(1 - $x * $x), $x ) }
```

crypt $plaintext, $salt

Performs *trapdoor* encryption via the crypt() UNIX system call. To verify an existing encrypted string, you can use the encrypted text as the salt (e.g., compare crypt ($plain, $crypted) to the existing crypted string). This allows your code to work with the standard crypt() and with more exotic implementations.

defined EXPR
defined

Returns True if EXPR has a value other than the undefined value
"undef", and returns False if EXPR has the value "undef". If EXPR is not
present, $_ will be checked. Note that "undef" is not the same as 0 or
"", which are both defined values.

When used on a hash element, it tells you whether the value is
defined. It does not tell you if the key itself is defined in the hash. Use the
exists() function to determine if a particular key exists within a hash.

To determine whether or not a subroutine exists, use "defined
&myFuncName" without parentheses. Using defined() on whole hashes
and arrays can produce confusing results and is, therefore, of limited use-
fulness.

delete EXPR

Deletes the specified key(s) and their associated values from a hash.
Returns the deleted value(s) associated with the key(s), or returns the
undefined value if there was no such key in the hash. Deleting from the
environment variable hash $ENV{} modifies the environment in which
your program runs (e.g., deleting $ENV{'PATH'} would alter the directory
search path applied to any executed system commands). Deleting from a
hash tied to a DBM file deletes the entry from the DBM file.

For example:

```
# deletes the key 'something' and the value delete
# associated with it from the hash
$myHash{'something'};

# deletes everything from the hash
delete @myHash{keys %myHash};
```

However, the last statement is slower than just assigning the empty
list to the hash or undefining it, as shown in the following statement:

```
%myHash = ();
undef %myHash;
```

die $message

Stops execution, prints the $message to the standard error output device, and exits. If the string in $message does not end with a newline character, the name of the script and the line number stopped at are also printed. Including the special variable $!, which in a string context carries a system-produced error message, is frequently useful.

For example:

```
open MYFILE, "test.dat" or die "Can't open file: $!";
```
might produce

```
Can't open file: No such file or directory at test.pl line 5.
```

each %hash

Returns the key (and value) of the next element in the %hash. In a list context, returns a two-element list containing the key and value for the next element of a hash. When called in scalar context, returns just the key. Each successive call to each on the same hash will iterate through the contents of that hash, returning the *next* element(s). When the end of the hash is reached, a null array (in list context) or undef (in scalar context) is returned. Another call to each on the same hash would return the *first* element again.

NOTE

In general, you shouldn't rely on the order of the keys and values returned (because the order may change in future versions of Perl). You can, however, rely on the order returned by the keys() or values() functions being the same on the same, unmodified hash.

For example, the following code returns the keys and values of the current environment:

```
while (($key,$value) = each %ENV) {
    print "$key=$value\n";
}
```

See also keys(), values(), and sort().

eof FILEHANDLE

Returns 1 if the next read on FILEHANDLE will return end of file, or if FILEHANDLE is not open. FILEHANDLE may be an expression whose value gives the real filehandle. If FILEHANDLE is omitted, the last filehandle used is assumed.

exists $array{$key}

Returns True if the key specified by the contents of $key exists in the hash $array.

NOTE
There doesn't need to be a defined value corresponding to the key.

exit $status

Evaluates $status and exits the script with that value.

If $status is omitted, exits with status of 0 (no error). Typically, you use a status of 0 for a normal exit, and a status of 1 for an exit on error—although this may vary depending on your environment. *See also* die().

exp $power
exp

Returns *e* (the natural logarithm base) to the power of $power. If $power is omitted, gives exp($_).

fcntl FILEHANDLE,FUNCTION,SCALAR

Implements the fcntl(2) UNIX system function. To import the correct constant definitions, place

```
use Fcntl;
```

before the call to fctnl().

fcntl() will produce a fatal error if used on a machine that doesn't implement fcntl(2).

fileno FILEHANDLE

Returns the file descriptor for a filehandle. Returns undefined if the FILEHANDLE does not refer to an open file.

flock FILEHANDLE, $operation

Implements the flock(2) UNIX system call to lock access to the file specified by FILEHANDLE. Depending on your system environment, Perl may use an emulation of UNIX flock() to provide the same functionality. Returns True for success; returns False on failure. Produces a fatal error if the environment doesn't implement flock(2), fcntl(2) locking, or lockf(3).

The file locking mechanisms used are adhered to only if all other processes and programs accessing the file use flock().

$operation is defined as LOCK_SH, LOCK_EX, or LOCK_UN, possibly combined with LOCK_NB. To use these constants, you must place

    use Fcntl;

before the call to flock().

LOCK_SH requests a shared lock, LOCK_EX requests an exclusive lock, and LOCK_UN releases a previously requested lock. LOCK_NB is used to prevent the call to flock() from blocking while waiting for the lock to be granted.

Recent versions of Perl flush FILEHANDLE before locking or unlocking it.

fork

Performs a fork(2) UNIX system call to create a child process. Execution for the child process begins at the same point in the script at which the fork() call was made. It returns the process id (pid) of the child process to the parent, '0' to the child process, or undef if the call to fork() is unsuccessful.

NOTE
Not all system environments support fork().

format

Used to declare a picture format for use by the write() function.

getc FILEHANDLE
getc

Returns the next single character from the input file specified by FILE-HANDLE. Returns undef if FILEHANDLE is at the end of the file or if there was an error. If FILEHANDLE is omitted, getc reads from the standard input.

getlogin

Implements the getlogin() UNIX system call, which on most systems returns the current login name—if there is one. In most cases, using getpwuid($<) is preferable.

getpeername SOCKET

Returns the packed sockaddr address of the other end of the SOCKET connection.

getpgrp $pid

For systems that implement or emulate the getpgrp() UNIX system call, getpgrp $pid returns the current process group for the specified PID. For a $pid of 0, getpgrp $pid returns the current process group for the current process. If PID is omitted, getpgrp $pid returns the process group of the current process.

getppid

Returns the process id of the parent process.

getpriority $process_id
getpriority $uid

Returns the current priority for a process, a process group, or a user. If used on a system that doesn't implement the getpriority() UNIX system call, it will raise a fatal exception.

getpwnam NAME
getgrnam NAME
gethostbyname NAME
getnetbyname NAME
getprotobyname NAME
getpwuid UID
getgrgid GID
getservbyname NAME,PROTO
gethostbyaddr ADDR,ADDRTYPE
getnetbyaddr ADDR,ADDRTYPE
getprotobynumber NUMBER
getservbyport PORT,PROTO
getpwent
getgrent
gethostent
getnetent
getprotoent
getservent
setpwent
setgrent
sethostent STAYOPEN
setnetent STAYOPEN
setprotoent STAYOPEN

setservent STAYOPEN
endpwent
endgrent
endhostent
endnetent
endprotoent
endservent

These functions implement the UNIX system calls of the same names. On a UNIX system, see the networks(5) man page for details. The use of these functions on other systems may be emulated or unsupported.

getsockname SOCKET

Returns the packed sockaddr address from the local end of the SOCKET connection.

getsockopt SOCKET,LEVEL,OPTNAME

Like the UNIX system call, returns the socket option specified or returns undef if there is an error.

glob EXPR
glob

Returns the value of EXPR with filename expansions such as the standard UNIX shell /bin/csh would do. If EXPR is omitted, '$_' is used.

gmtime EXPR

In a list context, gmtime EXPR converts a time as returned by the time() function to a nine-element array with the time localized for the standard Greenwich time zone.

```
# 0   1   2    3     4    5     6     7     8
($sec,$min,$hour,$mday,$mon,$year,$wday,$yday,$isdst) =
gmtime(time);
```

Each array element is numeric and comes straight out of a struct tm (defined in /usr/include/time/h on UNIX systems). The month value $mon has the range 0 through 11. The weekday $wday has the range 0 through 6, starting with Sunday as day 0. The $year is the number of years since 1900; therefore, the $year for the year 2021 would be 121.

If EXPR is omitted, the current system time is assumed.

goto LABEL

Causes execution to jump to the statement with the unique LABEL preceeding it. It is not possible to jump into a subroutine or into the middle of a loop.

grep EXPR,@list

In a list context, this function returns a new list consisting of each element from @list for which EXPR evaluates to True. In a scalar context, it returns the number of times the expression was True.

For example:

```
# remove lines that begin with a '#'
@newlines = grep(!/^#/, @input_lines);
```

See also the map() function for an array composed of the results of EXPR.

hex EXPR
hex

Interprets EXPR as a hex string and returns the corresponding value. If EXPR is omitted, $_ is used.

For example:

```
print hex '0xA'; # prints '10'
print hex 'aF';   # same
```

index $string,$substring,$position
index $string,$substring

Returns the position of the first occurrence of $substring in $string at or after $position. If $position is omitted, this function starts searching from the beginning of the string. The return value is the position, starting at 0, for the first character of $string. If the substring is not found, it returns −1.

int EXPR
int

Returns the integer portion of EXPR, truncating any value after the decimal point. If EXPR is omitted, int uses $_. Note that this function does not perform rounding.

For example:

```
$a = int(5.94); # $a become '5'
```

ioctl FILEHANDLE,FUNCTION,SCALAR

Implements the ioctl() UNIX system call. *See* the ioctl UNIX man pages for details.

join EXPR,@list

Joins the separate strings of @list into a single string with fields separated by the value of EXPR, and returns that new string.

For example:

```
$fullpath = join('/', $relative_path, $myfile);
```
See also the split() function.

keys %hash

Returns an array whose members are all the keys of the named hash.

For example:

```
%hash = ( 'fish', 'yellowtail',
          'mammal', 'dolphin' );

@types = keys(%hash); # @types contains 'fish' and 'mammal'
```
See also each(), values(), and sort().

kill $signal, @list_of_processes

Sends a signal to a list of processes and returns the number of processes successfully signaled.

last LABEL
last

When used without LABEL, breaks out of the innermost loop being executed. If last is used with a LABEL, it jumps to the end of the block named by LABEL.

lc $string
lc

Returns the lowercase version of $string (or $_ if $string is omitted).

lcfirst $string
lcfirst

Returns the value of $string (or $_ if $string is omitted) with only the first character set in lowercase.

length $string
length

Returns the length in characters of the value of $string (or $_ if $string is omitted).

link OLDFILE, NEWFILE

Creates a new filename linked to the old filename. Returns True if successful; returns False if not.

listen SOCKET, QUEUESIZE

Implements the listen() UNIX system call, accepting connections on a predefined SOCKET. Returns True if it succeeded; returns False if it didn't.

localtime EXPR

Similar to the gmtime() function, but it uses the local time zone for the system rather than Greenwich mean time.

log EXPR
log

Returns the natural logarithm of EXPR (or $_ if EXPR is omitted). *See* the exp() function for the inverse operation.

lstat FILEHANDLE
lstat $filename
lstat

Similar to the stat() function (including setting the special '_' filehandle). However, in a symbolic link, it operates on the link itself instead of the file to which the link points. If symbolic links are unimplemented on your system, a normal stat() is performed.

If $filename is omitted, stats '$_' is performed.

map EXPR,@list

Evaluates EXPR for each element of the @list and returns the list value. In a scalar context, it returns the total number of elements generated.

For example:

```
# returns the names in all uppercase
@uppercased = map(uc, @names);
```

mkdir $filename, $mode

Creates the directory specified by $filename, with permissions specified by $mode (as modified by umask). If it succeeds, it returns True. If it doesn't succeed, it returns False and sets $! (errno).

msgctl ID, CMD, ARG
msgget KEY, FLAGS
msgsnd ID, MSG, FLAGS
msgrcv ID, VAR,SIZE, TYPE, FLAGS

Implements the UNIX System V system calls by the same names. *See* the respective man pages for details.

next LABEL
next

Skips to the loop within the block named by LABEL. If LABEL is omitted, next skips to the next iteration within the innermost loop.

oct EXPR
oct

Interprets EXPR as an octal string and returns the corresponding value. If EXPR begins with 0x, oct() interprets it as a hex string. If EXPR starts off with 0b, it is interpreted as a binary string. If EXPR is omitted, $_ is used.

open FILEHANDLE, $filename

Opens a file whose name is $filename and associates it with the FILE-HANDLE.

If the filename begins with "<" or nothing, the file is opened for input. If the filename begins with ">", the file is created if necessary, truncated, and opened for output. If the filename begins with ">>", the file is created if necessary and opened for appending. You can put a "+" in front of the ">" or "<" to indicate that you want both read and write access to the file. Therefore, "+<" is usually preferred for making read/write updates—

the "+>" mode would erase the file first. Normally, you can't use either read-write mode to update textfiles because they have variable-length records.

If the filename begins with "|", the filename is interpreted as a command to which output is to be piped. If the filename ends with a "|", the filename is interpreted as a command which pipes output to the invoking code.

opendir DIRHANDLE, $directory_name

Opens a directory named $directory_name for processing by the readdir(), telldir(), seekdir(), rewinddir(), and closedir() functions. Returns True if successful.

ord EXPR
ord

Returns the numeric ASCII value of the first character of EXPR. It returns $_ if EXPR is omitted. The chr() function performs the inverse operation.

pack $template, @list

Packs an @list into a binary structure determined by $template, returning a scalar string with the structure. The $template is a sequence of characters that determine the order and type of values that are aggregated to construct the return value and consists of the following character codes:

```
a    A string with arbitrary binary data, will be
     null padded.
A    An ASCII string, will be space padded.
Z    A null-terminated (ASCII) string, will be null-
     padded.

b    A bit string (ascending bit order, like vec()).
B    A bit string (descending bit order).
h    A hex string (low nybble first).
H    A hex string (high nybble first).

c    A signed char value.
C    An unsigned char value.
```

s   A signed short value.
S   An unsigned short value (exactly 16 bits).

i   A signed integer value.
I   An unsigned integer value (at least 32 bits,
     may be larger depending on system environment).

l   A signed long value.
L   An unsigned long value (exactly 32 bits).

n   A short in "network" (big-endian) order
     (exactly 16 bits).
N   A long in "network" (big-endian) order (exactly
     32 bits).
v   A short in "VAX" (little-endian) order (exactly
     16 bits).
V   A long in "VAX" (little-endian) order (exactly
     32 bits).

q   A signed quad (64-bit) value.
Q   An unsigned quad value (only on 64-bit integer
     capable systems).

f   A single-precision float in the native format.
d   A double-precision float in the native format.

p   A pointer to a null-terminated string.
P   A pointer to a structure (fixed-length string).

u   A uuencoded string.

w   A BER compressed integer. Its bytes represent
     an unsigned integer in base 128, most
     significant digit first, with as few digits as
     possible. Bit eight (the high bit) is set on
     each byte except the last.

x   A null byte.
X   Back up a byte.
@   Null fill to absolute position.

For example:

```
$foo = pack("CCCC",65,66,67,68);
# foo eq "ABCD"
$foo = pack("C4",65,66,67,68);
# same thing
```

```
$foo = pack("s2",1,2);
# "\1\0\2\0" on little-endian
# "\0\1\0\2" on big-endian

$foo = pack("a4","abcd","x","y","z");
# "abcd"

$foo = pack("aaaa","abcd","x","y","z");
# "axyz"

$foo = pack("a14","abcdefg");
# "abcdefg\0\0\0\0\0\0\0"
```

pop @array
pop

Removes and returns the last element from @array. The array is short-ened by one element. Returns undef if @array is empty. If @array is not specified, it uses the @ARGV array in the main program block or @_ in a subroutine block.

pos $scalar
pos

Returns the offset position where the last matched search was performed on the $scalar variable. If $scalar is omitted, then $_ is used.

print FILEHANDLE LIST
print LIST
print

Prints the contents of LIST as a string to the appropriate output. If FILE-HANDLE is specified, sends the output to the file specified by FILEHANDLE (assuming the file is open and able to be written to). If FILEHANDLE is omitted, the currently selected output device (STDOUT by default) is used. If LIST is omitted, the print function prints the contents of $_.

For example:

```
print MYFILE "save this for later\n";
print "i tried $count times to do it\n";
```

printf FILEHANDLE $format, LIST
printf $format, LIST

Analogous to the ANSI C language printf() function. The $format is parsed, and the values of the variables in LIST are substituted in place of the '%' markers. The most common markers are '%s' for string and '%d' for integer. Many other options are possible; however, so refer to a C language reference for more detail. As with print(), if FILEHANDLE is specified, the output goes to the file specified by FILEHANDLE. If FILE-HANDLE is omitted, the output goes to the currently selected output device. In general, print() is more efficient than printf().

For example:

```
$count = 5;
$thing = "sorting";
printf "i tried %d times to do %s\n", $count, $thing;
```

push @array, LIST

Appends the elements in LIST to the end of the @array, returning the new number of elements in the array. *See also* pop().

q/STRING/
qq/STRING/
qr/STRING/
qx/STRING/
qw/STRING/

Generalized quotes for strings.

quotemeta $string
quotemeta

Returns a copy of $string with all the nonalphanumeric characters backslashed. If $string is omitted, $_ is used.

rand $number
rand

Returns a random fractional number between 0 and the value of $number. The $number must be positive, and if omitted, '1' is used. *See also* srand().

read FILEHANDLE, $scalar, $length, $offset
read FILEHANDLE, $scalar, $length

Reads $length bytes of data into variable $scalar from the FILEHANDLE. Returns the number of bytes actually read, or it returns undef when there is an error. The $scalar will grow or shrink to the length actually read. If no $offset is specified, it is assumed to be 0.

readdir DIRHANDLE

Returns the next directory entry for a directory opened by opendir(). If used in a list context, readdir returns the rest of the entries in the directory. If there are no more entries, it returns an undefined value in a scalar context or a null list in a list context.

readlink EXPR
readlink

If symbolic links are implemented, readlink returns the value of a symbolic link. If symbolic links are not implemented, readlink gives a fatal error. If there is a system error, it returns the undefined value and sets '$!' (errno). If EXPR is omitted, it uses '$_'.

recv SOCKET, $scalar, $len, $flags

Receives a message on a socket. The data is read into the $scalar variable from the specified SOCKET filehandle up to $len bytes. The flags are defined in the recvfrom() UNIX system call.

redo LABEL
redo

The redo command restarts a loop block without reevaluating the conditional. The continue block, if there is one, is not executed. If the LABEL is omitted, the command refers to the innermost enclosing loop.

ref EXPR
ref

Returns True if EXPR is a reference; returns False if not. If EXPR is not specified, '$_' will be used.

rename $oldname, $newname

Changes the name of the file $oldname to $newname. Returns 1 for success and 0 for failure. This function does not work across file system boundaries.

reset EXPR
reset

Clears the value of variables whose names begin with the letters in EXPR. More than one letter can be specified using ranges. If EXPR is not specified, reset uses the special variable ?? (two question marks). The reset() function always returns True. If you use:

```
reset 'A-Z';
```

you will reset all of your environment variables ENV and ARGV, which is probably not what you want.

return EXPR
return

Used to return the list of arguments at the end of a subroutine's execution. If no return statement is found, a subroutine always returns the result of the last expression in it.

reverse @list
reverse $string

Reverses the order of elements in @list, or it reverses the order of characters in $string.

rewinddir DIRHANDLE

Resets the current position to the start of the directory for use with the readdir() function on DIRHANDLE.

rindex $str, $substring, $position
rindex STR, SUBSTR

Gets the position of the last occurrence of $substring in $str. Starts the search from the end of $string unless a position has been specified. If a position is specified, the function starts the search at the position from the end of the string.

rmdir $filename
rmdir

Removes the directory specified by $filename, but only if the directory is empty. Uses $_ if $filename is not specified. Returns 1 on success, and returns 0 on failure with the error code in $!.

scalar EXPR

Forces the EXPR to be interpreted in a scalar context, and returns the value of EXPR.

seek FILEHANDLE, $position,
$startingpoint

Similar to the seek() and fseek() UNIX system calls, seek sets the file pointer for FILEHANDLE. The values for $startingpoint are 0 to set the position from the beginning of the file, 1 to set the position relative to the current location in the file, and 2 to set the position relative to the end of file. Returns 1 upon success; returns 0 upon failure.

seekdir DIRHANDLE, $position

Moves the current position for the readdir() routine on DIRHANDLE to $position, which must be a value returned by telldir().

select FILEHANDLE
select

If FILEHANDLE is specified, select sets the *currently selected filehandle* to FILEHANDLE. If FILEHANDLE is omitted, select returns the currently selected filehandle. The currently selected filehandle is the filehandle to which all write() and print() statements will output if the filehandle isn't specified in the write() or print() statements.

semctl ID,SEMNUM,CMD,ARG
semget KEY,NSEMS,FLAGS
semop KEY,OPSTRING

Works just like the UNIX System V IPC functions of the same name. *See* the UNIX man pages for more detail.

send SOCKET,MSG,FLAGS,TO
send SOCKET,MSG,FLAGS

Sends a message on a SOCKET using the socket() UNIX system call.

setpgrp $pid, $pgrpid

Sets the current process group for the specified $pid. Use a $pid of 0 to imply the current process. Works only if the underlying system supports the operation.

setpriority $process, $group, $user

Sets the current priority for a process, a process group, or a user like the UNIX system call setpriority(). Only works if the underlying system supports it.

shift @array
shift

Removes the first value from the front of the @array and returns the value. The size of @array is reduced by one. If the @array is empty, it returns undef. If @array is not specified, shift uses @_. *See also* pop(), push(), and unshift().

shmctl ID,CMD,ARG
shmget KEY, SIZE, FLAGS

Works just like the UNIX System V IPC shared memory functions. *See* the UNIX man pages for more detail.

sin $radians
sin

Returns a double-precision scalar with the sine of the value of $radians. If $radians is omitted, $_ is used.

sleep $seconds
sleep

Makes the process do nothing for the number of $seconds specified. If $seconds is omitted or evaluates to NULL, the process sleeps forever. You should not mix calls to alarm() and sleep() in the same program.

sort SUBNAME @list
sort BLOCK @list
sort @list

Sorts the @list and returns the sorted list value. Empty values in arrays are removed. The SUBNAME and code BLOCK are pointers to user-defined functions that take two arguments and return an integer value of 1, 0, or −1. A 1 indicates that the first argument is greater than the second. A 0 indicates that the arguments are equal. A −1 indicates that the second argument is greater than the first.

splice @array, $offset, $length, @list
splice @array, $offset, $length
splice @array, $offset

Removes the elements at the position specified by the integer $offset and continuing for the number of items specified by $length from the @array and replaces them with the contents of @list. Returns the list of items removed from @array. The @array grows or shrinks as needed. If @list is not provided, nothing is inserted. If $length is not provided, all the elements from $offset onward are removed.

split /PATTERN/, $string, $limit
split /PATTERN/, $string
split /PATTERN/
split

Returns an array derived from splitting a $string into an array of strings of items equal to the number of elements in $limit. If $string is not provided, the $_ variable is used. The PATTERN may be more than one character long. If PATTERN is not specified, the function splits at white spaces after the leading white spaces have been removed. It returns the number of items up to the limit specified and leaves the remainder as one long list. A call to split() with no arguments is equivalent to a split(' ', $_) call. The PATTERN to a split() call can be a regular expression or a variable containing a regular expression.

sprintf FORMAT, LIST

Similar to the `printf()` function, but instead of sending the output to the currently selected output device, the output goes to the return value of the function.

For example:

```
$adjective = "nice";
$mystring = sprintf "this is %s", $adjective;
# now $mystring contains "this is nice"
```

sqrt $value
sqrt

Returns the square root of $value. If $value is omitted, $_ is used.

srand $seed
srand

Seeds the random number generator for rand() using $seed as a number. Explicitly calling srand() is usually not necessary because it is called implicitly when the rand() operator is first used. However, this was not the case in versions of Perl before 5.004. Therefore, if your script will run under older Perl versions, it should explicitly call srand().

stat FILEHANDLE
stat $filename
stat

Returns a 13-element list giving the status information for either the file opened via FILEHANDLE or named by $filename. If $filename is omitted, $_ is used. Returns a null list if the stat fails.

For example:

```
($dev,$ino,$mode,$nlink,$uid,$gid,$rdev,$size
$atime,$mtime,$ctime,$blksize,$blocks)
   = stat($filename);
```

Not all fields are supported on all filesystem types. The meanings of the fields by position in the returned array are as follows:

```
 0 dev      device number of filesystem
 1 ino      inode number
 2 mode     file mode  (type and permissions)
 3 nlink    number of (hard) links to the file
 4 uid      numeric user ID of file's owner
 5 gid      numeric group ID of file's owner
 6 rdev     the device identifier (special files only)
 7 size     total size of file, in bytes
 8 atime    last access time since the epoch
 9 mtime    last modify time since the epoch
10 ctime    inode change time (NOT creation time!) since
            the epoch (1/1/1970)
11 blksize  preferred block size for file system I/O
12 blocks   actual number of blocks allocated
```

substr $string, $offset, $length, $replacement
substr $string, $offset, $length
substr $string, $offset

Gets a substring from $string of up to $length characters and returns it. The first character to extract from $string is at position 0, unless a positive $offset is specified. If $offset is negative, the offset starts from the end of the string. If $length is not provided, everything up to the end of the string is returned. If $length is negative, it leaves that many characters off from the end of the $string. Using $replacement allows you to replace parts of $string with the contents of $replacement, returning what was in $string before the replacement, which is like a call to splice().

symlink $oldfile, $newfile

Creates a new filename symbolically linked to the old filename. Returns 1 for success; returns 0 for failure.

syscall LIST

Makes the system call, passing the remaining elements as arguments. Using unimplemented system calls will produce a fatal error. Strings are passed by reference and numbers are passed as integers.

sysread FILEHANDLE, $scalar, $length, $offset
sysread FILEHANDLE, $scalar, $length

Reads $length bytes of data into variable $scalar from the specified FILEHANDLE using the read() UNIX system call. Returns the number of bytes actually read. Returns undef in the case of an error. The $scalar grows or shrinks to the length actually read. The offset is used to read data at some place other than the first bytes in $scalar.

system $program $arguments...

Similar to exec(), but this function branches off and returns to the parent process when the child process is finished. Because 'system()' and backticks block 'SIGINT' and 'SIGQUIT', killing the program they are running won't interrupt your program.

syswrite FILEHANDLE, $scalar, $length, $offset
syswrite FILEHANDLE, $scalar, $length
syswrite FILEHANDLE, $scalar

Attempts to write $length bytes of data from variable $scalar to the specified FILEHANDLE using the UNIX system call write(). Returns the number of bytes actually written. Returns undef when an error occurs. An $offset is used to place the read data at the number of $offset at the beginning of the string in $scalar.

tell FILEHANDLE
tell

Gets the current file position for FILEHANDLE. If no FILEHANDLE is specified, it uses the last read file.

telldir DIRHANDLE

Returns the current position of the readdir() routines on DIRHANDLE. A value can be used with seekdir() to access a particular location in a directory.

time

Returns the number of non-leap seconds since the epoch (00:00:00 UTC, January 1, 1970). Used with gmtime() and localtime().

times

Returns a four-item array with the user and system times (in seconds) for this process and the children (if any) of this process.

truncate FILEHANDLE, $length
truncate $filename, $length

Truncates the file opened on FILEHANDLE (or the file specified by $filename) to the specified $length.

uc $string
uc

Returns an uppercased copy of $string (or $_ if $string is omitted).

ucfirst $string
ucfirst

Returns the value of $string (or $_ if $string is omitted) with the first character uppercased.

umask $value
umask

Sets the umask for the process to $value and returns the old value. If $value is omitted, this function just returns the current umask.

If umask(2) is not implemented on your system and you are trying to restrict access for *yourself* (i.e., (EXPR & 0700) > 0), umask produces a fatal error at runtime. If umask(2) is not implemented and you are not trying to restrict access for yourself, umask returns 'undef'.

undef EXPR

Removes any definition of EXPR, which can be a scalar, array, hash, or subroutine. Using undef on $hash{$key} is often more confusing than using delete().

unlink LIST
unlink

Deletes the files named in LIST (or in $_ if no list is specified). Returns the number of files successfully deleted. The unlink() will not delete directories (unless the program is run as root and used with the -U flag to Perl); use rmdir() to remove directories.

unpack $template, EXPR

The unpack() function does the reverse of pack(): It takes a string representing a structure and expands it, returning the array value. In a scalar context, it returns just the first value produced. The $template has the same format as the pack() function. *See also* pack.

unshift @array, @list

Performs the opposite of the shift() function—or the opposite of a push(), depending on how you look at it. Adds the contents of @list to the front of the @array and returns the new number of elements in the array.

utime $accesstime, $modificationtime, @files

Modifies the access and modification times on each file in a list of files. Returns the number of files successfully changed.

values %hash

Returns an array containing only the values of the %hash. The order in which the values are returned may be assumed to be random—although in fact the order is the same order that the keys() or each() function would produce on the same modified hash. *See also* keys().

wait

Waits for a child process to terminate and returns the pid of the deceased process. It returns −1 if there are no child processes. The status is returned in the $? special variable.

waitpid PID, FLAGS

Waits for a particular child process to terminate and returns the pid of the deceased process. It returns −1 if there is no such child process. The status is returned in $?.

wantarray

Returns True if the currently executing subroutine is looking for a list value, returns False if a scalar value is being looked for, and returns UNDEFINED if no value is being looked for.

warn LIST

Produces a message on STDERR similar to die(), but it doesn't exit or throw an exception.

write FILEHANDLE
write EXPR
write

Writes a formatted record to the specified file using the format associated with that file. *See also* print().

Appendix C
STANDARD PERL MODULES

This appendix describes how to use the modules included with a standard Perl installation (as of version 5.005). These modules (listed alphabetically) represent a small fraction of the modules publicly available for Perl. If you can't find what you need here, visit the CPAN archives (`http://www.cpan.org`), where you probably can find what you need.

AutoLoader

This module allows you to load subroutines only on demand instead of preloading them before your program executes.

Synopsis

```
package Foo;
use AutoLoader 'AUTOLOAD';
# import the default AUTOLOAD subroutine

package Bar;
use AutoLoader;
# don't import AUTOLOAD, define our own
sub AUTOLOAD {
    ...
    $AutoLoader::AUTOLOAD = "...";
    goto &AutoLoader::AUTOLOAD;
}
```

Description

The AutoLoader module works with the AutoSplit module and the '__END__' token to defer the loading of some subroutines until they are used instead of loading them all at once.

To use AutoLoader, the author of a module must place the definitions of subroutines to be autoloaded after an '__END__' token. (See the perldata manpage.) You can manually run the AutoSplit module to extract the definitions into individual files, which will be named according to the convention auto/funcname.al.

AutoLoader implements an AUTOLOAD subroutine. When an undefined subroutine is called in a client module of AutoLoader, AutoLoader's AUTOLOAD subroutine attempts to locate the subroutine in a file with a name related to the location of the file from which the client module was read. As an example, if POSIX.pm is located in /usr/local/lib/perl5/ POSIX.pm, AutoLoader will look for Perl subroutines POSIX in /usr/ local/lib/perl5/auto/POSIX/*.al, where the '.al' file has the same name as the subroutine, sans package. If such a file exists, AUTOLOAD will read and evaluate it, thereby (presumably) defining the needed subroutine. AUTOLOAD will then 'goto' the newly defined subroutine.

Once this process completes for a given function, it is defined, so future calls to the subroutine will bypass the AUTOLOAD mechanism.

Subroutine Stubs

In order for object method lookup and/or prototype checking to operate correctly even when methods have not yet been defined, you need to *forward declare* each subroutine (as in `'sub NAME;'`). See the "Synopsis" section in the `perlsub` manpage. Such forward declaration creates *subroutine stubs*, which are placeholders with no code.

The `AutoSplit` and `AutoLoader` modules automate the creation of forward declarations. The `AutoSplit` module creates an index file containing forward declarations of all the `AutoSplit` subroutines. When the `AutoLoader` module is used (run with `'use'`), it loads these declarations into its callers package.

Because of this mechanism, it is important that `AutoLoader` is always used and not required (run with `'require'`). In order to use AutoLoader's AUTOLOAD subroutine, you *must* explicitly import it:

```
use AutoLoader 'AUTOLOAD';
```

Overriding AutoLoader's AUTOLOAD Subroutine

Some modules, mainly extensions, provide their own AUTOLOAD subroutines. They typically need to check for special cases (such as constants) and then fall back to `AutoLoader`'s AUTOLOAD for the rest.

Such modules should *not* import AutoLoader's AUTOLOAD subroutine. Instead, they should define their own AUTOLOAD subroutines along these lines:

```
use AutoLoader;
use Carp;

sub AUTOLOAD {
  my $constname;
  ($constname = $AUTOLOAD) =~ s/.*:://;
  my $val = constant($constname, @_ ? $_[0] : 0);
  if ($! != 0) {
    if ($! =~ /Invalid/) {
      $AutoLoader::AUTOLOAD = $AUTOLOAD;
      goto &AutoLoader::AUTOLOAD;
```

```
    }
    else {
        croak "constant $constname is not defined";
    }
}
*$AUTOLOAD = sub { $val };
# same as: eval "sub $AUTOLOAD { $val }";
goto &$AUTOLOAD;
}
```

If any module's own AUTOLOAD subroutine has no need to fall back to the AutoLoader's AUTOLOAD subroutine (because it doesn't have any AutoSplit subroutines), then that module should not use AutoLoader.

Package Lexicals

Package lexicals declared with 'my' in the main block of a package using AutoLoader will not be visible to autoloaded subroutines, because the given scope ends at the '__END__' marker. A module using such variables as package globals will not work properly under the AutoLoader.

The 'vars' pragma (see the section on vars in the perlmod manpage) may be used in such situations as an alternative to explicitly qualifying all globals with the package namespace. Variables predeclared with this pragma will be visible to any autoloaded routines (but will not be invisible outside the package, unfortunately).

AutoLoader versus SelfLoader

The AutoLoader is similar in purpose to SelfLoader: they both delay the loading of subroutines.

SelfLoader uses the '__DATA__' marker rather than '__END__'. Although this means you don't need to use a hierarchy of disk files and the associated open and close for each routine loaded, SelfLoader is slower when parsing the lines after '__DATA__'. Once the lines are parsed at startup, routines are cached. SelfLoader can also handle multiple packages in a file.

AutoLoader reads code only as it is requested. In many cases this should make it faster than SelfLoader; however, AutoLoader requires that a mechanism like AutoSplit be used to create the individual files. The ExtUtils::MakeMaker manpage will invoke AutoSplit automatically if AutoLoader is used in a module source file.

Caveats

Prior to Perl 5.002, AutoLoaders had a slightly different interface. Any old modules that use AutoLoader should be changed to the new calling style. Typically, this means changing a require to a use, adding the explicit `AUTOLOAD` import, if needed, and removing AutoLoader from '@ISA'.

On systems with restrictions on filename length, the file corresponding to a subroutine may have a shorter name that the routine itself. This can lead to conflicting filenames. The AutoSplit package warns of these potential conflicts when used to split a module.

AutoLoader may fail to find the autosplit files (or may even find the wrong ones) when '@INC' contains relative paths, and the program uses 'chdir'.

See Also

The SelfLoader manpage—an autoloader that doesn't use external files.

Benchmark

The Benchmark provides ways to determine the amount of time needed to execute a block of code. It is useful for comparing different ways of doing the same thing and can help you optimize code.

```
timethis - run a chunk of code several times
timethese - run several chunks of code several times
timeit - run a chunk of code and see how long it goes
```

Synopsis

```perl
timethis ($count, "code");

# Use Perl code in strings...
timethese($count, {
  'Name1' => '...code1...',
  'Name2' => '...code2...',
});

# ... or use subroutine references.
timethese($count, {
  'Name1' => sub { ...code1... },
  'Name2' => sub { ...code2... },
});
```

```
$t = timeit($count, '...other code...')
print "$count loops of other code took:",timestr($t),"\n";
```

Description

The Benchmark module encapsulates a number of routines to help you figure out how long it takes to execute some code.

Methods

The following methods configure Benchmark for use.

new

The New command returns the current time. For example:

```
use Benchmark;
$t0 = new Benchmark;
# ... your code here ...
$t1 = new Benchmark;
$td = timediff($t1, $t0);
print "the code took:",timestr($td),"\n";
```

debug

The Debug command enables or disables debugging by setting the '$Benchmark::Debug' flag:

```
debug Benchmark 1;
$t = timeit(10, ' 5 ** $Global ');
debug Benchmark 0;
```

Standard Exports

The following routines will be available if you use the Benchmark module.

timeit (COUNT, CODE)

The COUNT argument is the number of times to run the loop, and CODE is the code to run. CODE may be either a code reference or a string to be evaluated; either way it will be run in the caller's package.

Returns: a Benchmark object.

timethis (COUNT, CODE, [TITLE, [STYLE]])

The COUNT argument is the number of times to run the loop, and CODE is the code to run. CODE may be a string to evaluate or a code reference; either way the CODE will run in the caller's package. Results will be printed to STDOUT as TITLE followed by the times. If the TITLE argument is omitted, the title defaults to "timethis COUNT." STYLE determines the format of the output, as described for timestr().

If the COUNT is negative, the number is interpreted to mean the *minimum number of CPU seconds* to run. A zero signifies the default of three seconds.

For example, to run for at least 10 seconds:

```
timethis(-10, $code)
```

or to run two pieces of code tests for at least three seconds:

```
timethese(0, { test1 => '...', test2 => '...'})
```

CPU seconds are, in UNIX terms, the user time plus the system time of the process itself, as opposed to the realtime (wall-clock time) and the time spent by the child processes. Less than 0.1 seconds is not accepted (for example, −0.01 as the count will cause a fatal runtime exception).

The CPU seconds is the minimum time. CPU scheduling and other operating system factors may complicate the attempt so that a little more time is spent. The benchmark output will, however, also list the number of '$code' runs/second, which should be a more interesting number than the actual seconds.

Returns: a Benchmark object.

timethese (COUNT, CODEHASHREF, [STYLE])

CODEHASHREF is a reference to a hash containing names as keys and either a string to evaluate or a code reference for each value. For each (KEY, VALUE) pair in the CODEHASHREF, this routine will call timethis(COUNT, VALUE, KEY, VALUE).

The routines are called in string comparison order of KEY. The COUNT can be zero or negative. *See* timethis().

timediff (T1, T2)

Timediff (T1, T2) returns the difference between two Benchmark times as a Benchmark object suitable for passing to timestr().

timesum (T1, T2)

This command returns the sum of two Benchmark times as a Benchmark object suitable for passing to timestr().

timestr (TIMEDIFF, [STYLE, [FORMAT]])

This routine returns a string that formats the times in the TIMEDIFF object in the requested STYLE. TIMEDIFF is expected to be a Benchmark object similar to the one returned by timediff().

STYLE can be 'all', 'noc', 'nop', or 'auto'. The 'all' command shows each of the five available times (wall-clock time, user time, system time, user time of children, and system time of children). The 'noc' command shows all the available times except the two children times. The 'nop' command shows only wall-clock time and the two children times. The 'auto' command (the default) will act as 'all' unless the children times are both zero, in which case it will act as 'noc'.

FORMAT is the printf(3) manpage-style format specifier (without the leading '%') used to print the times. It defaults to '5.2f'.

Caveats

Comparing evaluated strings with code references will give you inaccurate results. A code reference will show a slower execution time than the equivalent evaluated string.

The realtime timing is performed using time(2) and the granularity is, therefore, only one second.

Short tests may produce negative figures because Perl can appear to take longer to execute the empty loop than it takes to execute a short test. For example, try:

```
timethis(100,'1');
```

The system time of the null loop might be slightly more than the system time of the loop with the actual code; therefore, the difference might end up being less than 0.

CGI::Carp

This module provides routines for writing error and diagnostic messages to an HTTPD Web server's logs, rather than the standard error device.

Synopsis

```
use CGI::Carp;

die "dying because of fatal error.\n";

use CGI::Carp qw(cluck);
cluck "I wouldn't do that if I were you";

use CGI::Carp qw(fatalsToBrowser);
die "Fatal error messages are now sent to browser";
```

Description

CGI scripts have a nasty habit of leaving warning messages that are neither time stamped nor fully identified in the error logs. Tracking down the script that caused the error is a pain. CGI::Carp fixes the problem. Replace the usual

```
use Carp;
```

with

```
use CGI::Carp
```

The standard warn(), die (), croak(), confess(), and carp() calls will be replaced automatically with functions that write nicely time-stamped messages to the HTTP server error log.

For example:

```
[Fri Nov 17 21:40:43 1995] test.pl: I'm confused at test.pl
➡ line 3.
[Fri Nov 17 21:40:43 1995] test.pl: Got an error message:
➡ Permission denied.
[Fri Nov 17 21:40:43 1995] test.pl: I'm dying.
```

Redirecting Error Messages

By default, error messages are sent to STDERR. Most HTTPD servers direct STDERR to the server's error log. Some applications may keep private error logs, distinct from the server's error log, or they may direct error messages to STDOUT so that the browser will receive them.

The 'carpout()' function is provided for this purpose. Because carpout() is not exported by default, you must import it explicitly by saying

```
use CGI::Carp qw(carpout);
```

The `carout()` function requires one argument, which should be a reference to an open filehandle for writing errors. It should be called in a `BEGIN' block at the top of the CGI application so that compiler errors will be caught.

For example:

```
BEGIN {
  use CGI::Carp qw(carpout);
  open(LOG, ">>/usr/local/cgi-logs/mycgi-log") or
    die("Unable to open mycgi-log: $!\n");
  carpout(LOG);
}
```

The `carpout()`command does not handle file locking on the log for you at this point.

The real STDERR is not closed. It is moved to SAVEERR. Some servers, when dealing with CGI scripts, close their connection to the browser when the script closes STDOUT and STDERR. SAVEERR is used to prevent this from happening prematurely.

You can pass filehandles to `carpout()` in a variety of ways. The *correct way*, according to Tom Christiansen, is to pass a reference to a filehandle `glob`:

```
carpout(\*LOG);
```

The following syntaxes are also accepted:

```
carpout(LOG);
carpout(main::LOG);
carpout(main'LOG);
carpout(\LOG);
carpout(\'main::LOG');
```

. . . and so on.

`FileHandle` and other objects work as well.

Using `carpout()` is not great for performance; however, using it for debugging or moderate-use applications is recommended. Perhaps a future version of this module will delay the redirection of STDERR until one of the `CGI::Carp` methods is called to prevent the performance hit.

Making Perl Errors Appear in the Browser Window

If you want to send fatal (`die`, `confess`) errors to the browser, ask to import the special `"fatalsToBrowser"` subroutine:

```
use CGI::Carp qw(fatalsToBrowser);
die "Bad error here";
```

Fatal errors will now be echoed to the browser as well as to the log. CGI::Carp arranges to send a minimal HTTP header to the browser so that even errors that occur in the early compile phase will be seen. Nonfatal errors will be directed only to the log file (unless redirected with carpout).

Changing the Default Message

By default, the software error message is followed by a note to contact the Webmaster by e-mail with the time and date of the error. If you don't like this message, you can change it using the set_message() routine. This routine is not imported by default. You should import it on the use() line:

```
use CGI::Carp qw(fatalsToBrowser set_message);
set_message("It's not a bug, it's a feature!");
```

You may also pass a code reference to create a custom error message. At runtime, your code will be called with the text of the error message that caused the script to die. For example:

```
use CGI::Carp qw(fatalsToBrowser set_message);
BEGIN {
    sub handle_errors {
        my $msg = shift;
        print "<h1>Oh gosh</h1>";
        print "Got an error: $msg";
    }
    set_message(\&handle_errors);
}
```

In order to correctly intercept compile-time errors, you should call set_message() from within a BEGIN{} block.

CGI::Cookie

This module is a standard interface that provides reading, parsing, and writing of Netscape-style browser cookies.

Synopsis

```
use CGI qw/:standard/;
use CGI::Cookie;
```

```
# Create new cookies and send them
$cookie1 = new CGI::Cookie(-name=>'ID',-value=>123456);
$cookie2 = new CGI::Cookie(-name=>'preferences',
                           -value=>{ font => Helvetica,
                           size => 12 }
);
print header(-cookie=>[$cookie1,$cookie2]);

# fetch existing cookies
%cookies = fetch CGI::Cookie;
$id = $cookies{'ID'}->value;

# create cookies returned from an external source
%cookies = parse CGI::Cookie($ENV{COOKIE});
```

Description

CGI::Cookie is an interface to Netscape (HTTP/1.1) cookies. This innovation allows Web servers to store information on the browser's side of the connection so that it persists across multiple client requests. Although CGI::Cookie is intended to be used in conjunction with CGI.pm (and is used by it internally), you can use this module independently.

For full information on cookies see: http://www.ics.uci.edu/pub/ietf/http/rfc2109.txt.

Using CGI::Cookie

CGI::Cookie is object oriented. Each cookie object has a name and a value. The name is any scalar value. The value is any scalar or array value (associative arrays are also allowed). Cookies also have several optional attributes, including:

Expiration date   The expiration date tells the browser how long to hang onto the cookie. If the cookie specifies an expiration date in the future, the browser will store the cookie information in a disk file and return it to the server every time the user reconnects (until the expiration date is reached). If the cookie specifies an expiration date in the past, the browser will remove the cookie from the disk file. If the expiration date is not specified, the cookie will persist only until the user quits the browser.

Domain   This is a partial or complete domain name for which the cookie is valid. The browser will return the cookie to any host that matches the partial domain name. For example, if you specify a domain name of .capricorn.com, Netscape will return the cookie to Web servers running on any of the machines named www.capricorn.com, ftp.capricorn.com, feckless.capricorn.com, etc. Domain names must contain at least two periods to prevent attempts to match on top-level domains like .edu. If no domain is specified, the browser will return the cookie only to servers on the host from which the cookie originated.

Path If you provide a cookie-path attribute, the browser will check it against your script's URL before returning the cookie. For example, if you specify the path /cgi-bin, the cookie will be returned to each of the scripts /cgi-bin/tally.pl, /cgi-bin/order.pl, and /cgi-bin/customer_service/complain .pl, but not to the script /cgi-private/site _admin.pl. By default, path is set to backslash (/), which causes the cookie to be sent to any CGI script on your site.

Secure Flag If the secure attribute is set, the cookie will be sent to your script only if the CGI request is occurring on a secure channel, such as SSL.

Creating New Cookies

```
$c = new CGI::Cookie(-name    => 'foo',
                     -value   => 'bar',
                     -expires => '+3M',
                     -domain  => '.capricorn.com',
                     -path    => '/cgi-bin/database'
                     -secure  => 1
);
```

Create cookies from scratch with the new method. The -name and -value parameters are required. The name must be a scalar value. The value can be a scalar, an array reference, or a hash reference. (At some point in the future, cookies will support one of the Perl object serialization protocols for full generality.)

In addition to the required –name and –value parameters, the following optional parameters can be specified:

▶ Expires accepts any of the relative or absolute date formats recognized by CGI.pm (for example, "+3M" for three months in the future). See CGI.pm's documentation for details.

▶ Domain points to a domain name or to a fully qualified hostname. If not specified, the cookie will be returned only to the Web server that created it.

▶ Path points to a partial URL on the current server. The cookie will be returned to all URLs beginning with the specified path. If not specified, it defaults to '/', which returns the cookie to all pages at your site.

▶ If set to a True value, secure instructs the browser to return the cookie only when a cryptographic protocol is in use.

Sending the Cookie to the Browser

Within a CGI script you can send a cookie to the browser by creating one or more Set-Cookie: fields in the HTTP header. Here is a typical sequence:

```
my $c = new CGI::Cookie(-name    => 'foo',
                        -value   => ['bar','baz'],
                        -expires => '+3M');

print "Set-Cookie: $c\n";
print "Content-Type: text/html\n\n";
```

To send more than one cookie, create several Set-Cookie: fields. Alternatively, you may concatenate the cookies with "; " and send them in one field.

Internally, Cookie overloads the "" operator to call its as_string() method when incorporated into the HTTP header. The as_string() command turns the cookie's internal representation into an RFC-compliant text representation. You may call the as_string() command yourself if you prefer:

```
print "Set-Cookie: ",$c->as_string,"\n";
```

Recovering Previous Cookies

```
%cookies = fetch CGI::Cookie;
```

Fetch returns an associative array consisting of all the cookies returned by the browser. The keys of the array are the cookie names. You can iterate through the cookies this way:

```
%cookies = fetch CGI::Cookie;
foreach (keys %cookies) {
    do_something($cookies{$_});
}
```

In a scalar context, fetch() returns a hash reference, which may be more efficient if you are manipulating multiple cookies. CGI.pm uses the URL escaping methods to save and restore reserved characters in its cookies. If you are trying to retrieve a cookie set by a foreign server, this escaping method may trip you up. Instead use raw fetch(), which has the same semantics as fetch(), but performs no unescaping.

You may also retrieve cookies that were stored in some external form using the parse() class method:

```
$COOKIES = 'cat /usr/tmp/Cookie_stash';
%cookies = parse CGI::Cookie($COOKIES);
```

Manipulating Cookies

Cookie objects have a series of accessor methods to get and set cookie attributes. Each accessor has a similar syntax. Called without arguments, the accessor returns the current value of the attribute. Called with an argument, the accessor changes the attribute and returns its new value.

See Also

```
the CGI::Carp manpage, the CGI manpage =cut
```

Carp
Cluck
Croak
Confess

This module writes error or diagnostic info, but with more context information than warn() or die() provide.

Synopsis

```
use Carp;
croak "We're outta here!";

use Carp qw(cluck);
cluck "This is how we got here!";
```

Description

The Carp routines are useful in your own modules because they act like die() or warn(); however, they report where the error was in the code from which they were called. If a routine Foo()has a carp() in it, the carp() will report the error as occurring where Foo() was called, not where carp() was called.

Forcing a Stack Trace

As a debugging aid, you can force Carp to treat a croak as a confess and treat a carp as a cluck across *all* modules. In other words, you can force a detailed stack trace to be performed. This can be very helpful when you are trying to understand why, or from where, a warning or error is being generated.

This feature is enabled by saying:

```
perl -MCarp=verbose script.pl
```

or by including the string 'MCarp=verbose' in the PERL5OPT environment variable.

Bugs

Currently, the Carp routines don't handle exception objects. If called with a first argument that is a reference, they simply call die() or warn(), as appropriate.

Class::Struct

Provides a mechanism for declaring 'struct' and similar datatypes, while retaining Perl's notion of basic scalar, array, hash, and module types.

Synopsis

```
use Class::Struct;
# declare struct, based on array:
struct( CLASS_NAME => [ ELEMENT_NAME => ELEMENT_TYPE, ... ]);
# declare struct, based on hash:
struct( CLASS_NAME => { ELEMENT_NAME => ELEMENT_TYPE, ... });
```

```
package CLASS_NAME;
use Class::Struct;
# declare struct, based on array, implicit class name:
struct( ELEMENT_NAME => ELEMENT_TYPE, ... );

package Myobj;
use Class::Struct;
# declare struct with four types of elements:
struct( s => '$', a => '@', h => '%', c => 'My_Other_Class' );

$obj = new Myobj;                     # constructor

# scalar type accessor:
$element_value = $obj->s;             # element value
$obj->s('new value');                 # assign to element

# array type accessor:
$ary_ref = $obj->a;                   # reference to whole array
$ary_element_value = $obj->a(2);      # array element value
$obj->a(2, 'new value');              # assign to array element

$hash_ref = $obj->h;                  # reference to whole hash
$hash_element_value = $obj->h('x');   # hash element value
$obj->h('x', 'new value');            # assign to hash element

# class type accessor:
$element_value = $obj->c;             # object reference
$obj->c->method(...);                 # call method of object
$obj->c(new My_Other_Class);          # assign a new object
```

Description

'Class::Struct' exports a single function: 'struct'. Given a list of element names and types, and optionally a class name, 'struct' creates a Perl 5 class that implements a data structure similar to 'struct'.

The new class is given a constructor method, 'new', for creating struct objects.

Each element in the struct data has an accessor method, which is used to assign to the element and to fetch its value. The default accessor can be overridden by declaring a 'sub' of the same name in the package.

Each element's type can be scalar, array, hash, or class.

Cwd

This module allows you to determine the current working directory, without performing a system() call.

Synopsis

```
use Cwd;
$dir = cwd;

use Cwd;
$dir = getcwd;

use Cwd;
$dir = fastgetcwd;

use Cwd 'chdir';
chdir "/tmp";
print $ENV{'PWD'};

use Cwd 'abs_path';
print abs_path($ENV{'PWD'});

use Cwd 'fast_abs_path';
print fast_abs_path($ENV{'PWD'});
```

Description

The abs_path() function takes a single argument and returns the absolute path name for that argument. It uses the same algorithm as getcwd() (actually, getcwd() is abs_path(".")).

The fastcwd() function looks the same as getcwd(), but it runs faster. It's also more dangerous because it might chdir() you out of a directory that it can't chdir() you back into. If fastcwd encounters a problem, it will return undef; however, it will probably leave you in a different directory. For a measure of extra security, if everything appears to have worked, the fastcwd() function will verify that it leaves you in the same directory that it started in. If it has changed, it will 'die' with the message:

> Unstable directory path, current directory changed unexpectedly. That should never happen.

The fast_abs_path() function looks the same as abs_path(), but it runs faster and, like fastcwd(), is more dangerous.

The cwd() function looks the same as getcwd and fastgetcwd, but it is implemented using the most natural and safe form for the current architecture. For most systems, it is identical to 'pwd' (but without the trailing line terminator).

You should use cwd (or another *cwd() function) in *all* code to ensure portability.

If you ask to override your chdir() built-in function, your PWD environment variable will be kept up-to-date. It will only be kept up-to-date if all the packages that use chdir import it from Cwd.

See Also

See the "Overriding Built-in Functions" section in the perlsub manpage.

DB_File

DB_File enables access to Berkeley DB version 1.*x* database files using tie() functions.

Synopsis

```
use DB_File ;

[$X =] tie %hash,
            'DB_File',
            [$filename, $flags, $mode, $DB_HASH] ;
[$X =] tie %hash,
            'DB_File',
            $filename, $flags, $mode, $DB_BTREE ;
[$X =] tie @array,
            'DB_File',
            $filename, $flags, $mode, $DB_RECNO ;

$status = $X->del($key [, $flags]) ;
$status = $X->put($key, $value [, $flags]) ;
$status = $X->get($key, $value [, $flags]) ;
$status = $X->seq($key, $value, $flags) ;
$status = $X->sync([$flags]) ;
$status = $X->fd ;
```

```
# BTREE only
$count = $X->get_dup($key) ;
@list  = $X->get_dup($key) ;
%list  = $X->get_dup($key, 1) ;
$status = $X->find_dup($key, $value) ;
$status = $X->del_dup($key, $value) ;

# RECNO only
$a = $X->length;
$a = $X->pop ;
$X->push(list);
$a = $X->shift;
$X->unshift(list);

untie %hash ;
untie @array ;
```

Description

DB_File is a module that allows Perl programs to use the facilities provided by Berkeley DB version 1.x. (If you have a newer version of DB, see the "Using DB_File with Berkeley DB version 2" section.) You should have a copy of the Berkeley DB manual pages at hand when you read this documentation. The interface defined here closely mirrors the Berkeley DB interface.

Berkeley DB is a C library that provides a consistent interface to a number of database formats. DB_File provides an interface to all three of the database types currently supported by Berkeley DB.

The file types are:

DB_HASH   This database type allows arbitrary key/value pairs to be stored in data files. This is equivalent to the functionality provided by other hashing packages like DBM, NDBM, ODBM, GDBM, and SDBM. Remember though, the files created using DB_HASH are not compatible with any of the other packages mentioned.

A default hashing algorithm, which will be adequate for most applications, is built into Berkeley DB. If you do need to use your own hashing algorithm, you can write your own in Perl and have DB_File use it instead.

DB_BTREE   The BTREE format allows arbitrary key/value pairs to be stored in a sorted, balanced binary tree.

As with the DB_HASH format, you can provide a user-defined Perl routine to perform the comparison of keys. By default, though, the keys are stored in lexical order.

DB_RECNO   Allows both fixed-length and variable-length flat text files to be manipulated using the same key/value pair interface as in DB_HASH and DB_BTREE. In this case, the key will consist of a record (line) number.

Using DB_File with Berkeley DB Version 2

Although DB_File is intended to be used with Berkeley DB Version 1, it can also be used with Version 2. In this case, the interface is limited to the functionality provided by Berkeley DB 1.*x*. Anywhere the Version 2 interface differs, DB_File arranges for it to work like Version 1. This feature allows DB_File scripts that were built with Version 1 to be migrated to Version 2 without any changes.

If you want to use the new features available in Berkeley DB 2.*x*, use the Perl module Berkeley DB instead.

At the time of this writing, the Berkeley DB module is still alpha quality (the version number is less than 1.0) and, therefore, is unsuitable for use in any serious development work. (Once a version number is greater than or equal to 1.0, software is considered stable enough for real work.)

NOTE

The database file format has changed in Berkeley DB Version 2. If you cannot re-create your databases, you must dump any existing databases with the db_dump185 utility that comes with Berkeley DB. Once you have rebuilt DB_File to use Berkeley DB Version 2, your databases can be re-created using 'db_load'. Refer to the Berkeley DB documentation for further details.

Please read the "COPYRIGHT" section in the Berkeley DB distribution before using Version 2.*x* of Berkeley DB with DB_File.

Interface to Berkeley DB

DB_File allows access to Berkeley DB files using the tie() mechanism in Perl 5 (for full details, see the "tie()" entry in the perlfunc manpage). This facility allows DB_File to access Berkeley DB files using either an associative array (for DB_HASH and DB_BTREE file types) or an ordinary array (for the DB_RECNO file type).

In addition to using the `tie()` interface, you can also directly access most of the functions provided in the Berkeley DB API. See the "The API Interface" section.

Opening a Berkeley DB Database File

```
tie %array, 'DB_File', $filename, $flags, $mode, $DB_HASH ;
```

The `'filename'`, `'flags'` and `'mode'` parameters are the direct equivalent of their dbopen() counterparts. The final parameter ($DB_HASH) performs the function of both the `'type'` and `'openinfo'` parameters in dbopen().

In the previous example, $DB_HASH is a predefined reference to a hash object. DB_File has three of these predefined references: $DB_HASH, $DB_BTREE, and $DB_RECNO.

The keys allowed in each of these predefined references are limited to the names used in the equivalent C structure. For example, the $DB_HASH reference will allow only keys called `'bsize'`, `'cachesize'`, `'ffactor'`, `'hash'`, `'lorder'`, and `'nelem'`.

To change one of these elements, just assign to it like this:

```
$DB_HASH->{'cachesize'} = 10000 ;
```

The three predefined variables $DB_HASH, $DB_BTREE, and $DB_RECNO are usually adequate for most applications. If you do need to create extra instances of these objects, constructors are available for each file type.

Here are examples of the constructors and the valid options available for DB_HASH, DB_BTREE, and DB_RECNO.

```
$a = new DB_File::HASHINFO ;
$a->{'bsize'} ;
$a->{'cachesize'} ;
$a->{'ffactor'};
$a->{'hash'} ;
$a->{'lorder'} ;
$a->{'nelem'} ;
```

```perl
$b = new DB_File::BTREEINFO ;
$b->{'flags'} ;
$b->{'cachesize'} ;
$b->{'maxkeypage'} ;
$b->{'minkeypage'} ;
$b->{'psize'} ;
$b->{'compare'} ;
$b->{'prefix'} ;
$b->{'lorder'} ;

$c = new DB_File::RECNOINFO ;
$c->{'bval'} ;
$c->{'cachesize'} ;
$c->{'psize'} ;
$c->{'flags'} ;
$c->{'lorder'} ;
$c->{'reclen'} ;
$c->{'bfname'} ;
```

The values stored in the previous hashes are, for the most part, the direct equivalents of their C counterparts. Like their C counterparts, they are set to default values, meaning you don't have to set *all* of the values when you only want to change one. Here is an example:

```perl
$a = new DB_File::HASHINFO ;
$a->{'cachesize'} = 12345 ;
tie %y, 'DB_File', "filename", $flags, 0777, $a ;
```

A few of the options need extra discussion here. When used, the C equivalent of the keys `'hash'`, `'compare'`, and `'prefix'` store pointers to C functions. In DB_File, these keys are used to store references to Perl subs. Here are templates for each of the subs:

```perl
sub hash
{
    my ($data) = @_ ;
    ...
    # return the hash value for $data
    return $hash ;
}
```

```
sub compare
{
    my ($key, $key2) = @_ ;
    ...
    # return  0 if $key1 eq $key2
    #        -1 if $key1 lt $key2
    #         1 if $key1 gt $key2
    return (-1 , 0 or 1) ;
}

sub prefix
{
    my ($key, $key2) = @_ ;
    ...
    # return number of bytes of $key2 which are
    # necessary to determine that it is greater
    # than $key1
    return $bytes ;
}
```

See the "Changing the BTREE Sort Order" section for an example of using the 'compare' template.

If you are using the DB_RECNO interface and you intend to use 'bval', you should check the "The 'bval' Option" section.

Default Parameters

You can omit some or all of the final four parameters in the call to 'tie' and let them take default values. Because DB_HASH is the most common file format used, the call:

```
tie %A, "DB_File", "filename" ;
```

is equivalent to:

```
tie %A, "DB_File", "filename", O_CREAT|O_RDWR, 0666, $DB_HASH ;
```

You can also omit the filename parameter, so the call:

```
tie %A, "DB_File" ;
```

is equivalent to:

```
tie %A, "DB_File", undef, O_CREAT|O_RDWR, 0666, $DB_HASH ;
```

In-Memory Databases

Berkeley DB allows the creation of in-memory databases by using NULL (that is, a '(char *)0' in C) in place of the filename. DB_File uses 'undef' instead of NULL to provide this functionality.

DB_HASH

The DB_HASH file format is probably the most commonly used of the three file formats that DB_File supports. It is also very straightforward to use.

A Simple Example

This example shows how to create a database, add key/value pairs to the database, delete key/value pairs, and, finally, how to enumerate the contents of the database.

```
use strict ;
use DB_File ;
use vars qw( %h $k $v ) ;

tie %h, "DB_File", "fruit", O_RDWR|O_CREAT, 0640, $DB_HASH
    or die "Cannot open file 'fruit': $!\n";

# Add a few key/value pairs to the file
$h{"apple"} = "red" ;
$h{"orange"} = "orange" ;
$h{"banana"} = "yellow" ;
$h{"tomato"} = "red" ;

# Check for existence of a key
print "Banana Exists\n\n" if $h{"banana"} ;

# Delete a key/value pair.
delete $h{"apple"} ;

# print the contents of the file
while (($k, $v) = each %h)
  { print "$k -> $v\n" }

untie %h ;
```

Here is the output:

```
Banana Exists

orange -> orange
tomato -> red
banana -> yellow
```

Note that (like the ordinary associative arrays) the order of the keys retrieved is in an apparently random order.

DB_BTREE

The DB_BTREE format is useful when you want to store data in a given order. By default, the keys will be stored in lexical order; however, as you will see from the example shown in the next section, it is very easy to define your own sorting function.

Changing the BTREE Sort Order

This script shows how to override the default sorting algorithm that BTREE uses. Instead of using the normal lexical ordering, a case-insensitive compare function will be used.

```perl
use strict ;
use DB_File ;

my %h ;

sub Compare
{
    my ($key1, $key2) = @_ ;
    "\L$key1" cmp "\L$key2" ;
}

# specify the Perl sub that will do the comparison
$DB_BTREE->{'compare'} = \&Compare ;

tie %h, "DB_File",
        "tree", O_RDWR|O_CREAT, 0640, $DB_BTREE
    or die "Cannot open file 'tree': $!\n" ;

# Add a key/value pair to the file
$h{'Wall'} = 'Larry' ;
$h{'Smith'} = 'John' ;
$h{'mouse'} = 'mickey' ;
$h{'duck'}  = 'donald' ;

# Delete
delete $h{"duck"} ;

# Cycle through the keys printing them in order.
# Note it is not necessary to sort the keys as
# the btree will have kept them in order
# automatically.
foreach (keys %h)
  { print "$_\n" }

untie %h ;
```

Here is the output from the previous code:

```
mouse
Smith
Wall
```

Bear the following points in mind if you want to change the order in a BTREE database:

▶ The new `compare` function must be specified when you create the database.

▶ You cannot change the order once the database has been created. Therefore, you must use the same `compare` function every time you access the database.

Handling Duplicate Keys

The BTREE file type optionally allows a single key to be associated with an arbitrary number of values. This option is enabled by setting the flags element '$DB_BTREE' to R_DUP when you create the database.

Using the tied hash interface when you want to manipulate a BTREE database with duplicate keys can be difficult. Consider this code:

```
use strict ;
use DB_File ;

use vars qw($filename %h ) ;

$filename = "tree" ;
unlink $filename ;

# Enable duplicate records
$DB_BTREE->{'flags'} = R_DUP ;

tie %h, "DB_File", $filename, O_RDWR|O_CREAT, 0640,
        $DB_BTREE
    or die "Cannot open $filename: $!\n";

# Add some key/value pairs to the file
$h{'Wall'} = 'Larry' ;
$h{'Wall'} = 'Brick' ; # Note the duplicate key
$h{'Wall'} = 'Brick' ; # Note duplicate key & value
$h{'Smith'} = 'John' ;
$h{'mouse'} = 'mickey' ;
```

```
# iterate through the associative array
# and print each key/value pair.
foreach (keys %h)
  { print "$_  -> $h{$_}\n" }

untie %h ;
```

Here is the output:

```
Smith   -> John
Wall    -> Larry
Wall    -> Larry
Wall    -> Larry
mouse   -> mickey
```

As you can see, three records have been successfully created with key `'Wall'`. The only problem is that when they are retrieved from the database they *seem* to have the same value, namely `'Larry'`. The problem is caused by the way that the associative array interface works. Basically, when the associative array interface is used to fetch the value associated with a given key, it will retrieve only the first value.

Although it may not be immediately obvious from the previous code, the associative array interface can be used to write values with duplicate keys, but it cannot be used to read them back from the database.

The way to get around this problem is to use the Berkeley DB API method called `'seq'`. This method allows sequential access to key/value pairs. See the "The API Interface" section for details of both the `'seq'` method and the API.

Here is the previous script rewritten using the `'seq'` API method:

```
use strict ;
use DB_File ;

use vars qw($filename $x %h $status $key $value) ;

$filename = "tree" ;
unlink $filename ;

# Enable duplicate records
$DB_BTREE->{'flags'} = R_DUP ;

$x = tie %h, "DB_File", $filename, O_RDWR|O_CREAT,
                        0640, $DB_BTREE
    or die "Cannot open $filename: $!\n";
```

```
                    # Add some key/value pairs to the file
                    $h{'Wall'} = 'Larry' ;
                    $h{'Wall'} = 'Brick' ; # Note the duplicate key
                    $h{'Wall'} = 'Brick' ; # Note duplicate key & value
                    $h{'Smith'} = 'John' ;
                    $h{'mouse'} = 'mickey' ;

                    # iterate through the btree using seq
                    # and print each key/value pair.
                    $key = $value = 0 ;
                    for ($status = $x->seq($key, $value, R_FIRST) ;
                         $status == 0 ;
                         $status = $x->seq($key, $value, R_NEXT) )
                      { print "$key -> $value\n" }

                    undef $x ;
                    untie %h ;
```

It will print the following:

```
          Smith    -> John
          Wall     -> Brick
          Wall     -> Brick
          Wall     -> Larry
          mouse    -> mickey
```

This time we have all the key/value pairs, including the multiple values associated with the key 'Wall'.

To make life easier when dealing with duplicate keys, DB_File comes with a few utility methods.

The get_dup() Method

The 'get_dup' method assists in reading duplicate values from BTREE databases. The method can take the following forms:

```
          $count = $x->get_dup($key) ;
          @list  = $x->get_dup($key) ;
          %list  = $x->get_dup($key, 1) ;
```

In a scalar context, the method returns the number of values associated with the key '$key'.

In a list context, it returns all the values that match '$key'. Note that the values will be returned in an apparently random order.

In a list context, if the second parameter is present and evaluates True, the method returns an associative array. The keys of the associative array correspond to the values that matched in the BTREE and the values of the array are a count of the number of times that particular value occurred in the BTREE.

So assuming the previously created database, we can use `'get_dup'` as in the following code:

```
my $cnt  = $x->get_dup("Wall") ;
print "Wall occurred $cnt times\n" ;

my %hash = $x->get_dup("Wall", 1) ;
print "Larry is there\n" if $hash{'Larry'} ;
print "There are $hash{'Brick'} Brick Walls\n" ;

my @list = $x->get_dup("Wall") ;
print "Wall =>      [@list]\n" ;

@list = $x->get_dup("Smith") ;
print "Smith =>     [@list]\n" ;

@list = $x->get_dup("Dog") ;
print "Dog =>       [@list]\n" ;
```

and it will print the following:

```
Wall occurred 3 times
Larry is there
There are 2 Brick Walls
Wall =>      [Brick Brick Larry]
Smith =>     [John]
Dog =>       []
```

The find_dup() Method

```
$status = $X->find_dup($key, $value) ;
```

This method checks for the existence of a specific key/value pair. If the pair exists, the cursor is left pointing to the pair and the method returns 0. Otherwise, the method returns a nonzero value.

Assuming the database from the previous example, the following code:

```
use strict ;
use DB_File ;

use vars qw($filename $x %h $found) ;

my $filename = "tree" ;

# Enable duplicate records
$DB_BTREE->{'flags'} = R_DUP ;
```

```
$x = tie %h, "DB_File", $filename, O_RDWR|O_CREAT,
             0640, $DB_BTREE
    or die "Cannot open $filename: $!\n";

$found = ( $x->find_dup("Wall", "Larry") == 0 ? ""
                                          : "not") ;
print "Larry Wall is $found there\n" ;

$found = ( $x->find_dup("Wall", "Harry") == 0 ? ""
                                          : "not") ;
print "Harry Wall is $found there\n" ;

undef $x ;
untie %h ;
```

prints the following:

```
Larry Wall is there
Harry Wall is not there
```

The del_dup() Method

```
$status = $X->del_dup($key, $value) ;
```

This method deletes a specific key/value pair. It returns 0 if they exist and have been deleted successfully. Otherwise, the method returns a nonzero value.

Again, assuming the existance of the 'tree' database, the following code:

```
use strict ;
use DB_File ;

use vars qw($filename $x %h $found) ;

my $filename = "tree" ;

# Enable duplicate records
$DB_BTREE->{'flags'} = R_DUP ;

$x = tie %h, "DB_File", $filename, O_RDWR|O_CREAT,
             0640, $DB_BTREE
    or die "Cannot open $filename: $!\n";

$x->del_dup("Wall", "Larry") ;
```

```
$found = ( $x->find_dup("Wall", "Larry") == 0 ? ""
                                             : "not") ;
print "Larry Wall is $found there\n" ;

undef $x ;
untie %h ;
```

prints the following:

```
Larry Wall is not there
```

Matching Partial Keys

The BTREE interface has a feature that allows partial keys to be matched. This functionality is available *only* when the 'seq' method is used with the R_CURSOR flag. For example,

```
$x->seq($key, $value, R_CURSOR) ;
```

Here is the relevant quote from the dbopen manpage (Regents of the University of California), which defines the use of the R_CURSOR flag with seq:

For the DB_BTREE access method, the returned key is not necessarily an exact match for the specified key. The returned key is the smallest key greater than or equal to the specified key, permitting partial key matches and range searches.

In the following example script, the 'match' sub uses this feature to find and print the first matching key/value pair given a partial key:

```
use strict ;
use DB_File ;
use Fcntl ;

use vars qw($filename $x %h $st $key $value) ;

sub match
{
    my $key = shift ;
    my $value = 0;
    my $orig_key = $key ;
    $x->seq($key, $value, R_CURSOR) ;
    print "$orig_key\t-> $key\t-> $value\n" ;
}

$filename = "tree" ;
unlink $filename ;

$x = tie %h, "DB_File", $filename, O_RDWR|O_CREAT,
           0640, $DB_BTREE
    or die "Cannot open $filename: $!\n";
```

```perl
                    # Add some key/value pairs to the file
                    $h{'mouse'} = 'mickey' ;
                    $h{'Wall'} = 'Larry' ;
                    $h{'Walls'} = 'Brick' ;
                    $h{'Smith'} = 'John' ;

                    $key = $value = 0 ;
                    print "IN ORDER\n" ;
                    for ($st = $x->seq($key, $value, R_FIRST) ;
                         $st == 0 ;
                         $st = $x->seq($key, $value, R_NEXT) )

                      { print "$key -> $value\n" }

                    print "\nPARTIAL MATCH\n" ;

                    match "Wa" ;
                    match "A" ;
                    match "a" ;

                    undef $x ;
                    untie %h ;
```

Here is the output:

```
                    IN ORDER
                    Smith -> John
                    Wall  -> Larry
                    Walls -> Brick
                    mouse -> mickey

                    PARTIAL MATCH
                    Wa -> Wall  -> Larry
                    A  -> Smith -> John
                    a  -> mouse -> mickey
```

DB_RECNO

DB_RECNO provides an interface to flat text files. Both variable-length and fixed-length records are supported.

In order to make RECNO more compatible with Perl, the array offset for all RECNO arrays begins at 0 rather than 1, as in Berkeley DB.

As with normal Perl arrays, a RECNO array can be accessed using negative indexes. The index −1 refers to the last element of the array, −2 the second to the last, and so on. Attempting to access an element before the start of the array will cause a fatal run-time error.

The 'bval' Option

The operation of the bval option warrants some discussion. Here is the definition of bval from the Berkeley DB 1.85 recno manual page (Regents of the University of California):

The delimiting byte to be used to mark the end of a record for variable-length records, and the pad character for fixed-length records. If no value is specified, newlines ("\n") are used to mark the end of variable-length records and fixed-length records are padded with spaces.

The second sentence is wrong. In fact, bval will default to "\n" only when the openinfo parameter in dbopen is NULL. If a non-NULL openinfo parameter is used, the value that happens to be in bval will be used. That means you must always specify bval when using any of the options in the openinfo parameter. This documentation error will be fixed in the next release of Berkeley DB.

Now that Berkeley DB is clarified, what about DB_File? The behavior defined in the previous quote is quite useful, so DB_File conforms to it.

You can specify other options (e.g., cachesize) and still have bval default to "\n" for variable-length records and default to space for fixed-length records.

A Simple Example

Here is a simple example that uses RECNO. (If you are using a version of Perl prior to 5.004_57, this example won't work. See the "Extra RECNO Methods" section for a work-around.)

```
use strict ;
use DB_File ;

my @h ;
tie @h, "DB_File", "text", O_RDWR|O_CREAT, 0640,
        $DB_RECNO
    or die "Cannot open file 'text': $!\n" ;

# Add a few key/value pairs to the file
$h[0] = "orange" ;
$h[1] = "blue" ;
$h[2] = "yellow" ;
```

```
push @h, "green", "black" ;

my $elements = scalar @h ;
print "The array contains $elements entries\n" ;

my $last = pop @h ;
print "popped $last\n" ;

unshift @h, "white" ;
my $first = shift @h ;
print "shifted $first\n" ;

# Check for existence of a key
print "Element 1 Exists with value $h[1]\n"
   if $h[1] ;

# use a negative index
print "The last element is $h[-1]\n" ;
print "The 2nd last element is $h[-2]\n" ;

untie @h ;
```

Here is the output from the script:

```
The array contains 5 entries
popped black
unshifted white
Element 1 Exists with value blue
The last element is green
The 2nd last element is yellow
```

Extra RECNO Methods

If you are using a version of Perl earlier than 5.004_57, the tied array interface is quite limited. In the previous example script, 'push', 'pop', 'shift', and 'unshift' would not work with a tied array, nor would you be able to determine the array length of a tied array.

To make the interface more useful for older versions of Perl, a number of methods are supplied with DB_File to simulate the missing array operations. All these methods are accessed via the object returned from the tie call.

Here are the methods:

```
$X->push(list) ;
```

Pushes the elements of 'list' to the end of the array.

```
$value = $X->pop ;
```

Removes and returns the last element of the array.

```
$X->shift
```

Removes and returns the first element of the array.

```
$X->unshift(list) ;
```

Pushes the elements of 'list' to the start of the array.

```
$X->length
```

Returns the number of elements in the array.

Another Example

Here is a more complete example that uses some of the previously described methods. It also uses the API interface directly (see the "The API Interface" section).

```
use strict ;
use vars qw(@h $H $file $i) ;
use DB_File ;
use Fcntl ;

$file = "text" ;

unlink $file ;

$H = tie @h, "DB_File", $file, O_RDWR|O_CREAT,
            0640, $DB_RECNO
    or die "Cannot open file $file: $!\n" ;

# first create a text file to play with
$h[0] = "zero" ;
$h[1] = "one" ;
$h[2] = "two" ;
$h[3] = "three" ;
$h[4] = "four" ;


# Print the records in order.
#
# The length method is needed here
# because evaluating a tied
# array in a scalar context does
# not return the number of
# elements in the array.
```

```perl
print "\nORIGINAL\n" ;
foreach $i (0 .. $H->length - 1) {
    print "$i: $h[$i]\n" ;
}

# use the push & pop methods
$a = $H->pop ;
$H->push("last") ;
print "\nThe last record was [$a]\n" ;

# and the shift & unshift methods
$a = $H->shift ;
$H->unshift("first") ;
print "The first record was [$a]\n" ;

# Use the API to add a new record after record 2.
$i = 2 ;
$H->put($i, "Newbie", R_IAFTER) ;

# and a new record before record 1.
$i = 1 ;
$H->put($i, "New One", R_IBEFORE) ;

# delete record 3
$H->del(3) ;

# now print the records in reverse order
print "\nREVERSE\n" ;
for ($i = $H->length - 1 ; $i >= 0 ; - $i)
  { print "$i: $h[$i]\n" }

# same again, but use the API functions instead
print "\nREVERSE again\n" ;
my ($s, $k, $v) = (0, 0, 0) ;
for ($s = $H->seq($k, $v, R_LAST) ;
        $s == 0 ;
        $s = $H->seq($k, $v, R_PREV))
  { print "$k: $v\n" }

undef $H ;
untie @h ;
```

This is what it outputs:

```
ORIGINAL
0: zero
1: one
2: two
3: three
4: four

The last record was [four]
The first record was [zero]

REVERSE
5: last
4: three
3: Newbie
2: one
1: New One
0: first

REVERSE again
5: last
4: three
3: Newbie
2: one
1: New One
0: first
```

The API Interface

In addition to accessing Berkeley DB using a tied hash or array, you can also directly use most of the API functions defined in the Berkeley DB documentation.

To do this you need to store a copy of the object returned from the tie.

```
$db = tie %hash, "DB_File", "filename" ;
```

Once you have done that, you can access the Berkeley DB API functions as DB_File methods directly like this:

```
$db->put($key, $value, R_NOOVERWRITE) ;
```

If you saved a copy of the object returned from `'tie'`, the underlying database file will *not* be closed until the tied variable is untied *and* all copies of the saved object are destroyed.

```
use DB_File ;
        $db = tie %hash, "DB_File", "filename"
            or die "Cannot tie filename: $!" ;
        ...
        undef $db ;
        untie %hash ;
```

See the "The untie() Gotcha" section for more details.

All the functions defined in the dbopen manpage—except `close()` and `dbopen()`—are available. The `DB_File` method interface to the supported functions has been implemented to mirror the way Berkeley DB works whenever possible. In particular, note that:

▶ The methods return a status value. All methods return 0 on success. All methods return −1 to signify an error and set `'$!'` to the exact error code. The return code 1 generally (but not always) means that the key specified did not exist in the database. Other return codes are defined. Refer to the following and to the Berkeley DB documentation for details. The Berkeley DB documentation should be used as the definitive source.

▶ When a Berkeley DB function returns data via one of its parameters, the equivalent `DB_File` method does exactly the same.

▶ If you are careful, you can mix API calls with the tied hash/array interface in the same piece of code. Although only a few of the methods used to implement the tied interface currently use the cursor, you should always assume that the cursor has been changed any time the tied hash/array interface is used. As an example, this code will probably not do what you expect:

```
$X = tie %x, 'DB_File', $filename, O_RDWR|O_CREAT, 0777,
            $DB_BTREE
    or die "Cannot tie $filename: $!" ;

# Get the first key/value pair and set the cursor
$X->seq($key, $value, R_FIRST) ;

# this line will modify the cursor
$count = scalar keys %x ;
```

```
          # Get the second key/value pair.
          # oops, it didn't, it got the last key/value pair!
          $X->seq($key, $value, R_NEXT) ;
```

The previous code can be rearranged to get around the problem, like this:

```
          $X = tie %x, 'DB_File', $filename, O_RDWR|O_CREAT, 0777,
                       $DB_BTREE
               or die "Cannot tie $filename: $!" ;

          # this line will modify the cursor
          $count = scalar keys %x ;

          # Get the first key/value pair and set  the cursor
          $X->seq($key, $value, R_FIRST) ;

          # Get the second key/value pair.
          # worked this time.
          $X->seq($key, $value, R_NEXT) ;
```

All the constants defined in the dbopen manpage for use in the flags parameters in the following defined methods are also available. Refer to the Berkeley DB documentation for the precise meaning of the flags values.

Here is a list of the methods available:

```
          $status = $X->get($key, $value [, $flags]) ;
```

Given a key ('$key'), this method reads the value associated with it from the database. The value read from the database is returned in the '$value' parameter. If the key does not exist, the method returns 1. No flags are currently defined for this method.

```
          $status = $X->put($key, $value [, $flags]) ;
```

This method stores the key/value pair in the database. If you use either the R_IAFTER or R_IBEFORE flags, the '$key' parameter will have the record number of the inserted key/value pair set. Valid flags are R_CURSOR, R_IAFTER, R_IBEFORE, R_NOOVERWRITE, and R_SETCURSOR.

```
          $status = $X->del($key [, $flags]) ;
```

This method removes all key/value pairs with key '$key' from the database. A return code of 1 means that the requested key was not in the database. R_CURSOR is the only valid flag at present.

```
          $status = $X->fd ;
```

This method returns the file descriptor for the underlying database. See the "Locking Databases" section for an example of how to use the 'fd' method to lock your database.

```
          $status = $X->seq($key, $value, $flags) ;
```

This interface allows sequential retrieval from the database. See the dbopen manpage for full details. Both the `$key` and `$value` parameters will be set to the key/value pair read from the database. The flags parameter is mandatory. The valid flag values are R_CURSOR, R_FIRST, R_LAST, R_NEXT, and R_PREV.

```
$status = $X->sync([$flags]) ;
```

This method flushes any cached buffers to disk. R_RECNOSYNC is the only valid flag at present.

Data::Dumper

This module takes a Perl data structure and provides a text representation, suitable for persistent storage of data or objects.

Synopsis

```
use Data::Dumper;

# simple procedural interface
print Dumper($foo, $bar);

# extended usage with names
print Data::Dumper->Dump([$foo, $bar], [qw(foo *ary)]);

# configuration variables
{
  local $Data::Dump::Purity = 1;
  eval Data::Dumper->Dump([$foo, $bar], [qw(foo *ary)]);
}

# OO usage
$d = Data::Dumper->new([$foo, $bar], [qw(foo *ary)]);
...
print $d->Dump;
...
$d->Purity(1)->Terse(1)->Deepcopy(1);
eval $d->Dump;
```

Description

Given a list of scalars or reference variables, Data::Dumper writes their contents in Perl syntax. The references can also be objects. The contents of each variable is output in a single Perl statement. Data::Dumper correctly handles self-referential structures.

The return value can be evaluated to get back an identical copy of the original reference structure.

Any references that are the same as one of those passed will be named '$VAR'*n* (where *n* is a numeric suffix). Other duplicate references to substructures within '$VAR'*n* will be appropriately labeled using arrow notation. You can specify names for individual values to be dumped if you use the 'Dump()' method, or you can change the default '$VAR' prefix to something else. See '$Data::Dumper::Varname' and '$Data::Dumper::Terse'.

The default output of self-referential structures can be evaluated; however, the nested references to '$VAR'*n* will be undefined, because a recursive structure cannot be constructed using one Perl statement. You should set the 'Purity' flag to 1 to get additional statements that will correctly fill these references.

In the extended usage form, the references to be dumped can be given user-specified names. If a name begins with a '*', the output will describe the dereferenced type of the supplied reference for hashes and arrays, and coderefs. Where possible, output of names will be avoided if the 'Terse' flag is set.

In many cases, methods that are used to set the internal state of the object will return the object itself, so method calls can be conveniently chained together.

Several styles of output are possible, all controlled by setting the 'Indent' flag. See the "Configuration Variables or Methods" section for details.

Methods

PACKAGE->new(*ARRAYREF [*, *ARRAYREF]*)

This method returns a newly created 'Data::Dumper' object. The first argument is an anonymous array of values to be dumped. The optional second argument is an anonymous array of names for the values. The names do not need a leading '$' sign, and they must be comprised of alphanumeric characters. For ARRAY and HASH references, you can begin a name with an '*' to specify that the dereferenced type must be dumped instead of the reference itself.

The prefix specified by `'$Data::Dumper::Varname'` will be used with a numeric suffix if the name for a value is undefined.

`Data::Dumper` will catalog all references encountered while dumping the values. Cross-references (in the form of names of substructures in Perl syntax) will be inserted at all possible points, preserving any structural interdependencies in the original set of values. Structure traversal is depth-first and proceeds in order from the first supplied value to the last.

The following code:

```
*$OBJ*->Dump  *or*  *PACKAGE*->Dump(*ARRAYREF [*,
    *ARRAYREF]*)
```

returns the string form of the values stored in the object (preserving the order in which they were supplied to `'new'`), subject to the following listed configuration options. In an array context, it returns a list of strings corresponding to the supplied values.

The second form, for convenience, simply calls the `'new'` method on its arguments before immediately dumping the object.

```
*$OBJ*->Dumpxs  *or*  *PACKAGE*->Dumpxs(*ARRAYREF [*,
    *ARRAYREF]*)
```

This method is available if you were able to compile and install the XSUB extension to `'Data::Dumper'`. It is similar to the previous `'Dump'` method; however, it is about four to five times faster, because it is written entirely in C.

```
*$OBJ*->Seen(*[HASHREF]*)
```

This code queries or adds to the internal table of already encountered references. You must use `'Reset'` to explicitly clear the table if needed. Such references are not dumped; instead, their names are inserted wherever they are encountered. This technique is useful for properly dumping subroutine references.

This method expects an anonymous hash of name => value pairs. The same rules apply for names that apply for `'new'`. If no argument is supplied, it will return the `"seen"` list of name => value pairs, in an array context. Otherwise, it returns the object itself.

```
*$OBJ*->Values(*[ARRAYREF]*)
```

This code queries or replaces the internal array of values that will be dumped. When called without arguments, it returns the values. Otherwise, it returns the object itself.

```
*$OBJ*->Names(*[ARRAYREF]*)
```

This code queries or replaces the internal array of user-supplied names for the values that will be dumped. When called without arguments, it returns the names. Otherwise, it returns the object itself.

```
*$OBJ*->Reset
```

This code clears the internal table of "seen" references and returns the object itself.

Functions

```
Dumper(*LIST*)
```

This function returns the string form of the values in the list, subject to the following listed configuration options. The values will be named '$VAR'*n* in the output, where *n* is a numeric suffix. It will return a list of strings in an array context.

```
DumperX(*LIST*)
```

This function is similar to the 'Dumper()' function; however, it calls the XSUB implementation. It is available only if you were able to compile and install the XSUB extensions in 'Data::Dumper'.

Configuration Variables or Methods

Several configuration variables can be used to control the kind of output generated when the procedural interface is used. These variables are usually localized (run with 'local') in a block so that other parts of the code are not affected by the change.

These variables determine the default state of the object created by calling the 'new' method, but they cannot be used to alter the state of the object thereafter. Instead, the equivalent method names should be used to query or set the internal state of the object.

The method forms return the object itself when called with arguments, so that they can be chained together.

```
$Data::Dumper::Indent  *or*  *$OBJ*->Indent(*[NEWVAL]*)
```

This method controls the style of indentation. It can be set to 0, 1, 2, or 3. Style 0 spews output without any newlines, indentation, or spaces between list items. It is the most compact format possible that can still be called valid Perl. Style 1 outputs a readable form with newlines but no fancy indentation (each level in the structure is simply indented by a fixed amount of whitespace). Style 2 (the default) outputs a very readable form, which considers the length of hash keys (so the hash values line up). Style 3 is similar to Style 2, but it also annotates the elements of arrays with their indexes (The comments have their own lines, so array output consumes twice the number of lines). Style 2 is the default.

```
$Data::Dumper::Purity  *or*  *$OBJ*->Purity(*[NEWVAL]*)
```

This method controls the degree to which the output can be evaluated to re-create the supplied reference structures. Setting it to 1 will output additional Perl statements that will correctly re-create nested references. The default is 0.

```
$Data::Dumper::Pad  *or*  *$OBJ*->Pad(*[NEWVAL]*)
```

This method specifies the string that will be prefixed to every line of the output. Empty string is used by default if this method isn't used to specify something.

```
$Data::Dumper::Varname  *or*
        *$OBJ*->Varname(*[NEWVAL]*)
```

This method contains the prefix to use for tagging variable names in the output. The default is "VAR".

```
$Data::Dumper::Useqq  *or*  *$OBJ*->Useqq(*[NEWVAL]*)
```

When set, this method enables the use of double quotes to represent string values. Whitespace other than space will be represented as '[\n\t\r]', "unsafe" characters will be backslashed, and unprintable characters will be output as quoted octal integers. Because setting this variable imposes a performance penalty, the default is 0. The 'Dumpxs()' method does not honor this flag yet.

```
$Data::Dumper::Terse  *or*  *$OBJ*->Terse(*[NEWVAL]*)
```

When set, Data::Dumper will emit single, non-self-referential values as atoms/terms rather than statements. This means that the '$VAR'*n* names will be avoided when possible; however, the output may not always be parseable by 'eval'.

```
$Data::Dumper::Freezer  *or*
        $*OBJ*->Freezer(*[NEWVAL]*)
```

This variable can be set to a method name or to an empty string to disable the feature. Data::Dumper will invoke that method via the object before attempting to make it into a string. This method can alter the contents of the object (if, for instance, it contains data allocated from C) and even rebless (reuse the command bless) it in a different package. The client is responsible for making sure the specified method can be called via the object and that the object ends up containing only Perl data types after the method has been called. It defaults to an empty string.

```
$Data::Dumper::Toaster   *or*
        $*OBJ*->Toaster(*[NEWVAL]*)
```

This variable can be set to a method name or to an empty string to disable the feature. `Data::Dumper` will emit a method call for any objects that are to be dumped using the syntax `'bless(DATA, CLASS)-'METHOD()>`.This means that the method specified must perform any modifications required on the object (like creating a new state within it, and/or reblessing it in a different package) and then return it. The client is responsible for making sure the method can be called via the object, and that it returns a valid object. It defaults to an empty string.

```
$Data::Dumper::Deepcopy   *or*
        $*OBJ*->Deepcopy(*[NEWVAL]*)
```

This variable can be set to a Boolean value to enable deep copies of structures. Cross-referencing will then be performed only when absolutely essential (i.e., to break reference cycles). The default is 0.

```
$Data::Dumper::Quotekeys   *or*
        $*OBJ*->Quotekeys(*[NEWVAL]*)
```

This variable can be set to a Boolean value to control whether hash keys are quoted. A False value will prevent hash keys from quoting when it looks like a simple string. The default is 1, which will always enclose hash keys in quotes.

```
$Data::Dumper::Bless   *or*   $*OBJ*->Bless(*[NEWVAL]*)
```

This variable can be set to a string that specifies an alternative to the `'bless'` `builtin` operator used to create objects. A function with the specified name should exist and should accept the same arguments as the builtin. The default is `'bless'`.

Examples

Run these code snippets to get a quick feel for the behavior of this module. When you are through with these examples, you may want to add or change the various configuration variables previously described to see their behavior. (See the testsuite in the `Data::Dumper` distribution for more examples.)

```
use Data::Dumper;

package Foo;
sub new {bless {'a' => 1, 'b' => sub { return "foo" }}, $_[0]};

package Fuz;           # a weird REF-REF-SCALAR object
sub new {bless \($_ = \ 'fu\'z'), $_[0]};

package main;
$foo = Foo->new;
$fuz = Fuz->new;
$boo = [ 1, [], "abcd", \*foo,
{1 => 'a', 023 => 'b', 0x45 => 'c'},
\\"p\q\'r", $foo, $fuz];

########
# simple usage
########

$bar = eval(Dumper($boo));
print($@) if $@;
print Dumper($boo), Dumper($bar);
# pretty print (no array indices)

$Data::Dumper::Terse = 1;    # don't output names where
feasible
$Data::Dumper::Indent = 0;   # turn off all pretty print
print Dumper($boo), "\n";

$Data::Dumper::Indent = 1;   # mild pretty print
print Dumper($boo);

$Data::Dumper::Indent = 3;   # pretty print with array indices
print Dumper($boo);

$Data::Dumper::Useqq = 1;    # print strings in double quotes
print Dumper($boo);

########
# recursive structures
########
```

```
@c = ('c');
$c = \@c;
$b = {};
$a = [1, $b, $c];
$b->{a} = $a;
$b->{b} = $a->[1];
$b->{c} = $a->[2];
print Data::Dumper->Dump([$a,$b,$c], [qw(a b c)]);

$Data::Dumper::Purity = 1;  # fill in the holes for eval
print Data::Dumper->Dump([$a, $b], [qw(*a b)]); # print as @a
print Data::Dumper->Dump([$b, $a], [qw(*b a)]); # print as %b

$Data::Dumper::Deepcopy = 1;# avoid cross-refs
print Data::Dumper->Dump([$b, $a], [qw(*b a)]);


$Data::Dumper::Purity = 0;  # avoid cross-refs
print Data::Dumper->Dump([$b, $a], [qw(*b a)]);


########
# object-oriented usage
########

$d = Data::Dumper->new([$a,$b], [qw(a b)]);
$d->Seen({'*c' => $c});       # stash a ref without printing it
$d->Indent(3);
print $d->Dump;
$d->Reset->Purity(0);         # empty the seen cache
print join "--\n", $d->Dump;

########
# persistence
########

package Foo;
sub new { bless { state => 'awake' }, shift }
sub Freeze {
  my $s = shift;
  print STDERR "preparing to sleep\n";
  $s->{state} = 'asleep';
  return bless $s, 'Foo::ZZZ';
}
```

```
package Foo::ZZZ;
sub Thaw {
  my $s = shift;
  print STDERR "waking up\n";
  $s->{state} = 'awake';
  return bless $s, 'Foo';
}

package Foo;
use Data::Dumper;
$a = Foo->new;
$b = Data::Dumper->new([$a], ['c']);
$b->Freezer('Freeze');
$b->Toaster('Thaw');
$c = $b->Dump;
print $c;
$d = eval $c;
print Data::Dumper->Dump([$d], ['d']);

########
# symbol substitution (useful for recreating CODE refs)
########

sub foo { print "foo speaking\n" }
*other = \&foo;
$bar = [ \&other ];
$d = Data::Dumper->new([\&other,$bar],['*other','bar']);
$d->Seen({ '*foo' => \&foo });
print $d->Dump;
```

Bugs

Due to the limitations of Perl subroutine call semantics, you cannot pass an array or hash. Prepend it with a '\' to pass its reference instead. This limitation will be remedied with the arrival of prototypes in later versions of Perl. For now, you need to use the extended usage form, and prepend the name with an '*' to output it as a hash or an array.

'Data::Dumper' cheats with CODE references. If a code reference is encountered in the structure being processed, an anonymous subroutine that contains the string ' "DUMMY" ' will be inserted in its place, and a warning will be printed if 'Purity' is set. You can evaluate the result, but bear in mind that the anonymous sub that is created is just a place-holder. Perhaps someday, Perl will have a switch to cache-on-demand the string representation of a compiled piece of code. If you know all the code refs that your data structures are likely to have, you can use the `'Seen'` method to precede the internal reference table and make the dumped output point to them. See the previous Examples section .

The `'Useqq'` flag is not honored by `'Dumpxs()'` (it always outputs strings in single quotes).

DirHandle

`DirHandle` is an alternative interface for accessing and reading filesystem directory information.

Synopsis

```
use DirHandle;
➡ $d = new DirHandle ".";
if (defined $d) {
  while (defined($_ = $d->read)) { something($_); }
  $d->rewind;
                while (defined($_ = $d->read))
➡ { something_else($_); }
undef $d;
}
```

Description

The `'DirHandle'` method provides an alternative interface to the `opendir()`, `closedir()`, `readdir()`, and `rewinddir()` functions.

The only objective benefit to using `'DirHandle'` is that it prevents namespace pollution by creating `globs` to hold directory handles.

Env

Using Env enables a more convenient and familiar way to reference environment variables.

Synopsis

```
use Env;
use Env qw(PATH HOME TERM);
```

Description

Perl maintains environment variables in a pseudo-hash named %ENV. When this access method is inconvenient, you can use the Perl module 'Env' to treat environment variables as simple variables.

The Env::import() function ties environment variables with suitable names to global Perl variables with the same names. By default, it does so with all existing environment variables ('keys %ENV'). If the import function receives arguments, it treats them like a list of environment variables to tie; it's okay if they don't yet exist.

After an environment variable is tied, use it like a normal variable. You may access its value:

```
@path = split(/:/, $PATH);
```

or modify it:

```
$PATH .= ":.";
```

as you like. To remove a tied environment variable from the environment, assign it the undefined value:

```
undef $PATH;
```

File::Basename

This module provides ways to extract name and path information from complete file paths.

Synopsis

```
use File::Basename;

($name,$path,$suffix) = fileparse($fullname,@suffixlist)
fileparse_set_fstype($os_string);
$basename = basename($fullname,@suffixlist);
$dirname = dirname($fullname);

($name,$path,$suffix) =
fileparse("lib/File/Basename.pm","\.pm");
fileparse_set_fstype("VMS");
$basename = basename("lib/File/Basename.pm",".pm");
$dirname = dirname("lib/File/Basename.pm");
```

Description

These routines allow you to parse file specifications into useful pieces using the syntax of different operating systems.

fileparse_set_fstype

You select the syntax via the routine `fileparse_set_fstype()`.

If the argument passed to it contains one of the substrings `"VMS"`, `"MSDOS"`, `"MacOS"`, `"AmigaOS"`, or `"MSWin32"`, the file specification syntax of that operating system is used in future calls to `fileparse()`, `basename()`, and `dirname()`. If it contains none of these substrings, UNIX syntax is used. The pattern matching is case-insensitive. If you selected VMS syntax and the file specification you pass to one of these routines contains a `"/"`, the routine assumes you are using UNIX emulation and applies the UNIX syntax rules instead—for that function call only.

If the argument passed to it contains one of the substrings `"VMS"`, `"MSDOS"`, `"MacOS"`, `"AmigaOS"`, `"os2"`, `"MSWin32"`, or `"RISCOS"`, the pattern matching for suffix removal is performed without regard to case, because those systems are not case-sensitive when opening existing files (though some of them preserve case on file creation).

If you haven't called `fileparse_set_fstype()`, the syntax is chosen by examining the `builtin` variable `'$^O'` according to these rules.

fileparse

The `fileparse()` routine divides a file specification into three parts: a leading path, a filename, and a suffix. The path contains everything up to and including the last directory separator in the input file specification. The remainder of the input file specification is then divided into name and suffix based on the optional patterns you specify in `'@suffixlist'`. Each element of this list is interpreted as a regular expression and is matched against the end of name. If this succeeds, the matching portion of name is removed and prepended to the suffix. By properly using `'@suffixlist'`, you can remove file types or versions for examination.

If you concatenate path, name, and suffix in that order, the result will denote the same file as the input file specification.

Examples

Using UNIX file syntax:

```
($base,$path,$type) =
fileparse('/virgil/aeneid/draft.book7',
                                '\.book\d+');
```

would yield

```
        $base eq 'draft'
        $path eq '/virgil/aeneid/',
        $type eq '.book7'
```

Similarly, using VMS syntax:

```
($name,$dir,$type) =
fileparse('Doc_Root:[Help]Rhetoric.Rnh',
                                '\..*');
```

would yield

```
        $name eq 'Rhetoric'
        $dir  eq 'Doc_Root:[Help]'
        $type eq '.Rnh'
```

basename

The basename() routine returns the first element of the list produced by calling fileparse() with the same arguments, except that it always quotes metacharacters in the given suffixes. It is provided for program compatibility with the UNIX shell command basename(1).

dirname

The dirname() routine returns the directory portion of the input file specification. When using VMS or MacOS syntax, the result of the routine is identical to the second element of the list produced by calling fileparse() with the same input file specification. (Under VMS, if there is no directory information in the input file specification, then the current default device and directory are returned.) When using UNIX or MS-DOS syntax, the return value conforms to the behavior of the UNIX shell command dirname(1). This is usually the same as the behavior of fileparse(), but it differs in some cases. For example, for the input file specification lib/, fileparse() considers the directory name to be lib/, and dirname() considers the directory name to be '.'.

The dirname command runs a variety of file-test checks on directory trees.

File::CheckTree

This module performs standard file-test operations on one or more files.

Synopsis

```
use File::CheckTree;

$warnings += validate( q{
    /vmunix                 -e || die
    /boot                   -e || die
    /bin                    cd
        csh                 -ex
        csh                 !-ug
        sh                  -ex
        sh                  !-ug
    /usr                    -d || warn "What happened
➥ to $file?\n"
    });
```

Description

The `validate()` routine takes a single multiline string consisting of lines containing a filename plus a file test to try on it. (The file test may also be a `"cd"`, causing subsequent relative filenames to be interpreted relative to that directory.) After the file test you may put `'|| die'` to make it a fatal error if the file test fails. The default is `'|| warn'`. The file test may optionally have a `'!'` prepended to test for the opposite condition. If you perform a `cd` and then list some relative filenames, you may want to indent them slightly for readability. If you supply your own `die()` or `q` message, you can use `$file` to interpolate the filename.

File tests may be bunched: `"-rwx"` tests for `'-r'`, `'-w'`, and `'-x'`. Only the first failed test of the bunch will produce a warning.

The routine returns the number of warnings issued.

File::Compare

This module tests two files to see if they are the same.

Synopsis

```
use File::Compare;
```

```
        if (compare("file1","file2") == 0) {
            print "They're equal\n";
        }
```

Description

The `File::Compare::compare` function compares the contents of two sources, each of which can be a file or a filehandle. It is exported from `File::Compare` by default.

`File::Compare::cmp` is a synonym for `File::Compare::compare`. It is exported from `File::Compare` only by request.

Returns

`File::Compare::compare` returns 0 if the files are equal, 1 if the files are unequal, or −1 if an error was encountered.

File::Copy

This module copies or moves a file specified using a string filename or a filehandle.

Synopsis

```
        use File::Copy;

        copy("file1","file2");
        copy("Copy.pm",\*STDOUT);
        move("/dev1/fileA","/dev2/fileB");

        use POSIX;
        use File::Copy cp;

        $n=FileHandle->new("/dev/null","r");
        cp($n,"x");
```

Description

The `File::Copy` module provides two basic functions: `'copy'` and `'move'`, which are useful for getting the contents of a file from one place to another.

The `'copy'` function takes two parameters: a file from which to copy and a file to which to copy. Either argument may be a string, a `FileHandle` reference or a `FileHandle` glob. Obviously, if the first argument is a filehandle of some sort, it will be read from. If it is a *filename*, it will be opened for reading. Likewise, the second argument will be created if necessary and written to.

NOTE

Passing files as handles instead of names may cause information to be lost on some operating systems. You should use filenames whenever possible. Files are opened in binary mode where applicable. To obtain consistent behavior when copying from a filehandle to a file, use `'binmode'` on the filehandle.

An optional third parameter can be used to specify the buffer size used for copying. This parameter is the number of bytes from the first file that will be held in memory at any given time, before being written to the second file. The default buffer size depends on the file, but it will generally be the whole file (up to 2MB) or 1K for filehandles that do not reference files (e.g., sockets).

You may use the syntax `'use File::Copy "cp"'` to get at the `"cp"` alias for this function. The syntax is the same.

The `'move'` function also takes two parameters: the current name and the intended name of the file to be moved. If the destination is a directory that already exists and the source is not a directory, the source file will be renamed into the directory specified by the destination.

If possible, move() will simply rename the file. Otherwise, it copies the file to the new location and deletes the original. If an error occurs during this copy-and-delete process, you may be left with a copy or possibly a partial copy of the file under the destination name.

You may use the `"mv"` alias for this function in the same way that you use the `"cp"` alias for `'copy'`.

`File::Copy` also provides the `'syscopy'` routine, which copies the file specified in the first parameter to the file specified in the second parameter—preserving OS-specific attributes and file structure. For UNIX systems, this is equivalent to the simple `'copy'` routine. For VMS systems, this calls the `'rmscopy'` routine. For OS/2 systems, this calls the `'syscopy'` XSUB directly.

Returns

All functions return 1 on success and 0 on failure. $! will be set if an error was encountered.

File::DosGlob

A module that implements DOS-like globbing with a few enhancements.

Synopsis

```
require 5.004;

# override CORE::glob in current package
use File::DosGlob 'glob';

# override CORE::glob in ALL packages
# (use with extreme caution!)
use File::DosGlob 'GLOBAL_glob';

@perlfiles = glob  "..\\pe?l/*.p?";
print <..\\pe?l/*.p?>;

# from the command line (overrides only in main::)
> perl -MFile::DosGlob=glob -e "print <../pe*/*p?>"
```

Description

This module is largely compatible with perlglob.exe (the M$ setargv.obj version) in all but one respect: it understands wildcards in directory components.

For example, '<..\\l*b\\file/*glob.p?'> will work as expected (in that it will find something like '..\lib\File/DosGlob.pm'). Note that all path components are case-insensitive and that backslashes and forward slashes are both accepted and preserved. You may have to double the backslashes if you are putting them in literally, due to parsing of the pattern by Perl.

Spaces in the argument delimit distinct patterns, so 'glob('*.exe *.dll')' globs all filenames that end in '.exe' or '.dll'. If you want to put literal spaces in the glob pattern, you can escape them with either double quotes or backslashes—for example, 'glob('c:/"Program Files"/*/*.dll')', or 'glob('c:/Program\ Files/*/*.dll')'. The argument is tokenized using `'Text::ParseWords::parse_line()'`, so see the `Text::ParseWords` manpage for details of the quoting rules used.

File::Find

This module traverses a file tree, optionally depth-first, returning all filenames that match a set of criteria.

Synopsis

```
use File::Find;
find(\&wanted, '/foo','/bar');
sub wanted { ... }

use File::Find;
finddepth(\&wanted, '/foo','/bar');
sub wanted { ... }
```

Description

The first argument to `find()` is either a hash reference describing the operations to be performed for each file, a code reference, or a string that contains a subroutine name. If the argument is a hash reference, the value for the key `'wanted'` should be a code reference. This code reference is called the `wanted()` function.

Currently the only other supported key for the previous hash is `'bydepth'`. When it is used, the `directory walk-over` is performed depth-first. Entry point `finddepth()` is a shortcut for specifying `{bydepth = 1}` in the first argument of `find()`.

The `wanted()` function performs the verifications you specify. `$File::Find::dir` contains the current directory name, and `$_` contains the current filename within that directory. `$File::Find::name` contains `'"$File::Find::dir/$_"'`. The current working directory is changed to `$File::Find::dir` when the function is called. The function may set `$File::Find::prune` to prune the tree.

`File::Find` assumes that you don't alter the `$_` variable. If you do alter it, make sure you return it to its original value before exiting your function.

This library is useful for the `'find2perl'` tool, which when fed

```
find2perl / -name .nfs\* -mtime +7 \
    -exec rm -f {} \; -o -fstype nfs -prune
```

produces something like:

```
sub wanted {
    /^\.nfs.*$/ &&
    (($dev,$ino,$mode,$nlink,$uid,$gid) = lstat($_))
      &&
    int(-M _) > 7 &&
    unlink($_)
    ||
    ($nlink || (($dev,$ino,$mode,$nlink,$uid,$gid) =
      lstat($_))) &&
    $dev < 0 &&
    ($File::Find::prune = 1);
}
```

Set the variable $File::Find::dont_use_nlink if you're using AFS, since AFS cheats.

The 'finddepth' command is similar to 'find', except that it performs a depth-first search.

Here's another interesting function. It will find all the symlinks that don't resolve:

```
sub wanted {
  -l && !-e && print "bogus link $File::Find::name\n";
}
```

Bugs

There is no way to make find or finddepth follow symlinks.

File::Path

This module creates or removes a series of directories.

Synopsis

```
'use File::Path'

'mkpath(['/foo/bar/baz', 'blurfl/quux'], 1, 0711);'

'rmtree(['foo/bar/baz', 'blurfl/quux'], 1, 1);'
```

Description

The `mkpath` function provides a convenient way to create directories—even if your `mkdir` kernel call won't create more than one directory level at a time. The `mkpath` command takes three arguments:

▶ The name of the path to create or a reference to a list of paths to create.

▶ A Boolean value, which if True will cause `mkpath` to print the name of each directory as it is created (defaults to False).

▶ The numeric mode to use when creating the directories (defaults to 0777).

It returns a list of all directories (including intermediates determined using the UNIX `/` separator) created.

Similarly, the `rmtree` function provides a convenient way to delete a subtree from the directory structure, much like the UNIX command `rm - r`. The `rmtree` command takes three arguments:

▶ The root of the subtree to delete or a reference to a list of roots. All of the files and directories below each root, as well as the roots themselves, will be deleted.

▶ A Boolean value, which if True will cause `rmtree` to print a message (giving the name of the file and indicating whether it's using `rmdir` or `unlink` to remove it, or that it's skipping it) each time it examines a file. (Defaults to False.)

▶ A Boolean value, which if True will cause `rmtree` to skip any files to which you do not have delete access (if running under VMS) or write access (if running under another OS). In the future, this process will change when a criterion for delete permission under operating systems other than VMS is settled. (Defaults to False.)

It returns the number of files successfully deleted. Symlinks are treated as ordinary files.

NOTE

If the third parameter is not True, 'rmtree' is unsecure in the face of failure or interruption. Files and directories that were not deleted may be left with permissions reset to allow world read-and-write access. The occurrence of errors in rmtree is not apparent from the return value and can be determined only by trapping diagnostic messages using '$SIG{__WARN__}'. Therefore, it is best not to use 'rmtree($foo,$bar,0' in situations where security is an issue.

File::Spec

File::Spec allows filenames to be constructed in way that preserves functionality on a number of different operating system platforms.

Synopsis

```
'use File::Spec;'

'$x=File::Spec->catfile('a','b','c');'

which returns 'a/b/c' under Unix.
```

Description

This module is designed to support operations commonly performed on file specifications (such as concatenating several directory and filenames into a single path or determining whether a path is rooted). Although File::Spec is usually called *filenames*, do not confuse it with the contents of a file or with Perl's filehandles. It is based on code taken directly from MakeMaker 5.17, which is code written by Andreas König, Andy Dougherty, Charles Bailey, Ilya Zakharevich, Paul Schinder, and others.

Because these functions are different for most operating systems, each set of OS specific routines is available in a separate module, including:

```
File::Spec::Unix
File::Spec::Mac
File::Spec::OS2
File::Spec::Win32
File::Spec::VMS
```

The module appropriate for the current OS is automatically loaded by File::Spec. Because some modules (like VMS) use OS-specific facilities, it may not be possible to load all modules under all operating systems.

Because `File::Spec` is object-oriented, subroutines should not be called directly, as in:

```
File::Spec::catfile('a','b');
```

They should be called as class methods:

```
File::Spec->catfile('a','b');
```

For a reference of the available functions, consult the `File::Spec::Unix` manpage, which contains the entire set of functions, each of which is inherited by the modules for other platforms. For further information, see the `File::Spec::Mac` manpage, the `File::Spec::OS2` manpage, the `File::Spec::Win32` manpage, or the `File::Spec::VMS` manpage.

File::Spec::Mac

`File::Spec::Mac` is a subclass of `File::Spec`, which is used for handling file specifications on Mac OS.

Synopsis

```
'require File::Spec::Mac;'
```

Description

These methods are for manipulating file specifications.

Methods

The following methods are available when `File::Spec::MacOS` is used:

canonpath

On MacOS, there's nothing to be done. It returns what it's given.

catdir

This command concatenates two or more directory names to form a complete path ending with a directory. Put a trailing " : " on the end of the complete path if there isn't one, as you would in MacPerl's environment.

The fundamental requirement of this routine is that

```
File::Spec->catdir(split(":",$path)) eq $path
```

Due to the nature of Macintosh paths, you can obtain reasonable results for some common situations by utilizing additional possibilities. Here are the rules:

▶ Each argument must have its trailing " : " removed.

▶ Each argument, except the first, must have its leading " : " removed.

▶ They must be joined by a " : ".

For example:

```
File::Spec->catdir("a","b") = "a:b:"
File::Spec->catdir("a:",":b") = "a:b:"
File::Spec->catdir("a:","b") = "a:b:"
File::Spec->catdir("a",":b") = "a:b"
File::Spec->catdir("a","","b") = "a::b"
```

To obtain a relative path (one beginning with :), begin the first argument with : or put a " " as the first argument.

If you don't want to worry about these rules, only allow a ":" at the beginning of the first argument. Never allow a " : " at the beginning or end of any other arguments.

An additional ambiguity exists under MacPerl. In the following code:

```
File::Spec->catfile("LWP","Protocol","http.pm")
```

does the programmer intend the code to be relative or absolute? There's no way to tell, except by checking for the existence of LWP: or :LWP. The user may mean a dismounted volume or a relative path in a different directory (like in @INC). Because those checks aren't performed here, this routine will treat code as absolute.

catfile

This command concatenates one or more directory names and a filename to form a complete path ending with a filename. Because this command uses catdir, the same caveats regarding placement of colons apply. Note that the leading : is removed from the filename, so that

```
File::Spec->catfile($ENV{HOME},"file");
```

and

```
File::Spec->catfile($ENV{HOME},":file");
```

give the same answer, as one might expect.

curdir

This command returns a string representing the current directory.

rootdir

This command returns a string representing the root directory. Under MacPerl, it returns the name of the startup volume (because it's the closest in concept, although other volumes aren't rooted there). On any other platform, it returns ' ', because there's no common way to indicate the root directory across all Macs.

updir

This command returns a string representing the parent directory.

file_name_is_absolute

This command takes a path as its argument and returns True, if the path is an absolute path. When a name can be either relative or absolute (for example, a folder named "HD" in the current working directory on a drive named "HD"), relative wins. Use ":" in the appropriate place in the path if you want to distinguish without ambiguity.

path

This command returns the null list for the MacPerl application, because the concept is usually meaningless under MacOS. If you're using the MacPerl tool under MPW, it gives back $ENV{Commands} suitably split, as is done in :lib:ExtUtils:MM_Mac.pm.

See Also

The File::Spec manpage.

File::Spec::OS2

This module is a subclass of File::Spec, which is used for handling file specifications on OS/2.

Synopsis

```
use File::Spec::OS2; # Done internally by File::Spec if
➥ needed
```

Description

See `File::Spec::Unix` for documentation of the methods provided there. This package overrides the implementation of these methods, not the semantics.

File::Spec::Unix

This module is a subclass of `File::Spec`, which is used for handling file specifications on UNIX.

Synopsis

```
'require File::Spec::Unix;'
```

Description

These are methods for manipulating file specifications.

Methods

The following methods are available when using `File::Spec::Unix`:

canonpath

This command performs no physical check on the filesystem; however, it performs a logical cleanup of a path. On UNIX, it eliminates successive slashes and successive `"/."`

catdir

This command concatenates two or more directory names to form a complete path ending with a directory. You should remove the trailing slash from the resulting string, because it doesn't look good, isn't necessary, and confuses OS2. Of course, if this is the root directory, don't cut off the trailing slash.

catfile

This command concatenates one or more directory names and a filename to form a complete path ending with a filename.

curdir

This command returns a string representing the current directory—"." on UNIX.

rootdir

This command returns a string representing the root directory—"/" on UNIX.

updir

This command returns a string representing the parent directory—".." on UNIX.

no_upwards

Given a list of filenames, this command strips out those that refer to a parent directory. (It does not strip symlinks, it strips only '.', '..', and equivalents.)

file_name_is_absolute

This command takes a path as its argument and returns True, if the path is an absolute path.

path

This command takes no argument. It returns the environment variable PATH as an array.

join

Join is the same as catfile. It concatenates one or more directory names and a filename to form a complete path ending with a filename.

See Also

The File::Spec manpage.

File::Spec::VMS

This module is a subclass of File::Spec, which is used for handling file specifications on VMS.

Synopsis

```
use File::Spec::VMS; # Done internally by File::Spec if
➥ needed
```

Description

See `File::Spec::Unix` for documentation of the methods provided there. This package overrides the implementation of these methods, not the semantics.

Methods

The following methods are available when using `File::Spec::VMS`:

catdir

This command concatenates a list of file specifications, and it returns the result as a VMS-syntax directory specification.

catfile

This command concatenates a list of file specifications, and it returns the result as a VMS-syntax directory specification.

curdir (override)

This command returns a string representing the current directory.

rootdir (override)

This command returns a string representing the root directory.

updir (override)

This command returns a string representing the parent directory.

path (override)

This command translates the logical name DCL$PATH as a searchlist, rather than trying to split the string value of `'$ENV{'PATH'}'`.

file_name_is_absolute (override)

This command checks for VMS directory specifications and UNIX separators.

File::Spec::Win32

A subclass of File::Spec for handling file specifications on 32-bit Windows.

Synopsis

```
use File::Spec::Win32; # Done internally by File::Spec if needed
```

Description

See the `File::Spec::Unix` documentation for the methods provided. This package overrides the implementation of these methods, not the semantics.

Methods

The following methods are available when you use `File::Spec::Win32`:

catfile

This command concatenates one or more directory names and a filename to form a complete path ending with a filename.

canonpath

This command does not perform a physical check on the filesystem; however, it does perform a logical cleanup of a path. On UNIX, successive slashes and successive "/" combinations are eliminated.

File::stat

This method is an alternative, object-oriented interface to Perl's built-in `stat()` function.

Synopsis

```
use File::stat;
$st = stat($file) or die "No $file: $!";
if ( ($st->mode & 0111) && $st->nlink > 1) ) {
    print "$file is executable with lotsa links\n";
}
```

```
use File::stat qw(:FIELDS);
stat($file) or die "No $file: $!";
if ( ($st_mode & 0111) && $st_nlink > 1) ) {
    print "$file is executable with lotsa links\n";
}
```

Description

This module's default exports override the core stat() and lstat() functions, replacing them with versions that return "File::stat" objects. This object has methods that return the similarly named structure field name from the stat(2) function—namely dev, ino, mode, nlink, uid, gid, rdev, size, atime, mtime, ctime, blksize, and blocks.

You may also import all the structure fields directly into your namespace as regular variables using the :FIELDS import tag. (This still overrides your stat() and lstat() functions.) Access these fields as variables named with a preceding 'st_' in front of their method names. Thus, '$stat_obj->dev()' corresponds to $st_dev if you import the fields.

To access this functionality without the core overrides, pass the 'use' an empty import list, and then access functions with their full qualified names. The built-ins are still available via the 'CORE::' pseudo-package.

NOTE
Although this class currently is implemented using the Class::Struct module to build a class similar to struct, you shouldn't rely on this implementation.

FileCache

This module provides a way to keep more files open than the operating system permits.

Synopsis

```
cacheout $path;
print $path @data;
```

Description

The 'cacheout' function will make sure that a filehandle (with the path name you give it) is open and available for writing. It automatically closes and reopens files if you exceed your system file descriptor maximum.

Bugs

The system header file sys/param.h may have a 'NOFILE' definition that is ignored on some systems, so you may have to set $FileCache::cacheout_maxopen yourself.

FileHandle

This method is an alternative, object-oriented interface used to manipulate files via filehandles.

Synopsis

```
use FileHandle;

$fh = new FileHandle;
if ($fh->open("< file")) {
    print <$fh>;
    $fh->close;
}

$fh = new FileHandle "> FOO";
if (defined $fh) {
    print $fh "bar\n";
    $fh->close;
}

$fh = new FileHandle "file", "r";
if (defined $fh) {
    print <$fh>;
    undef $fh;      # automatically closes the file
}

$fh = new FileHandle "file", O_WRONLY|O_APPEND;
if (defined $fh) {
    print $fh "corge\n";
    undef $fh;      # automatically closes the file
}
```

```
$pos = $fh->getpos;
$fh->setpos($pos);

$fh->setvbuf($buffer_var, _IOLBF, 1024);

($readfh, $writefh) = FileHandle::pipe;

autoflush STDOUT 1;
```

Description

'FileHandle::new' creates a 'FileHandle', which is a reference to a newly created symbol (see the 'Symbol' package). If it receives any parameters, they are passed to 'FileHandle::open'. If the open fails, the 'FileHandle' object is destroyed. Otherwise, it is returned to the caller.

NOTE

This class is now a front-end to the IO::* classes.

'FileHandle::new_from_fd' creates a 'FileHandle' similarly to way 'new' creates one. It requires two parameters, which are passed to 'FileHandle::fdopen'. If the fdopen fails, the 'FileHandle' object is destroyed. Otherwise, it is returned to the caller.

'FileHandle::open' accepts one or two parameters. With one parameter, it is just a front-end for the built-in 'open' function. With two parameters, the first parameter is a filename that may include whitespace or other special characters, and the second parameter is the open mode, optionally followed by a file permission value.

If 'FileHandle::open' receives a Perl mode string (">", "+<", etc.) or a POSIX fopen() mode string ("w", "r+", etc.), it uses the basic Perl 'open' operator.

If 'FileHandle::open' is given a numeric mode, it passes that mode and the optional permissions value to the Perl 'sysopen' operator. For convenience, 'FileHandle::import' tries to import the O_XXX constants from the Fcntl module. If dynamic loading is not available, this may fail, but the rest of FileHandle will still work.

'FileHandle::fdopen' is similar to 'open' except that its first parameter is not a filename but rather a filehandle name, a FileHandle object, or a file descriptor number.

If the C functions fgetpos() and fsetpos() are available, then 'FileHandle::getpos' returns an opaque value that represents the current position of the FileHandle, and 'FileHandle::setpos' uses that value to return to a previously visited position.

If the C function setvbuf() is available, then 'FileHandle::setvbuf' sets the buffering policy for the FileHandle. The calling sequence for the Perl function is the same as its C counterpart, including the macros '_IOFBF', '_IOLBF', and '_IONBF', except that the buffer parameter specifies a scalar variable to use as a buffer.

WARNING

A variable used as a buffer by 'FileHandle::setvbuf' must not be modified until the FileHandle is closed or until 'FileHandle::setvbuf' is called again. If it is modified in any way, memory corruption may result!

See the perlfunc manpage for complete descriptions of each of the following supported 'FileHandle' methods, which are just front-ends for the corresponding built-in functions:

```
close
fileno
getc
gets
eof
clearerr
seek
tell
```

See the perlvar manpage for complete descriptions of each of the following supported 'FileHandle' methods:

```
autoflush
output_field_separator
output_record_separator
input_record_separator
input_line_number
format_page_number
format_lines_per_page
format_lines_left
format_name
format_top_name
format_line_break_characters
format_formfeed
```

For normal I/O, you might need the following methods:

$fh->print

See the `"print"` entry in the `perlfunc` manpage.

$fh->printf

See the `"printf"` entry in the `perlfunc` manpage.

$fh->getline

This method works similarly to `<$fh>`, which is described in the "I/O Operators" section in the `perlop` manpage. However, it's more readable and can be safely called in an array context and still returns just one line.

$fh->getlines

This method works like `<$fh>` when it is called in an array context to read the remaining lines in a file; however, it's more readable. It will also `croak()` if accidentally called in a scalar context.

Many other functions are available because `FileHandle` is descended from `IO::File`, `IO::Seekable`, and `IO::Handle`. Refer to those respective pages for documentation on more functions.

FindBin

This command is used to find the full path on the filesystem to the script currently running.

Synopsis

```
use FindBin;
use lib "$FindBin::Bin/../lib";
```

or

```
use FindBin qw($Bin);
use lib "$Bin/../lib";
```

Description

This method locates the full path to the script `bin` directory to allow the use of paths relative to the `bin` directory.

This method allows a user to set up a directory tree for software with directories <root>/bin and <root>/lib. The previous example will allow the use of modules in the lib directory without knowing where the software tree is installed.

If perl is invoked using the -e option or the perl script is read from 'STDIN', then FindBin sets both '$Bin' and '$RealBin' to the current directory.

Exportable Variables

```
$Bin - path to bin directory from where script was invoked
$Script - basename of script from which perl was invoked
$RealBin - $Bin with all links resolved
$RealScript - $Script with all links resolved
```

Known Bugs

If perl is invoked as

```
perl filename
```

and filename does not have executable rights and a program called filename exists in the users '$ENV{PATH}' (which satisfies both -x and –T), then FindBin assumes that it was invoked via the '$ENV{PATH}'.

The workaround invokes perl as:

```
perl ./filename
```

IO

This is a convenient class loader for some of the IO::* modules.

Synopsis

```
use IO;
```

Description

'IO' provides a simple mechanism to load some of the IO modules at once. Currently, this includes:

```
IO::Handle
IO::Seekable
IO::File
IO::Pipe
IO::Socket
```

For more information on any of these modules, refer to its respective documentation.

IO::File

This is an alternative, object-oriented interface used for accessing files.

Synopsis

```perl
use IO::File;

$fh = new IO::File;
if ($fh->open("< file")) {
    print <$fh>;
    $fh->close;
}

$fh = new IO::File "> file";
if (defined $fh) {
    print $fh "bar\n";
    $fh->close;
}

$fh = new IO::File "file", "r";
if (defined $fh) {
    print <$fh>;
    undef $fh;       # automatically closes the file
}

$fh = new IO::File "file", O_WRONLY|O_APPEND;
if (defined $fh) {
    print $fh "corge\n";

    $pos = $fh->getpos;
    $fh->setpos($pos);

    undef $fh;       # automatically closes the file
}

autoflush STDOUT 1;
```

Description

'IO::File' inherits from 'IO::Handle' and 'IO::Seekable'. It
extends these classes with methods that are specific to filehandles.

Constructor

Either of following constructors may be used to create a new File::IO
object.

new ([ARGS])

This constructor creates an 'IO::File'. If it receives any parameters,
they are passed to the method 'open'. If the open fails, the object is
destroyed. Otherwise, it is returned to the caller.

new_tmpfile

This constructor creates an 'IO::File' opened for read/write on a newly
created temporary file. On systems where this is possible, the temporary
file is anonymous (i.e., it is unlinked after creation, but held open). If the
temporary file cannot be created or opened, the 'IO::File' object is
destroyed. Otherwise, it is returned to the caller.

Methods

The following methods are available when using IO::File.

open(FILENAME [,MODE [,PERMS]])

The 'open' method accepts one, two, or three parameters. With one parameter, it is just a front-end for the built-in 'open' function. With two
parameters, the first parameter is a filename that may include whitespace
or other special characters, and the second parameter is the open mode,
optionally followed by a file permission value.

If 'IO::File::open' receives a Perl mode string (">", "+<", etc.) or a
POSIX fopen() mode string ("w", "r+", etc.), it uses the basic Perl
'open' operator.

If 'IO::File::open' is given a numeric mode, it passes that mode
and the optional permissions value to the Perl 'sysopen' operator. For
convenience, 'IO::File::import' tries to import the O_XXX constants

from the Fcntl module. If dynamic loading is not available, this may fail, but the rest of IO::File will still work.

See Also

The perlfunc manpage, the "I/O Operators" section in the perlop manpage, the IO::Handle manpage, and the IO::Seekable manpage

IO::Handle

This is an alternative, object-oriented interface for using filehandles.

Synopsis

```
use IO::Handle;

$fh = new IO::Handle;
if ($fh->fdopen(fileno(STDIN),"r")) {
    print $fh->getline;
    $fh->close;
}

$fh = new IO::Handle;
if ($fh->fdopen(fileno(STDOUT),"w")) {
    $fh->print("Some text\n");
}

use IO::Handle '_IOLBF';
$fh->setvbuf($buffer_var, _IOLBF, 1024);

undef $fh; # automatically closes the file if open

autoflush STDOUT 1;
```

Description

'IO::Handle' is the base class for all other IO handle classes. Objects of 'IO::Handle' were not intended to be created directly; instead 'IO::Handle' is inherited from several other classes in the IO hierarchy.

If you are looking for a replacement for the `FileHandle' package, refer to the documentation for 'IO::File'.

An 'IO::Handle' object is a reference to a symbol (see the 'Symbol' package).

Constructor

Either of the following constructors may be used to create a new 'IO::Handle' object.

new ()

This constructor creates a new 'IO::Handle' object.

new_from_fd (FD, MODE)

This constructor creates an 'IO::Handle' similarly to the way 'new' does. It requires two parameters, which are passed to the method 'fdopen'. If the fdopen fails, the object is destroyed. Otherwise, it is returned to the caller.

IO::pipe

This is an alternative, object-oriented interface used for handling pipes.

Synopsis

```
use IO::Pipe;

$pipe = new IO::Pipe;

if($pid = fork()) { # Parent
    $pipe->reader();

    while(<$pipe> {
        ....
    }

}
elsif(defined $pid) { # Child
    $pipe->writer();

    print $pipe ....
}
```

```
                or

                $pipe = new IO::Pipe;

                $pipe->reader(qw(ls -l));

                while(<$pipe>) {
                    ....
                }
```

Description

'IO::Pipe' provides an interface for creating pipes between processes.

Constructor

The following constructor is used to create a new IO::Pipe object.

new ([READER, WRITER])

This constructor creates an 'IO::Pipe', which is a reference to a newly created symbol (see the 'Symbol' package). 'IO::Pipe::new' optionally takes two arguments, which should be objects blessed into 'IO::Handle' or a subclass thereof. These two objects will be used for the system call to 'pipe'. If no arguments are given, the method 'handles' is called on the new 'IO::Pipe' object.

These two handles are held in the array part of the glob until either 'reader' or 'writer' is called.

Methods

The following methods are available when using IO::Pipe.

reader ([ARGS])

The object is reblessed into a subclass of 'IO::Handle', and it becomes a handle at the reading end of the pipe. If 'ARGS' are given, 'fork' is called and 'ARGS' are passed to exec.

writer ([ARGS])

The object is reblessed into a subclass of 'IO::Handle', and it becomes a handle at the writing end of the pipe. If 'ARGS' are given, 'fork' is called and 'ARGS' are passed to exec.

handles ()

This method is called during construction by `'IO::Pipe::new'` on the newly created `'IO::Pipe'` object. It returns an array of two objects blessed into `'IO::Pipe::End'`, or a subclass thereof.

IO::Seekable

This is a class that supplies seek-based methods to other objects based on IO::Handle.

Synopsis

```
use IO::Seekable;
package IO::Something;
@ISA = qw(IO::Seekable);
```

Description

`'IO::Seekable'` does not have a constructor of its own, because it is intended to be inherited by other objects based on `'IO::Handle'`. It provides methods that allow seeking of the file descriptors.

If the C functions fgetpos() and fsetpos() are available, then `'IO::File::getpos'` returns an opaque value that represents the current position of the IO::File, and `'IO::File::setpos'` uses that value to return to a previously visited position.

See the perlfunc manpage for complete descriptions of each of the following supported `'IO::Seekable'` methods (which are just front-ends for the corresponding built-in functions):

seek
tell

IO::Select

This is an object-oriented interface to the select() system call.

Synopsis

```
use IO::Select;

$s = IO::Select->new();
```

```
$s->add(\*STDIN);
$s->add($some_handle);

@ready = $s->can_read($timeout);

@ready = IO::Select->new(@handles)->read(0);
```

Description

The `IO::Select` package implements an object approach to the system `select`' function call. It allows the user to see what IO handles (see the `IO::Handle` manpage) are ready for reading, ready for writing, or have an error condition pending.

Constructor

The following constructor is used to create a new `IO::Select` object.

new ([HANDLES])

The constructor creates a new object and optionally initializes it with a set of handles.

Methods

The following methods are available when using `IO::Select`.

add (HANDLES)

This method adds the list of handles to the `IO::Select` object. These values will be returned when an event occurs. `IO::Select` keeps these values in a cache, which is indexed by the `fileno` of the handle; therefore, if more than one handle with the same `fileno` is specified, only the last one is cached.

Each handle can be an `IO::Handle` object, an integer, or an array reference where the first element is an `IO::Handle` or an integer.

remove (HANDLES)

This method removes all the given handles from the object. It also works by using the `fileno` of the handles. The exact handles that were added do not need to be passed; only handles that have an equivalent `fileno` need to be passed.

exists (HANDLE)

This method returns a True value (actually the handle itself) if the handle is present. It returns undef if the handle does not exist.

handles

This method returns an array of all registered handles.

can_read ([TIMEOUT])

This method returns an array of handles that are ready for reading. 'TIMEOUT' is the maximum amount of time to wait before returning an empty list. If 'TIMEOUT' is not given and any handles are registered, then the call will block.

can_write ([TIMEOUT])

This is similar to 'can_read'. It also checks for handles that can be written to.

has_error ([TIMEOUT])

This is similar to 'can_read'. It also checks for handles that have an error condition, for example EOF.

count ()

This method returns the number of handles that the object will check for when one of the 'can_' methods is called or the object is passed to the 'select' static method.

bits()

This method returns the bit string suitable as an argument to the core select() call.

bits()

This method returns the bit string suitable as an argument to the core select() call.

select (READ, WRITE, ERROR [, TIMEOUT])

The 'select' method is a static method (that is, you call it with the package name like `new`). 'READ', 'WRITE', and 'ERROR' are either 'undef' or 'IO::Select' objects. 'TIMEOUT' is optional and has the same effect as the core select call.

The result will be an array of three elements, each a reference to an array which will hold the handles that are ready for reading, are ready for writing, or that have error conditions. Upon error, an empty array is returned.

Example

This short example shows how 'IO::Select' could be used to write to a server that communicates with several sockets while also listening for more connections on a listen socket.

```perl
use IO::Select;
use IO::Socket;

$lsn = new IO::Socket::INET(Listen => 1,
                            LocalPort => 8080);
$sel = new IO::Select( $lsn );

while(@ready = $sel->can_read) {
    foreach $fh (@ready) {
        if($fh == $lsn) {
            # Create a new socket
            $new = $lsn->accept;
            $sel->add($new);
        }
        else {
            # Process socket

            # Maybe we have finished the socket
            $sel->remove($fh);
            $fh->close;
        }
    }
}
```

Math::BigFloat

This method offers a way to use floating-point numerals of arbitrary length.

Synopsis

```
use Math::BigFloat;
$f = Math::BigFloat->new($string);

$f->fadd(NSTR) return NSTR          addition
$f->fsub(NSTR) return NSTR          subtraction
$f->fmul(NSTR) return NSTR          multiplication
$f->fdiv(NSTR[,SCALE]) returns NSTR division to SCALE
➥ places
$f->fneg() return NSTR              negation
$f->fabs() return NSTR              absolute value
$f->fcmp(NSTR) return CODE          compare
➥ undef,<0,=0,>0
$f->fround(SCALE) return NSTR       round to SCALE digits
$f->ffround(SCALE) return NSTR      round at SCALEth
➥ place
$f->fnorm() return (NSTR)           normalize
$f->fsqrt([SCALE]) return NSTR      sqrt to SCALE places
```

Description

All basic math operations are overloaded if you declare your big floats as:

```
$float = new Math::BigFloat
         "2.123123123123123123123123123123123";
```

Number Format

Canonical strings have the form /[+-]\d+E[+-]\d+/ . Input values can have embedded whitespace.

Error Returns 'NaN'

An input parameter was "Not a Number," or an attempt was made to divide by zero or take the square root of a negative number.

   Division is computed to
`'max($div_scale,length(dividend)+length(divisor))'` digits
by default. This method is also used for default sqrt scale.

Math::BigInt

This method offers a way to use integers of arbitrary size.

Synopsis

```
use Math::BigInt;
$i = Math::BigInt->new($string);

$i->bneg return BINT              negation
$i->babs return BINT              absolute value
$i->bcmp(BINT) return CODE        compare numbers
(undef,<0,=0,>0)
$i->badd(BINT) return BINT        addition
$i->bsub(BINT) return BINT        subtraction
$i->bmul(BINT) return BINT        multiplication
$i->bdiv(BINT) return (BINT,BINT) division (quo,rem) just
quo if scalar
$i->bmod(BINT) return BINT        modulus
$i->bgcd(BINT) return BINT        greatest common divisor
$i->bnorm return BINT             normalization
```

Description

All basic math operations are overloaded if you declare your big integers as

```
$i = new Math::BigInt '123 456 789 123 456 789';
```

The actual math is done in an internal format consisting of an array whose first element is the sign (/^[+-]$/) and whose remaining elements are base 100,000 digits with the least significant digit first. The string 'NaN' is used to represent the result when input arguments are not numbers; it is also used to represent the result of dividing by zero.

Math::Complex

This package lets you create and manipulate complex numbers.

Synopsis

```
use Math::Complex;

$z = Math::Complex->make(5, 6);
$t = 4 - 3*i + $z;
$j = cplxe(1, 2*pi/3);
```

Description

By default, Perl limits itself to real numbers; however, an extra 'use' statement brings full, complex support, along with a full set of mathematical functions typically associated with and/or extended to complex numbers.

To create a complex number, use either:

```
$z = Math::Complex->make(3, 4);
```

or

```
$z = cplx(3, 4);
```

if you know the Cartesian form of the number. You can use

```
$z = 3 + 4*i;
```

if you like. To create a number using the polar form, use either:

```
$z = Math::Complex->emake(5, pi/3);
```

or

```
$x = cplxe(5, pi/3);
```

instead. The first argument is the modulus, the second is the angle (in radians, the full circle is 2*pi). (Remember that 'e' is used as a notation for complex numbers in the polar form.)

You could write:

```
$x = cplxe(-3, pi/4);
```

but that will be silently converted into '[3,-3pi/4]', because the modulus must be nonnegative (it represents the distance to the origin in the complex plane).

You could also have a complex number as the argument of either 'make' or 'emake'. The appropriate component of the argument will be used.

```
$z1 = cplx(-2, 1);
$z2 = cplx($z1, 4);
```

Here are some examples:

```
use Math::Complex;

$j = cplxe(1, 2*pi/3);  # $j ** 3 == 1
print "j = $j, j**3 = ", $j ** 3, "\n";
print "1 + j + j**2 = ", 1 + $j + $j**2, "\n";

$z = -16 + 0*i;                    # Force it to be a complex
print "sqrt($z) = ", sqrt($z), "\n";
```

```
$k = exp(i * 2*pi/3);
print "$j - $k = ", $j - $k, "\n";

$z->Re(3);                    # Re, Im, arg, abs,
$j->arg(2);                   # (the last two aka rho, theta)
                              # can be used also as mutators.
```

Net::Ping

This package provides a way to check the reachability of remote host over a network connection.

Synopsis

```
use Net::Ping;

$p = Net::Ping->new();
print "$host is alive.\n" if $p->ping($host);
$p->close();

$p = Net::Ping->new("icmp");
foreach $host (@host_array)
{
    print "$host is ";
    print "NOT " unless $p->ping($host, 2);
    print "reachable.\n";
    sleep(1);
}
$p->close();

$p = Net::Ping->new("tcp", 2);
while ($stop_time > time())
{
    print "$host not reachable ",
        scalar(localtime()), "\n"
        unless $p->ping($host);
    sleep(300);
}
undef($p);

# For backward compatibility
print "$host is alive.\n" if pingecho($host);
```

Description

This module contains methods to test the ability to reach remote hosts on a network. A ping object is created with optional parameters, a variable number of hosts may be pinged multiple times, and then the connection is closed.

You may choose one of three different protocols to use for the ping. With the "tcp" protocol, the ping() method attempts to establish a connection to the remote host's echo port. If the connection is successfully established, the remote host is considered reachable. No data is actually echoed. This protocol does not require any special privileges, but it has a higher overhead than the other two protocols.

Specifying the "udp" protocol causes the ping() method to send a udp packet to the remote host's echo port. If the echoed packet is received from the remote host and the received packet contains the same data as the packet that was sent, the remote host is considered reachable. This protocol does not require any special privileges.

If the "icmp" protocol is specified, the ping() method sends an icmp echo message to the remote host, which is what the UNIX ping program does. If the echoed message is received from the remote host and the echoed information is correct, the remote host is considered reachable. Specifying the "icmp" protocol requires that the program be run as root or that the program be setuid to root.

Functions

The following functions are available when using Net::Ping:

Net::Ping->new([$proto [, $def_timeout [, $bytes]]]);

Create a new ping object. All of the parameters are optional. The $proto command specifies the protocol to use when doing a ping. The current choices are "tcp", "udp", or "icmp". The default is "udp".

If a default timeout ($def_timeout) in seconds is provided, it is used when a timeout is not given to the ping() method (see the following listing). The timeout must be greater than 0 and the default, if not specified, is five seconds.

If the number of data bytes ($bytes) is given, that many data bytes are included in the ping packet sent to the remote host. The number of data bytes is ignored if the protocol is "tcp". The minimum (and default) number of data bytes is 1 if the protocol is "udp"; it is 0 if the protocol is not "udp". The maximum number of data bytes that can be specified is 1,024.

$p->ping($host [, $timeout]);

Ping the remote host and wait for a response. $host can be either the hostname or the IP number of the remote host. The optional timeout must be greater than 0 seconds and defaults to whatever was specified when the ping object was created. If the hostname cannot be found or there is a problem with the IP number, undef is returned. Otherwise, 1 is returned if the host is reachable and 0 if it is not. For all practical purposes, undef and 0 and can be treated as the same case.

$p->close();

Close the network connection for this ping object. The network connection is also closed by "undef $p". The network connection is automatically closed if the ping object goes out of scope (e.g., $p is local to a subroutine and you leave the subroutine).

pingecho($host [, $timeout]);

To provide backward compatibility with the previous version of Net:: Ping, a pingecho() subroutine is available with the same functionality as before. The pingecho() command uses the tcp protocol. The return values and parameters are the same as described for the ping() method. This subroutine is obsolete and may be removed in a future version of Net::Ping.

NOTE

The pingecho()command and a ping object with the tcp protocol use alarm() to implement the timeout. Therefore, don't use alarm() in your program while you are using pingecho() or a ping object with the tcp protocol. The udp and icmp protocols do not use alarm() to implement the timeout.

There will be less network overhead (and less efficiency in your program) if you specify either the udp or the icmp protocol. The tcp protocol will generate 2.5 times or more traffic for each ping than either udp or icmp. If many hosts are pinged frequently, you may want to implement a small wait (e.g., 25 milliseconds or more) between each ping to avoid flooding your network with packets.

The icmp protocol requires that the program be run as a root or that it be setuid to a root. The tcp and udp protocols do not require special privileges; however, not all network devices implement the echo protocol for tcp or udp.

Local hosts normally should respond to pings within milliseconds. However, on a very congested network, it may take up to three seconds or longer to receive an echo packet from the remote host. If the timeout is set too low under these conditions, it will appear that the remote host is not reachable (which is almost the truth).

Being able to be reached doesn't necessarily mean the remote host is actually functioning beyond its ability to echo packets.

Because of a lack of anything better, this module uses its own routines to pack and unpack ICMP packets. It would be better for a separate module that understands all of the different kinds of ICMP packets to be written.

Net::hostent

This is an alternative, object-oriented interface to Perl's built-in gethostbyname() and gethostbyaddr() functions.

Synopsis

```
use Net::hostnet;
```

Description

This module's default exports override the core gethostbyname() and gethostbyaddr() functions, replacing them with versions that return "Net::hostent" objects. This object has methods that return the similarly named structure field name from the C's hostent structure from netdb.h. These methods consist of: name(), aliases(), addrtype(), length(), and addr_list(). The aliases and addr_list methods return array reference; the rest return scalars. The addr method is equivalent to the zero placed element in the addr_list array reference.

You may also import all the structure fields directly into your namespace as regular variables using the :FIELDS import tag. (Note that this still overrides your core functions.) You access these fields as variables named with a preceding 'h_'. Therefore, '$host_obj->name()' corresponds to $h_name if you import the fields. Array references are available as regular array variables; for example, `'@{ $host_obj- >aliases() }'` would be simply @h_aliases.

The gethost() function is a simple front-end that forwards a numeric argument to gethostbyaddr() by way of Socket::inet_aton and forwards the rest of the arguments to gethostbyname().

To access this functionality without the core overrides, pass the empty import list to the `'use'`, and then access functions with their full qualified names. On the other hand, the built-ins are still available via the `'CORE::'` pseudo-package.

Examples

```
use Net::hostent;
use Socket;

@ARGV = ('netscape.com') unless @ARGV;

for $host ( @ARGV ) {

    unless ($h = gethost($host)) {
        warn "$0: no such host: $host\n";
        next;
    }

    printf "\n%s is %s%s\n",
            $host,
            lc($h->name) eq lc($host) ? "" : "*really* ",
            $h->name;

    print "\taliases are ", join(", ", @{$h->aliases}), "\n"
                if @{$h->aliases};

    if ( @{$h->addr_list} > 1 ) {
        my $i;
        for $addr ( @{$h->addr_list} ) {
            printf "\taddr #%d is [%s]\n", $i++, inet_ntoa($addr);
        }
    } else {
        printf "\taddress is [%s]\n", inet_ntoa($h->addr);
    }
```

```
        if ($h = gethostbyaddr($h->addr)) {
            if (lc($h->name) ne lc($host)) {
    printf "\tThat addr reverses to host %s!\n", $h->name;
                $host = $h->name;
                redo;
            }
        }
    }
```

NOTE

Although this class is currently implemented using the Class::Struct module to build a class of 'struct' and similar datatypes, you shouldn't rely on this.

Net::netent

This module provides an alternative, object-oriented interface to Perl's getnetbyname() and getnetbyaddr() functions.

Synopsis

```
use Net::netent qw(:FIELDS);
getnetbyname("loopback")            or die "bad net";
printf "%s is %08X\n", $n_name, $n_net;

use Net::netent;

$n = getnetbyname("loopback")       or die "bad net";
{ # there's gotta be a better way, eh?
    @bytes = unpack("C4", pack("N", $n->net));
    shift @bytes while @bytes && $bytes[0] == 0;
}
printf "%s is %08X [%d.%d.%d.%d]\n", $n->name,
    $n->net, @bytes;
```

Description

This module's default exports override the core getnetbyname() and getnetbyaddr() functions, replacing them with versions that return "Net::netent" objects. This object has methods that return the similarly named structure field name from the C's netent structure from netdb.h. These methods consist of name(), aliases(), addrtype(), and net().The aliases() method returns an array reference; the rest of the methods return scalars.

You may also import all the structure fields directly into your namespace as regular variables using the :FIELDS import tag. (Note that this still overrides your core functions.) You access these fields as variables named with a preceding 'n_'. Therefore, '$net_obj->name()' corresponds to $n_name if you import the fields. Array references are available as regular array variables—for example, '@{ $net_obj->aliases() }' would be simply @n_aliases.

The getnet() function is a simple front-end that forwards a numeric argument to getnetbyaddr() and forwards the rest of the arguments to getnetbyname().

To access this functionality without the core overrides, pass an empty import list to 'use', and then access functions with their full qualified names. On the other hand, the built-ins are still available via the 'CORE::' pseudo-package.

Examples

The getnet() functions perform the following in the Perl core:

```
sv_setiv(sv, (I32)nent->n_net);
```

The gethost() functions perform the following in the Perl core:

```
sv_setpvn(sv, hent->h_addr, len);
```

This means that the address comes back in binary for the host functions and as a regular Perl integer for the net ones. This seems to be a bug, but here's how to deal with it:

```
use strict;
use Socket;
use Net::netent;

@ARGV = ('loopback') unless @ARGV;

my($n, $net);

for $net ( @ARGV ) {

    unless ($n = getnetbyname($net)) {
        warn "$0: no such net: $net\n";
        next;
    }
```

```perl
        printf "\n%s is %s%s\n",
              $net,
              lc($n->name) eq lc($net) ? "" : "*really* ",
              $n->name;

    print "\taliases are ", join(", ", @{$n->aliases}), "\n"
                if @{$n->aliases};

    # this is stupid; first, why is this not in binary?
    # second, why am i going through these convolutions
    # to make it look right
    {
        my @a = unpack("C4", pack("N", $n->net));
        shift @a while @a && $a[0] == 0;
        printf "\taddr is %s [%d.%d.%d.%d]\n", $n->net, @a;
    }

    if ($n = getnetbyaddr($n->net)) {
        if (lc($n->name) ne lc($net)) {
    printf "\tThat addr reverses to net %s!\n", $n->name;
            $net = $n->name;
            redo;
        }
    }
}
```

NOTE

Although this class is currently implemented using the Class::Struct module to build a class of 'struct' and similar datatypes, you shouldn't rely on this.

Net::protoent

This method provides an alternative, object-oriented interface to Perl's built-in getprotoent(), getprotobyname(), and getnetbyport() functions.

Synopsis

```perl
use Net::protoent;
$p = getprotobyname(shift || 'tcp') || die "no proto";
printf "proto for %s is %d, aliases are %s\n",
    $p->name, $p->proto, "@{$p->aliases}";
```

```
use Net::protoent qw(:FIELDS);
getprotobyname(shift || 'tcp') || die "no proto";
print "proto for $p_name is $p_proto, aliases are
    @p_aliases\n";
```

Description

This module's default exports override the core getprotoent(), getprotobyname(), and getnetbyport() functions, replacing them with versions that return "Net::protoent" objects. They take default second arguments of "tcp". This object has methods that return the similarly named structure field name from the C's protoent structure from netdb.h. These methods consist of name(), aliases(), and proto().The aliases method returns an array reference; the rest of the methods return scalars.

You may also import all the structure fields directly into your namespace as regular variables using the :FIELDS import tag. (Note that this still overrides your core functions.) You access these fields as variables named with a preceding 'p_'. Therefore, '$proto_obj->name()' corresponds to $p_name if you import the fields. Array references are available as regular array variables. For example, '@{ $proto_obj- >aliases() }' would be simply @p_aliases.

The getproto() function is a simple front-end that forwards a numeric argument to getprotobyport() and forwards the rest of the arguments to getprotobyname().

To access this functionality without the core overrides, pass an empty list to the 'use', and then access functions with their full qualified names. On the other hand, the built-ins are still available via the 'CORE::' pseudo-package.

NOTE
Although this class is currently implemented using the Class::Struct module to build a class of 'struct' and similar datatypes, you shouldn't rely on this.

Net::servent

This is an alternative, object-oriented interface to Perl's built-in getservent(), getservbyname(), and getnetbyport() functions.

Synopsis

```
use Net::servent;
$s = getservbyname(shift || 'ftp') ||
        die "no service";
printf "port for %s is %s, aliases are %s\n",
    $s->name, $s->port, "@{$s->aliases}";

use Net::servent qw(:FIELDS);
getservbyname(shift || 'ftp') || die "no service";
print "port for $s_name is $s_port, aliases are
    @s_aliases\n";
```

Description

This module's default exports override the core getservent(), get-servbyname(), and getnetbyport() functions, replacing them with versions that return "Net::servent" objects. They take default second arguments of "tcp". This object has methods that return the similarly named structure field name from the C's servent structure from netdb.h. These methods consist of name(), aliases(), port(), and proto(). The aliases method returns an array reference; the rest of the methods return scalars.

You may also import all the structure fields directly into your namespace as regular variables using the :FIELDS import tag. (Note that this still overrides your core functions.) You access these fields as variables named with a preceding 'n_'. Therefore, '$serv_obj->name()' corresponds to $s_name if you import the fields. Array references are available as regular array variables; for example, '@{ $serv_obj- >aliases() }' would be simply @s_aliases.

The getserv() function is a simple front-end that forwards a numeric argument to getservbyport(), and forwards the rest of the arguments to getservbyname().

To access this functionality without the core overrides, pass an empty import list to the 'use', and then access functions with their full qualified names. On the other hand, the built-ins are still available via the 'CORE::' pseudo-package.

Examples

```
use Net::servent qw(:FIELDS);

while (@ARGV) {
    my ($service, $proto) = ((split m!/!, shift),
      'tcp');
    my $valet = getserv($service, $proto);
    unless ($valet) {
        warn "$0: No service: $service/$proto\n"
        next;
    }
    printf "service $service/$proto is port %d\n",
      $valet->port;
    print "alias are @s_aliases\n" if @s_aliases;
}
```

Safe

The Safe extension module allows the creation of compartments in which Perl code can be evaluated.

Synopsis

```
use Safe;

$compartment = new Safe;
$compartment->permit(qw(time sort :browse));
$result = $compartment->reval($unsafe_code);
```

Description

Each compartment has a new namespace and an operator mask.

The root of the namespace (i.e., "main::") is changed to a different package. The code evaluated in the compartment cannot refer to variables outside this namespace, even with runtime glob lookups and other tricks.

The code, which is compiled outside the compartment, can place variables into (or *share* variables with) the compartment's namespace. Only that data will be visible to code evaluated in the compartment.

By default, the only variables shared with compartments are the underscore variables $_ and @_ (and, technically, the less frequently used %_, _ filehandle, and so on). If variables other than these were shared, the Perl operators which default to $_ would not work, nor would the assignment of arguments to @_ on subroutine entry.

Each compartment has an associated *operator mask*. Recall that Perl code is compiled into an internal format before execution. Evaluating Perl code (e.g., via "eval" or "do 'file'") causes the code to be compiled into an internal format and then, provided there was no error in the compilation, executed. Code evaluated in a compartment compiles the subject to the compartment's operator mask. Attempting to evaluate code in a compartment that contains a masked operator will cause the compilation to fail with an error. The code will not be executed.

The default operator mask for a newly created compartment is the ':default' optag.

Make sure you read the Opcode(3) module documentation for more important information, especially the detailed definitions of opnames, optags, and opsets.

Because the operator mask applies only at the compilation stage, you can control access to potentially unsafe operations by having a handle to a wrapper subroutine (written outside the compartment) placed into the compartment. For example:

```
$cpt = new Safe;
sub wrapper {
    # vet arguments and perform potentially
    # unsafe operations
}
$cpt->share('&wrapper');
```

Search::Dict, Look

This method allows case-dependent or case-independent searching in a dictionary file.

Synopsis

```
use Search::Dict;
look *FILEHANDLE, $key, $dict, $fold;
```

Description

This method sets the file position in FILEHANDLE to be the first line greater than or equal (stringwise) to $key. It returns the new file position or −1 if an error occurs.

The flags specify dictionary order and case folding:

- ▶ If $dict is True, search by dictionary order (ignore everything except word characters and whitespace).
- ▶ If $fold is True, ignore case.

SelectSaver

SelectSaver provides a way to save and restore filehandles.

Synopsis

```
use SelectSaver;

{
    my $saver = new SelectSaver(FILEHANDLE);
    # FILEHANDLE is selected
}
# previous handle is selected

{
    my $saver = new SelectSaver;
    # new handle may be selected, or not
}
# previous handle is selected
```

Description

A 'SelectSaver' object contains a reference to the filehandle that was selected when it was created. If its new method gets an extra parameter, then that parameter is selected; otherwise, the selected filehandle remains unchanged.

When a 'SelectSaver' is destroyed, it reselects the filehandle that was selected when it was created.

SelfLoader

SelfLoader allows functions to be loaded only when they are used, not when the script is loaded for execution.

Synopsis

```
package FOOBAR;
use SelfLoader;

... (initializing code)

__DATA__
sub {....
```

Description

This module tells its users that functions in the FOOBAR package are to be autoloaded from after the '__DATA__' token. See also the "Autoloading" section in the Perlsub manpage.

The __DATA__ token

The '__DATA__' token tells the Perl compiler that the Perl code has finished compiling. Everything after the '__DATA__' token is available for reading via the filehandle FOOBAR::DATA (where FOOBAR is the name of the current package when the '__DATA__' token is reached). This works the same way that '__END__' does in the 'main' package—except that the data from the modules after '__END__' are not automatically retrievable, whereas data after '__DATA__' are automatically retrievable. The `__DATA__' token is not recognized in versions of Perl prior to 5.001m.

If a package is split across multiple files and more than one of those files contains a '__DATA__' token, the last `__DATA__' token encountered is the one that is accessible by the filehandle. Further, the '__DATA__' token of an included package supersedes the '__END__' tag of the main program, since the included package is encountered later in the compilation process.

SelfLoader Autoloading

To make the SelfLoader work, the user places the '__DATA__' token *after* the Perl code that needs to be compiled and run at 'require' time and *before* the subroutine declarations that can be loaded later—usually because they may never be called.

The SelfLoader will read from the FOOBAR::DATA filehandle to load the data after `__DATA__' and load any subroutine when it is called. The costs are the one-time parsing of the data after '__DATA__' and a load delay for the _first_ call of any autoloaded function. The benefits (hopefully) include a speeded up compilation phase, with no need to load functions that are never used.

The SelfLoader will stop reading from '__DATA__' if it encounters the '__END__' token—just as you would expect. If the '__END__' token is present and is followed by the token DATA, then the SelfLoader leaves the FOOBAR::DATA filehandle open on the line after that token.

The SelfLoader exports the 'AUTOLOAD' subroutine to the package using the SelfLoader, and this loads the called subroutine when it is first called.

There is no advantage to putting subroutines that will _always_ be called after the '__DATA__' token.

SelfLoader and AutoLoader

The SelfLoader can replace the AutoLoader. You just need to change 'use AutoLoader' to 'use SelfLoader'. (Note that the SelfLoader exports the AUTOLOAD function and the '__END__' token to '__DATA__'. If you have your own AUTOLOAD and are using the AutoLoader too, you probably know what you're doing.) You will need Perl version 5.001m (version 5.001 with all the patches up to m) or later to use this.

There is no need to inherit from the SelfLoader.

The SelfLoader works similarly to the AutoLoader, but it picks up the subs from after the '__DATA__' instead of picking them up from the 'lib/auto' directory. You achieve a maintenance gain because you do not need to run AutoSplit on the module at installation, and you achieve a runtime gain because you do not need to keep opening and closing files to load subs. You do accept a runtime loss from parsing the code after the '__DATA__'. Details of the AutoLoader and another view of these distinctions can be found in that module's documentation.

Socket, sockaddr_in, sockaddr_un, inet_aton, inet_ntoa

This module is just a translation of the C socket.h file.

Synopsis

```
use Socket;

$proto = getprotobyname('udp');
socket(Socket_Handle, PF_INET, SOCK_DGRAM, $proto);
$iaddr = gethostbyname('hishost.com');
$port = getservbyname('time', 'udp');
$sin = sockaddr_in($port, $iaddr);
send(Socket_Handle, 0, 0, $sin);

$proto = getprotobyname('tcp');
socket(Socket_Handle, PF_INET, SOCK_STREAM,
        $proto);
$port = getservbyname('smtp', 'tcp');
$sin = sockaddr_in($port,inet_aton("127.1"));
$sin = sockaddr_in(7,inet_aton("localhost"));
$sin = sockaddr_in(7,INADDR_LOOPBACK);
connect(Socket_Handle,$sin);

($port, $iaddr) =
    sockaddr_in(getpeername(Socket_Handle));
$peer_host = gethostbyaddr($iaddr, AF_INET);
$peer_addr = inet_ntoa($iaddr);

$proto = getprotobyname('tcp');
socket(Socket_Handle, PF_UNIX, SOCK_STREAM,
        $proto);
unlink('/tmp/usock');
$sun = sockaddr_un('/tmp/usock');
connect(Socket_Handle,$sun);
```

Description

Unlike the old mechanism, which required a translated socket.ph file, this mechanism uses the h2xs program (see the Perl source distribution material) and your native C compiler. This means that Perl has a far better chance of getting the numbers right—including all of the commonly used pound-defines like AF_INET, SOCK_STREAM, etc.—since the C compiler will include the header files from your particular system.

Some common socket newline constants are provided, including 'CR', 'LF', and 'CRLF', as well as '$CR', '$LF', and '$CRLF', which map to '\015', '\012', and '\015\012'. If you do not want to use the literal characters in your programs, then use the constants provided here. They are not exported by default, but they can be imported individually and with the `':crlf'` export tag, as shown here:

```
use Socket qw(:DEFAULT :crlf);
```

In addition, some structure manipulation functions are available:

inet_aton HOSTNAME

This command takes a string giving the name of a host, and it translates that string to the four-byte string (structure). It takes arguments of both the `'rtfm.mit.edu'` type and the `'18.181.0.24'` type. If the hostname cannot be resolved, it returns `undef`. For multihomed hosts (hosts with more than one address), the first address found is returned.

inet_ntoa IP_ADDRESS

This command takes a four-byte ip address (as returned by `inet_aton()`) and translates it into a string of the form `'d.d.d.d'`, where the d's are numbers less than 256 (the normal readable four-dotted number notation for internet addresses).

INADDR_ANY

INADDR_ANY returns a packed string and does not return a number. It returns the four-byte wildcard ip address which specifies any of the hosts ip addresses. (A particular machine can have more than one ip address, each address corresponding to a particular network interface. This wildcard address allows you to bind to all of them simultaneously.) Normally, it is equivalent to `inet_aton('0.0.0.0')`.

INADDR_BROADCAST

INAAR_BROADCAST does not return a number, but it returns a packed string. It returns the four-byte `'this-lan'` ip broadcast address. This can be useful for some protocols to solicit information from all servers on the same LAN cable. It is normally equivalent to `inet_aton('255.255.255.255')`.

INADDR_LOOPBACK

INADDR_LOOPBACK returns the four-byte loopback address and does not return a number. Normally, it is equivalent to `inet_aton('localhost')`.

INADDR_NONE

INADDR_NONE returns the four-byte 'invalid' ip address and does not return a number. Normally, it is equivalent to inet_aton('255.255.255.255')

sockaddr_in PORT, ADDRESS
sockaddr_in SOCKADDR_IN

In an array context, this command unpacks its SOCKADDR_IN argument and returns an array consisting of (PORT, ADDRESS). In a scalar context, it packs its (PORT, ADDRESS) arguments as a SOCKADDR_IN and returns it. If this is confusing, use pack_sockaddr_in() and unpack_sockaddr_in() explicitly.

pack_sockaddr_in PORT, IP_ADDRESS

This command takes two arguments, a port number and a four-byte IP_ADDRESS (as returned by inet_aton()). It returns the sockaddr_in structure with those arguments packed with AF_INET filled. For internet domain sockets, this structure is normally what you need for the arguments in bind(), connect(), and send(), and it is also returned by getpeername(), getsockname(), and recv().

unpack_sockaddr_in SOCKADDR_IN

This command takes a sockaddr_in structure (as returned by pack_sockaddr_in()) and returns an array of two elements: the port and the four-byte ip- address. It will croak if the structure does not have AF_INET in the right place.

sockaddr_un PATHNAME
sockaddr_un SOCKADDR_UN

In an array context, this command unpacks its SOCKADDR_UN argument and returns an array consisting of (PATHNAME). In a scalar context, it packs its PATHNAME arguments as a SOCKADDR_UN and returns it. If this is confusing, use pack_sockaddr_un() and unpack_sockaddr_un() explicitly. They are supported only if your system has <sys/un.h>.

pack_sockaddr_un PATH

This command takes one argument, a path name. It returns the sockaddr_un structure with that path packed with AF_UNIX filled. For UNIX domain sockets, this structure is normally what you need for the arguments in bind(), connect(), and send(). It is also returned by getpeername(), getsockname(), and recv().

unpack_sockaddr_un SOCKADDR_UN

This command takes a sockaddr_un structure (as returned by pack _sockaddr_un()) and returns the path name. It will croak if the structure does not have AF_UNIX in the right place.

Symbol

Symbol provides different ways for you to manipulate Perl's symbol table.

Synopsis

```
use Symbol;

$sym = gensym;
open($sym, "filename");
$_ = <$sym>;
# etc.

ungensym $sym;       # no effect

print qualify("x"), "\n";                    # "Test::x"
print qualify("x", "FOO"), "\n"              # "FOO::x"
print qualify("BAR::x"), "\n";               # "BAR::x"
print qualify("BAR::x", "FOO"), "\n";        # "BAR::x"
print qualify("STDOUT", "FOO"), "\n";        # "main::STDOUT"
(global)
print qualify(\*x), "\n";                     # returns \*x
print qualify(\*x, "FOO"), "\n";              # returns \*x

use strict refs;
print { qualify_to_ref $fh } "foo!\n";
$ref = qualify_to_ref $name, $pkg;

use Symbol qw(delete_package);
delete_package('Foo::Bar');
print "deleted\n" unless exists $Foo::{'Bar::'};
```

Description

'Symbol::gensym' creates an anonymous glob and returns a reference to it. This glob reference can be used as a file or directory handle.

For backward compatibility with older implementations that didn't support anonymous globs, 'Symbol::ungensym' is also provided. However, it doesn't do anything.

'Symbol::qualify' turns unqualified symbol names into qualified variable names (e.g., "myvar" -> "MyPackage::myvar"). If it is given a second parameter, 'qualify' uses it as the default package; otherwise, it uses the package of its caller. Regardless, global variable names (e.g., "STDOUT", "ENV", and "SIG") are always qualified with "main::".

Qualification applies only to symbol names (strings). References are left unchanged under the assumption that they are glob references, which are qualified by their nature.

'Symbol::qualify_to_ref' is similar to 'Symbol::qualify', except that it returns a glob reference rather than a symbol name; therefore, you can use the result even if 'use strict 'refs'' is in effect.

'Symbol::delete_package' wipes out a whole package namespace. This routine is not exported by default; therefore, you may want to import it explicitly.

Sys::Hostname

This module tries every conceivable method to get the system's hostname.

Synopsis

```
use Sys::Hostname;
$host = hostname;
```

Description

This module attempts several methods to get the system hostname and then caches the result. It tries 'syscall(SYS_gethostname)', ''hostname'', ''uname - n'', and the file /com/host. If all these attempts fails, it croaks.

All nulls, returns, and newlines are removed from the result.

Sys::Syslog, openlog, closelog, setlogmask, syslog

This is a Perl interface to the UNIX syslog(3) calls, which are used for logging error and diagnostic information to syslogd.

Synopsis

```
# all except setlogsock, or:
use Sys::Syslog;
# default set, plus setlogsock
use Sys::Syslog qw(:DEFAULT setlogsock);

setlogsock $sock_type;
openlog $ident, $logopt, $facility;
syslog $priority, $format, @args;
$oldmask = setlogmask $mask_priority;
closelog;
```

Description

Sys::Syslog is an interface to the UNIX 'syslog(3)' program. You can call `syslog()' with a string priority and a list of 'printf()' args just like you call 'syslog(3)'.

Syslog provides the following functions:

openlog $ident, $logopt, $facility

$ident is prepended to every message. $logopt contains zero or more of the following words: pid, ndelay, cons, and nowait. $facility specifies the part of the system.

syslog $priority, $format, @args

If $priority permits, this command logs ($format, @args) similarly to the way 'printf(3V)' would print it, except that %m is replaced with '"$!"' (the latest error message).

setlogmask $mask_priority

This command sets log mask $mask_priority and returns the old mask.

setlogsock $sock_type (added in 5.004_02)

This command sets the socket type to be used for the next call to `'open-log()'` or `'syslog()'`. It returns True on success, and it returns undef on failure.

A value of `'unix'` will connect to the UNIX domain socket returned by `'_PATH_LOG'` in `syslog.ph`. A value of `'inet'` will connect to an INET socket returned by `getservbyname()`. Any other value croaks.

The INET socket is used by default.

closelog

`Closelog` closes the log file.

Note that `'openlog'` now takes three arguments, just like `'openlog(3)'`.

Examples

```
openlog($program, 'cons,pid', 'user');
syslog('info', 'this is another test');
syslog('mail|warning', 'this is a better test: %d',time);
closelog();

syslog('debug', 'this is the last test');

setlogsock('unix');
openlog("$program $$", 'ndelay', 'user');
syslog('notice', 'fooprogram: this is really done');

setlogsock('inet');
$! = 55;
syslog('info', 'problem was %m'); # %m == $! in syslog(3)
```

Dependencies

Sys::Syslog needs syslog.ph, which can be created with `'h2ph'`.

See Also

The UNIX syslog(3) manpage.

Term::Cap

This module provides an interface to the terminal capabilities (termcap) database.

Synopsis

```
require Term::Cap;
$terminal = Tgetent Term::Cap {
                          TERM => undef,
                          OSPEED => $ospeed };
$terminal->Trequire(qw/ce ku kd/);
$terminal->Tgoto('cm', $col, $row, $FH);
$terminal->Tputs('dl', $count, $FH);
$terminal->Tpad($string, $count, $FH);
```

Description

These are low-level functions to extract and use capabilities from a terminal capability (termcap) database.

The Tgetent function extracts the entry of the specified terminal type TERM (defaults to the environment variable TERM) from the database.

It will look in the environment for a TERMCAP variable. If one is found and the value does not begin with a slash and the terminal type name is the same as the environment string TERM, the TERMCAPstring is used instead of reading a termcap file. If it does begin with a slash, the string is used as a path name of the termcap file to search. If TERMCAP does not begin with a slash and the name is different from TERM, Tgetent searches the files $HOME/.termcap, /etc/termcap, and /usr/share/misc/termcap, in that order—unless the environment variable TERMPATH exists, in which case it specifies a list of file path names (separated by spaces or colons) to be searched instead. Whenever multiple files are searched and a tc field occurs in the requested entry, the entry it names must be found in the same file or one of the succeeding files. If there is a ':tc=...:' in the TERMCAP environment variable string, it will continue the search in the files as previously described.

OSPEED is the terminal output bit rate (often mistakenly called the baud rate). OSPEED can be specified as either a POSIX termios/SYSV termio speed (where 9600 equals 9600) or an old BSD-style speed (where 13 equals 9600).

Tgetent returns a blessed object reference, which the user can then use to send the control strings to the terminal using Tputs and Tgoto. It calls 'croak' on failure.

Tgoto decodes a cursor addressing string with the given parameters.

The output strings for Tputs are cached for counts of 1 for performance. Tgoto and Tpad do not cache. '$self->{_xx}' is the raw termcap data, and '$self->{xx}' is the cached version.

Tgoto, Tputs, and Tpad return the string and also output the string to $FH if specified.

The extracted termcap entry is available in the object as '$self->{TERMCAP}'.

Examples

```perl
 # Get terminal output speed
require POSIX;
my $termios = new POSIX::Termios;
$termios->getattr;
my $ospeed = $termios->getospeed;

# Old-style ioctl code to get ospeed:
#     require 'ioctl.pl';
#     ioctl(TTY,$TIOCGETP,$sgtty);
#     ($ispeed,$ospeed) = unpack('cc',$sgtty);

# allocate and initialize a terminal structure
$terminal = Tgetent Term::Cap {
    TERM => undef, OSPEED => $ospeed };

# require certain capabilities to be available
$terminal->Trequire(qw/ce ku kd/);

# Output Routines, if $FH is undefined
# these just return the string

# Tgoto does the % expansion stuff with
# the given args
$terminal->Tgoto('cm', $col, $row, $FH);

# Tputs doesn't do any % expansion.
$terminal->Tputs('dl', $count = 1, $FH);
```

Term::Complete

This routine provides word completion on the list of words in the array
(or array reference).

Synopsis

```
$input = Complete('prompt_string', \@completion_list);
$input = Complete('prompt_string', @completion_list);
```

Description

This routine provides word completion on the list of words in the array
(or array ref).

The tty driver is put into raw mode using the system command 'stty
raw - echo' and restored using 'stty -raw echo'.

The following command characters are defined:

\<tab\>	Attempts word completion. Cannot be changed.
^D	Prints completion list. Defined by *$Term::Complete::complete*.
^U	Erases the current input. Defined by *$Term::Complete::kill*.
\<del\>, \<bs\>	Erases one character. Defined by *$Term::Complete::erase1* and *$Term::Complete::erase2.

Diagnostics

A bell sounds when word completion fails.

Bugs

The completion character \<tab\> cannot be changed.

Term::ReadLine

This module provides a coherent front-end interface to various 'Read-line' packages. If no real package is found, it substitutes stubs instead of basic functions.

Synopsis

```
use Term::ReadLine;
$term = new Term::ReadLine 'Simple Perl calc';
$prompt = "Enter your arithmetic expression: ";
$OUT = $term->OUT || STDOUT;
while ( defined ($_ = $term->readline($prompt)) ) {
  $res = eval($_), "\n";
  warn $@ if $@;
  print $OUT $res, "\n" unless $@;
  $term->addhistory($_) if /\S/;
}
```

Description

This package is just a front-end to some other packages. At the time of this writing, the only such package is Term-ReadLine, which is available on CPAN near you. The real target of this stub package is to set up a common interface to whatever Readline emerges with time.

It supports a minimal set of functions

All the supported functions should be called as methods—i.e., either as:

```
$term = new Term::ReadLine 'name';
```

or as:

```
$term->addhistory('row');
```

where $term is a return value of Term::ReadLine->Init.

`ReadLine'

This command returns the actual package that executes the commands. Possible values include: 'Term::ReadLine::Gnu', 'Term::ReadLine::Perl', and 'Term::ReadLine::Stub Exporter'.

`new'

This command returns the handle for subsequent calls to following functions. The argument is the name of the application. As an option, it can be followed by two arguments for `'IN'` and `'OUT'` filehandles. These arguments should be `globs`.

`readline'`

This command gets an input line, *possibly* with actual `'Readline'` support. The trailing newline is removed. It returns `'undef'` on `'EOF'`.

`addhistory'`

This command adds a line to the `input` history, from where it can be used if the actual `'Readline'` is present.

`IN', $`OUT'`

If `'Readline'` input and output cannot be used for Perl, this command returns the filehandles for input and output or `'undef'`.

`MinLine'`

If an argument is specified, MinLine specifies the minimum size line to be included in history. If no `argument` is specified, nothing should be included in the history. `MinLine` returns the old value.

`findConsole'`

This command returns an array with two strings that give the most appropriate names for files for input and output using the conventions `'"<$in"'` and `'">out"'`.

Attribs

This command returns a reference to a hash that describes the internal configuration of the package. The names of keys in this hash conform to standard conventions with the leading `'rl_'` stripped.

`Features'

This command returns a reference to a hash with keys that are present in the current implementation. Several optional features are used in the minimal interface:

- ▶ `'appname'` should be present if the first argument to `'new'` is recognized.

- ▶ `'minline'` should be present if the `'MinLine'` method is not dummy.

▶ 'autohistory' should be present if lines are put into history automatically ('autohistory' may be subject to 'MinLine')

▶ 'addhistory' should be present if the 'addhistory' method is not dummy.

If the 'Features' method reports that the feature 'attribs' is present, the method 'Attribs' is not dummy.

Additional Supported Functions

Actually, 'Term::ReadLine' can use some other package that will support a richer set of commands.

All these commands are callable via a method interface, and they have names that conform to standard conventions with the leading 'rl_' stripped.

The stub package included with the Perl distribution material allows these additional methods: 'tkRunning' and 'ornaments'.

`tkRunning`

This method makes the Tk event loop run while waiting for user input (i.e., during the 'Readline' method).

`ornaments`

This method makes the command line stand out by using termcap data. The argument to 'ornaments' should be 0, 1, or a string of the form '"aa,bb,cc,dd"'. Four components of this string should be names of terminal capacities. The first two will be issued to make the prompt standout; the last two will be issued to make the input line standout.

`newTTY`

This command takes two arguments: input filehandle and output filehandle. The default input and output filehandles are switched to use these filehandles.

You can check to see whether the currently loaded ReadLine package supports these methods by checking for the corresponding 'Features'.

Test

Test provides a simple framework for writing test scripts.

Synopsis

```perl
use strict;
use Test;

# use a BEGIN block so we print our plan
# before MyModule is loaded
BEGIN { plan tests => 14, todo => [3,4] }

# load your module...
use MyModule;

ok(0); # failure
ok(1); # success

ok(0); # ok, expected failure (see todo list, above)
ok(1); # surprise success!

ok(0,1);               # failure: '0' ne '1'
ok('broke','fixed'); # failure: 'broke' ne 'fixed'
ok('fixed','fixed'); # success: 'fixed' eq 'fixed'
ok('fixed',qr/x/);   # success: 'fixed' =~ qr/x/

ok(sub { 1+1 }, 2); # success: '2' eq '2'
ok(sub { 1+1 }, 3); # failure: '2' ne '3'
ok(0, int(rand(2))); # (just kidding :-)

my @list = (0,0);
ok @list, 3, "\@list=".join(',',@list); # diagnostics
    ok 'segmentation fault', '/(?i)success/';  # regex
match
    skip($feature_is_missing, ...);
    #do platform specific test
```

Description

The Test::Harness module expects to see particular output when it executes tests. This module aims to make writing proper test scripts just a little bit easier (and less error prone).

Test Types

You can choose among three different test types:

- ▶ Normal
- ▶ Skip
- ▶ Todo.

Normal tests are expected to succeed. If they don't, something's screwed up!

Skip is used for tests that may or may not be able to run, depending on the availability of platform specific features. The first argument should evaluate to True (think "yes, please skip") if the required feature is not available. After the first argument, skip works the same way as normal tests do.

Todo tests are designed to maintain an executable Todo list. These tests are expected fail. If a Todo test does succeed, the feature in question should not be on the Todo list.

Packages should *not* be released with successful Todo tests. As soon as a Todo test starts working, it should be promoted to a normal test and the newly working feature should be documented in the release notes or change log.

Return Value

In a scalar context, both 'ok' and 'skip' return True if their test succeeds and return False if it doesn't.

onfail

```
BEGIN { plan test => 4, onfail =>
    sub { warn "CALL 911!" } }
```

Although test failures should be enough, extra diagnostics can be triggered at the end of a test run. An array ref of hash refs that describe each test failure is passed to 'onfail'. Each hash will contain at least the following fields: 'package', 'repetition', and 'result'. (The file, line, and test number are not included because their correspondence to a particular test is tenuous.) If the test had an expected value or a diagnostic string, they will also be included.

The optional 'onfail' hook might be used simply to print the version of your package and/or how to report problems. It might also be used to generate extremely sophisticated diagnostics for a particularly bizarre test failure. However it's not a panacea. Core dumps and other unrecoverable errors prevent the 'onfail' hook from running. (It is run inside an 'END' block.) Besides, 'onfail' is probably overkill in most cases. (Your test code should be simpler than the code it is testing.)

Text::ParseWords

This module parses text into an array of tokens or an array of arrays.

Synopsis

```
use Text::ParseWords;
@lists = &nested_quotewords($delim, $keep, @lines);
@words = &quotewords($delim, $keep, @lines);
@words = &shellwords(@lines);
@words = &parse_line($delim, $keep, $line);
@words = &old_shellwords(@lines); # DEPRECATED!
```

Description

The &nested_quotewords() and &quotewords() functions accept a delimiter (which can be a regular expression) and a list of lines. They break those lines up into a list of words (ignoring delimiters that appear inside quotes). &quotewords() returns all of the tokens in a single long list. &nested_quotewords() returns a list of token lists corresponding to the elements of @lines. &parse_line() tokenizes a single string. The &*quotewords() functions simply call &parse_lines(); so if you're splitting only one line, you can call &parse_lines() directly and save a function call.

The $keep argument is a Boolean flag. If True, the tokens are split on the specified delimiter, but all other characters (quotes, backslashes, etc.) are kept in the tokens. If $keep is False, the &quotewords() functions remove all quotes and backslashes that are not themselves backslash-escaped or inside of single quotes (i.e., &quotewords() tries to interpret these characters just like the Bourne shell). These semantics are significantly different from the original version of this module shipped with Perl 5.000 through 5.004. As an additional feature, $keep may be the keyword "delimiters", which causes the functions to preserve the delimiters in each string as tokens in the token lists—in addition to preserving quote and backslash characters.

&shellwords() is written as a special case of &quotewords(), and it does token parsing with whitespace as a delimiter—similar to most UNIX shells.

Examples

Here's the sample program:

```
use Text::ParseWords;
@words = &quotewords('\s+', 0, q{this   is "a test" of\
quotewords \"for you});
$i = 0;
foreach (@words) {
    print "$i: <$_>\n";
    $i++;
}
```

Here is the previous program's output:

```
0: <this>
1: <is>
2: <a test>
3: <of quotewords>
4: <"for>
5: <you>
```

The previous program demonstrates the following:

```
0
a simple word
1
multiple spaces are skipped because of our $delim
2
use of quotes to include a space in a word
3
use of a backslash to include a space in a word
4
use of a backslash to remove the special meaning of a
double-quote
5
another simple word (note the lack of effect of the
backslashed double-quote)
Replacing '&quotewords('\s+', 0, q{this is...})' with
'&shellwords(q{this is...})' is a simpler way to
accomplish the same thing.
```

Text::Soundex

This is an implementation of the Soundex algorithm as described by
Donald Knuth.

Synopsis

```
use Text::Soundex;

$code = soundex $string; # get soundex code for a string
@codes = soundex @list;  # get list of codes for list of
                         # strings

# set value to be returned for strings without soundex code

$soundex_nocode = 'Z000';
```

Description

This module implements the Soundex algorithm as described by Donald Knuth in *The Art of Computer Programming, Volume 3* (Addison-Wesley Publishing © 1998). The algorithm is intended to hash words (in particular surnames) into a small space using a simple model that approximates the sound of the word when spoken by an English speaker. Each word is reduced to a four-character string, the first character being an uppercase letter and the remaining three characters being digits.

If there is no Soundex code representation for a string, the value of '$soundex_nocode' is returned. This is initially set to 'undef', but many people seem to prefer an *unlikely* value like 'Z000' (how unlikely this is depends on the data set being used.) Any value can be assigned to '$soundex_nocode'.

In a scalar context, 'soundex' returns the Soundex code of its first argument. In an array context, a list is returned in which each element is the Soundex code for the corresponding argument passed to 'soundex'.

For example:

```
@codes = soundex qw(Mike Stok);
```

leaves '@codes' containing '('M200', 'S320')'.

Examples

Knuth's examples of various names and the Soundex codes they map to are listed here:

```
Euler, Ellery -> E460
Gauss, Ghosh -> G200
Hilbert, Heilbronn -> H416
Knuth, Kant -> K530
Lloyd, Ladd ->.L300
Lukasiewicz, Lissajous -> L222
```

The following lines show the scalar and list use of 'soundex':

```
$code = soundex 'Knuth';  # $code contains 'K530'
@list = soundex qw(Lloyd Gauss);
# @list contains 'L300', 'G200'
```

Limitations

Because the Soundex algorithm was originally used a long time ago in the United States, it considers only the English alphabet and pronunciation.

Because it is mapping a large space (arbitrary length strings) onto a small space (single letter plus three digits), no inference can be made about the similarity of two strings that end up with the same Soundex code. For example, both Hilbert and Heilbronn end up with a Soundex code of 'H416'.

Text::Tabs

Text::Tabs provides a Perl interface to the UNIX expand() and unexpand() utilities.

Synopsis

```
use Text::Tabs;

$tabstop = 4;
@lines_without_tabs = expand(@lines_with_tabs);
@lines_with_tabs = unexpand(@lines_without_tabs);
```

Description

Text::Tabs does about what the UNIX utilities expand(1) and unexpand(1) do. Given a line with tabs in it, expand will replace the tabs with the appropriate number of spaces. Given a line with or without tabs in it, unexpand will add tabs when it can save bytes by doing so.

Bugs

Expand doesn't handle newlines very quickly. Do not feed an entire document to it in one string. Instead, feed it an array of lines.

Text::Wrap

Provides simple word wrapping to format paragraphs within a string.

Synopsis

```
use Text::Wrap

print wrap($initial_tab, $subsequent_tab, @text);
print fill($initial_tab, $subsequent_tab, @text);

use Text::Wrap qw(wrap $columns $huge);

$columns = 132;
$huge = 'die';
$huge = 'wrap';
```

Description

Text::Wrap::wrap() is a very simple paragraph formatter. It formats a single paragraph at a time by breaking lines at word boundaries. Indentation is controlled for the first line ($initial_tab) and all subsequent lines ($subsequent_tab) independently.

Lines are wrapped at $Text::Wrap::columns columns. $Text::Wrap::columns should be set to the full width of your output device.

When words longer than $columns are encountered, they are broken up. Previous versions of wrap() died (used die()). To restore the old (dying) behavior, set $Text::Wrap::huge to 'die'.

Text::Wrap::fill() is a simple multiparagraph formatter. It formats each paragraph separately, and then it joins them together when it's done. It will destroy any whitespace in the original text. It breaks text into paragraphs by looking for whitespace after a newline. In other respects, it acts like wrap().

Example

```
print wrap("\t","","This is a bit of text that forms a
➥ normal book-style paragraph");
```

Tie::Array

This module provides methods for array-tying classes.

Synopsis

```
package NewArray;
use Tie::Array;
@ISA = ('Tie::Array');

# mandatory methods
sub TIEARRAY { ... }
sub FETCH { ... }
sub FETCHSIZE { ... }

sub STORE { ... }
# mandatory if elements writeable
sub STORESIZE { ... }
# mandatory if elements can be added/deleted

# optional methods - for efficiency
sub CLEAR { ... }
sub PUSH { ... }
sub POP { ... }
sub SHIFT { ... }
sub UNSHIFT { ... }
sub SPLICE { ... }
sub EXTEND { ... }
sub DESTROY { ... }

package NewStdArray;
use Tie::Array;
```

```
            @ISA = ('Tie::StdArray');

            # all methods provided by default

            package main;

            $object = tie @somearray,Tie::NewArray;
            $object = tie @somearray,Tie::StdArray;
            $object = tie @somearray,Tie::NewStdArray;
```

Description

This module provides methods for array-tying classes. See the perltie manpage for a list of the functions required in order to tie an array to a package. The basic Tie::Array package provides stub 'DELETE' and 'EXTEND' methods and provides implementations of 'PUSH', 'POP', `SHIFT', 'UNSHIFT', 'SPLICE', and 'CLEAR' in terms of basic 'FETCH', 'STORE', 'FETCHSIZE', and 'STORESIZE'.

The Tie::StdArray package provides efficient methods required for tied arrays that are implemented as blessed references to an "inner" Perl array. It inherits from Tie::Array and should cause tied arrays to behave exactly like standard arrays, allowing for the selective overloading of methods.

For developers wanting to write their own tied arrays, the required methods arc briefly defined here. See the perltie manpage section for a more detailed description and example code.

TIEARRAY classname, LIST

The class method is invoked by the command 'tie @array, classname'. It associates an array instance with the specified class. 'LIST' would represent additional arguments (along the lines of the AnyDBM _File manpage and compatriots) needed to complete the association. The method should return an object of a class that provides the methods listed in the following text.

STORE this, index, value

This method stores datum *value* into *index* for the tied array associated with object *this*. If this makes the array larger, then class's mapping of 'undef' should be returned for new positions.

FETCH this, index

This method retrieves the datum in *index* for the tied array associated with object *this*.

FETCHSIZE this

This method returns the total number of items in the tied array associated with object *this*. (It is equivalent to `'scalar(@array)'`.)

STORESIZE this, count

This method sets the total number of items in the tied array associated with object *this* to be *count*. If this makes the array larger, then class's mapping of `'undef'` should be returned for new positions. If the array becomes smaller, then entries beyond count should be deleted.

EXTEND this, count

This is an informative call that array is likely to grow to have *count* entries. It can be used to optimize allocation. This method need do nothing.

CLEAR this

This command clears (removes, deletes) all values from the tied array associated with object *this*.

DESTROY this

This is the normal object destructor method.

PUSH this, LIST

This command appends elements of LIST to the array.

POP this

This command removes the last element of the array and returns it.

SHIFT this

This command removes the first element of the array (shifting other elements down) and returns it.

UNSHIFT this, LIST

This command inserts LIST elements at the beginning of the array, moving existing elements up to make room.

SPLICE this, offset, length, LIST

This command perform the equivalent of 'splice' on the array.

The *offset* is optional and defaults to zero, negative values count back from the end of the array. The *length* is optional and defaults to rest of the array.

LIST may be empty. It returns a list of the original *length* elements at *offset*.

Caveats

At present, tied @ISA is unsupported. There is a potential conflict between magic entries needed to flag a modification to @ISA, and those needed to implement 'tie'.

Very little consideration has been given to the behavior of tied array when '$[' is not set to default value of zero.

Tie::Handle

This module provides some skeletal methods for handle-tying classes.

Synopsis

```
package NewHandle;
require Tie::Handle;

@ISA = (Tie::Handle);

sub READ { ... }         # Provide a needed method
sub TIEHANDLE { ... }    # Overrides inherited method

package main;

tie *FH, 'NewHandle';
```

Description

This module provides some skeletal methods for handle-tying classes. See the perltie manpage for a list of the functions required to tie a handle to a package. The basic Tie::Handle package provides a new method, as well as methods 'TIESCALAR', 'FETCH', and 'STORE'. The new method is provided as a means of grandfathering for classes that forget to provide their own `'TIESCALAR'` method.

For developers wanting to write their own tied-handle classes, the methods are summarized in the following text. The `perltie` manpage section documents these methods and has sample code:

TIEHANDLE classname, LIST

This method is invoked by the command `'tie *glob, classname'`. It associates a new `glob` instance with the specified class. `'LIST'` would represent additional arguments (along the lines of the `AnyDBM_File` manpage and compatriots) needed to complete the association.

WRITE this, scalar, length, offset

This method writes *length* bytes of data from *scalar* starting at *offset*.

PRINT this, LIST

This method prints the values in LIST.

PRINTF this, format, LIST

This method prints the values in LIST using *format*.

READ this, scalar, length, offset

This method reads *length* bytes of data into *scalar* starting at *offset*.

READLINE this

This method reads a single line.

GETC this

This method gets a single character.

DESTROY this

This method frees the storage area associated with the tied handle referenced by *this*. This method is rarely needed, as Perl manages its memory quite well. But the option exists, should a class need to perform specific actions upon the destruction of an instance.

Tie::Hash
Tie::StdHash

This module provides some skeletal methods for hash-tying classes.

Synopsis

```
package NewHash;
require Tie::Hash;

@ISA = (Tie::Hash);

sub DELETE { ... }      # Provides needed method
sub CLEAR { ... }       # Overrides inherited method


package NewStdHash;
require Tie::Hash;

@ISA = (Tie::StdHash);

# All methods provided by default, define only
# those needing overrides
sub DELETE { ... }

package main;

tie %new_hash, 'NewHash';
tie %new_std_hash, 'NewStdHash';
```

Description

This module provides some skeletal methods for hash-tying classes. See the perltie manpage for a list of the functions required to tie a hash to a package. The basic Tie::Hash package provides a 'new' method, as well as methods 'TIEHASH', 'EXISTS', and 'CLEAR'. The Tie::StdHash package provides most methods required for hashes in the perltie manpage. It inherits from Tie::Hash and causes tied hashes to behave exactly like standard hashes, allowing for selective overloading of methods. The 'new' method is provided as grandfathering in case a class forgets to include a 'TIEHASH' method.

For developers wanting to write their own tied hashes, the required methods are briefly defined in the following sections. See the `perltie` manpage section for a more detailed description, as well as example code.

TIEHASH classname, LIST

This is the method invoked by the command `'tie %hash, classname'`. It associates a new hash instance with the specified class. `'LIST'` would represent additional arguments (along the lines of the `AnyDBM_File` manpage and compatriots) needed to complete the association.

STORE this, key, value

This method stores the datum *value* into *key* for the tied hash *this*.

FETCH this, key

This method retrieves the datum in *key* for the tied hash *this*.

FIRSTKEY this

This method returns the (`key`, `value`) pair for the first key in the hash.

NEXTKEY this, lastkey

This method returns the next key for the hash.

EXISTS this, key

This method verifies that *key* exists with the tied hash *this*.

DELETE this, key

This method deletes the key *key* from the tied hash *this*.

CLEAR this

This method clears all values from the tied hash *this*.

Caveats

The `perltie` manpage documentation includes a method called `'DESTROY'` as a necessary method for tied hashes. Neither `Tie::Hash` nor `Tie::StdHash` define a default for this method. This is a standard for class packages, but it may be omitted in favor of a simple default.

More Information

The packages relating to various DBM-related implementations (DB_File, NDBM_File, etc.) show examples of general tied hashes, as does the Config manpage module. Although they do not utilize Tie::Hash, they serve as good working examples.

Tie::RefHash

This module provides the ability to use references as hash keys.

Synopsis

```
require 5.004;
use Tie::RefHash;
tie HASHVARIABLE, 'Tie::RefHash', LIST;

untie HASHVARIABLE;
```

Description

This module provides the ability to use references as hash keys if you first 'tie' the hash variable to this module.

It is implemented using the standard Perl TIEHASH interface. Please see the 'tie' entry in Perlfunc(1) and perltie(1) for more information.

Example

```
use Tie::RefHash;
tie %h, 'Tie::RefHash';
$a = [];
$b = {};
$c = \*main;
$d = \"gunk";
$e = sub { 'foo' };
%h = ($a => 1, $b => 2, $c => 3, $d => 4, $e => 5);
$a->[0] = 'foo';
$b->{foo} = 'bar';
for (keys %h) {
    print ref($_), "\n";
}
```

Tie::Scalar
Tie::StdScalar

This module provides some skeletal methods for scalar-tying classes.

Synopsis

```
package NewScalar;
require Tie::Scalar;

@ISA = (Tie::Scalar);

sub FETCH { ... }       # Provides a needed method
sub TIESCALAR { ... }   # Overrides inherited method


package NewStdScalar;
require Tie::Scalar;

@ISA = (Tie::StdScalar);

# All methods provided by default,
# so define only what
# needs be overridden
sub FETCH { ... }

package main;

tie $new_scalar, 'NewScalar';
tie $new_std_scalar, 'NewStdScalar';
```

Description

This module provides some skeletal methods for scalar-tying classes. See the perltie manpage for a list of the functions required to tie a scalar to a package. The basic Tie::Scalar package provides a 'new' method—as well as methods 'TIESCALAR', 'FETCH', and 'STORE'. The Tie::Std-Scalar package provides all the methods specified in the perltie manpage. It inherits from Tie::Scalar and causes scalars tied to it to behave exactly like the built-in scalars, allowing for selective overloading of methods. The 'new' method is provided as a means of grandfathering for classes that forget to provide their own 'TIESCALAR' method.

For developers wanting to write their own tied-scalar classes, the methods are summarized in the following sections. The `perltie` man-page section documents these and has sample code as well:

TIESCALAR classname, LIST

This is the method invoked by the command `'tie $scalar, classname'`. It associates a new scalar instance with the specified class. `'LIST'` would represent additional arguments (along the lines of the `AnyDBM_File` manpage and compatriots) needed to complete the association.

FETCH this

This method retrieves the value of the tied scalar referenced by *this*.

STORE this, value

This method stores data *value* in the tied scalar referenced by *this*.

DESTROY this

This method frees the storage associated with the tied scalar referenced by *this*. This method is rarely needed, because Perl manages its memory quite well. But the option exists, should a class want to perform specific actions upon the destruction of an instance.

The `perltie` manpage section uses a good example of tying scalars by associating process IDs with priority.

Tie::SubstrHash

This module provides fixed-table-sized, fixed-key-length hashing functions.

Synopsis

```
require Tie::SubstrHash;

tie %myhash,
    'Tie::SubstrHash',
    $key_len,
    $value_len,
    $table_size;
```

Description

The Tie::SubstrHash package provides a hash-table-like interface to an array of determinate size, with constant key size and record size.

Upon tying a new hash to this package, the developer must specify the size of the keys that will be used, the size of the value fields that the keys will index, and the size of the overall table (in terms of key-value pairs, not size in hard memory). *These values will not change for the duration of the tied hash.* The newly allocated hash table may now have data stored and retrieved. Efforts to store more than '$table_size' elements will result in a fatal error—as will efforts to store a value not exactly '$value_len' characters in length or efforts to reference through a key not exactly '$key_len' characters in length. Although these constraints may seem excessive, the result is a hash table that uses much less internal memory than an equivalent freely allocated hash table.

Caveats

Because the current implementation uses the table and key sizes for the hashing algorithm, there is no means by which to dynamically change the value of any of the initialization parameters.

Time::Local

This module provides ways to efficiently compute time from local and GMT time.

Synopsis

```
$time = timelocal($sec,$min,$hours,$mday,$mon,$year);
$time = timegm($sec,$min,$hours,$mday,$mon,$year);
```

Description

These routines are quite efficient, and yet they are always guaranteed to agree with localtime() and gmtime(). The most notable points are that the year is *the year minus 1900* and the month is *a number from 0 to 11.* We manage this by caching the start times of any months we've seen before. If we know the start time of the month, we can always calculate any time within the month. The start times themselves are guessed by successive approximation starting at the current time, since most dates seen in practice are close to the current date. Unlike algorithms that do a binary search (calling gmtime once for each bit of the time value, resulting in 32 calls), this algorithm calls it at most six times—and usually only once or twice. If you hit the month cache, of course, it doesn't call it at all.

Timelocal is implemented using the same cache. We just assume that we're translating a GMT time, and then fudge it when we're done for the timezone and daylight savings arguments. The timezone is determined by examining the result of localtime(0) when the package is initialized. The daylight savings offset is currently assumed to be one hour.

Both routines return −1 (negative one) if the integer limit is hit (i.e., for dates after the 1st of January, 2038 on most machines).

Time::gmtime

This module provides an alternative, object-oriented interface to Perl's built-in gmtime() function.

Synopsis

```
use Time::gmtime;
$gm = gmtime();
printf "The day in Greenwich is %s\n",
 (qw(Sun Mon Tue Wed Thu Fri Sat Sun))[ gm->wday() ];

use Time::gmtime w(:FIELDS;
printf "The day in Greenwich is %s\n",
 (qw(Sun Mon Tue Wed Thu Fri Sat Sun))[ gm_wday() ];

$now = gmctime();

use Time::gmtime;
use File::stat;
$date_string = gmctime(stat($file)->mtime);
```

Description

This module's default exports override the core gmtime() function, replacing it with a version that returns "Time::tm" objects. This object has methods that return the similarly named structure field name from the C's tm structure from time.h. These methods consist of sec(), min(), hour(), mday(), mon(), year(), wday(), yday(), and isdst().

You may also import all the structure fields directly into your namespace as regular variables using the `:FIELDS` import tag. (Note that this still overrides your core functions.) You access these fields as variables named with a preceding `'tm_'` in front their method names. Therefore, `'$tm_obj->mday()'` corresponds to $tm_mday if you import the fields.

The `gmctime()` function provides a way of getting at the scalar sense of the original `CORE::gmtime()` function.

To access this functionality without the core overrides, pass an empty import list to the `'use'`, and then access functions with their full qualified names. On the other hand, the built-ins are still available via the `'CORE::'` pseudo-package.

Time::localtime

This module provides an alternative, object-oriented interface to Perl's built-in `localtime()` function.

Synopsis

```
use Time::localtime;
printf "Year is %d\n", localtime->year() + 1900;

$now = ctime();

use Time::localtime;
use File::stat;
$date_string = ctime(stat($file)->mtime);
```

Description

This module's default exports override the core `localtime()` function, replacing it with a version that returns "Time::tm" objects. This object has methods that return the similarly named structure field name from the C's tm structure from `time.h`. These methods consists of `sec()`, `min()`, `hour()`, `mday()`, `mon()`, `year()`, `wday()`, `yday()`, and `isdst()`.

You may also import all the structure fields directly into your namespace as regular variables using the `:FIELDS` import tag. (Note that this still overrides your core functions.) You access these fields as variables named with a preceding `'tm_'` in front their method names. Therefore, `'$tm_obj->mday()'` corresponds to $tm_mday if you import the fields.

The ctime() function provides a way of getting at the scalar sense of the original CORE::localtime() function.

To access this functionality without the core overrides, pass an empty import list to the 'use', and then access function functions with their full qualified names. On the other hand, the built-ins are still available via the 'CORE::' pseudo-package.

NOTE
Although this class is currently implemented using the Class::Struct module to build a class of 'struct' and similar datatypes, you shouldn't rely on this.

Time::tm

This module is an internal base class used by Time::gmtime and Time::localtime.

Synopsis

Don't use this module directly.

Description

This module is used internally as a base class by Time::localtime and Time::gmtime functions. It creates a Time::tm struct object that is addressable just like's C's tm structure from time.h—namely with sec, min, hour, mday, mon, year, wday, yday, and isdst.

This class is an internal interface only.

User::grent

This module provides an alternative, object-oriented interface to Perl's built-in getgrent(), getgruid(), and getgrnam() functions.

Synopsis

```
use User::grent;
$gr = getgrgid(0) or die "No group zero";
if ( $gr->name eq 'wheel' && @{$gr->members} > 1 ) {
    print "gid zero name wheel, with other members";
}
```

```
use User::grent qw(:FIELDS;
getgrgid(0) or die "No group zero";
if ( $gr_name eq 'wheel' && @gr_members > 1 ) {
    print "gid zero name wheel, with other members";
}

$gr = getgr($whoever);
```

Description

This module's default exports override the core getgrent(), get-gruid(), and getgrnam() functions, replacing them with versions that return "User::grent" objects. This object has methods that return the similarly named structure field name from the C's passwd structure from grp.h. These methods consists of name(), passwd(), gid(), and members() (not mem). The first three methods return scalars: the last method returns an array reference.

You may also import all the structure fields directly into your namespace as regular variables using the :FIELDS import tag. (Note that this still overrides your core functions.) You access these fields as variables named with a preceding 'gr_'. Therefore, '$group_obj->gid()' corresponds to $gr_gid if you import the fields. Array references are available as regular array variables, so '@{ $group_obj->members() }' would be simply @gr_members.

The getpw() function is a simple front-end that forwards a numeric argument to getpwuid() and forwards the rest of the arguments to get-pwnam().

To access this functionality without the core overrides, pass an empty import list to the 'use', and then access functions with their full qualified names. On the other hand, the built-ins are still available via the 'CORE::' pseudo-package.

User::pwent

This module provides an alternative, object-oriented interface to Perl's built-in getpwent(), getpwuid(), and getpwnam() functions.

Synopsis

```
use User::pwent;
$pw = getpwnam('daemon') or die "No daemon user";
if ( $pw->uid == 1 && $pw->dir =~ m#^/(bin|tmp)?$# ) {
    print "gid 1 on root dir";
}

use User::pwent qw(:FIELDS);
getpwnam('daemon') or die "No daemon user";
if ( $pw_uid == 1 && $pw_dir =~ m#^/(bin|tmp)?$# ) {
    print "gid 1 on root dir";
}

$pw = getpw($whoever);
```

Description

This module's default exports override the core getpwent(), getpwuid(), and getpwnam() functions, replacing them with versions that return "User::pwent" objects. This object has methods that return the similarly named structure field name from the C's passwd structure from pwd.h— namely name, passwd, uid, gid, quota, comment, gecos, dir, and shell.

You may also import all the structure fields directly into your name-space as regular variables using the :FIELDS import tag. (Note that this still overrides your core functions.) Access these fields as variables named with a preceding 'pw_' in front their method names. Therefore, '$passwd_obj->shell()' corresponds to $pw_shell if you import the fields.

The getpw() function is a simple front-end that forwards a numeric argument to getpwuid() and forwards the rest of the arguments to getpwnam().

To access this functionality without the core overrides, pass an empty import list to the `use', and then access functions with their full quali-fied names. On the other hand, the built-ins are still available via the 'CORE::' pseudo-package.

Index

Note to Reader: In this index, **boldfaced** page numbers refer to primary discussions of the topic; *italics* page numbers refer to figures.

B

G

H

L

About the Contributors

James Jaworski has written five books on Java and JavaScript, including *Java 2 Unleashed* and *The Java Developer's Guide.* He also writes the "SuperScripter" column for CNET's popular Web site for Webmasters, Builder.com.

Eric Herrmann is president of Application Software Solutions, Inc. (ASSI), which builds business Internet solutions in Perl, JavaScript, and other languages. The author of the best-selling *Teach Yourself CGI Programming With Perl 5 in a Week,* he has an MS in computer science and more than ten years of programming experience.

Deborah S. Ray and Eric J. Ray are owners of RayComm, Inc., a technical communications consulting firm that specializes in cutting-edge Internet and computing technologies. Together they have co-authored more than 10 computer books, including the first and second editions of *Mastering HTML 4: Premium Edition* from Sybex. They also write a syndicated computer column, which is available in newspapers across North America, and serve as Technology Review Editors for *Technical Communication, the Journal of the Society for Technical Communication.*

Erik Strom herds computers and their users as an assistant managing editor at *The Denver Post.* He was a freelance writer, editor, and systems consultant in his previous life.

Joseph Schmuller a Senior Systems Analyst at Barnett Technologies, is the author of *ActiveX: No experience required,* also from Sybex. Editor-in-Chief of *PC AI* magazine from 1991 through 1997, he has written numerous articles and reviews on advanced computing technology. He is also a partner in Adcomtec, a firm specializing in Web site design for mass media organizations, and is an Adjunct Professor at the University of North Florida

Nathan Moser is a Senior Software Engineer at Critical Path, an advanced messaging technology firm in San Francisco. Previous to this, he developed some of the first internal Web applications at Netscape Communication. In his spare time, Nathan composes and performs digital music.